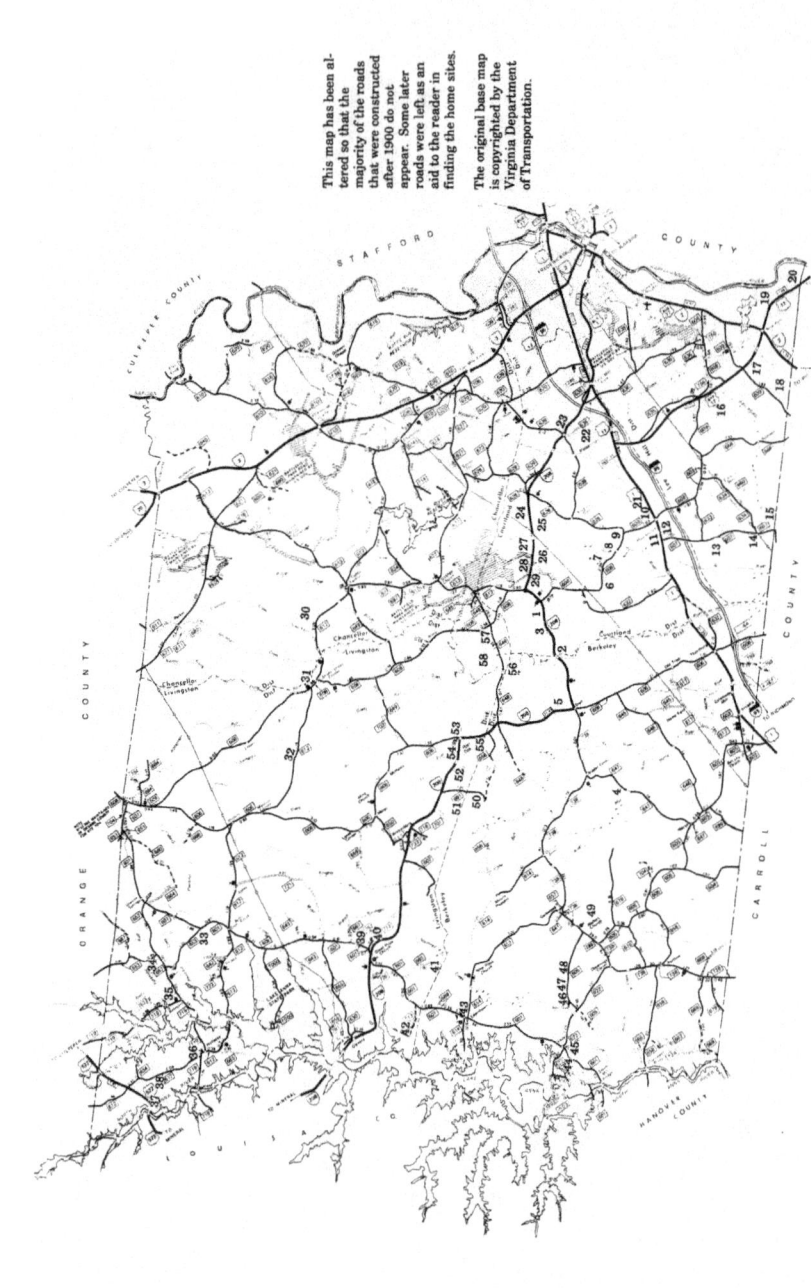

This map has been altered so that the majority of the roads that were constructed after 1900 do not appear. Some later roads were left as an aid to the reader in finding the home sites.

The original base map is copyrighted by the Virginia Department of Transportation.

MARRIAGES IN VIRGINIA

Spotsylvania County,
1851–1900
and
Orange County,
1851–1867

Therese A. Fisher

HERITAGE BOOKS
2012

HERITAGE BOOKS
AN IMPRINT OF HERITAGE BOOKS, INC.

Books, CDs, and more—Worldwide

For our listing of thousands of titles see our website at
www.HeritageBooks.com

Published 2012 by
HERITAGE BOOKS, INC.
Publishing Division
100 Railroad Ave. #104
Westminster, Maryland 21157

Copyright © 1992 Therese A. Fisher

All rights reserved. No part of this book may be reproduced or transmitted in any form or by any means, electronic or mechanical, including photocopying, recording or by any information storage and retrieval system without written permission from the author, except for the inclusion of brief quotations in a review.

International Standard Book Numbers
Paperbound: 978-1-55613-570-5
Clothbound: 978-0-7884-9440-6

TABLE OF CONTENTS

Abbreviations	v
Introduction	vii
Itinerary	xv
Husbands' Index	1
Wives' Index	352
Births Index	391

ABBREVIATIONS USED IN THIS BOOK

POB...Place of Birth
POR...Place of Residence
POM...Place of Marriage
POC...Person of Color
NA....Native American
S/O...Son of
D/O...Daughter of
B.D...Birth Date
D.D...Death Date
S.....Single (as stated by the bride or groom)
W.....Widower or Widow
D.....Divorced
Co....County
Ch....Church
FMR...Fredericksburg Ministers Return found in the Fredericksburg, Va. Circuit Court. Generally attached to the marriage license after 1864
FML...Fredericksburg Marriage License found in the files of the Fredericksburg Va. Circuit Court. Found after 1850. Those after about 1855 contain more genealogical information than the previous forms.
OMR...Orange County Minister's Return. The originals and excellent indexes compiled by clerks of the court are in the Orange County Court House Circuit Clerk's Office. This minister's return is generally attached to the marriage license after 1864.
OML...Orange County Marriage License. Found in the files of the Clerk of the Circuit Court, Orange, Virginia. This was the form that was used after about 1854 and contains excellent genealogical data. It appears to be completed by the clerk of the court using information supplied by the prospective bride and groom.
SPMR..Spotsylvania County Ministers Returns found in the Circuit Court Clerk's Office at the Court House in Spotsylvania. Generally attached to the marriage license after 1864
SPML..Spotsylvania County Marriage License found in the files of the Spotsylvania Circuit Court Clerk's Office. Not used before 1850. Forms used between 1850 and 1853 have very little genealogical data. Forms used between 1854 and 1855 are a little more detailed but it isn't until 1856 that the forms consistantly contain superlative genealogical material.

SPBR..Spotsylvania Birth Record. Register of
       births created by the Clerk of the Court
       from 1853 to 1867. No births were
       recorded during the Civil War. In 1868, the
       job of collecting birth information was
       given to the Commissioner of Revenue.
GBSP..Guardian Bonds of Spotsylvania. Found in
       the Clerk of the Circuit Court's office,
       Spotsylvania Court House.
CBC...Craigs Baptist Church in Spotsylvania Co.
SGMC..Shady Grove Methodist Church in Spotsylvania
       County.
M.E...Methodist Episcopal Church. The previous
       name that the United Methodist Church of
       today was known.
StGF..St.George's Episcopal Church located in
       Fredericksburg.
PCF...Presbyterian Church located in
       Fredericksburg
TCF...Trinity Church now located in
       Fredericksburg. At one time the church was
       considered to be in Spotsylvania County
FN....Fredericksburg News published biweekly.
       Partially indexed by Robert Hodge.
       Microfilmed. Located in the Central
       Rappahannock Regional Library and in
       the library at Mary Washington College,
       Fredericksburg
Lt....Lieutenant
Sgt...Sargeant
Pvt...Private
W.....White
M.....Male
F.....Female

I have eliminated the state designation for the
city of Fredericksburg and the counties of
Stafford, Orange & Spotsylvania. Whenever these
political jurisdictions appear it is to be
understood that the state of Virginia is implied.
Any county that has no state designation is
considered in the commonwealth of Virginia. Keep
in mind that the state of West Virginia was a part
of the commonwealth of Virginia and so counties
that are now in West Virginia may have been
considered a part of Virginia at the time of
marriage or at the time of birth.

INTRODUCTION

With this continuation of records from the counties surrounding Fredericksburg as well as from Fredericskburg, we begin to get a clearer picture of how the present population came to be as well as some interesting insights into lifestyles, patterns of migration and family "alliances". Rather than rehash all the material that I covered in the introduction of the first book on Fredericksburg, Spotyslvania, Stafford and Orange, I'd like to pick up where we left off.

I have found that there are some significant changes in population mergings that have effected the content of this book.

The first and most noticable change is with Orange County. As I began to compile the marriages from the Orange County records, I discovered that there were fewer and fewer marriages that took place between Orange County residents and the inhabitants of Spotsylvania, Stafford and Fredericskburg. The marriagables seemed to find their marriage partners in Orange, Culpeper, Madison and Albemarle counties more than previously and almost to the exclusion of Spotsylvania, Stafford and Fredericksburg. As a result of this finding, I terminated my research in Orange County. The records that I am including in this book include all the marriages recorded in Orange County through 1867. I sincerely hope that this will not anger families whose ancestors trace back to Orange County in the later part of the nineteenth century. To continue with those records would have been counterproductive to the purpose of this book, which was to compile in one place those families who intermarried and to show some continuation of family lines.

A second change in records that was brought forcefully to my attention was the importance of reviewing the records of all known brothers and sisters. Unlike earlier documents, licenses and ministers returns after 1854 contain a wealth of genealogical data. Siblings would occasionally provide slightly different data on parental names. An example would be one sibling who stated his father's name with initials only, while another gave a first given name while still another provided a first initial and a middle name in full. It is also possible to get an approximation of immigration dates from the birth places stated by siblings of different ages.

I found that caution needs to be used in relying solely on the bride or groom's statements of marital status, birth dates or parents' names.

There were numerous examples of a bride or groom who stated his or her marital status as single, when the entry immediately following or previous shows a previous marriage. It is probably that individuals considered themselves single if they were no longer living with their spouse. As far as ages of the bride, we need to take the bride's statement of her age with a grain of salt on occasion. There was a tremendously amusing entry in Spotsylvania County where the marriage license was completed and the court clerk scratched out the age stated by the bride and wrote in an age about seven years older. He then noted next to the age that the change was made at the insistance of the bride's brothers!

The condition of the records after 1850 is, naturally, much better than that of earlier documents. Writing is clearer and there are few tears or ink blots. There still is, however, some difficulty in deciphering handwriting. Where there was a large doubt in my mind as to the accuracy of my transcription of the handwriting I followed the entry with a (?).

Records after 1850 from Spotsylvania County are an interesting mixture of gratifying completeness and annoying gaps in information. It is said that when the battle of Spotsylvania Court House was imminent, the county clerk buried the records of the county out behind the court house so that the fate of Stafford County records would not befall them. It is because of this foresight that we are fortunate to have as much data from the founding of the county forward as we have. The annoying gaps are the abbreviated forms that were used in the early 1850's that basically gave the names of the parties and the date of the ceremony. There are also more perplexing gaps in the quantity of marriages recorded and the number of documents preserved. It appears that some unknown fate effected about 30% of the marriage licenses and ministers returns from 1850 through 1863 after they were recorded in the clerk's book. Those who typed or wrote the data from the documents into the marriage register book occasionally used abbreviations or initials in place of the name of the participant or parent. Without the original document, it is difficult to accurately determine the correct name. I also found that when subsequent information on the marriage popped up, there arose some question as to the accuracy of the transcription in some cases. In a number of instances, I was able to locate a name by researching other documents stored at the courthouse. But in others, there was nothing else available to research. I hope that the descendants of these "initialed" individuals are determined and resourceful enough to find the gaps of information based on what has been provided in this book.

I have used the title Dr. wherever it has been given and there has been no other indication to specify the type of Dr. implied, whether it was a physician or a PhD. I have also indicated that a lady was previously married if her name was preceeded by a Mrs. but there was no other indication as to her widowhood or divorced state. Occasionally the place of marriage was given as the residence of a person. If I could ascertain the political jurisdiction in which the person resided, I gave the place of marriage as the county or city. If the marriage license or the church record or the newspaper article specified that the marriage took place at a specific church, I included the name of the church. I made no assumptions based on which church had recorded the marriage. A number of marriages were recorded at one church while the marriage actually took place in another church and in another county or city.

There are differences in the information contained on records from varying sources. I found differences in given names, ages and residences. I cannot choose which of these records is the more accurate or the correct one for each family. It is hoped that the researcher will have some additional information, whether it is census records, family Bibles or oral tradition to determine which of the records is correct.

There are some references to military units during the War Between the States years (1861-1865). There was also a military "peace keeping" presence that remained in the Fredericksburg area for several years after the war ended. I included any military unit affiliation that was stated in the marriage document.

Church records in the area are not as complete as one could wish for. Shiloh Baptist Church, while mentioned numerous times in the Fredericksburg records after 1866 lost all their early church records in a flood in 1945. Fredericksburg Baptist Church, probably the more dominant Baptist Church in Fredericksburg, kept its marriage records with the private papers of each individual minister. These records were retained by the minister and, if still extant, are among the private papers of the minister. St. George's Episcopal Church, whose records stretched back to the eighteenth century, sent their pre-war records to Richmond for safekeeping. There they were burned along with numerous other church and civil records during the attacks on Richmond. St. John's Episcopal Church merged with Christ Church in Spotsylvania County in the 1840's. Any marriage records from either church before 1900 are not known to be in the area. St. Mary's Catholic Church, the only Catholic church in the area until after 1900, does not permit access to their records. However, the Catholic population in this area was not a large one. The main center of Catholicism seemed to be with the Brent family in Stafford County and some of the Irish and German families that immigrated to Fredericksburg after the Civil War. It appears that most if not all marriages that took place where the bride was resident of the included political jurisdictions are included in the civil records, i.e. marriage licenses.

Church records from Stafford are annoyingly absent. Aquia Church (formerly Overwharton Parish) has the largest number of records but these are not as complete as one would expect from a church as old as Aquia. Apparently mismanagement of documents in early days allowed many records to be destroyed or lost. Records are now maintained in locked conditions and have been well preserved. Hartwood church records, also among the oldest, are not available in Stafford. They may be among the session minutes preserved on microfilm at Union Theological Seminary in Richmond.

Shady Grove Methodist Church in Spotsylvania did not maintain separate church records. Apparently any marriage records that exist are in the possesion of ministers' families or in collections under the minister's name.

Piney Branch Baptist Church in Spotsylvania follows the Baptist tradition of ministers maintaining any marriage or christening records in their private papers. The only Piney Branch records that I am aware of are those of the Rev. Jeremiah Chandler who was minister to that congregation in the early 1800's. His papers are on file at the Virginia State Archives, Richmond, Va.

Researchers will find that there is a great deal of mobility that takes place in the second half of the nineteenth century. One can find a parent's place of residence in Fredericksburg and the child's place of residence in New York. When this difference was noted in one of the records, I so distinguished this difference by including the parents' place of residence in parentheses after their names while the son or daughter's place of residence is stated as POR without parentheses.

There are a large number of records for people of African heritage contained in the records of Fredericksburg, Spotsylvania and Stafford as well as some in Orange. These brides and grooms are generally designated with the abbreviation "POC". There are exceptions. Before approximately 1870 there was no place to designate race or color on the marriage license. I did not assume any race. However, it seems safe to believe that if the marriage took place in a church designated as a "Colored Baptist Church" or if the parents or children of the couple were indicated to be "persons of color" in other documents or if one of the couple was designated as a person of color in a later marriage, that that person or couple was of African heritage. Frequently one or both parents of the bride or groom were stated as unknown. However, searching voter registration rolls for Fredericksburg, particularly the listing of "Colored Voters", occasionally will turn up a previously unknown parental connection.

County clerks usually did not record the parents of a child born without benefit of a sanctioned marriage between the parents. In these cases there generally is the absence of a father's name. It was not unusual for African-Americans to be unfamiliar with their parents' names. The early demise of parents or separation from birth parents at an early age could have caused this lack of knowledge as well as the court clerk's restrictions on designating a parent from a marriage that took place in a non-conventional fashion.

The years immediately following the War Between the States were an exciting time in genealogical histories. Blacks who had been slaves acquired last names, numerous immigrants flooded into the area and many soldiers who had apparently spent some time in the area, returned and married local girls. It was a time of rebuilding...of both homes and families.

With the mobility that came about after the war in particular, there are a surprising number of individuals that came from many different states to either settle in the area or claim their spouses and move on. There are a number of instances, particularly in Fredericksburg, where neither the husband nor the wife appear to have any connections in the area, but have married in local churches or courthouses. Based on the lack of progeny in later records, we may assume that they did not settle in the area, rather they went on to their previous place of residence or followed the husband's job demands.

On the subject of jobs: the marriage license forms leave no place for the woman's occupation. Some women worked at a job, others did not. We cannot assume that just because no occupation was stated for the wife on the form, none was held by her. In fact, a large number of women did hold jobs. A perusal of the newspapers of the time show a number of women advertising as teachers or milliners. Other records (census records for example)and histories show still more women working as house servants, cooks and other jobs.

Abbreviated forms of names as well as nicknames were still being used on civil documents. I have found Kitty used for Catherine, Polly for Mary, Patsy for Martha, Sandy for Alexander, Fannie for Frances and Maggie for Margaret. I don't mean to imply that these are the only nicknames used; these just seem to be used more often.

I have included birth dates for individuals when these have been included as a part of the information of the marriage license. I included a small section on Spotsylvania births in the back of this book. Spotsylvania births were recorded in a birth registration book from 1853 to 1868, and do not include births that took place during the War Between the States. Those births that are included are helpful but by no means can the few births that I have recorded be considered to be complete. I understand that there are a number of Spotsylvania births that are available from 1868 to 1896 or so. If this is the case, there is a wealth of information available beyond what I have here. Fredericksburg birth records were compiled in a book by Robert Hodge and are available at the court house as well. According to the court clerk, most of these birth records were taken from school records.

I have also found some of the married couples buried side by side in cemetaries in Spotsylvania. When I have located a couple or an individual with no doubt in my mind as to their idenity, I have recorded the date found on the tombstone.

While I have personally thanked the Clerks of the Court in Spotsylvania and Orange, I would like to publicly acknowledge their helpful assistance and kind permission to extract the documents they have in their possesion. Margaret Cook of Spotsylvania is now retired, but her help and interest in my project will not be forgotten. Mr. Joiner of Orange was wonderfully enthusiastic and interested in the material that I was gathering. He was quite aware of the benefits of utilizing modern technology to preserve and expedite use of the data passed to us from his predecessors. Sonya Harvison of the Spotsylvania Historical Museum was responsible for creating the Itineraries and the map of Spotsylvania County home sites. I am grateful for the time and knowledge that she put into their creation. I would like to thank Barbara Willis of the Central Rappahannock Regional Library for inspiring this book. The staffs at the Spotsylvania and Orange Court Houses were also helpful. The numerous ministers and church secretaries that answered questions and helped me locate documents also deserve a heartfelt thank you. I wish to thank the members of the Jawbones Society in Fredericksburg for helping me find data and encouraging me when I became overwhelmed by the amount of information I obtained. And last but not least I wish to thank my husband for giving me the freedom to pursue this book. Without his support, this would not have been possible.

ITINERARY

This itinerary is part of a study conducted by Sonya Harvison, current director of the Spotsylvania Museum. Two other studies were used to supplement her work: "HH" indicates the study titled "Historic Homes", and "VHLC" indicates the study conducted by the Virginia Historic Landmark Commission. Both are available for viewing at the Spotsylvania Museum. A map with these sites marked appears at the beginning of the book.

1. ZION CHURCH - Liberty Methodist Class organized November, 1850. Name changed to Zion Methodist Episcopal Church at the start of the Civil War. Located west side Rt. 208 at its intersection with Rt. 608 east. (HH) Church; brick, five course American bond; 1 story; gable roof with lunette; built ca. 1859, late Greek Revival period; additions include late nineteenth-century apse. (VHLC)

2. SNOW HILL - Original structure built ca. 1770. Early owners, Benjamin Alsop, Revolutionary War soldier, and Stapleton Crutchfield III, Clerk of Court 1836-1848. Snow Hill #2 built 1910 by Eustace Gordon. Located east of Rt. 208, north of Po River, 2 miles south of Spotsylvania Court House. (HH)

3. KENMORE (WOODS) - ca. 1830. Home of Dr. Hubbard T. Minor and his wife Malvina Crutchfield. Two-story brick dwelling. Located west of Rt. 208, one mile south of Spotsylvania Court House. (HH) Farmhouse; brick, Flemish bond; 1 1/2 stories; gambrel roof; interior end chimneys; center-hall plan; built late eighteenth century, early Federal period. (VHLC)

4. GREENBRANCH (Delos) - ca. 1833. Built for Oscar Crutchfield, Member, Virginia House of Delegates, 1834-1843; 1850-1851 (Barbara Willis). Located south of Rt. 647, north of Mat River, entrance to private drive approximately 0.5 mile east of intersection of Rts. 738 and 647. (HH) Plantation house; brick, Flemish bond; 2 stories; gable roof; interior end chimneys; side-hall, double-pile plan enlarged to center-hall, double-pile plan; built early nineteenth century, Federal period; additions include numerous alterations. A magnificent example of Federal period plantation architecture. (VHLC)

5. LINDEN HALL (LINDEN, LINDEN FOREST) - ca. 1830. Built for Martha Ann Crutchfield and her husband James Nalle. Located north side Rt. 208, 0.2 mile west of Snell. (HH) Farmhouse; brick, 3 course American bond; 2 stories; gable roof; interior end chimneys; center-hall plan; built early nineteenth century, Federal period; additions include modern frame wing. Linden Hall bears a remarkable similarity to La-Vue both in plain exterior detailing and brickwork. (VHLC)

6. SALEM (SALEM FARM) - Original structure built late eighteenth century; one-and one-half stories, large chimneys on each end. The home of the Rev. Addison M. Lewis. In 1831, home of Rev. John A. Billingsley and his wife Sarah Duerson. Present structure has an addition, duplicating the original structure, joined by a hallway. Located south side of Rt. 608, 3 miles east of intersection of Rts. 608 and 208 on the Ni River. (HH)

7. HICKORY POINT - Original house built by Samuel Alsop prior to 1818; present dwelling believed to have been built ca. 1870-1890. Located north side Rt. 608, two miles east of intersection of Rts. 608 and 208. (HH)

8. RIVERSIDE (RIVERSIDE MILLS, ANDERSON MILL, COVENTRY) - Built prior to Civil War. Inherited in 1904 by Frederick Lee Frazer from the estate of his father, James Lewis Frazer. Property contained the family's grist mill, saw mill and old miller's house. In 1917 a flour mill was added and the name Riverside Flour Mill was used for the first time. Stayed in operation until ca. 1930. None of the old miller's house is in existence. Current structure, 1904. Mills were washed out in the 1941 flood. Located north of the Ni River, northwest of Rt. 608 east, 1.5 miles west of Massaponax Church. (HH)

9. BUNKER HILL - Richard W. Colbert family home from 1863 until 1987 when the descendants of George C. Rawlings, Sr. and Marguerite Colbert, his wife, sold the house and remaining acreage to Otis T. Light. Located west of Rt. 608 at intersection of Rts. 608 and 628. (HH)

10. MASSAPONAX BAPTIST CHURCH - ca. 1788. Served as rest area for both the Union and the Confederate troops; a register of soldiers' names and addresses can still be read on the balcony and stairwell walls. Grant and his generals met in the churchyard following the Battle of Spotsylvania Court House. Located northwest corner of intersection of U.S. Rt. 1 and Rt. 608 east. (HH) Church; brick, stretcher bond; one story; gable roof with pedimented gable-end front; built mid-nineteenth century; additions include modern brick wing. Although the present church dates from the mid-nineteenth century, the congregation was established as early as 1788. (VHLC)

11. BONNIE HOME

12. STIRLING - ca. 1860. Large, brick home built by Taverner Holladay for his brother John Holladay. 1987 home of his great-great-grandson, Carroll C. Hayden. Located north side of Rt. 607, 0.5 mile east of U.S. Rt. 1, on Cropp's Lane. (HH) Plantation house; brick, 5 course American bond; 2 stories; hipped roof; interior end chimneys; center-hall double-pile plan; built ca. 1850, Greek revival. Of particular note on this well-preserved ante-bellum plantation house is the gracefully executed Doric porch. (VHLC)

13. LA VISTA - 1838. Boulware home. Located south side of Rt. 607, 1.6 miles east of U.S. Rt. 1. (HH)

14. WESTWOOD - 1818. Gift from Samuel Alsop to his grandson, William Samuel Chandler. Wing added to house, 1952. 1862 headquarters of General Pickett, CSA. Located north of Ni River on south side of Rt. 607 just before its junction with Rt. 634. (HH)

15. NYLAND - ca. 1850. Built by Joseph Campbell Chandler on gift of land from his grandfather, Samuel Alsop. Joseph was a practicing physician during the Civil War. Located on north side Rt. 607 near Caroline County Line. (HH) Farmhouse; frame with beaded weatherboard; 2 stories; gable roof with 2-story porch; exterior end chimneys, brick, 3 course American bond; center-hall, double-pile plan; built mid-nineteenth century, Greek revival period. Badly deteriorated, Nyland still retains a great deal of its ante-bellum grandeur. Complemented by fine interior woodwork and original exterior detailing, Nyland is worthy of preservation. (VHLC)

16. LA VUE - Bulit 1818 by George Alsop. Well-preserved brick home. Alsop family cemetery (Prospect View) north of house. Located south of Rt. 608 and west of Richmond, Fredericksburg and Potomac Railroad. (HH) Farmhouse; brick, 3 course American bond; 2 stories; hipped roof; interior end chimneys; L plan; built early nineteenth century, Federal period; additions include later brick wing. Despite its large and impressive plan, the exterior detailing of La-Vue is quite plain. (VHLC)

17. ST. JULIEN - ca. 1804. Home of Francis Taliaferro Brooke (1763-1851). Listed in Virginia Landmarks Register and National Register of Historic Places, 1975. Located 6 miles south of Fredericksburg, 0.5 mile west of Rt. 2, 1 mile southwest of intersection of Rts. 2 and 17. (HH) Plantation house; brick, Flemish bond; 2 stories; hipped roof with recessed 2-story porch and pedimented central bay; interior end chimneys; center-hall plan with rear ell; built early eighteenth century, Federal period. With its stone jack arches, recessed central bays and splendid interiors, Saint Julien is one of the finest Federal country houses in Virginia. (VHLC)

18. MARENGO - ca. 1800. A Taliaferro home for 100 years. Traditionally headquarters of Confederate General John H. Hood before the Battle of Fredericksburg. Located approximately 1.2 miles south of intersection of Rts. 2 and 17 at New Post. (HH)

19. NOTTINGHAM - ca. 1790. Home of Gen'l Alexander Spotswood, grandson of Lt. Gov. Alexander Spotswood. Remained in Spotswood family until 1844. Located 6 miles south of Fredericksburg on north side Rt. 17, east side Massaponax Creek, across the creek from Newpost. (HH) Plantation house; brick, Flemish bond; 2 stories; gable roof with pedimented frame gables; interior chimneys; center-hall, double-pile plan; built early nineteenth century, Federal; additions include later 2-story tetrastyle portico. Despite the additions of a portico and frame wing, Nottingham retains much of its original architectural character. (VHLC)

20. BELVIDERE (BELVIDERA) - ca. 1760. Brick, Flemish bond, home of Col. Wm. Daingerfield, Cdr. 7th Regiment of Virginia, during the Revolutionary War. Located on Rappahannock River, off Tidewater Trail (Rt. 17) at Caroline County line. (HH) Plantation house; brick, Flemish bond; 2-1/2 stories; pedimented gable roof with dormer windows; interior end chimneys; built mid-eighteenth century, early Federal style; additions include later brick wings. Well-preserved in a dramatic setting, Belvidere is one of Spotsylvania County's most important historic houses. The Rappahannock River plantation was the home of the Dangerfield family. (VHLC)

21. WESTERN VIEW (MARTIN'S MANOR) - A Samuels family home. Manor Flea Mart, 1987. Located west side Rt. 1, approximately 1 mile north of intersection of Rts. 1 and 608. (HH)

22. BREEZELAND (FAIRVIEW) - ca. 1837. Large brick home, built by Samuel Alsop. (Now in Breezewood subdivision.) Located south of Rt. 208 approximately 0.5 mile east of Rt. 639. (HH) Farmhouse; brick, American bond; 2 stories; gable roof with handsomely detailed cornice; interior end chimneys; built circa 1837, early Greek revival; additions include period Greek Revival 1-story porch with balustrade. With its delicate Greek revival detailing and well-executed brickwork, Breeze Land reflects a high level of craftsmanship of ante-bellum Spotsylvania County. (VHLC)

23. SUNNYSIDE - Part of the Fontaine Maury tract in 1796. Home of Mrs. Beth Barton French in 1860. Civil War dignitaries, including Generals Lee and Jackson, were frequent visitors here. In the 1970s, mansion and dependencies were restored by Sidney L. Shannon, founder of Shannon Airport, Shannon Air Museum and Aviation Library. Also, ancestral home of Jean Wakeman Jones, first woman member of the Spotsylvania County Board of Supervisors. Located northeast of intersection of Rts. 208 and 639. (HH)

24. BLOOMSBURY (BLOOMSBERRY) - ca. 1750. Located west side Rt. 208, 2.5 miles north of Spotsylvania Court House. (HH)

25. ROSEMONT - ca. 1750-1770. Plantation house; two-story frame with weatherboard. A Gayle home since 1848. Located east of Rt. 208, north of Ni River. (HH) Plantation house; frame with weatherboard; 2 stories; gable roof with modillion cornice; exterior end chimneys, brick, Flemish bond; built late eighteenth century, early Federal period; outbuildings include early frame pyramidal roof smokehouse. Rosemount and its outbuildings are in a fine state of preservation. (VHLC)

26. WHIG HILL - ca. 1750. Farm house, frame with weatherboard; headquarters of General Warren during the Battle of Spotsylvania Court House. Located east of Rt. 208, one mile north of Spotsylvania Court House. (HH) Farmhouse; frame with weatherboard; 1 1/2 stories; gambrel roof; interior chimneys, brick; center-hall, ell plan; built late eighteenth century; additions include numerous frame wings and alterations. The name Whig Hill is reportedly derived from several meetings of the Whig party at the house during the eighteenth century. (VHLC)

27. DIXIE - prior to Civil War. A Beverley home, a part of the Whig Hill Estate. Located west of Rt. 208, one mile north of Spotsylvania Court House. (HH)

28. DABNEY FARM - ca. 1840. Three-story, brick dwelling; home of R. C. Dabney, Clerk of Court 1860-1876. Located north side Rt. 208, 0.25 mile east of Spotsylvania Court House. (Included in the Spotsylvania Court House Historic District.) (HH) Farmhouse; brick, Flemish bond facade with American bond rear and end walls; 2 stories; gable roof; interior end chimney; side hall plan; built circa 1840, Greek revival; additions include late nineteenth century frame wing; outbuildings include brick smokehouse and frame center chimney plan kitchen-washhouse. (VHLC)

29. CONFEDERATE CEMETERY - Over 600 Confederate soldiers, representing 10 Confederate states, rest here. Cemetery is operated by the Trustees of the Confederate Memorial Association. Located east side of Rt. 208, 0.25 mile north of Spotsylvania Court House. (Included in the Spotsylvania Court House Historic District.) (HH)

30. OAKLEY - 1817. Built by Samuel Alsop. Owned by the Beals family since 1926. Located west side Rt. 612, north of Corbin Bridge (Po River). (HH) Plantation house; brick, Flemish bond, 2 stories; gable roof with modillion and dentil cornice; semi-exterior end chimneys; side hall, double-pile plan; built early nineteenth century, Federal period; additions include 1 story brick Flemish bond wing with a 3 course American bond end wall. Beautifully restored and maintained, Oakley is one of Spotsylvania's finest examples of Federal architecture. The interior woodwork is unusually elaborate. (VHLC)

31. SHADY GROVE METHODIST CHURCH - Original church built 1841; present building erected 1908. Located north of Rt. 608, at intersection of Rts. 608 and 612. (HH)

32. GRINDSTONE HILL ROAD - Currently Firetower Road. (Runs through grids 30, 43 and 44.) Rt. 612 from Shady Grove Corner to Mastins Corner (junction of Rts. 612 and 606).

32. GRINDSTONE HILL TRACT - 1800. Original 1560 acres owned by Robert Patton and Ann G. Patton, his wife. Appears to have been investment property. Was advertised as "Gold Land For Sale" when it was sold in 1833 to satisfy lien against the remaining 920 acres. Located northwest corner junction of Rts. 612 and 606.

32. GRINDSTONE MINE (HILL MINE) - 1905, possibly earlier. Gold mine, also silver, pyrite, lead and zinc ore potential. Located 0.4 mile north northeast of Rt. 612, 1.35 miles by road east of junction with Rt. 606.

33. GLEN EREDINE SITE AND POWELL CEMETERY - 1853. A part of Leavett's Level built by William H. Mansfield, grandfather of James Roger Mansfield. Cemetery includes graves of 3 Civil War soldiers: James L. Powell, John G. Powell and Robert D. Powell, grandsons of Ptolemy Powell; death dates from 1870. Located south side Rt. 653, 1 mile east of intersection of Rts. 652 and 653. Recently purchased and being restored by the Gabardy family. (HH)

34. WALNUT HILL AND CEMETERY - ca. 1820. Original owner, Jonathan (Nathan) Johnson, II. Home of Mr. and Mrs. Richard Morrow, 1975; currently owned and being restored by ____. Located west side Rt. 652, east of Foremost Run, approximately 0.5 mile north of intersection of Rts. 652 and 653. (HH) Farmhouse; frame with weatherboard; 2 stories; hipped roof; interior end chimneys, brick; center-hall plan with frame ell; built ca. 1860; additions include porch and later wings. Walnut Hill is visually complimented by its interesting doorway and well-preserved interior detailing. (VHLC)

35. MT. HERMON BAPTIST CHURCH - Organized 1812. Located northwest of intersection of Rts. 652 and 719. (HH) Frame with weatherboard; 2 stories; hipped roof; built mid-nineteenth century, Greek revival. This ante-bellum church with its austere detailing reflects the simplicity a country church could assume. (VHLC)

36. PROSPECT HILL AND CEMETERY - ca. 1806. Home of Waller Holladay. Listed on Virginia Landmarks Register May, 1982; listed on National Register of Historic Places October, 1982. Located north side Rt. 612, south of Pamunkey Creek, west of intersection of Rts. 612 and 719. (HH) Plantation house: frame with weatherboard; 2 stories; gable roof with modillion cornice; interior chimneys; center-hall, double-pile plan; built circa 1780, late Georgian; outbuildings include log saddle-back granary and numerous other structures. With its fine collection of early outbuildings Prospect Hill is an interesting example of a late eighteenth century plantation complex. (VHLC)

37. CHERRY GROVE #1 AND CEMETERY - Land grant, 1723. Original home built in 1700s for William Quarles. Site of a Washington-Lafayette conference during the Revolution. Currently owned by the Harris family, 1987. Located south side Rt. 612, north of Lake Anna, east of Rt. 522. (HH) Farmhouse; frame with beaded weatherboard; 2 stories; gable roof with modillion cornice; exterior end chimney, brick, Flemish bond; side hall plan; built ca. 1810, Federal style; additions include later wings; outbuildings include frame smokehouse. Designed as a simple side-hall plan farmhouse. Cherry Grove is distinguished by its period exterior detailing and fine interior paneling. (VHLC)

38. KIRK O'CLIFF PRESBYTERIAN CHURCH - Built 1876 on a cliff on the north bank of the North Anna River, which forms the boundary between the counties of Louisa and Spotsylvania. In 1911, the church was dismantled, relocated and rebuilt at its present location. Located on Rt. 612, 0.4 mile east of intersection of Rts. 612 and 654. (HH) Church; brick, American bond; 1 story, gable roof; built late nineteenth century. This simple church is an unusual example of a small brick Victorian era country church. (VHLC)

39. ANDREWS TAVERN - Original log structure built by John Andrews in 1793; brick dwelling built by Samuel Andrews, 1826; frame addition built and licensed as tavern, 1836; has been used as a store, post office, polling place and militia muster. Placed on Virginia Landmarks Register and National Register of Historic Places, 1976. Owned by Taylor family, 1987. Located east side of Rt. 601, approximately 0.6 mile northwest of intersection of Rts. 601 and 208. (HH) Plantation house and

Ordinary; brick, Flemish bond facade with 3 course American bond rear and end walls; 2 stories; gable roof; semi-interior end chimneys; built early nineteenth century, Federal style; outbuildings include diamond notched log storage building and frame smokehouse. Reputedly built by John Andrews (Samuel), Andrew's Tavern with its beautiful exterior detailing and elaborate Federal period interiors is a well-preserved and well-documented early nineteenth century county landmark. (VHLC)

40. BROOKS STORE (LEACHEY BROOKS) - Early 1900s. Representative architecture of early country store. Located north of intersection of Rts. 601 and 208. (HH) Store; frame with weatherboard; 2 stories; gable roof; built early twentieth century, vernacular; additions include 1-story wing. Situated at a rural crossroads, the Brooks Store is a typical example of the early twentieth-century rural store complex common to Spotsylvania County. (VHLC)

41. BELLE FONTE AND CEMETERY - Original grant 1702; present structure built ca. 1848-1850; believed to have been built on site of original home. Court met here while first courthouse was being built on Rt. 648. DAR marker (Washington-Lewis Chapter) on grave site of Maj. Lewis Holladay, Revolutionary War soldier. Located south side of east Northeast Creek east of Rt. 601, at end of Rt. 665. (HH) Farmhouse: frame; 2 stories; gable roof; exterior end chimneys, brick, 5 course American bond; built mid-nineteenth century, vernacular; outbuildings include late nineteenth century frame barns. (VHLC)

42. LIVINGSTON - Major Lewis Holladay of "Belle Fonte" purchased land in 1803; original house has had many additions. Has been in the Boggs family since the marriage of the Rev. Hugh C. Boggs to Ann Holladay, daughter of Major Lewis Holladay. Current owner Waller Boggs, 1987. Located south on Rt. 713, off Rt. 601, first house on right. (HH) Farmhouse; frame with weatherboard; 2 stories; hipped roof; exterior end chimneys, brick; center-hall, double-pile plan: built mid-nineteenth century; additions include numerous frame wings; outbuildings include pyramidal roofed smokehouse. (VHLC)

43. WALLER'S TAVERN - (Lewiston) Prior to 1805. Located at the intersection of Rts. 601 and 614. (Still standing, 1987.)
    LEWIS STORE POST OFFICE - 1805-1891.
    LEWISTON POST OFFICE - 1891+
    Known as Duke's Store, 1987, unoccupied. (HH)

44. RED HOUSE #1 - ca. 1855. Home of the Capt. Thomas Roderick Dew, III family. (A son, Thomas Welch Dew, was a medical doctor and also Superintendent of Spotsylvania County Public Free Schools, 1905-1907; a daughter, Kate, married Judge Robert Emmett Waller.) The house, a large, frame, vernacular structure has just had a new coat of paint - red! Current owner, Lewis Fielding Luck, 1987. Located east of Rt. 622, approximately 1.0 mile southwest of intersection of Rts. 601 and 622. (HH) Farmhouse, frame with weatherboard; 2 stories; gable roof; exterior end chimney, brick; center-hall plan; built mid-nineteenth century, vernacular. (VHLC)

45. LEVY - Name derived from Leon Levy (b. 1809) and Arabella Moss Levy family. Seated at the intersection of Rts. 622 and 601. Mildred A. Levy married John B. Harris in 1878 and the house (southeast corner of the intersection) became known as the Harris House. The sixth generation, the A. Miller Arritt, III family is currently in residence, 1987. (HH)

46. ASPINWALL AND CEMETERY - Site of Aspinwall Tavern and home of the Charles Young family from 1802-1918; until recently, the home of three generations of the A. Miller Arritt family. Located northwest of intersection of Rts. 605 and 622. (HH)

47. HILLSBOROUGH (HILLS PLANTATION) - Prior to 1844. Wedding gift to Nelson S. Waller and his bride, Mary Hampton DeJarnette, grandparents of the present owner, Judge A. Nelson Waller, 1987. Original house burned in 1948. Located west side Rt. 605, 0.5 mile north of intersection of Rts. 605 and 622. (HH)

48. WILDWOOD AND CEMETERY - Was the home of Judge Robert Emmet Waller (b. Dec. 10, 1846) and his second wife, Kate Dew Waller. The house is standing but uninhabited. The cemetery is fenced, contains inscribed stones and is located on opposite side of Rt. 605. Located west side of Rt. 605, between Rts. 738 and 622, approximately 1.5 miles from Waller's Church. (HH)

49. WALLERS BAPTIST CHURCH - Constituted 1769. Original structure frame; second structure brick, burned after Civil War; present structure erected 1874. Located at intersection of Rts. 738 and 605. (HH) Church; brick, American bond; 1 story; gable roof with frame gables and lunette, and projecting tetrastyle Doric portico; built mid-nineteenth century; Greek revival period. (VHLC)

50. TOWLES MILL - Located on Black Rock Run, west of Rt. 656 and south of Mt. Airy house site. (HH)

51. BLACK ROCK SITE - Original structure prior to 1832; story-and-a-half frame dwelling. Present building story-and-a-half brick dwelling. Has been in Turnley family since 1864. Current owner Robert J. Turnley, 1987. Located south side Rt. 691 (Black Rock Drive), approximately one mile east of intersection of Rts. 208 and 691. (HH)

52. COOL SPRING - Smith/Massey family home. Cemetery established 1857 and is still being used (1987). Current owner Robert A. Massey, 1987. Located east side of Rt. 208, south side Ta River. (HH)

53. POST OAK - (Part of Maple Grove) built by J. F. Z. Billingsley, founder of Travelers Rest Baptist Church (ca. 1900) at Snell. Is being restored by current owner, 1987. Located north side of Rt. 606 at its intersection with Rt. 208 west. (HH)

54. POST OAK FARM - Home and general store of the Arthur Lewis Blanton family in 1912. Store building razed in 1972. Owned by Col. Kerry L. Lane in 1987. Located southwest corner of intersection of Rts. 208 and 606. (HH)

54. POST OAK POST OFFICE - 1880-1883; 1884-1930+ (*Virginia Genealogist*, Vol. 22. no. 4, 1978). Opened February 13, 1883 by John A. B. Gordon, first postmaster (Mansfield - "LocustGrove Pantation"). (Clover Green 1850-1866; 1883-1884.) Located southwest corner of intersection of Rts. 208 and 606. (HH)

55. LOCUST GROVE #1 AND HERNDON-GORDON-MORTON CEMETERY - (23 graves) Death dates: 1871 to 1989. Negro burying ground southeast of residence. Founded ca. 1752 by Edward Herndon. Home of Mansfield family 1904-1982. Home of Roger Mansfield, author of *A History of Early Spotsylvania*, c. 1977. Owner, Wilson Smith, 1987. Located south of Rt. 208, approximately one mile west of intersection of Rts. 648 and 208. (HH)

56. SPOTSYLVANIA COUNTY COURT HOUSE (OLD SITE, 1781-1839) - Court House Lot Marker, dated 1819, is currently being used as a foundation support for the Warren House front porch. Located east of Rt. 648, north of Po river, north of Warren House, 1987. (HH)

57. BLOCK HOUSE SITE - Early fort. Located southwest corner intersection of Rts. 608 and 648. (HH)

58. MILLBROOK - Established ca. 1750. The 1795 home of Betty Washington Lewis (widow of Fielding Lewis). Current owner, Bill Vakos, 1987. Located north side Po River on Rt. 747, off Rt. 608 west. (HH)

ABELL, John H. s/o
Edward S.& Annie
M.Abell age 24 S
farmer POB
St.Mary's Co,Md
POR St.Mary's
Co,Md & **TOMPKINS**,
Eva W. d/o Frank
& Rebecca
M.Tompkins age 24
S POB & POR
Spotsylvania; POM
Ormsby,Caroline
Co 6 Sep 1882
SPMR 4 Sep 1882
SPML

ABELL, John H. s/o
E.S.& A.M.Abell
age 24 S farmer
POB & POR
St.Mary's Co, Md
& **THOMPKINS**, Eva
W. d/o F.&
R.M.Thompkins age
24 S POB & POR
Spotsylvania; POM
Caroline Co 6 Sep
1882 SPMR

ACORS, George s/o
Henry & Sarah
Acors age 23 S
POB & POR
Spotsylvania POC
& **COOK**, Dansy d/o
William & Emily
Cook age 21 S POB
& POR
Spotsylvania POC;
POM Spotsylvania
20 Jun 1900 SPMR

ACORS, J.T. s/o Henry
& Sarah Acors age
21 S laborer POB
& POR
Spotsylvania POC
& **LEWIS**, Mary E.
d/o Virginia
Lewis age 22 S
POB & POR
Spotsylvania POC;
14 Apr 1888 SPMR

ACORS, James s/o H.&
S.Acors age 22 S
laborer POB & POR

Spotsylvania POC
& **JACKSON**, Fannie
d/o N.& Polly
Jackson age 18 S
POB & POR
Spotsylvania POC;
POM Spotsylvania
15 Jun 1897 SPMR

ACORS, John M. &
BROOK, Margaret
E. d/o Granvill
Brook age 15; 8
Jan 1876
SPConsent

ACORS, Mason J. s/o
Mary Acors age 32
S farmer POB &
POR Spotsylvania
& **BROOKS**, Louisa
d/o T.W. & Maria
Brooks age 24 S
POB & POR
Spotsylvania; POM
Spotsylvania 21
Feb 1893 SPMR

ACORS, Robert H. s/o
Henry & Sarah
Acors age 24 S
POB & POR
Spotsylvania POC
& **WEEDON**, M.E.
d/o Beverly &
Rose Weedon age
24 S POB
Spotsylvania POC;
POM Spotsylvania
24 Mar 1883 SPMR

ACORS, Thomas s/o
William & Fanny
Acors age 60 W
farmer POB & POR
Spotsylvania POC
& **LEWIS**,
Georgiana d/o
Sally Lewis age
25 S POB & POR
Spotsylvania POC;
POM Spotsylvania
17 Apr 1887 SPMR

ACRES, J.T. s/o Henry
& Sarah Acres age
34 W farmer POB &
POR Spotsylvania
POC & **WOODWARD**,

Mattie d/o Kate Gibson age 19 S POB & POR Spotsylvania POC; POM Spotsylvania 3 May 1900 SPMR

ACRES, John Minor s/o John & Mary Acres age 23 S farmer POB & POR Spotsylvania & **BROOKE**, Margaret E. d/o Granville & Rebecca Brook age 15 S POB & POR Spotsylvania; POM Spotsylvania 9 Jan 1876 SPMR 8 Jan 1876 SPML

ACRES, Thomas s/o William Acres & F.Fryer age 40 S laborer POB & POR Spotsylvania POC & **BUNDY**, Either L. d/o H.Dotson & C.Bundy age 40 S POB & POR Spotsylvania POC; POM Spotsylvania 21 Sep 1878 SPMR 20 Sep 1878 SPML

ADAMS, Festus S. s/o Robert Adams & Mildred Mason age 19 S farmer POB & POR Orange & **CHILDRESS**, Virginia C. d/o Giles R.Childress & Sarah Patton age 18 S POB Spotsylvania POR Orange; POM Orange 6 Mar 1866 OMR 26 Feb 1866 OML

ADAMS, John Q. s/o Robert Adams & Mildred Mason age 22 S farmer POB & POR Orange & **BROOKING**, Lucy J. d/o Charles R.Brooking & Susan Sanders age 20 S POB & POR Orange; POM Orange 15 Feb 1866 OMR 13 Feb 1866 OML

ADAMS, Robert Jr. & **MASON**, Lucy A.; 12 Nov 1860 OML

ADKINS, Robert s/o Robert & America Adkins age 21 S laborer POB & POR Spotsylvania POC & **JACKSON**, Margaret d/o Thomas & Mary Jackson age 18 S POB & POR Spotsylvania POC; POM Spotsylvania 17 Nov 1881 SPMR 16 Nov 1881 SPML

ALDRIDGE, John R. s/o Wessell & Mary Ann Aldridge age 36 W farmer POB New Castle, Delaware POR Spotsylvania & **DECKER**, Prudence Ann d/o John & Letitia Decker age 30 S POB Warren, New Jersey POR Spotsylvania; POM Spotsylvania 1 Dec 1867 SPMR 30 Nov 1867 SPML

ALEXANDER, Archy s/o Lewis & Martha Alexander age 23 S laboere POB & POR Spotsylvania POC & **STUART**, Malinda d/o Jim & Celey Stuart age 21 S POB Botetourt Co POR Spotsylvania POC; POM Spotsylvania

26 May 1877 SPMR
21 May 1877 SPML
ALEXANDER, Manvil
parents deceased
age 25 W laborer
POB Campbell
Co,Va POR
Spotsylvania POC
& **ROY**, Nelly d/o
Peter & Matilda
Roy age 20 S POB
& POR
Spotsylvania POC;
POM Spotsylvania
29 Oct 1876 SPMR
28 Oct 1876 SPML
ALEXANDER, Peter s/o
Peter & Julia
Alexander age
21y3mo S laborer
POB & POR
Fredericksburg
POC & **CHILDS**,
Sallie d/o Sallie
Childs age 25 S
POB Caroline Co
POR
Fredericksburg
POC; POM
Fredericksburg 26
Jan 1893 FMR 25
Jan 1893 FML
ALLEN, David W. s/o
James Allen &
Alexandria Long
age 36 S farmer
POB Botetout Co
POR Augusta Co &
WALLACE, Martha
A. d/o Jesse
D.Wallace & Ellen
Cochran age 36 S
POB Rockingham Co
POR Orange; POM
Orange C.H. 4 Sep
1863 OMR OML
ALLEN, George s/o
Henry T.&
Margaret Allen
age 21 S farmer
POB & POR
Spotsylvania &
POWELL, Fanny d/o
John M.& Florinda

Powell age 17 S
POB & POR
Spotsylvania; POM
Spotsylvania 12
Oct 1888 SPMR 11
Oct 1888 SPML
ALLEN, Henry Thomas
s/o William & Ann
Allen age 21 S
nothing
particular POB &
POR Spotsylvania
& **BALLARD**,
Margaret d/o
James & Maria
Ballard age 20 S
POB & POR
Spotsylvania; POM
Spotsylvania 19
Apr 1855 SPMR
SPML
ALLEN, J.H.Jr s/o
J.H.& E.A.Allen
age 30 S merchant
POB & POR Essex
Co & **SWIFT**, M.E.
d/o W.T.&
O.A.Swift age 20
S POB
Fredericksburg
POR Spotsylvania;
POM Spotsylvania
19 Nov 1891 SPMR
ALLEN, James s/o
J.Tanner Allen &
Anna Carey age 25
S servant POB &
POR Orange POC &
BRAMHAM, Laura
d/o Giles Bramham
age 22 S POB &
POR Orange POC;
POM Orange 2 Nov
1867 OMR 1 Nov
1867 OML
ALLEN, John F. s/o
John & Almira
Allen age 33 S
teacher POB
Sandisfield, Mass
POR Henry Co,
Alabama & **ATKINS**,
Eliza F. d/o
Joseph & Mary

Atkins age 25 S
POB & POR Orange;
POM Orange 20 Aug
1857 OMR OML
ALLEN, Peter s/o Mary
Allen age 21 S
laborer POB & POR
Spotsylvania POC
& **JOHNSON**, Mary
d/o Dolly
Poindexter age 17
S POB & POR
Spotsylvania; POM
Spotsylvania 23
Aug 1898 SPMR
ALLEN, William L. s/o
J.C.& E.Allen age
23 S farmer POB
Louisa Co POR
Caroline Co &
PENDLETON, Rosa
L. d/o William
M.& A.E.Pendleton
age 20 S POB &
POR Spotsylvania;
POM Massaponax,
Spotsylvania 23
Dec 1880 SPMR 20
Dec 1880 SPML
ALLISON, John William
s/o Robert &
Maria Allison age
20 S spinning POB
Culpeper POR
Orange & **SMITH**,
Jane d/o Harris &
Susan Smith age
21 S POB Stafford
POR Orange; POM
Orange 17 Aug
1854 OMR
ALMOND, Addison S. age
38 S POB
Spotsylvania &
BROOKS, Fanny age
16 S POB
Spotsylvania; POM
Spotsylvania 25
Feb no year. type
of form used from
about 1855
through 1867 SPMR

ALMOND, James & **CLARK**,
Elizabeth; 27 Apr
1854 SPML
ALMOND, Linton V. s/o
M.B.& J.G.Almond
age 48 W clerk
POB & POR
Spotsylvania &
FAULKNER, J.M.
d/o Lewis &
Elizabeth
Faulkner age 50 S
POB & POR
Spotsylvania; POM
Spotsylvania 16
Jan 1891 SPMR
ALMOND, Oscar s/o
Henry & Josie
Almond age 32 S
farmer POB & POR
Spotsylvania &
SOUTHERLIN,
Elizabeth d/o
William & Sarah
Southerlin age 20
S POB & POR
Orange; POM
Orange 2 Dec 1858
OMR 26 Nov 1858
OML
ALRICH, Samuel W. s/o
John R.& J.(?)
Alrich age 24 S
farmer POB
Delaware POR
Spotsylvania &
LANDRUM, Annie F.
d/o John W.&
M.L.Landrum age
23 S POB & POR
Spotsylvania; POM
Spotsylvania 12
Nov 1879 SPMR 10
Nov 1879 SPML
ALSOP, A.A. s/o J.M.&
S.J.Alsop age 43
S farmer POB &
POR Spotsylvania
& **PRITCHETT**, A.B.
d/o P.B.&
A.E.Pritchett age
37 S POB & POR
Spotsylvania; POM

Spotsylvania 21
Apr 1897 SPMR
ALSOP, Archy s/o Henry
& Mary Alsop age
26 S laborer POB
& POR Caroline Co
POC & **TEMPLE**,
Ella d/o Q.L. &
M.Temple age 19 S
POB & POR
Spotsylvania POC;
POM Spotsylvania
12 Oct 1876 SPMR
10 Oct 1876 SPML
ALSOP, Armstead s/o
Henry & Mary Ann
Alsop age 23 S
farmer POB & POR
Spotsylvania POC
& **MOSS**, Lucy Ann
d/o Richard &
Mariah Moss age
22 S POB & POR
Spotsylvania POC;
POM Spotsylvania
21 Dec 1882 SPMR
SPML
ALSOP, Armstead s/o
Henry & Mary
A.Alsop age 23 S
farmer POB & POR
Spotsylvania POC
& **MOSS**, Lucy A.
d/o Richard &
Maria Moss age 22
S POB & POR
Spotsylvania POC;
POM Spotsylvania
21 Dec 1882 SPMR
ALSOP, Arthur M. s/o
John S.& A.Alsop
age 24 S farmer
POB & POR
Spotsylvania &
HARRIS, Susan M.
d/o J.C.&
L.A.Harris age 22
S POB Delaware
POR Spotsylvania;
POM Bethel Ch,
Spotsylvania 26
Sep 1880 SPMR 25
Sep 1880 SPML

ALSOP, Aubrey s/o
Henry & Mary Ann
Alsop age 23 S
laborer POB & POR
Spotsylvania &
THORNTON, Nelly
d/o Fazao & Jenny
Thornton age 21 S
POB Caroline Co
POR Spotsylvania;
POM Spotsylvania
23 Dec 1875 SPMR
21 Dec 1875 SPML
ALSOP, James S. s/o
J.M.& S.J.Alsop
age 30 S farmer
POB & POR
Spotsylvania &
JONES, Lelia E.
d/o W.L.& Betty
Jones age 19 S
POB & POR
Spotsylvania; POM
Spotsylvania 6
Feb 1889 SPMR
ALSOP, John F. s/o
John S.&
D.A.Alsop age 26
S farmer POB &
POR Spotsylvania
& **TALLEY**, Mollie
E. d/o L.M.&
M.A.Talley age 23
S POB & POR
Spotsylvania; POM
Spotsylvania 11
Jun 1876 SPMR 9
Jun 1876 SPML
ALSOP, John s/o Janus
A.(or James A.) &
Sue M.Alsop age
28 S POB & POR
Spotsylvania &
CHARTTERS, F.H.
d/o H.H.&
E.W.Chartters age
21 S POB
Middlesex Co POR
Spotsylvania; POM
Spotsylvania 5
May 1889 SPMR
ALSOP, Thomas J. s/o
F.I. & E. Alsop
age 31 S farmer

POB Spotsylvania
& **STEPHENS**, A.
d/o E. Stephens
(father)age 19 S
POB Spotsylvania;
27 Oct 1855 SPML
ALSOP, Thomas s/o Josh
& E.V.Alsop age
27 POB Caroline
Co POR
Spotsylvania POC
& **COLEMAN**, L.L.
d/o G.& Sally
Coleman age 21 S
POB Washington
D.C. POR
Spotsylvania POC;
POM Spotsylvania
28 Dec 1891 SPMR
ALSOP, William J. s/o
J.M.& Susan
J.Alsop age 27 S
machinist POB &
POR Spotsylvania
& **OSWALD**, Annie
A. d/o William &
Annie Oswald age
28 S POB
Baltimore, Md POR
Spotsylvania; POM
Tabernacle Ch,
Spotsylvania 27
Aug 1890 SPMR
ALSOP, William J. s/o
Willis & Amanda
Alsop age 28 SW
laborer POB
Caroline Co POR
Spotsylvania POC
& **COLEMAN**, Lettie
d/o Buckner &
Polly Coleman age
21 S POB & POR
Spotsylvania POC;
POM Spotsylvania
21 Nov 1889 SPMR
ALTENBURG, David F.
s/o David W.&
Salinda
S.Altenburg age
20 S farmer POB
Tuscola Co,
Michigan POR
Spotsylvania &

PULLIAM, Cora V.
d/o Thomas C.&
Harriet L.Pulliam
age 19 S POB &
POR Spotsylvania;
POM Zion M.E.Ch
S.,Spotsylvania 7
Dec 1886 SPMR 3
Dec 1886 SPML
ALTENBURG, David F.
s/o David W.&
Salinda
S.Altenburg age
20 S POB Michigan
POR Spotsylvania
& **PULLIAM**, Cora
V. d/o Thomas C.&
Harriet L.Pulliam
age 17 S POB &
POR Spotsylvania;
POM Spotsylvania
7 Dec 1886 SPMR 3
Dec 1886 SPML
ALTENBURG, David W.
s/o James P.&
Julia Altenburg
age 63 W farmer
POB Monroe Co,
N.Y. POR
Spotsylvania &
WILSON, Laura J.
d/o A.H.& Sarah
Wilson age 36 S
POB & POR
Spotsylvania; POM
Spotsylvania 25
Jan 1894 SPMR 23
Jan 1894 SPML
AMISS, William L. s/o
Redwood L. & Mary
E. Amiss of
Culpeper Co.,Va.
age 25 POR
Fredericksburg &
FLEMING, Nellie
E. d/o David E. &
Alice Fleming of
Fredericksburg
age 27 POR
Fredericksburg;
POM
Fredericksburg 1
Jun 1892 TCF

AMOS, Jackson s/o
Estes Amos & Mary
Darnell age 35 S
miller POB & POR
Madison Co &
DARNELL, Frances
d/o Fielding
Darnell age 34 W
POB Madison Co
POR Orange; POM
Orange 23 Jul
1865 OMR 14 Jul
1865 OML
ANDERSON, C.Harper s/o
M.S.&
S.S.Anderson age
23 S farmer POB &
POR Albemarle Co
& SCOTT, Sallie
T.S. d/o James
M.& Sarah Scott
age 24 S POB &
POR Spotsylvania;
POM Bel
Air,Spotsylvania
15 Feb 1872 SPMR
14 Feb 1872 SPML
ANDERSON, Edmond s/o
Edmund & Keziah
Anderson age 51 W
laborer POB & POR
Caroline Co POC &
JOHNSON, Nicey
d/o David &
Patience Johnson
(POR Caroline
Co)age 28 S POB &
POR Spotsylvania
POC; POM Caroline
Co 8 Nov 1883
SPMR 5 Nob 1883
SPML
ANDERSON, Fountain s/o
Elijah & Charlott
Anderson age 24 S
farming POB & POR
Spotsylvania POC
& CARTER, Amanda
d/o Frank (dec)&
Betsy (dec)Carter
age 21 S POB &
POR Spotsylvania
POC; POM
Spotsylvania 6
Apr 1874 SPMR
SPML
ANDERSON, H.W. s/o
R.C.& F.Anderson
age 39 W
physician POB
Prince Edward Co
POR Covington &
SMITH, A.O. d/o
Z.W.& O.V.Smith
age 22 S POB &
POR Spotsylvania;
POM Caroline Co
14 Aug 1895 SPMR
ANDERSON, Henry
Watkins s/o
Robert C.& Fannie
Anderson age 39 W
physician POB
Prince Edward Co,
Va POR Covington,
Va & SMITH, Anne
Olivia d/o
Z.W.Smith &
Olivia V.Smith
age 22 S POB &
POR Spotsylvania;
POM County Line
Ch, Caroline Co
14 Aug 1895
Caroline MR 12
Aug 1895 SPML
ANDERSON, James s/o
John & Sarah
Anderson age 21 S
laborer POB & POR
Spotsylvania POC
& COLES, Jennie
d/o Alex & Sarah
Coles age 18 S
POB & POR
Spotsylvania POC;
POM Spotsylvania
4 Nov 1897 SPMR
ANDERSON, James W. s/o
Henry Anderson &
Martha Gaines age
26 S printer POB
Franklin CO,Ga
POR Covington, Ga
& BICKERS,
Henrietta S. d/o
William H.Bickers
& Elizabeth

7

Hawkins age 23 S
POB & POR Orange;
POM Orange 21 Jan
1866 OMR 19 Jan
1866 OML
ANDERSON, John K. s/o
J.& K.Anderson
age 26 S laborer
POB & POR
Spotsylvania POC
& **TAYLOR**, Willie
Ann d/o Cyrus &
M.Taylor age 23 S
POB & POR
Spotsylvania; POM
Spotsylvania 23
Feb 1879 SPMR 21
Feb 1879 SPML
ANDERSON, Jordon s/o
Isaac & Katy
Anderson age 23 S
farmer POB & POR
Spotsylvania POC
& **HART**, Melvina
d/o" M.d"(?) &
Fanny Hart age 20
S POB & POR
Spotsylvania POC;
POM Spotsylvania
31 Dec 1868 SPMR
21 Dec 1868 SPML
ANDERSON, Robert s/o
Isaac & Katy
Anderson age 26 S
farmer POB & POR
Spotsylvania POC
& **BOXLEY**,
Hardinia d/o
Isaac & Mary
Boxley age 18 S
POB & POR
Spotsylvania; POM
Spotsylvania 7
Jan 1875 SPMR 5
Jan 1875 SPML
ANDREWS, B.T. s/o John
L. & M.E.Andrews
age 36 S farmer
POB & POR
Spotsylvania &
DABNEY, M.E. d/o
R.C.& M.M.Dabney
age 29 S POB &
POR Spotsylvania;

POM Spotsylvania
27 Aug 1889 SPMR
ANDREWS, Buford T. s/o
John L.&
M.E.Andrews age
40 D farmer POB
Orange POR
Spotsylvania &
SCOTT, Irene D.
d/o W.T.&
E.M.Scott age 20
S POB & POR
Spotsylvania; POM
Goshen Ch,
Spotsylvania 15
Nov 1893 SPMR
SPML
ANDREWS, C.R. s/o John
L.& M.E.Andrews
age 32 W farmer
POB & POR
Spotsylvania &
HARRIS, Bertie K.
d/o T.A. &
M.E.Harris age 21
S POB & POR
Spotsylvania; POM
Zion M.E.Ch,
Spotsylvania 19
Dec 1889 SPMR
ANDREWS, Edwin s/o
Edward G. &
H.Andrews age 38
S farmer POB &
POR Essex Co &
FERNEYHOUGH,
Sallie M. d/o
John &
E.Ferneyhough age
25 S POB & POR
Spotsylvania; POM
Sligo,
Spotsylvania 25
Nov 1873 SPMR 24
Nov 1873 SPML
ANDREWS, George T. s/o
James & Mary
J.V.Andrews age
20 S farmer POB &
POR Essex Co &
CHESLEY, Frances
E. d/o William
S.& Mary
A.Chesley age 22

S POB
Fredericksburg
POR Spotsylvania;
POM Spotsylvania
25 Nov 1873 SPMR
24 Nov 1873 SPML
ANTHONY, James s/o Kit
& Jane Anthony
age 30 W farmer
POB Goochland Co
POR Spotsylvania
POC & **ROLLINS**,
Frances d/o Sam &
Amy Coleman age
33 W POB & POR
Spotsylvania POC;
POM Cherry Grove,
Spotsylvania 23
Dec 1886 SPMR
SPML
ANTHONY, James s/o Kit
& Jane Anthony
age 30 W farmer
POB Goochland Co
POR Spotsylvania
POC & **ROLLINS**,
Frances d/o Sam &
Annie Coleman age
33 W POB & POR
Spotsylvania POC;
POM Cherry
Grove,Spotsylvani
a 23 Dec 1886
SPMR SPML
APPERSON, A. s/o Eli &
Mary Apperson age
26 S farmer POB
Spotsylvania POR
Orange & **WEBB**,
Annie E. d/o
J.A.& S.B.Webb
age 19 S POB
Orange POR
Spotsylvania; POM
Spotsylvania 13
Jun 1900 SPMR
APPERSON, Eli s/o
Alfred & Malinda
Apperson age 24 S
farmer POB & POR
Orange &
DAVENPORT, Mary
Catherine d/o
William & Sarah
Davenport age 19
S POB Albemarle
Co POR
Spotsylvania; POM
Spotsylvania 24
Dec 1873 SPMR 22
Dec 1873 SPML
APPLER, Jacob E. s/o
David & Rachel
Appler age 44 W
clerk POB
Washington D.C.&
CHANCELLOR, Ann
E. d/o George &
Ann Chancellor
age 32 S POB
Spotsylvania; 12
Aug 1856 SPML
ARMISTEAD, Adam s/o
Adam & F.
Armistead age 30
S POB Stafford
POR Spotsylvania
POC & **THORNTON**,
Grace d/o James &
Julia Thornton
age 22 S POB &
POR Spotsylvania
POC; 20 Dec 1888
SPMR
ARMISTEAD, E.L. s/o
Frances Armistead
age 27 S farmer
POB Stafford POR
Spotsylvania POC
& **ROSS**, Hattie
d/o Archie &
Agnes Ross age 18
S POB & POR
Spotsylvania POC;
POM Spotsylvania
6 Feb 1890 SPMR
ARMISTEAD, P. s/o L.&
F.Armistead age
27 S laborer POB
& POR
Spotsylvania POC
& **LEWIS**,
Elizabeth d/o
Caesar & Rachel
Lewis age 27 S
POB & POR
Spotsylvania 30
Sep 1897 SPMR

ASHBY, Charles William s/o William Ashby & Lucy Strauther age 43 S physician POB Rappahannock Co POR Rappahannock Co & **DICKINSON**, Sally E. d/o William Dickinson & J.Buckner age 25 S POB Caroline Co POR Caroline Co; POM Spotsylvania 27 Apr 1855 SPMR SPML

ASHBY, William W. s/o James & S.J.Ashby age 28 S merchant POB Washington D.C. POR Spotsylvania & **DABNEY**, Clara d/o Robert C.& M.M.Dabney age 21 S POB & POR Spotsylvania; POM Spotsylvania C.H. 7 Mar 1877 SPMR SPML

ASHTON, John T. s/o Charles H. & Julia A. Ashton age 25 S farmer POB King George Co POR King George Co & **WIATT**, Hannah d/o F.J. & E.W. Wiatt age 24 S POB & POR Spotsylvania; POM Spotsylvania 17 Nov 1859 SPMR SPML

ASHTON, John T. s/o Charles M.& Julia A.Ashton age 25 S farmer POB & POR King George Co & **WIATT**, Hannah d/o F.J.& E.W.Wiatt age 24 S POB & POR Spotsylvania;

POM Spotsylvania 17 Nov 1859 SPMR SPML

ATKINS, Edward s/o Robert & America Atkins age 21 S farmer POB & POR Spotsylvania POC & **TYLER**, Sarah d/o Abby Rodgers age 19 S POB & POR Spotsylvania POC; POM Spring Hill, Spotsylvania 21 Jan 1875 SPMR 13 Jan 1875 SPML

ATKINS, J.B. s/o Frank & E.Atkins age 22 S POB & POR Spotsylvania & **HAREFIELD**, Nellie d/o Thad & Martha Harefield age 17 S POB & POR Spotsylvania; POM Spotsylvania 21 Mar 1899 SPMR

ATKINS, James E. s/o Louisa Atkins age 24 S laborer POB & POR Spotsylvania POC & **CARTER**, Annie d/o A.& America Carter age 20 S POB & POR Spotsylvania POC; POM Spotsylvania 29 Dec 1897 SPMR

ATKINS, James R. s/o Charles D.& Mary Atkins age 25 S farmer POB & POR Orange & **WHITLOCK**, Mary F. d/o George W.& Jane C.Whitlock age 22 S POB Orange POR Spotsylvania; POM Spotsylvania 3 Oct 1875 SPMR 2 Oct 1875 SPML

ATKINS, Richard M. s/o
William L.& Mary
F.Atkins age 27 S
farmer POB & POR
Spotsylvanioa &
LUCK, Mary E. d/o
Alfred &
Catherine Luck
age 27 S POB &
POR Spotsylvania;
POM Spotsylvania
20 Jan 1886 SPMR
12 Jan 1886 SPML

ATKINS, Robert F. s/o
William B. &
Eliza Atkins age
29 S farmer POB &
POR Spotsylvania
& **PAYNE**, Emma C.
d/o James & Mary
Payne age 21 S
POB & POR
Spotsylvania; POM
Spotsylvania 12
Apr 1868 SPMR 9
Apr 1868 SPML

ATKINS, Robert F. s/o
William B.& Eliza
Atkins age 29 S
POB & POR
Spotsylvania &
PAYNE, Emma C.
d/o James & Mary
Payne age 21 S
POB & POR
Spotsylvania; POM
Spotsylvania 12
Apr 1868 SPMR 9
Apr 1868 SPML

ATKINS, William E. s/o
Frank & Emma
Atkins age 23 S
POB & POR
Spotsylvania &
BROOKS, Hattie V.
d/o William H.&
Sophie Brooks age
16 S POB & POR
Spotsylvania; POM
Spotsylvania 11
Dec 1894 SPMR

ATKINS, William L. s/o
W.B. & E. Atkins
age 35 S mechanic
POB Spotsylvania
& **LUCK**, M.F. d/o
T. & E. Luck age
33 S POB
Spotsylvania; POM
Spotsylvania 29
Oct 1855 SPMR
SPML

ATKINS, William W. POR
Spotsylvania &
HARRISS, Martha
C. d/o Lucy
A.Harriss POR
Spotsylvania; 5
Aug 1871
SPConsent

ATKINS, William W. s/o
William L.& Sarah
Atkins age 23 S
mechanic POB &
POR Spotsylvania
& **HARRIS**, Martha
A. d/o James O.&
Lucy A.Harris age
17 S POB & POR
Spotsylvania; POM
Spotsylvania 6
Aug 1871 SPMR 4
Aug 1871 SPML

ATKINSON, E.L. s/o
L.B.& Elizabeth
J.Atkinson age 32
W POB & POR
Louisa Co &
WHEELER, Betty A.
d/o James A.& Ann
E.Wheeler age 33
S POB & POR
Spotsylvania; POM
Spotsylvania 21
Nov 1886 SPMR 9
Nov 1886 SPML

ATKINSON, E.L. s/o
L.B.& Elizabeth
J.Atkinson age 32
W farmer POB &
POR Louisa Co &
WHEELER, Betty A.
d/o James A. &
Ann E.Wheeler age
33 S POB & POR
Spotsylvania; POM
Spotsylvania 21

AUSTIN, Samuel G. s/o
William Austin &
Susan Thompson
age 29 S farmer
POB & POR Orange
& **BOND**, Lucy A.
d/o Joseph Bond &
Mildred Whitlock
age 24 S POB
Louisa Co POR
Orange; POM
Orange 23 Feb
1863 OMR 21 Feb
1863 OML
AUSTIN, William H. s/o
Charles & Ellen
Austin age 33 S
farmer POB & POR
Spotsylvania POC
& **BROOKS**, Mary E.
d/o Sarah West
age 23 S POB &
POR Spotsylvania
POC; POM
Spotsylvania 19
Feb 1889 SPMR
BAGGETT, John W. s/o
Samuel I.Baggett
Jr.& Addie
B.Baggett age 22
S farmer POB &
POR Spotsylvania
& **WILKERSON**,
Maggie d/o W.A.&
Leah A. Wilkerson
age 22 S POB &
POR Spotsylvania;
POM
Fredericksburg 19
Dec 1900 FMR 18
Dec 1900 SPML
BAIERS, John s/o Jacob
& Rosa Baiers age
23 S turner POB
Pennsylvania POR
Spotsylvania &
CROUSE, Mary d/o
Felix & Sofa
Crouse age 26 S
POB Germany POR
Spotsylvania; POM
Spotsylvania C.H.

29 Jun 1882 SPMR
SPML
BAILEY, C.B. s/o C.&
J.P.Bailey age 25
S farmer POB &
POR Spotsylvania
& **FRAZER**, E.J.
d/o James L.&
C.M.Frazer age 22
S POB & POR
Spotsylvania; POM
Spotsylvania 7
Oct 1886 SPMR
BAILEY, Samuel &
PURKS, Martha;
POM Orange 3 Feb
1853 OMR 1 Feb
1853 OML
BAINES, John Robert
s/o Robert &
Emily Baines age
28 S bookkeeper
POB Oakham,
England POR
Baltimore, Md &
NEWTON, Edith d/o
Thomas G.&
Frances Newton
age 23 S POB
Liverpool,
England POR
Spotsylvania; POM
Goshen Ch,
Spotsylvania 8
Nov 1889 SPMR
BAKER, A.U. s/o
E.G.A.& Margaret
Baker age 27 S
mechanic POB
Baltimore,Md POR
Virginia &
MARTIN, Amanda
d/o L.& Eliza
Martin age 23 S
POB Fauquier Co
POR Spotsylvania;
POM Spotsylvania
4 Dec 1864 SPMR 3
Dec 1864 SPML
BAKER, A.U. s/o E.G.A.
& Margarett Baker
age 27 S mechanic
POB Baltimore, Md
POR Virginia &

MARTIN, Amanda d/o L. & Eliza Martin age 23 S POB Fauquire Co POR Spotsylvania; POM Spotsylvania 4 Dec 1864 SPMR 3 Dec 1864 SPML
BAKER, Oscar A. s/o Aaron & Kesiah Baker age 27 S railraod man POB Minnesota POR Washington D.C. & **JETT**, Emma d/o John T. & Sarah F. Jett age 22 S POB & POR Spotsylvania; POM Spotsylvania 27 Dec 1892 SPMR 26 Dec 1892 SPML
BAKER, Thomas S. s/o William & Lucinda Baker age 31 S farmer POB & POR Louisa Co & **DAVIS**, Maria Jane d/o William J. & Elizabeth Davis S POB & POR Orange; POM Orange 25 May 1858 OMR 21 May 1858 OML
BAKER, William J. s/o B.W. & Mattie Baker age 20 S POB Louisa Co POR Spotsylvania & **SAMUEL**, L.M. d/o A.J. & M.E. Samuel age 15 S POB Essex Co POR Spotsylvania; POM Spotsylvania 29 Dec 1884 SPMR
BALL, James C. s/o James C. & Elizabeth Ball age 23 S farmer POB & POR Spotsylvania & **PEYTON**, Mattie A.E. d/o Walter & Elizabeth Peyton age 23 S POB & POR Spotsylvania; POM Spotsylvania 5 May 1867 SPMR 2 May 1867 SPML
BALL, James C. W farmer & **HUMPHRIES**, Jane S POB Spotsylvania; POM Spotsylvania 20 Dec 1853 SPMR SPML
BALL, James W. & **PEYTON**, Mattie A.E. age 21; May 1867 SPConsent
BALL, Willie s/o Thomas & Martha Ball age 25 S farmer POB King & Queen Co POR Hanover Co & **HICKS**, Annie d/o John R. & M.C. Hicks age 24 S POB & POR Spotsylvania; POM Spotsylvania 22 Jan 1896 SPMR SPML
BALLARD, A. s/o Thomas & Mary Ballard age 28 S farmer POB & POR Spotsylvania & **LEITCH**, Ida A. d/o William & Virginia Leitch age 21 S POB & POR Spotsylvania; POM Spotsylvania 16 Oct 1881 SPMR
BALLARD, Arthur s/o Thomas & Mary Ballard age 28 S farmer POB & POR Spotsylvania & **LEITCH**, Ida A. d/o William Leitch & Virginia Berry age 21 S POB & POR Spotsylvania; POM

Spotsylvania 16 Oct 1881 SPMR 14 Oct 1881 SPML
BALLARD, Elias W. s/o Edward & Lora A. Ballard age 20 S farmer POB Louisa Co POR Orange & **CLARK**, Mildred d/o William & Lucy Clark age 30 S POB & POR Orange; POM Orange 22 Apr 1856 OMR 14 Apr 1856 OML
BALLARD, James A. s/o F.T.& V.W. Ballard age 23 S farmer POB & POR Stafford & **SMITH**, Addie E. d/o Charles C.& E.C. Smith age 25 S POB Essex Co POR Spotsylvania; POM Spotsylvania 5 Jun 1877 SPMR 31 May 1877 SPML
BALLARD, William F. & **CHILES**, M.E. POR Spotsylvania; POM Spotsylvania 3 Oct 1853 SPMR & SPML
BALLARD, William S. s/o Edwin Ballard & Lora Ann Harris age 21 S farmer POB & POR Orange & **SCHYLER**, Mary E. d/o William Schyler & Mary A. Sovill age 25 S POB & POR Orange; POM Orange 16 Oct 1866 OMR 8 Oct 1866 OML
BANK, Marshall s/o Edgar & Mary Banks age 21 S laborer POB & POR Spotsylvanuia POC & **LEWIS**, Ester d/o A.& M. Lewis age 21 S POB & POR Spotsylvania POC; POM Spotsylvania 28 Dec 1876 SPMR SPML
BANK, Marshel & **LEWIS**, Easter d/o Margaret Lewis; 27 Dec 1876 SPConsent
BANKHEAD, Charles L. s/o Charles S.& Mary Ann Bankhead age 22 S farmer POB Albemarle Co POR Orange &
BANKHEAD, Mary C. d/o William & Dorothea Bankhead age 23 S POB Caroline Co POR Orange; POM Orange 26 Sep 1855 OMR 25 Sep 1855 OML
BANKHEAD, Edgar s/o H.& L. Bankhead age 25 S laborer POB & POR Spotsylvania POC & **WASHINGTON**, M.E. d/o Lewis & Lucy Washington age 18 S POB & POR Spotsylvania POC; POM Spotsylvania C.H. 7 Dec 1886 SPMR
BANKS, Buck s/o James & Mary Banks age 27 S laborer POB & POR Caroline Co POC & **WILKINS**, Mollie d/o William & Lucinda Wilkins age 26 S POB & POR Spotsylvania POC; POM Spotsylvania 19 Jan 1899 SPMR 18 Jan 1899 SPML

BANKS, Charles s/o Z.&
M.Quarles age 27
S laborer POB &
POR Spotsylvania
POC & **LEWIS**,
Frances s/o
Willis & Jennie
Taylor age 39 W
POB & POR
Spotsylvania; POM
Cherry Grove,
Spotsylvania 6
Mar 1879 SPMR 5
Mar 1879 SPML
BANKS, Frederick s/o
Frank Turner &
Mary Quarles age
21 S POB & POR
Spotsylvania POC
& **LAUSON**. Fanny
d/o Charles &
Rosetta Gordon
age 21 S POB &
POR Spotsylvania;
POM Spotsylvania
19 Feb 1871 SPMR
18 Feb 1871 SPML
BANKS, Robert s/o Mary
Banks age 23 S
laborer POB & POR
Spotsylvania POC
& **LIPSCOMB**,
Amanda d/o Susan
Lipscomb age 19 S
POB & POR
Spotsylvania POC;
POM Spotsylvania
8 Aug 1889 SPMR 7
Aug 1889 SPML
BANKS, William s/o S.&
M.E.Banks age 25
S laborer POB &
POR Spotsylvania
POC & **JONES**,
Jennie d/o Rich.
Jones age 25 S
POB & POR
Spotsylvania POC;
POM Spotsylvania
2 Dec 1886 SPMR
BAPTIST, E.G. s/o
Edward & Eliza
J.C.Baptist age
41 W minister POB
Powhatan Co POR
Maringo Co,
Alabama &
DUERSON, Sarah A.
d/o Henry & Sarah
Duerson age 29 S
POB & POR
Spotsylvania; POM
Spotsylvania 11
Nov 1869 SPMR 8
Nov 1869 SPML
BAPTIST, E.G. s/o Ed.
& C.C.Baptist age
28 S minister POB
Powhatan Co POR
Spotsylvania &
DUERSON, Maria E.
d/o James &
C.A.Duerson age
19 S POB & POR
Spotsylvania; POM
Spotsylvania 13
Jan 1857 SPMR
SPML
BARBOUR, Philip D. POR
Kentucky &
NEWMAN, Fanny B.
d/o James Newman;
POM Orange 11 Mar
1852 OMR 8 Mar
1852 OML
BARKS, Oliver s/o Mike
& America Barks
age 21 S laborer
POB & POR
Spotsylvania POC
& **COLEMAN**, Jane
d/o Lindsay &
Jane Coleman age
21 S POB & POR
Spotsylvania POC;
POM Spotsylvania
13 Feb 1873 SPMR
11 Feb 1873 SPML
BARNES, William M. age
22 S farmer POB
Beaver Co, Pa POR
Spotsylvania &
MOORE, Catherine
d/o Joseph & Mary
Moore age 16 S
POB Beaver Co, Pa
POR Spotsylvania;

POM Spotsylvania
21 Oct 1883 SPMR
BARNETT, James s/o
John & Rebecca
Barnett age 31 S
miner POB England
POR Spotsylvania
& **LEWIS**, Nannie
d/o William &
Huldah Lewis age
26 S POB & POR
Spotsylvania; POM
M.E.Ch,
Fredericksburg 30
Apr 1866 FMR SPML
BARNETT, John & **LEWIS**,
H.E. POB
Spotsylvania; POM
Spotsylvania 3
Oct 1853 SPMR
BARTLESON, Edward S.
s/o J.W.& Susan
R.Bartleson age
24 S milling POB
Bucks Co,Pa POR
Spotsylvania &
PULLIAM, Annie C.
d/o John J.&
Melissa A.Pulliam
age 20 S POB &
POR Spotsylvania;
POM Spotsylvania
5 Jun 1889 SPMR 4
Jun 1889 SPML
BATTAILE, B.A. s/o
Alfred & Mary
Battaile age 36 S
saddler POB
Orange Co POR
Orange Co &
GRAVES, Rosa L.
d/o Colby & Jane
Graves age 33 S
POB & POR
Spotsylvania; POM
Spotsylvania 15
Dec 1864 SPMR 10
Dec 1864 SPML
BATTAILE, B.A. s/o
Alfred & Mary
Battaile age 36 S
saddler POB & POR
Orange & **GRAVES**,
Rosa L. d/o Colby
& Jane Graves age
33 S POB & POR
Spotsylvania; POM
Spotsylvania 15
Dec 1864 SPMR 10
Dec 1864 SPML
BATTAILE, James R. s/o
Richard Battaile
& Mary Wright age
28 S saddler POB
& POR Orange &
NEWMAN, Jane E.
d/o Morris
D.Newman & Mary
A.Tatum age 21 S
POB Madison Co
POR Orange; POM
Orange 27 Jul
1865 OMR 25 Jul
1865 OML
BATTAILE, Lawrence s/o
Lucy Hopkins age
30 S farmer POB
Caroline Co POR
Spotsylvania POC
& **LOMAX**, Maria
d/o Washington &
Betsy Lomax age
24 S POB & POR
Spotsylvania POC;
POM Spotsylvania
22 Feb 1872 SPMR
16 Feb 1872 SPML
BAXTER, Jacob s/o
Charles & Ann E.
Baxter age 24 S
farmer POB & POR
Spotsylvania &
SULLIVAN, Emily
F. d/o W.F.& Ann
Sullivan age 19 S
POB & POR
Spotsylvania; POM
Spotsylvania 24
Dec 1885 SPMR
BAXTER, Robert s/o
Charles & Ann
Eliza Baxter age
28 S farmer POB &
POR Spotsylvania
& **MORRIS**,
Margaret d/o Mary
Morris age 16 S
POB & POR

Spotsylvania; POM
Spotsylvania C.H.
5 Jun 1887 SPMR
BEADLES, R.B. s/o John
& N.Beadles age
26 S minister POB
King William Co
POR Spotsylvania
& **HOLLADAY**, R.R.
d/o W.&
K.Holladay age 25
S POB & POR
Spotsylvania; POM
Spotsylvania 27
Oct 1858 SPMR
SPML
BEALE, John G. s/o
John G.Beale &
Eliza Diggs age
22 S farmer POB &
POR Fauquier Co &
GORDON, Susan V.
d/o Reuben
L.Gordon & Eliza
Beale age 20 S
POB Albemarle Co
POR Orange; POM
Orange 27 Nov
1867 OMR 18 Nov
1867 OML
BEALE, Nathaniel J.
s/o Charles &
Mary Beale age 26
S farmer POB
Orange POR
Gordonsville &
SIBERT, Diana R.
d/o Robert J.&
Elizabeth Sibert
age 19 S POB
Shenandoah POR
Gordonsville; POM
Orange 28 Oct
1858 OMR 27 Oct
1858 OML
BEALS, James D. s/o
D.L.& C.A.Beals
age 24 S stone
mason POB & POR
Loudon Co &
HEISLOP, Laura
d/o James A.&
D.Heislop age 17
S POB & POR

Spotsylvania; POM
Spotsylvania 18
Dec 1878 SPMR 17
Dec 1878 SPML
BEAZLEY, C.L. s/o John
G.& Betty Beazley
age 23 S farmer
POB Caroline Co
POR Hanover Co &
WILKERSON, Mary
d/o Thomas J.&
C.A.Wilkerson age
20 S POB & POR
Spotsylvania; POM
Spotsylvania 16
Oct 1878 SPMR 14
Oct 1878 SPML
BEAZLEY, Henry T. s/o
Duerson &
C.Beazley age 31
S plasterer POB &
POR Spotsylvania
& **BURRUSS**, Emma
L. d/o W.L.&
Martha Burruss
age 20 S POB
Caroline Co POR
Spotsylvania; POM
Spotsylvania 12
Mar 1883 SPMR
BEAZLEY, James A. &
MORTON, Sallie
A.; 6 Mar 1860
OML
BEAZLEY, John A. s/o
John & Laura
Beazley age 46 W
farmer POB Essex
Co POR Middlesex
Co & **HOLLADAY**,
Jemima P. d/o
William & Kitty
Holladay age 33 S
POB & POR
Spotsylvania; POM
Rose Hill,
Spotsylvania 4
Dec 1872 SPMR 3
Dec 1872 SPML
BEAZLEY, John s/o W.&
M.Beazley age 30
W farmer POB
Caroline Co POR
Spotsylvania &

LOVING, Jane d/o
M.& S.Loving age
18 S POB Caroline
Co POR Louisa Co;
POM Spotsylvania
1 Mar 1858 SPMR
BEAZLEY, Melvin T. s/o
Luther S.& Cenia
W.Beazley age 22
S machinist POB
Caroline Co POR
Richmond,Va &
CARTER, Annie E.
d/o George W.&
Mollie M.Beazley
age 19 S POB
Caroline Co POR
Spotsylvania; POM
Spotsylvania 30
Mar 1899 SPMR
SPML
BEAZLEY, William H.
s/o William &
M.A.Beazley age
24 S laborer POB
& POR
Spotsylvania POC
& COLES, Louisa
d/o F.Coles age
22 S POB Caroline
Co POR
Spotsylvania POC;
POM Mt.Zion Ch,
Spotsylvania 25
Dec 1878 SPMR
SPML
BECKHAM, John S. s/o
William & Sallie
Beckham age 25 W
farmer POB Orange
& ELLEY, Ann d/o
Ed & Sarah Elley
age 23 S POB
Spotsylvania; POM
Spotsylvania 14
Jul 1851 SPMR
SPML
BELL, Elijah H. &
LUMSDEN, Jane
Elizabeth; 17 Dec
1855 SPML
BELL, Granville s/o
John B.Bell &
Mary Brock age 28

S farmer POB &
POR Orange &
WRIGHT, Sally Ann
d/o Dabney Wright
& Jane M.Estes
age 26 POB Louisa
Co POR Orange;
POM Orange 7 Mar
1867 OMR 4 Mar
1867 OML
BELL, James A. s/o H.&
J.Bell age 21 S
farmer POB & POR
Spotsylvania &
MARTIN, Parthenia
d/o L.& G.(or
S.)Martin age 27
S POB Orange POR
Spotsylvania; POM
Bell's Cross
Roads,
Spotsylvania 19
Feb 1879 SPMR 15
Feb 1879 SPML
BELL, James R. s/o
Henry C.& Betsy
Ann Bell age 19 S
school teacher
POB & POR Orange
& PAYNE, Mary E.
d/o Charles &
Mary Payne age 18
S POB & POR
Orange; POM
Orange 5 Feb 1857
OMR 27 Jan 1857
OML
BELL, Nelson H. s/o
John H.&
Elizabeth Bell
age 30 S merchant
POB Augusta Co
POR Baltimore,Md
& CAVE, Hannah
Jane d/o Richard
& Maria Cave age
26 S POB & POR
Orange; POM
St.Thomas Ch,
Orange 10 Oct
1854 OMR
BELL, Orville s/o John
B.& Mary Bell age
20 S farmer POR

Orange & **ESTES**, Mary T. d/o James & Elizabeth B.Estes age 17 S POR Orange; POM Orange 27 Dec 1858 OMR OML

BELL, Robert H. s/o James & Catherine Bell age 21 S shoemaker POB & POR Spotsylvania & **PROCTOR**, M.E. d/o William & E.Proctor age 22 S POB & POR Spotsylvania; POM Spotsylvania 6 Aug 1857 SPMR SPML

BELL, Thomas s/o Ralph Bell & Dorcus age 23 S farmer POB Orange POR Adams Co, Pa POC & **WRIGHT**, Amanda age 21 S POB & POR Orange POC; POM Orange C.H.22 Nov 1865 OMR OML

BELL, William L. s/o James & Catherine P.Bell age 21 S POB Spotsylvania & **MORGAN**, Mary E. d/o Henry & Mildred J.Morgan age 17 S POB Caroline Co; POM Spotsylvania 20 Sep 1853 SPMR SPML

BELLAMY, James & **LONG**, Jane F.; 14 Feb 1852 OML

BETTELHEIM, A.S.(Dr.) s/o Samuel & Eve Bettleheim age 38 W rabbi POB Hungary, Austria POR Richmond,Va & **ISEMAN**, Levinia d/o Isaac & Charlotte Iseman age 27 S POB Nash Co, N.C.POR Spotsylvania; POM Spotsylvania 12 Feb 1873 SPMR 5 Feb 1873 SPML

BEVERLEY, Charles s/o Thornton & Malinda Beverley age 22 S laborer POB & POR Spotsylvania POC & **JACKSON**, Edna d/o Andrew & Daphney Jackson age 23 S POB & POR Spotsylvania POC; POM Spotsylvania 6 Jul 1892 SPMR SPML

BEVERLEY, William s/o Thornton & Melinda Beverley age 21 S laborer POB & POR Spotsylvania POC & **REDMAN**, Mary d/o Harriet Redman POB & POR Spotsylvania POC; POM Spotsylvania C.H.17 Oct 1895 SPMR SPML

BEVERLY, F.C. s/o M.K.& J.Beverly age 33 S farmer POB Caroline Co POR Spotsylvania & **GAYLE**, M.A. d/o J.P. & F.Gayle age 19 S POB Caroline Co POR Spotsylvania; POM Spotsylvania 22 Jul 1857 SPML

BEVERLY, William s/o George & Julia Beverley age 37 S laborer POB & POR Caroline Co POC & **WORMLEY**, Hannah d/o Moses & Mary Wormley age 22 S

POB & POR
Spotsylvania POC;
POM Spotsylvania
18 Feb 1892 SPMR
BIBB, A.B. s/o E.&
M.F.Bibb age 26 S
farmer POB Louisa
Co POR Louisa Co
& **MASSEY**, S.E.
d/o B.& J.Massey
age 21 S POB &
POR Spotsylvania;
POM Spotsylvania
26 Apr 1860 SPML
BICKERS, Samuel s/o
Thomas & Judy
Bickers age 61 W
farm laborer POB
& POR Louisa Co
POC & **DICKINSON**,
Nelly age 39 S
POB & POR Orange
POC; POM 27 Dec
1866 OMR 24 Dec
1866 OML
BILLINGSLEY, J.P. s/o
J.P. &
J.D.Billingsley
age 22 S merchant
POB Spotsylvania
& **GORDON**, B.S.
d/o J.A. &
J.S.Gordon age 20
S POB
Spotsylvania; POM
Spotsylvania 6
Nov 1853 SPMR
SPML
BILLINGSLEY, Joseph F.
s/o Joseph A.&
Mary
M.Billingsley age
60 W minister of
the gospel POB
Spotsylvania POR
Westmoreland Co &
BOXLEY, Judith D.
d/o John & Mary
Lipscomb age 59 W
POB & POR
Spotsylvania; POM
Spotsylvania 14
Jul 1899 SPMR 8
Apr 1899 SPML

BIRD, Lemuel L. s/o
Emeline Bird age
26 S POB & POR
Spotsylvania POC
& **ACORS**, Addie
d/o Thomas &
Melinda Acors age
20 S POB & POR
Spotsylvania POC;
POM Spotsylvania
21 Dec 1885 SPMR
BISCOE, Thomas Lawson
s/o William E.&
Catharine Biscoe
age 20 S farmer
POB & POR
Spotsylvania &
JONES, Virginia
A. d/o Eli M. &
Mary Elizabeth
Jones age 16 S
POB & POR
Spotsylvania; POM
Spotsylvania 29
Dec 1870 SPMR 26
Dec 1870 SPML
BISCOE, William E.&
WRIGHT, Susan R.;
27 Nov 1854 OML
BLACK, Benjamin F. s/o
Jerry & Martha
Black age 38 W
laborer POB
Augusta Co POR
Spotsylvania POC
& **WILLIAMS**,
Nannie d/o
Caroline Williams
age 34 W POB &
POR Spotsylvania
POC; POM New Hope
Ch, Spotsylvania
9 Oct 1898 SPMR
14 Sep 1898 SPML
BLACK, Joseph s/o
Andrew & Sarah
Black age 24 S
miller POB & POR
Spotsylvania &
BEAZLEY, Nannie
d/o Davison &
Clementina
Beazley age 19 S
POB & POR

Spotsylvania; POM
Spotsylvania 5
Feb 1874 SPMR 2
Feb 1874 SPML
BLACK, Lee s/o Andrew
& S.E.Black age
24 S farmer POB &
POR Sptsylvania &
DODD, Willie d/o
William Dodd &
Julia Hogan age
22 S POB & POR
Spotsylvania; POM
Spotsylvania 5
Dec 1886 SPMR
BLACKLEY, George W.
s/o George D. &
Sarah Blackley
age 23 S farmer
POB Richmond Co
POR Spotsylvania
& **SOUTHWORTH**,
Annie E. d/o
James Southworth
age 18 S POB &
POR Spotsylvania;
POM Spotsylvania
15 Nov 1866 SPMR
12 Nov 1866 SPML
BLACKMAN, Taliaferro
s/o E.&
W.Blackman age 23
S laborer POB &
POR Spotsylvania
POC & **DORRON**,
Maria d/o R.&
P.Dorran age 22 S
POB & POR
Spotsylvania POC;
POM Spotsylvania
12 Aug 1880 SPMR
SPML
BLACKMAN, Thornton s/o
E.& W.Blackman
age 25 S laborer
POB Fauquier Co
POR Spotsylvania
POC & **DERSON**,
Georgeanna d/o
Richmond &
P.Derson age 23 S
POB & POR
Spotsylvania POC;
POM Spotsylvania

1 Oct 1876 SPMR
16 Sep 1876 SPML
BLACKWELL, Francis
E.s/o James D.&
Emma Blackwell
age 43 S farmer
POB & POR
Fauquier Co &
SMITH, Bessie
R.H. d/o Robert &
Mary Smith age 38
S POB Fauquier Co
POR Spotsylvania;
POM
Fredericksburg 16
Oct 1895 FMR 15
Oct 1895 SPML
BLANK, William P.s/o
Robert Blank &
Amanda Smithson
age 34 S merchant
POB Campbell Co
POR Gordonsville
& **PARROTT**, Sallie
A. d/o Samuel
H.Parrott & Mary
Hartsook age 24 S
POB Madison Co
POR Orange; POM
Orange 21 Dec
1865 OMR 18 Dec
1865 OML
BLANKENBAKER, John E.
s/o John A. &
Harriet
A.Blankenbaker
age 21 S farmer
POB Madison Co
POR Spotsylvania
& **CLORE**, Frances
d/o William H.&
Margaret A.Clore
age 18 S POB
Madison Co POR
Spotsylvania; POM
Spotsylvania 28
Dec 1893 SPMR 27
Dec 1893 SPML
BLANTON, John W. s/o
James W.& Emaline
Blanton age 35 S
railraod employee
POB Caroline Co
POR Spotsylvania

& **BULLOCK**,
Alberta d/o B.B.
& Mollie Bullock
age 32 S POB &
POR Spotsylvania;
POM Spotsylvania
26 Apr 1899 SPMR
22 Apr 1899 SPML
BLANTON, Richard A.
s/o John T.&
A.E.Blanton age
31 S farmer POB &
POR Caroline Co &
DURRETT, Kate B.
d/o E.V.&
M.L.Durrett age
21 S POB Louisa
Co POR
Spotsylvania; POM
Spotsylvania 12
Dec 1877 SPMR 5
Dec 1877 SPML
BLAYDES, R.C. s/o
H.F.& M.E.Blaydes
farmer POB & POR
Spotsylvania &
WILSON, Cary Lee
d/o W.L.&
S.L.Wilson age 22
S POB & POR
Spotsylvania; POM
St.Clair Hotel,
Richmond,Va 22
Oct 1884 SPMR 15
Oct 1884 SPML
BLAYDES, R.Coleman s/o
H.F.& M.E.Blaydes
age 22 S farmer
POB & POR
Spotsylvania &
WILSON, Ora
Washington d/o
W.S.& S.S.Wilson
age 17 S POB &
POR Spotsylvania;
POM Green Branch,
Spotsylvania 15
Dec 1875 SPMR 13
Dec 1875 SPML
BLEDSOE, Benjamin F.
s/o John Bledsoe
& Margaret Perry
age 25 W farmer
POB Culpeper Co

POR Orange &
DAVIS, Harriet E.
d/o John Davis &
Lucinda M.Lyle
age 18 S POB
Tennessee POR
Orange; POM
Orange 11 Apr
1861 OMR 10 Apr
1861 OML
BLEDSOE, Franklin s/o
John & Margaret
Bledsoe age 20 S
farmer POB
Culpeper POR
Orange & **PROCTOR**,
Madaline d/o
Thomas & Frances
Proctor age 22 S
POB & POR Orange;
POM Orange 17 Aug
1856 OMR 14 Aug
1856 OML
BLEDSOE, John T. s/o
Howard Bledsoe &
Julia Yager age
49 W tailor POB
Madison Co POR
Orange &
THOMPSON, Amanda
C. d/o Samuel
S.Thompson & Lucy
A,M.Snell age 24
S POB Davidson
Co,Tennessee POR
Orange; POM
Orange 11 Mar
1863 OMR 9 Mar
1863 OML
BLEDSOE, Moses G. s/o
Moses & Sidney
Bledsoe age 24 S
carpenter POB &
POR Orange &
SANDERS, Mary C.
d/o Hansford &
Mary V.Sanders
age 25 S POB &
POR Orange; POM
Orange 18 Jan
1859 OMR 17 Jan
1859 OML
BLEDSOE, William J. &
SOMMERVILLE, Jane

E.; 7 Dec 1857
OML
BOGGS, William s/o
J.S.Williams &
Nicey Boggs age
25 S laborer POB
& POR
Spotsylvania POC
& **ELLIS**, Mary d/o
George & Jane
Ellis age 24 S
POB & POR
Spotsylvania POC;
POM Spotsylvania
22 Mar 1900 SPMR
SPML
BOLANDER, Charles J.
s/o C.G.&
M.A.Bolander age
42 S farmer POB
New York City POR
Spotsylvania &
FAULCONER, Annie
E. d/o W.&
K.A.Faulconer age
23 S POB & POR
Spotsylvania; POM
Spotsylvania 3
Jan 1878 SPMR 26
Dec 1877 SPML
BOLLING, Lawrence T.
s/o Thornton &
Elizabeth Bolling
age 30 S farmer
POB & POR
Spotsylvania &
TAPP, Sarah E.
d/o Vincent &
Catherine Tapp
age 25 S POB &
POR Spotsylvania;
POM
Fredericksburg 19
Dec 1868 FMR 17
Dec 1868 SPML
BOLLS, Franklin s/o
William Bolls &
Elizabeth Lebow
age 24 S farmer
POB Cleveland Co,
Tennessee POR
Union Co,
Tennessee & **SEE**,
Lucy Ellen d/o

John H.See &
Frances Hughes
age 17 S POB &
POR Orange; POM
Orange 29 Apr
1864 OMR 28 Apr
1864 OML
BOND, Joseph W. &
GROOM, Virginia
Ann; 8 May 1858
OML
BOND, Thomas W. &
KINGER, Virginia
W.; POM Orange 6
Mar 1851 OMR 4
Mar 1851 OML
BOON, Shepherd s/o
Calvin &
Henrietta Boon
age 22 S laborer
POB & POR
Spotsylvania POC
& **ELLEY**,
Saphronia d/o
Sam.& Margaret
Elley age 21 S
POB & POR
Spotsylvania POC;
POM Spotsylvania
31 Dec 1895 SPMR
SPML
BOONE, Calvin s/o
Allen & Willie
Boone age 25 S
farmer POB
Southampton Co,Va
POR Spotsylvania
POC ("born free")
& **SHEPHERD**,
Henrietta d/o
Gilbert &
Margaret Shepherd
age 15 S POB &
POR Spotsylvania
POC; POM
Spotsylvania 26
Dec 1865 SPMR 22
Dec 1865 SPML
BOOTEN, R.Sinclair s/o
Richard C.& Lucy
Booten age 28 S
farmer POB & POR
Madison Co &
WILLIAMS, Mildred

P. d/o Lewis B.&
Mary Williams age
21 S POB & POR
Orange; POM
Orange 6 Dec 1860
OMR OML
BOSTON, James N. s/o
William B.Boston
& Sarah Powell
age 22 S farmer
POB & POR Orange
& **BRAGG**, Mary Y.
d/o Joseph Bragg
& Sarah
F.Broughan age 17
S POB Albemarle
Co POR Orange;
POM Orange 11 Jul
1867 OMR 10 Jul
1867 OML
BOSWELL, John s/o John
& Margaret
Boswell age 23 S
laborer POB & POR
Spotsylvania POC
& **WASHINGTON**,
Mary d/o Jarrett
& Patsy
Washington age 25
S POB & POR
Spotsylvania POC;
POM New Hope
Baptist Ch 26 Dec
1899 SPMR SPML
BOUGHAN, Nathaniel J.
s/o John Boughan
& Polly Snelson
age 44 S
carpenter POB &
POR Louisa Co &
McMULLEN, Ann B.
d/o William
B.Boston & Sarah
Powell age 28 W
POB & POR Orange;
POM Orange 28 Feb
1867 OMR 25 Feb
1867 OML
BOULWARE, Richard S.
s/o Ewell
Boulware & Mary
R.Raglon age 63 W
farmer POB Louisa
Co POR Orange &

TOWELLS, Julia
Ann d/o Thomas
Towells &
Catherine
Stubblefield age
47 S POB
Spotsylvania POR
Orange; POM
Orange 30 Sep
1862 OMR 29 Sep
1862 OML
BOUSE (or Boase),
Simon s/o James
Bouse & Eliza
Yaron age 21 S
miner POB England
POR Orange &
SANDERS, Virginia
d/o Nathaniel &
Ann Sanders age
21 S POB & POR
Orange; POM
Orange 31 Dec
1867 OMR 27 Dec
1867 OML
BOUTWRIGHT, John L.
s/o John
H.Boutwright &
Mary E. Lord (or
Sorel)age 21 S
lieutenant in
regular
Confederate Army
POB & POR
Columbia, South
Carolina &
TALIAFERRO, Annie
P. d/o Edmund
T.Taliaferro &
Octavia
H.Robertson age
19 S POB & POR
Orange; POM
Orange C.H.25 Aug
1863 OMR OML
BOWERING, A.B. s/o
Benjamin &
Lucinda Bowering
age 50 W
commissioner of
revenue POB
Patterson, New
Jersey POR
Fredericksburg &

JONES, Maggie A.
d/o A.B.& E.R.
Jones age 22 S
POB & POR
Spotsylvania; POM
Salem Ch,
Spotsylvania 18
Oct 1893 SPMR 16
Oct 1893 SPML
BOWERING, Andrew B.
s/o Benjamin &
Lucinda Bowering
age 57 W comm.of
revenue POB
Patterson N.J.
POR
Fredericksburg &
JONES, Annie
Laurie d/o Andrew
B.& Ellen R.Jones
age 30 S POB &
POR Spotsylvania;
POM Salem Ch 25
Oct 1899 SPMR 23
Oct 1899 SPML
BOWIE, A. Dr. &
TURNLEY, Sarah M.
(of age) 27 Apr
1865 Meadow Farm
SPConsent
BOWIE, A. s/o Dr.S.W.&
Julia R.Bowie age
34 W physician
POB Edgefield
C.H., S.C. POR
Sounds Co,
Alabama &
TURNLEY, Sarah M.
d/o Edmund & Mary
Turnley age 26 S
POB & POR
Spotsylvania; POM
Spotsylvania 30
Apr 1865 SPMR 28
Apr 1865 SPML
BOWLER, George W. &
SAUNDERS, Sarah
J. age over 21
POR Orange; 20
Feb 1854 OML
BOWLER, William H. s/o
George W.& Sarah
J.Bowler age 22 S
farmer POB Orange

Co POR Orange Co
& **MASSEY**, Lillie
R. d/o A.B.Mastin
age 16 S POB &
POR Spotsylvania;
POM Spotsylvania
22 Jun 1882 SPMR
17 Jun 1882 SPML
BOWLER, William H. s/o
G.W.& S.J.Bowler
age 22 S farmer
POB Orange POR
Spotsylvania &
MASSEY, Lellis R.
d/o A.B.Mastin
age 16 S POB &
POR Spotsylvania;
POM Spotsylvania
22 Jun 1882 SPMR
BOWLING, Arthur s/o
Thornton &
Elizabeth Bowling
age 22 S POB &
POR Spotsylvania
& **SATTERWHITE**,
Mary Ann d/o Hugh
& Lucinda
Satterwhite age
25 S POB Caroline
Co POR
Spotsylvania; POM
Spotsylvania 24
Dec 1868 SPMR 23
Dec 1868 SPML
BOWLING, E.V. s/o
L.T.& Sarah
E.Bowling age 26
S laborer POB &
POR Spotsylvania
& **WHARTON**, Mary
F. d/o Milton &
Mary Wharton age
19 S POB & POR
Spotsylvania; POM
Spotsylvania 9
Mary 1898 SPMR
SPML
BOWLING, John Dominick
s/o John &
C.J.Bowling age
25 S farmer POB &
POR Prince George
Co, Md & **NALLE**,
Mildred Wallace

d/o Edmund P.&
Mildred S.Wallace
age 26 S POR
Spotsylvania; POM
Catholic Ch
Fredericksburg 12
Jun 1894 FMR SPML
BOWLING, John F. s/o
Silas & ELizabeth
Bowling age 23 S
farmer POB & POR
Spotsylvania &
POWELL, Mary Ann
d/o Thornton &
Elizabeth Powell
age 22 S POB &
POR Spotsylvania;
POM Spotsylvania
14 Apr 1870 SPMR
11 Apr 1870 SPML

BOWLING, R.W. s/o R.&
E. Bowling age 22
S farmer POB &
POR Spotsylvania
& JETT, C.A. d/o
P.& C.Jett age 22
S POB Stafford
POR Spotsylvania;
POM Spotsylvania
19 Feb 1861 SPML
BOWMAN, L.A. s/o H.D.&
J.Bowman age 23 S
railroad POB
Carolien Co POR
Spotsylvania &
MANN, W.M. d/o
E.T.& A.E.Mann
age 23 S POB
Hanover Co POR
Spotsylvania; POM
Spotsylvania 1
Aug 1887 SPMR
BOXLEY, Isaac G. s/o
George & Drisilla
Boxley age 78 W
farmer POB Louisa
Co POR
Spotsylvania &
LIPSCOMB, Judy D.
d/o John & Mary
Lipscomb age 41 S
POB & POR
Spotsylvania; POM

Spotsylvania 10
Nov 1880 SPMR 1
Nov 1880 SPML
BOXLEY, James age 22 S
POB & POR
Spotsylvania POC
& COLEMAN, Louisa
age 23 S POB &
POR Spotsylvania
POC; POM
Tolville, Louisa
Co 26 Dec 1877
SPMR 3 Dec 1877
SPML
BOXLEY, Patterson s/o
Pat & Amy Boxley
age 26 S merchant
POB & POR
Spotsylvania POC
& LEWIS, Lucy d/o
Rich & M.Lewis
age 22 S POB &
POR Spotsylvania
POC; POM
Spotsylvania
C.H.26 Dec 1878
SPMR SPML
BOXLEY, Ralph &
CRUCHFIELD, Ellen
d/o Harriet
Cruchfield age
22; 22 Feb 1877
SPConsent
BOXLEY, Ralph s/o
Isaac & Matilda
Boxley age 22 S
laborer POB & POR
Spotsylvania POC
& CRUTCHFIELD,
Ellen d/o Peter &
Harriet
Crutchfield age
22 S POB Orange
POR Spotsylvania
POC; POM Branch
Fork Ch,
Spotsylvania 24
Feb 1877 SPMR 23
Feb 1877 SPML
BOYD, C.A. s/o
Alexander & Betsy
E.Boyd age 22 S
farmer POB
Sullivan Co, N.Y.

POR Spotsylvania
& **FILE**, Delia A.
d/o John H.&
C.A.File age 19 S
POB New York City
POR Spotsylvania;
POM Spotsylvania
14 Nov 1872 SPMR
SPML

BOYKIN, Robert
Virginius s/o
Robert M.Boykin &
Sarah V.B.Young
age 31 S formerly
ch.clk naval
store Gosport
navy yard & capt.
A.C.of C.S.A.POB
Isle of Wight Co
POR Portsmouth,Va
& **CHAPMAN**, Emma
d/o John
M.Chapman & Susan
Cole age 20 S POB
& POR Orange; POM
Orange C.H. 25
Feb 1864 OMR OML

BRADLEY, Braxton S.
s/o William H.&
Lucy E.Bradley
age 28 S farmer
POB & POR
Spotsylvania &
OLIVER, Rosa d/o
Chester &
M.Virginia Oliver
age 23 S POB &
POR Spotsylvania;
27 Aug 1900 SPML

BRADLEY, Edwin B. s/o
William & Nelly
Bradley age 46 W
merchant POB
Madison Co &
TALIAFERRO, Lucy
W. d/o Hay &
Milly Taliaferro
age 44 S POB
Orange; POM
Orange 8 Sep 1859
OMR OML

BRADLEY, W.H. s/o
Thornton H.&
Frances Bradley

age 28 S mechanic
POB Caroline Co
POR Spotsylvania
& **CARTER**, Lou E.
d/o Metzi &
Ab.Carter age 21
S POB Caroline Co
POR Spotsylvania;
POM Spotsylvania
28 Dec 1869 SPMR
21 Dec 1869 SPML

BRADLEY, William s/o
Richard Bradley &
Sarah Lloyd age
26 S farmer POB
Bedford Co POR
Orange &
BATTAILE,
Elizabath B. d/o
Mary Battaile age
19 S POB & POR
Orange; POM
Orange 9 May 1865
OMR 8 May 1865
OML

BRADSHAW, Alexander &
LEE, Willieann;
17 Nov 1860 OML

BRAGG, Joseph M. s/o
Joseph Bragg &
Sarah F.Boughan
age 22 S farmer
POB & POR Orange
& **BOSTON**,
Clementine V. d/o
William B.Boston
& Sarah Powell
age 20 S POB &
POR Orange; POM
Orange 28 Feb
1867 OMR 25 Feb
1867 OML

BRANCH, James C. s/o
John J.& Virginia
Branch age 29 S
farmer POB
Occonee Co,
Georgia POR
Georgia &
RAWLINGS, Edmonia
F. d/o Alfred &
Judith A.Rawlings
age 32 S POB &
POR Spotsylvania;

POM Spotsylvania
4 Feb 1891 SPMR 2
Feb 1891 SPML
BRANCH, S.C. s/o J.J.&
V.Branch age 25 S
farmer POB & POR
Georgeia &
RAWLINGS, Clara
L. d/o A.&
J.A.Rawlings age
25 S POB & POR
Spotsylvania; POM
Ellengolan,
Spotsylvania 13
Oct 1880 SPMR 12
Oct 1880 SPML
BRANCH, Walker s/o
Nelson Branch &
Malinda Ward age
26 W blacksmith
POB Culpeper Co
POR Orange POC &
BOWLER, Ellen d/o
Addison & Winney
Bowler age 21 S
POB & POR Orange
POC; POM Orange 3
Oct 1867 OMR 28
Sep 1867 OML
BRANHAM, John H. &
DADE, Ann W. d/o
Albert G.Dade;
POM Orange 7 Feb
1851 OMR 4 Feb
1851 OML
BRAXTON, Carter M. s/o
Carter M.Braxton
& Elizabeth Mayo
age 28 S civil
engineer POB
Norfolk,Va POR
Fredericksburg &
HUME, Fannie P.
d/o David Hume &
Fannie Dade age
26 S POB & POR
Orange ; POM
Orange 16 Feb
1865 OMR OML
BRAXTON, Dallas s/o
Baptist Freeman &
Ellen Braxton age
22 S laborer POB
& POR

Spotsylvania &
CATLETT, Lydia
d/o Emily Catlett
age 22 S POB &
POR Spotsylvania;
POM Spotsylvania
19 Dec 1875 SPMR
16 Dec 1875 SPML
BRAXTON, William s/o
William & Mary
Braxton age 21 S
laborer POB
Henrico Co POR
Spotsylvania POC
& **WOOLFOLK**, Milly
d/o Reuben &
E.Woolfolk age 21
S POB & POR
Spotsylvania POC;
POM Spotsylvania
26 Dec 1878 SPMR
23 Dec 1878 SPML
BRENT, George Lee s/o
William Brent
Jr.& Winifred
B.Lee age 37 S
lawyer POB
Fairfax Co POR
Richmond,Va &
JOHNSON, Betsy S.
d/o Benjamin
V.Johnson &
Amanda Duke age
18 S POB & POR
Orange; POM
Montebello,
Orange 11 Jan
1865 OMR 9 Jan
1865 OML
BRIGGS, Henderson s/o
L.& R.Briggs age
24 W laborer POB
& POR
Spotsylvania POC
& **HENDERSON**, Mary
d/o S.& P.Alsop
age 27 W POB &
POR Spotsylvania
POC; POM
Spotsylvania 24
Jan 1880 SPMR 21
Jan 1880 SPML
BRIGHTWELL, John D.Jr.
s/o John

D.Brightwell Sr.
& Drucilla
Pulliam age 35 S
farmer POB
Spotsylvania POR
Orange & **COOPER**,
Malvina D. d/o
Owen Cooper &
Jane Humphries
age 32 S POB &
POR Orange; POM
Orange 21 Mar
1867 OMR 20 Mar
1867 OML

BRISCOE, William D.
s/o L.John &
Sarah D.Briscoe
age 34 S farmer
POB & POR
Jefferson Co,Va &
GOODLOE, Evie d/o
George P.& Mary
E.Goodloe age 18
S POB & POR
Spotsylvania; POM
Spotsylvania 27
Nov 1866 SPMR 24
Nov 1866 SPML

BRISTOW, J.B. s/o
J.S.& L.Bristow
age 24 S minister
POB Madison Co
POR Middlesex Co
& **RAWLINGS**,A.E.
d/o J.R &
A.E.Rawlings age
21 S POB Amherst
Co POR
Spotsylvania; POM
Spotsylvania 19
Sep 1861 SPMR

BRISTOW, Lewis S. s/o
Lewis S.& Frances
Bristow age 40 W
farmer POB & POR
Middlesex Co &
DECKER, Mary A.
age 36 S POR
Spotsylvania; POM
Gravel Hill,
Spotsylvania 1
Nov 1877 SPMR 24
Oct 1877 SPML

BROADDUS, James H. s/o
Thomas &
Catherine
Broaddus age 27 S
laborer POB & POR
Spotsylvania POC
& **WHITE**, Winnie
B. d/o Peter &
Sarah White age
17 S POB & POR
Spotsylvania POC;
POM Spotsylvania
24 Dec 1891 SPMR
23 Dec 1891 SPML

BROADDUS, James J. s/o
G.W.&
L.R.Broaddus age
28 S farmer POB &
POR Caroline Co &
MANSFIELD, Louise
F. d/o William
H.& Cordelia
Mansfield age 25
S POB & POR
Spotsylvania; POM
Spotsylvania 17
Oct 1894 SPMR 16
Oct 1894 SPML

BROADDUS, John E. s/o
M.W. & E.Broaddus
age 21 S farmer
POB Caroline Co
POR Spotsylvania
& **GAYLE**, B.M. d/o
J.P. & F.Gayle
age 22 S POB
Caroline Co POR
Spotsylvania; POM
Spotsylvania 23
Mar 1858 SPML
SPMR

BROADDUS, Pleasant s/o
John H.&
C.Broaddus age 24
S POB & POR
Spotsylvania POC
& **LEWIS**, Susan
d/o A.& M.Lewis
age 24 S POB &
POR Spotsylvania
POC; POM New Hope
Ch, Spotsylvania
30 May 1878 SPMR
29 May 1878 SPML

BROADDUS, William S
POC & **WILLIS**,
Rosa age 21 S
POC; 3 Dec 1877
SPML

BROADDUS, William S.
s/o Pleasant &
Sarah Broaddus
age 32 S POB &
POR Spotsylvania
POC & **MOSS**, Mary
L. d/o Kellis &
Dena Moss age 22
S POB & POR
Spotsylvania 29
Dec 1898 SPMR 28
Dec 1898 SPML

BROADDUS, Willis s/o
Andrew & Agnes
Broaddus age 28 S
farmer POB Louisa
Co POR Orange POC
& **WEEDON**, Rosa
d/o Beverley &
Rosa Weedon age
23 S POB & POR
Spotsylvania POC;
POM Spotsylvania
1 Oct 1896 SPMR
28 Sep 1896 SPML

BROCK, Ja.H. s/o John
& Mary Brock age
48 S farmer POB &
POR Spotsylvania
& **LEWIS**, Virginia
A. d/o James &
E.Lewis age 35 S
POB & POR
Spotsylvania; POM
Spotsylvania 31
Dec 1861 SPMR

BROCK, Robert S. s/o
John C. &
Elizabeth Brock
age 25 S
carpenter POB &
POR Hanover Co &
DAVIS, Margaret
R. d/o William
J. & Elizabeth
Davis age 21 POB
Orange POR
Gordonsville,
Orange Co; POM
Orange 13 Apr
1854 OMR 12 Apr
1854 OML

BROCK, Soloman s/o
Nathaniel H.&
Polly Brock age
56 S POB & POR
Spotsylvania POC
& **POINDEXTER**,
Louisa d/o
Alexander & Maria
Poindexter age 30
S POB Orange POR
Spotsylvania; POM
Spotsylvania C.H.
13 Aug 1889 SPMR
SPML

BROCK, Thomas s/o
Solomon & Ellen
Brock age 21 S
laborer POB & POR
Spotsylvania POC
& **THOMPSON**,
Maggie d/o Arch &
Fanny Thompson
age 21 S POB &
POR Spotsylvania
POC; POM
Spotsylvania 4
Feb 1892 SPMR 2
Feb 1892 SPML

BROCK, Thomas s/o
Solomon & Ellen
Brock age 21 S
laborer POB & POR
Spotsylvania POC
& **THOMPSON**,
Maggie d/o Arch &
Fannie Thompson
age 21 S POB &
POR SPotsylvania
POC; POM
Spotsylvania 4
Feb 1892 SPMR 2
Feb 1892 SPML

BROCKENBROUGH, William
Gray s/o Mr.&
Mrs.W.A.
Brockenbrough age
31 S farmer POB &
POR Richmond Co &
DENT, Parke P.
d/o Thomas &
Minnie W.Dent age

23 S POB Caroline Co POR Spotsylvania; POM Waller's Baptist Ch 4 Oct 1899 SPMR 26 Sep 1899 SPML

BROCKMAN, Albert T. s/o Samuel Brockman & Frances Graves age 24 S farmer POB & POR Orange & **BURRUSS**, Alice d/o Robert B.Burruss & Ann Graves age 18 S POB & POR Orange; POM Orange 27 Nov 1866 OMR 24 Nov 1866 OML

BROCKMAN, Belfield & **DOLEN**, Julia P. niece of H.Houck; 2 Jan 1851 OML

BROCKMAN, Joshua L.& **GRAVES**, Ann E.; 8 Nov 1852 OML

BROCKMAN, Lucian T. s/o William L.Brockman & Elizabeth Graves age 21 S farmer POB & POR Orange & **SAMUEL**, Adaline C. d/o Trenton E.Samuel & Bettie Coleman age 21 S POB & POR Orange; POM Orange 12 Jan 1863 OMR OML

BROCKMAN, William A. s/o William L.& Elizabeth C.Brockman age 30 S farmer POB & POR Orange & **MOORE**, Elizabeth T. d/o Robert & Harriet Moore age 18 S POB & POR Orange; POM Orange 6 Dec 1855 OMR 5 Dec 1855 OML

BROCKMAN, William s/o Asa Brockman & Lucy Quisenberry age 39 S farmer POB & POR Orange & **BICKERS**, Lucy M. d/o William Bickers & Elizabeth Hawkins age 25 S POB & POR Orange; POM Orange 20 Dec 1866 OMR 18 Dec 1866 OML

BROOK, Essex s/o Albert & Patty Brook age 25 S farmer POB Essex Co POR Spotsylvania POC & **MILES**, Siller d/o Patience Miles age 19 S POB & POR Spotsylvania POC; POM Spotsylvania 26 Jan 1869 SPMR 15 Jan 1869 SPML

BROOKING, James M. s/o Robert U.Brooking & Mildred Wilhoit age 24 S farmer POB & POR Orange & **WILHOIT**, Sarah E. d/o Curtis Wilhoit & Moriah E.Harrison age 25 S POB & POR Orange; POM Orange 17 Nov 1859 OMR 16 Nov 1859 OML

BROOKING, William F. & **PETTIS**, Eliza S.; POM Orange 22 Jan 1851 OMR 20 Jan 1851 OML

BROOKMAN, Marshall s/o Pleasant & Helen Brookman age 35 S farmer POB & POR Orange & **CARTER**,

Isabelle d/o
W.F.& Letitia
Carter age 24 S
POB & POR
Spotsylvania; POM
Spotsylvania 14
Jun 1899 SPMR
SPML
BROOKS, A.O. s/o J.R.&
Mary Brooks age
24 S miner POB &
POR Spotsylvania
& **HAREFIELD**,
Myrtle d/o Thad.&
Martha Harefield
age 17 S POB &
POR Spotsylvania;
POM Spotsylvania
16 Dec 1897 SPMR
SPML
BROOKS, Albert &
DUNAWAY, Emila A.
d/o Jordan
Dunaway (POR
Spotsylvania); 1
Apr 1862
SPConsent
BROOKS, Albert s/o
Dabney &
Elizabeth Brooks
age 24 S miller &
DUNAWAY, Emily
d/o Jordon &
Delphia Dunaway
age 22 S POB &
POR Spotsylvania;
POM Spotsylvania
3 Apr 1862 SPMR 2
Apr 1862 SPML
BROOKS, Albert T. s/o
Thomas & Esther
Brooks age 22 S
blacksmith POB &
POR Spotsylvania
POC & **HART**,
Fannie E. d/o
Matcholm & Amy
Hart age 21 S POB
& POR
Spotsylvania POC;
POM Spotsylvania
8 Dec 1874 SPMR 7
Dec 1874 SPML

BROOKS, Alexander D.
s/o Dabney &
Elizabeth Brooks
age 24 S farmer
POB & POR
Spotsylvania &
BROOKS, Lucy M.
d/o Granville &
Rebecca Brooks
age 23 S POB &
POR Spotsylvania;
POM Spotsylvania
2 Jan 1867 SPMR 1
Jan 1867 SPML
BROOKS, Aurelius s/o
A.C.& M.A.Brooks
age 29 S mechanic
POB & POR
Spotsylvania &
WHEELER, Bettie
J. d/o E.L.&
M.T.Wheeler age
17 S POB & POR
Spotsylvania; POM
Spotsylvania 24
Nov 1880 SPMR 15
Nov 1880 SPML
BROOKS, Benjamin F.
s/o George W.&
Izzie D.Brooks
age 25 S miner
POB & POR
Spotsylvania &
HAREFIELD, Clara
A. d/o Thad C.&
Martha
J.Harefield age
22 S POB & POR
Spotsylvania; POM
Spotsylvania 21
May 1894 SPMR 20
May 1894 SPML
BROOKS, Charles A. s/o
G.& Emily
A.Brooks age 31 W
railroading POB
Spotsylvania POR
Culpeper &
HERRING, Fannie
d/o Robert &
Sallie Sorrell
age 25 S POB &
POR Spotsylvania;
POM Spotsylvania

20 Oct 1896 SPMR
19 Oct 1896 SPML
BROOKS, Charles s/o
A.& J.Brooks age
23 S laborer POB
& POR Culpeper
POC & **COOK**, Julia
d/o William &
C.Cook age 18 S
POB & POR
Spotsylvania POC;
POM Spotsylvania
26 Dec 1878 SPMR
24 Dec 1878 SPML
BROOKS, Clarence A.
s/o Alexander &
Lucy M.Brooks age
20 S farmer POB &
POR Spotsylvania
& **BROOKS**, Nettie
Lee d/o Luther &
Ella Brooks age
19 S POB & POR
Spotsylvania; POM
Spotsylvania 21
Aug 1898 SPMR 20
Aug 1898 SPML
BROOKS, D.W. s/o T.W.&
M.Brooks age 19 S
POB & POR
Spotsylvania &
CARR, Annie D.
d/o J.D.&
M.A.Carr age 19 S
POB & POR
Spotsylvania; POM
Spotsylvania 25
Jun 1884 SPMR
BROOKS, George s/o
Aron & Ellen
Brooks age 40 S
farmer POB & POR
Spotsylvania POC
& **MORIS**, Doratha
Ellen d/o Cubid &
Lucy Hall age 27
W POB & POR
Spotsylvania POC;
POM Poor House,
Spotsylvania 17
Feb 1876 SPMR 9
Feb 1876 SPML
BROOKS, George W. s/o
Alfred & Eliza
A.Brooks age 18y
4mo S farmer POB
& POR
Spotsylvania &
BROOKS, Isadora
d/o Granville &
Rebecca Brooks
age 16 S POB &
POR Spotsylvania;
POM Spotsylvania
4 Apr 1867 SPMR 2
Apr 1867 SPML
BROOKS, George W. s/o
Eliza A.Brooks
(under age) &
BROOKS, Isadora
B. d/o Granvill
Brooks; 2 Apr
1867 SPConsent
BROOKS, Jackson s/o
W.H.& Sophia
Brooks age 22 S
miner POB & POR
Spotsylvania &
TRAYNHAM, Menta
d/o Sam.& Lucy
Traynham age 21 S
POB & POR
Spotsylvania; POM
Spotsylvania 16
Dec 1897 SPMR
SPML
BROOKS, James &
FISHER, Mary; 9
Aug 1853 OML
BROOKS, James R. s/o
Allen C.& Mary
A.Brooks age 27 S
farmer POB & POR
Spotsylvania &
JONES, Mary C.
d/o William & Ann
T.Brumley age 35
W POB & POR
Spotsylvania; POM
Spotsylvania 8
Aug 1872 SPMR 7
Aug 1872 SPML
BROOKS, James T. s/o
Albert & Eliza
Brooks age 21 S
farmer POB & POR
Spotsylvania &
HAREFIELD, Mary

d/o Thad & M.
Harefield age 19
S POB & POR
Spotsylvania; POM
Spotsylvania 16
Nov 1884 SPMR
BROOKS, Jesse s/o
Alfred & Eliza
Brooks age 22 S
miner POB & POR
Spotsylvania &
BROOKS, Judy d/o
Dabney &
Elizabeth Brooks
age 25 S POB &
POR Spotsylvania;
POM Spotsylvania
2 Jun 1882 SPMR
SPML
BROOKS, Jessee s/o
Alfred & Eliza
Brooks age 22 S
miner POB & POR
Spotsylvania &
BROOKS, Judy d/o
D.& E.Brooks age
25 S POB & POR
Spotsylvania; POM
Spotsylvania 2
Jun 1882 SPMR
BROOKS, John A. s/o
Alfred & Eliza
A.Brooks age 24 S
farmer POB & POR
Spotsylvania &
HARFIELD, Eleanor
d/o T.&
M.Harfield age 20
S POB & POR
Spotsylvania; POM
Spotsylvania 12
Oct 1880 SPMR 9
Oct 1880 SPML
BROOKS, John s/o
Addison & Julia
Brooks age 23 S
laborer POB
Culpeper Co POR
Orange POC &
SMITH, Ailsy G.
d/o Isaac & Sally
Smith age 22 S
POB & POR
Spotsylvania POC;

POM Pilgrim
Colored Baptist
Ch, Orange 13 Jan
1889 SPMR 10 Jan
1889 SPML
BROOKS, John Z. s/o
A.C.& M.A.Brooks
age 32 S mechanic
POB & POR
Spotsylvania &
WILLOUGHBY,
Sallie E. d/o
John &
L.Willoughby age
26 S POB & POR
Spotsylvania; POM
Spotsylvania 14
Oct 1880 SPMR 11
Oct 1880 SPML
BROOKS, Joseph H. s/o
A.C.& M.A.Brooks
age 27 S mechanic
POB & POR
Spotsylvania &
BROOKS, Delia d/o
William & Nancy
Brooks age 23 S
POB & POR
Spotsylvania; POM
Spotsylvania 28
May 1884 SPMR
BROOKS, Joseph s/o A.&
S.Brooks age 24 S
laborer POB & POR
Spotsylvania POC
& WIGLESWORTH,
Anna d/o W.&
M.Wiglesworth age
21 S POB & POR
Spotsylvania POC;
POM New Hope Ch,
Spotsylvania 5
Feb 1880 SPMR 30
Jan 1880 SPML
BROOKS, Luther s/o
Allen C.& Mary
J.Brooks age 27 S
miner POB & POR
Spotsylvania &
BROOKS, Ellen L.
d/o Alfred &
Eliza A.Brooks
age 17 S POB &
POR Spotsylvania;

BROOKS, Melvin P. s/o
A.& J.Brooks age
21 S laborer POB
Culpeper POR
Spotsylvania POC
& **ACRES**, Fannie
d/o H.& S.Acres
age 20 S POB &
POR Spotsylvania
POC; POM
Spotsylvania 18
Apr 1880 SPMR 15
Apr 1880 SPML

BROOKS, O.L. s/o Tandy
W.& Maria
L.Brooks age 21 S
miner POB & POR
Spotsylvania &
BROOKS, Ollie V.
d/o W.H.& Sophia
Brooks age 18 S
POB & POR
Spotsylvania; POM
Spotsylvania 14
Aug 1892 SPMR 6
Aug 1892 SPML

BROOKS, O.L. s/o Tandy
W.& Maria
L.Brooks age 21 S
miner POB & POR
Spotsylvania &
BROOKS, Allie V.
d/o W.H. & Sophia
Brooks age 18 S
POB & POR
Spotsylvania; POM
Spotsylvania 14
Aug 1892 SPMR 6
Aug 1892 SPML

BROOKS, Oceola s/o
Allan C.& Mary
A.Brooks age 28 S
farmer POB & POR
Spotsylvania &
HARFIELD, Daisy
V. d/o Thaddeus &
Martha Harfield
age 20 S POB &
POR Spotsylvania;
POM Spotsylvania
C.H.29 Mar 1895
SPMR SPML

BROOKS, Olander s/o
Tandy W.& Maria
Brooks age 24 S
farmer POB & POR
Spotsylvania &
BROOKS, Nannie O.
d/o George W.&
Isadora Brooks
age 17 S POB &
POR Spotsylvania;
POM Spotsylvania
26 Dec 1895 SPMR
SPML

BROOKS, Reuben s/o A.&
S.Brooks age 27 S
laborer POB & POR
Spotsylvania POC
& **MORSE**,
Elizabeth d/o
Richard & M.Morse
age 21 S POB &
POR Spotsylvania
POC; POM
Spotsylvania 11
Sep 1879 SPMR 8
Sep 1879 SPML

BROOKS, Robert &
JONES, Mary C.
age 35 W POR
Spotsylvania;
undated SPConsent

BROOKS, T.W. s/o G.&
R.Brooks age 20 S
carpenter POB &
POR Spotsylvania
& **HAREFIELD**, M.S.
d/o J.&
A.Harefield age
23 S POB & POR
Spotsylvania; POM
Spotsylvania 25
Dec 1858 SPMR

BROOKS, Thomas F. s/o
Mary E.Carr (nee
Brooks) age 20 S
farmer POB & POR
Spotsylvania &
WILLIAMS, Julia
d/o Mrs.Ella
Williams age 15 S
POB & POR
Spotsylvania; POM

Spotsylvania 16 Jan 1896 SPMR SPML

BROOKS, W.T. s/o William J. & Nancy Brooks age 35 S farmer POB & POR Spotsylvania & **WHEELER**, M.J. d/o Ed & M.J. Wheeler age 28 S POB & POR Spotsylvania; POM Spotsylvania 22 Dec 1886 SPMR

BROOKS, Walter R. s/o Alex & Lucy Brooks age 21 S miner POB & POR Spotsylvania & **BROOKS**, Lilly W. d/o Luther & Ella Brooks age 17 S POB & POR Spotsylvania; POM Spotsylvania 8 Jun 1890 SPMR

BROOKS, William D. & **DUNAWAY**, Delpha O. d/o Jordan Dunaway; 19 Feb 1867 SPConsent

BROOKS, William F. s/o A.C. & M.A. Brooks age 25 S farmer POB & POR Spotsylvania & **CARR**, Sallie M. d/o J.D. & L.M. Carr age 22 S POB & POR Spotsylvania; POM Spotsylvania C.H. 17 Mar 1886 SPMR

BROOKS, William H. s/o Alfred & Eliza A. Brooks age 33 S miner POB & POR Spotsylvania & **BROOKS**, Sophia d/o Granville & Rebecca Brooks sister of James M. Brooks age 16 S POB & POR Spotsylvania; POM Spotsylvania 25 Dec 1873 SPMR 24 Dec 1873 SPML

BROOKS, William I. W POB Orange & **McGARY**, Lucy A. S POB Spotsylvania; POM Spotsylvania 8 Jun 1853 SPMR

BROOKS, William P. s/o Alexander & Lucy Brooks age 23 S miner POB & POR Spotsylvania & **BROOKS**, Quincy I. d/o F.W. & Mariah Brooks age 17 S POB & POR Spotsylvania; POM Spotsylvania 12 Aug 1894 SPMR 11 Aug 1894 SPML

BROWN, Arthur s/o George & Milly Brown age 21 S laborer POB Caroline Co POR Spotsylvania POC & **SMITH**, Sally d/o Nancy Smith age 19 S POB & POR Spotsylvania POC; POM Spotsylvania 13 Jan 1871 SPMR 10 Jan 1870 SPML

BROWN, Arthur s/o John & Sarah Brown age 24 S farmer POB & POR Caroline Co POC & **SCOTT**, Mary J. d/o Robert & Minnie Scott age 27 S POB & POR Spotsylvania POC; POM Spotsylvania 3 Apr 1898 SPMR 31 Mar 1898 SPML

BROWN, Augustus F. s/o Richard & Mary H. Brown age 33 S farmer POB & POR Stafford &

WHARTON, Jennie C. d/o James R.& Ann E.Wharton age 18 S POB & POR Spotsylvania; POM Spotsylvania C.H. 27 Jan 1891 SPMR SPML

BROWN, Bazil s/o Ralph & Selina Brown age 28 S laborer POB Caroline Co POR Spotsylvania & **JACKSON**, Sarah J. d/o Henry & Sarah Jackson age 20 S POB Caroline Co POR Spotsylvania; POM Spotsylvania 18 Dec 1889 SPMR SPML

BROWN, Benjamin s/o Benjamin & Anna Brown age 23 S laborer POB & POR Spotsylvania POC & **LEWIS**, Hettie d/o Milly Lewis age 20 S POB & POR Spotsylvania POC; POM Spotsylvania C.H. 20 Sep 1893 SPMR SPML

BROWN, Calvin s/o Benjamin & Martha Brown age 40 W laborer POB & POR Spotsylvania POC & **BOON**, Elizabeth d/o Calvin & Henrietta Boon age 18 S POB & POR Spotsylvania POC; POM Spotsylvania 7 Jul 1897 SPMR SPML

BROWN, Charles s/o Maron & Mary I.Brown age 25 S farmer POB & POR Tompkins Co, N.Y. & **FISHER**, Sarah E. d/o Elijah & Elizabeth A. Fisher age 25 S POB Luzern Co, Pa POR Spotsylvania; POM Spotsylvania 25 Oct 1867 (possible clerk's error in year) SPMR 25 Oct 1870 SPML

BROWN, Daniel & **JOHNSON**, (aka Johnston) Mary d/o Elizabeth Johnston; POM Orange 19 Mar 1852 OMR 18 Mar 1852 OML

BROWN, Edward Samuel s/o Isaac & Maria Brown age 25 S carpenter POB & POR Spotsylvania POC & **LEWIS**, Maria d/o Jacob & Kesiah Lewis age 24 S POB & POR Spotsylvania POC; POM Brechnock, Spotsylvania 31 Dec 1891 SPMR 29 Dec 1891 SPML

BROWN, Harry G. s/o J.T.& Mary E.Brown age 19 S miner POB & POR Louisa Co & **LEWIS**, Emma C. d/o Fred.A.& Edith E.Lewis age 21 S POB & POR Spotsylvania; POM Good Hope, Spotsylvania 30 Sep 1900 SPMR 27 Sep 1900 SPML

BROWN, Jacob s/o Jeff & Eliza Brown age 27 S laborer POB & POR Oakville, Spotsylvania POC & **DAWSON**, Mary

Rose age 18 S POB
& POR Oakville,
Spotsylvania POC;
POM Spotsylvania
5 Aug 1875 SPMR 3
Aug 1875 SPML

BROWN, James s/o
Easter Brown age
27 S laborer POB
& POR
Spotsylvania POC
& **COLEMAN**, Susan
d/o Easter
Coleman age 21 S
POB & POR
Spotsylvania POC;
POM Spotsylvania
29 Nov 1894 SPMR
SPML

BROWN, James s/o J.&
P.Brown age 21 S
laborer POB & POR
Spotsylvania POC
& **SCOTT**, Iris d/o
W.H.& J.Scott age
21 S POB & POR
Spotsylvania POC;
POM Branch Fork
Ch, Spotsylvania
23 Sep 1877 SPMR
22 Sep 1877 SPML

BROWN, James W. s/o
James O.Brown &
Sarah M.Cooper
age 23 S farmer
POB & POR Orange
& **BOWLER**, Mary E.
d/o Robert Bowler
& Caroline E.
Bolling age 22 S
POB & POR Orange;
POM Orange 29 Mar
1866 OMR 26 Mar
1866 OML

BROWN, John s/o Martha
Tyler age 21 S
laborer POB & POR
Stafford POC &
WILLIAMS, Lucy
d/o M.Williams
POB & POR
Spotsylvania POC:
POM Spotsylvania
28 Oct 1883 SPMR

BROWN, R.J. s/o Henry
& Polly Brown age
32 S farmer POB &
POR Spotsylvania
POC & **COMFORT**,
Fannie d/o Emily
Comfort age 34 S
POB & POR
Spotsylvania POC;
POM Spotsylvania
9 Apr 1883 SPMR

BROWN, Robert J. POC &
COMFORT, Fannie
POC; POM Branch
Fork Ch,
Spotsylvania 9
Apr 1883 SPMR 3
Apr 1883 SPML

BROWN, Thomas s/o
Isaac & Maria
Brown age 22 S
laborer POB & POR
Spotsylvania POC
& **GOODLOE**,
Georgeanna d/o
George & Jane
Ellis age 32 W
POB & POR
Spotsylvania POC;
POM Spotsylvania
28 Dec 1897 SPMR
SPML

BROWNING, Cornelius R.
s/o Joshua
Browning & Lilly
Goddin age 24 S
POB Brooks Co,Ga
POR Colquett Co,
Ga farmer &
JONES, Frances A.
d/o John Jones &
Susan Bickers age
26 S POB & POR
Orange; POM
Orange 22 Dec
1863 OMR 21 Dec
1863 OML

BROWNING, John A. s/o
Willis &
Elizabeth
Browning age 25 S
farmer POB & POR
Rappahannock Co &
WILLIS, Mary

Lewis d/o George
& Martha P.Willis
age 18 S POB
Florida POR
Orange; POM
Orange 5 Oct 1853
OMR 4 Oct 1853
OML
BRUFF, David T. s/o
William W.& Sarah
A.Bruff age 27 S
druggist POB &
POR Talbot Co,Md
& **SMITH**, Ida L.
d/o John L.& Mary
E.Smith age 27 S
POB Talbot Co,Md
POR Spotsylvania;
POM Spotsylvania
9 Mar 1882 SPMR 8
Mar 1882 SPML
BRUFF, David T. s/o
William W.& Sarah
Bruff age 27 S
druggist & **SMITH**,
Ida L. d/o John
L. & Mary E.Smith
age 27 S POB
Talbot Co, Md POR
Spotsylvania; POM
Spotsylvania 9
Mar 1882 SPMR
BRUMLEY, Benjamin R.
s/o William & Ann
T.Brumley age 24
S mechanic POB
Spotsylvania &
DILLARD, Mary T.
d/o Thomas &
Elizabeth Dillard
age 25 S POB
Spotsylvania; POM
Spotsylvania 28
Feb 1853 SPMR
SPML
BRUMLEY, James H. s/o
William & Ann
Brumley age 36 S
mechanic POB &
POR Spotsylvania
& **WHITLOCK**,
Sallie B. d/o
E.L.& Elethea
Whitlock age 36 S

POB Louisa Co POR
Spotsylvania; POM
Spotsylvania C.H.
28 Nov 1882 SPMR
SPML
BRUMLEY, William T.
s/o R.B.&
M.F.Brumley age
28 S mechanic POB
& POR
Spotsylvania &
TAYLOR, Isa B.
d/o William &
F.E.Taylor age 26
S POB & POR
Spotsylvania; POM
Spotsylvania 27
Sep 1887 SPMR
BRUNNELL, William H.
s/o A.J.&
Sommerville
Brunnell age 32 S
farmer POB
Fredericksburg
POR Spotsylvania
& **JOHNSON**, Annie
E. d/o William
T.& Susan Johnson
age 26 S POB &
POR Spotsylvania;
POM Zion Ch,
Spotsylvania 21
May 1890 SPMR
BRYANT, John s/o
William Bryant &
Elizabeth Glassim
age 31 S miner
POB England POB
Orange & **SMITH**,
Ann E. d/o
William Smith &
Sarah Hawkins age
17 S POB Fauquier
Co POR Orange;
POM Orange 26 Nov
1867 OMR 23 Nov
1867 OML
BUCKNER, Dandridge s/o
E. & M.Dorson age
28 S laborer POB
& POR
Spotsylvania POC
& **CARTER**, Luella
d/o Sol &

M.Carter age 22 S POB & POR Spotsylvania POC; POM Spotsylvania 5 Jan 1881 SPMR SPML

BULLOCK, B.B. s/o Thomas & S.Bullock age 29 S farmer POB & POR Spotsylvania & BELL, Mary M. d/o J.& C.Bell age 19 S POB & POR Spotsylvania; POM Spotsylvania 5 Nov 1857 SPMR SPML

BULLOCK, B.F. & BULLOCK, Kate E. age 27 POR Spotsylvania; 28 Oct 1868 SPConsent

BULLOCK, Benjamin F. s/o Thomas & Susan R. Bullock age 32 S teacher POB & POR Spotsylvania & BULLOCK, Kate E. d/o Joseph & Catherine Kyle age 27 W POB Mobile, Alabama POR Spotsylvania; POM Fredericksburg 29 Oct 1868 FMR 28 Oct 1868 SPML

BULLOCK, Gus A. s/o John & H. Bullock age 22 S farmer POB & POR Spotsylvania & JONES, Leanna d/o George & A.Jones age 21 S POB & POR Spotsylvania; POM Spotsylvania 3 Jul 1856 SPMR 27 Jun 1857 SPML

BULLOCK, Oswald s/o William R.& Sophia Bullock age 23 S student POB & POR Orange & QUISENBERRY, Ann F. d/o Hezakiah & Emily Quisenberry age 21 S POB & POR Orange; POM Orange 27 Nov 1855 OMR 26 Nov 1855 OML

BULLOCK, R. s/o J.& H.Bullock age 30 S farmer POB & POR Spotsylvania & DUERSON, M. d/o J.& C.Duerson age 27 S POB & POR Spotsylvania; POM Spotsylvania 23 Dec 1858 SPMR SPML

BULLOCK, T.L. s/o B.B.& M.A.Bullock age 25 S railroad POB Caroline Co POR Spotsylvania & EUBANK, Lucy B. d/o Isaac & Virginia Eubank age 23 S POB Caroline Co POR Spotsylvania; POM Summit, Spotsylvania 30 Jul 1889 SPMR

BULLS, Alfred age 40 W farm laborer POB Essex Co POR Albemarle Co POC & JACKSON, Ellen age 26 W POB & POR Orange POC; POM Orange 17 Nov 1866 OMR

BUMPASS, Howard T. s/o H.O.& A.T. Bumpass age 24 S farmer POB & POR Louisa Co & CAFFREY, Carrie C. d/o R.S.& Sarah Caffrey age

21 S farmer POB & POR Spotsylvania; POM Spotsylvania 23 Feb 1893 SPMR 20 Feb 1893 SPML

BUNNELL, A.J. s/o L.& A.Bunnell age 59 W mechanic POB & POR Spotsylvania & **STEWART**, Martha T. d/o James & L.Stewart age 50 S POB & POR Spotsylvania; POM Spotsylvania 29 Jan 1879 SPMR 27 Jan 1879 SPML

BUNNELL, Andrew J. s/o Luther & Ann Bunnell age 46 W mechanic POB & POR Spotsylvania & **HART**, Bettie E. d/o Arch'd & Ann R.Hart age 32 S POB Baltimore POR Spotsylvania; POM Hartwood, Spotsylvania 4 Apr 1866 SPMR 3 Apr 1866 SPML

BURCH, William s/o Ira & Adelene Burch age 40 W farmer POB Herkimore Co, N.Y. POR Romy, N.Y. & **SHERMAN**, Sylvia A. d/o Asa & Cordelia Sherman age 19 S POB Durhamville, N.Y. POR Spotsylvania; POM Spotsylvania 15 May 1870 SPMR 14 May 1870 SPML

BURKE, G.B. s/o Thomas J.Burke age 21 S farmer POB & POR Spotsylvania & **PERRY**, Isabell d/o E.A.Perry POB & POR Spotsylvania age 15 S; POM Spotsylvania 1 Mar 1860 SPMR SPML

BURKLEY, Peter s/o Daniel & Patience Burkley age 70 W farmer POB Orange POR Spotsylvania POC & **QUARLES**, Mary age 50 W POB & POR Spotsylvania POC; POM City Road Ch, Spotsylvania 13 Jun 1875 SPMR 10 Jun 1875 SPML

BURLEY, A. s/o Sam & B.Burley age 55 W POB & POR Spotsylvania POC & **WHITE**, Maria d/o Ann Washington age 35 S POB Culpeper POR Spotsylvania; POM Spotsylvania 29 Dec 1886 SPMR

BURNAM, Charles s/o Charles Burnam & Mercie Weimer age 39 S farmer POB Canada POR Orange & **GABBOT**, Lucinda d/o James Gabbot POB & POR Orange; POM Orange 13 Jun 1867 OMR 12 Jun 1867 OML

BURROUS, L.C. s/o J.& C.Burrous age 20 S farmer POB & POR Spotsylvania & **SHACKLEFORD**, G.G. d/o J.& A.Shackleford age 22 S POB & POR Spotsylvania; POM Spotsylvania 20 Nov 1859 SPMR SPML

BURRUS, Ben s/o John & Clara Burrus age 22 S farmer POB &

POR Spotsylvania
& **ACORS**,
Catherine d/o H.&
E.Acors age 23 S
POB & POR
Spotsylvania; POM
Spotsylvania 12
Dec 1858 SPMR
SPML
BURRUS, Henry s/o
Gloucester &
Martha Burruss
age 27 S laboraer
POB & POR
Spotsylvania POC
& **RICHARDSON**,
Daisy d/o John &
Julia Richardson
age 18 S POB &
POR Spotsylvania
POC; POM Mt.Zion
Baptist Ch 19 Jan
1898 SPMR 18 Jan
1898 SPML
BURRUS, Joseph E. s/o
J.T.& P.P.Burruss
age 22 S farmer
POB & POR
Spotsylvania &
SHULTZ, Lena d/o
Henry & Elizabeth
Schultz age 20 S
POB & POR
Spotsylvania; POM
Spotsylvania 25
Jan 1882 SPMR 23
Jan 1882 SPML
BURRUSS, H.C. s/o
Robert B. &
A.E.Burruss age
25 S farmer POB &
POR Orange &
KENDALL, Rosa V.
d/o Robert G.&
Virginia
A.Kendall age 18
S POB & POR
Spotsylvania; POM
Spotsylvania 26
Oct 1875 SPMR 30
Sep 1875 SPML
BURRUSS, John D. s/o
Leon & Gabriella
Burruss age 34 S
farmer POB & POR
Spotsylvania &
SACRA, Nannie M.
d/o O.M.& Fanny
Sacra age 23 S
POB & POR
Spotsylvania; POM
Spotsylvania 24
Apr 1898 SPMR 20
Apr 1898 SPML
BURRUSS, Nelson L. s/o
William E.L.&
Martha H.Burruss
age 35 S farmer
POB Caroline Co
POR Spotsylvania
& **HOCKADAY**, Ella
N. d/o E.W.&
E.H.Hockaday age
21 S POB & POR
Spotsylvania; POM
Spotsylvania 4
Oct 1899 SPMR
SPML
BURRUSS, Thomas s/o
Gloucester &
Martha Burruss
age 22 S laborer
POB & POR
Spotsylvania POC
& **GRAY**, Ellen d/o
Willis & Malinda
Gray age 18 S POB
& POR
Spotsylvania POC:
POM Spotsylvania
2 Jun 1896 SPMR
SPML
BURRUSS, William T.
s/o Joseph
Burruss & Nancy
Terrill age 34 S
farmer POB & POR
Orange & **SEE**,
Almyra A. d/o
James See &
Gracie E.Proctor
age 20 S POB &
POR Orange; POM
Orange 2 Feb 1865
OMR OML
BURRUSS, Willie Nelson
s/o Leon C.&
Gabriella Burruss

age 25 S farmer POB & POR Spotsylvania & **CRAWFORD**, Virgie L. d/o William L.& Sarah M.Crawford age 23 S POB & POR Spotsylvania; POM Waller's Ch, Spotsylvania 15 Dec 1897 SPMR 13 Dec 1897 SPML

BURTON, Beverly s/o M.& J.Burton age 26 S farmer POB Stafford POR Spotsylvania & **FLEMING**, Octavia B. d/o B.S.& Lucy Fleming age 24 S POB & POR Spotsylvania; POM Spotsylvania 11 Sep 1878 SPMR SPML

BURTON, Emmet H. s/o Ab.S.& F.E.Burton age 24 S farmer POB & POR Spotsylvnania & **DUNAVANT**, Amelda d/o A.M. & M.Dunavant age 21 S POB & POR Spotsylvania; POM Spotsylvania 13 Feb 1877 SPMR 9 Feb 1877 SPML

BURTON, George W. & **JOHNSON**, Virginia S. d/o Mary A.C.Johnson; 23 Dec 1867 SPConsent

BURTON, George W. s/o William S.& Margaret A.Burton age 42 W farmer POB Fauquier Co POR Spotsylvania & **JOHNSON**, Virginia S. d/o John & Mary A.C.Johnson age 30 S POB & POR Spotsylvania; POM Spotsylvania 26 Dec 1867 SPMR 24 Dec 1867 SPML

BURTON, Hezekiah C. s/o A.S.& S.E.Burton age 29 S blacksmith POB Culpeper Co POR Fredericksburg & **STRATTEN**, Lula L. d/o John W.& Louisa A.Stratton age 21 S POB & POR Spotsylvania; POM Fredericksburg 26 Dec 1889 SPMR 25 Dec 1889 SPML

BURWELL, Moody s/o George & Rose Burwell age 22 S laborer POB King George Co POR Spotsylvania POC & **WHITE**, Mollie d/o Edie White age 20 S POB & POR Spotsylvania POC; POM Mount Pleasant, Spotsylvania 29 Dec 1892 SPMR 28 Dec 1892 SPML

BURWELL, Moody s/o George & Rose Burwell age 22 S POB King George Co POR Spotsylvania POC & **WHITE**, Molly d/o Eddie White age 20 S POB & POR Spotsylvania POC; POM Spotsylvania 29 Dec 1892 SPMR

BUTLER, Alexander F. & **ANDREWS**, Elizabeth Ann d/o Lewis Andrews; 23 Feb 1852 OML

BUTLER, Edward &
 RENOLS, Alice d/o
 James & Lucy Ann
 Renols; Dec 1872
 SPConsent
BUTLER, Edward s/o S.&
 J.Butler age 44 W
 POB King William
 Co POR
 Spotsylvania POC
 & SMITH, Betsy
 d/o H.& M.Winsley
 age 40 W POB &
 POR Spotsylvania
 POC; POM
 Spotsylvania 27
 Dec 1876 SPMR
 SPML
BUTLER, Eliga s/o
 Eliga Butler &
 Mary A. Chewning
 age 29 S POB &
 POR Spotsylvania
 & CHEWNING, Susan
 F. d/o Garland S.
 Chewning age 24 S
 POB & POR
 Spotsylvania; POM
 Spotsylvania 8
 Dec 185_ SPMR
BUTLER, George E. s/o
 J.M.& S.E.Butler
 age 24 S lawyer
 POB & POR Louisa
 Co & LACY, Clara
 E. d/o Z.T.&
 Ellen Lacy age 16
 S POB Essex Co
 POR Spotsylvania;
 POM Spotsylvania
 23 Dec 1885 SPMR
BUTLER, Oscar &
 CATLETT, Mary d/o
 Archie Catlett
 age 21; 3 Feb
 1877 SPConsent
BUTLER, Oscar s/o
 Barnett & Eve
 Butler age 21 S
 laborer POB & POR
 Spotsylvania POC
 & CATLETT, Mary
 d/o Archie &
 R.Catlett age 21

S POB & POR
 Spotsylvania POC;
 POM Spotsylvania
 3 Feb 1877 SPMR
 SPML
BUTZNER, William J.
 s/o George &
 Ellen Butzner age
 25 S farmer POB &
 POR Spotsylvania
 & DECKER, Lucy J.
 d/o John &
 L.B.Decker age 30
 S POB & POR
 Spotsylvania; POM
 Gravel Hill,
 Spotsylvania 29
 Aug 1877 SPMR
 SPML
BUZZELL, Ruel T. s/o
 Noah & Olive
 Buzzell age 25 S
 salesman POB
 Manlius (?),N.Y.
 POB Boston &
 SNOWDON, Caroline
 V. d/o Edward &
 Catherine Snowdon
 age 23 S POB N.Y.
 POR Spotsylvania;
 POM Spotsylvania
 17 Apr 1873 SPMR
 SPML
BYERS, Charles s/o
 John & Sallie
 Byers age 22 S
 laborer POB & POR
 Spotsylvanaia POC
 & WHITE, Vicie
 d/o Landora White
 age 19 S POB &
 POR Spotsylvania
 POC; POM
 Spotsylvania 28
 Dec 1898 SPMR 28
 Nov 1898 SPML
BYERS, David H.s/o
 David Myers &
 Nancy Mumly(?)
 age 35 W merchant
 POB Albemarle Co
 POR Orange &
 KEITH, Helen J.
 d/o Daniel Keith

age 32 S POB &
POR Orange; POM
Orange 23 May
1867 OMR 22 May
1867 OML

BYIERS, John s/o Jacob
& Rosa Byiers age
25 W turner POB
Pennsylvania POR
Spotsylvania &
SMITH, Sarah M.
d/o Joseph &
Martha Smith age
21 S POB & POR
Spotsylvania; POM
Spotsylvania 26
Nov 1884 SPMR

BYRD, Booker s/o
Gabriel & Jenny
Byrd age 22 S
farmer POB Essex
Co POR
Spotsylvania POC
& **PARKER**, Mary
d/o Henry & Jane
Parker age 18 S
POB & POR
Spotylvania POC;
POM Spotsylvania
16 Oct 1873 SPMR
15 Oct 1873 SPML

CADOT, Seymour Sinton
s/o Lemuel &
Catherine Cadot
of Ohio age 46
POR Richmond, Va.
& **COLBERT**,
Lillian Lyndall
d/o J.W. & B.A.
Colbert of
Fredericksburg
age 24 POR
Fredericksburg;
POM
Fredericksburg 18
Jun 1896 TCF

CAHOE, Patrick s/o
Richard & Nancy
Cahoe age 25 S
laborer POB
County Waterford,
Ireland POR
Orange & **STITZER**,
Elizabeth d/o
William &
Elizabeth Stitzer
age 24 S POB &
POR Orange; POM
Orange 9 Oct 1855
OMR

CAMELL, John L. s/o
Thomas Camel &
Nancy Thacker age
21 S overseer POB
Caroline Co POR
Orange & **THACKER**,
Julia d/o
Benjamin Thacker
& Lucy Lowrey age
22 S POB & POR
Orange; POM
Orange 10 Nov
1861 OMR 28 Oct
1861 OML

CAMMACK, Horace A. s/o
Durrett &
Elizabeth Cammack
age 54 W farmer
POB & POR
Spotsylvania &
RAWLINGS, Junie
D. d/o Alfred &
Judith A.Rawlings
age 37 S POB &
POR Spotsylvania;
POM Spotsylvania
28 Sep 1887 SPMR
22 Sep 1887 SPML

CAMMACK, Robert J. s/o
Robert J.& Lucy
J.Cammack age 40
S farmer POB &
POR Spotsylvania
& **DAY**, Fanny W.
d/o John L.& Mary
E.Andrews age 39
W POB & POR
Spotsylvania; POM
Spotsylvania 13
Dec 1900 SPMR 12
Dec 1900 SPML

CAMP, Grant s/o
William &
Carolline Camp
age 22 S laborer
POB & POR
Spotsylvania POC
& **LAWSON**, Fanny

d/o Dabney & Ellen Lawson age 17 S POB & POR Spotsylvania POC; POM Spotsylvania C.H. 15 Mar 1894 SPMR SPML

CAMPBELL, French s/o Warner & Courtney Campbell age 23 S laborer POB Caroline Co POR Spotsylvania POC & **RAWLINGS**, Fanny d/o Richard & Caroline Rawlings age 23 S POB Caroline Co POR Spotsylvania POC; POM Spotsylvania C.H.28 May 1891 SPMR SPML

CAMPBELL, William s/o Lewis & Sara Campbell age 48 W minister of the gospel POB & POR Spotsylvania POC & **YOUNG**, Ellen d/o William Cook age 32 W POB & POR Spotsylvania; POC; POM Spotsylvania 3 Dec 1885 SPMR SPML

CAMPER, William H.s/o John Camper & Mary J.Jones age 30 S minister POB Botetout Co POR Orange & **JERDONE**, Mary C. d/o Francis Jerdone & Eliza M.Watkins age 22 S POB & POR Orange; POM Orange 18 Dec 1866 OMR 12 Dec 1866 OML

CANADAY, James D. s/o James Canaday & Ann Tinder age 26 S farmer POB & POR Orange & **MASON**, Ellen A. d/o Charles Mason & Lucy Jones age 24 S POB & POR Orange; POM Orange 25 Jan 1866 OMR 23 Jan 1866 OML

CANADAY, Melvin Lorenzo s/o A.A. & Virginia Canaday of Spotsylvania Co. & **WATSON**, Ida d/o Charles & Agnes Watson of Spotsylvania Co age 23 POR Spotsylvania Co.; POM Spotsylvania Co. 17 Apr 1895 TCF

CANNON, John H. s/o Phil Cannon age 40 W POB Stafford POR Spotsylvania & **PERRY**, Mildred A. d/o William Perry age 25 S POB & POR Spotsylvania; POM Spotsylvania 12 Jul 1856 SPMR

CANNON, John S. s/o Ira & Elizabeth Cannon age 42 W farmer POB & POR Spotsylvania & **ALSOP**, Emma O. d/o William Alsop age 35 S POB & POR Spotsylvania; POM Spotsylvania 17 Feb 1887 SPMR 14 Feb 1887 SPML

CANNON, John S. s/o Ira & Elizabeth Cannon age 23 S farmer POB & POR Spotsylvania & **CLARKE**, Sarah J. d/o John H.& Marah F.Clarke

age 22 S POB &
POR Spotsylvania;
POM Spotsylvania
5 Mar 1867 SPMR 4
Mar 1867 SPML
CANNON, Richard M. s/o
Joseph &
Elizabeth Cannon
age 34 W stone
mason POB
Caroline Co &
JONES, Lucy Ann
d/o George & Jane
Jones age 22 S
POB Caroline Co;
POM Spotsylvania
7 Mar 1855 SPMR
CAPNER, William J. s/o
William J.&
C.Capiner age 21
S mechanic POB
Newe Jersey POR
Spotsylvania &
JOHNSON, Harriet
E. d/o Mary
Robertson age 17
S POB
Pennsylvania POR
Spotsylvania; POM
Presbyterian Ch,
Fredericksburg 19
Jun 1878 FMR 17
Jun 1878 SPML
CAPNIE, William J. &
JOHNSON, Harriet
E. d/o father
deceased & mother
now Mrs.
Robertson (age
39)(POR
Pittsburg,
Pa)ward of
I.C.Kingsley age
16 b.d.26 Jul
1878 ; 17 Jun
1878 SPConsent
CARBERRY, Patrick s/o
William &
Margaret
Carberrry W
laborer POB
Ireland POR
Orange & **JOHNSON**,
Susan d/o William

B.& Martha Lewis
W POB & POR
Orange; POM
Orange 16 Feb
1856 OMR 15 Feb
1856 OML
CARDWELL, R.L. s/o
James & Lucy
A.Cardwell age 26
S machinist POB &
POR Richmond, Va
& **TRIBBLE**, M.H.
d/o William &
Mary A.Tribble
age 25 S POB &
POR Spotsylvania;
POM River Hill 23
Dec 1890 SPMR 22
Dec 1890 SPML
CARNAHAN, E.W. s/o W.&
L.Carnohan age 27
W farmer POB &
POR Spotsylvania
& **ARNOLD**, Sallie
W. d/o R.Arnold
age 31 S POB
Caroline Co POR
Spotsylvania; POM
Spotsylvania 25
Dec 1879 SPMR 18
Dec 1879 SPML
CARNAHAN, Joseph W.
s/o Warren & Lucy
A.Carnohan age 50
W farmer POB &
POR Spotsylvania
& **HUMPHRIES**,
Bettie J. d/o
James E. &
Rebecca Humphries
age 46 S POB &
POR Spotsylvania;
POM Spotsylvania
19 Nov 1899 SPMR
18 Nov 1899 SPML
CARNEAL, Atwell P. &
JONES, Mary C.;
25 Jul 1860 SPML
CARNEAL, Atwell R. &
JONES, Mary C.;
25 Jul 1860 OML
CARNEAL, E. s/o K.&
A.Carneal age 32
S carpenter POB &

POR Caroline Co
&**JONES**, Sarah d/o
T.R.& A.Jones age
18 S POB & POR
Spotsylvania; POM
Spotsylvania 4
Apr 1858 SPMR

CARNEAL, Edgar S. s/o
Isaac & Elizabeth
Carneal age 26 S
farmer POB & POR
Spotsylvania &
JONES, Martha T.
d/o Thomas R. &
Ann J.Jones age
21 S POB & POR
Spotsylvania; POM
Baptist Ch,
Spotsylvania 26
Apr 1866 SPMR
SPML

CARNEAL, Edward s/o
Thomas & Pamelia
I.Carneal age 20
S farmer POB &
POR Spotsylvania
& **CANNON**,
Virginia A. d/o
Ira & Elizabeth
Cannon age 23 S
POB & POR
Spotsylvania; POM
Spotsylvania 6
Dec 1870 SPMR
SPML

CARNEAL, Edward T. s/o
Thomas V. &
Pamilia Carneal
age 37 W farmer
POB & POR
Spotsylvania &
HAYNES, Alice d/o
Robert & Sallie
Haynes age 21 S
POB & POR
Spotsylvania; POM
Spotsylvania C.H.
11 Apr 1888 SPML
SPMR

CARNEAL, George s/o
Eulistus & Sarah
Carneal age 29 S
farmer POB & POR
Spotsylvania &

SACRA, Alice d/o
James C. & Mary
J. Sacra age 28 S
POB & POR
Spotsylvania; POM
Spotsylvania 21
Jun 1888 SPMR
SPML

CARNEAL, John s/o
Thomas & Nannie
Carneal age 44 W
farmer POB
Hanover Co POR
Culpeper Co &
BROOKS, Sarah
Mium d/o Albert
G. & Emily A.
Brooks age 18 S
POB Hanover Co
POR Spotsylvania;
POM Spotsylvania
C.H.2 Oct 1888
SPMR SPML

CARNEAL, Monroe J. s/o
R.H.& Mary
Carneal age 24 S
farmer POB & POR
Caroline Co &
HAYNES, Amma M.
d/o Joseph S.&
Mildred D.Haynes
age 24 S POB
Caroline Co POR
Spotsylvania;POM
Spotsylvania 6
Apr 1899 SPMR 1
Apr 1899 SPML

CARNEAL, Robert Lee
s/o Lee & Sallie
Carneal age 23 S
driver POB
Spotsylvania POR
Fredericksburg &
STEVENS, Emma d/o
Lewis & Ella
Stevens age 19 S
POB & POR
Spotsylvania; POM
Spotsylvania 22
Apr 1891 SPMR
SPML

CARNEEL, John s/o
James Carneel &
Betsy Wright age

57 W farmer POB & POR Caroline Co & **THACKER**, Ann d/o Benjamin Thacker & Lucy Lowry age 35 S POB Hanover Co POR Orange; POM Orange 20 Oct 1867 OMR 18 Oct 1867 OML

CARNER, Corree A. s/o John W.& Annie Carner age 23 S farmer POB & POR Spotsylvania & **CARTER**, Anna K. d/o Festus E.& Pamelia Carter age 15 S POB & POR Spotsylvania; POM Spotsylvania 12 Apr 1893 SPMR 8 Apr 1893 SPML

CARNER, Henry A. s/o Allen & Elizabeth Carner age 28 S farmer POB North Carolina POR Kentucky & **JOHNSON**, Lucy F. d/o Thomas & Jane Johnson age 19 S POB & POR Spotsylvania; POM Spotsylvania 20 Dec 1875 SPMR 15 Dec 1875 SPML

CARNER, John W. & **JONES**, Anna E.; 9 Dec 1867 SPConsent

CARNER, John W. s/o Allan & Elizabeth A.Carner age 23 S farmer POB & POR Spotsylvania & **JONES**, Anna E. d/o William E.& Elizabeth Ann Jones age 17 S POB & POR Spotsylvania; POM Spotsylvania 12 Dec 1867 SPMR

CARNOHAN, Ca.E. s/o W.& F.Carnohan age 29 S overseeing POB Spotsylvania POR Louisa Co & **PIERCE**, R.R. d/o W.& N.Pierce age 21 S POB & POR Spotsylvania; POM Spotsylvania 22 Mar 1860 SPMR

CARNOHAN, Charles E. s/o Willis & F.Carnohan age 47 W farmer POB & POR Spotsylvania & **WHEELER**, Martha Jane d/o Anderson & A.Wheeler age 33 S POB & POR Spotsylvania; POM Spotsylvaia 9 Sep 1877 SPMR 3 Sep 1877 SPML

CARNOHAN, Edward s/o Warren & Lucy A.Carnohan age 19 S farmer POB & POR Spotsylvania & **HOPE**, Elton Placett d/o Ed L.& Mary C.Hope age 18 S POB & POR Spotsylvania; POM Spotsylvania 22 Dec 1870 SPMR 17 Dec 1870 SPML

CARNOHAN, Edward W. s/o Waller & Lucy Carnohan age 32 W farmer POB & POR Spotsylvania & **LONG**, Elizabeth H. d/o Henry C.& Elizabeth H.Sutton age 38 W POB Caroline Co POR Spotsylvania; POM Spotsylvania 27 Jan 1885 SPMR 23 Jan 1885 SPML

CARNOHAN, George S. s/o Warren & Lucy

A.Carnohan age 25 S farmer POB & POR Spotsylvania & **CARNOHAN**, Fanny d/o Charles E.& Rebecca R.Carnohan age 20 S POB & POR Spotsylvania; POM Spotsylvania C.H. 7 Jan 1886 SPMR 6 Jan 1886 SPML
CARNOHAN, Joseph W. s/o Warren & Lucy A.Carnohan age 48 W farmer POB & POR Spotsylvania & **PEYTON**, Sallie M. d/o George H.& Betty Peyton age 37 S POB & POR Spotylvania; POM Spotsylvania 1 Dec 1897 SPMR 26 Nov 1897 SPML
CARNOHAN, Robert B. s/o Warren & Lucy A.Carnohan age 30 S farmer POB & POR Spotsylvania & **LONG**, Ophelia E. d/o John G.& Elizabeth Long (now Elizabeth H.Carnohan) age 17 S POB & POR Spotsylvania; POM Spotsylvania 21 Jan 1886 SPMR 20 Jan 1886 SPML
CARPENTER, F. s/o T.F.& J.Carpenter age 47 W farmer POB Louisa Co POR Tennessee & **BLAYDES**, Barbara M. d/o J.C.& P.Blaydes age 40 S POB & POR Spotsylvania; POM Spotsylvania 16 Aug 1859 SPMR
CARPENTER, William J. s/o Jonathan &

Anne E.Carpenter age 37 S farmer POB & POR Rappahannock Co & **BEAZLEY**, Ann E. d/o Thomas K.& Anne E.Beazley age 30 S POB & POR Spotsylvania; POM Spotsylvania 13 May 1873 SPMR SPML
CARPENTER, Willis H. s/o Jonas Carpenter age 25 S farmer POB & POR Madison Co & **MURRAY**, Carolina S. d/o Joseph & Lutecia Murry age 20 S POB Dublin, Ireland POR Orange; POM Orange 7 Sep 1854 OMR OML
CARR, Charles M. s/o John S.& M.E.Carr age 25 S farmer POB & POR Caroline Co & **LEVELY**, Annie M. d/o Thomas & Mary Levely age 22 S POB Caroline Co POR Spotsylvania; POM Massaponax Ch, Spotsylvania 20 Jun 1880 SPMR 19 Jun 1880 SPML
CARR, Hosea J. s/o John D. & Lucy Mary Carr age 23 S miner POB & POR Spotsylvania & **BROOKS**, Lucy A. d/o William & Ann Brooks age 22 S POB & POR Spotsylvania; POM Spotsylvania 23 Jul 1893 SPMR 15 Jul 1893 SPML
CARR, Jeter S. s/o John J. & Martha

Carr age 36 W
farmer POB
Caroline Co POR
Spotsylvania &
BAKER, Lillie C.
d/o Bushrod &
Mattie Baker age
26 S POB Louisa
Co POR
Spotsylvania; POM
Spotsylvania 31
Jul 1888 SPMR
SPML
CARR, John D. s/o
Betsy Carr age 54
W farmer POB &
POR Spotsylvania
& **BROOKS**,
Henrietta d/o
Allen C.& Mary
Ann Brooks age 34
S POB & POR
Spotsylvania; POM
Spotsylvania 7
Feb 1889 SPMR 1
Feb 1889 SPML
CARR, John P. s/o John
D.& Lucy M. Carr
age 29 S farmer
POB & POR
Spotsylvania &
BROOKS, Mary E.
d/o William &
Nancy Brooks age
38 S POB & POR
Spotsylvania; POM
Spotsylvania
C.H.30 Dec 1889
SPMR SPML
CARR, John s/o Betsy
Carr age 22 S
farmer POB
Spotsylvania &
HAREFIELD, Lucy
M. d/o Jordon W.&
Ann E.Harefield
age 21 S POB
Orange; POM
Spotsylvania 24
Dec 1854 SPMR
CARTER, Abram s/o F.&
Nancy Carter age
57 W farmer POB &
POR Spotsylvania

POC &
CRUTCHFIELD,
Nannie d/o
Georgie
Crutchfield age
25 S POB & POR
Spotsylvania POC;
POM Spotsylvania
9 Jan 1900 SPMR 2
Jan 1900 SPML
CARTER, Alexandria s/o
Alexandria &
Fannie Carter age
87 W farmer POB
Culpeper Co POR
Spotsylvania POC
& **SCOTT**, Nancy
d/o Martha
Johnson age 28 S
POB Louisa Co POR
Spotsylvania POC;
POM Spotsylvania
25 Mar 1895 SPMR
23 Mar 1895 SPML
CARTER, Benjamin S.
s/o George & Ann
Carter age 62 W
farmer POB
Caroline Co POR
Spotsylvania &
DICKEN, Martha A.
d/o Edmond & Mary
Dicken age 56 POB
Caroline Co POR
Spotsylvania; POM
Spotsylvania 31
Aug 1882 SPMR 30
Aug 1882 SPML
CARTER, Benjamin S.
s/o George & Ann
Carter age 62 W
farmer POB
Caroline Co POR
Spotsylvania &
DICKEN, M.A. d/o
Edmund & Mary
Dicken age 56 S
POB Caroline CO
POR Spotsylvania;
POM Spotsylvania
30 Aug 1882 SPMR
CARTER, Cassius s/o
William Fitzhugh
& Elizabeth Lucy

Carter age 30 S physician POB & POR Fairfax & **TALIAFERRO**, Jane A. d/o Charles & Louisa G.Taliaferro age 17 S POB Caroline Co POR Orange; POM Orange 18 Jun 1856 OMR OML

CARTER, Festus E. s/o Edward & Mary Carter age 28 S mechanic POB Caroline Co POR Spotsylvania & **LEWIS**, Pamilia d/o Herndon & Mahala Learndow age 24 W POB Orange POR Spotsylvania; POM Spotsylvania 8 Feb 1866 SPMR 31 Jan 1866 SPML

CARTER, John E. s/o Woodford & Elizabeth P.Carter age 33 S farmer POB Caroline Co POR Spotsylvania & **JONES**, Rebecca L. d/o Thomas R.& Ann J.Jones age 26 S POB & POR Spotsylvania; POM Spotsylvania C.H.21 Feb 1884 SPMR SPML

CARTER, John H. s/o Lewis & Louisa Carter age 22 S laborer POB & POR Spotsylvania POC & **CHEWNING**, Alice d/o William Campbell & Rachel Chewning age 23 S POB & POR Spotsylvania POC; POM Spotsylvania

20 Dec 1900 SPMR SPML

CARTER, John Melza s/o Melza & Abergail Carter age 25 S farmer POB Caroline Co POR Spotsylvania & **PAYNE**, Texanar d/o John M.& Elizabeth Payne age 22 S POB & POR Spotsylvania; POM Spotsylvania 26 Dec 1872 SPMR 23 Dec 1872 SPML

CARTER, Lewis s/o William & Caroline Carter age 23 S farmer POB & POR Spotsylvania POC & **ATKINS**, Louisa d/o Robert & America Atkins age 22 S POB & POR Spotsylvania POC: POM Spring Forest, Spotsylvania 9 Dec 1874 SPMR SPML

CARTER, Nelson V. s/o Festus E.& Pamilia Carter age 23 S carpenter POB & POR Spotsylvania & **HALL**, Hattie V. d/o Horace C.& Jane E.Hall age 16 S POB & POR Spotsylvania; POM Spotsylvania C.H.4 Jun 1891 SPMR SPML

CARTER, Waller Z. & **ALMOND**, Laticia d/o Lewis Almond age 21 ; 2 Aug 1871 SPConsent

CARTER, Warner s/o Peggy Carter age 22 S farmer POB &

POR Spotsylvania
& **HOLMES**, Edele
d/o Daniel &
Martha Holmes age
19 S POB & POR
Spotsylvania; POM
Spotsylvania 11
Apr 1869 SPMR 10
Apr 1869 SPML
CARTER, William B. s/o
Hazlewood & Emily
Carter age 43 W
farmer POB & POR
Caroline Co &
PAYNE, Anna G.
d/o E.T.& Harriet
Payne age 20 S
POB Caroline Co
POR Spotsylvania;
POM Spotsylvania
20 Dec 1898 SPMR
SPML
CARTER, William B. s/o
Nicholas H.&
E.E.Carter age 26
S farmer POB
Caroline Co POR
Spotsylvania &
ACORS, Calahan
d/o Thomas A.&
Elinnia Acors age
23 S POB Caroline
Co POR
Spotsylvania; POM
Spotsylvania C.H.
22 Dec 1881 SPMR
SPML
CARTER, William H. &
HERNDON, Ann E.
age 24 W POR
Spotsylvania; 26
Dec 1865
SPConsent
CARTER, William s/o
William &
Henrietta Carter
age 23 S laborer
POB Orange POR
Spotsylvania POC
& **TERRELL**,
Charlotte d/o
John & Eliza
Terrell age 23 S
POB & POR

Spotsylvania POC;
POM Spotsylvania
26 Jan 1879 SPMR
23 Jan 1879 SPML
CARTER, Willie J. s/o
Waller F.&
L.Carter age 24 S
farmer POB & POR
Spotsylvania &
MASTIN, Bettie L.
d/o James B.&
V.L.Mastin age 18
S POB King George
Co POR
Spotsylvania; POM
Spotsylvania 18
Dec 1895 SPMR
SPML
CARY, Benjamin s/o L.&
W.Cary age 21 S
farmer POB & POR
Spotsylvania POC
& **JONES**,
Georgeana age 22
S POB & POR
Spotsylvania POC;
POM Mt.Zion Ch,
Spotsylvania 23
Dec 1877 SPMR 22
Dec 1877 SPML
CASEY, Michael C. s/o
Michael &
Catharine Casey
S clerk POB
Ireland POR
Fulton Co,
Georgia &
MALSBERGER, Emily
W. d/o Thomas &
Mary Woodall W
POB Maryland POR
Spotsylvania; POM
Spotsylvania
(catholic priest
named R.S.
Andrews) 6 Oct
1864 SPMR SPML
CASEY, Michael C. s/o
Michael &
Catherine Casey
clerk S POB
Ireland POR
Fulton Co, Ga &
MALSBERGER, Emily

W. d/o Thomas &
Mary Woodall W
POB Maryland POR
Spotsylvania; POM
Catholic Ch,
Spotsylvania 6
Oct 1864 SPMR
SPML
CASON, James W. s/o
Thomas Cason &
Anna Withers age
22 S farmer POB
Georgia POR
Alabama & RILEY,
Ophelia d/o Jacob
Riley & Mary
Hicks age 16 S
POB Spotsylvania
POR Orange; POM
Orange 12 Oct
1862 OMR 7 Oct
1862 OML
CATES (possibly
Cotes), David S.
s/o David H.Cates
& Elizabeth
Morris age 30 S
boot & shoemaker
POB & POR Orange
& HUTCHISON,
Mattie E. d/o
William
F.Hutchison &
Martha L.Brawner
age 21 S POB
Fauquier Co POR
Orange; POM
Orange 6 Dec 1866
OMR OML
CATLETT, Archie s/o
Jackson Howard &
Emily Catlett age
21 S POB & POR
Spotsylvania POC
& SAMUEL, Abbie
d/o Phil & Mary
Samuel age 19 S
POB & POR
Spotsylvania POC;
POM Spotsylvania
18 Aug 1886 SPMR
SPML
CATLETT, Charles s/o
Richard Parker &
Emily Catlett age
19 S laborer POB
& POR
Spotsylvania POC
& LEWIS, Fairy
Belle d/o James &
Sarah Lewis age
18 S POB & POR
Spotsylvania POC;
POM Spotsylvania
13 Dec 1898 SPMR
SPML
CATLETT, E.H. s/o
T.L.& N.G.Catlett
age 28 S
telegraph
operator POB
Caroline Co POR
Richmond &
EUBANK, Nellie G.
d/o J.L.&
Virginia Eubank
age 24 S POB
Caroline Co POR
Spotsylvania; POM
Spotsylvania 28
Nov 1893 SPMR 27
Nov 1893 SPML
CATLETT, Jackson s/o
Arch Catlett &
Lavenia Croxton
age 24 S laborer
POB & POR
Spotsylvania POC
& COLEMAN, Jane
d/o Milly Coleman
age 23 S POB
Spotsylvania POR
Fredericksburg
POC; POM Pine
Hill,
Spotsylvania 7
Aug 1881 SPMR 6
Aug 1881 SPML
CATLETT, Jefferson s/o
Sarah Catlett
("not married")
age 23 S farm
laborer POB & POR
Spotsylvania POC
& COMFORT, Susan
d/o Charles &
Lucy Comfort age
19 S POB & POR

Spotsylvania POC; POM Brockville, Spotsylvania 30 Apr 1888 SPMR SPML

CATLETT, Richard & **OLIVER**, Mary d/o Betty Oliver; 1 Jan 1877 SPConsent

CATLETT, Richard S. s/o James & Maria Catlett age 23 S farmer POB & POR Spotsylvania & **OLIVER**, Mary A. d/o John & Catherine Oliver age 17 S POB & POR Spotsylvania; POM Spotsylvania 4 Jan 1877 SPMR 1 Jan 1877 SPML

CATLETT, Thomas s/o Emily Catlett age 22 S laborer POB & POR Spotsylvania POC & **SMITH**, Bettie d/o Rose Smith age 21 S POB & POR Spotsylvania POC; POM Spotsylvania 13 Aug 1881 SPMR SPML

CAVE, L.W. s/o R.P.& S.F.Cave age 23 S farmer POB Greene Co POR Orange & **ANDREWS**, E.S. d/o L.& S.Andrews age 19 S POB Orange POR Spotsylvania; POM Spotsylvania 8 Jan 1861 SPMR

CAVE, Robert C.s/o Robert P.Cave & Sarah F.Lindsay age 20 S farmer POB & POR Orange & **DANIEL**, Fannie S. d/o William F.Daniel & Julia Terrill age 18 S POB & POR Orange; POM Sycamore Ch, Richmond,Va 15 Jan 1863 Richmond MR 12 Jan 1863 OML

CAVE, Thomas B. s/o Richard Cave & Maria Porter age 56 S farmer pOB Madison Co POR Orange & **DOWNER**, Lucy F. d/o Robert Downer & Frances Daniel age 32 S POB & POR Orange; POM Orange 27 Jul 1865 OMR 24 Jul 1865 OML

CAW, Jeter S. s/o John & M.Caw age 28 S farmer POB & POR Caroline Co & **BAKER**, Caroline d/o B.Baker age 25 S POB Louisa Co POR Spotsyvlania; POM Spotsylvania 23 Dec 1880 SPMR 22 Dec 1880 SPML

CHANCELLOR, James E. s/o G.& A.Chancellor S doctor POB & POR Spotsylvania & **ANDERSON**, D.J. d/o T.& J.P.Anderson S POB & POR Spotsylvania; POM Spotsylvania 18 Nov 1853 SPMR

CHANDLER, Boyd D. s/o Thomas K. & A.P.Chandler age 21 S railroad official POB Fredericksburg POR Richmond & **FRAZER**, Jennie C. d/o James L.&

Mattie Frazer age
21 S POB
Buckingham Co POR
Spotsylvania; POM
Coventry,
Spotsylvania 1
Nov 1881 SPMR
SPML
CHAPMAN, James Henry
s/o Edmund
Chapman &
Phinella Wood age
22 S POB & POR
Orange POC &
ROBINSON,
Caroline age 18 S
POR Orange POC;
POM Orange 28 Dec
1867 OMR 25 Dec
1867 OML
CHAPMAN, Nathaniel s/o
Pearson Chapman &
S.M.Alexander age
25 S POB & POR
Charles Co, Md &
CHAPMAN, Mary d/o
John M.Chapman &
Susan Cole age 24
S POB & POR
Orange; POM
Orange 23 Oct
1867 OMR 22 Oct
1867 OML
CHAPMAN, William Henry
& **STANARD**, Mary
E.; POM Orange 1
Apr 1852 OMR 31
Mar 1852 OML
CHARTTERS, Charles J.
s/o Thomas R.&
Julia D.Chartters
age 39 S farmer
POB Spotsylvania
POR Stafford &
MORRISON, Ella
d/o Robert R.&
Mary A.Morrison
age 30 S POB &
POR Spotsylvania;
POM Spotsylvania
23 Nov 1892 SPMR
18 Nov 1892 SPML
CHARTTERS, Thomas E.
s/o Thomas R.&

Julia D.Charters
age 25 S farmer
POB & POR
Spotsylvania &
LANDRAM, Bettie
G. d/o William &
Lucy P.Landram
age 26 S POB &
POR Spotsylvania;
POM Spotsylvania
25 Nov 1873 SPMR
12 Nov 1873 SPML
CHATTEN, John s/o
Thomas & Rebecca
Chatten age 60 W
farmer POB
Maryland POR
Spotsylvania &
BALLARD, Maria
d/o Sanford &
Susan F.Ballard
age 21 S POB &
POR Spotsylvania;
POM Spotsylvania
24 Feb 1886 SPMR
23 Feb 1886 SPML
CHESLEY, H.G. s/o
William S.& Mary
Chesley age 24 S
farmer POB
Fredericksburg
POR Stafford &
FURNEYHOUGH, Mary
S. d/o Robert W.&
F.G. Furneyhough
age 22 S POB
Essex Co POR
Spotsylvania; POM
Spotsylvania 27
Nov 1867 SPMR
SPML
CHESLEY, William S.
s/o Robert &
Elizabeth Chesley
age 42 W saddler
POB King George
Co POR
Spotsylvania &
CAWTHORNE, M.A.
d/o A.&
M.Cawthorne age
41 S POB Essex Co
POR Spotsylvania;

CHEW, Benjamin F. s/o Minor & Charity Chew age 24 S farmer POB & POR Spotsylvania POC & **SCOTT**, Lina A. d/o Robert & Winnie Scott age 20 S POB & POR Spotsylvania POC; POM Beulah Ch 27 Dec 1899 SPMR 26 Dec 1899 SPML

CHEW, George s/o Hillard & Betsy Chew age 27 S laborer POB & POR Spotsylvania & **HOWARD**, Susan d/o Daniel Howard & Lucy Tyler age 23 S POB & POR Spotsylvania; POM Spotsylvania 7 Nov 1869 SPMR 6 Nov 1869 SPML

CHEW, Melvin s/o Trenton & Emily Chew age 24 S laborer POB & POR Spotsylvania POC & **GOODLOE**, Maudy d/o Robert & Sallie Goodloe age 23 S POB & POR Spotsylvania POC; POM Spotsylvania 20 Dec 1882 SPMR 18 Dec 1882 SPML

CHEW, Minor s/o John & Caroline Chew age 39 W farmer POB & POR Spotsylvania POC & **DAY**, Linda age 39 S POB Caroline Co POR Spotsylvania POC; POM Spotsylvania C.H. 28 Dec 1886 SPMR SPML

CHEW, Minor s/o John & Caroline Chew age 22 S farmer POB & POR Spotsylvania POC & **WEBB**, Charity d/o Ben & Maria Lucas Webb age 21 S POB & POR Spotsylvania POC; POM Spotsylvania 18 Dec 1867 SPMR 14 Dec 1867 SPML

CHEWNING, Absalom s/o George W. & Delila Chewning age 32 S carpenter POB & POR Spotsylvania & **SWIFT**, Anna C. d/o William & Olympia Swift age 19 S POB & POR Spotsylvania; POM Greenwood, Spotsylvania 16 Dec 1884 SPMR 1 Dec 1884 SPML

CHEWNING, Charles M. s/o C.S. & H. Chewning age 29 S school teacher POB & POR Spotsylvania & **TOMPKINS**, Nannie R. d/o Edm. & H. Tompkins age 23 S POB & POR Spotsylvania; POM Spotsylvania 28 Jan 1874 SPMR 17 Jan 1874 SPML

CHEWNING, Don F. s/o George W. & Alice S. Chewning age 20 S carpenter POB & POR Spotsylvania & **SWIFT**, Emma J. d/o William T. & Olympia Swift age 22 S POB Fredericksburg POR Spotsylvania; POM Antioch Ch, Orange 24 Dec

CHEWNING, Eddie B. POR Spotsylvania & **CHEWNING** E---nd J. POR Spotsylvania; undated SPConsent

CHEWNING, Edward B. s/o C.L.& M.O.Chewning age 21 S farmer POB & POR Spotsylvania & **CHEWNING**, Emma d/o J.E.& Virginia Chewning age 19 S POB & POR Spotsylvania; POM Spotsylvania 15 Sep 1878 SPMR 4 Sep 1878 SPML

CHEWNING, George W. s/o Henry & Branchy Chewning age 24 S POR Louisa Co & **DIGGS**, Mary age 18 S; POM Orange 27 Dec 1853 OMR 26 Dec 1853 OML

CHEWNING, George W. S POR Spotsylvania & **VANNCETTER**, Nancy M. d/o Aaron Vanncetter S POR Spotsylvania; POM Spotsylvania 10 Nov 1853 SPMR

CHEWNING, H.K. s/o Hiram & Ann E.Chewning age 33 S farmer POB & POR Spotsylvania & **JERRELL**, Josie d/o Joseph & Louisa Jerrell age 33 S POB & POR Spotsylvania; POM Mine Road Baptist Ch, Spotsylvania 14 Feb 1894 SPMR 1 Feb 1894 SPML

1896 OMR 21 Dec 1896 SPML

CHEWNING, James s/o Liston Almond & Rachel Chewning age 24 S farmer POB & POR Spotsylvania & **JONES**, Mary E.V. d/o Thomas & Mary Ann Jones age 20 S POB & POR Spotsylvania; POM Spotsylvania 23 Dec 1895 SPMR SPML

CHEWNING, Jasper T. s/o John T.& Margaret Chewning age 24 S farmer POB Orange POR Spotsylvania & **LEWIS**, Carrie E. d/o Stephen L.& Carrie E.Lewis age 19 S POB & POR Spotsylvania; POM Spotsylvania 6 Sep 1899 SPMR 5 Sep 1899 SPML

CHEWNING, John S. s/o William N.& Permelia Chewning age 23 S farmer POB & POR Spotsylvania & **TINDER**, Margaret d/o George W. & Sarah Tinder age 20 S POB & POR Orange; POM Orange 25 Sep 1859 SPMR 23 Sep 1859 OML

CHEWNING, Lester B. s/o John T.& Margaret F.Chewning age 29 S farmer POB Orange POR Spotsylvania & **DEMPSEY**, Laura A. d/o David A.& Edmonia Dempsey age 17 S POB Orange POR

Spotsylvania; POM the Wilderness 11 Oct 1899 SPMR SPML

CHEWNING, Lucius C. s/o John T. & M.T.Chewning age 22 S carpenter POB Orange POR Spotsylvania & **DULIN**, Dicy A. d/o E.T. & Sophia J.Dulin age 22 S POB Madison Co POR Spotsylvania; POM Spotsylvania 19 Feb 1890 SPMR 14 Feb 1890 SPML

CHEWNING, Marcus A. s/o William & Susan Chewning age 24 S farmer POB Orange POR Spotsylvania & **BISCOE**, Sallie Bettie d/o William E.& Catherine R.Biscoe age 19 S POB & POR Spotsylvania; POM Spotsylvania 3 Dec 1865 SPMR 28 Nov 1865 SPML

CHEWNING, Marcus A. & **BISCOE**, Sallie Bettie d/o William Biscoe (who had a broken leg at this time); 27 Nov 1865 SPConsent

CHEWNING, Melvin M. s/o Oscar L.& Mary O.Chewning age 35 W farmer POB & POR Spotsylvania & **DAVIS**, Ellie B. d/o James L.& Ann Davis age 26 S POB & POR Spotsylvania; POM Waller's Ch,

Spotsylvania 15 Jan 1889 SPMR 10 Jan 1889 SPML

CHEWNING, Melvin M. s/o S.& F.Chewning age 22 S POB & POR Spotsylvania & **CHEWNING**, Fanny L. d/o Joseph E. & Virgia(?) Chewning age 21 S POB & POR Spotsylvania; POM Spotsylvania 3 May 1876 SPMR 2 May 1876 SPML

CHEWNING, Melvin M. & **CHEWNING**, Fannie L. age 21; 2 May 1876 SPConsent

CHEWNING, Melvin M. & **JOHNSON**, Lucie F. d/o Thomas Johnson; 25 Nov 1875 SPConsent

CHEWNING, R.W. s/o William V.& Pamelia Chewning age 78 W farmer POB Spotsylvania POR Orange & **JONES**, Mary E. d/o Garland Chewning age 65 W POB & POR Spotsylvania; POM Spotsylvania 31 Jan 1893 SPMR 30 Jan 1893 SPML

CHEWNING, Russell A. s/o A.H.& Medora Chewning age 22 S farmer POB & POR Spotsylvania & **McGEE**, Mattie L. s/o Absalom & Frances McGee age 23 S POB & POR Spotsylvania; POM Spotsylvania C.H.26 Nov 1891 SPMR SPML

CHEWNING, Thomas S. s/o Oscar S. & Theldah M.Chewning age 26 S farmer POB & POR Spotsylvania & **PARTLOW**, Matta L. d/o Lancelot & Nancy H.Partlow age 24 S POB & POR Spotsylvania; POM Spotsylvania 23 Jan 1866 SPMR 12 Jan 1866 SPML

CHEWNING, William s/o Liston Almond & Rachel Chewning age 17 S farmer POB & POR Spotsylvania & **JONES**, Martha Olivia d/o Thomas & Mary Ann Jones age 20 S POB & POR Spotsylvania; POM Spotsylvania C.H. 27 Mar 1888 SPML SPML

CHEWNING, William s/o O.S.& M.Chewning age 23 S teacher POB & POR Spotsylvania & **FLEMING**, C.S.(or Q.) d/o B.S.& S.A.Fleming age 17 S POB & POR Spotsylvania; POM Spotsylvania 22 May 1860 SPMR

CHILDRESS, Henry P. s/o Giles R.Childres & Sarah E.Pottes(?) age 24 S farmer POB Spotsylvania POR Orange & **TINDER**, Virginia E. d/o George W.Tinder & Sarah Quisenberry age 24 S POB & POR Orange; POM Orange 6 Mar 1862 OMR 28 Feb 1862 OML

CHILDRESS, John W. s/o Robert M. & Lucy A.Childress age 28 S POB Albemarle Co POR King William Co & **TOMPKINS**, Frances B. d/o Robert & Jane Tompkins age 22 S POB Caroline Co POR Spotsylvania; POM Spotsylvania 6 Nov 1872 SPMR 4 Nov 1872 SPML

CHILDRESS, William A. s/o William Childress & Elizabeth Ellis age 47 S carpenter POB Louisa Co POR Orange & **CHILDRESS**, Wilhelma C. d/o Archibald Shiflett & Barlinda Vaughn POB Louisa Co POR Orange; POM Orange 28 Dec 1865 OMR 18 Dec 1865 OML

CHILDS, Jackson s/o Daniel & Lucinda Childs age 22 S laborer POB Caroline Co POR Spotsylvania POC & **SCOTT**, Charlotte Ann Elizabeth d/o Shadrack (POR Fauquier Co)& Mary Scott age 22 S POB Culpeper Co POR Spotsylvania POC; POM Spotsylvania 14 Apr 1873 SPMR SPML

CHILDS, Winston s/o Daniel & Lucinda Childs age 25 S laborer POB Caroline Co POR Spotsylvania POC & **SLAUGHTER**, Courtney d/o George & Kitty Coleman age 27 W POB & POR Spotsylvania POC; POM Spotsylvania 28 Dec 1882 SPMR 27 Dec 1882 SPML

CHILES, R.W. s/o W.& P.Chiles age 23 S POB & POR Spotsylvania POC & **COLEMAN**, Martha A. d/o Humphrey Coleman & Easter Chiless age 19 S POB & POR Spotsylvania POC; POM New Hope Ch, Spotsylvania 18 Jan 1880 SPMR 21 Jan 1880 SPML

CHINN, John E. age 26 POR Stafford Co. & **MONTEITH**, Ella age 25 POR Stafford Co.; POM Stafford Co. 4 Dec 1890 TCF

CHRISTIAN, Joseph s/o Toby & Sally Christian age 23 S laborer POB & POR Louisa Co POC & **DIGGS**, Mildred d/o John & Ellen Diggs age 21 S POB Louisa Co POR Spotsylvania POC; POM Spotsylvania 4 Jan 1877 SPMR 1 Jan 1877 SPML

CLAIBORNE, A.G. s/o Jesse & Maria Claiborne age 28 W farmer POB & POR Caroline Co POC & **WASHINGTON**, Mary Frances D. d/o Benjamin & Sarah Washington age 20 S POB & POR Spotsylvania POC; POM Spring Hill, Spotsylvania 26 May 1875 SPMR 17 May 1875 SPML

CLARK, A.L. s/o John H.& Martha Clark age 37 W mechanic POB Spotsylvania POR Orange & **HERRING**, Fronie J. d/o Robert Herring & Sallie E.Sorrell age 23 S POB & POR Spotsylvania; POM Spotsylvania 7 Jan 1901 SPMR 15 Dec 1900 SPML

CLARK, Ernest J. s/o Wyatt A.& Izora L.Clark age 21 S farmer POB Orange POR Spotsylvania & **MITCHELL**, Maggie B. d/o John C. & Ella Mitchell age 23 S POB & POR Spotsylvania; POM S.A.Christian Ch, Spotsylvania 27 Nov 1898 SPMR 25 Nov 1898 SPML

CLARK, George G. & **MCGEE**, Anie Bell d/o J. & Louise A.Stratton; 4 Jun 1877 SPConsent

CLARK, John T. d/o J.M.Clark & Aleitha Emerson age 25 S house carpenter POB Charles Co, Md POR Orange C.H. & **GRAHAM**, Josephine d/o Isaac

F.Graham & Rosetta Larmand age 19 S POB Richmond POR Orange C.H.; POM Orange 22 Jan 1861 OMR 21 Jan 1861 OML

CLARK, John Z. s/o John H.Clark & Martha E.Conner age 22 S carpenter POB & POR Spotsylvania & **JONES**, Amanda S. d/o Churchill Jones & Emiline Long age 22 S POB & POR Orange; POM Orange 9 Feb 1865 OMR 30 Jan 1865 OML

CLARK, William O. s/o S.T.& Susan Clark age 24 S farmer POB & POR Orange & **JONES**, Angelina d/o John & Susan Jones age 32 S POB & POR Orange; POM Orange 5 Nov 1857 OMR 4 Nov 1857 OML

CLARK, Willis s/o Willis & Martha Clarke age 37 W blacksmith POB & POR Spotsylvania POC & **MURPHY**, Maggie L. d/o J.H.& Julia Murphy age 22 S POB & POR Spotsylvania POC; POM Spotsylvania 24 Dec 1896 SPMR 7 Sep 1896 SPML

CLARKE, A. s/o A.& M.Clarke age 26 S farmer POB & POR Spotsylvania & **ALMOND**, M. d/o H.& J.Almond age 23 S POB & POR Spotsylvania; POM Spotsylvania 26 May 1858 SPMR

CLARKE, Frank s/o James & Martha Clarke age 26 S laborer POB & POR Spotsylvania POC & **COLEMAN**, Martha J. d/o Gundy & Eliza E.Coleman age 27 S POB & POR Spotsylvania POC; POM Spotsylvania 17 Mar 1887 SPMR 14 Mar 1887 SPML

CLARKE, George G. s/o George & Mary Clarke age 38 S boot & shoemaker POB Maine POR Chesterfield Co & **McGEE**, Annie Belle d/o Ebenezer & Louisa McGee (now Louisa Stratton) age 18 S POB & POR Spotsylvania; POM Spotsylvania 10 Jun 1877 SPMR 9 Jun 1877 SPML

CLARKE, George W. s/o John H.& Martha F.Clarke age 23 S farmer POB & POR Spotsylvania & **BULLOCK**, Esther V. age 19 S POB & POR Spotsylvania; POM Spotsylvania 2 Feb 1869 SPMR 1 Feb 1869 SPML

CLARKE, Strother W. s/o John H. & Martha F.Clarke age 23 S farmer POB & POR Spotsylvania & **CANNON**, Mary E. d/o Ira & Elizabeth Cannon age 21 S POB &

POR Spotsylvania;
POM Spotsylvania
13 Feb 1872 SPMR
14 Feb 1872 SPML
CLARKE, W.F. s/o
Richard & Patsy
Clarke age 37 S
farmer POB & POR
Spotsylvania POC
& **GORDON**, Mary F.
d/o George &
Matilda Gordon
age 25 S POB &
POR Spotsylvania
POC; POM Beulah
Ch 21 Dec 1899
SPMR SPML
CLARKE, William s/o
Washington &
Malvina Clarke
age 2_ S farmer
POB & POR
Spotsylvania &
OAKS, Belvedary
d/o John &
Dariame Oaks age
23 S POB & POR
Spotsylvania; POM
Orange 4 Aug 1866
SPMR 30 Jul 1866
SPML
CLAXTON, Benjamin s/o
Reuben Claxton &
Nancy Taylor age
23 S farm laborer
POB & POR Orange
POC & **TAYLOR**,
Catherine d/o
Bennet Taylor &
Barbara Jackson
age 21 S POB &
POR Orange POC;
POM Orange 9 Nov
1867 OMR 4 Nov
1867 OML
CLAY, John s/o Thomas
& Emily Clay age
25 S farmer POB
Culpeper Co POR
Fauquier Co POC &
ACORS, Fanny d/o
Thomas &
Athelinda Acors
age 22 S POB &

POR Spotsylvania
POC; POM at their
residence,
Spotsylvania 1
Sep 1881 SPMR 31
Aug 1881 SPML
CLORE, Henry L. s/o
William B.& Mary
E.Clore age 43 W
farmer POB
Madison Co POR
Spotsylvania &
HAWKINS, Rosa L.
d/o A.B.& Lucy
M.Hawkins age 24
S POB & POR
Spotsylvania; POM
Spotsylvania 30
Jun 1897 SPMR 29
Jan 1897 SPML
CLORE, James L. s/o
James W.& Frances
Clore age 24 S
farmer POB
Madison Co, Va
POR Spotsylvania
& **POWELL**, Annie
L. d/o J.T.&
L.E.Powell age 20
POB & POR
Spotsylvania; POM
Spotsylvania 24
Dec 1885 SPMR 22
Dec 1885 SPML
COATES, William Henry
s/o Warfield &
Matilda Coats age
25 S pork packer
POB Spotsylvania
POR Washington
D.C. POC & **MINOR**,
Julia d/o John &
Emily Minor age
23 S POB & POR
Spotsylvania POC;
POM New Hope Ch,
Spotsylvania 14
Aug 1898 SPMR 13
Aug 1898 SPML
COATS, John s/o John &
Minerva Coats age
23 S farm laborer
POB & POR
Spotsylvania POC

& **HARRIS**, Elsie d/o Patsy Harris age 22 S POB & POR Spotsylvania POC: POM Spotsylvania 16 May 1869 SPMR 13 May 1869 SPML

COBB, Mont T. s/o O.& R.Cobb age 22 S farmer POB & POR Caroline Co & **FAULKNER**, M.A. d/o P.E.& F.A.Faulkner age 21 S POB & POR Spotsylvania; POM Spotsylvania 4 Nov 1861 SPMR

COCHRAN, John s/o Patrick & Ann Cochran age 33 S chopping wood & digging ditches POB Ireland POR Orange & **LEATHERS**, Betsy d/o J.T.& Lucy Ann Leathers age 26 S POB & POR Orange; POM Orange 31 Mar 1860 OMR 30 Mar 1860 OML

COFFMAN, Andrew E. s/o Andrew Coffman & Polly Charlton age 27 S farmer POB & POR Rockingham Co & **HEATWELL**, Bettie G. d/o David Heatwell & Eliza Garrison age 27 S POB Rockingham Co POR Orange; POM Orange 17 Oct 1861 OMR 16 Oct 1861 OML

COGHILL, David s/o G.& R.Coghill age 40 S merchant POB & POR Richmond & **HATCHER**, Emma T. d/o P.A.& E.M.Hatcher age 21 S POB Petersburg POR Spotsylvania; POM Spotsylvania 20 Nov 1861 SPMR

COGHILL, Granville s/o Thomas & Briny Coghill age 26 S laborer POB Caroline Co POR Spotsylvania POC & **COLEMAN**, Margaret d/o James & Kitty Coleman age 20 S POB Caroline Co POR Spotsylvania POC; POM Spotsylvania 15 Dec 1881 SPMR 13 Dec 1881 SPML

COGHILL, Warner s/o Warner & Rose Coghill age 22 S laborer POB & POR Spotsylvania POC & **WARE**, Lucy d/o Lucy Ware age 22 S POB & POR Spotsylvania POC; POM Spotsylvania C.H. 5 Sep 1893 (probable error in month by minister) SPMR 5 Oct 1893 SPML

COLBERT, Chastine W. s/o R.W.& M.E.Colbert age 28 S merchant POB & POR Spotsylvania & **MASSEY**, Ella Maude d/o A.W.& Lucy Massey age 21 S POB & POR Spotsylvania; POM Spotsylvania 21 Dec 1897 SPMR 17 Dec 1897 SPML

COLBERT, Lucian R. s/o R.W.& M.E.Colbert

age 21 S lumber dealer POB & POR Spotsylvania & **BULLOCK**, Daisy M. d/o Benjamin F.& Kate E.Bullock age 21 S POB & POR Spotsylvania; POM Massaponax Ch, Spotsylvania 20 Dec 1892 SPMR SPML

COLBERT, R.W. s/o T.B.& A.C.Colbert age 26 S merchant POB Culpeper POR Fauquier & **BEAZLEY**, M.E. d/o J.M.& M.E.Beazley age 21 S POB & POR Spotsylvania; POM Spotsylvania 1 Dec 1859 SPMR

COLEMAN, Addison Lee s/o Gundy & Eliza Ellen Coleman age 31 S farmer POB & POR Spotsylvania POC & **CRUMP**, Celia d/o Nelson Jackson age 30 W POB & POR Spotsylvania POC; POM Spotsylvania 14 Mar 1895 SPMR 13 Mar 1895 SPML

COLEMAN, Addison s/o Daniel & Celia Coleman age 22 S farmer POB & POR Spotsylvania POC & **SMITH**, Margaret d/o Davy & Ann Tucker Smith age 23 S POB & POR Spotsylvania POC; POM Spotsylvania 27 May 1871 SPMR 23 May 1871 SPML

COLEMAN, Alley s/o Glendy(?) & Hannah Coleman age 22 S laborer POB & POR Spotsylvania POC & **WALKER**, Rhoda d/o George & Leanna Walker age 22 S POB & POR Spotsylvania POC; POM Spotsylvania 9 Dec 1889 SPMR 2 Dec 1889 SPML

COLEMAN, Buckner s/o Major & Eliza Coleman age 21 W laborer POB & POR Spotsylvania POC & **CONNER**, Sarah d/o George & Ellen Conner age 20 S POB & POR Spotsylvania POC; POM Bethany Ch, Spotsylvania 18 Nov 1866 SPMR 16 Nov 1866 SPML

COLEMAN, Burrell s/o Ambrose Coleman & Fanny Hillman age 43 S blacksmith POB & POR Orange & **SMITH**, Sarah L. d/o James Smith & Sarah A.Hawkins age 21 S POB Fauquier CO POR Orange; POM Indiantown, Orange 4 Mar 1864 OMR 2 Mar 1864 OML

COLEMAN, Chancellor s/o James & Ann Coleman age 26 S laborer POB & POR Spotsylvania POC & **GUSS**, Emma d/o Thomas & Hannah Guss age 27 S POB & POR Spotsylvania POC; POM Spotsylvania 18 Jul 1896 SPMR SPML

COLEMAN, Charles B. s/o Humphrey & Easter Coleman

age 24 S laborer POB & POR Spotsylvania POC & **DIGGS**, Lyla d/o Sam & Rose Diggs age 24 S POB & POR Spotsylvania POC; POM Spotsylvania 6 Apr 1899 SPRM 4 Apr 1899 SPML

COLEMAN, Cyrus age 23 POR Spotsylvania & **WALKER**, Eliza J. age 20 POR Spotsylvania; undated SPConsent

COLEMAN, Cyrus s/o Sam & Amy Coleman age 23 S laborer POB Caroline Co POR Spotsylvania POC & **WALKER**, Eliza J. d/o Mary Walker POC age 20 S POB & POR Spotsylvania POC; POM Spotsylvania 28 Feb 1868 SPMR 26 Feb 1868 SPML

COLEMAN, Dabney s/o Sam & Amy Coleman age 20 S farmer POB Caroline Co POR Spotsylvania POC & **COATES**, Sarah d/o John & Maranda Coates age 22 S POB Caroline Co POR Spotsylvania POC; POM Spotsylvania 15 Jan 1869 SPMR 4 Jan 1869 SPML

COLEMAN, Fountain s/o S.& F.Coleman age 50 W laborer POB & POR Spotsylvania POC & **ELLIS**, Laura d/o J.& T.Ellis age 26 S POB & POR Spotsylvania POC; POM

Spotsylvania 23 Apr 1876 SPMR 21 Apr 1876 SPML

COLEMAN, Frank s/o Frank & Sophia Coleman age 25 S laborer POB & POR Caroline Co POC & **HOLMES**, Martha d/o Richard & Millie Holmes age 20 S POB & POR Spotsylvania POC; POM Spotsylvania 23 Jan 1890 SPMR 20 Jan 1890 SPML

COLEMAN, Gundy s/o Balston & Dilsy Coleman age 64 W farmer POB & POR Spotsylvania POC & **WHITE**, Georgeanna d/o Ben & Lina White age 32 S POB & POR Spotsylvania POC; POM Spotsylvania 18 Apr 1900 SPMR SPML

COLEMAN, Henry s/o Matilda Coleman age 23 S laborer POB & POR Spotsylvania POC & **CRUTCHFIELD**, Louisa d/o Robert & Lucy Crutchfield age 18 S POB & POR Spotsylvania POC: POM Spotsylvania 4 Jan 1883 SPMR 1 Jan 1883 SPML

COLEMAN, Horace & **GREEN**, Jenney (not 21) mother's POR Oakville, Spotsylvania; 24 May 1875 SPConsent

COLEMAN, I.W. s/o S.& M.D.Coleman age 35 S physician

POB & POR
Caroline Co &
DUERSON, S.A. d/o
J.& C.Duerson age
27 S POB & POR
Spotsylvania; POM
Spotsylvania 28
Nov 1860 SPMR
COLEMAN, James s/o
M.Gray age 24 S
laborer POB & POR
Spotsylvania POC
& **ACRES**, Martha
d/o T.& E.Acres
age 19 S POB &
POR Spotsylvania
POC; POM
Spotsylvania 12
Jan 1881 SPMR
SPML
COLEMAN, James W. s/o
Lammuel & Clara
Coleman age 26 S
farmer POB Louisa
Co POR
Spotsylvania POC
& **MANUEL**, Betty
d/o Philip & Lucy
Manuel age 21 S
POB & POR
Spotsylvania POC;
POM Spotsylvania
25 Jan 1896 SPMR
24 Jan 1896 SPML
COLEMAN, John A. s/o
George & Martha
Ross age 30 S
farmer POB & POR
Spotsylvania POC
& **COLEMAN**, Sally
A. d/o Harrison &
Jane Coleman age
24 S POB & POR
Spotsylvania POC;
POM Spotsylvania
24 Feb 1881 SPMR
19 Feb 1881 SPML
COLEMAN, John s/o
David & Eliza
Coleman age 22 S
laborer POB & POR
Spotsylvania POC
& **BURLEY**, Leonora
d/o Absalom &
Polly Burley age
20 S POB & POR
Spotsylvania POC;
POM Spotsylvania
21 Dec 1886 SPMR
18 Dec 1886 SPML
COLEMAN, John s/o
Fountain & Rose
Coleman age 24 S
farmer POB & POR
Spotsylvania POC
& **COMFORT**, Mary
d/o Lavenia
Woolfolk age 23 W
POB & POR
Spotsylvania POC;
POM Spotsylvania
29 Dec 1890 SPMR
SPML
COLEMAN, John s/o
Miner & Louisa
Coleman age 21 S
laborer POB & POR
Spotsylvania POC
& **TAYLOR**, Sallie
d/o Scy & Amelia
Taylor age 18 S
POB & POR
Spotsylvania POC;
POM Spotsylvania
C.H.19 Nov 1890
SPMR SPML
COLEMAN, John T.Jr
s/o John
T.Coleman Sr.&
Emilly L.Coleman
age 32 S farmer
POB & POR
Spotsylvania &
HARRIS, Carrie O.
d/o Clement M.&
M.S.Harris age 29
S POB & POR
Spotsylvania; POM
Spotsylvania
C.H.7 Dec 1890
SPMR 5 Dec 1890
SPML
COLEMAN, Lewis s/o
Daniel & Celia
Coleman age 37 W
farmer POB & POR
Spotsylvania POC
& **SAMUEL**, Ann d/o

Katy Wortham age 38 W POB & POR Spotasylvania POC; POM Spotsylvania 22 Mar 1894 SPMR 21 Mar 1894 SPML

COLEMAN, Lewis s/o James & Catherine Coleman age 25 W farmer POB & POR Spotsylvania POC & **FORTS**, Fanny d/o William & Rebecca Forts age 17 S POB & POR Spotsylvania POC; POM Spotsylvania 11 Jan 1900 SPMR SPML

COLEMAN, Lewis s/o James & Kitty Coleman age 20 S laborer POB & POR Spotsylvania POC & **LINDSAY**, Susan d/o George Lindsay age 22 S POB & POR Spotsylvania POC; POM Spotsylvania C.H. 27 Jul 1893 SPMR SPML

COLEMAN, Lewis s/o Daniel & C.Coleman age 26 S laborer POB & POR Spotsylvania POC & **DUDLEY**, Rosetta d/o M.& P.Dudley age 21 S POB Nelson Co POR Spotsyvlania POC; POM Spotsyvlania 13 May 1880 SPMR 11 May 1880 SPML

COLEMAN, Littleton L. s/o Reuben L.Coleman & Mary Walker age 25 S POB Spotsylvania POR Orange & **SAMUEL**, Carrie V. d/o Thornton

V.Samuel & Bettie Coleman age 18 S POB & POR Orange; POM Orange 20 Dec 1866 OMR 18 Dec 1866 OML

COLEMAN, Major s/o Horace & Jannie Coleman age 24 S laborer POB & POR Spotsylvania POC & **LEWIS**, Annie d/o Peter & Mary Lewis age 19 S POB & POR Spotsylvania POC; POM Beaulah, Spotsylvania 8 Oct 1900 SPMR 7 Oct 1900 SPML

COLEMAN, Nicholas P. s/o John & Frances Coleman age 25 S farmer POB & POR Orange & **FRAZER**, Huldah M. d/o Herndon & Martha Frazer age 21 S POB & POR Spotsylvania; POM Spotsylvania 6 Nov 1872 SPMR 4 Nov 1872 SPML

COLEMAN, Oscar & **ADKINS**, Dabna(?) Nancy d/o James B.Adkins; 12 Mar 1874 SPConsent

COLEMAN, Oscar s/o Deimis & Sally Coleman age 23 S POB & POR Spotsylvania POC & **ADKINS**, Nannie d/o James R.& America Adkins age 23 S POB & POR Spotsylvania POC; POM Spring Forest, Spotsylvania 19 Mar 1874 SPMR no date on SPML

COLEMAN, Otho s/o
Addison &
Margaret Coleman
age 21 S farmer
POB & POR
Spotsylvania POC
& **HART**, Norma
Estella d/o Henry
& Nora Hart age
21 S POB & POR
Spotsylvania POC;
POM Spotsylvania
2 Jan 1900 SPMR 1
Jan 1900 SPML

COLEMAN, R.W. s/o
Thomas S. & __.
N.Coleman age 35
S farmer &
BLAYDES, Edna d/o
H.F.& M.E.Blaydes
age 18 S; POM
Spotsylvania 26
May 1875 SPMR 24
May 1875 SPML

COLEMAN, Reuben L. s/o
Reuben L.Coleman
& Mary Waller age
28 farmer POB
Spotsylvania POR
Orange &
BROCKMAN, Adaline
d/o Trenton
V.Samuel & Bettie
Coleman age 25 W
POB & POR Orange;
POM Orange 28 Feb
1867 OMR OML

COLEMAN, Robert
Lafayette s/o
Whitehead &
Elizabeth Coleman
age 32 S school
teacher POB
Spotsylvania &
POWELL, Nancy
Smith d/o William
R. & Mary S.
Powell age 24 S
POB Spotsylvania;
POM Clover Green,
Spotsylvania 25
Sep 1856 SPMR 24
Sep 1856 SPML

COLEMAN, Robert L. s/o
Louisa Coleman
age 26 S laborer
POB & POR
Spotsylvania POC
& **MICKENS**, Lula
d/o William &
Easter Mickens
age 21 S POB &
POR Spotsylvania
POC; POM
Hardenburgh,
Spotsylvania 20
Feb 1890 SPMR 18
Feb 1890 SPML

COLEMAN, Robert s/o
Addison L.& Maria
Coleman age 42 W
farmer POB
Caroline Co POR
Spotsylvania &
HART, Elizabeth
d/o Robert J.&
Margaret Hart age
24 S POB & POR
Spotsylvania; POM
Spotsylvania C.H.
30 Nov 1881 SPMR
3 Nov 1881 SPML

COLEMAN, S.A. s/o
A.L.& M.Coleman
age 27 S railroad
POB & POR
Caroline Co &
COLEMAN, Julia A.
d/o H.& J.Coleman
age 16 S POB &
POR Spotsylvania;
POM Spotsylvania
21 May 1880 SPMR
SPML

COLEMAN, Seth s/o
Willis & Martha
Coleman age 22 S
laborer POB & POR
Spotsylvania POC
& **CLARKE**, Sue d/o
John & Mary
Clarke age 23 S
POB Washington
D.C. POR
Spotsylvania POC;
POM Spotsylvania
C.H.27 Feb 1892

69

SPMR SPML
CROWN, James H.
s/o J.S.& Mary
F.Crown age 26 S
farmer POB Tenley
Town, D.C. POR
Florida & **WALLER**,
Laura May d/o
A.B.& Minerva
Waller age 19 S
POB & POR
Spotsylvania; POM
Spotsylvania 31
Aug 1892 SPMR 30
Aug 1892 SPML
COLEMAN, Solon T. s/o
Thomas S.&
Angelina
H.Coleman age 26
S farmer POB &
POR Spotsylvania
& **BLAYDES**, Nannie
B. d/o Hugh F.&
Mary E.Blaydes
age 18 S POB &
POR Spotsylvania;
POM Spotsylvania
16 Dec 1869 SPMR
10 Dec 1869 SPML
COLEMAN, Taylor s/o
Billy & Easther
Coleman age 20y
9mo S farmer POB
& POR
Spotsylvania POC
& **JOHNSON**, Martha
d/o Daniel &
Patience Johnson
age 25 W POB &
POR Spotsylvania
POC; POM
Lombardy,
Spotsylvania 5
Jan 1869 SPMR 2
Mar 1868 SPML
COLEMAN, Taylor s/o
William & Clary
Coleman age 24 S
laborer POB & POR
Spotsylvania POC
& **LEWIS**, Ruther
d/o Albert &
Nelly Hambleton
age 21 S POB &
POR Spotsylvania
POC; POM
Spotsylvania 22
Dec 1875 SPMR 21
Dec 1875 SPML
COLEMAN, Warren s/o
Walker &
M.Coleman age 21
S laborer POB &
POR Spotsylvania
POC & **JACKSON**,
Laura D. d/o Tom
& Mary Jackson
age 18 S POB &
POR Spotsylvania
POC; 2 May 1877
SPML
COLEMAN, William J.
s/o J.T.&
E.L.Coleman age
23 S POB & POR
Spotsylvania &
BAILEY, L.E. d/o
C.& J.Bailey age
20 S POB & POR
Spotsylvania; POM
Spotsylvania 14
Apr 1880 SPMR 13
Apr 1880 SPML
COLEMAN, Winfield S.
s/o H.&
J.F.Coleman age
27 S farmer POB &
POR Spotsylvania
& **LANDRAM**,
Georgeanna A. d/o
William &
J.A.Shepherd age
25 W POB Caroline
Co POR
Spotsylvania; POM
Spotsylvania 7
Sep 1876 SPMR 2
Sep 1876 SPML
COLEMAN, Wyatt & **ROSS**,
Virginia ("they
having been
living together
as man and wife
for some
time..."); 1 Mar
1867 SPConsent
COLEMAN, Wyatt s/o
Anthony & Amelia

Dawson age 27 S
farmer POB
Spotsylvania POC
& **ROSS**, Virginia
d/o George &
Martha Ross age
15 S POB
Spotsylvania POC;
POM Spotsylvania
3 Mar 1867 SPMR 1
Mar 1867 SPML
COLES, Alexander s/o
William & Ann
Coles age 36 S
laborer POB
Louisa Co POR
Spotsylvania POC
& **PENDLETON**,
Virginia d/o
Frank & Harriet
Pendleton age 27
S POB & POR
Spotsylvania POC;
POM Mt Olivet,
Spotsylvania 29
Dec 1882
(probable
minister's error
in year) SPMR 5
Dec 1892 SPML
COLES, Alexander s/o
Charles & Fanny
Coles age 23 S
laborer POB & POR
Spotsylvania POC
& **MADISON**, Sally
s/o George &
Sophia Madison
age 23 S POB &
POR Spotsylvania
POC; POM
Spotsylvania 6
Aug 1876 SPMR 4
Aug 1876 SPML
COLLINS, C.F. s/o
George T.& Ann
J.Collins age 22
S farmer POB &
POR Caroline Co &
RAWLINGS, N.J.
d/o Alfred &
J.A.Rawlings age
23 S POB & POR
Spotsylvania; POM

Waller's Ch,
Spotsylvania 25
Oct 1881 SPMR 24
Oct 1881 SPML
COLLINS, E.B. s/o
George T.& Ann
J.Collins age 21
S farmer POB &
POR Caroline Co &
BAPTIST, F.C. d/o
E.G.& Maria
E.Baptist age 21
S POB & POR
Spotsylvania; POM
Waller's Ch,
Spotsylvania 25
Oct 1881 SPMR 24
Oct 1881 SPML
COLLINS, Henry s/o
Joseph & Adeline
Collin age 25 S
laborer POB & POR
Spotsylvania POC
& **FRAZIER**, Rachel
d/o William
Frazier age 20 S
POB & POR
Spotsylvania POC;
POM Spotsylvania
5 Nov 1885 SPMR 2
Nov 1885 SPML
COLLINS, John s/o
Dennis & Amanda
Collins age 25 S
farmer POB & POR
Spotsylvania &
WILKERSON, Eliza
d/o W.A.&
L.A.Wilkerson age
16 S POB & POR
Spotsylvania; POM
Spotsylvania
C.H.22 Feb 1893
SPMR 22 Feb 1893
SPML
COLLINS, Lewis s/o
John & Johanna
Collins age 52 S
farmer POB
Ireland POR
Spotsylvania &
ENNIS, Amanda d/o
Catherine Ennis
age 21 S POB

Stafford POR Spotsylvania; POM Spotsylvania 15 Jan 1865 SPMR 12 Jan 1865 SPML

COLLINS, Peter s/o Peter & Elizabeth Collins age 31 W miner POB England POR Orange & **WILLIAMS**, Ann C. d/o James & Elizabeth Williams age 27 S POB England POR Orange; POM Orange 24 Aug 1856 OMR 22 Aug 1856 OML

COLLIS, J.W. s/o Hezekiah & Margaret Collis age 28 S carpenter POB Fauquier Co POR Spotsylvania & **PROCTOR**, Ellen d/o Lewis Proctor age 24 S POB & POR Spotsylvania; POM Spotsylvania 11 Oct 1865 SPMR SPML

COLSTON, Wallace s/o William Colston & Harriet Baylor age 25 S laborer on farm POB Albemarle Co POR Orange POC & **BROCK**, Courtney d/o Alex.Brock & Grace Jones age 23 S POB & POR Orange POC; POM Orange 8 Sep 1866 OMR 6 Sep 1866 OML

COLVIN, Eilliam F. s/o John D.& Frances Colvin age 20 S carpenter POB & POR Culpeper & **HAWLEY**, Lucy M.

d/o Thomas & L.A.Hawley age 22 S POB Culpeper POR Orange; POM Orange 15 Feb 1855 OMR

COMFORT, Beverley s/o George & Dinah Comfort age 25 S laborer POB & POR Spotsylvania POC & **SOUTHALL**, Emma d/o Mike & Celia Southall age 19 S POB & POR Spotsylvania POC; POM Branch Fork Ch, Spotsylvania 23 Dec 1884 SPMR 15 Dec 1884 SPML

COMFORT, Beverley s/o George & Dinah Comfort age 35 S laborer POB & POR Spotsylvania POC & **KING**, Ida d/o Joseph & Amanda King age 22 S POB & POR Spotsylvania POC ; POM Spotsylvania 1 Apr 1897 SPMR SPML

COMFORT, Charles s/o Wilson & L.Comfort age 50 W laborer POB & POR Spotsylvania POC & **LEWIS**, Fanny s/o John & Effie Lewis age 40 W POB & POR Spotsylvania POC; POM Spotsylvania 25 Dec 1880 SPMR SPML

COMFORT, Frank s/o J.D.Brightwell & Emily Comfort age 25 W laborer POB & POR Spotsylvania POC & **BROWN**, Susanna

s/o William &
Susan Brown age
20 S POB & POR
Spotsylvania POC;
POM Branch Fork,
Spotsylvania 26
Sep 1875 SPMR 1
Sep 1875 SPML

COMFORT, Lucian s/o
Fanny Comfort age
26 W carpenter
POB & POR
Spotsylvania POC
& **HOLLADAY**,
Maggie (aka
Maggie Taylor)
d/o Henry & Mary
Holladay age 18 S
POB & POR
Spotsylvania POC;
POM Spotsylvania
31 Dec 1890 SPMR
29 Dec 1890 SPML

COMFORT, Lucian s/o
Fanny Comfort age
33 W carpenter
POB & POR
Spotsylvania POC
& **GORDON**, Blanche
d/o Anthony &
Laura Gordon age
16 S POB & POR
Spotsylvania POC;
POM Spotsylvania
24 Mar 1897 SPMR
11 Mar 1897 SPML

COMFORT, Lucian s/o
William Lewis &
Fanny Comfort age
21 S laborer POB
& POR
Spotsylvania POC
& **MOSS**, Ida d/o
Richard & Maria
Moss age 19 S POB
& POR
Spotsylvania POC;
POM Spotsylvania
18 Dec 1884 SPMR
15 Dec 1884 SPML

COMFORT, Thomas H. s/o
Wilson & Sarah
Ann Comfort age
22 S laborer POB
& POR
Spotsylvania POC
& **WOOLFOLK**, Mary
d/o Levenia
Woolfolk age 17 S
POB & POR
Spotsylvania POC;
POM Branch Fork
Ch, Spotsylvania
23 Dec 1884 SPMR
15 Dec 1884 SPML

COMFORT, William s/o
George & Dinah
Comfort age 26 S
laborer POB & POR
Spotsylvania POC
& **SMITH**, Mary d/o
Thomas & Frances
Smith age 23 S
POB Orange POR
Spotsylvania; POM
Spotsylvania 23
Aug 1898 SPMR
SPML

COMFORT, Wilson s/o
Charles & Fannie
Comfort age 22 S
laborer POB & POR
Spotsylvania POC
& **ACORS**, Sarah A.
d/o Henry & Sarah
Acors age 20 S
POB & POR
Spotsylvania POC;
POM Spotsylvania
16 Dec 1888 SPMR
13 Dec 1888 SPML

COMMACK, H.A. s/o D. &
E.Commack age 27
S farmer POB &
POR Spotsylvania
& **ANDREWS**, E.F.
d/o L.& S.Andrews
age 23 S POB
Orange POR
Spotsylvania; POM
Spotsylvania 27
Feb 1861 SPMR

CONDON, John s/o David
& Mary Condon age
33 S laborer POB
Ireland POR
Orange & **BROWN**,
Sarah F. d/o

William & Mary
Brown age 24 S
POB & POR Orange;
POM Orange 24 Dec
1853 OMR OML
CONNER, Henry s/o
Frank & Patsy
Conner age 26 S
laborer POB & POR
Spotsylvania POC
& **ROBINSON**, Annie
d/o Trenton Chew
& Florence Minor
age 25 S POB &
POR Spotsylvania
POC; POM
Spotsylvania 12
Dec 1883 SPMR
SPML
CONNER, Richard s/o
D.Conner age 50 W
farmer POB
Stafford POR
Spotsylvania &
POWELL, Surella
June d/o Thornton
& E.Powell age 25
S POB & POR
Spotsylvania; POM
Spotsylvania 22
May 1879 SPMR 19
May 1879 SPML
CONNER, William s/o
John Conner &
Nancy Wiggerton
age 54 W planter
POB Rappahannock
Co POR Tennessee
& **TERRILL**, Sallie
J. d/o Edmund
Terrill & Susan
Smith age 31 S
POB & POR Orange;
POM Orange 21 May
1861 OMR 20 May
1861 OML
CONWAY, Peter V.D. s/o
W.P. & Margaret
E. Conway age 52
POR
Fredericksburg &
STANSBURY,
Letitia Y. d/o
John I. & Mary O.
Stansbury age 36
POR
Fredericksburg;
POM
Fredericksburg 6
Mar 1895 TCF
CONWAY, R.M. &
HOLLADAY, Kate L.
d/o Henry
A.Holladay; 9 Feb
1867 SPConsent
(marriage to take
place on 14 Feb
1867)
CONWAY, R.M. s/o W.P.&
M.E.Conway age 26
S POB Stafford
POR Spotsylvania
& **HOLLADAY**, Kate
L. d/o H.A.&
M.F.Holladay age
17 S POB & POR
Spotsylvania; 9
Feb 1867 SPML (ML
states that the
marriage date
will be 14 Feb
1867)
COOK, Carl s/o
Gottfried &
Martha Cook age
25 S restaurant
keeper POB
Milhausen,Germany
POR
Fredericksburg &
MARTELS, Elfride
M. d/o Carl &
Mina Martels POB
Caestaug,Germany
age 25 S POR
Spotsylvania; POM
Spotsylvania 20
Sep 1887 SPMR 19
Sep 1887 SPML
COOK, William age 85 W
farmer POB & POR
Spotsylvania POC
& **HERNDON**, Susan
age 22 S POB &
POR Spotsylvania
POC; POM
Spotsylvania 14

Jan 1886 SPMR SPML
COOK, William J. s/o Marshall & Susan Cook age 24 S bricklayer POB Culpeper POR Orange & **SMITH**, Angelina d/o Caleb & Elizabeth Smith age 20 S POB & POR Orange; POM Orange 19 Feb 1856 OMR 14 Feb 1856 OML
COOMBS, Homer J. s/o Joseph Combs & Mary A. Burruss age 26 S POB Caroline Co POR Spotsylvania POC & **ALSOP**, Mary E. d/o Henry & Mary A. Alsop age 21 S POB & POR Spotsylvania POC; POM Spotsylvania 3 Jan 1884 SPMR 28 Dec 1883 SPML
COOPER, Elijah A. s/o Elijah Cooper & Julia A. Browning age 25 S seaman POB Gloucester Co POR Hampton, Va & **CLARK**, Martha E. d/o William Clark & Frances Estes age 17 S POB & POR Orange; POM Orange 21 Feb 1865 OMR 20 Feb 1865 OML
COOPER, James B. s/o Barnett A. & Lucinda Cooper age 20 S farmer POB & POR Stafford & **DUNAVANT**, Mary L. d/o Jacob & Mary Dunavant age 18 S POB & POR Spotsylvania; POM Spotsylvania 21 Dec 1893 SPMR 20 Dec 1893 SPML

COOPER, James M. s/o Dallas & Mary Cooper age 23 S farmer POB Stafford POR Spotsylvania & **HANEY**, Angie d/o J.T. & Louisa Haney age 19 S POB & POR Spotsylvania; POM Spotsylvania C.H. 20 Mar 1895 SPMR 18 Mar 1895 SPML

COOPER, James S. s/o Edward & Louisa Cooper age 21 farmer POB Stafford POR Spotsylvania & **BAKER**, Sophelia d/o William & Electra Baker age 22 POB Stafford POR Spotsylvania; POM Spotsylvania 19 Nov 1869 SPMR SPML

COOPER, Thomas s/o Fleming & Martha Cooper age 25 S laborer POB & POR Spotsylvania POC & **STREET**, Maggie d/o James & Bettie Street age 18 S POB & POR Spotylvania POC; POM Little Road Ch, Spotsylvania 20 Apr 1890 SPMR 19 Apr 1890 SPML

COOPER, William J. & **BROCKMAN**, Sarah E. d/o Asa Brockman; 10 Nov 1853 OML

COOPER, William J. s/o Owen & Jane Cooper age 28 W

farmer POB & POR Orange & **GRAVES**, Mary Walker d/o Isaac W. & Eliza E. Walker age 24 S POB & POR Orange; POM Orange 29 Mar 1860 OMR 24 Mar 1860 OML
CORBIN, Henry s/o James & B. Corbin age 21 S laborer POB & POR Spotsylvania POC & **RENNOLDS**, Rachael d/o E. & F. Rennolds age 20 S POB & POR Spotsylvania POC; POM Spotsylvania 30 Dec 1880 SPMR 27 Dec 1880 SPML
CORTHON, James s/o C.L. & M.E. Corthon age 24 W laborer POB Ohio POR Spotsylvania & **MASTIN**, Cordelia d/o Linsfield Mastin sister in law to Mr. Bell age 24 S POB & POR Spotsylvania; POM Spotsylvania 10 Aug 1884 SPMR 4 Aug 1884 SPML
COVINGTON, James s/o R.N. & Mary W. Covington age 21 S farmer POB Caroline Co POR Spotsylvania & **ROSE**, Olivia d/o M.A. & Bettie Rose age 17 S POB & POR Spotsylvania; POM Spotsylvania 9 Mar 1890 SPMR 3 Mar 1890 SPML
COVINGTON, Thomas s/o Robert & Mary Covington age 22 S farmer POB & POR Spotsylvania

& **THACKER**, Martha d/o Elijah & Mildred Thacker age 24 S POB & POR Spotsylvania; POM Spotsylvania C.H. 18 May 1900 SPMR SPML
COWHERD, Charles P. s/o Frank & Charlotte L. Cowherd age 31 S farmer POB & POR Orange & **HOLLADAY**, Emily Gertrude d/o John M. & Lizzie L. Holladay age 23 S POB & POR Spotsylvania; POM Trinity Ch, Louisa 2 Nov 1898 Louisa MR 14 Oct 1898 SPML
COWHERD, Coleby & **COWHERD**, Mary Jane; POM Orange 4 Nov 1852 OMR 2 Nov 1852 OML
COX, John Benjamin & **LUMSDEN**, Sarah M.; 29 Jun 1857 SPML
COX, Joseph W. & **MARTIN**, Mary J. W; 30 Mar 1867 SPConsent
COX, Joseph W. s/o George & S.A. Cox age 33 S farmer POB & POR Spotsylvania & **MARTIN**, Mary J. d/o Shederack & Elizabeth Martin age 38 W POB & POR Spotsylvania; POM Spotsylvania 3 Apr 1867 SPMR 1 Apr 1867 SPML
COX, Mortimer s/o James & Lucy A. Cox age 63 W farmer POB King

George Co POR Spotsylvania & **McWHIRT**, Annie d/o Silas & Agnes McWhirt age 32 S POB & POR Spotylvania; POM Spotsylvania 1 Dec 1881 SPMR 28 Nov 1881 SPML

CRAFTON, William M. s/o William T.& Mary E.Crafton age 31 S farmer POB Louisa Co POR Spotsylvania & **BULLOCK**, Virgie W. d/o Dr.Robert M. & Anne E.Bullock age 26 S POB & POR Spotsylvania; POM Spotsylvania 12 Jul 1899 SPMR 5 Jul 1899 SPML

CRANE, Jonas & **BURRUSS**, Catharine S.F. ward of Thomas F.Burruss; POM Orange 7 Jul 1853 OMR 6 Jul 1853 OML

CRANK, J.H. s/o J.B.& S.M.Crank age 21 S farmer POB & POR Louisa Co & **CAMMACK**, Willie E. d/o H.A.& E.F.Cammack age 18 S POB & POR Spotsylvania; POM Spotsylvania 19 Oct 1886 SPMR 4 Oct 1886 SPML

CRAWFORD, William S. s/o John P.& Jemimah Crawford age 42 W farmer POB & POR Spotsylvania & **TATE**, Sarah M. d/o Andrew Tate age 38 S POB

Hanover Co POR Spotsylvania; POM Spotsylvania 14 Jan 1873 SPMR 6 Jan 1873 SPML

CREBBS, John C. s/o John & Hannah Crebbs age 30 W architect/builder POB Winchester,Va POR Louisa Co & **BICKERS**, Bettie A. d/o William & Elizabeth Bickers age 22 S POB & POR Orange; POM Orange 11 Feb 1858 OMR 8 Feb 1858 OML

CRISMOND, Austin s/o C.& M.Crismond age 23 S school teacher POB King George Co POR Spotsylvania & **COLEMAN**, Mary Frances d/o James & Lucy Stuart Coleman age 34 S POB & POR Spotsylvania; POM Spotsylvania 16 Feb 1858 SPMR

CRISMOND, Joseph P. s/o John & Jane Crismond age 21 S farmer POB Caroline Co POR Spotsylvania & **CARNOHAN**, Sallie I. d/o William Carnohan age 23 S POB & POR Spotsylvania; pOM Spotsylvania 26 Jun 1866 SPMR SPML

CROCKETT, Thomas R. s/o Thomas J.Crockett & Margaret Robinson age 30 S bricklayer POB District of

77

Columbia POR Orange & **SACRA**, Sarah A. d/o Thomas J.Sacra & Lucinda Robinson age 18 S POB Spotsylvania POR Orange; POM Orange 9 Aug 1864 OMR 8 Aug 1864 OML
CRONIE, William Henry s/o H.B. & Mary A. Cronie of Caroline Co. age 42 POR Washington D.C. & **BERRYMAN**, Ella Lane d/o Montgomery & Eliza L. Slaughter of Fredericksburg age 30 POR Fredericksburg; POM Fredericksburg 30 Dec 1895 TCF
CROPP, George W. s/o John & Eliza Cropp age 31 S farmer POB Stafford POR Spotsylvania & **HOLLADAY**, C.E. d/o John & Elizabeth Holladay age 23 S POB & POR Spotsylvania; POM Spotsylvania 27 Mar 1856 SPMR
CROPP, W.S. s/o J.S.Cropp age 70 W farmer POB Stafford POR Spotsylvania & **DUERSON**, S.M. d/o J.& N.Duerson age 38 S POB & POR Spotsylvania; POM Spotsylvania 3 Mar 1859 SPMR
CROSS, Charles H. s/o George Cross & Rosa A.Betts age 27 S farmer POB England POR Orange & **HANSFORD**, Mary G. d/o John Hansford & Sarah King age 30 S POB & POR Orange; POM Orange 30 Nov 1865 OMR 24 Nov 1865 OML
CROSS, William G. s/o G.& E.Cross age 34 S minister POB Morgan POR Spotsylvania & **SPINDLE**, E.A. d/o William & E.Spindle age 30 S POB Orange Co POR Spotsylvania; POM Spotsylvania 1854 SPMR
CROW, John T. s/o John N.& Eliza J.Crow age 25 S merchant POB & POR Essex Co & **GREEN**, Lucilla E. d/o William E.& Ann E.Green age 30 S POB & POR Spotsylvania; POM Massaponax Ch, Spotsylvania 3 Jan 1889 SPMR 1 Jan 1889 SPML
CRUMP, Barnett s/o Barnett & Mary Crump age 21 S farmer POB & POR Spotsylvania POC & **ALSOP**, Kitty d/o Henry & Mary Ann Alsop age 21 S POB & POR Spotsylvania POC; POM Spotsylvania 4 Aug 1867 SPMR 30 Jul 1867 SPML
CRUMP, Minor s/o Peter & Betsy Crump age 23 S laborer POB

& POR Spotsylvania POC & **JACKSON**, Celia d/o Nelson & Clara Jackson age 19 S POB & POR Spotsylvania POC; POM Spotsylvania 15 Dec 1881 SPMR SPML

CRUMP, Paul s/o Ben & Hannah Crump age 41 W farmer POB & POR Spotsylvania & **TYLER**, Milley d/o Dick & Mary Tyler age 25 W POB & POR Spotsylvania; POM Spotsylvania 28 Dec 1866 SPMR 27 Dec 1866 SPML

CRUMP, William Henry s/o Barnett & Kitty Crump age 25 S farmer POB & POR Spotsylvania POC & **CARTER**, Abbie d/o Warner & Eadie Carter age 24 S POB & POR Spotsylvania POC; POM Spotsylvania 21 Mar 1900 SPMR 19 Mar 1900 SPML

CRUSON, Thomas s/o Richard & Betty Cruson age 22 S dentist POB Richmond Co POR Philadelphia, Penn & **HART**, Martha d/o Malcolm & Betty Hart age 22 S POB & POR Spotsylvania POC; POM New Hope Ch, Spotsylvania 15 Apr 1894 SPMR 13 Apr 1894 SPML

CRUTCHFIELD, C. s/o S.& S.A.Crutchfield age 22 1/2 S farmer POB & POR Spotsylvania & **FRAZER**, M.M. d/o F.& M.B.Frazer age 20 S POB & POR Spotsylvania; POM Spotsylvania 7 Feb 1861 SPMR

CRUTCHFIELD, John s/o Robert & Lucy Crutchfield age 26 S farmer POB & POR Spotsylvania POC & **BROADDUS**, Mary R. d/o Pleasant & Sarah Broaddus age 23 S POB & POR Spotsylvania POC; POM Spotsylvania 25 Jan 1894 SPMR 20 Jan 1894 SPML

CRUTCHFIELD, Reuben s/o Crager Smith & Lucy Crutchfield age 21 S farmer POB & POR Spotsylvania & **COLEMAN**, Hettie d/o Daniel & Celia Coleman age 21 S POB & POR Spotsylvania; POM Spotsylvania 25 Dec 1869 SPMR 21 Dec 1869 SPML

CRUTCHFIELD, Robert s/o Robert & L.Crutchfield age 23 S laborer POB & POR Spotsylvania POC & **GORDON**, Ann d/o L.& L.Gordon age 21 S POB & POR Spotsylvania POC; POM Spotsylvania 12 Jan 1881 SPMR 11 Jan 1881 SPML

CULLEN, George Jr.s/o George & Barbara Cullen age 23 S

jeweler POB & POR Orange C.H.& **HANSBROUGH**, Martha S. d/o Alexander Hamilton & Elizabeth Hansbrough age 18 S POB Culpeper C.H. POR Orange C.H.; POM Orange 15 Jun 1858 OMR 14 Jun 1858 OML

CUMMINGS, Edgar F. s/o John & Hannah Cummings age 23 S horticulturist POB & POR Loudon Co & **ROOSA**, Annie G. d/o R.B.& Annie K.Roosa age 26 S POB Sullivan Co, N.Y. POR Spotsylvania; POM Waller's Baptist Ch, Spotsylvania 29 Jun 1898 SPMR 15 Jun 1898 SPML

CUNNINGHAM, A.B. s/o Solomon & Polly Cunningham age 60 W farmer POB Otsego Co, N.Y. POR Spotsylvania & **CARNOHAN**, Dora A. d/o Warren & L.A.Carnohan age 36 S POB & POR Spotsylvania; POM Spotsylvania 19 Dec 1892 SPMR 17 Dec 1894 SPML

CURTIS, Calvin H. s/o Jeff & Sallie Curtis age 26 S farmer POB & POR Spotsylvania & **PERRY**, Mary A. d/o Robert & Lavinia Perry age 17 S POB & POR Spotsylvania; POM Spotsylvania C.H.
1 Dec 1886 SPMR SPML

CURTIS, James A. s/o Jeff & Sallie Curtis age 21 S farmer POB & POR Spotsylvania & **SORRELL**, Edmonia M. d/o John R.& Amanda J.Sorrell age 19 S POB Orange POR Spotsylvania; POM Post Oak, Spotsylvania 29 Dec 1896 SPMR 28 Dec 1896 SPML

CURTIS, Jefferson s/o Thomas & Ann Curtis age 22 S wheelwright POB & POR Spotsylvania & **HICKS**, Sally Ann d/o Peter & Mary Ann Hicks age 24 S POB & POR Spotsylvania; POM Spotsylvania 26 Dec 1854 SPMR

CURTIS, Jefferson T. s/o Thomas & Ann Curtis age 34 W mechanic POB & POR Spotsylvania & **DICKINSON**, Sarah A. d/o John & Emily Dickinson age 28 S POB & POR Spotsylvania; POM Spotsylvania Nov 1867 SPMR 4 Nov 1867 SPML

CURTIS, John B. s/o John & Mary Curtis age 29 S tailor POB Westmoreland Co POR Orange & **HALEY**, Maria P. d/o James & Mary Stephens age 31 W POB & POR Orange; POM Orange 4 Oct

1859 OMR 3 Oct
1859 OML
CURTIS, John s/o
Jefferson & Sarah
Curtis age 21 S
farmer POB & POR
Spotsylvania &
SORRELL, Luella
d/o John & Amanda
Sorrell age 16 S
POB & POR
Spotsylvania; POM
Spotsylvania C.H.
11 Sep 1890 SPMR
SPML
CURTIS, John T. s/o
Thomas & Ann
Curtis age 32 S
mechanic POB &
POR Spotsylvania
& **ALSOP**, Jane F.
d/o Thomas &
Elizabeth Alsop
age 34 S POB &
POR Spotsylvania;
POM Spotsylvania
11 Feb 1868 SPMR
SPML
CURTIS, Nepoleon s/o
Charles & Jane
Curtis age 21 S
farmer POB & POR
Spotsylvania &
SMALLWOOD,
Evelina d/o
Thomas & Betsy
Alsop age 24 W
POB & POR
Spotsylvania; POM
Spotsylvania 2
Apr 1868 SPMR 27
Mar 1868 SPML
CURTIS, T.J. s/o
Jefferson & Sarah
Curtis age 27 S
farmer POB
Fredericksburg
POR Spotsylvania
& **HAISLOP**, Annie
O. d/o R.B.& Lucy
D. Haislop age 18
S POB & POR
Spotsylvania; POM
Spotsylvania 26
Nov 1885 SPMR 24
Nov 1885 SPML
CURTIS, William G. s/o
Jefferson &
Sallie E.Curtis
age 20 S farmer
POB & POR
Spotsylvania &
FAY, Dora E. d/o
John & Emilly Fay
age 22 S POB &
POR Spotsylvania;
POM Spotsylvania
C.H. 5 Oct 1892
SPMR SPML
DADE, Albert G. s/o
Langhorn Dade &
Ann Harrison age
50 W farmer POB
King George Co
POR Orange &
BROOKING, Mary R.
d/o Jacob Walters
& _____ Brooking
(Belinda was
written in at a
later date) age
34 W POB & POR
Orange; POM
Orange 15 May
1866 OMR 9 May
1866 OML
DAFFAU, William P. s/o
James A.& Ann
M.Daffau age 25 S
farmer POB & POR
Stafford &
PEMBERTON, Lizzie
S. d/o William &
Maggie
E.Pemberton age
22 S POB Culpeper
Co POR
Spotsylvania; POM
Beach Grove Ch,
Spotsylvania 25
Dec 1884 SPMR 23
Dec 1884 SPML
DALEY, Alexander s/o
John Daley &
Elizabeth Dunn
age 53 W leather
dealer POB Kings
Co, Ireland POR

Orange &
RAWLINGS, Sarah
J. d/o Richard
Rawlings & Lucy
S.Rawlings age 41
S POB & POR
Orange; POM
Spotsylvania 28
May 1863 SPMR 26
May 1863 OML
DANDRIDGE, Charles &
LEWIS, Mary Ann
age 19 (as of 1
Jun 1867);
undated SPConsent
DANDRIDGE, Woodford
s/o Byrd &
Margaret
Dandridge age 37
W laborer POB &
POR Spotsylvania
POC & **COLEMAN**,
Hattie d/o Minor
& Louisa Coleman
age 24 D POB &
POR Spotsylvania
POC; POM
Spotsylvania 23
Nov 1897 SPMR 22
Nov 1897 SPML
DANIEL, Beverley R.Jr.
s/o Z.C.& Fanny
Daniel age 21 S
farmer POB & POR
Spotsylvania &
PULLIAM, Ivy S.
d/o Dr. John D.&
Lucy N.Pulliam
age 17 POB & POR
Spotsylvania; POM
Spotsylvania 3
Oct 1894 SPMR
SPML
DARE, Andrew J. s/o
John & Jane
M.Dare age 67 S
farmer POB & POR
Spotsylvania &
CRAWFORD, Eva
M.d/o Jerome &
Maria Sisler age
39 W POB Seneca
Falls, N.Y.POR
Spotsylvania; POM

Spotsylvania 21
May 1899 SPMR 19
May 1899 SPML
DARLINGTON, John T.
s/o Henry
Darlington &
Charlotte Bledso
age 21 S
newspaper
publisher POB
Edgefield
District, S.C.
POR Elbert Co,Ga
& **ADAMS**, Arianna
H. d/o Thomas
J.Adams & Martha
Owens age 15 S
POB & POR Orange;
POM
Verdiersville,
Orange 19 Mar
1863 OMR 17 Mar
1863 OML
DARNELL, Benjamin L.
s/o Moses & Sarah
Darnell age 52 S
farmer POB & POR
Spotsylvania &
MAZE, Ann Matilda
d/o Elizabeth
Maze age 23 S POB
& POR
Spotsylvania; POM
Spotsylvania
1864 SPMR1 Sep
1864 SPML
DARNELL, Benjamin L.
s/o Moses & Sarah
Darnell age 52 S
farmer POB & POR
Spotsylvania &
MAZE, Ann Matilda
d/o Elizabeth
Maze age 23 S POB
& POR
Spotsylvania; POM
Spotsylvania 1864
SPMR 1 Sep 1864
SPML
DAVENPORT, Charles E.
s/o William S.&
Sarah A.Davenport
age 21 S farmer
POB & POR

Spotsylvania &
JONES, Ida L. d/o
James A. &
M.L.Jones age 21
S POB & POR
Spotsylvania; POM
Spotsylvania 18
Dec 1888 SPMR 15
Dec 1888 SPML
DAVENPORT, Dorsey W.
s/o W.D.& Ella
Davenport age 21
S farmer POB &
POR Spotsylvania
& **HALL**, Clara I.
d/o L.W.& Maggie
Hall age 19 S POB
& POR
Spotsylvania; POM
Spotsylvania
C.H.12 Feb 1895
SPMR SPML
DAVENPORT, John Tanner
s/o Peter &
Martha Davenport
age 24 S painter
POB & POR
Richmond & **BELL**,
Mary Margaret d/o
Francis & Mary
Bell age 19 S POB
& POR Orange; POM
Orange 27 May
1856 OMR 26 May
1856 OML
DAVENPORT, Lewis s/o
William Davenport
& Phebe Day age
28 S carpenter
POB New York City
POR Orange &
LOURY, Sarah C.
d/o Jefferson
Wright & Sarah
Wright age 21 S
POB & POR Orange;
POM Orange 26 Dec
1865 OMR OML
DAVENPORT, Walker G.
s/o W.S.& Sarah
Davenport age 22
S miner POB
Albemarle Co POR
Spotsylvania &

POOLE, Bertie H.
d/o W.M.& Lucy
M.Poole age 17 S
POB & POR
Spotsylvania; 22
Dec 1892 SPML
DAVENPORT, Walter D.
s/o Huldah
Davenport age 22
S farmer POB &
POR Spotsylvania
& **EUBANK**, Ella W.
d/o John & Katy
Eubank age 23 S
POB Albemarle Co
POR Spotsylvania;
POM Clover Green,
Spotsylvania 12
Nov 1872 SPMR 4
Nov 1872 SPML
DAVIDSON, W.S. s/o S.&
E. Davidson age
43 S farmer POB
Campbell POR
Appomattox &
LANDRAM, M.A. d/o
W.& S.Landram age
24 S POB & POR
Spotsylvania; POM
Spotsylvania 26
Jan 1860 SPMR
DAVIS, Andrew J. &
FERNEYHOUGH,
Susan E. d/o
Elizabeth
Ferneyhough; POM
Orange 2 Feb 1852
OMR 22 Dec 1851
OML
DAVIS, Andrew s/o
Benjamin & Katie
Davis age 30 S
farmer POB & POR
Spotsylvania POC
& **CARR**, Betsy d/o
Dabney & Polly
Carr age 20 S POB
& POR
Spotsylvania; POM
Spotsylvania 28
Jul 1866 SPMR
SPML
DAVIS, Dudley s/o
Jacob Davis &

Sarah Howard age 22 S laborer POB Louisa Co POR Spotsylvania & **HOWARD**, Maria d/o Silas Minor & Rachel Minor age 19 S POB & POR Spotsylvania; POM Spotsylvania 29 Mar 1877 SPMR 28 Mar 1877 SPML

DAVIS, Edward A. s/o Abraham Davis & Sarah Smith age 42 S carpenter POB Colinton District, S.C. POR Orangeburg District, S.C. & **BROWN**, Mary D. d/o Robinson Brown & Ann Bishop age 28 S POB Culpeper Co POR Orange; POM Walnut Farm, Orange married by chaplain of 27th Va Infantry, Stonewall Brigade 18 Mar 1864 OMR 17 Mar 1864 OML

DAVIS, Edward s/o Parke B. Davis & Maria King age 35 S farmer POB & POR King William Co & **BROCKMAN**, Fannie d/o William L. Brockman & Elizabeth C. Graves age 27 S POB & POR Orange; POM Orange 1 Mar 1866 OMR 28 Feb 1866 OML

DAVIS, George s/o Anderson & Ailey Davis age 21 S laborer POB & POR Louisa Co POC & **JOHNSON**, Drucilla d/o Solomon & Mary Johnson age 19 S POB & POR Spotsylvania POC; POM Spotsylvania C.H. 20 Dec 1888 SPMR SPML

DAVIS, George s/o George & Mahala Kendall age 22 S farmer POB Louisa Co POR Spotsylvania POC & **BOYD**, Betsy Ann d/o Reuben & Margaret Boyd age 23 S POB Louisa Co POR Spotsylvania POC; POM Spotsylvania 29 Dec 1870 SPMR 27 Dec 1870 SPML

DAVIS, George W. s/o Thomas & Susan Davis age 24 S carpenter POB Orange POR Green Co & **CASON**, Sallie M. d/o Benjamin & Elizabath Cason age 23 S POB & POR Orange; POM Orange 15 Apr 1858 OMR 14 Apr 1858 OML

DAVIS, I.M. s/o H.E. & S.E. Davis age 30 S physician POB & POR Spotsylvania & **DAVIS**, Drucilla G. d/o George W. & Virginia Davis age 18 S POB & POR Spotsylvania; POM Spotsylvania 8 Mar 1866 SPMR 5 Mar 1866 SPML

DAVIS, James s/o Robert Davis & Harriet Sanders age 25 S shoemaker POB Madison Co POR

Orange POC &
SNEED, Milly d/o
Winston Sneed &
Lucy Carter age
22 S POB & POR
Orange POC; POM
Orange 11 Oct
1866 OMR 10 Oct
1866 OML
DAVIS, Lemuel E. s/o
R.L.& L.C.Davis
age 21 S farmer
POB Hanover Co
POR Spotsylvania
& **GOODMAN**, Ethel
d/o C.W.& Mary
C.Goodwin age 24
S POB POR
Spotsylvania; POM
Spotsylvania 31
Dec 1896 SPMR
SPML
DAVIS, Richard R. &
BLEDSOE, Martha
A.; undated
Orange Co ML (was
found in 1859 ML)
DAVIS, Robert P. s/o
Parks B.& Martha
Davis age 41 S
housebuilder POB
King William Co
POR Richmond &
KENDALL, Octavia
A. d/o Thomas G.&
Eliza Kendall age
28 S POB
Spotsylvania POR
Orange; POM
Orange 3 May 1859
OMR 2 May 1859
OML
DAVIS, Robert s/o
Andrew & Melissa
Davis age 23 S
laborer POB & POR
Spotsylvania POC
& **MANUEL**, Fannie
d/o Jackson &
Lucinda Manuel
age 21 S POB
Caroline Co POR
Spotsylvania POC;
11 Dec 1884 SPML

DAVIS, Thomas J. &
JACKSON, Mary E.;
26 Jan 1857 OML
DAVIS, Thornton s/o
Benjamin & Nelly
Davis age 25 S
laborer on farm
POB & POR Orange
POC & **MAGRUDER**,
Judy d/o Peter &
Phoebe Magruder
age 21 S POB &
POR Orange POC:
POM Orange 19 Oct
1867 OMR 16 Oct
1867 OML
DAVIS, William H. s/o
Maria Davis age
26 S farmer POB &
POR Spotsylvania
POC & **JOHNSON**,
Lottie R. d/o
Louis & Delia
Johnson age 22 S
POB & POR
Spotsylvania POC;
POM Spotsylvania
23 Jan 1900 SPMR
SPML
DAWSON, Addison s/o
Edward & Martha
Dawson age 34 S
laborer POB & POR
Spotsylvania POC
& **TYLER**, Delilah
d/o Edward & Rena
Tyler age 30 S
POB & POR
Spotsylvania POC;
POM Spotsylvania
17 Jan 1894 SPMR
SPML
DAWSON, Charles M. s/o
William M. & Mary
F.Dawson age 21 S
farmer POB & POR
Loudon Co &
RICHESON,
Parthania S. d/o
Nancy Richeson
age 21 S POB &
POR Spotsylvania;
POM Spotsylvania

6 Aug 1873 SPMR 5 Aug 1873 SPML

DAWSON, Erasmus s/o Edward & Martha Dawson age 25 W laborer POB & POR Spotsylvania POC & **TYLER**, Jane d/o Edward & Rena Tyler age 27 S POB & POR Spotsylvania POC; POM Spotsylvania 31 Jan 1900 SPMR SPML

DAWSON, Lewis s/o Lewis & Evelina Dawson age 26 S laborer POB & POR Spotsylvania POC & **GARNETT**, Lelia d/o Mollie Garnett age 17 S POB & POR Spotsylvania POC; POM Spotsylvania 4 Jan 1899 SPMR 2 Jan 1899 SPML

DAWSON, Matt s/o Edmund & Caroline Dawson age 25 S farmer POB & POR Spotylvania POC & **CARY**,Evelina d/o Woodson & Charlott Cary age 22 S POB Caroline Co POR Spotsylvania POC; POM Spotsylvania 26 Apr 1873 SPMR SPML

DAWSON, Ras s/o Edward & Martha Dawson S laborer POB & POR Spotsylvania POC & **TAYLOR**, Julia d/o James Taylor S POB & POR Spotsylvania POC; POM Cherry Grove, Spotsylvania 9 Jul 1896 SPMR SPML

DAWSON, Robin s/o Robin & Eliza Dawson age 36 W laborer POB North Caroline POR Spotsylvania POC & **WORMSLEY**, Elzie d/o Toby & Daphney Gibbs age 36 W POB & POR Spotsylvania POC; POM Spotsylvania C.H.19 Jan 1886 SPMR SPML

DAY, George W. s/o Harriet Day age 28 S laborer POB & POR Spotsylvania POC & **WIGGLESWORTH**, Ellen d/o Walker & Mary Jane Wigglesworth age 22 S POB & POR Spotsylvania POC; POM New Hoep Ch, Spotsylvania 17 Dec 1885 SPMR 8 Dec 1885 SPML

DAY, William L.(Captain) s/o John A. & Mary R.Day age 50 S farmer POB & POR Spotsylvania & **ANDREWS**, Fanny W. d/o John L.& Mary E.Andrews age 28 S POB & POR Spotsylvania; POM Spotsylvania 12 Mar 1890 SPMR 4 Mar 1890 SPML

DAY, William R. & **FLETCHER**, Margaret d/o Sarah Fletcher; 8 Sep 1877 SPConsent

DAY, William R. s/o Benjamin & E.Day age 27 S carpenter POB Maryland POR

Spotsylvania &
FLETCHER,
Margaret d/o
Madison & Sarah
Fletcher age 19 S
POB & POR
Spotsylvania; POM
Spotsylvania 9
Sep 1877 SPMR 8
Sep 1877 SPML
DEASMAN, Francis M.
s/o William &
Diantha Deasman
age 26 S farmer
POB & OR Tompkins
Co, N.Y. &
FISHER, Hannah M.
d/o Elijah &
Elizabeth
A.Fisher age 27 S
POB Luzern Co, Pa
POR Spotsylvania;
POM Spotsylvania
25 Oct 1867
(possible error
in year by
minister) 25 Oct
1870 SPML
DECKER, M.E. s/o J.&
S.Decker age 26 S
teacher POB
Warren Co,N.J.
POR Spotsylvania
& **DUERSON**, A.E.
d/o D.& A.Duerson
age 25 S POB &
POR Spotsylvania;
4 Dec 1860 SPML
DECKER, Walker J. s/o
John & Letitia
Decker age 45 W
minister POB
Spotsylvania POR
Orange & **CHESLEY**,
Mary S. d/o W.A.&
Mary A.Chesley
age 26 S POB
Fredericksburg
POR Spotsylvania;
POM Spotsylvania
1 Jun 1886 SPMR
31 May 1886 SPML
DEJARNETTE, A.H. s/o
James C.& Lucy
Mary Dejarnette
age 31 S farmer
POB & POR
Caroline Co &
MORTON, Fenton W.
d/o Jeremiah &
Charlotte
W.Morton age 25 S
POB Culpeper Co
POR Spotsylvania;
POM Spotsylvania
24 Feb 1886 SPMR
23 Feb 1886 SPML
DEMAINE, Charles W.
s/o William
Demaine &
Elizabeth Mankin
age 21 S fireman
on O.& A.railroad
POB Alexandria
City POR Orange &
MUSE, Annie E.
d/o Edward & Mary
Muse age 21 S POB
New York City POR
Orange; POM
Gordonsville 15
Mar 1864 OMR 11
Mar 1864 OML
DEMPSEY, James A. &
SMITH, Elizabeth;
20 Dec 1852 OML
DEMPSEY, Pleasant O.
s/o James A.&
Elizabeth Dempsey
age 21 S farmer
POB & POR Orange
& **WAYLAND**, Kate
H. d/o Robert &
Susie Wayland age
21 S POB Madison
Co POR
Spotsylvania; POM
Spotsylvania
C.H.27 Oct 1890
SPMR SPML
DEMPSEY, William A. &
MORRIS, Margaret
F.; POM Orange 6
Jan 1852 OMR 2
Jan 1852 OML
DEMPSEY, William s/o
James A.&
Elizabeth Dempsey

age 27 S farmer POB & POR Orange & **CHILTON**, Almira F. d/o John F.& Hester A.Chilton age 27 S POB Stafford POR Spotsylvania; POM Spotsylvania 18 Dec 1884 SPMR SPML

DEMPSY, David A. s/o P.R.& N.Dempsy age 28 S farmer POB Orange POR Spotsylvania & **CHILDRESS**, Sarah d/o Robert & L.Childress age 18 S POB Orange POR Spotsylvania; POM Spotsylvania 15 Jan 1879 SPMR 14 Jan 1879 SPML

DESPARD, Edward s/o M.& L.Despard age 22 S POB & POR Spotsylvania POC & **CRUTCHFIELD**, Sarah d/o Robert & L.Crutchfield age 20 S POB & POR Spotsylvania POC; POM Branch Fork Ch, Spotsylvania 30 Jan 1879 SPMR 23 Jan 1879 SPML

DESPER, James Henderson s/o Murry & Louisa Desper age 21y 6mo S farmer POB & POR Spotsylvania POC & **BROCK**, Nancy d/o Richard & Agnes Brock age 18 S POB & POR Spotsylvania POC; POM Spotsylvania 29 Aug 1874 SPMR 28 Aug 1874 SPML

DESREAUX, George s/o John & Ann Desreaux of Isle of Jersey age 70 POR Stafford Co. & **WALLER**, Fannie Elizabeth d/o Robert & Elizabeth Waller of Spotsylvania age 45 POR Fredericksburg; POM Fredericksburg 10 May 1893 TCF

DICKERSON, Hiram B. s/o Thomas H. & Clara E.Dickinson age 39 S farmer POB & POR Spotsylvania & **TOWLES**, Carrie C. d/o T.T.& Elizabeth Towles age 27 S POB & POR Spotsylvania; POM Spotsylvania 28 Nov 1894 SPMR 26 Nov 1894 SPML

DICKERSON, John R. s/o John & Emilly Dickinson age 58 W carpenter POB Spotsylvania POR Fredericksburg & **HALL**, Lucy Mary d/o Horace C.& Lucy Hall age 43 S POB & POR Spotsylvania; POM Spotsylvania C.H.26 Sep 1892 SPMR SPML

DICKERSON, Levi s/o Frayser (?) & Mary Dickerson age 25 S laborer POB & POR Spotsylvania POC & **WILLIS**, Nannie d/o Julia Dickerson age 19 POB & POR Spotsylvania POC;

POM Spotsylvania C.H. 7 Jan 1884 SPMR SPML

DICKERSON, Walker s/o George & Clara Dickerson age 21 S farmer POB Caroline Co POR Spotsylvania & GARNET, Chany d/o Rhoda Garnet age 25 S POB Caroline Co POR Spotsylvania; POB Spotsylvania Jun 1867 SPMR 24 Jun 1867 SPML

DICKINSON, Albert T. s/o Thomas H. & Clara E. Dickinson age 25 S farmer POB Caroline Co POR Spotsylvania & HAILEY, Anna B. d/o J.B. & L. Hailey age 21 S POB & POR Spotsylvania; POM Spotsylvania 26 Feb 1874 SPMR (possible error in year) 25 Dec 1874 SPML

DICKINSON, Bowie C. s/o R.H. & M.F. Dickinson age 24 S farmer POB & POR Spotsylvania & WRIGHT, Emma C. d/o John W. & Catherine Wright age 18 S POB & POR Spotsylvania; POM Spotsylvania 10 Nov 1897 SPMR 4 Nov 1897 SPML

DICKINSON, Charles S. s/o Robert Q. & Susan E. Dickinson age 30 S student POB & POR Richmond, Va & GOODWIN, Fanny D. d/o John & Fanny Goodwin age 24 S POB Texas POB Spotsylvania; POM County Line Ch, Caroline Co 31 Aug 1893 Caroline MR 23 Aug 1893 SPML

DICKINSON, F.P. s/o H.M. & S.C. Dickinson ge 35 S farmer POB & POR Spotsylvania & ULLIAM, A. Myrtle d/o Dr. J.D. & L.N. Pulliam age 19 S POB & POR Spotsylvania; POM Spotsylvania 20 Dec 1893 SPMR 4 Dec 1893 SPML

DICKINSON, George s/o Ann Turner age 23 S railroad hand POB & POR Spotsylvania POC & WASHINGTON, Josephine d/o Jarratt & Patsy Washington age 22 S POB & POR Spotsylvania POC; POM Spotsylvania C.H. 7 May 1887 SPMR SPML

DICKINSON, J.Y. s/o William B. & Emma Dickinson age 22 S merchant POB & POR Caroline Co & DICKINSON, Annie M. d/o James C. & Annie M. Dickinson age 23 S POB & POR Spotsylvania; POM Grace Ch, Caroline Co 8 Jun 1898 Caroline MR 6 Jun 1898 SPML

DICKINSON, James C. s/o William J. & June Dickinson

age 28 S farmer
POB & POR
Caroline Co &
SMITH, Nannie M.
d/o William M. &
Harriet Smith age
23 S POB
Fredericksburg
POR Spotsylvania;
POM St George Ch,
Fredericksburg 11
Jul 1867 FMR 10
Jul 1867 SPML
DICKINSON, James s/o
William Dickinson
& Matilda
Matthews age 48 W
farmer POB Essex
Co POR Richmond
Co & **TAYLOR**, Ann
M. d/o Richard
S.Taylor &
Eleanor Gwathway
age 43 S POB King
William Co POR
Orange; POM
Orange 31 Oct
1867 OMR 30 Oct
1867 OML
DICKINSON, John R. s/o
Robert H.& Mary
Ann Dickinson age
21 S farmer POB &
POR Spotsylvania
& **EDENTON**,
Florence L. d/o
J.P.& Agnes
Edenton age 23 S
POB & POR
Spotsylvania; POM
Spotsylvania 23
Mar 1898 SPMR 22
Mar 1898 SPML
DICKINSON, M.H. s/o
Robert H.& Mary
F.Dickinson age
23 S merchant POB
& POR
Spotsylvania &
ROBINSON, Lillie
May d/o Michael &
Jenny Robinson
age 17 S POB &
POR Spotsylvania;
POM Spotsylvania
8 Apr 1891 SPMR 3
Apr 1891 SPML
DICKINSON, Richard J.
s/o Robert &
Emily Dickinson
age 27 S farmer
POB Caroline Co
POR Spotsylvania
& **CRUTCHFIELD**,
Mary J. d/o
William & Jane C.
Crutchfield age
28 S POB & POR
Spotsylvania; POM
Spotsylvania 8
Aug 1867 SPMR 7
Aug 1867 SPML
DICKINSON, Robert H.
s/o John & Emily
Dickinson age 24
S mechanic POB &
POR Spotsylvania
& **HICKS**, Mary F.
d/o Robert &
Bettie Hicks age
28 S POB & POR
Spotsylvania; POM
Spotsylvania 21
Sep 1865 SPMR 14
Sep 1865 SPML
DICKINSON, William C.
s/o Hugh M.&
S.C.Dickinson age
26 S farmer POB &
POR Spotsylvania
& **COLEMAN**, Julia
W. d/o Reuben S.&
Mary B.Coleman
age 24 S POB &
POR Spotsylvania;
POM Spotsylvania
1868 (no day or
month on MR) 17
Dec 1868 SPML
DICKMAN, John s/o
Edward & Sarah
Dickman age 74 W
farmer POB
Albemarle Co POR
Spotsylvania &
MARTIN, Lavinia
E. age 40 S POB
Caroline Co POR

Spotsylvania; 10 Nov 1876 SPML (ML states the date of the marriage to be 11 Nov 1876)

DIGGS, Henry s/o Harum & Lucy Diggs age 52 W farmer POB Louisa Co POR Spotsylvania POC & **QUARLES**, Susan d/o Ab.& Frances Quarles age 45 S POB & POR Spotsylvania POC; POM Spotsylvania C.H.4 Oct 1892 SPMR SPML

DILLAN, Alexander W. s/o Thomas & Elizabeth Dillan age 42 W mechanic POB & POR Spotsylvania & **LIPSCOMB**, Virginia C. d/o Ira E. & Ann F.Lipscomb age 29 S POB & POR Spotsylvania; POM 14 Mar 1874 SPMR 13 Mar 1874 SPML

DILLARD, Alexander W. & **COLLINS**, Emily L.; POM Spotsylvania 30 Mar 1854 (no day on MR)SPML

DILLARD, Benjamin L. s/o George W.& Lucy J.Dillard age 35 S physician POB & POR Albemarle Co & **BAPTIST**, Maude G. d/o E.G.& Sarah D.Baptist age 22 S POB & POR Spotsylvania; POM Glanville, Spotsylvania 19 Sep 1893 SPMR 18 Sep 1893 SPML

DILLARD, Benjamin s/o John R.& Mary Dillard age 24 S farmer POB & POR Spotsylvania & **HAILEY**, Sallie d/o Benjamin & Louisa F.Hailey age 16 POB & POR Spotsylvania; POM Spotsylvania C.H. 4 Sep 1884 SPMR SPML

DILLARD, Ferdidnand E. s/o Isaiah J.& Julia A.E.Dillard age 22 S farmer POB & POR Spotsylvania & **DILLARD**, Lottie R. d/o A.W.& Emilly L.Dillard age 24 S POB & POR Spotsylvania; POM Spotsylvania 12 Oct 1892 SPMR 10 Oct 1892 SPML

DILLARD, George B. s/o James D.& L.P.Dillard age 33 S physician POB & POR Spotsylvania & **PEAKE**, Lucy A. d/o James B.& E.J.Peake age 19 S POB & POR Spotsylvania; POM Spotsylvania 17 Nov 1857 SPMR

DILLARD, Isaiah J. s/o John R.& Mary E.Dillard age 19 S farmer POB & POR Spotsylvania & **JONES**, Julia A. d/o Eli M.& Mary E.Jones age 17 S POB Orange POR Spotsylvania; POM Spotsylvania 25 Oct 1866 SPMR 17 Oct 1866 SPML

DILLARD, James A. s/o
Isaiah & Julia
Dillard age 28 S
farmer POB & POR
Spotsylvania &
SEAY, Emma L. d/o
James L.& Lucy
Ellen Seay age 22
S POB & POR
Spotsylvania; POM
Maple Grove,
Spotsylvania 15
Apr 1896 SPMR 13
Apr 1896 SPML
DILLARD, James A. s/o
James T.& Martha
E.Dillard age 23
S farmer POB &
POR Spotsylvania
& HICKS, Mollie
J. d/o James
T.Hicks age 16 S
POB & POR
SPotsylvania; POM
Spotsylvania 29
Jan 1885 SPMR 24
Jan 1885 SPML
DILLARD, James T. S
POR Spotsylvania
& GIBSON, Martha
A.F. S POR
Spotsylvania; POM
Spotsylvania 15
Nov 1853 SPMR
DILLARD, Lewis O. s/o
A.W.& M.L.Dillard
age 23 S farmer
POB & POR
Spotsylvania &
FLEMING, Olivia
J. d/o Bozel S.&
Lucy A.Fleming
age 19 S POB &
POR Spotsylvania;
POM Spotsylvania
9 Nov 1881 SPMR 7
Nov 1881 SPML
DILLARD, Ryland T. s/o
W.M.& Hardenia
A.Dillard age 32
S farmer POB &
POR Spotsylvania
& HALL, Nettie C.
d/o William W.&
Jennnie F.Hall
age 22 S POB &
POR Spotsylvania;
POM Waller's Ch,
Spotsylvania 26
May 1891 SPMR 21
May 1891 SPML
DILLARD, Thomas &
DICKERSON,
Lucindy M.; 27
Feb 1865
SPConsent
DILLARD, Thomas s/o
John & Polly
Dillard W farmer
POB & POR
Spotsylvania &
DICKINSON,
Lucinda d/o John
Dickinson S POB &
POR Spotsylvania;
POM Spotsylvania
9 Mar 1865 SPMR 7
Mar 1865 SPML
DILLARD, William M.
s/o William &
Elizabeth Dillard
age 24 S farmer
POB Spotsylvania
& PARTLOW,
Hidenia d/o L.&
Nancy H.Partlow
age 19 S POB
Spotsylvania; 10
Apr 1856 SPML
DISMUKES, Benjamin &
HORD, Lucy; 22
Dec 1859 SPML
DIXON, George W. s/o
Jacob & Martha
J.Dixon age 26 S
miner POB Nelson
Co POR
Spotsylvania &
PERRY, Ida F. d/o
William H.&
Virginia A.Perry
age 18 S POB &
POR Spotsylvania;
POM Spotsylvania
17 May 1883 SPMR
SPML
DOBYNS, James W. s/o
John W.& Amelia

Dobyns age 20 S
cooper POB & POR
Spotsylvania &
ALMOND, A.N. d/o
Lewis & Susan
Almond age 17 S
POB & POR
Spotsylvania; POM
Spotsylvania 10
Aug 1884 SPMR 8
Aug 1884 SPML
DOBYNS, John H. s/o
G.H.& J.E.Dobyns
age 50 W farmer
POB Essex Co POR
Spotsylvania &
SMITH, Susan J.
d/o Warner &
Susan A.Kent age
44 W POB Fluvanna
Co POR
Spotsylvania; POM
Spotsylvania C.H.
15 Oct 1899 SPMR
SPML
DODDS, Wesley D. s/o
Joseph & Margaret
Dodds age 21 S
farmer POB Owen
Sound, Ont. POR
Caroline Co &
SCHULZE, Anna E.
d/o Henry &
Elizabeth Schulze
age 28 S POB &
POR Spotsylvania;
POM County Line
Baptist Ch,
Caroline Co 29
May 1900 Caroline
MR 17 Apr 1900
SPML
DODSON, Harrison age
70 S laborer POB
& POR
Spotsylvania POC
& **CUNNINGHAM**,
Fanny age 50 S
POB & POR
Spotsylvania POC;
POM Spotsylvania
24 May 1879 SPMR
19 May 1879 SPML

DOGGETT, ANdrew C. s/o
Ic R.B. & Lucy
Doggett of
Fredericksburg
age 41 POR
Fredericksburg &
RICHARDS, Emilie
LeG. d/o Wm. H. &
Emilie H.
Richards of
Fredericksburg
age 28 POR
Fredericksburg;
POM
Fredericksburg 21
Jan 1895 TCF
DOGGETT, James M. s/o
Lemuel & Sarah
Doggett age 64 S
POB & POR
Spotsylvania &
PRUETT, Martha E.
d/o Ann Pruett
age 41 S POB &
POR Spotsylvania;
POM Spotsylvania
C.H. 30 Sep 1885
SPMR SPML
DOLLY, James C. s/o
Rev.S.B.&
M.C.Dolly age 30
S teacher POB
Highland Co POR
Loudon Co &
TURNLEY, Mary M.
d/o Ira P.&
Cornelia Turnley
age 25 S POB &
POR Spotsylvania;
POM Black Rock,
Spotsylvania 18
Jun 1896 SPMR 17
Jun 1896 SPML
married by the
groom's father
DOOLEY, Harden B. s/o
Thomas Dooley &
Susan Dooley age
19 S farmer POB &
POR Bedford Co &
BOWLER, Harriet
A. d/o Robert
Bowler & Caroline
V.Bowling age 21

SA POB & POR Orange; POM Orange 16 Feb 1864 OMR 12 Feb 1864 OML

DORSON, Albert s/o E.& L.Dorson age 28 S laborer POB & POR Spotsylvania POC & BROOKE, Fanny d/o M.Hart age 25 W POB & POR Spotsylvania POC; POM Spotsylvania 7 Jan 1881 SPMR 3 Jan 1881 SPML

DORSON, Daniel s/o R.& P.Dorson age 23 S laborer POB & POR Spotsylvania POC & LOMAX, Sarah d/o Sally Lomax age 22 S POB & POR Spotsylvania POC; POM Spotsylvania C.H.17 Nov 1878 SPMR 16 Nov 1878 SPML

DOTTS, Daniel s/o Daniel & E.Dotts age 21 S laborer POB & POR Spotsylvania POC & ROLLINS, Catherine d/o James & Jane Rollins age 20 S POB Caroline Co POR Spotsylvania; POM New Hope Ch, Spotsylvania 26 Dec 1878 SPMR SPML

DOWELL, Maj.M. & DOWELL, Mary M.; 26 Oct 1857 OML

DOWNER, Charles M. s/o Larkin & Mary Downer age 30 S farmer POB Spotsylvania POR Orange & DOWNER, Mary B. d/o Robert & Frances A.Downer age 23 S POB Louisa Co POR Orange; POM Orange 22 Feb 1859 OMR 18 Feb 1859 OML

DOWNER, James s/o R.C.& M.C.Downer age 23 S farmer POB & POR Orange & BULLOCK, Eva I. d/o R.M.& Ann Bullock age 23 S POB & POR Spotsylvania; POM Gold Mine Ch, Louisa Co 10 May 1893 Louisa MR 1 May 1893 SPML

DOWNER, Reuben C. s/o Robert G.Downer & Frances A.Daniel age 24 S bricklayer/plasterer POB & POR Orange & DANIEL, Mary C. d/o James B.Daniel & Margaret Besme (?) age 16 S POB & POR Orange; POM Orange 7 Jan 1864 OMR 1 Jan 1864 OML

DOWNER, Thomas W. s/o Larkin & M.Downer age 34 S farming POB Locust Hill, Spotsylvania & HAWKINS, Martha F. d/o Thomas & Mary Hawkins age 38 S POB Springfiled, Spotsylvania; POM Spotsylvania 5 Oct 1853 SPMR

DOWNER, Thomas W. s/o Larkin & Mary Downer age 51 W farmer POB & POR Spotsylvania & TODD, Sallie W.

d/o Charles &
Matilda Todd age
36 S POB & POR
Spotsylvania; POM
Spotsylvania 17
Oct 1871 SPMR 14
Oct 1871 SPML
DOWNER, William W. &
  REYNOLDS, Lucy
  Mary ward of
  Robert
  E.Reynolds; POM
  Orange 15 Dec
  1852 OMR 13 Dec
  1852 OML
DUDLEY, Jefferson, s/o
  Reuben & Alcie
  Dudley age 23 S
  farmer POB & POR
  Spotsylvania POC
  & **LEWIS**, Susan
  d/o Lawrence &
  Martha Lewis age
  18 S POB & POR
  Spotsylvania POC:
  POM Spotsylvania
  17 May 1873 SPMR
  16 May 1873 SPML
DUDLEY, John s/o James
  & Mary Dudley age
  53 W laborer POB
  New York City,
  N.Y. POR
  Spotsylvania POC
  & **TERRELL**,
  Harriet A. d/o
  Armistead & Mary
  Jenkins age 56 W
  POB & POR
  Spotsylvania POC;
  POM Spotsylvania
  10 Apr 1900 SPMR
  9 Apr 1900 SPML
DUERSON, Charles D. &
  HICKS, Sedona Ann
  d/o Th.S.Hicks; 6
  Mar 1862
  SPConsent
DUERSON, Daniel F. S
  POR Spotsylvania
  & **LEITCH**, Ellen
  E. S POR
  Spotsylvania; POM

Spotsylvania 13
Apr 1854 SPMR
DUERSON, William R.
  s/o Robert C.&
  C.K.Duerson age
  29 S merchant POB
  & POR
  Spotsylvania &
  TOWLES, Emma V.
  d/o Thomas T.&
  E.S.Towles age 25
  S POB & POR
  Spotsylvania; POM
  Spotsylvania 6
  Apr 1876 SPMR 4
  Apr 1876 SPML
DUERSTON, John F. s/o
  F.F.& Charlotte
  A.Duerston age 31
  S telegraph
  operator POB &
  POR Powhatan Co &
  SOUTHWORTH,
  Louise d/o C.B.&
  Mary F.Southworth
  age 27 S POB &
  POR Spotsylvania;
  POM Bethany
  Baptist Ch,
  Spotsylvania 29
  Apr 1896 SPMR 27
  Apr 1896 SPML
DUKE, William G. &
  BLAYDES, Mary E.;
  POM Spotsylvania
  18 Jul 1855 SPMR
DUNAVANT, Hezekiah s/o
  Hezekiah & Mary
  Dunavant age 62 W
  farmer POB Louisa
  Co POR
  Spotsylvania &
  BOWLING, Jane d/o
  R.& Mary Bowling
  age 48 S POB &
  POR Spotsylvania;
  POM Spotsylvania
  8 Mar 1855 SPMR
DUNAWAY, Joseph E. s/o
  J.H.& Dulcie
  B.Dunaway age 21
  S farmer POB &
  POR Spotsylvania
  & **DULIN**, Martha

E. d/o E.T.&
L.E.Dulin age 24
S POB Madison Co
POR Spotsylvania;
POM Spotsylvania
3 Apr 1895 SPMR 1
Apr 1895 SPML

DUNAWAY, William F.
s/o Jarvis & Jane
Dunaway age 29 W
Tool keeper POB
Henrico Co &
PROCTOR, Mary A.
d/o John & Nancy
Proctor age 25 S
POB Spotsylvania;
POM Spotsylvania
16 Oct 1856 SPMR

DUNAWAY, Wistar W. s/o
Archie & Mary
Dunnavant age 35
S farmer POB &
POR Spotsylvania
& BURTON, Lula
d/o Wesley &
Louisa Stratton
age 30 W POB &
POR Spotsylvania;
POM Spotsylvania
2 May 1900 SPMR
SPML

DUNN, Benjamin F. s/o
John Dunn &
Mildred Watts age
47 S physician
POB & POR Louisa
Co & GRAVES,
Hattie F. d/o
Abner Graves &
Pamela Edwards
age 27 S POB
Chesterfield Co
POR Orange; POM
Orange 19 Dec
1867 OMR 7 Dec
1867 OML

DUNN, E.L.R. s/o E.S.&
I.L.Dunn age 24 S
merchant POB &
POR Caroline Co &
CAFFREY, Mary d/o
P.S.& S.Caffrey
age 21 S POB New
Jersey POR
Spotsylvania; POM
Spotsylvania 19
Dec 1878 SPMR 2
Dec 1878 SPML

DUNN, E.S. age 55 W
farmer POB
Caroline Co POR
Caroline Co &
BURRUSS, Sallie
E. d/o John
E.Burruss age 38
S POB Caroline Co
POR Spotsylvania;
POM Caroline Co 9
Mar 1882 SPMR 6
Mar 1882 SPML

DUNN, James B. s/o A.&
H.Dunn age 25 S
carpenter POB
Caroline Co POR
Richmond,Va &
PROCTOR, D.E. d/o
William Proctor
age 22 S POB &
POR Spotsylvania;
30 May 1860 SPML

DUNNAVANT, Allen E.
s/o John H.&
Dulcie
B.Dunnavant age
21 S farmer POB
Stafford POR
Spotsylvania &
DULIN, Mary E.
d/o E.T.& Louisa
E.Dulin age 18 S
POB Madison Co
POR Spotsylvania;
POM Spotsylvania
22 Dec 1890 SPMR
SPML

DUNNAVANT, John H. s/o
Archie M.& Mary
Dunnavant age 22
S farmer POB &
POR Spotsylvania
& JETT, Dulcie
d/o James &
Catherine Jett
age 23 S POB &
POR Spotsylvania;
POM Spotsylvania
28 Feb 1867 SPMR
26 Feb 1867 SPML

DUNNAWAY, Jacob s/o
    Archie & Mary
    Dunnaway age 32 S
    farmer POB & POR
    Spotsylvania &
    JETT, Mary L. d/o
    James & Catherine
    Jett age 24 S POB
    & POR
    Spotsylvania; POM
    Spotsylvania 22
    Feb 1874 SPMR 19
    Feb 1874 SPML
DURRETT, A.E. s/o
    J.J.& Margaret
    J.Durrett age 21
    S faremer POB &
    POR Spotsylvania
    & CHEWNING, Mary
    V. d/o M.M.&
    Fanny S.Chewning
    age 20 S POB &
    POR Spotsylvania;
    POM Waller's
    Baptist Ch,
    Spotsylvania 9
    Jun 1897 SPMR 7
    Jun 1897 SPML
DURRETT, A.L. s/o H.&
    L.Durrett age 37
    W physician POB
    Caroline Co POR
    Spotsylvania &
    FRAZER, Fannie C.
    d/o F.& M.Frazer
    age 32 S POB &
    POR Spotsylvania;
    POM Spotsylvania
    31 Jan 1860 SPMR
DURRETT, Addsion S.
    s/o Harry & Letty
    Durrett age 37 W
    physician POB
    Caroline Co POR
    Spotsylvania &
    FRAZER, Fannie C.
    d/o Frulk(?) &
    Mary B.Frazer age
    32 S POB & POR
    Spotsylvania; POM
    Snow Hill,
    Coventry,
    Spotsylvania 31

Jan 1865 SPMR 23
Jan 1865 SPML
DURRETT, Cecil B. s/o
    A.L.& L.Durrett
    age 24 S
    machinist POB &
    POR Spotsylvania
    & LEAVELL, Mollie
    A. d/o B.L.&
    R.E.Leavell age
    20 S POB & POR
    Spotsylvania; POM
    Massaponax Ch,
    Spotsylvania 15
    Jan 1878 SPMR
    SPML
DURRETT, Elliott V.
    s/o Albert &
    Nancy Durrett age
    32 S farmer POB &
    POR Caroline Co &
    BLANTON, Mary A.
    d/o William & Ann
    Blanton age 26 S
    POB Caroline Co
    POR Spotsylvania;
    6 May 1867 SPML
DURRETT, Everett V.
    s/o E.V.& Mary
    Durrett age 23 S
    farmr POB & POR
    Spotsylvania &
    YOUNG, Emma D.
    d/o M.L.&
    Virginia Young
    age 28 S POB &
    POR Spotsylvania;
    POM Spotsylvania
    15 Jan 1896 SPMR
    9 Jan 1896 SPML
DURRETT, Frank H.
    mechanic POR
    Spotsylvania &
    SHACKLEFORD,
    Elizabeth A. S
    POR Spotsylvania;
    POM Spotsylvania
    Aug 1853 SPMR
DURRETT, Henry D. s/o
    R.A.& E.Durrett
    age 27 S farmer
    POB Caroline Co
    POR Spotsylvania
    & SHACKLEFORD,

Betty J. d/o
L.W.& E.M.
Shackleford age
16 S POB & POR
Spotsylvania; POM
Spotsylvania 26
Dec 1878 SPMR 24
Dec 1878 SPML
DURRETT, Thomas B. s/o
William W.&
Allentine Durrett
age 23 S railraod
engineer POB
Spotsylvania POR
Huntington, W.Va
& **MANN**, Lula L.
d/o E.B.& A.E
Mann age 18 POB
Hanover Co POR
Spotsylvania; POM
Spotsylvania 20
Feb 1883 SPMR 15
Feb 1883 SPML
DUVALL, Alexander
Robert s/o Robert
& Martha Duvall
age 32 S farmer
POB & POR
Spotsylvania &
CAMMACK, Maria T.
d/o Robert &
Elizabeth Cammack
age 40 S POB &
POR Cole Hill,
Spotsylvania; POM
Spotsylvania 5
Apr 1853 SPMR
DUVALL, E.M. s/o C.&
M.Duvall age 35 W
farmer POB
Spotsylvania POR
Scott Co, Ky. &
JERRELL, S.G. d/o
William Cropp age
22 W POB Stafford
POR Spotsylvania;
9 Aug 1860 SPML
DYE, Filmore s/o
George & Julia
Dye age 24 S
farmer POB
Stafford POR
Spotsylvania &
DUNNAVANT, Louisa

d/o Archie (dec)
& Mary Dunnavant
age 22 S POB &
POR Spotsylvania;
POM Spotsylvania
21 May 1882 SPMR
1 May 1882 SPML
EARNEST, Joseph
minister &
TAYLOR, Betsy
Hord; POM Orange
30 Dec 1851 OMR
OML
EASTBURN, B.F. s/o
Oliver & Annie
Eastburn age 26 S
farmer POB New
Castle Co,
Delaware POR
Spotsylvania &
WHITE, Jennie L.
d/o William A.&
Harriet S.White
age 28 S POB &
POR Spotsylvania;
POM Tabernacle
Ch, Spotsylvania
17 Oct 1883 SPMR
15 Oct 1883 SPML
EDDINS, William A. s/o
A.J.Eddins &
Amanda J.Miller
age 23 S clerk in
store POB
Rockingham Co POR
Albemarle Co &
GLENN, Susan C.
d/o William Glenn
& Samantha Taylor
age 18 S POB Page
Co POR Orange;
POM Orange 31 May
1866 OMR OML
EDENTON, Benjamin J.
s/o John B.& Mary
Edenton age 26 S
farmer POB & POR
Spotsylvania &
SACRA, Mary E.
d/o Oscar M.&
Frances B.Sacra
age 22 S POB &
POR Spotsylvania;
POM 13 Apr 1890

SPMR 10 Apr 1890 SPML
EDENTON, Ellis E. d/o J.P.& A.A.Edenton age 21 S farmer POB & POR Spotsylvania & **HAILEY**, Martha A. d/o Benjamin & Louisa Hailey age 18 S POB & POR Spotsylvania; POM Spotsylvania 21 Apr 1892 SPMR 19 Apr 1892 SPML
EDENTON, James P. s/o S.J.& Huldah E.Edenton age 22 S farmer POB & POR Spotsylvania & **KENDIG**, Agness A. d/o Urias & Isabella W.Kendig age 17 S POB Louisa Co POR Spotsylvania; POM Spotsylvania 1 Mar 1868 SPMR 27 Feb 1868 SPML
EDENTON, John J. s/o Stephin & Huldah E.Edenton age 29 S farmer POB & POR Spotsylvania & **SACROW**, Mary E. d/o John B.& Clara Burruss age 28 W POB & POR Spotsylvania; POM Spotsylvania 9 Nov 1865 SPMR 7 Nov 1865 SPML
EDENTON, Joseph H. s/o Stephen & Huldah Edenton age 38 S farmer POB & POR Spotsylvania & **PAYNE**, Sarah H.B. d/o John M.& Elizabeth F.Payne age 38 S POB & POR Spotsylvania; POM Spotsylvania 15 Nov 1885 SPMR 2 Nov 1885 SPML
EDENTON, Thadeus N. s/o John B.& Mary E.Edenton age 24 S POB & POR Spotsylvania & **WRENN**, Mary E. d/o Thomas & Frances Wrenn age 23 S POB & POR Spotsylvania; POM Spotsylvania 22 Dec 1874 SPMR 16 Dec 1874 SPML
EDENTON, V.J. s/o Sally E.Edenton age 24 S farmer POB & POR Spotsylvania & **EDENTON**, Sally B. d/o William B.& Mary A.Edenton age 20 S POB & POR Spotsylvania; POM Spotsylvania 25 Jan 1887 SPMR 21 Jan 1887 SPML
EDENTON, W.B. s/o S.B.& H.Edenton age 23 S farmer POB & POR Spotsylvania & **LUCK**, M.A. d/o W.T.& S.Luck age 19y 6mo S POB & POR Spotsylvania; POM Spotsylvania 31 Jan 1858 SPMR
EDINGTON, Charles A. s/o John & Mary Edington age 22 S farmer POB & POR Spotsylvania & **DURRETT**, Addie d/o F.H.& N.A.Durrett sister of James F.Durrett age 21 S POB & POR Spotsylvania; POM Spotsylvania 6 Feb 1879 SPMR 3 Feb 1879 SPML

EDINGTON, Joseph
H.(aka John) s/o
John & Mary
Edington age 23 S
farmer POB & POR
Spotsylvania &
SACRA, Mary S.
d/o John & Mary
Sacra age 26 S
POB & POR
Spotsylvania; POM
Spotsylvania 1
Mar 1876 SPMR 28
Feb 1876 SPML
EDINTON, John J. s/o
John B.& Mary
E.Edinton age 28
S farmer POB &
POR Spotsylvania
& **PAYNE**, Betty
d/o Albert &
Margaret Payne
age 23 S POB &
POR Spotsylvania;
POM Spotsylvania
24 May 1876 SPMR
20 May 1876 SPML
EDLER, Thomas s/o
Samey & Rose
Edler age 30 S
laborer POB & POR
Spotsylvania POC
& **JOHNSON**, Mary
d/o Henry & Betsy
Johnson age 24 S
POB & POR
Spotsylvania POC:
POM Spotsylvania
14 Jul 1872 SPMR
13 Jul 1872 SPML
EDWARD, Wilson s/o
Edward & Lydia
Edward age 30 S
laborer POB
Cumberland Co,Va
POR Spotsylvania
POC & **HARRIS**,
Martha Ellen d/o
Samuel & Frances
Harris age 17 S
POB & POR
Spotsylvania POC;
POM Glencoe,
Spotsylvania 25
Nov 1855 SPMR 24
Nov 1866 SPML
EDWARDS, John s/o E.&
A.Edwards age 37
S farmer POB
Fredericksburg
POR Spotsylvania
& **MASON**, A.E. d/o
W.& A.Mason age
26 S POB Culpeper
POR Spotsylvania;
POM Spotsylvania
24 Mar 1859 SPMR
EDWARDS, John s/o S.&
E.Edwards age 38
S farmer POB
Culpeper POR
Spotsylvania &
BOWLING, M.E. d/o
T.R. & E.Bowling
age 25 S POB &
POR Spotsylvania;
POM Spotsylvania
7 Jan 1858 SPMR
EFFREIG, Anthony s/o
Martin & Mary
Effreig age 41 W
painter POB
Elless, Germany
POR Spotsylvania
& **HILLMAN**, Emma
T. d/o John A.&
Nancy J.Hillman
age 36 S POB &
POR Louisa Co ;
POM Louisa Co 15
May 1894 Louisa
MR SPML
EGGLESTON, Robert I.
s/o Richard
S.Eggleston &
Jane Saunders age
24 S farmer POB
New Kent Co POR
Charles City Co &
EDDINS, Emma J.
d/o A.Eddins &
Julia Stanard age
16 S POB Powhatan
Co POR Orange;
POM Orange 2 Nov
1865 OMR OML
EIPPER, Austin J. s/o
Christopher &

Lucinda Eipper age 25 S blacksmith POB Luzerne Co,Penn POR Spotsylvania & **STEPHENS**, Jennie V. d/o L.H.& Sarah Stephens age 18 S POB New York POR Spotsylvania; POM Spotsylvania 4 Oct 1883 SPMR 3 Oct 1883 SPML

ELAM, T.Poindexter s/o W.C.& D.A.P.Elam age 28 S postal clerk U.S.R.R.Service POB & POR Louisa Co & **HOLLADAY**, Julia R. d/o John M.& L.L.W.Holladay age 18 S POB & POR Spotsylvania; POM Trinity Baptist Ch, Louisa Co 15 Oct 1896 Louisa MR 29 Sep 1896 SPML

ELAM, Thomas J. s/o Odiga Elam & Mary J.Davenport age 22 S farmer POB Trout Co,Ga POR Steward Co,Ga & **LANCASTER**, Sarah Jane d/o James M.Jacobs & Lucy Finney age 18 W POB & POR Orange; POM Orange 9 Jul 1863 OMR 6 Jul 1863 OML

ELAM, Thomas W. s/o T.J.& S.J.Elam age 21 S farmer POB & POR Orange & **DAVENPORT**, Eva P. d/o W.D.& Ella Davenport age 19 S POB & POR Spotsylvania; POM Spotsylvania 8 Mar 1899 SPMR SPML

ELLERSON, James Roy s/o Mr. & Mrs. Ellerson of Hanover Co., Va.age 36 POR Richmond, Va. & **MURDOUGH**, Lucy T. d/o Rev E.C. & Roberta Murdough of Fredericksburg age 28 POR Fredericksburg; POM Fredericksburg 29 Oct 1890 TCF

ELLIS, Alexander s/o Nelson Ellis & Sady Hill age 25 S laborer POB & POR Orange POC & **GILES**, Eliza d/o Edmund & Maria Giles age 28 S POB & POR Orange POC; POM Orange 17 Deec 1866 OMR OML

ELLIS, Anderson s/o Jane Ellis age 28 S POB & POR Spotsylvania POC & **THRASHLY**, Isabella d/o Jennie Thrashly age 23 S POB & POR Spotsylvania POC; POM Spotsylvania 2 Feb 1898 SPMR SPML

ELLIS, Charles s/o James & Martha E.Ellis age 26 S POB & POR Spotsylvania POC & **STANARD**, Fanny d/o Major & Adeline Stanard age 20 S POB & POR Spotsylvania POC; POM

Spotsylvania 27 Mar 1890 SPMR SPML

ELLIS, DeWitt C. s/o Samuel & Elizabeth Ellis age 33 S farmer POB Ottseyo Co,N.Y. POR Fredericksburg & **HAYS**, Mary J. d/o William & Elizabeth Hays age 22 S POB Albany Co, N.Y. POR Spotsylvania; POM Eastern View, Spotsylvania 12 Jan 1871 SPMR 11 Jan 1871 SPML

ELLIS, Edmond s/o Lucy Ellis age 30 S laborer POB & POR Spotsylvania POC & **CAMP**, Ella d/o William & Caroline Camp age 23 S POB & POR Spotsylvania POC: POM Spotsylvania 3 Sep 1896 SPMR SPML

ELLIS, Harrison s/o Edmund Ellis & Nancy Dade age 20 S laborer POB Orange C.H. POR Orange POC & **HUGHES**, Alice d/o Ellen Waugh age 22 S POB & POR Orange POC; POM Orange C.H. 29 Sep 1866 OMR OML

ELLIS, Hezekiah s/o George & C.Lewis(possible clerk error in last name) age 22 S laborer POB & POR Spotsylvania POC & **LEWIS**, Nancy d/o Mat & M.Lewis age 232 S

POB & POR Spotsylvania POC; POM Spotsylvania 19 Dec 1878 SPMR SPML

ELLIS, Horace age 23 S farm laborer POB & POR Orange POC & **PRESLEY**, Emily age 25 S POB & POR Orange POC; POM Orange 26 Dec 1867 OMR OML

ELLIS, James E. s/o George & Jane Ellis age 24 S laborer POB & POR Sptosylvania POC & **CAMMACK**, Julia d/o James & Columbia Cammack age 22 S POB & POR Spotsylvania POC; POM Mount Olive Ch, Spotsylvania 26 Jan 1893 SPMR 23 Jan 1893 SPML

ELLIS, Joseph s/o Billy & Lucy Ellis age 23 S laborer POB & POR Spotsylvania POC & **CHEW**, Nannie d/o Claiborne & Patsy Chew age 15 S POB & POR Spotsylvania POC; 30 Jun 1884 SPML

ELLIS, Joseph s/o William & Lucy Ellis age 24 S laborer POB & POR Spotsylvania POC & **CAMMACK**, Emily d/o M.& B.Cammack age 21 S POB & POR Spotsylvania POC; POM Spotsylvania 6 Oct 1878 SPMR 3 Oct 1878 SPML

ELLIS, Lewis B. s/o Hezekiah Ellis &

Malinda Carries age 25 S farmer POB & POR Prince William Co & **BROWN**, Philippa J. d/o John G.Brown & Patsy F.Holbert age 18 S POB & POR Orange; POM Orange 7 Dec 1865 OMR 6 Dec 1865 OML

ELLIS, Washington s/o Tom & Joanna Ellis age 27 D laborer POB & POR Spotsylvania POC & **JOHNSON**, Lydia d/o Henry & Sarah Johnson age 17 S POB & POR Spotsylvania POC; POM Branch Fork Ch, Spotsylvania 27 Oct 1883 SPMR 18 Oct 1883 SPML

ELLIS, Washington, s/o Tom & Joanna Ellis age 24 S laborer POB & POR Spotsylvania POC & **HETER**, Catherine age 25 S POB & POR Spotsylvania POC; POM Branch Fork, Ch, Spotsylvania 26 May 1877 SPMR 7 May 1877 SPML

ELLIS, William s/o James & Martha Ellis age 29 S laborer POB & POR Spotsylvania POC & **GREEN**, Rose Lee age 21 S POB & POR Spotsylvania POC; POM Spotsylvania 3 Apr 1884 SPMR 2 Apr 1884 SPML

ELY, Samuel s/o Moses & Patsy Ely age 24 S laborer POB & POR Spotsylvania POC & **WALKER**, Margaret d/o Charles & F.Walker age 21 S POB & POR Spotsylvania POC; POM Spotsylvania 20 Nov 1875 SPMR 19 Nov 1875 SPML

EMBREY, Beauanerges s/o Isaac & Catherine Embrey age 32 S farmer POB & POR Spotsylvania & **SMITH**, Arianna V. d/o William C.& Sarah E.Smith age 21 S POB & POR Spotsylvania; POM Spotsylvania 26 Nov 1884 SPMR 24 Nov 1884 SPML

EMBREY, John A. s/o Joseph Embrey & Catherine Peyton age 23 S farmer POB Rappahannock Co POR Culpeper & **PRIEST**, Eliza A. d/o Fellows Priest & Lucy Hickerson age 23 S POB Culpeper Co POR Orange; POM Orange 5 Dec 1865 OMR 27 Nov 1865 OML

EMBREY, Joseph H. s/o Isaac & Catherine Embrey age 39 S farmer POB Culpeper Co POR Spotsylvania & **CURTIS**, Mattie L. d/o Jesse & Mary Curtis age 24 S POB Culpeper Co POR Spotsylvania; POM Fredericksburg 20

Apr 1887 SPMR SPML

EMMONS, James s/o James S.& Ann Emmons age 21 S farmer POB & POR Fauquier Co & **COLLINS**, Rebecca E. d/o Francis & Margaret Collins age 27 S POB Madison Co POR Orange; POM Orange 23 Dec 1856 OMR 16 Dec 1856 OML

ENNIS, Davis s/o Jackson & Maria Ennis age 39 W livery owner POB Cumberland Co, Va POR Fredericksburg POC & **REDMOND**, Jane Willie d/o Henry & Martha Redmond age 21 S POB & POR Spotsylvania POC; POM Fredericksburg 10 Nov 1897 SPMR 9 Nov 1897 SPML

ESQUE, William (possibly William Essex) & **BICKERS**, Mary F.; POM Orange 23 Dec 1851 OMR

ESTES, Andrew F. s/o Robert Estes & Sally E.Cosby age 22 S farmer POB Louisa Co POR Orange & **HAYES**, Lucy C. d/o Thomas Hayes & Bettie Brockman age 19 S POB & POR Orange; POM Orange 24 Jan 1867 OMR 22 Jan 1867 OML

ESTES, John C. s/o Robert Estes & Sally Cosley (aka Sarah Estes) age 22 S POB Albemarle Co POR Orange & **WRIGHT**, Mildred F. d/o Dabney Wright & Ann Maria Estes (aka Jane M.Wright) age 16 S POB Louisa Co POR Orange; POM Orange 22 Jan 1861 OMR 18 Jan 1861 OML

ESTES, Richard s/o D.& C.Estes age 25 S moulder POB Louisa Co POR Fredericksburg & **DAVENPORT**, Jennie d/o William & S.Davenport age 22 S POB Albemarle Co POR Spotsylvania; POM Spotsylvania 1 Jan 1881 SPMR 31 Dec 1880 SPML

ESTES, Thomas B. s/o Thomas Estes age 48 S farmer POB & POR Orange & **ESTES**, Mary E. d/o John Estes age 38 S POB & POR Orange; POM Orange 10 Dec 1866 OMR

ESTES, William T. s/o Robert Estes & Sally Cosby age 24 S farmer POB Louisa Co POR Orange & **WRIGHT**, Mary V. d/o Dabney Wright & Jane M.Estes age 23 S POB & POR Orange; POM Orange 18 Apr

1867 OMR 9 Apr
1867 OML
EUBANK, Elias D. s/o George W.Eubank & Mary C.Hill age 23 S farmer POB & POR Nelson Co & **BECKHAM**, Mary O. d/o James Beckham & Sarah Canaday age 16 S POB & POR Orange; POM Gordonsville,Orange 5 Nov 1863 OMR 4 Nov 1863 OML
EUBANK, Isaac L.Jr. s/o Isaac L. & Virginia E.Eubank age 25 S telegraph operator POB & POR Spotsylvania & **NUSSEY**, Mary J. d/o F.C.& Ellen Nussey age 20 S POB Wintersett, England POR Spotsylvania; POM Union Chapel, Spotsylvania 16 Dec 1896 SPMR 15 Dec 1896 SPML
EVANS, James R. s/o John A.& Maria J.Evans age 24 S clerk POB Stafford POR Fredericksburg & **PENDLETON**, Lily M. d/o T.W.& Helen B.Holladay age 23 W POB & POR Spotsylvania; POM Zion M.E. Ch, Spotsylvania 25 Apr 1894 SPMR 18 Apr 1894 SPML
EVANS, John D. s/o Tandy & Mildred Ann Evans age 30 W farmer POB Madison Co POR Hanover Co & **BROOKS**, Lucy d/o Albert & Emily Brooks age 23 S POB & POR Spotsylvania; POM Spotsylvania 29 Oct 1891 SPMR SPML
EVANS, Lewis s/o Tandy & Mildred Evans age 23 S farmer POB & POR Louisa Co & **BROOKS**, Betty A. d/o Allen C.& Mary Ann Brooks age 22 S POB & POR Spotsylvania; POM Spotylvania 25 Jul 1886 SPMR 19 Jul 1886 SPML
FAIRCHILD, Alfred L. s/o William C. Gordon & Lottie Fairchild age 21 S laborer POB & POR Spotsylvania POC & **GARNETT**, Alberta d/o Archie & Lettie Garnett age 21 S POB & POR Spotsylvania POC; POM Spotsylvania 11 Jan 1899 SPMR SPML
FAIRFAX, Edward s/o Minor Fairfax & Malinda Tansel age 21 S engineer POB Prince William Co POR Gordonsville & **DICKINSON**, Flora J. d/o Robert W.Dickinson & Julia Craig age 17 S POB Augusta Co POR Gordonsville; POM Gordonsville, Orange 19 Jan 1864 OMR 18 Jan 1864 OML

FALLIN, John A. s/o
H.H.Fallin &
Eleanor S.Walters
age 28 S
farmer/cost
engineer POB
Halifax Co, Va
POR Danville,Va &
ROGERS, Elizabeth
F. d/o Joseph
Rogers & Malinda
Newman age 23 S
POB & POR Orange;
POM Orange 30 Oct
1865 OMR 28 Oct
1865 OML

FANTLEROY, A. s/o
Riland & Miria
Fantleroy age 21
S farmer POB
Essex Co POR
Spotsylvania POC
& **KING**, Mary d/o
Horace & Sally
King age 21 S POB
& POR
Spotsylvania POC;
POM Spotsylvania
27 Apr 1875 SPMR
26 Apr 1875 SPML

FANTROZE, William s/o
R.& M.Fantroze
age 22 S
goldminer POB &
POR Spotsylvania
POC & **ROBERSON**,
Mandy d/o D.&
C.Roberson age 19
S POB & POR
Spotsylvania POC;
POM Spotsylvania
25 Dec 1879 SPMR
22 Dec 1879 SPML

FARISH, George s/o
Jarrott & Mary
Farish age 31 W
farmer POB & POR
Spotsylvania POC
& **GAINES**, Julia
d/o Anthony &
Polly Gaines age
18 S POB & POR
Spotsylvania POC;
POM Spotsylvania
17 Aug 1871 SPMR
15 Aug 1871 SPML

FARMER, Robert F. s/o
Robert & N.Farmer
age 25 S farmer
POB Caroline Co
POR Spotsylvania
& **CANNON**, E.A.
d/o Ira &
E.Cannon age 23 S
POB & POR
Spotsylvania; POM
Newington,
Spotsylvania 16
Feb 1876 SPMR 15
Feb 1876 SPML

FARMER, William C. s/o
Robert & Nancy
Farmer age 25 S
farmer POB & POR
Spotsylvania &
ALSOP, Mollie E.
d/o Benjamin P.&
Margaret A.Alsop
age 27 S POB &
POR Spotsylvania;
POM Spotsylvania
25 Mar 1885 SPMR
23 Mar 1885 SPML

FARRAR, David S. s/o
Garland & Mary
L.Farrar age 32 S
teacher POB
Goochland Co POR
Fluvanna &
ATKINS, Martha J.
d/o Joseph & Mary
Atkins age 27 S
POB & POR Orange;
POM Orange 18 Oct
1857 OMR 27 Oct
1857 OML

FAULCONER, E.N. s/o
Alfred Faulconer
& Madaline Bocock
age 25 S
carpenter POB &
POR Orange &
HANSFORD, Sallie
J. d/o William
Terrill & Fanny
Boston age 25 W
POB & POR Orange;
POM Orange 30 Aug

1866 OMR 27 Aug
1866 OML
FAULCONER, Frederick
W. s/o Alfred
M.Faulconer &
Madaline Bocock
age 23 S farmer
POB & POR Orange
& **APPERSON**,
Evelina d/o
Thomas Apperson &
Eveline Salmer
age 22 S POB
Culpeper Co POR
Orange; POM
Orange 31 Oct
1867 OMR
FAULCONER, George s/o
William &
Elizabeth
Faulconer age 37
W day laborer POB
& POR Orange &
WATSON, Sarah J.
d/o Benjamin &
Fannie Watson age
20 S POB & POR
Orange; POM
Orange 15 Mar
1858 OMR OML
FAULCONER, James F.
s/o James
F.Faulconer &
Priscilla Tinder
age 29 W farmer
POB Culpeper POR
Orange &
CANNADAY, Bettie
D. d/o James
Cannaday & Ann
Tinder age 21 S
POB & POR Orange;
POM Orange 14 Dec
1865 OMR 13 Dec
1865 OML
FAULCONER, James T.H.
s/o James
T.Faulconer age
22 S farmer POB
Culpeper Co &
TINDER, Susan S.
d/o John Tinder
age 21 S POB
Culpeper Co; POM

Orange 27 Dec
1859 OMR 8 Dec
1859 OML
FAULCONER, John C. s/o
Alfred
N.Faulconer &
Madaline Bocock
age 32 S
carpenter POB &
POR Orange &
PETITT, Columbia
F. d/o Fountain
P.Pettit & Martha
A.Roach age 20 S
POB & POR Orange;
POM Orange 19 Dec
1867 OMR 18 Dec
1867 OML
FAULCONER, Robert B.
s/o Carter B.&
Nannie Faulconer
age 45 S
carpenter POB &
POR Orange &
KENNEDY, Fannie
d/o Hiram
P.Kennedy & Mary
Faulconer age 34
S POB & POR
Orange; 14 Apr
1867 OML
FAULCONER, Silas H.
s/o Benjamin &
Mary Faulconer
age 22 S farmer
POB & POR Orange
& **HERRING**, Sally
F. d/o Ben &
L.Herring age 22
S POB & POR
Spotsylvania; POM
Spotsylvania 5
Apr 1877 SPMR 2
Apr 1877 SPML
FAULCONER, Thomas E.
s/o W.&
K.A.Faulconer age
24 S laborer POB
Orange POR
Spotsylvania &
HAWKINS, Bell d/o
T.A.(or H.) &
P.Hawkins age 29
S POB & POR

Spotsylvania; POM
Spotsylvania 6
Jan 1880 SPMR 5
Jan 1880 SPML
FAULCONER, William A.
s/o James
T.Faulconer S
farmer POB & POR
Orange & **TINDER**,
Lucy F. d/o John
Tinder S POB &
POR Orange; POM
Orange 20 Dec
1860 OMR 26 Nov
1860 OML
FAULKNER, George P.
s/o Pleasant E.&
Frances
A.Faulkner age 38
S farmer POB &
POR Spotsylvania
& **DAVIS**, Emma d/o
James L.& Mary
Davis age 35 S
POB & POR
Spotsylvania; POM
Waller's Baptist
Ch, Spotsylvania
23 Dec 1896 SPMR
19 Dec 1896 SPML
FAULKNER, William
Henry s/o
Pleasant E.&
Frances Faulkner
age 27 S farmer
POB & POR
Spotsylvania &
JERRELL, Louisa
A. d/o Joseph H.&
Louisa B.Jerrell
age 23 S POB &
POR Spotsylvania;
POM Spotsylvania
29 Nov 1870 SPMR
21 Nov 1870 SPML
FAUNTLEROY, Charles
s/o Randall &
Maria Fauntleroy
age 21 S farmer
POB & POR
Spotsylvania POC
& **WILLIAMS**, Annie
d/o Jefferson &
Jane Williams age

23 S POB & POR
Spotsylvania POC;
POM Spotsylvania
28 Sep 1882 SPMR
21 Sep 1882 SPML
FAWCETT, Thomas s/o
Thomas & Lydia
Fawcett age 44 S
farmer POB
Montgomery Co,Md
POR Spotsylvania
& **CHILDS**, Susan
J. d/o Frank &
Nancy Childs age
31 S POB & POR
Spotsylvania; POM
Spotsylvania 1874
SPMR 6 Apr 1874
SPML
FEARNEY, Lough Lewis &
JOHNS, Sarah d/o
Mason Johns; POM
Orange May 1851
OMR 6 May 1851
OML
FELTNER, George W. s/o
John D. Feltner &
Jane E.Talley age
23 S blacksmith
POB & POR
Jefferson Co, Va
& **WOOD**,
Louisianna d/o
Thomas Wood &
Sarah F.Berry age
23 S POB & POR
Orange; POM
Orange C.H.17 Sep
1863 OMR OML
FERGERSON, George s/o
Burwell & Ann
Fergerson age 31
S railroad
laborer POB & POR
Spotsylvania POC
& **PRICE**, Sarah
d/o Robert &
Franky Price age
21 S POB & POR
Spotsylvania POC;
POM New Hope Ch,
Spotsylvania; 27
Dec 1881 SPMR

FERGUSON, Edmund s/o Burwell & Ann Ferguson age 26 S POB & POR Spotsylvania POC & **LEWIS**, Lucy A. d/o Edie Anderson age 23 S POB & POR Spotsylvania POC; POM Spotsylvania 18 Mar 1886 SPMR 17 Mar 1886 SPML

FERGUSON, George s/o Burwell & Ann Ferguson age 43 W laborer POB & POR Spotsylvania POC & **WASHINGTON**, Rose d/o Charles & Ann Hill age 33 W POB Richmond Co, Va POR Spotsylvania POC; POM Spotsylvania C.H. 10 Apr 1895 SPMR SPML

FERGUSON, Jacob s/o Burrell & Ann Ferguson age 43 W farmer POB Caroline Co POR Spotsylvania POC & **DAWSON**, Rena d/o William & Susan Taylor age 27 W POB & POR Spotsylvania POC; POM Spotsylvania 22 Dec 1891 SPMR SPML

FERGUSON, William H. s/o Elijah & Barbara Ferguson age 48 W farmer POB Delaware Co,N.Y. POR Spotsylvania & **MARTIN**, Amanda E. d/o Thomas & Betsy Martin age 24 S POB & POR Spotsylvania; POM Spotsylvania 19 Jan 1873 SPMR 6 Jan 1873 SPML

FERNEYHOUGH, John s/o John Ferneyhough & Elizabeth Jones age 44 W farmer POB & POR Orange & **KEETON**, Mildred L. d/o Horace Keeton & Lucy M.Jennings age 26 S POB Green Co POR Orange; POM Orange 19 Dec 1861 OMR 16 Dec 1861 OML

FICKLIN, W.F. s/o A.(?)B. & A.E.Ficklin age 23 S merchant/miller POB & POR Stafford & **STANSBERRY**, Julia Bell d/o John S. & Mary O.Stansberry age 22 S POB Maryland POR Spotsylvania; POM St George Ch, Fredericksburg 19 Oct 1875 FMR 15 Oct 1875 SPML

FILLMORE, Stape s/o George & Caroline Fillmore age 24 S POB Spotsylvania POR Spotsylvania POC & **COLEMAN**, Lizzie d/o Gundy & Eliza Coleman age 18 A POB & POR Spotsylvania POC; POM Spotsylvania 20 Dec 1882 SPMR 23 Dec 1882 SPML

FINNEY, P.G. s/o Thomas W. & Julia F.Finney age 24 S farmer POB & POR Spotsylvania & **POOLE**, Allie K. d/o Alfred &

Nannie Poole age 26 S POB & POR Spotsylvania; POM Spotsylvania 1 Jan 1896 SPMR 31 Dec 1895 SPML

FINNEY, Page D. s/o Dr.T.W.& J.D.Finney age 23 S farmer POB & POR Spotsylvania & **HOLLADAY**, Nannie S. d/o T.W.& Helen Holladay age 18 S POB & POR Spotsylvania; POM Spotsylvania 23 Nov 1893 SPMR 20 Nov 1893 SPML

FINNY, Thomas Watkins s/o Page R.& Jane J.Finny age 36 S physician POB Culpeper Co POR Spotsylvania & **TWYMAN**, Julia D. d/o Claiborne & Mary Duvall age 34 W POB & POR Spotsylvania; POM Spotsylvania 17 Dec 1868 SPMR 15 Dec 1868 SPML

FISHER, Daniel A. s/o Daniel Fisher & Malinda Reagan age 22 S farmer POB Rockingham Co POR Orange & **COLE**, Josephine C. d/o Philip Cole & Edith Bryan age 21 S POB Rockingham Co POR Orange; POM Orange 19 Jun 1866 OMR 16 Jun 1866 OML

FISHER, Sylvanus s/o Sylvanus & Betsy Fisher age 70 W farmer POB & POR Spotsylvania POC & **CARTER**, Georgia d/o Phoebe Carter age 32 S POB & POR Spotsylvania POC; POM Spotsylvania 20 Jun 1900 SPMR SPML

FITCHTIG, Lewis J. age 45 W POR Baltimore, Md & **SMITH**, Mary L. age 35 W POB & POR Spotsylvania; POM 2 Oct 1899 SPMR 29 Aug 1899 SPML

FITZGERALD, Thomas F. s/o John & Alice Fitzgerald age 26 S cooper POB Ireland POR Spotsylvania & **MOORE**, E.Belle d/o Joseph & Mary Moore age 18 S POB Beaver Co,Penn POR Spotsylvania; POM Spotsylvania C.H. 19 Dec 1883 SPMR 17 Dec 1883 SPML

FLEMING, John J. s/o Bozwell & Lucy A.Fleming age 35 S farmer POB & POR Spotsylvania & **ROBINSON**, Capitola B. d/o Eli M.& Mary E.Jones age 24 W POB & POR Spotsylvania; POM Spotsylvania C.H.22 Jan 1884 SPMR SPML

FLEMING, Patrick H. s/o Boswell S.& Lucy A.Fleming age 22 S saddler POB Spotsylvania POR Amherst Co & **POOL**, Roberta A. d/o Alford (?) &

Roberta C. Pool age 17 S POB & POR Spotsylvania; POM Spotsylvania 16 Aug 1868 SPMR 15 Aug 1868 SPML

FLETCHER, Allen s/o Martha Fletcher age 26 S farmer POB & POR Spotsylvania & **SACRA**, Mary V. d/o C.R. & Amanda Sacra age 15 S POB & POR Spotsylvania; POM Spotsylvania 25 Dec 1900 SPMR 20 Dec 1900 SPML

FLETCHER, Leroy s/o Madison & Sarah Fletcher age 24 S farmer POB & POR Spotsylvania & **MARTIN**, Lucy Ellen d/o Linfield & Frances Martin age 17 S POB & POR Spotsylvania; POM Belair, Spotsylvania 4 Jan 1877 SPMR 1 Jan 1877 SPML

FLIPPO, Banks s/o Major & A.F. Flippo age 27 S farmer POB & POR Spotsylvania & **FITZPATRICK**, Maggie d/o Patrick Fitzpatrick age 24 S POB & POR Spotsylvania; POM Catholic Rectory, Fredericksburg 14 Oct 1891 FMR 13 Oct 1891 SPML

FLIPPO, J.D. s/o John J. & E.H. Flippo age 25 S farmer POB & POR Caroline Co &

EDENTON, M.E. d/o T.N. & Mary E. Edenton age 18 S POB & POR Spotsylvania; POM Waller's Ch, Glanville, Spotsylvania 5 Jun 1895 SPMR 1 Jun 1895 SPML

FLIPPO, John B. s/o John & Haseltine age 25 S farmer POB & POR Spotsylvania & **WHITLOCK**, S.L. d/o William & Sallie Whitlock S POB & POR Spotsylvania; POM Spotsylvania 11 Mar 1900 SPMR 5 Mar 1900 SPML

FLIPPO, Thomas J. s/o Jefferson & A.W. Flippo age 26 S farmer POB & POR Caroline Co & **POUND**, M.E. d/o Richard & Mary Pound age 19 S POB & POR Spotsylvania; POM Spotsylvania 27 Feb 1884 SPMR 25 Feb 1884 SPML

FLIPPO. William E. s/o John J. & E.H. Flippo age 23 S farmer POB Caroline Co POR Spotsylvania & **SACRA**, Nettie B. d/o Oscar M. & Frances B. Sacra age 21 S POB & POR Spotsylvania; POM Spotsylvania 5 Mar 1899 SPMR 2 Mar 1899 SPML

FONT, Larkin Jr. s/o Larkin & Mary Font age 24 S laborer POB & POR

Spotsylvania POC & **PRICE**, Catherine d/o Robert & F.Price age 23 S POB & POR Spotsylvania POC; POM Spotsyvlania 7 Oct 1876 SPMR SPML

FORT, Adolphus s/o Joseph W. Johnson & Lucy Towles age 22 S laborer POB & POR Spotsylvania POC & **YOUNG**, Lizzie d/o Humphrey & Mary Young age 25 S POB & POR Spotsylvania POC; POM Pine Branch Ch, Spotsylvania 7 Jan 1883 SPMR 1 Jan 1883 SPML

FORT, Albert s/o Larkin & Mary Fort age 34 S laborer POB & POR Spotsylvania POC & **WHITE**, Amelia d/o Joseph & Margaret White age 23 S POB & POR Spotsylvania POC; POM Spotsylvania 27 Feb 1881 SPMR 26 Feb 1881 SPML

FORT, Larkin s/o Christ & Courtney Fort age 28 W POB & POR Spotsylvania POC & **COMFORT**, Nancy d/o Gilbert Baylor age 24 S POB & POR Spotsylvania POC; 12 Mar 1867 SPMR 4 Mar 1867 SPML

FORT, William s/o L.& M.Fort age 26 S laborer POB & POR Spotsylvania POC & **BAYLOR**, Rebecca d/o John & F.Baylor age 22 S POB Caroline Co POR Spotsylvania POC; POM Spotsylvania 4 Nov 1880 SPMR 3 Nov 1880 SPML

FORTS, William s/o Larkin & Mary Forts age 39 W farmer POB & POR Spotsylvania POC & **HANCOCK**, Eliza d/o Benjamin & Sarah Johnson age 30 W POB Appomattox Co POR Spotsylvania POC; POM Spotsylvania C.H. 17 Jan 1895 SPMR SPML

FOSTER, Andrew & **SHIFLETT**, Sarah; 5 Oct 1852 OML

FOSTER, J.W. s/o J.W.& Mary E.Foster age 22 S miner POB & POR Louisa Co & **WILLOUGHBY**, Georgie age 21 S POB & POR Spotsylvania; POM Louisa Co 25 Dec 1895 Louisa MR 23 Dec 1895 SPML

FOSTER, Powhatan T. s/o William E. & E.A.Foster age 36 S merchant POB & POR Spotsylvania & **KNIGHTON**, Virginia E. d/o Robert S.& Georgianna Knighton age 22 S POB Orange POR Spotsylvania; POM Spotsylvania 18 Oct 1883 SPMR 15 Oct 1883 SPML

FOSTER, William B. s/o
W.E.& Engedi
Foster age 31 S
farmer POB & POR
Sposylvania &
McGARY, Lena E.
d/o H.A.& Susan
C.McGary age 23 S
POB & POR
Spotsylvania; POM
Good Hope Ch 7
Jun 1893 MR 5 Jun
1893 SPML

FOX, C.W. s/o Jacob &
Bettie Fox age 25
S laborer POB &
POR Spotsylvania
POC & **ANDERSON**,
Fannie d/o George
& Agnes Anderson
age 18 S POB &
POR Spotsylvania
POC; POM
Spotsylvania 19
Dec 183 SPMR 18
Dec 1883 SPML

FRANCIS, French s/o
Joe & Lizzy
Francis age 46 W
blacksmith POB
Culpeper Co POR
Orange POC &
TAYLOR, Rebecca
d/o Ben Taylor &
Barbara Jackson
age 24 S POB &
POR Orange POC;
POM Orange 21 Sep
1867 OMR OML

FRANSY, Thomas J. s/o
Thomas & Ann
Fransy age 33 W
clerk POB New
City POR
Fredericksburg &
LEWIS, Ann age 33
W POB & POR
Spotsylvania; POM
Spotsylvania Sep
1865 SPMR 21 Sep
1865 SPML

FRANTZ, John W. s/o
George & Keziah
A. Frantz age 31

W farmer POB
Luzern Co,Pa POR
Caroline Co &
ROBERTS, Julia
d/o Ebenezer &
Sarah Roberts age
22 S POB
Catanaugus
Co,N.Y. POR
Spotsylvania; POM
Spotsylvania 22
Oct 1873 SPMR 18
Oct 1873 SPML

FRAZER, David M.C. s/o
Samuel & Emeline
Frazer age 27 S
farmer POB New
Castle Co,
Delaware POR
Spotsylvania &
DECKER, Emma Iren
d/o John &
G.Decker age 21 S
POB & POR
Spotsylvania; POM
Spotsylvania 16
Dec 1869 SPMR 6
Dec 1869 SPML

FRAZER, Ferrell s/o
Ceazar & Fanny
Frazer age 27 S
laborer POB & POR
Spotsylvania POC
& **JOHNSTON**, Sally
d/o William &
Martha Johnston
age 26 S POB
Louisa Co POR
Spotsylvania POC;
POM Spotsylvania
26 Dec 1868 SPMR
24 Dec 1868 SPML

FRAZER, John s/o
William S.Frazer
& Ann Burruss age
29 S farmer POB &
POR Orange &
MORTON, Susan M.
d/o George
W.Morton & Susan
Terrill age 25 S
POB & POR Orange;
POM Orange 18 Dec

1866 OMR 12 Dec
1866 OML
FRAZER, John T. s/o
Thomas &
Margarett Frazer
age 52 S farmer
POB Shenandoah Co
POR Spotsylvania
& **CHANCELLOR**,
Mary E. d/o
Sanford & Fannie
L.Chancellor age
47 S POB & POR
Spotsylvania; POM
Spotsylvania 6
Jan 1875 SPMR 2
Jan 1875 SPML
FRAZER, Joseph &
DAUSEN, Julean
d/o Charles &
Luly(?) Dausen
(POR
Fredericksburg)
age 19 POR
Spotsylvania; 28
Mar 1868
SPConsent
FRAZER, Robert s/o
Harrison & Eliza
Frazer age 25 S
farmer POB & POR
Spotsylvania &
GORDON, Martha A.
d/o Charles &
Caroline Gordon
age 22 S POB &
POR Spotsylvania;
POM Spotsyvania
31 Mar 1866 SPMR
30 Mar 1866 SPML
FRAZER, Thomas A. s/o
James L.&
C.M.Frazer age 27
S farmer POB &
POR Spotsylvania
& **HARRIS**, Musette
C. d/o T.A.& Mary
E.Harris age 21 S
POB & POR
Spotsylvania; POM
Spotsylvania 27
May 1896 SPMR 26
May 1896 SPML

FRAZIER, Alexander s/o
William & Mary
Frazier age 54 W
laborer POB & POR
Spotsylvania POC
& **HOLMES**, Mary W
POB & POR
Spotsylvania POC;
POM Spotsylvania
4 Jan 1899 SPMR
SPML
FREEMAN, Thomas POC &
CLARK, Louisa
POC; 2 Jun 1853
OML
FROST, E.H. s/o L.C.&
M.C. Frost age 24
S farmer POB New
York City POR
Orange & **BURKE**,
Lizzie T. d/o
George & Isabella
Burke age 23 S
POB & POR
Spotsylvania; POM
Glenvilla,
Spotsylvania 2
Aug 1889 SPMR 1
Aug 1889 SPML
FULTON, Willie H. s/o
E.S.& Elizabeth
S.Fulton age 28 S
farmer POB & POR
Grayson Co, Va &
POOL, Ida A. d/o
Alfred & Nannie
Pool age 24 S POB
& POR
Spotsylvania; POM
Shady Grove
M.E.Ch,
Spotsylvania 22
Oct 1884 SPMR 21
Oct 1884 SPML
FURNEYHOUGH, M.A. s/o
R.W. &
F.B.Furneyhough
age 32 S farmer
POB Essex Co POR
Stafford &
HOWARD, C.L. d/o
James &
M.R.Howard age 24
S POB & POR

Spotsylvania; POM Spotsylvania 14 Nov 1878 SPMR 7 Nov 1878 SPML
GALISPIE, John N. s/o Jonathan & Matilda Gillispie, age 22 S wheelwright POB Albemarle POR Orange & **WRIGHT**, Lavinia A. d/o Dabney & Matilda Wright age 25 S POB & POR Orange; POM Orange 15 Jan 1857 OMR 13 Jan 1857 OML
GANNETT, Philip s/o Mefrow(?) & Mary S.Gannett age 21 S farmer POB & POR Caroline Co & **TAYLOR**, Ann E. d/o William & Nancy Taylor age 23 S POB & POR Spotsylvania; POM Spotsylvania 6 Dec 1871 SPMR 4 Dec 1871 SPML
GARDNER, George W. s/o Nathan & Eunice Gardner age 44 W farmer POB New York POR Spotsylvania & **COATS**, Martha V. d/o John Coats & Jane Willoughby age 36 S POB & POR Spotsylvania; POM Spotsylvania C.H. 5 Apr 1883 SPMR SPML
GARDNER, George W. s/o N.& M.E.Gardner age 22 S farmer POB & POR Spotsylvania & **PAYTES**, Virginia A. d/o A.& C.Paytes age 21 S POB & POR Spotsylvania; POM Spotsylvania 2 Mar 1879 SPMR 26 Feb 1879 SPML
GARDNER, John R. s/o Nathan & Martha Gardner age 24 S farmer POB & POR Spotsylvania & **COLLINS**, Lizzie d/o Dennis & Aman- Collins age 22 S POB & POR Spotsylvania; POM Spotsylvania 3 May 1893 SPMR SPML
GARDNER, Nathan M.Jr. s/o Nathan & Martha Gardner age 33 S merchant POB & POR Spotsylvania & **PATES**, Henrietta d/o Augustus & Clemintine Pates age 23 S POB & POR Spotsylvania; POM Spotsylvania C.H.9 Aug 1894 SPMR SPML
HARFIELD, Parker R. s/o Thad.M.& Martha Harfield age 23 S miner POB & POR Spotsylvania & **BROOKS**, Rosa L. d/o W.T.& Martha Brooks age 16 S POB & POR Spotsylvania; POM Spotsylvania C.H.17 Oct 1894 SPMR SPML
GARLICK, Dabney s/o W.& M.Garlick age 26 S laborer POB & POR Spotsylvania POC & **WILSON**, Judy d/o B.& L.William age 22 S POB & POR Spotsylvania

POC; POM New Hope Ch, Spotsylvania 4 Jul 1878 SPMR 3 Jul 1878 SPML
GREEN, William G. s/o T.S.& E.A.Green age 27 S farmer POB Rappahannock Co POR Culpeper Co & **HERRING**, Annie E. d/o B.H.& L.E.Herring age 18 S POB & POR Spotsylvania; POM Spotsylvania 6 Nov 1878 SPMR 4 Nov 1878 SPML
GARNETT, Archy s/o Arch & Lettie Garnett age 23 S laborer POB & POR Spotsylvania POC & **STANARD**, Winnie d/o Robert & Dolly Stanard age 16 S POB & POR Spotsylvnai POC; POM Spotsylvnai 30 Apr 1896 SPMR SPML
GARNETT, George s/o Henry & Annie Garnett age 48 W laborer POB Essex Co POR Spotsylvania POC & **JONES**, Mollie d/o William & Mandy Jones age 28 S POB & POR Spotsylvania POC; POM Spotsylvania C.H. 20 Sep 1888 SPMR SPML
GARNETT, Henry s/o George & Ellen Garnett age 18 S laborer POB & POR Spotsylvania POC & **JONES**, Lizzie d/o Fanny Jones age 21 S POB & POR Spotsylvania

POC; POM Spotsylvania 27 Nov 1899 SPMR SPML
GARNETT, Jeremiah K. s/o John G.& Elizabeth Garnett age 61 S miner POB Madison Co POR Spotsylvania & **PROCTOR**, R.F. d/o Austin & Northanna Proctor age 22 S POB & POR Spotsylvania; POM Spotsylvania 10 Feb 1876 SPMR 7 Feb 1876 SPML
GARNETT, Joel s/o James & Elizabeth Garnett age 33 S farmer POB & POR Culpeper & **SCOTT**, Ann E. d/o John & Ann Scott age 31 S POB & POR Orange; POM Orange 16 Oct 1855 OMR
GARNETT, Milton s/o James & Elizabeth Garnett age 33 S farmer POB Culpeper Co POR Orange & **COBBS**, Mary Ann d/o Peter N.& Courtney Cobbs age 22 S POB Albemarle Co POR Orange; POM Orange 3 Nov 1857 OMR 2 Nov 1857 OML
GARNETT, Mortimore s/o Wallace & Rosa Garnett age 35 S farmer POB Essex Co POR Spotsylvania POC & **WARD**, Fannie d/o Henry & Patsy Ward age 18 S POB & POR

Spotsylvania; POM Zoan, Spotsylvania 4 Sep 1870 SPMR 3 Sep 1870 SPML
GARNETT, Moses s/o Henry & Annie Garnett age 22y6mo S farmer POB Essex Co POR Spotsylvania POC & **CARTER**, Sarah N. d/o Aggy Carter age 25 W POB & POR Spotsylvania POC; POM Spotsylvania 20 Sep 1867 SPMR 19 Sep 1867 SPML
GARRETT, Charles M. s/o M.& E.Garrett age 22 S mechanic POB Pennsylvania POR Spotsylvania & **ANNS**, Lizzie J. d/o P.& L.Anns age 17 S POB Pennsylvania POR Spotsylvania; POM Spotsylvania 5 Jun 1879 SPMR 4 Jun 1879 SPML
GARRETT, Preston L. s/o P.H.& J.A.Garrett age 26 S railraod employee POB & POR Hanover Co & **PAYNE**, Sallie N. d/o T.B.& L.M. Payne age 21 S POB & POR Spotsylvania (sister in law to a Mr.Mastin); POM Spotsylvania 26 Jan 1888 SPMR 23 Jan 1888 SPML
GATEWOOD, Jarrett s/o Jarrett Gatewood & Eliza Harrison age 23 S farmer POB Caroline Co POR Spotsylvania POC & **WILLIAMS**, Mary d/o Troy & Martha Williams age 23 S POB & POR Spotsylvania POC; POM Spotsylvania C.H. 3 Jan 1883 SPMR SPML
GATEWOOD, Josephus s/o Bartlett & Frances Gatewood age 51 W farmer POB & POR Caroline Co & **DILLARD**, Hardinia A. d/o Lancelot & Nancy Partlow age 29 W POB & POR Spotsylvania; POM Spotsylvania 18 Sep 1866 SPMR 15 Sep 1866 SPML
GATEWOOD, Thomas H. s/o William L.& Lucy A.Gatewood age 24 S attorney POB Essex Co POR Middlesex & **CRUTCHFIELD**, Sally d/o Stap. & Sally A.Crutchfield age 18 S POB & POR Spotsylvania; POM St George Ch Fredericksburg 16 Oct 1861 FMR 10 Oct 1861 SPML
GATTON, Lewis W. s/o Henry E.& Ann Gatton age 37 S POB & POR Washington D.C. carpenter & **HONSER**, Bettie T. d/o Peter C.& Bettie T.Honser age 22 S POB & POR Spotsylvania; POM Kingsley's Chapel 25 Sep 1889 SPMR SPML

GAYLE, Thomas B. s/o
Josiah P.&
Frances M.Gayle
age 50 W farmer
POB Caroline Co
POR Spotsylvania
& **BULLOCK**, Lily
W. d/o Slaughter
& Bullock age 37
S POB Hanover Co
POR Spotsylvania;
POM Ashland, Va
27 Jun 1894
Hanover MR 25 Jun
1894 SPML

GAYLE, Thomas B. s/o
Jeriah P.&
Frances M.Gayle
age 23 S farmer
POB Caroline Co
POR Spotsylvania
& **SANFORD**,
Virginia d/o
Joseph & Agness
Sanford age 20 S
POB
Fredericksburg
POR Spotsylvania;
POM Spotsylvania
8 Jun 1865 SPMR 6
Jun 1865 SPML

GEIGER, Charles F.s/o
Frederick &
Louise Geiger age
25 S printer POB
Abingen
Wertemburg
Germany POR
Philadelphia,
Penn. & **CAFFREY**,
Jenetta A. d/o
P.S.& Sarah
Caffrey age 25 S
POB Portland
City, Oregon POR
Spotsylvania; POM
Spotsylvania 22
Sep 1886 SPMR 20
Sep 1886 SPML

GENTRY, John R. &
MANSFIELD, Mary
Jane d/o Thomas
M.Mansfield; 17
Feb 1851 OML

GEORGE, O.C. s/o
Peyton &
A,P.George age 28
S farmer POB &
POR Fauquier Co &
CROPTS, Bettie B.
d/o Silas F.&
C.M.Cropts age 22
S POB Fauquier Co
POR Spotsylvania;
POM "Benvenud",
Spotsylvania 29
Nov 1866 SPMR
SPML

GIBBS, Albert s/o Toby
& Daphney Gibbs
age 23 S farmer
POB Caroline Co
POR Spotsylvania
POC & **LEE**, Ann
d/o Dick &
Charity Lee age
25 W POB Caroline
Co POR
Spotsylvania POC;
POM Spotsylvania
18 Dec 1867 SPMR
14 Dec 1867 SPML

GIBBS, Alex.L. s/o
John & Pinkston
A.Gibbs age 27 S
merchant POB
Richmond Co POR
Fredericksburg &
MALLORY, Eveline
T. d/o Philip &
Sarah C.Mallory
age 28 S POB &
POR Orange; POM
Orange 28 Jan
1858 OMR 28 Dec
1857 OML

GIBSON, Charles
laborer POB & POR
Spotsylvania POC
& **GORDON**, Louisa
S POB & POR
Spotsylvania POC;
POM Graves Farm,
Spotsylvania 23
Sep 1882 SPMR 20
Sep 1882 SPML

GIBSON, E.Dorsey s/o
Thomas G.Gibson &

Puryfee(?) Gray age 34 S physician POB Orange POR Culpeper Co & **TOWLES**, Bettie C. d/o Thomas W.Gray & Sallie Lucas age 28 W POB & POR Orange; POM Orange C.H. 10 Oct 1865 OMR OML

GIBSON, Joseph s/o John & Charlotte Gibson age 20 S farmer POB Louisa Co POR Spotsylvania POC & **WILLIAMS**, Lavinia d/o Jeff & Caroline Williams age 19 S POB Louisa Co POR Spotsylvania; POM Spotsylvania 14 Jul 1872 SPMR 13 Jul 1872 SPML

GIBSON, Joseph s/o John Gibson & C.Boxley age 24 S laborer POB & POR Spotsylvania POC & **WHITE**, Cornelia d/o H.& C.White age 18 S POB & POR Spotsylvania POC; POM Spotsylvania 31 May 1877 SPMR 21 May 1877 SPML

GIBSON, Nathan & **GIBSON**, Mary Jane d/o Burwell Gibson; 3 Oct 1854 OML

GIBSON, Thomas s/o Charles & T.Gibson age 223 S laborer POB & POR Spotsylvania POC & **JACKSON**, Emma d/o Sam & Mary F. Jackson age 19 S POB &
POR Spotsylvania POC; POM Spotsylvania 16 Apr 1881 SPMR 15 Apr 1881 SPML

GILCHRIST, John K. s/o David & Mary Gilchrist age 33 S railroad engineer POB Greensburg, Pennsylvania POR Fredericksburg & **EUBANK**, S.H. d/o J.L.& Jennie Eubank age 23 S POB Caroline CO POR Summit, Spotsylvania; POM Summit, Spotsylvania 8 Dec 1881 SPMR 2 Dec 1881 SPML

GILDED, Thomas Burke s/o John B.& Mary Gilded age 35 S miller POB Manchester, England POR Spotsylvania & **FLIPPO**, Septimia d/o Major Flippo & Aurelia F.Heislop age 17 S POB Caroline Co POR Spotsylvania; POM Trinity Ch, Spotsylvania 28 Aug 1877 SPMR 27 Aug 1877 SPML

GILLIAM, William & **PARROTT**, Martha A. d/o George Parrott; 9 Jun 1851 OML

GILLISPIE, William G.& **DOUGLAS**, Sarah A. d/o William Douglas; 28 Apr 1851 OML

GIPPER, C.Lewis s/o Christopher & Lucinda Gipper age 23 S mechanic

POB Pennsylvania POR Spotsylvania & **THOMPSON**, Delia d/o J.R.Thompson age 22 S POB New York POR Spotsylvania; POM Spotsylvania 3 Apr 1881 SPMR 23 Mar 1881 SPML

GOFF, James M. s/o James Goff & Martha Jones age 33 W house carpenter /ship joiner POB Richland District, S.C. POR Clarke Co, Alabama & **SKINNER**, Eliza A. d/o William Skinner & Jane Webb age 25 S POB Madison Co POR Orange; POM Orange 10 Aug 1864 OMR 6 Aug 1864 OML

GOFFNEY, Ebenezer s/o William Goffney & Leanna Thornton age 26 S POB & POR Orange POC & **JACKSON**, Anna d/o Monroe & Eliza Jackson age 19 S POB & POR Orange POC; POM Orange 28 Dec 1867 OMR 26 Dec 1867 OML

GOOCH, William E. s/o William Gooch & Mary E.Young age 27 S farmer POB Orange POR Spotsylvania & **GRAVES**, Minie A. d/o Garrett & Jane Graves age 29 S POB & POR Spotsylvania; POM Spotsylvania 30 Aug 1882 SPMR 26 Aug 1882 SPML

GOODLOE, Charles s/o George P.& Mary E.Goodloe age 21 S farmer POB & POR Spotsylvania & **DUERSON**, Edwina C. d/o Henry & Emily Duerson age 23 S POB & POR Spotsylvania; POM Locust Grove, Spotsylvania 20 Nov 1872 SPMR 4 Nov 1872 SPML

GOODLOE, James s/o Robert & Sallie Goodloe age 25 S laborer POB & POR Spotsylvania POC & **ELLIS**, Georgeanna age 22 S POB & POR Spotsylvania POC; POM New Hop Ch,(possible minister's error may be New Hope Ch) Spotsylvania 6 May 1886 SPMR 5 May 1886 SPML

GOODLOE, Sym B. s/o S.B.& R.M.Goodloe age 23 S clerk salesman POB Caroline Co POR Spotsylvania & **POUND**, Mattie A. d/o Richard & Mary Pound age 20 S POB & POR Spotsylvania; POM Spotsylvania 24 Feb 1887 SPMR 22 Feb 1887 SPML

GOODMAN, Charles G. s/o Christopher C.& Virginia Goodman age 27 S farmer POB & POR Hanover Co & **SEAY**, Mary C. d/o Wyatt & Lucinda

S.Seay age 23 S
POB & POR
Spotsylvania; POM
Spotsylvania 27
Feb 1868 SPMR 22
Feb 1868 SPML
GOODMAN, Jacob L.s/o
Samuel W.& Mary
W.Goodman age 22
S farmer POB
Albemarle Co POR
Spotsylvania &
SACRA, Martha A.
d/o John L.&
Sarah C.Sacra age
22 S POB & POR
Spotsylvania; POM
Partlow,
Spotsylvania 29
Dec 1891 SPMR 24
Dec 1891 SPML
GOODWIN, Charles E.
s/o John & Mary
Ann Goodwin age
25 S gangsman on
railroad POB
Prince William Co
POR Orange &
MASON, Sarah
Margaret d/o
Sanders &
Catherine Mason
age 20 S POB
Rockingham Co POR
Orange; POM
Orange 20 Dec
1855 OMR 19 Dec
1855 OML
GOODWIN, James A. s/o
John & Mary Ann
Goodwin age 23 S
farmer POB Prince
William Co POR
Orange & **MASON**,
Emily Frances d/o
Sanders &
Catherine Mason
age 18 S POB
Rockingham, Va
POR Orange; POM
Orange 4 Sep 1856
OMR OML
GOODWIN, John F. s/o
John & Mary

A.Goodwin age 25
S POB Prince
William Co POR
Orange & **DUVALL**,
Sarah E. d/o
William L. &
Comfort Duvall
age 19 S POB
Annarundle Co,Md
POR Orange; POM
Orange 18 Jun
1857 OMR OML
GOODWIN, John T. s/o
Dr. William &
Frances Goodwin
age 27 farmer POR
Louisa Co &
TERRILL, Betsy
Veranda d/o Dr.
William Terrill
age 18; POM
Orange 22 Dec
1853 OMR 12 Dec
1853 OML
GOODWIN, John T. s/o
Dr.William &
Frances Goodwin
age 27 farmer POR
Louisa Co &
TERRILL, Betty O.
d/o Dr.U.Terrill
age 18 POR
Orange; POM
Orange 22 Dec
1853 OMR
GOODWIN, Minor s/o
Alex & Charlotte
Goodwin age 22 S
laborer POB
Louisa Co POR
Hanover Co POC &
WIGGLESWORTH,
Elizabeth d/o
William & Sarah
Wigglesworth age
21 S POB & POR
Spotsylvania POC;
POM Partlow, Va
13 Dec 1885 SPMR
7 Dec 1885 SPML
GOODWIN, Richard T.
s/o Semple &
S.D.Goodwin age
26 S farmer POB &

POR Louisa Co & **COLEMAN**, Emma S. d/o John T. & Emma Coleman age 22 S POB & POR Spotsylvania; POM Spotsylvania 22 Dec 1875 SPMR 6 Dec 1875 SPML
GOODWIN, Robert J. s/o John Goodwin & Mary A.Arnold age 28 S engineer on O.& A.railroad POB Prince William Co POR Orange & **DAVIS**, Bettie W. d/o William J.Davis age 22 S POB & POR Orange; POM Orange 5 Sep 1867 OMR 3 Sep 1867 OML
GOODWIN, William P. s/o John T. & Ann E. Goodwin age 25 S farmer POB Oakley, Caroline Co POR Caroline Co & **GOODWIN**, Mary Byrd d/o William M.B.& Nannie S.Goodwin age 17 S POB Rose Hill, Spotsylvania POR Spotsylvania; POM Rose Hill, Spotsylvania 21 Nov 1871 SPMR 20 Nov 1871 SPML
GORDON, C.E.s/o Joseph H.& Hannah E.Gordon age 29 S farmer POB & POR Spotsylvania & **TOWLES**, Lizzie W. d/o Dr.T.T.& E.S.Towles age 25 S POB & POR Spotsylvania; POM Spotsylvania 18

Jan 1887 SPMR 17
Jan 1887 SPML
GORDON, Edward H.s/o Hugh & Hannah Gordon age 54 S farmer POB Newburg, Orange Co, N.Y.POR Spotsylvania & **ALMOND**, Alverda d/o Barnett & Anne Almond age 50 S POB & POR Spotsylvania; POM Spotsylvania 15 Jun 1896 SPMR 22 May 1896 SPML
GORDON, George F.s/o Cosmo & Adeline Gordon age 22 S farmer POB & POR Spotsylvania & **BECK**, Maggie T. d/o John E.& Margaret E.Beck age 22 S POB & POR Spotsylvania; POM Spotsylvania C.H. 21 Nov 1887 SPMR SPML
GORDON, George s/o Sam & Suckey Gordon age 55 W POB & POR Spotsylvania POC & **DAINGERFIELD**, Matilda d/o Bob & Mariah Johnson age 38 W POB & POR Spotsylvania POC; POM Spotsylvania 27 Dec 1871 SPMR 18 Dec 1871 SPML
GORDON, Henry F. s/o S.& P.Gordon age 49 S farmer POB & POR Caroline Co & **BOULWARE**, Irene d/o A.M.& M.Boulware age 33 S POB King William Co POR Spotsylvania; POM

Belvedere,
Spotsylvania 12
Feb 1879 SPMR 6
Feb 1879 SPML
GORDON, John A.B. s/o
John A.& Jane
L.Gordon age 46 W
farmer POB & POR
Spotsylvania &
LIPSCOMB, Sallie
L. d/o John L.&
Mary E.Andrews
age 44 W POB &
POR Spotsylvania;
POM Spotsylvania
22 Jul 1890 SPMR
21 Jul 1890 SPML
GORDON, John A.B. s/o
John A.Gordon &
Jane Herndon age
23 S farmer POB &
POR Spotsylvania
& **GORDON**, Fanny
F. d/o Edward
Gordon & Fanny
Herndon age 23 S
POB Culpeper Co
POR Orange; POM
Orange 12 Nov
1867 OMR 4 Nov
1867 OML
GORDON, Joseph H. s/o
John A.& Jane
Gordon age 23 S
farmer POB & POR
Spotsylvania &
WILLIS, Hannah E.
d/o James &
Elizabeth Willis
age 24 S POB &
POR Orange; POM
Orange 3 Mar 1857
OMR 2 Mar 1857
OML
GORDON, Leland s/o
Charles &
R.Gordon age 22 S
laborer POB & POR
Spotsylvania POC
& **SMITH**, Agnes
s/o Lewis &
L.Smith age 23 S
POB & POR
Spotsylvania POC;
POM Spotsylvania
5 Feb 1880 SPMR 4
Feb 1880 SPML
GORDON, Linsey s/o
Ralph & Caroline
Gordon age 24 S
laborer POB & POR
Spotsylvania POC
& **WOOLFOLK**,
Bettie d/o
Barnett & Ellen
Woolfolk age 23 S
POB & POR
Spotsylvania POC;
POM Rubenwood
Fork,
Spotsylvania 28
Feb 1877 SPMR 26
Feb 1877 SPML
GORDON, Oliver s/o
George & Ellen
Gordon age 21 S
farmer POB & POR
Spotsylvania POC
& **DANGERFIELD**,
Diana d/o Beverly
& Matilda
Dangerfield age
19 S POB & POR
Spotsylvania POC;
POM Cherry Grove,
Spotsylvania 9
Jan 1874 SPMR
SPML
GORDON, Robert s/o
James & Eliza
Gordon age 22 S
laborer POB & POR
Spotsylvania POC
& **LEWIS**, Amanda
d/o Rich &
Matilda Lewis age
21 S POB & POR
Spotsylvania; POM
Spotsylvania 19
Feb 1880 SPMR 18
Feb 1880 SPML
GORDON, Samuel Jr.s/o
Samuel & Patsy
F.Gordon age 36 S
pork packer POB
Caroline Co POR
St.Louis, MO &
YERBY, Alice D.

d/o Thomas P. &
Jane D. Yerby age
20 S POB & POR
Spotsylvania; POM
Belle Voir,
Spotsylvania 10
Jan 1882 SPMR 6
Jan 1882 SPML

GORDON, Thomas C. s/o
John A. Gordon &
Jane S. Herndon
age 26 S farmer
POB & POR
Spotsylvania &
BALLARD, Lucy J.
d/o Charles
B. Ballard & Sarah
Chancellor age 23
S POB
Spotsylvania POR
Orange; POM
Orange 9 Nov 1865
OMR 27 Oct 1865
OML

GORDON, William C. s/o
Sam & Jane Gordon
age 25 S
blacksmith POB &
POR Spotylvania
POC & **ALSOP**,
Georgeanna d/o
Henry & Mary Ann
Alsop age 17 S
POB & POR
Spotylvania POC;
POM Spotsylvania
24 Dec 1873 SPMR
23 Dec 1873 SPML

GOSS, Jessee H. s/o
J.H. & Mary Goss
age 27 S lawyer
POB Georgia POR
LaGrange, Georgia
& **NEWMAN**, Julia
d/o J.B. &
S.B. Newman age 25
S POB & POR
Orange; POM
Orange 2 Sep 1857
OMR 1 Sep 1857
OML

GOSS, John W. & **MACON**,
Sarah F.; POM
Orange 15 Sep
1853 OMR 13 Sep
1853 OML

GRADY, George D. s/o
George T. & Roanna
G. Grady age 22 S
farmer POB & POR
Spotsylvania &
TALLEY, Maud Z.
d/o James M. Lucy
Talley age 22 S
POB & POR
Spotsylvania; POM
Spotsylvania
C.H. 6 Jun 1894
SPMR 31 May 1894
SPML

GRADY, George T. s/o
William A. & E.R.
Grady age 23 S
farmer POB & POR
Spotsylvania &
SMITH, Rowenna G.
d/o Benj. & Julia
Smith age 21 S
POB Stafford POR
Spotsylvania; POM
Spotsylvania 30
Jan 1862 SPMR 29
Jan 1862 SPML

GRADY, John W. s/o
Preston & Kate
Grady age 21 S
mechanic POB
Louisa Co POR
Orange & **COX**,
S.A. d/o John &
Sarah Cox age 23
S POB & POR
Spotsylvania; POM
Orange 9 Jan 1883
OMR 1 Jan 1883
SPML

GRAHAM, Walter C. s/o
J.W. & Mary Graham
age 22 S farmer
POB Montgomery
Co, Va POR
Spotsylvania &
CAMPBELL, Maggie
d/o O.H. & Sarah
Campbell age 23 S
POB Washington
Co, Va POR
Spotsylvania; POM

Spotsylvania 22 Jul 1896 SPMR SPML

GRANINGER, Sabastian s/o Sabastian & Mary C.Graninger age 41 S farmer POB Illinois POR Stafford & **MULLEN**, Mary Agnes d/o David & Rosa Mullen age 24 S POB Maryland POR Spotsylvania; POM St.Mary's Ch, Fredericksburg 18 Jan 1893 FMR 16 Jan 1893 SPML

GRANT, Decker s/o Mary Grant age 19 S laborer POB & POR Louisa Co POC & **POINDEXTER**, Maria L. d/o Charles & Ella Poindexter age 17 S POB & POR Spotsylvania POC; POM Spotsylvania 24 Feb 1893 SPMR SPML

GRAVATT, Ellis W. s/o John C.& Anada Gravatt age 24 S coach trimmer POB Caroline Co POR Fredericksburg & **TERRILL**, Mary T. d/o Oliver & Susan E.Terrill age 19 S POB & POR Orange; POM Orange 23 Dec 1856 OMR 8 Dec 1856 OML

GRAVES, Benjamin age 24 S laborer POB Orange POR Spotsylvania POC & **ROBINSON**, Matilda d/o Frank & Mary Robinson age 23 S POB & POR Spotsylvania POC; POM Branch Fork Ch, Spotsylvania 25 Nov 1875 SPMR 24 Nov 1875 SPML

GRAVES, Benton V. s/o Colby Graves & Jane Ferguson age 33 S farmer POB & POR SPotsylvania & **STUBBLEFIELD**, Susan d/o Thomas Stubblefield & Mary Hilman age 29 S POB & POR Orange; POM Orange 19 Dec 1865 OMR 14 Dec 1865 OML

GRAVES, George W. s/o Paschal & Elizabeth C.Graves age 24 S farmer POB Page Co POR Green Co & **PRICE**, Louisa H. d/o Curtis Wilhoit & Maria Louisa Harrison age 24 W POB & POR Orange; POM Orange 17 Jan 1861 OMR 14 Jan 1861 OML

GRAVES, Isaac S. s/o Lewis & Frances Graves age 51 W farmer POB & POR Orange & **BLAYDES**, Isabella M. d/o William Blaydes age 38 S POB & POR Spotsylvania; POM Louisa Co 1 Sep 1875 SPMR 26 Aug 1875 SPML

JUDD, H.B. s/o J.E.G. & E.B.Judd age 37 W engineer POB Birmington, N.Y. POR Palmira, N.Y. & **CLARKE**, Allice B. d/o J.H.& M.F. Clarke

age 24 S POB &
POR Spotsylvania;
POM Spotsylvania
5 May 1875 SPMR 3
May 1875 SPML
GRAVES, John S. s/o
Lewis Graves &
Fanny White age
34 S farmer POB &
POR Orange &
MEREDITH, Ursula
d/o Thomas
G.Kendall &
Elizabeth
Meredith age 34 W
POB Spotsylvania
POR Orange; POM
Orange 6 Mar 1862
OMR 3 Mar 1862
OML
GRAVES, Johnson s/o
Melissa Graves
age 27 S laborer
POB & POR
Spotsylvania POC
& **THOMPSON**,
Virgie d/o
Solomon & Mary
Johnson age 19 S
POB & POR
Spotsylvania POC;
POM Spotsylvania
15 Feb 1891 SPMR
14 Feb 1891 SPML
GRAVES, Joseph H.ls/o
J.L.& Amanda
Graves age 26 S
farmer POB Orange
POR Spotsylvania
& **BULLOCK**, Maud
Gabriella d/o
R.M.& Ann
E.Bullock age 22
S POB Louisa Co
POR Spotsylvania;
POM Spotsylvania
10 Jan 1884 SPMR
29 Dec 1883 SPML
GRAVES, Joseph H.s/o
Isaac L.& Amanda
M.Graves age 42 W
farmer POB & POR
Orange &
CHEWNING, Dallie

d/o George W.&
Alice Chewning
age 21 S POB &
POR Spotsylvania;
POM Spotsylvania
21 May 1899 SPMR
17 May 1899 SPML
GRAVES, Nelson s/o
Abram & Melissa
Graves age 24 S
laborer POB
Louisa Co POR
Louisa Co POC &
TAYLOR, Polly d/o
William & Rachel
Taylor age 21 S
POB & POR
Spotsylvania POC;
POM Spotsylvania
28 Jan 1882 SPMR
(probably error
of date by
minister) 25 Feb
1882 SPML
GRAVES, Richard P. s/o
Richard P.& Lucy
F.Graves age 26 S
farmer POB & POR
Orange &
DICKINSON, Emma
M. d/o Hugh M.&
Susan Dickinson
age 20 S POB &
POR Spotsylvania;
15 Oct 1874 SPML
GRAVES, Sandy P.s/o
Garrett & Jane
F.Graves age 26 S
farmer POB & POR
Spotsylvania &
TALLEY, Mary
Alice d/o James
M.& Lucy Talley
age 24 S POB &
POR Spotsylvania;
POM Spotsylvania
13 Dec 1882 SPMR
8 Dec 1882 SPML
GRAVES, Thomas E. s/o
Lewis Graves &
Fanny White age
22 S farmer POB &
POR Orange &
BROCKMAN, Lou d/o

Samuel Brockman & Frances A.Graves age 29 S POB & POR Orange; POM Orange 26 Dec 1867 OMR 23 Dec 1867 OML

GRAVES, Thomas S. s/o John S.& Emily Graves age 37 S farmer POB & POR Stafford & **SMITH**, Sallie A. d/o Benjamin & Julia A. Smith age 23 S POB Stafford POR Spotsylvania; POM Spotsylvania 13 Jan 1867 SPMR 11 Jan 1867 SPML

GRAY, Willis s/o J.& N.Gray age 40 W laborer POB King George Co POR Spotsylvania POC & **CARR**, Malinda age 40 W POB & POR Spotsylvania POC; POM Mt.Zion Ch, Spotsylvania 23 Sep 1877 SPMR 22 Sep 1877 SPML

GRAYSON, John A. s/o Joel & Delia Grayson age 26 S farmer POB Lafayette, Mississippi POR Spotsylvania & **ALSOP**, Martha A. d/o Benjamin & Maria Wilson age 29 W POB & POR Spotsylvania; POM M.E.Ch, Fredericksburg 18 Mar 1866 FMR 17 Mar 1866 SPML

GREEN, Edmund s/o George & Jenny Green age 61 S farmer POB & POR Spotylvania POC & **RAWLINGS**, Kitty age 50 W POB Orange POR Spotsylvania POC; POM Spotsylvania 26 Jul 1873 SPMR SPML

GREEN, George s/o Simon & Nancy Green age 35 W POB & POR Caroline Co POC & **COLEMAN**, Jennie d/o George & Martha Ross age 26 W POB & POR Spotsylvania POC; POM Spotsylvania 16 Feb 1881 SPMR 14 Feb 1881 SPML

GREEN, John C. s/o W.E.& Ann E. Green age 21 S farmer POB Stafford POR Spotsylvania & **WOOD**, Lizzie G. d/o Peter & Sarah Jane Wood age 21 S POB & POR Spotsylvania; POM Spotsylvania 31 Dec 1884 SPMR SPML

GREEN, Lewis s/o John & Harriett Green age 21 S farmer POB & POR Spotsylvania POC & **CORNICAN**, Rose d/o Matt & Fanny Carnican age 23 S POB & POR Spotsylvania POC; POM Mt.Zion Baptist Ch, Spotsylvania 13 May 1875 SPML 22 May 1875 SPML

GREEN, Nelson s/o Thornton & Agnes Green age 26 S farmer POB & POR Spotsylvania POC & **BUNLEY**, Matilda

d/o Solomon &
Bettie Bunley age
21 S POB Louisa
Co POR
Spotsylvania POC;
POM Branch Fork
Ch, Spotsylvania
26 Dec 1875 SPMR
SPML

GREEN, Robert s/o
Harrison &
Caroline Green
age 21 S farm
laborer POB & POR
Orange POC &
JACKSON, Caroline
age 24 S POB &
POR Orange POC;
POM Orange 29 Dec
1866 OMR 27 Dec
1866 OML

GREEN, Stephen &
RECTOR, Martha;
21 Oct 1854 OML

GREEN, Stephen G. s/o
George Green &
Sally Brimmer age
35 W POB
Westmoreland Co
POR Culpeper &
PIERCE, Delphia
A. d/o John
Pierce & Frances
Tamplin age 30 S
POB Spotsylvania
POR Orange; POM
Orange 20 Dec
1866 OMR 19 Dec
1866 OML

GREEN, T.J.s/o William
E.& Ann E.Green
ge 27 S farmer
POB & POR
Spotsylvania &
BURWELL, Susie J.
d/o Andrew J.&
Summerville
Burwell age 24 S
POB
Fredericksburg
POR Spotsylvania;
POM Massaponax
Baptist Ch,
Spotsylvania 28
Feb 1883 SPMR 26
Feb 1883 SPML

GREEN, Thornton s/o
William & Maria
Green age 21 S
laborer POB & POR
Spotsylvania POC
& **ELLIS**, Maud d/o
George & Jane
Ellis S POB & POR
Spotsylvania POC;
POM New Hope Ch,
Spotsylvania 8
Jul 1883 SPMR 2
Jul 1883 SPML

GREEN, William C. s/o
Charles & Mary
Green age 27 S
farmer POB Essex
Co, Va POR
Spotsylvania &
BEVERLEY, Matilda
d/o Thornton &
Malinda Beverly
age 28 S POB &
POR Spotsylvania;
POM Spotsylvania
C.H. 5 Dec 1893
SPMR SPML

GREY, Henry s/o
Altheus & Ellen
Grey age 22 S
farmer POB & POR
Spotsylvania POC
& **BOXLEY**, Jane
d/o Thornton &
Martha Boxley age
19 S POB & POR
Spotsylvania POC;
POM Spotsylvania
17 Dec 1868 SPMR
16 Dec 1868 SPML

GRIFFE, John s/o
Harris Griffe &
Sethe Wood age 19
S farmer POB &
POR Dekalb Co,Ga
& **PIERCE**, Eliza
H. d/o John
W.Pierce age 19 S
POB & POR Orange;
POM Orange 4 Sep
1863 OMR 2 Sep
1863 OML

GRIFFIN, James H. s/o James Griffin & Ann Oglesby age 46 S blacksmith POB Buford District, S.C. POR Irvine Co,Ga & **SMITH**, Mary A. d/o John & Patience Smith age 47 W POB Culpeper Co POR Orange; POM Orange 23 Jun 1864 OMR 20 Jun 1864 OML

GRIFFIS, George B. s/o Samuel H.& Mary Ann Griffis age 30 S merchant POB & POR Stafford & **McGEE**, Olivia D. d/o Absalom & Frances McGee age 22 S POB & POR Spotsylvania; POM Spotsylvania 14 Oct 1884 SPMR 6 Oct 1884 SPML

GRIMSLEY, James R. s/o C.D.& Lucy A.Grimsley age 21 S farmer POB Stafford POR Spotsylvania & **BOWLING**, Ophelia S. d/o Lawrence T.& S.E.Bowling age 18 S POB & POR Spotsylvania; POM Spotsylvania C.H.21 Mar 1889 SPMR SPML

GRIMSLEY, Richard s/o George & Pollie Grimsley age 21 S overseer POB Rappahannock POR Culpeper & **SMITH**, Ellen d/o Harison & Susan Smith age 25 S POB Culpeper POR Orange; POM Orange 3 Dec 1854 OMR

GROOMS, James M. s/o John C.& Mary E.Grooms age 25 S miner POB & POR Louisa Co & **WILLOUGHBY**, Cornelia d/o Margaret L.Willoughby age 20 S POB & POR Spotsylvania; POM Spotsylvania 1 May 1895 SPMR SPML

GRYMES, Benjamin A. & **BEALE**, Harriet H.; POM Orange 5 Jan 1853 OMR 3 Jan 1853 OML

GRYMES, Jeffery s/o Jeffery & Molly Grymes age 65 W farmer POB & POR Spotsylvania POC & **BROOKS**, Esther d/o Ben & Rose Lewis age 64 W POB & POR Spotsylvania POC: POM Spotsylvania 1 Sep 1872 SPMR 31 Aug 1872 SPML

GULLY, Patrick H.s/o John H.& Margaret A.Gulley age 26 S mechanic POB Massachussettes POR Louisa & **SCHOOLER**, Mattie A. d/o Thomas C.& Elizabeth Schooler age 23 S POB & POR Spotsylvania; POM Methodist Pasonage, Sulpher Mines,Louisa 22 Dec 1892 Louisa MR 19 Dec 1892 SPML

GUY, Charles B. s/o Ambrose & Mary

Guy age 33 W
farmer POB
Washington Co,
N.Y. POR Orange &
CHARTTERS, Lucy
P. d/o James P.&
Susan P.Chartters
age 19 S POB
Spotsylvania POR
Orange; POM
Orange 18 Feb
1860 SPMR 17 Feb
1860 OML

HAHN, William s/o
Charles &
Caroline Hahn age
24 S farmer POB
Hesse, Germany
POR Spotsylvania
& **LEITCH**, Eliza
F. d/o William &
Ellen Leitch age
22 S POB Stafford
POR Spotsylvania;
POM Spotsylvania
4 Nov 1869 SPMR 3
Nov 1869 SPML

HAILEY, Benjamin B. &
HAILEY, Louisa
previously
married; POM
Spotsylvania
(undated MR) 10
Feb 1861 SPML

HAILEY, Isaiah s/o
Benjamin & Louisa
F.Hailey age 20 S
farmer POB & POR
Spotsylvania &
WHEELER, Eddie J.
d/o Edward & Mary
Jane Wheeler age
21 S POB & POR
Spotsylvania; POM
Spotsylvania
C.H.20 Aug 1884
SPMR SPML

HAILEY, John L. s/o
John L.& Louisa
Hailey age 22 S
farmer POB & POR
Spotsylvania &
JONES, Mary Susan
d/o John & Susan

Jones age 23 S
POB Hanover Co
POR Spotsylvania;
POM Spotsylvania
16 Jan 1877 SPMR
11 Jan 1877 SPML

HAILEY, Wallace s/o
John L.& Mary
S.Hailey age 23 S
farmer POB & POR
Spotsylvania &
EDENTON, Mary L.
d/o John J.&
Betty Edenton age
19 S POB & POR
Spotsylvania; POM
Spotsylvania 23
Sep 1900 SPML 21
Sep 1900 SPML

HAINES, Henry R. s/o
John & Sarah
Haines age 34 S
POB Denbigh Hall,
England POR
Spotsylvania &
KING, Mary P. d/o
John & Sarah
Haines age 17 S
POB Orange POR
Spotsylvania; POM
Tabernacle
Methodist Ch 21
Apr 1884 SPMR 17
Apr 1884 SPML

HAISLIP, Norman F. s/o
Frank & Aurelia
F.Haislip age 26
S farmer POB &
POR Spotsylvania
& **SHELTON**, Susie
J. d/o W.A.&
Susan E. Shelton
age 24 S POB &
POR Spotsylvania;
POM Spotsylvania
C.H. 23 Dec 1897
SPMR 20 Dec 1897
SPML

HAISLIP, Silas E. s/o
A.J.& Agnes
B.Haislip age 25
S merchant POB
Fairfax Co, Va
POR

Fredericskburg & **SHADLE**, Edna A. d/o Samuel J.& Rachel S.Shadle age 22 S POB Lycomming Co, Penn POR Spotsylvania; POM Baptist Ch, Fredericksburg 25 Feb 1885 FMR 23 Feb 1885 SPML

HALE, Daniel W. s/o Jacob Hale & Elizabeth Ermon age 28 S blacksmith POB Rockingham Co POR Orange & **DAVIS**, Mary E. d/o William J.Davis age 29 S POB & POR Orange; POM Gordonsville, Orange 20 Dec 1866 OMR 17 Dec 1866 OML

HALL, Benjamin O. s/o Benjamin & Lurinda Hall age 21 S farmer POB & POR Stafford & **HUMPHRY**, Mary E. d/o John & Jane Humphries age 28 S POB & POR Spotsylvania; POM Spotsylvania 2 Nov 1869 SPMR 1 Nov 1869 SPML

HALL, Benjamin T. s/o B.O.& Mary E.Hall age 23 S farmer POB Stafford POR Spotsylvania & **MORRISON**, Eliza A. d/o R.R.& Mary A.Morrison age 33 S POB Alexandria, Va POR Spotsylvania; POM Spotsylvania 23 Nov 1898 SPMR 16 Nov 1898 SPML

HALL, Burton B. s/o Horace C.& Jane Hall age 22 S farmer POB & POR Spotsylvania & **JONES**, Myrdie D. d/o James A.& M.L.Jones age 17 S POB & POR Spotsylvania ; POM Spotsylvania C.H.9 May 1888 SPMR SPML

HALL, Clarence O. s/o Addison & Virginia A.Hall age 22 S farmer POB & POR Spotsylvania & **McGARY**, Eunice L. d/o Henry A.& Susan McGary age 18 S POB & POR Spotsylvania; POM Spotsylvania 25 Nov 1886 SPMR 22 Nov 1886 SPML

HALL, Everett C. s/o Horace C.& Jane E. Hall age 23 S farmer POB & POR Spotsylvania & **WHEELER**, Isabel B. d/o James W.& Mary W.Wheeler age 18 S POB & POR Spotsylvania; POM Spotsylvania 25 Oct 1893 SPMR SPML

HALL, H.C. & **BELL**, Jane E.; 29 Apr 1865 SPConsent

HALL, Henry s/o Wilson & Patsy Hall age 26 S laborer POB & POR Louisa Co POC & **WATSON**, Evelina d/o Henry & Margaret Watson age 20 S POB & POR Spotsylvania POC; POM Spotsylvania 27

Sep 1866 SPMR 27
Aug 1866 SPML
HALL, Horace C. s/o
Thomas &
Elizabeth Hall
age 54 W farmer
POB & POR
Spotsylvania &
BELL, Jane E. d/o
Henry & Catherine
Lumsden age 28 W
POB & POR
Spotsylvania; POM
Spotsylvania May
1865 SPMR 1 May
1865 SPML
HALL, John L. s/o
H.J.& J.A.Hall
age 23 S farmer
POB & POR
Spotsylvania &
TALLEY, Rosa May
d/o James M.&
L.T.Talley age 22
S POB & POR
Spotsylvania; POM
Wilderness Ch,
Spotsylvania 8
Jan 1896 SPMR 6
Jan 1896 SPML
HALL, John W. s/o
Benjamin O.& Mary
E.Hall age 25 S
farmer POB & POR
Stafford &
BEVERLEY, Bertie
C. d/o F.C.& M.A.
Beverley age 28 S
POB & POR
Spotsylvania; POM
Spotsylvania 28
Oct 1896 SPMR 26
Oct 1896 SPML
HALL, Joseph s/o
Hasten & Lucy
Hall age 26 S
farmer POB
Albemarle Co POR
Green Co & **RINER**,
Mary E. d/o Jacob
& Matilda Riner
age 18 S POB &
POR Orange; POM
Orange 25 Feb
1858 OMR 22 Feb
1858 OML
HALL, Littleburg W.
s/o Littleton W.&
Maggie Hall age
22 S farmer POB &
POR Spotsylvania
& **DAVENPORT**,
Della d/o W.D.&
Ella Davenport
age 21 S POB &
POR Spotsylvania;
POM Spotsylvania
30 Dec 1896 SPMR
28 Dec 1896 SPML
HALL, Littleton W. s/o
Horace & Lucy
Hall age 27 S
farmer POB & POR
Spotsylvania &
TRUEL, Margaret
L. d/o James &
Addiline Truel
age 24 S POB &
POR Spotsylvania;
POM Louisa Co 7
Jun 1866 SPMR 2
Jun 1866 SPML
HALL, William W. s/o
Benjamin & Lamint
Hall age 21 S
farmer POB & POR
Stafford &
SMITH, Virginia
T. d/o John &
Julia Curtis age
27 W POB Stafford
POR Spotsylvania;
POM Spotsylvania
22 Oct 1867 SPMR
21 Oct 1867 SPML
HANBACK, James
W.(possibly
Hauback)s/o James
H.& Martha
A.Hanback age 27
S farmer POB
Fauquire Co POR
Fauquire Co &
BAKER, Maggie M.
d/o J.W.& Mary
Baker age 24 S
POB Stafford POR
Spotsylvania; POM

Spotsylvania 28 Mar 1882 SPMR 27 Mar 1882 SPML
HANCOCK, John F. s/o William T.& Barbara Hancock age 50 S carpenter & contractor POB & POR Fredericksburg & **JETT**, Susie D. d/o John A.& Louisa Jett age 30 S POB Stafford POR Spotsylvania; POM Fredericksburg 11 Sep 1895 FMR 9 Sep 1895 SPML
HANCOCK, William T. s/o William T.& Barbara Hancock age 44 W carpenter POB & POR Fredericksburg & **JETT**, Mary Lou d/o John & Mary L.Jett age 33 S POB Stafford POR Spotsylvania; POM Fredericksburg 17 Dec 1890 FMR SPML
HANES, Robert s/o John M.& Oney H. Hanes age 30 S farmer POB & POR Caroline Co & **CARNEAL**, Sallie J. d/o Thomas & Virginia Jones age 26 W POB & POR Spotsylvania; POM Baptist Ch, Spotsylvania 26 Apr 1866 SPMR 21 Apr 1866 SPML
HANEY, B.L. s/o J.F.& Louisa J.Haney age 22 S farmer POB & POR Spotsylvania & **CARTER**, Anna Lee d/o John & Teck Carter age 23 S POB & POR Spotsylvania; 10 Sep 1900 SPML
HANEY, Jeremiah T. s/o Reuben & Matilda Haney age 26 S farmer POB & POR Spotsylvania & **LEWIS**, Louisa J. d/o Robert & Jane Haney age 20 S POB & POR Spotsylvania; POM Spotsylvania 8 Dec 1868 SPMR 5 Dec 1868 SPML
HANEY, William J. s/o John J.Haney & Huldah Jacobs age 27 S POB Orange POR Albemarle Co & **HARLOW**, Lucy Mary d/o Julius B.Harlow & Winney P.Crooks age 24 S POB & POR Orange; POM Orange 15 Jan 1867 OMR OML
HANKINS, D.R. s/o Matthew C.Hankins & M.P.Grissim age 34 S POB Wilson Co, Tennessee POR Lebanon, Tennessee & **CLARK**, Novella V. d/o William D.Clark & Jane M.Eliason age 22 S POB & POR Orange; POM Orange 6 Jun 1866 OMR OML
HANSBROUGH, John S. s/o Alexander Hamilton & Elizabeth Hansbrough age 25 S teacher POB Culpeper POR Fredericksburg & **BALLARD**, Mary E.

d/o Garland &
Georgianna
Ballard age 22 S
POB & POR Orange;
POM Orange 5 Aug
1856 OMR OML
HAOGLAND, George H.
s/o Peter L.&
Jane Hoagland age
32 D government
employee POB
Morristown, N.J.
POR Washington
D.C.& **WOOD**, Maria
J. d/o Peter &
Sarah J.Wood age
28 S POB Penn POR
Spotsylvania; POM
Spotsylvania 19
Oct 1885 SPMR
SPML
HARDING, H.P. s/o
P.C.& Hardenia
Harding age 24 S
farmer POB
Fauquier Co POR
Spotsylvania &
MARTIN, Sallie B.
d/o Richard H.&
Bettie L.Martin
age 19 S POB &
POR Spotsylvania;
POM Craig's
Baptist Ch,
Spotsylvania 22
Aug 1894 SPMR 18
Aug 1894 SPML
HARDING, P.C. s/o
Lewis & Eliza
J.Harding age 57
W farmer POB
Mississippi POR
Spotsylvania &
GARDNER, Flossie
d/o A.Z.&
E.C.Gardner age
23 S POB Orange
POR Spotsylvania;
POM Spotsylvania
13 Dec 1896 SPMR
12 Dec 1896 SPML
HARDY, Charles W. s/o
William J.Hardy &
Ann Trueblood age

29 S merchant POB
& POR Norfolk,Va
& **TALIAFERRO**,
Victoria d/o
Edmund
P.Taliaferro &
Octavia
H.Robertson age
26 S POB Culpeper
Co POR Orange;
POM Orange C.H.24
Oct 1865 OMR OML
HAREFIELD, James W.
s/o Thaddeus &
Martha Harefield
age 32 S farmer
POB & POR
Spotsylvania &
WHEELER, Laura
d/o James W.&
Mary W. Wheeler
age 22 S POB &
POR Spotsylvania;
POM Spotsylvania
17 Jan 1894 SPMR
16 Jan 1894 SPML
HARFIELD, Ferlandd s/o
Ed Harfield &
Malvina Bowler
age 22 S farmer
POB & POR
Spotsylvania &
TYLER, Agnes A.
d/o Robert & Emma
F.Tyler age 17 S
POB & POR
Spotsylvania; POM
Spotsylvania 15
Jul 1877 SPMR 14
Jul 1877 SPML
HARING, John E. s/o
Garrett R.&
C.A.Haring age 29
S civil engineer
POB Bergue(?) Co,
N.J. POR
Hillsdale, N.J. &
HARDENBERRY, Cora
A. d/o Charles &
Phoebe
Hardenberry age
21 S POB Sullivan
Co, N.Y. POR
Spotsylvania; POM

Spotsylvania 26
Jun 1895 SPMR
SPML
HARLEY, Batt & **MURPHY**,
Joanna; 17 Oct
1853 OML
HARLOW, Joseph C. s/o
Julius B.Harlow &
Winney B.Crooks
age 21 S miller
POB & POR Orange
& **ESTES**, Eliza M.
d/o William
B.Estes & Sarah
Bruce age 22 S
POB Madison Co
POR Orange; POM
Orange 13 Feb
1866 OMR 10 Feb
1866 OML
HARLOW, Lucian M. s/o
Richard & Rebecca
Harlow age 26 S
farmer POB Louisa
Co POR Orange &
BICKERS, Serena
d/o Proctor &
Lucy Bickers age
29 S POB & POR
Orange; POM
Orange 3 Feb 1858
OMR 2 Feb 1858
OML
HARRELL, Theodore s/o
Richard Harrell &
Sarah Adams age
26 S carpenter
POB Loudon Co POR
Fauquier Co &
GRAVES, Nannie B.
d/o Isaac
W.Graves & Eliza
Brockman age 18 S
POB & POR Orange;
POM Orange 6 Dec
1865v OMR 14 Nov
1865 OML
HARRIS, Charles E.S.
s/o W.B.&
L.M.Harris age 27
S farmer POB
Clarke Co POR
Clarke Co &
BEVERLEY, Lucy V.
d/o F.C.& M.A.
Beverley age 22 S
POB & POR
Spotsylvania; POM
Whig
Hill,Spotsylvania
4 Jan 1881 SPMR
SPML
HARRIS, James A. s/o
R.M.C. & Mary
F.Harris age 23 S
merchant POB &
POR Spotsylvania
& **FOSTER**, Edmonia
B. d/o William E.
& Engielis (?)
E.A.Foster age 21
S POB & POR
Spotsylvania; POM
Spotsylvania 30
Oct 1872 SPMR 29
Oct 1872 SPML
HARRIS, James D. s/o
T.A.& Mary
E.Harris age 25 S
merchant POB &
POR Spotsylvania
& **PENDLETON**,
Edith May age 21
S POB & POR
Spotsylvania; POM
Zion M.E.Ch,
Spotsylvania 19
Sep 1900 SPMR
SPML
HARRIS, James H. s/o
William H.& Betty
A. Harris age 23
S farmer POB &
POR Spotsylvania
& **DICKINSON**,
Bertie A. d/o
R.H.&
M.F.Dickinson age
24 S POB & POR
Spotsylvania; POM
Zion M.E.Ch,
Spotsylvania 14
Sep 1898 SPMR 12
Sep 1898 SPML
HARRIS, James L. s/o
James & Lucy
A.Harris age 30 S
farmer POB Louisa

Co POR
Spotsylvania &
PRITCHETT, Sarah
C. d/o B.W.&
Milly Pritchett
age 17 S POB &
POR Spotsylvania;
POM Spotsylvania
7 Jun 1883 SPMR
31 May 1883 SPML
HARRIS, John B. s/o
William C.&
M.F.Harris age 34
S POB Albemarle
Co POR
Spotsylvania &
LEVY, Millie A.
d/o Leon & A.Levy
age 23 S POB &
POR Spotsylvania;
POM Caroline Co 3
Mar 1878 SPMR 1
Dec 1877 SPML
HARRIS, John s/o
Overton & Dorcas
Harris age 22 S
laborer POB
Louisa Co POR
Spotsylvania POC
& **TURNER**, Mollie
d/o Edmond & Ann
Turner age 29 S
POB & POR
Spotsylvania POC;
POM Spotsylvania
5 Jan 1882 SPMR 3
Jan 1882 SPML
HARRIS, L.W. s/o John
T.& C.C.Harris
age 22 S farmer
POB & POR Newe
Kent Co & **HARRIS**,
Ida L. d/o C.M.&
M.S.Harris age 22
S POB & POR
Spotsylvania; POM
Spotsylvania 31
Dec 1878 SPMR 30
Dec 1878 SPML
HARRIS, Lee A. s/o
R.M.C.& Mary
F.Harris age 27 S
farmer POB & POR
Spotsylvania &

BARTLESON,
Alithia C. d/o
J.W.& Susan
R.Bartleson age
24 S POB Bucks
Co, Penn POR
Spotsylvania; POM
Spotsylvania
C.H.12 Mar 1884
SPMR SPML
HARRIS, Massey V. s/o
Charles M.&
Margarette
V.Harris age 22 S
farmer POB Orange
POR Spotsylvania
& **SWIFT**, Irene I.
d/o John H.&
Mildred Jane
Swift age 23 S
POB & POR
Spotsylvania; POM
Spotsylvania 3
Nov 1895 SPMR 31
Oct 1895 SPML
HARRIS, R.B. s/o
R.M.C.&
M.F.Harris age 20
S farmer POB &
POR Spotsylvania
& **FOSTER**, Bettie
J. d/o E.W.&
A.E.Foster age 21
S POB & POR
Spotsylvania; POM
Spotsylvania 24
Apr 1878 SPMR 1
Apr 1878 SPML
HARRIS, Richard H. s/o
Calvin D.Harris &
Mary F.Bowler age
25 S carpenter
POB & POR Orange
& **DAVIS**, Lucy M.
d/o William
I.Davis & Bettie
Bolles age 24 S
POB & POR Orange;
POM Gordonsville,
Orange 22 Jan
1863 OMR OML
HARRIS, Thomas A. s/o
R.M.C.&
M.F.Harris age 47

W sheriff of Spotsylvania Co POB & POR Spotsylvania & **EASTBURN**, Lizzie J. d/o Oliver & A.E.Eastburn age 39 S POB Delaware POR Spotsylvania; POM Tabernacle M.E.Ch 23 Sep 1891 SPMR 22 Sep 1891 SPML

HARRIS, Thomas A. s/o R.M.C.& Mary F.Harris age 22 S mechanic POB & POR Spotsylvania & **POOL**, Mary E. d/o Alfred & Roberta C.Pool age 21 S POB & POR Spotsylvania; POM Spotsylvania 14 Apr 1867 SPMR 13 Apr 1867 SPML

HARRIS, Thomas H. s/o C.M.& M.S.Harris age 27 S POB & POR Spotsylvania & **GRADY**, Lillie L. d/o W.A.& E.R.Grady age 25 S POB & POR Spotsylvania; POM Clifton, Spotsylvania 26 Oct 1881 SPMR 24 Oct 1881 SPML

HARRIS, Thomas H. s/o C.M.& Mary S.Harris age 44 W merchant POB Caroline Co POR Spotsylvania & **ALRICH**, Mary Ella d/o John R.& Jane Alrich age 40 S POB Delaware POR Spotsylvania; POM Tabernacle Ch, Spotsylvania 11 Jan 1899 SPMR 9 Jan 1899 SPML

HARRIS, Washington D. s/o William H.& Bettie A. Harris age 19 S farmer POB & POR Spotsylvania & **TALLEY**, Sarah E. d/o William E.& Mollie E. Talley age 25 S POB & POR Spotsylvania; POM Spotsylvania 28 Mar 1893 SPMR SPML

HARRIS, William D.& **FAULCONER**, Rachel V.; 11 Jun 1856 OML

HARRIS, William H. s/o James O.& Lucy A.Harris age 24 S farmer POB Louisa Co POR Spotsylvania & **SIMMS**, Betty A. d/o James & Ann E.Simms age 18 S POB Louisa Co POR Spotsylvania; POM Spotsylvania 9 Nov 1873 SPMR 27 Oct 1873 SPML

HARRIS, William s/o Robert M.C.& Mary Harris age 33 W farmer POB Warren Co, N.J. POR Spotsylvania & **BUCHANAN**, Mary A. d/o William & Florenda Buchanan age 32 S POB & POR Spotsylvania ; POM Spotsylvania 12 Oct 1870 SPMR 3 Oct 1870 SPML

HARRIS, Willis s/o Herbert & Eliza Harris age 35 W farmer POB & POR Spotsylvania & **WIGLESWORTH**, Matilda d/o

William & Sarah Wiglesworth age 27 S POB & POR Spotsylvania; POM Partlow, Spotsylvania 19 Jan 1893 SPMR 13 Jan 1893 SPML

HARRIS, Willis s/o Hubbard & Eliza Harris (now Coleman) age 21 S farmer POB & POR Spotsylvania POC & **CONNER**, Martha d/o Charles & Levinia Conner sister of Lucy Conner age 21 S POB & POR Spotsylvania POC; POM Waller's Ch, Spotsylvania 1 May 1870 SPMR 29 Apr 1870 SPML

HARRISON, Ralph F. s/o Ralph & Delia Harrison age 26 S laborer POB Caroline Co POR Washington D.C. POC & **COATES**, Bettie M. d/o John & Minerva Coates age 23 S POB Caroline Co POR Spotsylvania POC; POM Beulah Ch,Spotsylvania 18 Aug 1881 SPMR 17 Aug 1881 SPML

HARRISON, William H. & **SULLIVAN**, Mary; 7 Jun 1852 SPML

HARRISON, William H. & **SULLIVAN**, Mary; 7 Jun 1852 SPML

HARRY, B.G. s/o William T.& Eliza J.Harry age 26 S machinist POB England POR Richmond,Va & **PALMORE**, Sallie L. d/o J.P.& E.A.Palmore age 29 S POB Goochland Co POR Spotsylvania; POM Spotsylvania 24 Jun 1896 SPMR 23 Jun 1896 SPML

HART, Ferdinand H. s/o Arthier R.& Evelina C.S.Hart age 23 S farmer POB & POR Spotsylvania & **LIPSCOMB**, Isabella F. d/o John & Mary Lipscomb age 21 S POB & POR Spotsylvania; POM Spotsylvania 18 Dec 1867 SPMR 14 Dec 1867 SPML

HART, Henry H. s/o John & S.Hart age 28 S farmer POB & POR Spotsylvania & **BAPTIST**, Kate E. d/o E.G.& M.E.Baptist age 22 S POB & POR Spotsylvania; POM Spotsylvania 9 Mar 1880 SPMR 4 Mar 1880 SPML

HART, Henry s/o Jack & Sally Hart age 25 S farmer POB & POR Spotsylvania POC & **WASHINGTON**, Nora d/o Mary Washington age 21 S POB & POR Spotsylvannia POC; POM Spotsylvania 1 Jan 1873 (possible error in year by minister) SPMR 31 Dec 1873 SPML

HART, Henry s/o John & Elizabeth Hart age 51 S farmer

POB & POR Louisa Co & **RYAN**, Judith A. d/o Thomas E.& Elizabeth Ryan age 35 S POB & POR Spotsylvania; POM Spotsylvania 18 Nov 1873 SPMR 13 Nov 1873 SPML
HART, James T. s/o Mac & Anny Hart age 23 S POB & POR Spotsylvania POC & **LAURENCE**, Sally d/o Mac & Bettie Hart (possibly a clerk error) POB & POR Spotsylvania POC; POM Spotsylvania 31 Dec 1875 SPMR 28 Dec 1875 SPML
HART, John L. s/o Robert J.& Martha J.Hart age 25 W farmer POB & POR Spotsylvania & **SMITH**, Martha A. d/o Joseph & Martha J.Smith age 21 S POB & POR Spotsylvania; POM Spotsylvania C.H. 15 Aug 1881 SPMR SPML
HART, John s/o Joe & Milly Hart age 60 W farmer POB & POR Spotsylvania POC & **CHILDS**, Mary d/o Gabril & Tempy Childs age 55 W POB & POR Spotsylvania POC; POM Bethany Ch, Spotsylvania 4 Jul 1869 SPMR 1 Jul 1869 SPML
HART, Joseph s/o William T.& Virginia Hart age 22 S farmer POB & POR Spotsylvania & **MORRIS**, Carrie d/o Eliza Morris age 18 S POB & POR Spotsylvania; POM Spotsylvania 14 Jul 1897 SPMR SPML
HART, P.B. s/o Robert J.& M.M.Hart age 22 S farmer POB & POR Spotsylvania & **THOMAS**, E.E. d/o Alex & Lucy Thomas age 22 S POB Hanover Co POR Spotsylvania; POM Fredericksburg 23 Mar 1876 FMR 23 Mar 1876 SPML
HART, William G. s/o Arthur R. & Evelina S. Hart age 21 S farmer POB Fauquier Co POR Spotsylvania & **SANFORD**, Agness d/o Joseph & Agness Sanford age 20 S POB Fredericksburg POR Spotsylvania; POM Spotsylvania C.H. 15 Dec 1868 SPMR 12 Dec 1868 SPML
HART, William H. s/o James C.& Mary E.Hart age 24 S farmer POB & POR Spotsylvania & **WALLER**, Martha P. d/o John M. & Martha P.Waller age 21 S POB & POR Spotsylvania; POM Cedar Point, Spotsylvania 1 Feb 1872 SPMR 27 Jan 1872 SPML
HART, William T. s/o Robert J. & Margaret Hart age 50 W farmer POB & POR Spotsylvania

& **McALLISTER**, Catherine d/o Henry & Martha McAllister age 21 S POB Louisa Co POR Spotsylvania; POM Spotsylvania 29 Aug 1895 SPMR SPML

HATCH, William s/o J.D.& M.Hatch age 64 W farmer POB New York POR Hanover Co & **CHEWNING**, Nannie M. d/o O.L.& Mary O.Chewning sister in law to Mr.Z.Smith age 32 S POB & POR Spotsylvania; POM Spotsylvania 4 Sep 1883 SPMR 17 Aug 1883 SPML

HATCH, William s/o J.D.& M.Hatch age 60 W farmer POB New York POR Hanover Co & **CHEWNING**, Ella V. d/o D.L.& H.M.Chewning age 36 W POB & POR Spotsylvania; POM Spotsylvania 6 Feb 1879 SPMR 3 Feb 1879 SPML

HATCHER, Hilary E. s/o Uriel Hatcher & Susan Witt age 33 S minister POB Bedford Co, Va POR Orange & **JONES**, Gillie Frances d/o James L.Jones & Martha A.Porter age 26 S POB & POR Orange; POM Beaumont, Orange 2 Oct 1866 OMR 27 Sep 1866 OML

HATCHER, Patrick A. s/o Archibald & Annie Hatcher (Archibald was a farmer) age 65 W farmer POB Dinwiddie Co,Va POR Spotsylvania & **CLARK**, Addie V. d/o John & Louisa A.Clark (John was a farmer) age 35 S POB Dinwiddie Co,Va POR Spotsylvania; POM Spotsylvania 24 Mar 1874 SPMR 20 Mar 1874 SPML

HAWKINS, Alexander B.(SP Consent and MR give his name as Alexander B. ML Gives his name as Alexander W.Hawkins) s/o James H.& Fanny Hawkins age 24 S farmer POB & POR Spotsylvania & **TRIGG**, Lucy M. d/o Joseph W.& Amanda Trigg age 19 S POB & POR Spotsylvania; POM Spotsylvania 3 Dec 1868 SPMR 2 Dec 1868 SPML

HAWKINS, Alexander s/o Nicholas & Betty Hawkins age 74 W farmer POB Spotsylvania POR Orange & **HUME**, Ann d/o Francis & Lucy Hume age 34 S POB & POR Orange; POM Orange 27 May 1859 OMR

HAWKINS, E.P. s/o Thomas R.& Matilda Hawkins age 58 W minister of the gospel POB Orange POR Louisa Co & **HERNDON**,

Huldah F. d/o Alexander & Ann Herndon age 46 S POB & POR Spotsylvania; POM Maple Grove, Spotsylvania 18 Aug 1885 SPMR 17 Aug 1885 SPML

HAWKINS, John H. s/o J.W.& M.F.Hawkins age 25 S lumber dealer POB Madison C.H.,Va POR Spotsylvania & **BURTON**, C.M. d/o George W.& Virginia S.Burton age 19 S POB & POR Spotsylvania; POM Spotsylvania 20 Oct 1887 SPMR 18 Oct 1887 SPML

HAWKINS, Thomas C. s/o E.P. & Martha J.Hawkins age 27 S railraod employee POB Louisa Co POR Spotsylvania & **HERNDON**, Maria F. d/o Thomas & Nannie S.Herndon age 27 S POB & POR Spotsylvania; POM Maple Grove, Spotsylvania 5 Jul 1898 SPMR 4 Jul 1898 SPML (married by the groom's father)

HAWLEY, George W. s/o Abram & Mary A.Hawley age 44 W POB Albemarle Co POR Orange & **CROOKS**, Elvira S. d/o Joseph Bond & Catherine Crooks age 40 S POB & POR Orange; POM Orange 28 May 1857 OMR 25 May 1857 OML

HAYES, Joseph s/o Albert D.& Mary F.Hayes age 23 S carpenter POB & POR Hanover Co & **TAYLOR**, Doratha M. d/o Frances Taylor age 18 S POB & POR Spotsylvania; POM Spotsylvania 10 Aug 1871 SPMR 8 Aug 1871 SPML

HAYWARD, Alexander F. s/o Thomas & Margaret Hayward age 26 S merchant POB Maryland POR Florida & **WILLIS**, Isabella d/o George & Martha Willis age 20 S POB Florida POR Orange; POM Orange 4 Jun 1859 OMR OML

HAZLEHURST, William s/o Robert Hazelhurst & Frances S.Nuslow age 29 S banker & broker POB Glynn Co,Ga POR Macon, Ga & **CROCKFORD**, Rosa E. d/o John Crockford & Ellen Wendham age 24 S POB Alexandria,Va POR Orange; POM Woodley,Orange 14 Dec 1865 OMR 13 Dec 1865 OML

HEATWELL, Isaac B. s/o David & Eliza Heatwell age 23 S wheelwright POB Rockingham Co & **SMITH**, Margaret L. d/o James O.& Eliza A.Smith age 18 S POB Orange; POM Orange 1 Nov 1860 OMR 25 Oct 1850 OML

HEFLIN, Charles G. s/o C.G.& Alice Heflin age 24 S carpenter POB & POR Fredericksburg & **BIRDSALL**, Florence D. d/o A.J.& Julia Birdsall age 19 S POB Otsego Co, N.Y. POR Spotsylvania; POM Baptist Ch, Fredericksburg 17 Dec 1891 FMR 16 Dec 1891 SPML

HEFLIN, George W. s/o George W.& M.Heflin age 20 S farmer POB Fauquire Co POR Orange & **DEMPSEY**, Lucy E. d/o James & Catherine Dempsey age 22 S POB & POR Orange; POM Orange 30 Sep 1858 OMR 20 Sep OML

HEFLIN, John J. s/o C.G.& Ellen Heflin age 21y 3mo S mechanic POB Orange POR Frederickburg & **LEITCH**, Elizabeth A. d/o William J. & Ellen Leitch age 21y 4mo S POB Stafford POR Spotsylvania; POM Spotsylvania 8 Feb 1872 SPMR 7 Feb 1872 SPML

HEFLIN, John W. s/o Walter & Sarah Heflin age 26 S miner POB Stafford POR Louisa Co & **EDENTON**, Alice R. d/o William B.& Mary A.Edenton age 24 S POB & POR Spotsylvania; POM Spotsylvania C.H.4 May 1892 SPMR SPML

HEISLOP, John J. s/o Joseph A.& Dorothy A.Heislop age 27 S farmer POB & POR Spotsylvania & **GALLINGER**, Lucy A. d/o Cyrenius & Ann Amelia Gallinger age 17 S POB Lapeer Co, Michigan POR Spotsylvania; POM Spotsylvania 17 Feb 1887 SPMR 15 Feb 1887 SPML

HENDERSON, Arthur s/o James & Eilain Henderson of Stafford Co.age 21 POR Stafford Co. & **SULLIVAN**, Lenora d/o Woodson & Ann I. Sullivan of Stafford Co. age 16 POR Stafford Co.; POM Fredericksburg 21 Nov 1895 TCF

HENDERSON, Henry s/o Charles & Louisa Henderson age 25 W farmer POB & POR Spotsylvania POC & **ALSOP**, Mary d/o Sam & Patty Alsop age 16 S POB & POR Spotsylvania POC; POM Spotsylvania 22 Feb 1866 SPMR 21 Feb 1866 SPML

HENDERSON, John s/o Henry & Mary Henderson age 21 S laborer POB & POR Spotsylvania POC & **TALIAFERRO**,

Mary d/o Jerry &
Huldah Taliaferro
age 17 S POB &
POR Spotsylvania
POC; POM
Spotsylvania C.H.
28 Dec 1887 SPMR
SPML

HENDERSON, Joseph M.
s/o John & Sarah
Henderson age 21-
22 S farmer POB &
POR Orange &
ELLIS, Sarah E.
d/o Robert S.&
Emily A.Ellis age
17-18 S POB & POR
Orange; POM
Orange 9 May 1854
OMR 2 May 1854
OML

HENDERSON, Joseph s/o
John Henderson &
Sarah Quisenberry
age 26 W farmer
POB & POR Orange
& **TERRILL**,
H.Irvin d/o
U.Terrill & Jane
Lovell age 26 S
POB & POR Orange;
POM Orange 23 Dec
1858 OMR 20 Dec
1858 OML

HENDERSON, Levi s/o
John & Harriet
Henderson age 58
W laborer POB
Pennsylvania POR
Spotsylvania POC
& **TYLER**, Rachel
E. d/o Charles &
Judy Tyler age 25
S POB & POR
Spotsylvania POC;
POM Spotsylvania
25 Feb 1887 SPMR
SPML

HENDERSON, William s/o
John & Sally
Henderson age 42
W farmer POB &
POR Orange &
YOUNG, Sarah E.

d/o Curtis &
Nancy Brockman
age 36 W POB &
POR Orange; POM
Orange 24 Oct
1854 OMR 23 Oct
1854 OML

HENDLEY, William M.
s/o James Hendley
& Margaret May
age 50 S farmer
POB Western
Virginia POR
Orange & **EVANS**,
Sarah d/o John
V.Evans & Nancy
King age 35 S POB
& POR Orange; POM
Orange 13 Dec
1860 OMR 12 Dec
1860 OML

HENSHAW, John S. s/o
Philip T. & Sarah
A.Henshaw age 27
W farmer POB &
POR Oldham Co,
Kentucky & **COLE**,
Ann E. d/o
William & Mary
F.Cole age 23 S
POB & POR Orange;
POM Orange 28 Nov
1854 OMR 27 Nov
1854 OML

HENSHAW, Thomas P.G.
s/o Edward & Jane
Henshaw (now
Mrs.Royster) age
26 S farmer POB &
POR Richmond,Va &
PORTER, Virginia
O.S. d/o William
& Mary Ann Porter
age 32 S POB &
POR Orange; POM
Orange 5 Apr 1855
OMR

HERD, Walker J. &
HILLMAN, Louisa;
18 Jun 1858 SPML

HERNDON, Albert s/o
Zachary Herndon &
Betty Lewis age
28 S laborer POB

& POR
Spotsylvania POC
& **TAYLOR**, Amelia
d/o Sigh & Amelia
Taylor age 19 S
POB & POR
Spotsylvania POC;
POM Spotsylvania
4 Apr 1900 SPMR
SPML

HERNDON, Alex s/o
George &
A.Herndon age 24
S laborer POB &
POR Spotsylvania
POC & **WILLIAMS**,
Sallie d/o Robert
& H.Williams age
18 S POB & POR
Spotsylvania POC;
POM Greenwood,
Spotsylvania 11
Feb 1880 SPMR
SPML

HERNDON, Benjamin Jr.
of age POR Orange
& **ANDERSON**, Sally
age over 21 POR
Orange; POM
Orange 26 Jan
1854 OMR 25 Jan
1854 OML

HERNDON, Davis C. s/o
Benjamin Herndon
& Hannah Bledsoe
age 26 S farmer
POB & POR Orange
& **APPERSON**, Lucy
P. d/o Joseph
Apperson &
Lucinda Perry age
25 S POB & POR
Orange; POM
Orange 1 Jan 1867
OMR 31 Dec 1866
OML

HERNDON, Edward F. s/o
James & Esther
Herndon age 25 S
farmer POB & POR
Madison Co &
WAYLAND, Julia A.
d/o William &
Frances W.Wayland

age 19 S POB &
POR Orange; POM
Orange 27 Jul
1858 OMR 24 Jul
1858 OML

HERNDON, Harrison s/o
John & Mahala
Herndon age 24 S
mechanic POR
Orange POR North
Carolina & **MASON**,
Aby d/o Charles &
Lucy B.Mason age
18 S POB & POR
Orange; POM
Orange 5 Nov 1854
OMR

HERNDON, James C. &
FAULCONER, Emily
J.; POM Orange 3
Aug 1853 OMR 2
Aug 1853 OML

HERNDON, James s/o
James & Elizabeth
Hernson age 24 S
mechanic POB &
POR Orange &
PEACHER, Mary F.
d/o Alexander &
Nicy Peacher age
19 S POB & POR
Orange; POM
Orange 15 Oct
1854 OMR

HERNDON, Joel s/o
Francis Herndon
age 53 W
shoemaker POB &
POR Orange &
JAMES, Ruth d/o
George Sizer &
Nancy Hicks age
49 W POB & POR
Orange; POM
Orange 9 Apr 1860
OMR OML

HERNDON, John B. s/o
John Herndon Jr.&
Mahala Landrum
age 20 S
millwright POB &
POR Orange &
WEBB, Sarah A.E.
d/o Richard

C.Webb & Mary S.Lancaster age 22 S POB & POR Orange; POM Orange 21 Dec 1865 OMR 27 Nov 1865 OML

HERNDON, John s/o William & Susan Herndon age 59 W farmer POB & POR Orange & **COLEMAN**, Elizabeth d/o Ambrose & Frances Coleman age 46 S POB & POR Orange; POM Orange 31 Jan 1860 OMR 23 Jan 1860 OML

HERNDON, John W. & **MIDDLEBROOK**, Lucy C.; 9 Jan 1851 OML

HERNDON, Reuben G. s/o John Herndon & Mahala Landrum age 28 S carpenter POB & POR Orange & **MASON**, Susan S. d/o Saunders Mason & Catherine Jones age 20 S POB Rockingham Co POR Orange; POM Orange 14 Jan 1862 OMR 10 Jan 1862 OML

HERNDON, Robert N. s/o Richard T.Herndon & Ellen W.Hutchison age 26 S farmer POB & POR Orange & **BLEDSOE**, Georgianna F. d/o John Bledsoe & Jane Wood age 23 S POB Madison Co POR Orange; POM Orange 13 Dec 1866 OMR 19 Dec 1866 OML

HERNDON, Thomas & **BELL**, Elizabeth; 3 Aug 1852 OML

HERNDON, William L. s/o John Herndon Jr.& Mahala Landrum age 21 S bricklayer POB & POR Orange & **WRIGHT**, Bettie E. d/o John Wright age 19 S POB Spotsylvania POR Orange; POM Orange 28 Apr 1861 OMR OML

HERRING, Frederick s/o George & Sarah Herring age 27 S mechanic POB Orange POR Spotsylvania & **HATCH**, Leona S.W. d/o John A.Hatch age 24 S POB Culpeper POR Spotsylvania; POM Spotsylvania 12 Sep 1865 SPMR 11 Sep 1865 SPML

HERRING, Richard T. s/o George & Sallie Herring age 31 S carpenter POB Madison Co & **HERRING**, Apphia d/o Benjamin & Frances C. Herring age 23 S POB Orange Co; POM Forest Hill, Spotsylvania 24 Oct 1854 SPMR 14 Oct 1854 SPML

HERRING, Robert E. s/o George & Sally Herring age 27 S farmer POB & POR Orange & **KNIGHTEN**, Barbara A. d/o R.Taliaferro Knighten age 27 S

POB Louisa Co POR
Orange; POM
Orange 8 Dec 1859
OMR 7 Dec 1859
OML

HERTH, Cudlip s/o
Frederick &
Frederica Herth
age 28 S farmer
POB Werthenberg,
Germany POR
Spotsylvania &
WALLACE, Margaret
S. d/o John &
Margaret Wallace
age 24 S POB &
POR Spotsylvania;
POM Spotsylvania
2 Apr 1867 SPMR 1
Apr 1867 SPML

HESLOP, Rice B. s/o
James & Lucy
Heslop age 45 W
carpenter POB
Spotsylvania POR
Richmond City &
BEAZLEY, Lucy D.
d/o Duerson &
Clemintine
Beazley age 22 S
POB & POR
Spotsylvania; POM
Spotsylvania 28
Dec 1866 SPMR 25
Dec 1866 SPML

HESTER, James E. s/o
Ro.F.& Rebecca
M.Hester age 28 S
farmer POB Louisa
Co POR
Spotsylvania &
CHEWNING, Eugenia
H. d/o Garland
S.& Mary
A.Chewning age 22
S POB & POR
Spotsylvania; POM
Spotsylvania 31
Jan 1867 SPMR 30
Jan 1867 SPML

HESTER, James L. s/o
Benjamin H.& Ann
E.Hester age 25 S
farmer POB & POR

Spotsylvania &
WHITLOCK, Mary E.
d/o E.L.&
M.Whitlock age 24
S POB Louisa Co
POR Spotsylvania;
POM Spotsylvania
30 Mar 1876 SPMR
29 Mar 1876 SPML

HESTER, John E. s/o
Benjamin & Ann
Hester age 25 S
farmer POB & POR
Spotsylvania &
CHEWNING, Amanda
M. d/o Garland &
Mary Chewning age
22 S POB & POR
Spotsylvania; POM
Spotsylvania 28
Dec 1865 SPMR 26
Dec 1865 SPML

HESTER, Robert L. s/o
John E. & Amanda
Hester age 22 A
farmer POB & POR
Spotsylvania &
HAILEY, Virginia
T. d/o Benjamin &
Louisa Hailey age
20 S POB & POR
Spotsylvania; POM
Spotsylvania C.H.
9 Oct 1890 SPMR
SPML

HESTER, Thomas J. s/o
John E. & Amanda
M.Hester age 22 S
faremr POB & POR
Spotsylvania &
HAILEY, Mary C.
d/o Benjamin &
Louisa F.Hailey
age 19 S POB &
POR Spotsylvania;
POM Spotsylvania
29 Dec 1892 SPMR
28 Dec 1892 SPML

HEWLETT, Alan B. s/o
Thomas B.&
Frances Hewlett S
farmer POB & POR
Spotsylvania &
SEAY, Annie E.

d/o Wyatt &
Lucinda Seay S
POB Louisa Co POR
Spotsylvania; POM
Spotsylvania 6
Mar 1865 SPMR
HEWLETT, Alexander B.
& **SEAY**, Annie E.
d/o Wyatt Seay
(POR
Spotsylvania); 28
Feb 1865
SPConsent
HICKS, Charles M. s/o
Andrew T. & Mary
Hicks age 57 W
farmer POB & POR
Spotsylvania &
DUNAWAY, Mary E.
d/o Jordpn &
Delphia M.Dunaway
age 32 S POB &
POR Spotsylvania;
7 Sep 1874 SPML
HICKS, Charles M. s/o
Andrew T.& Mary
Hicks age 45 W
mechanic POB &
POR Spotsylvania
& **DUNAWAY**, Sally
J. d/o Jordan &
Delphia Dunaway
age 34 S POB &
POR Spotsylvania;
POM Spotsylvania
Dec 1867 SPMR 24
Dec 1867 SPML
HICKS, George P. s/o
Joseph S.&
Pamelia V. Hicks
age 22 S farmer
POB Louisa Co POR
Spotsylvania &
WILLOUGHBY, Lucy
F. d/o Joseph &
Ann E.Willoughby
age 22 S POB &
POR Spotsylvania;
POM Spotsylvania
28 Dec 1892 SPMR
23 Dec 1892 SPML
HICKS, John H. s/o
James T.& Nancy
E.Hicks age 29 S
farmer POB & POR
Spotsylvania &
PARKER, Mollie M.
d/o Edgar & Susan
Parker age 22 S
POB & POR
Spotsylvania; POM
Spotsylvania
C.H.12 Mar 1890
SPMR SPML
HICKS, John R. s/o
Robert Hicks &
Bettie Whitlock
age 25 S POB &
POR Spotsylvania
farmer & **BOND**,
Martha C. d/o
Joseph Bond &
Mildred Whitlock
age 21 S POB
Louisa Co POR
Orange; POM
Orange 15 Mar
1866 OMR 5 Mar
1866 OML
HICKS, Nathan S. s/o
Robert & M. Hicks
age 24 S POB &
POR Spotsylvania
& **WILLOUGHBY**,
Eddie W. d/o John
B.& L.Willoughby
age 23 S POB &
POR Spotsylvania;
POM Spotsylvania
24 Feb 1881 SPMR
23 Feb 1881 SPML
HICKS, Peter W. s/o
Robert Hicks &
Marina Whitlock
age 22 S farmer
POB Spotsylvania
POR Orange &
BOND, Lucy M. d/o
Thomas W.Bond &
Virginia Kinzer
age 14 S OIB &
POR Orange; POM
Orange 7 Feb 1867
OMR 6 Feb 1867
OML
HICKS, Robert L. s/o
James T.& Nancy
E.Hicks age 24 S

farmer POB & POR Spotsylvania & **MASTIN**, Nancy C. d/o Benjamin & E.A.Mastin age 20 S POB & POR Spotsylvania; POM Spotsylvania C.H. 26 Oct 1892 SPMR 24 Oct 1892 SPML

HICKS, Thomas s/o John F.& Virginia E.Hicks age 21 S farmer POB & POR Madison Co & **HOPKINS**, Sallie A. d/o Henry W.& Eliza I.Hopkins age 18 S POB & POR Spotsylvania; POM Spotsylvania 20 Mar 1883 SPMR 19 Mar 1883 SPML

HICKS, Werter G. s/o W.S.& S.E.Hicks age 23 S farmer POB & POR Spotsylvania & **JONES**, Isadora d/o T.M.& Marietta Jones age 19 S POB & POR Spotsylvania; POM Olivet M.E.Ch 29 Dec 1897 SPMR 27 Dec 1897 SPML

HICKS, William J. s/o Charles M. & Lucy J.Hicks age 20 S farmer POB & POR Spotsylvania & **DUNAWAY**, Elizabeth d/o Jordan & Delphia Dunaway age 16 S POB Louisa Co POR Spotsylvania; POM Spotsylvania 21 Mar 1866 (possible error in year by minister) 20 Mar 1867 SPML

HIGGINBOTHAM, C.D. s/o James A.& Mary M.Higgenbotham age 37 W merchant POB Amherst Co POR Augusta Co & **BUCHANAN**, Laura T. d/o William S.& Amanda M.Buchanan age 37 S POB & POR Spotsylvania; POM Spotsylvania 18 Jun 1890 SPMR SPML

HIGHLAND, Franklin Earl s/o J.E.& Lucy E.Highland age 23 S merchant POB West Milford, W.Va POR Clarksburg, W.Va & **POWELL**, Alene Estelle age 22 S POB Green _____, Spotsylvania POR Spotsylvania; POM Spotsylvania 16 Dec 1896 SPMR 12 Dec 1896 SPML

HILL, Archibald s/o Garlick & Rebecca Hill age 25 S farmer POB & POR Caroline Co & **RICHESON**, Sallie D. d/o William P.& Ann Richeson age 22 S POB & POR Spotsylvania; POM Spotsylvania 232 Dec 1873 SPMR 5 Dec 1873 SPML

HILL, Benjamin F. s/o Samuel & Sucky Hill age 27 S farm laborer POB Culpeper Co POR Orange POC & **MURPHY**, Lucinda d/o John & Polly Murphy age 21 S POB & POR Orange POC; POM Orange

C.H. 27 Dec 1866 OMR OML
HILL, Horace s/o Edward Shepherd & Martha Banks age 19 S laborer on farm POB & POR Orange POC & **OWENS**, Mary J. d/o Lewis & Matilda Owens age 18 S POB & POR Orange POC; POM Orange 24 Dec 1866 OMR OML
HILL, Thomas Jr. & **GOSS**, Sarah F.; POM Orange 21 Nov 1860 OMR 20 Nov 1860 OML
HILLDRUP, E.T. s/o Robert & Elizabeth L.Hilldrup age 24 S farmer POB Caroline Co POR Spotsylvania & **SMITH**, Mary E. d/o Dr.Austin & Mary M.Smith age 20 S POB King George Co POR Spotsylvania; POM Prot.Epis.Ch,Spotsylvania 14 Jan 1866 SPMR SPML
HILLDRUP, Richard B. s/o Robert & E.Hilldrup age 33 S POB Port Royal,Va POR Spotsylvania & **HOUSER**, Lydia M. d/o P.C.& B.T.Houser age 24 S POB & POR Spotsylvania; POM Spotsylvania 27 Oct 1880 SPMR 24 Oct 1880 SPML
HILLIARD, Arthur s/o Thomas & Nancy Hilliard age 21 S laborer POB & POR

Spotsylvania POC & **JACKSON**, Josephine d/o Fanny Montague age 20 S POB & POR Spotsylvania POC; POM Spotsylvania 20 Sep 1900 SPMR 19 Sep 1900 SPML
HILLIARD, Thomas s/o William & Phoebe Hilliard age 24 S farmer POB Caroline Co POR Spotsylvania POC & **GARNETT**, Louisa d/o George & Hannah Garnett age 22 S POB Caroline Co POR Spotsylvania POC; POM Spotsylvania Mar 1867 11 Mar 1867 SPML (ML states that the date of marriage will be 21 Mar 1867)
HILLYARD, Baylor s/o William & Ophelia Hillyard age 24 S POB Essex Co POR Spotsylvania POC & **GARNETT**, Lucy E. d/o George & Hannah Garnett age 16 S POB Essex Co POR Spotsylvania POC; POM Spotsylvania 7 Feb 1867 SPMR 30 Jan 1867 SPML
HILLYARD, William s/o Robin & Nancy Hillyard age 50 W farming POB King William Co POR Spotsylvania & **JOHNSON**, Maria d/o Moses & Juna Coleman age 40 W POB Caroline Co POR Spotsylvania;

HINES, S.D. s/o J.A. &
P.D.Hines age 27
S carpenter POB
Hanover Co POR
Richmond &
BOXLEY, Fanny d/o
John W. &
M.A.Boxley age 22
S POB Louisa Co
POR Spotsylvania;
POM Spotsylvania
27 Nov 1879 SPMR
26 Nov 1879 SPML

HIRSH, Isaac s/o
Kaufman & Hannah
Hirsh age 28 S
merchant POB
Baden, Germany
POR
Fredericksburg &
ISEMAN, Hannah
d/o Isaac
Charlott Iseman
age 20 S POB
Richmond City POR
Spotsylvania; POM
Congregation
Bayth Ahaba,
Richmond 11 Dec
1867 SPMR 18 Nov
1867 SPML

HITE, Carter s/o Major
Hite & Harriet
Coons age 25 S
farm laborer POB
& POR Orange POC
& RUCKER,
Columbia d/o
Legrand Rucker &
Harriet
E.Washington age
18 S POB & POR
Orange POC; POM
Orange 26 Dec
1867 OMR 23 Dec
1867 OML

HOAGLAND, George H.
s/o P.L. &
J.Hoagland age 24
S farmer POB New
Jersey POR
Caroline Co &
4 Aug 1867 SPMR
31 Jul 1867 SPML

JONES, Susan H.
d/o A.W. & C.Jones
age 18 S POB
Delaware POR
Spotsylvania; POM
Spotsylvania 31
Jan 1878 SPMR 7
Jan 1878 SPML

HOAGLAND, George H. &
HOAGLAND, Susie
H. divorce decree
entered 29 Oct
1883 at
Spotsylvania

HOCKADAY, Robert L.
s/o Walter W. &
Catherine
C.Hockaday age 21
S farmer POB &
POR Spotsylvania
& HART, Leah d/o
William T. &
Virginia A. Hart
age 21 POB & POR
Spotsylvania; POM
Spotsylvania C.H.
24 Jan 1889 SPMR
SPML

HODGSON, William B.
s/o Joseph
Hodgson &
PANNILL, Louisa
D. d/o George
Pannill Jr.; 28
Apr 1851 OML

HOFF, William V. s/o
Philip H. & Mary
Hoff age 24 S
dairy man POB
Warren Co POR
Washington D.C. &
PULLIAM,
Josephine L. d/o
Thomas C. &
Harriet Pulliam
age 24 S POB &
POR Spotsylvania;
POM Spotsylvania
20 Dec 1900 18
Dec 1899 SPML

HOGANS, William F. s/o
James W. & Susan
H.Hogans age 25 S
farmer POB & POR

Spotsylvania &
WILSON, Mittie M.
d/o A.H.& Sarah
M.Wilson age 24 S
POB & POR
Spotsylvania; POM
Spotsylvania 14
Jan 1891 SPMR 10
Jan 1891 SPML

HOILE, James s/o
Charles Hoile &
Sally Kilsh age
24 S farmer POB
North Caroline
POR Orange &
GILLABERT, Mary
A. d/o Peter
Gillabert &
Frances Gardner
age 17 S POB &
POR Orange; POM
Orange 2 Aug 1866
OMR 30 Jul 1866
OML

HOLLADAY, George s/o
Waller Holladay &
Rachel Stewart
age 20 S farmer
POB & POR
Spotsylvania &
FRAZIER, Martha
step daughter of
Robert Johnson
age 16 S POB
Bottetout Co POR
Spotsylvania; POM
Spotsylvania 20
Dec 1868 SPMR 9
Dec 1868 SPML
SPConsent

HOLLADAY, Henry T. s/o
Lewis S.Hollasay
& Jane Thompson
age 36 W miller
POB Spotaylvania
POR Orange &
PORTER, Fannie W.
d/o John A.Porter
& Mary Crump age
26 S POB & POR
Orange; POM
Orange 3 May 1865
OMR 28 Apr 1865
OML

HOLLADAY, John W. s/o
James M.& Lucy
D.Holladay age 26
S farmer POB &
POR Spotsylvania
& **HARRIS**, Mary C.
d/o A.N.&
Victoria M.Harris
age 23 S POB
Louisa Co POR
Spotsylvania; POM
Kirk O the Cliff,
Louisa Co 5 Nov
1890 Louisa MR 27
Oct 1890 SPML

HOLLADAY, Lewis L. s/o
Waller Holladay &
Huldah Lewis age
61 W physician
POB Spotsylvania
POR Orange &
GARNETT, Mary E.
d/o Larkin Willis
& Mary Gordon age
38 W POB & POR
Orange; POM
Locust Dale,
Madison Co 24 Jun
1864 Madison MR
23 Jun 1864 OML

HOLLADAY, Samuel J.
s/o William
Holladay & Martha
Wright age 23 S
farmer POB & POR
Butler Co,
Alabama & **CLARK**,
Mary H. d/o
William Clark &
Frances Estes age
18 S POB & POR
Orange; POM
Orange 1 Jun 1865
OMR 30 May 1865
OML

HOLLADAY, Taverner W.
s/o William &
Catherine
Holladay age 35 W
mechanic POB &
POR Spotsylvania
& **YOUNG**, Helen
d/o William &
Sarah Young age

21 S POB & POR Spotsylvania; POM Spotsylvania 7 Feb 1866 SPMR 5 Feb 1866 SPML

HOLLADAY, Waller L. s/o L.L.& Jane Holladay age 29 W dentist/farmer POB Spotsylvania POR Orange & **HENDERSON**, Mary J. d/o William & Elizabeth Henderson age 17 S POB Casewell, N.C. POR Orange; POM Orange 28 Oct 1858 OMR 25 Oct 1858 OML

HOLLADAY, William H. s/o Dr.Waller L.& Mary J.Holladay age 28 S farmer POB & POR Orange & **YERBY**, Affie F. d/o John P.& Ella Yerby age 28 S POB & POR Spotsylvania; POM Grace Ch,Caroline Co 27 Nov 1889 Caroline Co MR 26 Nov 1889 SPML

HOLLADAY, William s/o William & Rebecca Holladay age 65 W farmer POB & POR Spotsylvania & **PENDLETON**, Lucy E. d/o Henry & Catherine Pendleton age 50 S POB & POR Spotsylvania; POM Spotsylvania 3 Jan 1867 SPMR 2 Jan 1867 SPML

HOLLIDAY, Waller L. & **TALIAFERRO**, Elizabeth; 22 May 1852 OML

HOLLINS, Robert s/o Henry & Martha Hollins age 28 S laborer POB & POR Spotsylvania POC & **LEWIS**, Mary Belle d/o John & Adaline Lewis age 23 S POB & POR Spotsylvania POC; POM Spotsylvania (at the residence of the parties) 24 Apr 1895 SPMR SPML

HOLLOMAN, Thomas s/o H.& M.Holloman age 48 W farmer POB Alabama POR Spotsylvania & **OLIVER**, Catherine Ann d/o Thomas & M.Grinstone age 42 W POB & POR Spotsylvania; POM their home, Spotsylvania 13 Sep 1879 SPMR 12 Sep 1879 SPML

HOLLOWAY, Robert Esmond s/o R.G. & L.S. Holloway age 25 POR Norfolk, Va. & **LEAVELL**, Ida Gayle d/o W.T. & F.G. Leavell age 22 POR Fredericksburg; POM Fredericksburg 5 Apr 1899 TCF

HOLMES, Henry s/o Major & Marah Holmes age 22 S laborer POB & POR SPotsylvania POC & **POINDEXTER**, Ann d/o Hannah Poindexter (father dead) age 25 S POB & POR Spotsylvania POC; POM Spotsylvania 7 Apr 1883 SPMR 6 Apr 1883 SPML

HOLMES, Lewis s/o Claiborne Holmes & Rose Baggett age 38 S laborer POB & POR Spotsylvania POC & **DANDRIDGE**, Celia d/o Addison & Mary Lewis age 31 W POB & POR Spotsylvania POC; POM Spotsylvania 22 Nov 1900 SPMR SPML

HOLMES, Russell s/o Jacob Holmes & Nancy Taylor age 22 S farm laborer POB Hanover Co POR Orange POC & **THORNTON**, Rebecca d/o Moses Thornton age 16 S POB Albemarle Co POR Orange POC; POM Gordonsville, Orange 29 Dec 1866 OMR 27 Dec 1866 OML

HOLMES, William s/o Richard & Milly Holmes age 30 W laborer POB & POM Spotsylvania POC & **JOHNSON**, Bettie d/o Nicey Johnson age 18 S POB & POR Spotsylvania POC; POM Spotsylvania 29 Dec 1887 SPMR 14 Dec 1887 SPML

HOLT, William W. s/o Joel Holt & Sarah Parkerson age 23 S wheelwright POB Pulaski Co,Ga POR Dooly Co,Ga & **BOSTON**, Mary E. d/o John P.Boston & Frances Waugh age 17 S POB & POR Orange; POM Orange 15 Mar 1864 OMR OML

HOMES, Abraham s/o Paul Homes & Vina Powell age 26 S laborer POB & POR Orange POC & **BROCK**, Alice age 25 S POB & POR Orange POC; POM Gordonsville 20 Oct 1866 OMR 19 Oct 1866 OML

HOPKINS, Henry s/o Sil Schooler & Delphia Hopkins age 21 S laborer POB & POR Spotsylvania POC & **CARTER**, Rosa d/o Addison Samuel & Barbara Carter age 16 S POB & POR Spotsylvania POC; POM Spotsylvania 17 Apr 1899 SPMR SPML

HOPKINS, J.C. s/o Henry W.& Eliza T.Hopkins age 22 S farmer POB & POR Spotsylvania & **CHILTON**, Annie E. d/o John F.& Hester Ann Chilton age 22 S POB Stafford POR Spotsylvania; POM Spotsylvania 24 Mar 1881 SPMR 23 Mar 1881 SPML

HOPKINS, Marshall s/o Lawson Hopkins & Lucinda Chewning age 22 S farmer POB Spotsylvania POR Orange & **HUGHES**, Jane J. d/o James Ford & Ellen Hughes age 21 S POB & POR Orange; POM Orange 18 Oct

1866 OMR 16 Oct
1866 OML
HOPKINS, Samuel C. s/o
Lawson Hopkins &
Lucinda Hopkins
age 23 S farmer
POB Spotsylvania
POR Orange &
BOSTON, Susan F.
d/o John Boston &
Jane F.WAugh age
18 S POB & POR
Orange; POM
Orange 7 Apr 1863
OMR 6 Apr 1863
OML
HOPKINS, Zebulen s/o
John Hopkins &
Lucinda Overton
age 23 S POB
Spotsylvania POR
Orange & **DOOLEY**,
Harriet A. d/o
Robert Bowler age
25 W POB & POR
Orange; POM
Orange 26 Dec
1865 OMR 25 Dec
1865 OML
HOPLEY, Dennis S. s/o
Dennis S.Hopley &
Mary E.Spragle
age 22 S patent
maker POB & POR
Vickburg,
Mississippi &
CLARK, Minerva A.
d/o James T.Clark
& Mary A.
Wiltshire age 22
S POB & POR
Orange; POM
Unionville,
Orange 15 Sep
1863 OMR 14 Sep
1863 OML
HOSSLEY, Dennis S. s/o
Dennis Hossley &
Mary E.Spangler
age 26 W
wheelwright POB
Warren Co,
Mississippi POR
Orange & **AUSTIN**,
Sallie B. d/o
William C.Austin
& Susan Thompson
age 22 S POB &
POR Orange; POM
Orange 24 Sep
1867 OMR OML
HOUSER, William B. s/o
P.C.& Bettei
F.Houser age 33 S
farmer POB & POR
Spotsylvania &
COLE, Lizzie F.
d/o William H.&
Harriet G.Cole
age 31 S POB &
POR Spotsylvania;
POM Spotsylvania
16 Sep 1891 SPMR
SPML
HOUSEWORTH, Joseph H.
s/o V.M.&
S.W.Houseworth
age 23 S
gentleman POB &
POR Orange &
BRENT, Harriet M.
d/o George P.&
Harriet Brent age
25 S POB & POR
Orange; POM
Orange 12 Mar
1857 OMR 9 Maar
1857 OML
HOWARD, A. Randolph
s/o W. Kay &
Clara R. Howard
of King George
Co.,Va. age 24
POR
Fredericksburg &
SMITH, Fanny L.
d/o Wm. Aug. &
H.F. Smith of
Fredericksburg
age 20 POR
Fredericksburg;
POM
Fredericksburg 24
Jun 1891 TCF
HOWARD, Charles J. s/o
Joseph J.& Mary
R.Howard age 27 S
farmer POB & POR

Spotsylvania &
JENNINGS, Susie
E. d/o J.C.&
E.V.Jennings POB
Fauquire Co POR
Spotsylvania; POM
Spotsylvania 16
Sep 1886 SPMR 6
Sep 1886 SPML
HOWARD, Charles s/o
Cato & Ann Howard
age 22 S farmer
POB & POR
Spotsylvania POC
& **JACKSON**, Tamor
d/o William &
Mary Jackson age
22 S POB Caroline
Co POR
Spotsylvania POC;
POM Spotsylvania
19 Sep 1874 SPMR
18 Sep 1874 SPML
HOWARD, Constant s/o
Manuel & Dinah
Thornton (parents
names possibly
reversed by
clerk)age 23 S
shoemaker POB
Spotsylvania POR
Washington D.C. &
THORNTON, Malvina
d/o Bonifant &
Ellenor Howard
(clerk may have
reversed parents'
names) age 20 S
POB & POR
Spotsylvania; POM
Spotsylvania 5
Jan 1871 SPMR 5
Jan 1870 SPML
(possible clerk
error in year)
HOWARD, Jackson s/o
Jefferson & Nancy
Howard age 36 W
laborer POB & POR
Spotsylvania POC
& **LEWIS**, Aggie
d/o Richard &
Martha Lewis age
35 S POB & POR

Spotsylvania POC;
24 Oct 1866 SPML
HOWARD, John J. s/o
Jackson & Agnes
Howard age 29 S
laborer POB & POR
Spotsylvania POC
& **HOWARD**, Annie
L. d/o Cuistance
& Melvina Howard
age 28 S POB &
POR Spotsylvania
POC; POM
Spotsylvania 21
Dec 1898 SPMR 19
Dec 1898 SPML
HOWARD, Willie s/o
William & Sofa
Howard age 23 S
farmer POB & POR
Caroline Co &
MARSHALL,
Isabelle d/o
Albert S.&
Elizabeth Fugett
age 18 W POB
Stafford POR
Spotsylvania; POM
Spotsylvania 27
Dec 1883 SPMR 26
Dec 1883 SPML
HOWISON, John s/o
Samuel &
H.Howison age 67
W farmer POB
Fredericksburg
POR Spotsylvania
& **RAWLINGS**, Lucy
M. d/o James B.&
Ann Rawlings age
34 S POB & POR
Spotsylvaia; POM
Spotsyvlania 7
Dec 1876 SPMR 4
Dec 1876 SPML
HUCKABEE, John s/o
Younger & Nancy
Huckabee age 26 S
farmer POB
Marlboro, S.C.
POR Spotsylvania
& **BAKER**, Ann
Eliza d/o John &
Mary J.Baker age

16 S POB Louisa Co POR Spotsylvania; POM Spotsylvania 22 Feb 1866 SPMR 20 Feb 1866 SPML

HUDSON, Charles H. s/o J. & Lucinda Hudson age 32 S farmer POB & POR Spotsylvania & **HICKS**, Ludona A. d/o Thomas S. & Ann A. Hicks age 22 S POB & POR Spotsylvania; POM Spotsylvania 6 Mar 1862 SPMR SPML

HUDSON, Charles H. s/o J. & L.A.Hudson age 36 W farmer POB King George Co POR Spotsylvania & **SHELTON**, Mary James d/o William A. & S.E.Shelton age 23 S POB & POR Spotsylvania; POM Spotsylvania 28 Nov 1877 SPMR 27 Nov 1877 SPML

HUDSON, Charles L. s/o Charles H.& Sedonia Hudson age 23 S coal miner POB & POR Spotsylvania & **CHILTON**, Maggie T. d/o John F.& H.A.Chilton S POB Stafford POR Spotsylvania; POM Spotsylvania 23 Feb 1886 SPMR 20 Feb 1886 SPML

HUDSON, Thomas F. s/o Landon & Louisa Hudson age 21 S farmer POB Spotsylvania POR Caroline Co & **HART**, Maggie M.

d/o Robert J.& Margaret M.Hart age 19 S POB & POR Spotsylvania; POM Spotsylvania 13 Sep 1876 SPMR 12 Sep 1876 SPML

HUFFMAN, Kenney J. s/o James & Agnes Huffman age 22 S miner POB Rockingham Co POR Louisa Co & **TRAYNHAM**, Mary d/o Sam & Lucy Traynham age 19 S POB & POR Spotsylvania; POM Good Hope, Spotsylvania 3 Jul 1900 SPMR 25 Jun 1900 SPML

HUGHES, Edmund Bennet s/o Nancy Hughes age 21y 3mo S carpenter POB & POR Orange & **SHIPLETT**, Mildred Ann d/o James & Frances Shiplett age 21y 4mo S POB Orange POR Madison Co; POM Orange 1 Sep 1859 OMR

HUGHES, George H. s/o Pancy Wood age 24 S carpenter POB & POR Orange & **HERNDON**, Virginia d/o L.& Jane Herndon age 22 S POB & POR Orange; POM Orange 11 Feb 1858 OMR 10 Feb 1858 OML

HUGHES, Hugh s/o R.& C.Hughes age 24 S laborer POB & POR Spotsylvania POC & **CARTER**, Milly d/o S.Carter age 21 S POB & POR Spotsylvania POC;

POM Spotsylvania 11 Jan 1879 SPMR 6 Jan 1879 SPML
HUGHES, Jefferson & **HERNDON**, Mary A.; POM Orange 17 Mar 1853 OMR OML
HUGHES, John s/o Amstead & Sarah A. Hughes age 21 S farmer POB & POR Orange & **LEE**, Harriet E. d/o John H.& Sarah F.Lee age 16 S POB & POR Orange; POM Orange 20 Dec 1859 OMR 16 Dec 1859 OML
HUME, Benjamin s/o Frank & Lucy Hume age 30 S cooper POB Orange & **HUME**, Eliza d/o John & Nancy Hume age 25 S POB Orange; POM Orange 7 Sep 1860 OMR OML
HUME, Charles F. s/o Francis & Lucy Hume age 25 S carpenter POB & POR Orange & **HAYNES**, Sarah N. d/o John & Jane L.Bourne age 30 W POB & POR Orange; POM Orange 13 Nov 1856 OMR 11 Nov 1856 OML
HUME, Charles W.& **KENNEDY**, Louisa W.S.; POM Orange 12 Apr 1853 OMR OML
HUME, Francis s/o John Hume & Nancy Jones age 34 W miller POB Rockingham Co POR Orange & **CHEWNING**, Amanda P. d/o P.Wesley Chewning age 26 S POB & POR Orange; POM Orange 31 Dec 1865 OMR 29 Dec 1865 OML
HUME, Frank & **BATTAILE**, Martha Ann d/o Mary Battle; POM Orange 1 Sep 1852 OMR 30 Aug 1852 OML
HUME, Joseph H. s/o George A.& Susan H.Hume age 47 S farmer POB & POR Fauquier Co & **HOLLADAY**, Ida M. d/o William A.& Mary Jennings age 42 W POB Orange POR Spotsylvania; POM Orange 29 Jul 1900 OMR 3 Jul 1900 SPML
HUMPHREYS, William C. s/o William & F.Humphreys age 23 S farmer POB & POR Spotsylvania & **DAVIS**, Fanny K. d/o T.L.& U.F.Davis age 20 S POB & POR Spotsylvania 30 May 1876 SPMR 22 May 1876 SPML
HUMPHRIES, Charles L. s/o Robert & E.S.Humphries age 34 S farmer POB & POR Spotsylvania & **WRIGHT**, Virginia E. d/o James & L.Wright age 29 S POB & POR Spotsylvania; POM Spotsylvania 6 Aug 1878 SPMR 7 Aug 1878 SPML
HUMPHRIES, James Edwin s/o James E. & Rebecca Humphries age 20 S farmer

POB & POR
Spotsylvania &
SHACKLEFORD, Mary
Ann d/o L.W.&
Lucinda
Shackleford age
22 S POB & POR
Spotsylvania; POM
Spotsylvania 26
Jan 1869 SPMR 21
Jan 1869 SPML
HUMPHRIES, Joseph A.
s/o William &
Fanny Humphries
age 23 S farmer
POB & POR
Spotsylvania &
RICHESON, Frances
D. d/o William
P.& Ann Richeson
age 21 S POB &
POR Spotsylvania;
POM Spotsylvania
23 Dec 1873 SPMR
5 Dec 1873 SPML
HUMPHRIES, Robert H.
s/o R.&
E.F.Humphries age
27 S farmer POB &
POR Spotsylvania
& **BRUMLEY**, Mary
E. d/o Robert B.&
M.F.Brumley age
22 S POB & POR
Spotsylvania; POM
Spotsylvania 17
Aug 1879 SPMR 9
Aug 1879 SPML
HUMPHRIES, Waller M.
s/o William &
F.Humphries age
23 S farmer POB &
POR Spotsylvania
& **RICHARDSON**,
Kate A.d/o
William &
A.Richardson age
26 POB & POR
Spotsylvania; POM
Spotsylvania 2
Jan 1881 SPMR 30
Dec 1880 SPML
HUNTER, Stephen s/o
Jim & Ann Hunter
age 24 S farmer
POB Culpeper Co
POR Orange POC &
TAYLOR, Drusilla
d/o William &
Rachel Taylor age
22 S POB & POR
Spotsylvania POC;
POM Spotsylvania
28 May 1872 SPMR
23 May 1872 SPML
HUSBANDS, W.A.C. s/o
James Husbands &
Rebecca Lewis age
22 S physician
POB
Charlston,S.C.POR
Dallas Co,
Alabama &
MALLORY, Columbia
d/o Ichabod
Mallory & Mary
Kennedy age 16 S
POB & POR Orange;
POM Orange C.H. 7
Jan 1864 OMR 6
Jan 1864 OML
HUSTON, David s/o
Joseph & Sarah
Huston age 21 S
farmer POB
Hillsboro, Ohio
POR Spotsylvania
& **COX**, Isabella
d/o John & Sallie
Cox age 19 S POB
& POR
Spotsylvania; POM
Spotsylvania 20
Mar 1884 SPMR
SPML
HYER, Henry s/o Henry
& Catherine Hyer
age 23 S gunsmith
POB Richmond,Va
POR Petersburg &
LIPSCOMB, Martha
F. d/o Fitzhugh &
Martha Lipscomb
age 17 S POB &
POR Orange C.H.;
POM Orange 5 Aug
1856 OMR 4 Aug
1856 OML

IRVIN, John s/o David & Mary Irvin age 38 S farmer POB New Jersey POR Spotsylvania & **ADAMS**, Harriet d/o Thomas & Delia Adams age 25 S POB Hanover Co POR Spotsylvania; POM Spotsylvania C.H.21 Jul 1881 SPMR SPML

JACKSON, A. s/o G.& J.Jackson age 25 S laborer POB & POR Spotsylvania POC & **WATSON**, Grace d/o H.& M.Watson age 22 S POB & POR Spotsylvania POC; 8 Jan 1880 SPML

JACKSON, Albert S. s/o William S.& Ann M.Jackson age 24 S farmer POB & POR Spotsylvania & **GRAY**, Ella M. d/o Alfred & Ellen Gray age 22 S POB & POR Spotsylvania mulatto; POM Fredericksburg 21 Dec 1876 FMR 20 Dec 1876 SPML

JACKSON, Albert s/o Thom & Mary Jackson age 23 S farmer POB Spotsylvania POR Caroline Co POC & **LEWIS**, Frances d/o Charles & Nelly Lewis age 22 S POB & POR Spotsylvania; POM Spotsylvania 27 Dec 1869 SPMR 20 Dec 1869 SPML

JACKSON, Andrew s/o Noah & Dolly Jackson age 26 S laborer POB, Spotsylvania POR Parkers POC & **JACKSON**, Annie Bell d/o Samuel & Mary Frances Jackson age 26 S POB Spotsylvania POR Parkers POC; POM Spotsylvania 21 Dec 1899 SPMR SPML

JACKSON, Andrew s/o John & Mariah Rawlings age 21 S farmer POB & POR Spotsylvania POC & **STANARD**, Elizabeth d/o Jack & Betsy Stanard age 21 S POB Caroline Co POR Spotsylvania POC: POM Spotsylvania 27 Nov 1873 SPMR 26 Nov 1873 SPML

JACKSON, Charles s/o Thornton & Eliza Jackson age 22 S farmer POB Culpeper Co POR Spotsylvania POC & **LEWIS**, Mary Eliza d/o Claiborne & Mary Lewis age 19 S POB & POR Spotsylvania POC; POM Piney Branch Ch, Spotsylvania 3 Oct 1886 SPMR 1 Oct 1886 SPML

JACKSON, Charles s/o Andrew Jackson age 23 S farm laborer POB & POR Orange POC & **PORTER**, Alice d/o Allen Long age 17 S POB & POR Orange POC; POM Orange 9 Nov 1867

JACKSON, Claiborne s/o Josephine Minor age 23 S laborer POB Stafford POR Spotsylvania POC & **MINOR**, Addie age 20 S POB & POR Spotsylvania POC; POM Spotsylvania C.H.10 Jan 1894 SPMR SPML OMR 4 Nov 1867 OML

JACKSON, Dudley s/o Noah & Polly Jackson age 23 S laborer POB & POR Spotsylvania POC & **CARTER**, Josephine d/o Addison Samuel & Barbara Carter age 17 S POB & POR Spotsylvania POC; POM Spotsylvania 11 Aug 1898 SPMR SPML

JACKSON, Frederick s/o Susan Jackson age 20 S laborer POB & POR Spotsylvania POC & **CRUTCHFIELD**, Lula d/o Reuben & Betty A.Crutchfield age 20 S POB & POR Spotsylvania POC; POM Spotsylvania 4 Jan 1899 SPMR SPML

JACKSON, George s/o Thornton & Eliza Jackson age 22 S laborer POB Culpeper Co POR Spotsylvania POC & **GRAHAM**, Ellen d/o Hugh & Dolly Graham age 25 S POB & POR Spotsylvania POC; POM Spotsylvania 9 Apr 1882 SPMR 7 Apr 1882 SPML

JACKSON, George s/o Thornton & Eliza Jackson age 33 D laborer POB Culpeper Co POR Spotsylvania POC & **JOHNSON**, Louisa d/o George & Martha Johnson age 28 S POB & POR Spotsylvania POC; POM Spotsylvania C.H.20 Aug 1894 SPMR SPML

JACKSON, Grandson s/o Sam & Livinia Jackson age 22 S farmer POB & POR Spotsylvania POC & **SCOTT**, Susan d/o Daniel & Rachel Scott age 24 S POB & POR Spotsylvania POC: POM Spotsylvania 31 Dec 1873 SPMR SPML

JACKSON, Henry N. s/o Nelson & Mary Jackson age 30 S farmer POB & POR Spotsylvania POC & **BROADDUS**, Mattie A. d/o Pleasant & Sarah Broaddus age 25 S POB & POR Spotsylvania POC; POM New Hope Baptist Ch, Spotsylvania 27 Dec 1899 SPMR 26 Dec 1899 SPML

JACKSON, Henry s/o William & C.Jackson age 21 S laborer POB & POR Spotsylvania POC & **FRAZER**, Mary Ann d/o

R.Frazer age 20 S
POB & POR
Spotsylvania POC;
POM Spotsylvania
26 Dec 1878 SPMR
21 Dec 1878 SPML
JACKSON, J.E. age 50 W
minister POB New
York POR
Manchester,Va &
PUGSLEY, Mary d/o
Benjamin & Ann
Adams age 37 W
POB England POR
Spotsylvania; POM
Manchester,Va 21
May 1887 SPMR 28
Apr 1887 SPML
JACKSON, Jacob s/o
George & Mary
Jackson age 30 W
farmer POB Louisa
Co POR
Spotsylvania &
CAMMACK, Hannah
d/o George &
Annie Cammack age
25 S POB & POR
Spotsylvania; POM
New Market,
Spotsylvania 20
Feb 1871 SPMR 4
Feb 1871 SPML
JACKSON, James H. s/o
Jefferson &
Charlotte Jackson
age 38 W farmer
POB Caroline Co
POR Caroline Co
POC & BROWN,
Elvira d/o Ralph
& Selina Brown
age 23 S POB
Caroline Co POR
Spotsylvania POC;
POM Spotsylvania
30 Dec 1881 SPMR
28 Dec 1881 SPML
JACKSON, Jesse s/o
Noah & Polly
Jackson age 21 S
laborer POB & POR
Spotsylvania POC
& CARTER, Lydia

d/o Barbara
Carter age 20 S
POB & POR
Spotsylvania POC;
POM Spotsylvania
29 Jun 1898 SPMR
SPML
JACKSON, John age 28 S
in U.S.government
service,
Gordonsville POB
& POR Orange POC
& WALKER, Mary
age 30 W POB
Albemarle Co POR
Orange POC; POM
Orange 25 Dec
1867 OMR OML
JACKSON, John s/o
Samuel & Mary
F.Jackson age 29
S POB & POR
Spotsylvania POC
& YOUNG, Mary d/o
Humphrey & Mary
Young age 22 S
POB & POR
Spotsylvania POC;
POM Spotsylvania
31 Mar 1897 SPMR
SPML
JACKSON, Marshall M.
age 28 S
bricklayer POB &
POR Louisa Co POC
& WILLIAMS,
Hardenia age 18 S
POB & POR Orange
POC; POM Orange
20 Dec 1866 OMR
17 Dec 1866 OML
JACKSON, Nelson s/o
Celia Jackson age
38 W farmer POB &
POR Spotsylvania
POC & THORNTON,
Mary d/o Manuel &
Dina Thornton age
35 W POB & POR
Spotsylvania POC;
POM Spotsylvania
14 Mar (no year)
SPMR 12 Mar 1869
SPML

JACKSON, Nelson s/o M.& A.Jackson age 22 laborer POR B& POR Spotsylvania POC & **PETTIS**, Grace d/o W.& M.Pettis age 18 POB & POR Spotsylvania POC; POM Spotsylvania 10 Jul 1879 SPMR 7 Jul 1879 SPML

JACKSON, Noah s/o Noah & Polly Jackson age 21 S laborer POB & POR Spotsylvania POC & **GIBSON**, Martha d/o Louisa Gibson age 20 S POB & POR Spotsylvania POC; POM Spotsylvania C.H. 15 Sep 1898 SPMR SPML

JACKSON, Oscar s/o John Jackson & Gabriella Taylor age 19 S laborer on farm POB & POR Orange POC & **MILLS**, Alice d/o Edgar & Lucilla Mills age 18 S POB Louisa Co POR Orange POC; POM Orange 18 May 1867 OMR OML

JACKSON, Philip Martin s/o Jos.S.& Mary Jackson age 21 S blacksmith & **HOWARD**, Lucy Ann d/o Thomas & Elizabeth Howard age 19 S POB & POR Spotsylvania; POM Spotsylvania 22 Feb 1855 SPMR

JACKSON, Samuel s/o Adam & Amanda Jackson age 21 S laborer POB Lynchburg,Va POR Spotsylvania POC & **WINSTON**, Mary d/o Lucy Winston age 17 S POB & POR Spotsylvania POC; POM Spotsylvania 18 Oct 1883 SPMR SPML

JACKSON, Samuel s/o Washington Stewart & Rachel Tucker age 60 W laborer POB & POR Spotsylvania POC & **OVERTON**, Hannah age 35 W POB Caroline Co POR Spotsylvania POC; POM Spotsylvania 24 Nov 1892 SPMR 23 Nov 1892 SPML

JACKSON, Thomas s/o R.& M.Jackson age 37 S laborer POB Orange POR Spotsylvania POC & **FRAZER**, Martha A. d/o Caroline Frazer age 30 W POB & POR Spotsylvania POC; POM Spotsylvania 23 Dec 1880 SPMR 22 Dec 1880 SPML

JACKSON, Walter age 25 S POB Louisa Co POR Spotsylvania POC & **COLEMAN**, Lucy Ann d/o Fountaine & Laura Coleman age 16 S POB & POR Spotsylvania POC; 22 Oct 1891 SPMR 20 Oct 1891 SPML

JACKSON, Washington s/o Washington & Betty Jackson age 21 S laborer POB & POB Louisa Co & **POINDEXTER**, Betty d/o Pleasant & Rebecca

Poindexter age 21 S POB Louisa Co POR Spotsylvania POC; POM Spotsylvania 19 Apr 1886 SPMR 10 Apr 1886 SPML

JACKSON, William s/o John Jackson & Malinda Willis age 22 S laborer POB & POR Orange POC & **LEE**, Alice d/o Jeny Lee & Maria Stately age 15 S POB & POR Orange POC; POM Orange C.H. 1 Dec 1866 OMR OML

JACKSON, William s/o N.& M.Jackson age 24 S laborer POB Caroline Co POR Spotsylvania POC & **TURNER**, Rose d/o James & E.Turner age 22 S POB & POR Spotsylvania POC; POM New Hope Ch, Spotsylvania 26 Dec 1878 SPMR 23 Dec 1878 SPML

JACOBS, Absalom E. s/o Nathaniel Jacobs & Mary Strong age 25 W blacksmith POB & POR Orange & **BLEDSOE**, Sarah Jane d/o John Bledsoe & Peggy Perry age 33 S POB Culpeper POR Orange; POM Orange 28 Feb 1861 OMR 12 Feb 1861 OML

JACOBS, Benjamin & **JACOBS**, Elizabeth; 22 Aug 1859 OML

JACOBS, Richard F. s/o James M.Jacobs & Lucy Morris age 20 S miller POB & POR Orange & **FAULCONER**, Susan J. d/o William Faulconer & Elizabeth Jacobs age 25 S POB & POR Orange; POM Orange 24 Dec 1867 OMR 23 Dec 1867 OML

JACOBS, Solomon & **FAULCONER**, Margaret ward of George Faulconer; 3 Oct 1854 permission certificate, Orange

JACOBS, William s/o George & Catherine Jacobs age 26 S farmer POB & POR Orange & **RICHARDSON**, Sarah F. d/o Josiah & Sarah Richardson age 28 S POB & POR Orange; POM Orange 6 Jul 1856 OMR 5 Jul 1856 OML

JACOBS. Absalom E. s/o Nathaniel & Nancy H.Jacobs age 20 S blacksmith POB & POR Orange & **FAULCONER**, Margaret Elizabeth d/o William & Elizabeth Faulconer age 20 S POB & POR Orange; POM Orange 5 Oct 1854 OMR

JAMES, Abijah s/o A.& Jane James age 20 S laborer POB Delaware Co,Delaware POR Spotsylvania POC

& **TAYLOR**, Rosa A.
d/o Minor & Maria
Taylor age 17 S
POB & POR
Spotsylvania POC;
POM Spotsylvania
26 Dec 1888 SPMR
24 Dec 1888 SPML

JAMES, Henry s/o
Charles & Martha
James age 22 S
blacksmith POB &
POR Spotsylvania
POC & **RAWLINGS**,
Octavia d/o Jinny
Rawlings age 22 S
POB & POR
Spotsylvania POC;
POM Spotsylvania
30 Dec 1870 SPMR
27 Dec 1870 SPML

JAMES, Joseph s/o
Joseph & Sarah
James age 32 W
farmer POB & POR
Caroline Co &
JAMES, Bettie d/o
Garden & Mary
James age 27 S
POB Caroline Co
POR Spotsylvania;
POM Spotsylvania
16 Apr 1884 SPMR
14 Apr 1884 SPML

JAMES, Woodson s/o
Gordon & Mary
A.James age 36 W
farmer POB
Caroline Co POR
Spotsylvania &
BUTLER, Annie d/o
William & Mary
A.Butler age 37 S
POB & POR
Spotsylvania; POM
Spotsylvania 15
Dec 1895 SPMR 14
Dec 1895 SPML

JEFFERSON, Henry s/o
Moses & Jane
Jefferson age 24
S laborer POB
Orange POR
Spotsylvania POC

& **THOMAS**, Laura
d/o Henrietta
Thomas age 21 S
POB & POR
Spotsylvania POC;
POM Spotsylvania
11 Jan 1883 SPMR
3 Jan 1883 SPML

JEFFERSON, Monroe s/o
Maria Burton age
25 S laborer POB
& POR
Spotsylvania POC
& **SMITH**, Polly
d/o Rose Smith
age 19 S POB &
POR Spotsylvania
POC; POM
Spotsylvania 28
Dec 1885 SPMR 26
Dec 1885 SPML

JENKINS, Arther H. s/o
J.H.& Margarett
Jenkins age 50 W
farmer POB
Westmoreland Co
POR Spotsylvania
& **STEVENS**, Ann M.
d/o Ro.E.& Lucy
Stevens age 36 S
POB & POR
Spotsylvania; POM
Spotsylvania 31
Jun 1865 SPMR 27
May 1865 SPML

JENKINS, Benjamin F.
s/o Albert G.&
Catherine Jenkins
age 30 S farmer
POB Louisa Co POR
Spotsylvania &
BRIGHTWELL,
Bittie (aka
Bettie) d/o John
D.& Drucilla
Brightwell age 25
S POB & POR
Spotsylvania; POM
Spotsylvania 18
Mar 1868 SPMR 16
Mar 1868 SPML

JENKINS, Benjamin F. &
BRIGHTWELL,
Bettie d/o

J.D.Brightwell;
16 Mar 1868
SPConsent
JENKINS, William s/o
John & Betsey
Jenkins age 50 W
farmer POB
Richmond Co,Va
POR Spotsylvania
& **HANEY**, Mary d/o
Addison & Lucy
Haney age 30 S
POB & POR
Spotsylvania; POM
Spotsylvania 4
Oct 1873 SPMR
SPML
JENNINGS, James s/o
James & Nancy
Jennings age 39 W
gunsmith POB
Spotsylvania POR
Fredericksburg &
WHEELER, Lucy Ann
d/o James B.&
Mary Wheeler age
28 S POB & POR
Spotsylvania; POM
Spotsylvania 28
Apr 1867 SPMR 15
Apr 1867 SPML
JENNINGS, James s/o
James & Nancy
Jennings age 39 W
gunsmith POB
Spotsylvania POR
Fredericksburg &
WHEELER, Lucy Ann
d/o James B.&
Mary Wheeler age
28 S POB & POR
Spotsylvania; POM
Spotsylvania 28
Apr 1867 SPMR 15
Apr 1867 SPML
JERREL, Joseph H. s/o
R.H.& Nannie
Jerrell age 24 S
farmer POB
Christian Co,
Kentucky POR
Spotsylvania &
CARNER, Maud L.
d/o John W. &

Annie Carner age
28 S POB & POR
Spotsylvania; POM
Good Hope Baptist
Ch, Spotsylvania
1 Nov 1893 SPMR
26 Oct 1893 SPML
JERRELL, E.W. s/o B.&
M.Jerrell age 28
S POB
Spotsylvania POR
Texas &
HUMPHRIES, M.T.
d/o George &
E.Humphries age
24 S POB & POR
Spotsylvania; POM
Spotsylvania 20
Dec 1857 SPMR
JERRELL, John B. s/o
Joseph & Louisa
B.Jerrell age 29
S POB & POR
Spotsylvania &
SCOTT, Mary H.
d/o William D.&
J.F.Scott age 30
S POB & POR
Spotsylvania; POM
Spotsylvania 6
Feb 1877 SPMR 29
jan 1877 SPML
JERRELL, Robert H. s/o
Joseph H. &
Louisa B.Jerrell
age 21 S farmer
POB & POR
Spotsylvania &
JOHNSON, Nannie
d/o Marshal &
Sarah A.Johnson
age 21 S POB &
POR Spotsylvania;
15 Oct 1865 SPML
JERRELL, Roy s/o B.&
M.Jerrell age 24
S farming POB
Spotsylvania POR
Texas & **PEYTON**,
T.A.R. d/o M.&
A.Peyton age 22 S
POB & POR
Spotsylvania; POM

Spotsylvania 22 Nov 1855 SPMR
JERRELL, Thomas J. s/o W.J.& L.M.Jerrell age 28 S farmer POB Caroline Co POR New Kent Co & **BLAYDES**, Mary S. d/o Joseph F.& A.V.Blaydes age 21 S POB & POR Spotsylvania; POM Spotsylvania 28 Oct 1879 SPMR 27 Oct 1879 SPML
JERRELL, V.M. s/o J.C. & M.Jerrell age 24 S physician POB & POR Spotsylvania & **CROPP**, S.G. d/o W.T.& J.Cropp age 22 S POB Stafford POR Spotsylvania; POM Spotsylvania 4 May 1859 SPMR
JETT, Andrew s/o James & Catherine Jett age 21 S mechanic POB & POR Spotsylvania & **PERREY**, Elizabeth d/o John F.Perrey age 23 S POB & POR Spotsylvania; POM Spotsylvania 7 Oct 1855 SPMR
JETT, Gilson s/o Thomas & Delila Jett age 20 S farmer POB & POR Spotsylvania & **FAIRCHILD**, Laura d/o Samuel & Caroline Fairchild age 22 S POB New Jersey POR Spotsylvania; POM Spotsylvania 2 Dec 1875 SPMR SPML
JETT, Herbert W. s/o Norvell & Elizabeth Jett age 26 W farmer POB & POR Stafford & **McWHIRT**, Kate d/o Franklin & Cornelia F.McWhirt age 22 S POB & POR Spotsylvania; POM Spotsylvania 20 May 1897 SPMR 17 May 1897 SPML
JETT, J.T. s/o P.& C.Jett age 24 S farmer POB Stafford POR Spotsylvania & **BOWLING**, S.F. d/o R.& E. Bowling age 22 S POB & POR Spotsylvania; 7 Feb 1860 SPMR
JETT, James M. & **MCGEE**, Amanda R.; 5 Feb 1866 SPConsent
JETT, James M. s/o James & Catherine Jett age 23 S blacksmith POB & POR Spotsylvania & **MCGEE**, Amanda R. d/o Reuben & Margaret McGee age 21 S POB & POR Spotsylvania; POM M.E.Ch Fredericksburg 22 Feb 1866 FMR 5 Feb 1866 SPML
JETT, Robert s/o Thomas & Delila Jett age 25 S farmer POB & POR Spotsylvania & **CARTER**, Maria S. d/o Benjamin S.& Emily C.Carter age 25 S POB & POR Spotsylvania; POM Spotsylvania 16 Jan 1873 SPMR 15 Jan 1873 SPML

JETT, Roscoe T. s/o John T. & Sarah F. Jett age 36 S farmer POB & POR Spotsylvania & **MULLEN**, Maggie L. d/o Daniel & Rosa Mullen age 26 S POB Kent Co, Md POR Spotsylvania; POM Fredericksburg 27 Jan 1897 FMR 26 Jan 1897 SPML

JOHNSON, A.S. s/o William E. & Sarah F. Johnson age 25 S farmer POB & POR Culpeper Co & **GRIMSLEY**, Mary Elizabeth d/o Charles D. & Lucy A. Grimsley age 18 S farmer POB Washington D.C. POR Spotsylvania; POM Spotsylvania 13 Dec 1883 SPMR 10 Dec 1883 SPML

JOHNSON, Allen s/o Henry & Betsy Johnson age 22 S farmer POB & POR Spotsylvania POC & **JACKSON**, Jane d/o Moses & Mary Jackson age 24 S POB & POR Spotsylvania; POM Spotsylvania 29 Jan 1874 SPMR 28 Jan 1874 SPML

JOHNSON, Andrew s/o Solomon & Mary Johnson age 24 S laborer POB & POR Spotsylvania POC & **WHITUS**, Nannie d/o Michael & Georgiana Whitus age 22 S POB Louisa Co POR Spotsylvania POC; POM Spotsylvania C.H. 2 Jul 1891 SPMR SPML

JOHNSON, Andrew T. s/o George & Nancy P. Johnson age 26 S farmer POB & POR Hanover Co & **SPINDLE**, Willie E. d/o Edmund I. & Mary Spindle age 18 S POB & POR Spotsylvania; POM Spotsylvania 18 Dec 1873 SPMR 8 Dec 1873 SPML

JOHNSON, Bradley s/o Solomon & Mary Johnson age 20 S laborer POB & POR Spotsylvania POC & **BROOKS**, Mary d/o Mary Shelton ("not born in wedlock") age 18 S POB Goochland Co POR Spotsylvania POC; POM Spotsylvania C.H. 20 Dec 1888 SPMR SPML

JOHNSON, Charles s/o William & Patience Johnson age 23 S laborer POB & POR Spotsylvania POC & **MINOR**, Kitty Ann d/o Warner & Rose Minor age 18 S POB Caroline Co POR Spotsylvania POC; POM Spotsylvania 22 Mar 1883 SPMR 21 Mar 1883 SPML

JOHNSON, Claborne & **WILLIAMS**, Bettie; 1 Jul 1868 SPConsent

JOHNSON, Claiborn s/o Robert & Maria Johnson age 38 W laborer POB & POR Spotsylvania POC

& **WILLIAMS**,
Bettie d/o Sarah
Williams age 22 S
POB & POR
Spotsylvania POC;
POM Spotsylvania
(no date on
MR)SPMR 1 Jul
1868 SPML
JOHNSON, Daniel s/o
Daniel & Patience
Johnson age 29 S
farmer POB & POR
Spotsylvania &
WIGLESWORTH,
Milly d/o William
& Sarah
Wiglesworth age
22 S POB & POR
Spotsylvania; POM
Spotsylvania 6
Nov 1881 SPMR 2
NOv 1881 SPML
JOHNSON, Daniel s/o
Lewis & Catherine
Johnson age 35 S
laborer POB
Prince Edward Co
POR Spotsylvania
POC & **LILLY**,
Eliza d/o George
& Grace Lilly age
30 S POB Caroline
Co POR
Spotsylvania POC;
POM Spotsylvania
10 Oct 1883 SPMR
2 Oct 1883 SPML
JOHNSON, David s/o
David & Lina
Johnson age 21 S
farmer POB & POR
Spotsylvania &
MILES, Maria d/o
Miers & Patience
Miles age 21 S
POB & POR
Spotsylvania POC;
POM Spotsylvania
28 Dec 1867 SPMR
26 Dec 1867 SPML
JOHNSON, David s/o
David & Lina
Johnson age 21 S
farmer POB & POR
Spotsylvania POC
& **MILES**, Maria
d/o Miers &
Patience Miles
age 21 S POB &
POR Spotsylvania
POC; POM
Spotsylvania 28
Dec 1867 SPMR
JOHNSON, Edgar M. s/o
Marshall & Sarah
Johnson age 50 W
farmer POB & POR
Spotsylvania &
LANDRAM, Mary F.
d/o Willis &
Sarah Landram age
50 S POB & POR
Spotsylvania; POM
Brockenburg,
Spotsylvania 9
May 1889 SPMR 3
May 1889 SPML
JOHNSON, Eliphalet &
CHEWNING, America
E. d/o William
H.; 30 Dec 1870
SPConsent
JOHNSON, Eliphalet s/o
Thomas & Jane
F.Johnson age 21y
8mo S farmer POB
Orange POR
Spotsylvania &
CHEWNING, America
E. d/o William
H.& Ann Eliza
Chewning age 20 S
POB & POR
Spotsylvania; POM
Spotsylvania 3
Jan 1871 SPMR 31
Dec 1870 SPML
JOHNSON, Frank s/o
Aaron Johnson &
Lilly Homes age
28 W farm laborer
POB & POR Orange
POC & **MASON**,
Cally age 21 S
POB Madison Co
POR Orange POC;
POM Gordonsville,

Orange 27 Dec
1866 OMR 24 Dec
1866 OML
JOHNSON, Frank s/o G.&
C.Johnson age 36
W laborer POB
Orange Co POR
Orange POC &
COOK, Martha d/o
William & C.Cook
age 24 S POB &
POR Spotsylvania
POC; POM Zion
Hill Ch,
Spotsylvania 30
Jan 1881 SPMR 28
Jan 1881 SPML
JOHNSON, French s/o
Robert Johnson &
Ann Washington
age 21 S farmer
POB & POR
Spotsylvania POC
& **BROWN**, Lilly
d/o Joe Brown &
Polly Scott age
18 S POB & POR
Spotsylvania POC;
POM Branch Fork
Ch, Spotsylvania
24 Oct 1874 SPMR
23 Oct 1874 SPML
JOHNSON, Henry s/o
Henry & Polly
Johnson age 35 S
laborer POB & POR
Spotsylvania POC
& **FORD**, Caroline
d/o Chess &
Courtney Ford age
25 S POB & POR
Spotsylvania POC:
POM Spotsylvania
4 Oct 1875 SPMR
SPML
JOHNSON, Henry s/o
Daniel & Patience
Johnson age 22 S
farmer POB & POR
Spotsylvania POC
& **COLEMAN**, Martha
d/o Wilson Green
& Esther Chew age
25 W POB & POR

Spotsylvania POC:
POM Lombardy,
Spotsylvania 5
Jan 1869 SPMR 4
Jan 1868 SPML
JOHNSON, Isaac L. s/o
George T.Johnson
& Zalinda
L.Johnson age 47
W house painter
POB & POR
Lynchburg, Va &
GRAVATT, Mary T.
d/o Oliver
Terrill & Susan
Proctor age 30 W
POB & POR Orange;
POM Orange 19 Jun
1867 OMR 18 Jun
1867 OML
JOHNSON, J.M. s/o S.&
J.D.Johnson age
22 S army officer
POB & POR
Spotsylvania &
BOGGS, Eliza H.
d/o S.A.&
M.A.Boggs age 22
S POB & POR
Spotsylvania; POM
Spotsylvania 10
May 1860 SPMR
JOHNSON, Jacob s/o
Hardy
Johnson(mother)
age 19 S laborer
POB & POR
Spotsylvania POC
& **HOWARD**, Maggie
d/o Jackson &
Agnes Howard age
17 S POB & POR
Spotsylvania POC;
POM Spotsylvania
14 Mar 1894 SPMR
12 Mar 1894 SPML
JOHNSON, James B. s/o
Belfield & Eliza
Johnson age 24 S
merchant POB
Barboursville POR
Culpeper C.H. &
MARSHALL, Sarah
Cordelia d/o

James Marshall age 18 S POB Orange C.H. POR Barboursville; POM Orange 9 Jun 1858 OMR 4 Jun 1858 OML

JOHNSON, James M. s/o Joseph & Ellen Johnson age 44 S cooper POB & POR Spotsylvania & **BECKHAM**, Susan Ella d/o John & Nancy Beckham age 27 S POB & POR Spotsylvania; POM Spotsylvania C.H. 26 May 1884 SPMR SPML

JOHNSON, James M. s/o Thomas & Jane F.Johnson age 32 S tanner POB & POR Orange & **PENDLETON**, Bettie E. d/o Jackson & Maria Pendleton age 27 S POB & POR Spotsylvania; POM Spotsylvania 15 Jan 1874 SPMR 12 Jan 1874 SPML

JOHNSON, James S. s/o William & Elizabeth Johnson age 23 S farmer POB & POR Orange & **SULLIVAN**, Mary F. d/o Q.& Serepta Sullivan age 24 S POB & POR Spotsylvania; POM Spotsylvania 19 Dec 1889 SPMR 18 Dec 1889 SPML

JOHNSON, James S. s/o Richard Johnson & Priscilla Jones age 35 S farmer POB & POR Orange & **CHEWNING**, Anna S. d/o Pereguine W.Chewning &

Ellen A.Hopkins age 21 S POB Spotsylvania POR Orange; POM Orange 24 Oct 1867 OMR 21 Oct 1867 OML

JOHNSON, James s/o Carter Johnson & Charlotte A.Charity age 32 W laborer on farm POB & POR Orange POC & **GRAVES**, Lucinda d/o Dick & Dinah Richards age 31 W POB & POR Orange POC; POM Orange 18 Aug 1867 OMR 14 Aug 1867 OML

JOHNSON, John Alvin s/o James A.& Susan Johnson age 22 S farmer POB Orange POR Spotsylvania & **MINNICK**, Minerva Jane s/o John & Charlotte Minnick age 18 S POB Orange POR Spotsylvania; POM Spotsylvania C.H. 22 Jun 1892 SPMR SPML

JOHNSON, John C. s/o Aquilla & Dorcus Johnson age 48 S farmer POB & POR Spotsylvania & **DUERSON**, Virginia C. d/o John F.& N.Duerson age 38 S POB & POR Spotsylvania; POM Spotsylvania 25 Nov 1874 SPMR 20 Nov 1874 SPML

JOHNSON, John L. s/o Eliphalet & Sarah Johnson age 39 S farmer POB Orange POR Spotsylvania

& **PARKER**, Ann
Maria d/o George
S.& Hardenia
Parker age 25 S
POB & POR
Spotsylvania; POM
Spotsylvania 21
Jan 1866 SPMR 19
Jan 1866 SPML

JOHNSON, John S. s/o
John B.& Nancy
Johnson age 23 S
farmer POB & POR
Spotsylvania &
CARNEAL, Martha
d/o Isaac & Betsy
Carneal age 29 S
POB & POR
Spotsylvania; POM
Spotsylvania 17
Jan 1867 SPMR 15
Jan 1867 SPML

JOHNSON, John S. s/o
John B.& Nancy
Johnson age 23 S
farmer POB & POR
Spotsylvania &
CARNEAL, Martha
d/o Isaac & Betsy
Carneal age 29 S
POB & POR
Spotsylvania; POM
Spotsylvania 17
Jan 1867 SPMR 15
Jan 1867 SPML

JOHNSON, John s/o
James & Mary
Johnson age 25 S
laborer POB & POR
Spotsylvania POC
& **WILLIAMS**, Sarah
age 22 W POB &
POR Spotsylvania
POC; POM
Spotsylvania 21
Jul 1897 SPMR
SPML

JOHNSON, John s/o
Reubin & Lucy
Johnson age 20 S
laborer POB & POR
Spotsylvania POC
& **DAVIS**, Anna d/o
Alonzo & Sarah
Howard age 20 S
POB Louisa Co POR
Spotsylvania POC;
POM Spotsylvania
30 Aug 1877 SPMR
SPML

JOHNSON, John s/o
Rubin Johnson &
DAVIS, Anner age
20; 27 Aug 1877
SPConsent

JOHNSON, John T. s/o
Richard &
P.U.Johnson age
25 S POB & POR
Orange & **JOHNSON**,
Mary d/o John B.
Johnson age 22 S
POB & POR Orange;
POM Orange 26 Dec
1854 OMR

JOHNSON, Joseph H. s/o
William &
F.Johnson farmer
POB Spotsylvania
POR Orange &
ANDREWS, E.E. d/o
William H.Andrews
POB & POR
Spotsylvania; POM
Spotsylvania 14
Dec 1853 SPMR

JOHNSON, Joseph R. s/o
E.M.& Sallie
Johnson age 21 S
farmer POB & POR
Spotsylvania &
PRITCHETT,
Lillian May d/o
William P.&
Olivia
B.Pritchett age
21 S POB & POR
Spotsylvania; POM
Spotsylvania 16
Sep 1897 SPRM 14
Sep 1897 SPML

JOHNSON, Landon s/o
David & Patience
Johnson age 25 W
farmer POB & POR
Spotsylvania POC
& **CHEW**, Nicey d/o
Ellen Chew age 21

S POB & POR Spotsylvania POC; POM Spotsylvania 22 Mar 1874 SPMR 21 Mar 1874 SPML

JOHNSON, Lanzil s/o Daniel & Pacia Johnson age 22 S laborer POB & POR Spotsylvania POC & HOLMES, Mary Ann d/o Richard & Milly Holmes age 18 S POB & POR Spotsylvania POC; POM County Line Meeting House, Spotsylvania 19 Nov 1866 SPMR 2 Nov 1866 SPML

JOHNSON, Lewis J. s/o Lewis & Delia Johnson age 23 S laborer POB & POR Spotsylvania POC & BROWN, Julia d/o Easter Brown age 20 S POB & POR Spotsylvania POC; POM Spotsylvania 10 Dec 1896 SPMR SPML

JOHNSON, Matt s/o Edward & Fanny Johnson age 22 laborer POB Orange Co POR Spotsylvania POC & SMITH, Nancy d/o Landon & Levenia Smith age 21 S POB Orange POR Spotsylvania POC; POM Spotsylvania C.H. 13 Nov 1885 SPMR SPML

JOHNSON, Melzi S. s/o William E..& Sarah Johnson age 25 S farmer POB Culpeper Co POR Spotsylvania &
BECKHAM, Lovely V. d/o John L.& Nancy Beckham age 26 S POB Culpeper Co POR Spotsylvania; POM Spotsylvania 1 Nov 1883 SPMR 28 Sep 1883 SPML

JOHNSON, Morris s/o Lewis & Ella Holladay age 21 S POB & POR Hanover Co railroad POC & DAVIS, Alice d/o George Davis (mother dead) age 21 S POB Albemarle Co POR Spotsylvania POC; POM Cedar Point,Spotsylvania 28 Dec 1886 SPMR 22 Dec 1886 SPML

JOHNSON, Peter T. physician & CLARK, Nancy; POM Orange 24 Mar 1853 OMR 22 Mar 1853 OML

JOHNSON, Peter T.(Dr.) s/o David Johnson & Mary Tinsley age 48 W farmer POB Louisa Co POR Orange & CAVE, Georgianna V. d/o Richard & Maria Cave S POB & POR Orange; POM Orange 27 Apr 1859 OMR 25 Apr 1859 OML

JOHNSON, Philip s/o William Johnson & Milly Green age 21 S ditcher POB & POR Orange POC & MADISON, Ellen age 22 S POB & POR Orange POC; POM Orange 26 Dec

1867 OMR 24 Dec 1867 OML

JOHNSON, Randall age 24 farm laborer POB & POR Orange POC & **McINTOSH**, Alvia d/o Gus McIntosh & Lucinda Henderson age 17 S POB & POR Orange POC; POM Orange 29 Dec 1867 OMR 23 Dec 1867 OML

JOHNSON, Reuben s/o Grandison & Ann Johnson age 46 W laborer POB & POR Spotsylvania POC & **WHITE**, Laura d/o Henry & Celia White age 21 S POB & POR Spotsylvania POC; POM Little Mine Road B.Ch, Spotsylvania 19 Oct 1884 SPMR 14 Oct 1884 SPML

JOHNSON, Richard I. s/o Marshal & Sarah Johnson age 24 S farmer POB & POR Spotsylvania & **JERRELL**, Margaret F. d/o Joseph H. & Louisa A. Jerrell age 17 S POB & POR Spotsylvania; POM Spotsylvania 23 Jan 1868 SPMR 11 Jan 1868 SPML

JOHNSON, Robert s/o Stephen & Patsy Johnson age 40 W farmer POB Caroline Co POR Spotsylvania POC & **HARRIS**, Patsy age 40 W POB & POR Spotsylvania POC: POM Spotsylvania 27 Dec 1873 SPMR 26 Dec 1873 SPML

JOHNSON, Samuel s/o R. & C. Johnson age 23 S laborer POB Caroline Co POR Spotsylvania POC & **LEWIS**, Sarah d/o R. & A. Taylor age 21 S POB & POR Spotsylvania POC; POM Spotsylvania 26 Dec 1878 SPMR 19 Dec 1878 SPML

JOHNSON, Thomas s/o Jacob Johnson & Nancy Jarrell age 66 W farmer POB & POR Spotsylvania & **MARTIN**, Julia d/o William Martin & Malinda Faulconer age 23 S POB & POR Orange; POM Orange 4 Apr 1865 OMR 3 Apr 1865 OML

JOHNSON, W.T. s/o A. & D. Johnson age 29 S farmer POB & POR Spotsylvania & **DUERSON**, S.J. d/o D. & A. Duerson age 31 S POB & POR Spotsylvania; POM Spotsylvania 17 Dec 1857 SPMR

JOHNSON, William M. s/o J.P. Johnson & Martha Floyd age 22 S farmer POB Coveta Co, Ga POR Whitfield Co, Ga & **SOUTHERLAND**, Mary E. d/o Alex Southerland & Dinah Howard age 21 S POB & POR Orange; POM Orange 15 Jan

1863 OMR 12 Jan
1863 OML
JOHNSON, William S.
s/o William S.&
Sarah Johnson age
23 S farmer POB
Spotsylvania POR
Culpeper &
BURTON, Mary E.
d/o George W. &
Virginia Burton
age 22 S POB &
POR Spotsylvania;
POM Spotsylvania
30 Dec 1875 SPMR
27 Dec 1875 SPML
JOHNSON, William S.
s/o William E.&
Sarah F.Johnson
age 32 W saw mill
laborer POB
Culpeper Co POR
Spotsylvania &
HICKS, Anna H.
d/o Wade H.&
Leatha Hicks age
22 S POB
Fredericksburg
POR Spotsylvania;
POM Spotsylvania
C.H.15 Sep 1884
SPMR SPML
JOHNSON, William s/o
Ben Carter &
Gracie Williams
age 25 S laborer
POB & POR Orange
POC & **TIBBS**,
Frances d/o
Charles Bowler &
Mary Hoomes age
40 W POB & POR
Orange POC; POM
Orange C.H. 22
Aug 1866 OMR OML
JOHNSON, William s/o
Garrick Johnson &
Mary A.Richardson
age 25 S working
at saw mill POB
Savannah, Ga POR
Orange POC &
ROBINSON, Ann d/o
Beverley Robinson

& Harriet Tibbs
age 19 S POB &
POR Orange POC;
POM Orange 26 Dec
1867 OMR 23 Dec
1867 OML
JOHNSON, William T.
s/o F.& Jane
Johnson age 23 S
POB & POR
Spotsylvania POC
& **LUDLEY**, Mary
d/o Henry &
Martha Ludley age
21 S POB & POR
Spotsylvania POC;
POM Spotsylvania
29 Dec 1870 SPMR
23 Dec 1870 SPML
JOHNSON, Willie s/o
William & Mary
Johnson age 23 S
laborer POB & POR
Spotsylvania POC
& **LAWSON**, Maggie
d/o Isaac & Julia
Lawson age 23 S
POB & POR
Spotsylvania POC;
POM Spotsylvania
C.H. 17 Sep 1896
SPMR SPML
JOHNSON, Woody K. s/o
John C.& Virginia
C. Johnson age 23
S farmer POB &
POR Spotsylvania
& **MARSHALL**, Lucy
F. d/o A.L. &
Estelle
C.Marshall age 25
S POB Culpeper Co
POR Spotsylvania;
POM Spotsylvania
26 Oct 1897 SPMR
19 Oct 1897 SPML
JOHNSTON, William s/o
Lafayette & Jane
Johnston age 52 W
laborer POB & POR
Spotsylvania POC
& **CONNER**, Queen
d/o Charles &
Phoebe Conner age

35 S POB & POR
Spotsylvania POC;
POM Spotsylvania
16 Mar 1899 SPMR
13 Mar 1899 SPML
JOHNSTON, Henry &
COLDMAN, Martha;
4 Jan 1869
SPConsent
JONES, Aaron T. s/o
Jane Jones age 32
S farmer POB &
POR Delaware
Co,Delaware POC &
LEWIS, Frances
d/o Absalom &
Margaret Lewis
age 22 S POB &
POR Spotsylvania
POC; POM
Spotsylvania 1
Jan 1896 SPMR 31
Dec 1895 SPML
JONES, Alfred s/o
J.H.& S.Jones age
35 S minister POB
Ohio Co, West
Virginia POR
Petersburg,Va &
LACY, Elizabeth
Bryan d/o J.H.&
B.C.Lacy age 23 S
POB Stafford POR
Spotsylvania; POM
Ellwood,
Spotsylvania 4
Jun 1879 SPMR 3
Jun 1879 SPML
JONES, Andrew B. s/o
James S.& Agness
Jones age 23 S
farmer POB
Culpeper Co POR
Stafford &
PROCTOR, Ellen R.
d/o George W.&
Martha S.Proctor
age 18 S POB &
POR Spotsylvania;
POM Spotsylvania
1 Oct 1868 SPMR
30 Sep 1868 SPML
JONES, Bazell G. &
MILLS, Josephine

d/o F.S.Mills; 5
Dec 1868
SPConsent
JONES, Bony, s/o Sam &
Dina Jones age 28
S POB & POR
Spotsylvania POC
& **BANKS**, Fanny
d/o Malinda Banks
age 26 S POB &
POR Spotsylvania
POC; POM
Spotsylvania 7
Jan 1897 SPMR
SPML
JONES, Charles W. s/o
Charles H. & Lucy
Jones age 26 S
farmer POB & POR
Stafford &
THOMAS, Ellen
Douglas d/o
William T.&
Jeannette Thomas
age 20 S POB
Stafford POR
Spotsylvania; POM
Spotsylvania
C.H.10 Oct 1894
SPMR SPML
JONES, Churchill s/o
F.& Mary Jones
age 39 W farmer
POB Spotsylvania
& **ALMOND**, Jane
d/o N.Sullivan
age 22 W POB
Spotsylvania; POM
Spotsylvania 17
Aug 1856 SPMR
JONES, Edward s/o
Jerry & June
Jones age 32 S
laborer POB Essex
Co POR
Spotsylvania POC
& **TAYLOR**, Malvina
d/o Henry Smith &
Emma Taylor age
25 S POB Essex Co
POR Spotsylvania
POC; POM
Spotsylvania 27

Dec 1877 SPMR 21
Dec 1877 SPML

JONES, G.W. s/o
Thad.M.& Maretta
J.Jones age 23 S
merchant POB &
POR Spotsylvania
& **JENKINS**, Carrie
May d/o T.F.&
Alice Rosa
Jenkins age 18 S
POB & POR
Spotsylvania; POM
Spotsylvania 9
Oct 1895 SPMR 3
Oct 1895 SPML

JONES, George E. s/o
Henry & Elizabeth
Jones age 22 S
laborer POB
Spotsylvania POR
Fredericksburg &
KING, Geneva C.
d/o Thomas King
age 19 S POB
Stafford POR
Spotsylvania; POM
Spotsylvania 6
Jun 1875 SPMR 3
Jun 1875 SPML

JONES, George Edward
POR
Fredericksburg &
KING, Gineva
Chase ward of
T.Walker Landram;
undated SPConsent

JONES, George S. s/o
Benjamin P.&
Sarah F.Jones age
23 S farmer POB
Madison Co POR
Orange & **TALLEY**,
Mary J. d/o
Meriwether &
Delilah Talley
age 19 S POB &
POR Orange; POM
Orange 12 Jun
1855 OMR

JONES, George W. s/o
M.P. Jones age 22
S POB Orange &
JOHNSON, Emily J.

d/o J.B. &
N.Johnson age 25
S POB Orange; POM
Spotsylvania 28
Sep 1856 SPMR

JONES, Henry s/o
William & M.Jones
age 21 S laborer
POB Essex Co POR
Spotsylvania POC
& **JACKSON**,
Virginia d/o Ben
& C.(or O.)
Jackson age 27 S
POB Caroline Co
POR Spotsylvania
POC; POM New Hope
Ch, Spotsylvania
12 Oct 1877 SPMR
11 Oct 1877 SPML

JONES, Isaac s/o
Fielding & Mary
Jones age 22 S
blacksmith POB
Orange Co &
SULLIVAN,
Virginia F. d/o
Woodson Q. & Lucy
M. Sullivan age
20 S POB
Spotsylvania; POM
Spotsylvania 17
Jun 1857 SPMR 8
Jun 1857 SPML

JONES, James A. &
MILLS, Francis
Jane d/o
W.G.Mills (POR
Belmont Co, Ohio)
age 17; 16 Nov
1876 SPConsent

JONES, James A. &
NOLAN, Mary; 1
Jan 1866
SPConsent

JONES, James A. s/o
William R. &
Elizabeth Jones
age 21 S farmer
POB & POR
Spotsylvania &
NOLAN, Mary A.
d/o Z.W.&
Elizabeth Nolan

age 15 S POB & POR SPotsylvania; POM Spotsylvania 4 Jan 1866 SPMR 1 Jan 1865 SPML (possible error in year by clerk)
JONES, James A. s/o William R.& E.M.Jones age 29 W farmer POB & POR Spotsylvania & **MILLS**, Frances Jane d/o W.J.Mills age 17 S POB Louisa Co POR Spotsylvania; POM Louisa Co 5 Mar 1876 Louisa MR 23 Feb 1876 SPML
JONES, James L. s/o Thomas R.& Ann Jane Jones age 20y 9mo S farmer POB & POR Spotsylvania & **ACORS**, Dorothea d/o George & Maria Acors age 21 S POB & POR Spotsylvania; POM Spotsylvania 29 Jul 1869 SPMR 28 Jul 1869 SPML
JONES, James M. s/o Churchill Jones & ____ Cage age 24 S farmer POB & POR Spotsylvania & **PROCTOR**, Bettie A. age 22 S POB & POR Orange; POM Orange 21 Nov 1868 OMR 20 Nov 1868 SPML
JONES, James M. s/o James & M. Jones age 24 S farmer POB & POR Spotsylvania & **OLIVER**, V.S. d/o Mary Oliver age 20 S POB & POR Spotsylvania; POM Spotsylvania 7 Aug 1857 SPMR
JONES, James W. s/o Fielding & Kitty Jones age 21 S farmer POB Culpeper Co POR Spotsylvania & **JONES**, Annie J. d/o Churchill & Jane Jones age 22 S POB & POR Spotsylvania; POM Wilderness, Spotsylvania 27 Feb 1883 SPMR 26 Feb 1883 SPML
JONES, James W. s/o James S.& Agnes Jones age 26 S farmer POB & POR Spotsylvania & **BUNNELL**, Sallie A. d/o A.J.& S.Bunnell age 20 S POB & POR Spotsylvania; POM Fair View, Spotsylvania 13 Dec 1866 SPMR 12 Dec 1866 SPML
JONES, John E. s/o Edward & Mary A.Jones age 31 S farmer POB & POR Spotsylvania & **PILCHER**, Edmonia B. d/o E.M.& Mary E.Pilcher age 22 S POB & POR Spotsylvania 6 Jan 1870 SPMR 31 Dec 1869 SPML
JONES, John I. s/o Rich'd. R. & Hester Jones of Spotsylvania Co. age 24 POR Spotsylvania Co. & **JETT**, Rosa Catherine d/o James M. & Amanda Jett of

Spotsylvania Co. age 21 POR Spotsylvania Co.; POM Fredericksburg 2 Jan 1895 TCF

JONES, John J. s/o Richard R. & Hester Jones age 24 S farmer POB & POR Spotsylvania & **JETT**, Rosa Catherine d/o James M. & Amanda Jett age 21 S POB & POR Spotsylvania; POM Fredericksburg 2 Jan 1895 FMR 26 Dec 1894 SPML

JONES, John W. s/o Micajah & Susan Jones age 21 S blacksmith POB Madison Co POR Orange & **HEATWELL**, Eliza d/o David & Eliza Heatwell age 18 S POB Rockingham Co POR Orange; POM Orange 15 Jan 1857 OMR 14 Jan 1857 OML

JONES, John W.F. s/o Thomas & Susan S. Jones age 50 W minister POB Bedford Co POR Spotsylvania & **QUIMBY**, Mary J. d/o Charles & Harriet L. Stewart age 26 W POB & POR Spotsylvania; POM Lebanon, Spotsylvania 13 Mar 1870 SPMR 11 Mar 1870 SPML

JONES, Lucian M. s/o E.D. & S.A. Jones age 29 S farmer POB Louisa Co POR Spotsylvania &

EDENTON, Blanche A. d/o William B. & M.A. Edenton age 21 S POB & POR Spotsylvania; POM Spotsylvania 24 Jan 1894 SPMR 17 Jan 1894 SPML

JONES, Nathaniel S. s/o John R. & Elizabeth Jones age 38 W overseer POB Orange & **PAYNE**, Bettie d/o Charles & Lucy Payne age 36 S POB Orange; POM Orange 27 Jun 1860 SPMR 13 Jun 1860 OML

JONES, Richard & **ELLY**, Esther POB & POR Spotsylvanial POM Spotsylvania 3 Oct 1853 SPMR

JONES, Richard s/o Peter & Jennie Jones W laborer POB & POR Spotsylvania POC & **BROOKS**, Mary d/o Mat & Tamar Brooks S POB & POR Spotsylvania POC; POM Spotsylvania C.H. 18 Sep 1886 SPMR SPML

JONES, Robert L. s/o Thomas & Mary A. Jones age 23 S farmer POB & POR Spotsylvania & **OAKS**, Ella D. d/o F.B. & Elizabeth Oaks age 17 S POB & POR Spotsylvania; POM Spotsylvania 20 May 1884 SPMR 5 May 1884 SPML

JONES, Robert L. s/o Thomas & Mary Ann Jones age 25 W

farmer POB & POR
Spotsylvania &
CLARKE, Cornelia
A. d/o William &
Belvedelia Clarke
age 19 S POB &
POR Spotsylvania;
POM Spotsylvania
C.H. 24 Aug 1886
SPMR SPML
JONES, Robert T. s/o
R.A.& Mary
R.Jones age 25 S
farmer POB & POR
Spotsylvania &
DOWNS, Lucie
Elinor d/o Thomas
& Amanda E.Downs
age 23 S POB
Stafford POR
Spotsylvania; POM
Spotsylvania 27
Mar 1892 SPMR 26
Mar 1892 SPML
JONES, Roy A. s/o Roy
& Elzira Jones
age 28 S farmer
POB Stafford POR
Spotsylvania &
HOWARD, Mary R.
d/o Charles &
Caroline Todd age
27 W POB & POR
Spotsylvania; POM
Spotsylvania 30
Jan 1862 SPMR 27
Jan 1862 SPML
JONES, Roy A. s/o Roy
& Eliza Jones age
28 S farmer POB
Stafford POR
Spotsylvania &
HOWARD, Mary R.
d/o Charles &
Har. Todd age 27
W POB & POR
Spotsylvania; POM
Spotsylvania 30
Jan 1862 SPMR
JONES, S.T. s/o
M.R.Jones age 42
W school teacher
POB Henrico Co
POR Spotsyvania &

BRUMLEY, M.C. d/o
William & Ann
Brumley age 21 S
POB & POR
Spotsylvania; POM
Spotsylvania 22
Apr 1857 SPMR
JONES, T.M. s/o John &
Lucy Ann Jones
age 30 S farmer
POB & POR
Spotsylvania &
HARFIELD,
Florence d/o
Thaddeaus &
Martha Harfield
age 24 S POB &
POR Spotsylvania;
POM Spotsylvania
C.H. 21 Nov 1893
SPMR SPML
JONES, Thomas &
TAYLOR, Betty d/o
Ryland Taylor; 29
Mar 1869
SPConsent
JONES, Thomas B. s/o
F.& M.Jones age
22 S POB & POR
Orange & **PAYTES**,
M.A. age 17 S POB
& POR
Spotsylvania; POM
Spotsylvania 13
May 1859 SPMR
JONES, Thomas E. s/o
Eli M.& Mary
E.Jones age 22 S
farmer POB & POR
Spotsylvania &
WELCH, Mary A.
d/o Thomas &
Annie Welch age
25 S POB Doublin,
Ireland POR
Spotsylvania; POM
Spotsylvania 24
Jan 1875 SPMR 18
Jan 1875 SPML
JONES, Thomas s/o
Charles & Esther
Jones age 30 W
farmer POB Essex
Co POR

Spotsylvania POC & **TAYLOR**, Betty d/o Ryland & Ann Taylor age 15 S POB Essex Co POR Spotsylvania POC; POM Spotsylvania 4 Apr 1868 SPMR 3 Apr 1868 SPML

JONES, Thomas T. s/o A.B.& J.E.Jones age 25 S merchant POB Fauquier Co POR Memphis, Tennessee & **COLEMAN**, Lucie B. d/o J.T.& Emily(?) Coleman age 20 S POB & POR Spotsylvania; POM Spotsylvania 17 Oct 1871 SPMR 16 Oct 1871 SPML

JONES, Wallace s/o James & Maria Jones age 23 S restaurant keeper POB "Bodetourt" POR Baltimore, Md & **BROADUS**, Margaret d/o Samuel & Jenny Broadus age 22 S POB & POR Spotsylvania; POM Clifton, Spotsylvania 24 Feb 1870 SPMR 21 Feb 1870 SPML

JONES, Walter M. s/o George & Emily G.Jones age 23 S farmer POB & POR Spotsylvania & **JONES**, Pricilla S. d/o James S.& Agness Jones age 21 S POB & POR Spotsylvania; POM Spotsylvania 15 Oct 1873 SPMR 13 Oct 1873 SPML

JONES, Walter s/o James & Betty Jones age 22 S farmer POB Culpeper Co POR Spotsylvania & **BLANKENBECKER**, Mollie d/o John & Eliza Blankenbecker age 25 S POB Madison Co POR Spotsylvania; POM Spotsylvania 26 Dec 1900 SPMR SPML

JONES, William A. s/o Sarah Jones age 36 W farmer POB & POR Orange & **JONES**, Mary Jane d/o John Jones & Susan Bickers age 35 S POB & POR Orange; POM Orange 8 Jan 1862 OMR OML

JONES, William L. s/o James S. & Agnes A.Jones age 43 W farmer POB & POR Spotsylvania & **McCONCHIE**, Emma L. d/o William A.& Eliza A.McConchie age 40 S POB Fauquire Co POR Spotsylvania; POM Spotsylvania 23 May 1888 SPMR 21 May 1888 SPML

JONES, William L. s/o James S.& Agness Jones age 25 S farmer POB & POR Spotsylvania & **TALLEY**, Sarah E. d/o Nathan & Rhoda A.Talley age 19 S POB Louisa Co POR Spotsylvania; POM Spotsylvania 17 Dec 1868 SPMR 14 Dec 1868 SPML

JONES, William S. s/o William I.& Sally Jones age 27 S farmer POB Rankin Co, Mississippi POR Caroline Co & **SMITH**, Columbia C. d/o Charles C.& Emily C.Smith age 22 S POB Essex Co, Va POR Spotsylvania; POM Spotsylvania 26 Mar 1867 SPMR Mar 1867 SPML

JONES, William S. s/o William & Salley Jones age 27 S farmer POB Rankin Co, Mississippi POR Caroline Co & **SMITH**, Columbia C. d/o Charles C.& Emily C.Smith age 22 S POB Essex Co POR Spotsylvania; POM Spotsylvania 26 Mar 1867 SPMR Mar 1867 SPML

JORDON, John M. & **GENTRY**, Susan A. d/o Sarah Gentry; POM Orange 30 Jun 1853 OMR 27 Jun 1853 OML

JUDSON, Jud s/o Samuel H.& Sarah M.Judson age 30 S blacksmith POB Port Colburn, Canada West POR Spotsylvania & **COLEMAN**, Bettie S. d/o Fountan & Ann E.Coleman age 20 S POB & POR Spotsylvania; POM Spotsylvania 29 Apr 1871 SPMR 24 Apr 1871 SPML

KALE, Fielden s/o John Kale & Jane Gordon age 25 S laborer POB & POR Spotsylvania POC & **COLEMAN**, Milly d/o Lindsay & Sallie Coleman age 28 S POB & POR Spotsylvania POC; POM Mt.Hermon Meeting House, Spotsylvania 21 Oct 1866 SPMR 20 Oct 1866 SPML

KEENIN, Robert s/o James & Jane W.Keenin age 24 S laborer POB Ireland POR Orange & **TAMPLIN**, Sarah d/o Peter Magoverin & Sarah Tamplin age 28 S POB & POR Orange; POM Orange 26 Sep 1853 OMR OML

KEEPER, Charles H. s/o W.A.& M.L.Keeper age 26 S dentist POB & POR Louisa Co & **TAYLOR**, Mary Ella d/o William & F.Taylor age 23 S POB & POR Spotsylvania; POM Spotsylvaia 10 Sep 1879 SPMR 9 Sep 1879 SPML

KEEPER, William C. s/o C.H.& Mary E.Keeper age 23 S machinist POB Cincinnati, Ohio POR Orange & **HAILEY**, Virgie Lee age 19 S POB & POR Spotsylvania; POM Spotsylvania 27 Dec 1899 SPMR 20 Dec 1899 SPML

KEETON, James P. s/o Horace & Lucy Keeton age 24 S carpenter POB

Green Co POR
Orange & **GRUBBS**,
Ann E. d/o
Matthew G.&
Angelina R.Grubbs
age 17 S POB
Louisa Co POR
Orange; POM
Orange 10 Feb
1859 OMR 5 Feb
1859 OML
KEGS, Charles M. s/o
Thomas Kegs &
Lucy Wright age
24 S engineer on
O.& A.railroad
POB Prince
William Co POR
Alexandria,Va &
KING, Music D.
age 20 S POB &
POR Orange; POM
Orange 26 Sep
1867 OMR 21 Sep
1867 OML
KELLAM, Sam s/o
T.Curtis &
S.Kellam age 22 S
farmer POB Orange
POR Spotsylvania
& **DANDRIDGE**,
Louisa C. d/o
Byrd &
M.Dandridge age
13 S POB Caroline
Co POR
Spotsylvania; POM
Spotsylvania 31
Dec 1870 SPMR 30
Dec 1870 SPML
KELLAM, Samuel &
DANDRIDGE, Louisa
C. d/o Byrd
Dandridge age 13;
30 Dec 1879 (or
1870, the final
number is
unclear)
SPConsent
KELLY, John P. s/o
Granville J.&
Harriet E.Kelly
age 24 S farmer
POB Fauquier Co

POR Culpeper Co &
SHEETS, Mary
Isabella Frances
d/o Felix
T.Sheets (POR
Augusta Co)age
18y 4mo b.d.15
Dec 1853 POB
Augusta Co POR
Spotsylvania; POM
Spotsylvania 2
Apr 1873 SPMR 1
Apr 1873 SPML
KENDALL, Robert G. &
BROCKMAN,
Virginia A.; 12
Jan 1852 OML
KENDIE, Samuel E. s/o
W.& J.Kendie age
23 S farmer POB &
POR Spotsylvania
& **FLEMING**, E.D.
d/o B.Fleming age
22 S POB & POR
Spotsylvania; POM
Spotsylvania 4
Sep 1879 SPMR 1
Sep 1879 SPML
KENDIG, John W. s/o
Urias & Isabella
Kendig age 23 W
laborer in
foundry POB
Spotsylvania POR
Fredericksburg &
WREN, Louisa C.
d/o Edward P.&
Eveline Wren age
22 S POB & POR
Spotsylvania; POM
Spotsylvania C.H.
5 Jul 1882 SPMR
SPML
KENDIG, John W. s/o
Urias & I.W.
Kendig (possibly
Isabella W.) age
21 S farmer POB &
POR Spotsylvania
& **SHACKLEFORD**,
Pricilla M. d/o
L.W.&
L.Shackleford age
23 S POB & POR

Spotsylvania; POM Spotsylvania 25 Jan 1880 SPMR 23 Jan 1880 SPML
KENNEDY, Clinton s/o Sidney & E.N.Kennedy age 26 S farmer POB & POR Orange & **ALMOND**, Mary V. d/o Henry & Josephine Almond age 22 S POB & POR Spotsylvania; POM Spotsylvania 21 Feb 1867 SPMR 16 Feb 1867 SPML
KENNEDY, D.R. s/o William & Tabitha Kennedy age 25 S farmer POB Beaver Co, PEnn POR Spotsylvania & **KNIGHTON**, Roberta L. d/o Robert S.& G.B.Knighton age 22 S POB Orange POR Spotsylvania; POM Spotsylvania 8 Feb 1883 SPMR 5 Feb 1883 SPML
KENNEDY, Fountain & **PEYTON**, Eliza P.; POM Orange 24 Jan 1852 OMR OML
KENNEDY, Isaac & **BARTLEY**, Virginia A. d/o Oliver Bartley; 23 Apr 1852 OML
KENNEY, Clinton & **ALMOND**, Mary V. (of age); 16 Feb 1867 SPConsent
KENNEY, William H. s/o William H.Brockenbrough & America A. Kenney age 27 S carpenter POB & POR Albemarle Co POC & **MADISON**, Nelly d/o James & Louisa Madison age 18 S POB & OR Orange POC; POM Orange 12 Mar 1866 OMR OML
KENT, J.W. s/o W.& S.Kent age 21 S farmer POB Fluvanna POR Spotsylvania & **HICKS**, M.C. d/o R.& M.E.Hicks age 22 S POB & POR Spotsylvania; POM Spotsylvania 14 Feb 1861 SPMR
KENT, William F. s/o W.& S.A.Kent age 26 S farmer POB Fluvanna POR Spotsylvania & **CONLEY**, Lottie E. d/o H.& F.Conley age 22 S POB Chesterfield POR Spotsylvania; POM Spotsylvania 5 Dec 1878 SPMR 3 Dec 1878 SPML
KERFOOT, George C. s/o W.T.& E.M.Kerfoot age 23 S farmer POB & POR Clarke Co & **BEVERLEY**, Bessie G. d/o F.C.& M.A.Beverley age 23 S POB & POR Spotsylvania; POM Spotsylvania 8 Nov 1893 SPMR 6 Nov 1893 SPML
KEYS, Austin age 47 W farmer POB Louisa Co POR Spotsylvania POC & **CRUTCHFIELD**, Eliza age 35 W POB & POR Spotsylvania POC; POM Ebenezer Baptist Ch,Caroline Co 22 Oct 1882 Caroline

183

CoMR 20 Oct 1882
SPML
KEYS, Austin s/o
Sallie Keys age
68 W farmer POB &
POR Spotsylvania
POC & **JOHNSON**,
Leonora d/o Ralph
& Dinah Johnson
age 28 S POB &
POR Spotsylvania
POC; POM
Spotsylvania 7
Sep 1897 SPMR
SPML
KEYSER, William L. s/o
E.T. & Mary
J.Keyser age 25 S
farmer POB Page
Co POR
Rappahannock Co &
DeJARNETTE,
Callie H. d/o
Elliott H.& Era
M.DeJarnette age
25 S POB & POR
Spotsylvania; POM
Pine Forest,
Spotsylvania 11
Jun 1890 SPMR 10
Jun 1890 SPML
KING, George P. s/o
Samuel & Ann King
age 54 W farmer
POB Chester Co,
Pa POR Stafford &
CHANCELLOR,
Annastatia d/o
Melzi & Lucy
Chancellor age 28
S POB & POR
Spotsylvania; POM
Spotsylvania 25
Mar 1868 SPMR 24
Mar 1868 SPML
KING, S. s/o S.&
A.King age 35 W
farmer POB
Baltimore POR
Spotsylvania &
CHARLTON, A.E.
d/o J.P.&
S.P.Charlton age
21 S POB & POR
Spotsylvania; 19
May 1859 SPML
KING, Thomas s/o
Horace & Sallie
King age 27 W
miner POB & POR
Spotsylvania POC
& **CARTER**, Julia
d/o Eleck & Ellen
Carter age 25 S
POB & POR
Spotsylvania POC;
POM Spotsylvania
19 Apr 1883 SPMR
18 Apr 1883 SPML
KING, Thomas s/o
Horace & Sally
King age 35 W
farmer POB & POR
Spotsylvania POC
& **SMITH**, Laura
d/o Joe Smith age
26 S POB & POR
Spotsylvania POC;
POM Spotsylvania
18 Nov 1893 SPMR
13 Nov 1893 SPML
KING, Thomas s/o
Horace & Sally
King age 21 S
laborer POB & POR
Spotsylvania POC
& **ROBINSON**,
Martha d/o Dudley
& Charlotte
Robinson age 21 S
POB & POR
Spotsylvania POC;
POM Spotsylvania
5 Apr 1877 SPMR 4
Apr 1877 SPML
KING, William s/o
Albert & Matilda
King age 24 S
farmer POB & POR
Spotsylvania POC
& **ELLIS**, Maria
d/o James &
Martha Ellis age
24 S POB & POR
Spotsylvania POC;
POM Louisa Co 25
Dec 1884 Louisa

Co MR 24 Dec 1884 SPML
KINSEY, Edward W. s/o Dr.John & Margaret Kinsey age 41 W merchant POB Brooklyn, N.Y. POR Spotsylvania & **HALL**, Hattie J. d/o Thomas A. & Delia M. Hall age 25 S POB Chester Co, Penn POR Spotsylvania; POM Spotsylvania 21 Sep 1884 SPMR 20 Sep 1884 SPML

KINSEY, Nathaniel B. s/o E.W. & Sallie Kinsey age 24 S clerk POB Spotsylvania POR Washington D.C. & **BLACKLEY**, Lizzie C. d/o George W. & Annie Blackley age 21 S POB & POR Spotsylvania; POM Grace Lutheran Ch, Washington D.C. 31 Dec 1898 SPMR 30 Dec 1898 SPML

KINZER, John H. s/o Christian F. Kinzer & Mildred Sutton age 43 W farmer POB & POR Orange & **WAYLAND**, Susan C. d/o Clement Wayland age 37 S POB Madison Co POR Orange; POM Orange 7 Aug 1866 OMR 6 Aug 1866 OML

KIRBY, William s/o James Kirby age 60 W harness maker POB Spotsylvania &

WHARTON, Nancy d/o Thomas & Eliz. Thornton age 37 W POB Orange; POM Spotsylvania 24 Feb 1854 SPMR

KISHPAUGH, Asa B. s/o John & Phoebe A. Kishpaugh age 29 S lignon dealer POB & POR Spotsylvania & **PAYNE**, Estelle d/o Jesse & Catherine C. Payne age 19 S POB & POR Spotsylvania; POM Spotsylvania 15 Dec 1892 SPMR SPML

KNIGHTEN, Robert A. s/o Taliaferro & E. Watkins Knighten age 21 S mechanic POB & POR Orange & **HERRING**, Georgianna d/o George & Sarah Holbert Herring age 28 S POB & POR Orange; POM Orange 22 Oct 1857 OMR 5 Oct 1857 OML

KNIGHTEN, William s/o Mordecai & Frances Knighten age 30 W shoemaker POB & POR Orange & **SANFORD**, Nancy d/o Jefferson & Sarah Wright age 25 W POB & POR Orange; POM Orange 23 Jan 1855 OMR

KNIGHTON, S.C. s/o Robert A. & Georgianna Knighton age 24 S farmer POB Orange

POR Spotsylvania & **WILSON**, Lucy M. d/o Robert H.& Mary J.Wilson age 22 S POB & POR Spotsylvania; POM Spotsylvania 18 Feb 1891 SPMR 11 Feb 1891 SPML

KRAUSS, G.W. s/o J.& A.E,Krauss age 28 box maker POB Baltimore, Md POR King George Co & **JONES**, Lucie d/o G.& A.Jones age 26 S POB & POR Spotsylvania; POM Spotsylvania 12 Jan 1859 SPMR

KUBE, Lewis s/o John & Frederica Kube age 30 S farmer POB Spotsylvania POR Orange & **JOHNSON**, Mary T. d/o Thomas & Jane T.Johnson age 23 S POB Orange POR Spotsylvania; POM Spotsylvania 3 Apr 1870 SPMR 30 Mar 1870 SPML

KUBE,(aka Kuba) William s/o Henry & Katherine Kube age 25 S farmer POB Germany POR Orange & **DOWNEY**, Mildred C. d/o Sanders & Catherine Mason age 27 W POB & POR Orange; POM Orange 19 Nov 1857 OMR 18 Nov 1857 OML

KUNINGHAM, George F. s/o G.& M.Kuningham age 24 S farmer POB & POR Middlesex Co & **HOLLADAY**, Ida J. d/o T.W.& S.Holladay age 22 S POB Fredericksburg POR Spotsylvania; POM Spotsylvania 28 Nov 1877 SPMR SPML

LACY, Charles L. s/o Robert A.& Ann M.Lacy ge 24 S carpenter POB Albemarle Co POR Richmond, Va & **LACY**, E.Lee d/o John F.& Sallie Lacy age 21 S POB Goochland Co POR Spotsylvania; POM Spotsylvania 12 Apr 1883 SPMR 11 Apr 1883 SPML

LACY, Jeremiah s/o Jeremiah & Mary E.Lacy age 37 S farmer POB & POR Spotsylvania & **LUCK**, Mollie d/o Ira & Sarah Luck age 21 S POB & POR Spotsylvania; POM Spotsylvania C.H.27 Oct 1887 SPMR SPML

LACY, Marmaduke J. d/o John F.& S.J.Lacy age 39 W mechanic POB Goochland Co POR Spotsylvania & **SNEAD**, Sarah A. d/o E.C.& A.E.Snead age 17 S POB & POR Spotsylvania; POM Spotsylvania 1 Feb 1899 SPMR 30 Jan 1899 SPML

LACY, Thomas C. s/o Zachary T.& Eliza Lacy age 19 S lawyer POB Goochland Co POR Spotsylvania & **EDENTON**, Maria J. d/o William B.&

Mary A. Edenton age 22 S POB & POR Spotsylvania; POM Spotsylvania 13 Jan 1886 SPMR 9 Jan 1886 SPML

LAMB, Ezekiel & **WOOD**, Rebecka E.; POM Orange 24 Dec 1863 OMR

LANCASTER, Daniel M. s/o Jonathan & Sarah Lancaster age 25 S farmer POB Orange & **JACOBS**, Sarah J. d/o James M. & Lucy Jacobs age 15 S POB Orange; POM Orange 21 Nov 1860 OMR 20 Nov 1860 OML

LANCASTER, George E. s/o William C. & Mary F. Lancaster age 26 S farmer POB Orange POR Spotsylvania & **TINDER**, Bettie F. d/o James R. & Martha Tinder age 22 S POB Orange POR Spotsylvania; POM Spotsylvania 28 May 1874 SPMR 26 May 1874 SPML

LANCASTER, James G. s/o Edmund & Sarah Lancaster age 60 W farmer POB & POR Orange & **HERRING**, Susan F. d/o Benjamin & Fanny Herring age 42 S POB Orange POR Spotsylvania; POM Spotsylvania 8 Jan 1867 SPMR 3 Jan 1867 SPML

LANCASTER, Lucian F. s/o James M. & Eugenia Lancaster age 31 W farmer POB & POR Orange & **WEBB**, Maggie J. d/o James A. & Sallie Webb age 21 S POB & POR Spotsylvania; POM Spotsylvania 24 Nov 1900 SPMR SPML

LANCASTER, Morton s/o Robert & Catherine J. Lancaster age 21 S farmer POB & POR Orange & **TINDER**, Lunnuie(?) Irene d/o Thomas R. & Elizabeth J. Tinder age 23 S POB Orange POR Spotsylvania; POM New Hope Ch 7 Nov 1892 SPMR 29 Oct 1892 SPML

LANCASTER, Owen C. s/o Edmund Lancaster & Sarah Cooper age 42 W farmer POB & POR Orange & **HERNDON**, Mary d/o James Herndon & Elizabeth Quisenberry age 44 W POB & POR Orange; POM Orange 3 Oct 1865 OMR 25 Sep 1865 OML

LANCASTER, Paschal & **FAULCONER**, Catherine E.; 27 Feb 1860 OML

LANCASTER, Robinson S. s/o William C. Lancaster & Mary C. Oakes age 29 S farmer POB & POR Orange & **FAULCONER**, Catherine J. d/o James F. Faulconer & Priscilla Tinder age 33 S POB Culpeper Co

POR Orange; POM Orange 24 Dec 1866 OMR 19 Dec 1866 OML

LANCASTER, William s/o Jonathan & Sarah Lancaster age 25 S farmer POB & POR Orange & **TINDER**, Adaline Tutt d/o Thomas & Nancy Tinder age 19 S POB Orange POR Locust Hill; POM Orange 29 May 1856 OMR 28 May 1856 OML

LANDRAM, E.L. s/o Willis & Lucy Landram age 32 S farmer POB & POR Spotsylvania & **SCOTT**, Willie Etta d/o William D.& Jane Scott age about 23 POB & POR Spotsylvania; POM Spotsylvania 20 Dec 1883 SPMR 19 Dec 1883 SPML

LANDRUM, L.W. s/o J.N. & L.Landrum age 30 S mechanic POB & POR Spotsylvania & **FARISH**, E.J. d/o George R.& S.Farish age 31 S POB & POR Spotsylvania; POM Spotsylvania 29 Oct 1878 SPMR 26 Oct 1878 SPML

LANE, Ernest B. s/o Tandy & Philoma Lane age 26 S farmer POB & POR Spotsylvania & **DILLARD**, Frances E. d/o John R.& Mary Dillard age 24 S POB & POR Spotsylvania; POM Spotsylvania C.H. 17 Sep 1884 SPMR SPML

LANE, John William s/o Waller H.& Mary A.Lane age 19 S farmer POB & POR Spotsylvania & **MASTIN**, Eliza Ann d/o Lewis & Elizabeth Faulconer age 30 W POB & POR Spotsylvania; POM Spotsylvania 28 Dec 1865 SPMR 18 Dec 1865 SPML

LANE, S.P. s/o John & Mary R.Lane age 72 W farmer POB Maine POR Spotsylvania & **SIMMS**, Alverta V. d/o J.R.& M.A.Sims age 17 S POB & POR Spotsylvania; POM Spotsylvania C.H. 17 Jun 1886 SPMR SPML

LARMAND, John & **WRIGHT**, Ann C.; POM Orange 27 Apr 1852 OMR 26 Apr 1852 OML

LARMAND, John s/o Frances & Lucy Larmand age 38 W tinsmith POB Richmond,Va POR Orange C.H. & **BRADLEY**, Maria F. d/o William & Lucy Newman age 32 W POB & POR Orange; POM Orange 12 Apr 1855 OMR

LAURENCE, Thomas s/o H.& R.Laurence age 22 laborer POB & POR Louisa Co POC & **DIGGS**, Emily d/o J.&

E.Diggs age 18 S POB Louisa Co POR Spotsylvania POC; POM "rigenkeek", Spotsylvania 20 Dec 1877 SPMR 17 Dec 1877 SPML

LAWRENCE, Elijah s/o Sirus Lawrence & Betty Hart age 37 S farmer POB & POR Spotsylvania POC & **REDD**, Ella d/o Kato & Sarah Ware age 24 W POB & POR Spotsylvania POC; POM New Hope Ch, Spotsylvania 29 Dec 1896 SPMR 22 Dec 1896 SPML

LAWSON, Albert d/o John & Mary Ann Lawson age 34 S farmer POB Marim Co,W.Va POR Roanoke,Va & **SAMUEL**, Lula B. d/o A.J.& M.E.Samuel age 18 S POB Essex Co POR Spotsylvania; POM Spotsylvania 12 Mar 1888 SPMR 10 Mar 1888 SPML

LAWSON, Dabney & **BANKS**, Ellen d/o Mary Galls age 27; undated SPConsent

LAWSON, Dabney s/o Harry & Martha Lawson age 67 W laborer POB & POR Spotsylvania POC & **JOHNSON**, Judy d/o Elijah & Louisa Johnson age 40 W POB & POR SPotsylvania pOC; POM Spotsylvania C.H. 26 Jan 1883 SPMR SPML

LAWSON, Dabney s/o Harry & Martha Lawson age 54 W POB & POR Spotsylvania POC & **BANKS**, Ellen d/o Frank & Mary Banks age 24 S POB & POR Spotsylvania; POM James Smith Plantation, Spotsylvania 12 Jan 1873 SPMR 11 Jan 1873 SPML

LAWSON, Elmore s/o Isaac & Julia Lawson age 19 S laborer POB & POR Spotsylvania POC & **STANARD**, Cora d/o Robert & Dolly Stanard age 17 S POB & POR Spotsylvania POC; POM New Hope Baptist Ch, Spotsylvania 22 Nov 1900 SPMR 21 Nov 1900 SPML

LAWSON, Isaac s/o James & Lucy Lawson age 42 W laborer aPOB &POR Spotsylvania POC & **STANARD**, Dolly d/o Saul & Maria Carter age 40 W POB & POR Spotsylvania POC; POM Spotsylvania 1 Apr 1897 SPMR 31 Mar 1897 SPML

LAWSON, John D. s/o Daniel & Jane Lawson age 36 S commercial POB Orange Co, New York POR New York City & **BALLARD**, Helen Peyton d/o Garland & Georgiana Ballard age 25 S POB &

POR Orange; POM Orange 10 Jan 1855 OMR

LAWSON, Lanny s/o Sam & Nancy Lawson age 21 S farmer POB & POR Orange POC & **ARMISTEAD**, Hannah d/o Peter & Kizzy Armistead (Peter was a minister and he married Lanny & Hannah) age 22 S POB & POR Spotsylvania POC; POM Spotsylvania 9 May 1874 SPMR 7 May 1874 SPML

LAYTON, Marcus A. s/o James Layton & Maria L.Nelson age 23 S lawyer POB & POR Orange & **NEWMAN**, Lucy C. d/o Reuben Newman & Mary Clark age 17 S POB & POR Orange; POM Orange 22 Apr 1862 OMR OML

LEACH, James T. s/o William & Susan Leach age 33 W saw mill hand POB & POR Spotsylvania & **JONES**, Magdalene L. d/o Thomas & Mary Jones age 18 S POB & POR Spotsylvania; POM Spotsylvania C.H. 20 Mar 1890 SPMR SPML

LEATHERS, William E. s/o George W.& S.A.Leathers age 24 S farmer POB & POR Spotsylvania & **SHULZE**, Mary E. d/o Henry & Mary E.Shulze age 22 S POB & POR Spotsylvania; POM Spotsylvania 30 Mar 1876 SPMR SPML

LEATHERS. Levy & **YANCY**, Elizabeth; 17 Feb 1851 OML

LEAVELL, Benjamin L. s/o D.Leavell S merchant POB Spotsylvania POR Rappahannock Co. & **GAYLE**, Roberta E. d/o Josiah P.Gayle S POR Spotsylvania; 11 Oct 1853 SPMR

LEAVELL, William T. s/o John M. & S.M.Leavell age 26 S farmer POB Rappahannock POR Spotsylvania & **LEAVELL**, Fanny G. d/o B.S. & R.E.Leavell age 21 S POB & POR Spotsylvania; POM Fredericksburg 2 Dec 1875 FMR 1 Dec 1875 SPML

LEE, Davey & **LEWIS**, Mattie; 8 Jun 1876 SPConsent

LEE, David s/o Frank Lee & Frances Rollins age 32 S laborer POB Culpeper Co POR Spotsylvania POC & **TAYLOR**, Ella d/o Icy & Amelia Taylor age 16 S POB & POR Spotsylvania POC; POM Spotsylvania C.H.26 Mar 1885 SPMR SPML

LEE, David s/o Frank Lee & Frances Rollins age 26 S laborer POB Culpeper Co POR Spotsylvania POC

& **LEWIS**, Matty d/o Adison & Mary Lewis age 23 S POB & POR Spotsylvania POC; POM Spotsylvania 11 Jun 1876 SPMR 9 Jun 1876 SPML

LEE, James F. s/o George W.& AnnE.Lee age 21 S farmer POB Orange POR Spotsylvania & **BOWLING**, Irene C. d/o Lawrence T.& Sarah E.Bowling age 17 S POB & POR Spotsylvania; POM Spotsylvania C.H.6 Jul 1892 SPMR SPML

LEE, James s/o John H.& Sarah F.Lee age 18 S farming POB & POR Orange & **WOOD**, Martha J. d/o Thomas & Sarah F.Wood age 24 S POB & POR Orange; POM Orange 1 Dec 1859 OMR 30 Nov 1859 OML

LEE, Lafayette & **MASSEY**, Eliza; 24 Feb 1851 OML

LEE, Ned & **JACKSON**, Ann d/o Ann Jackson; 3 Jan 1876 SPConsent

LEE, Robert F. s/o Joseph T. Fanny T.Lee age 22 S farmer POB & POR King George Co & **WHARTEN**, Fannie P. d/o Robert & Catherine Wharten age 19 S POB & POR Spotsylvania; POM Beech Grove M.E.Ch 25 Mar 1890 24 Mar 1890 SPML

LEE, Samuel s/o John & Milly Lee age 69 W farmer POB Orange POR Spotsylvania & **PIERCE**, Jane d/o Richard & Amelia Pierce age 43 S POB & POR Spotsylvania; POM Spotsylvania 10 Nov 1867 SPMR 26 Oct 1867 SPML

LEE, Tolman Edward s/o Lewis & Ellen Lee age 30 S laborer POB & POR Spotsylvania POC & **RUSSELL**, Catherine d/o John L.& Eliza Russell age 20 S POB & POR Spotsylvania POC; POM Spotsylvania 19 Jan 1888 SPMR SPML

LEIGH, George C. s/o Richerson & Martha Leigh age 25 S merchant POB King William Co POR Ayletts, King William Co & **WILLIAMS**, Mary Blair d/o Lewis B.& Mary Williams age 23 S POB & POR Orange; POM Orange 8 Nov 1859 OMR 7 Nov 1859 OML

LEITCH, Bazil M. s/o William & Virginia Leitch age 27 S farmer POB & POR Spotsylvania & **PAYTES**, Sarah Frances d/o Agusta & Clementina Paytes

age 21 S POB &POR
Spotsylvania;'
POM Spotsylvania
C.H.3 Dec 1885
SPMR 2 Dec 1885
SPML

LEITCH, Frank s/o
William &
V.Leitch age 29 S
farmer POB & POR
Spotsylvania &
MILLS, Ella age
19 S POB & POR
Spotsylvania; POM
Fredericksburg 6
Feb 1881 FMR 4
Feb 1881 SPML

LEITCH, John B. s/o
William &
Charlotte Leitch
age 51 S farmer
POB King George
Co POR
Spotsylvania &
SIMPSON,
Elizabeth d/o
Frances Shelton
age 35 W POB &
POR Spotsylvania;
POM Spotsylvania
31 Dec 1854 SPMR

LEITCH, Thomas S. s/o
Thomas M.& Martha
S.Leitch age 30 S
farmer POB & POR
Buckingham Co &
SMITH, Inez V.
d/o E.W.& Mary
E.Smith age 20 S
POB & POR
Spotsylvania; POM
Belle Fonte,
Spotsylvania 26
Jun 1895 SPMR 17
Jun 1895 SPML

LEITCH, William s/o
William Leitch
age 38 S farmer
POB & POR
Spotsylvania &
ALMOND, Susan J.
d/o Jefferson
Almond age 17 S
POB & POR

Spotsylvania; POM
Spotsylvania 18
May 1854 SPMR

LEVI, Philip s/o
Joseph & Bettie
Levi age 30 S
merchant POB &
POR Baltimore, Md
& **IREMAN**, Sallie
d/o Isaac &
Charlotte Ireman
age 26 S POB
Germany POR
Spotsylvania; POM
Fredericksburg 19
Feb 1879 SPMR 15
Feb 1879 SPML

LEWIS Marcellus s/o
Ben & Amanda
Lewis age 23 S
farmer POB & POR
Spotsylvania POC
& **CAMMACK**, Lucy
d/o William &
Caroline Cammack
age 24 S POB &
POR Spotsylvania
POC; POM
Spotsylvania 22
Mar 1873 SPMR 21
Mar 1873 SPML

LEWIS, A.J. s/o W.&
Catherine Lewis
age 25 S farmer
POB & POR Orange
& **TAPP**, Harriet
C. d/o V.&
Catherine Tapp
age 23 S POB &
POR Spotsylvania;
18 Aug 1859 SPML

LEWIS, Addison s/o
James & Nellie
Lewis age 54 W
laborer POB & POR
Spotsylvania POC
& **CRUTCHFIELD**,
Betty Ann age 40
W POB & POR
Spotsylvania POC;
POM Mount Airy,
Spotsylvania 9
Apr 1891 SPMR 4
Apr 1891 SPML

LEWIS, Addison s/o
Anaky Lewis age
30 S blacksmith
POB & POR
Spotsylvania POC
& **MERCER**, Martha
d/o Keeling &
Judy Mercer age
18 S POB & POR
Spotsylvania POC;
POM Spotsylvania
12 Feb 1874 SPMR
9 Feb 1874 SPML
LEWIS, Alfred s/o
Robert & Jane
Lewis age 25 S
farmer POB & POR
Spotsylvania &
COOPER, Mary M.
d/o Richard &
Sarah Brown age
35 W POB Stafford
POR Spotsylvania;
POM Spotsylvania
17 Sep 1884 SPMR
12 Sep 1884 SPML
LEWIS, Allen &
JOHNSON, Mattie
d/o Lucy Jane
Johnson; 29 Dec
1875 SPConsent
LEWIS, Allen s/o B.&
Amy Lewis age 22
S laborer POB &
POR Spotsylvania
POC & **JOHNSON**,
Mattie d/o Ben &
Lucy Jane Johnson
age 15 S POB &
POR Spotsylvania
POC; POM
Spotsylvania 30
Dec 1875 SPMR 28
Dec 1875 SPML
LEWIS, Armistead age
21 S laborer POB
& POR
Spotsylvania POC
& **CHEW**, Elizabeth
age 21 S POB &
POR Spotsylvania
POC; POM
Spotsylvania 15
Mar 1894 SPMR
SPML
LEWIS, Arthur s/o
Albert & Nelly
Hambleton age 24
S laborer POB &
POR Spotsylvania
POC & **CHEW**, Maria
F. d/o Claiborne
& Patsy Chew age
17 S POB & POR
Spotsylvania POC;
POM Spotsylvania
7 Jul 1876 SPMR 5
Jul 1876 SPML
LEWIS, Barber s/o
William &
Charlotte Lewis
age 22 S farmer
POB Orange POR
Spotsylvania &
TYLER, Melvina
d/o Richard &
Clara Tyler age
18 S POB & POR
Spotsylvania; POM
Branch Fork Ch,
Spotsylvania 26
Dec 1875 SPMR
LEWIS, Braxton s/o
Addison & Mary
Lewis age 21 S
laborer POB & POR
Spotsylvania POC
& **SMITH**, Elnora
d/o Henry & Angy
Smith age 17 S
POB & POR
Spotsylvania POC;
20 May 1896 SPML
LEWIS, Caesar J. s/o
Ceasar & Mary
Lewis age 52 W
laborer POB & POR
Spotsylvania POC
& **SCOTT**, Lucy J.
d/o Peter &
Caroline Frazier
age 45 W POB &
POR Spotsylvania
POC; POM
Spotsylvania C.H.
12 Feb 1891 SPMR
SPML

LEWIS, Charles A. s/o
William & Mary
F.Lewis age 48 S
farmer POB & POR
Spotsylvania &
JENKINS, Sarah J.
d/o Arthur
Jenkins age 21 S
POB & POR
Spotsylvania; POM
Spotsylvania 10
Dec 1865 SPMR 9
Dec 1865 SPML
LEWIS, Charles J. s/o
Fleetwood & Jane
E.Lewis age 27 S
farmer POB & POR
Spotsylvania &
STEWART, Mary W.
d/o W.C.& Frances
R.Stewart age 18
S POB Fauquier Co
POR Spotsylvania;
POM Zion M.E.Ch,
Spotsylvania 30
Apr 1885 SPMR
SPML
LEWIS, Charles s/o
Alexander &
Melvina Lewis age
20 S laborer POB
& POR
Spotsylvania POC
& **GORDON**, Mary
Alice d/o
Claiborne & Mary
E.Lewis age 18 S
POB Maryland POR
Spotsylvania POC;
POM Spotsylvania
21 Dec 1898 SPMR
SPML
LEWIS, Charles s/o
Peter & Malvina
Lewis age 21 S
farmer POB & POR
Spotsylvania POC
& **LEWIS**, Lucy Ann
d/o Thornton &
Mary Lewis age 20
S POB & POR
Spotsylvania POC;
POM Spotsylvania

28 Dec 1869 SPMR
25 Dec 1869 SPML
LEWIS, Charles s/o
William F.Lewis &
JENINGS, Sarah
H.; 5 Dec 1865
SPConsent
LEWIS, Charles s/o Ben
& Isabella Lewis
age 57 W
carpenter POB &
POR Spotsylvania
POC & **FLIPPO**,
Frances d/o
Willis & Jenny
Taylor age 40 W
POB Caroline Co
POR Spotsylvania
POC; POM
Spotsylvania 10
Dec 1868 SPMR 7
Dec 1868 SPML
LEWIS, Eddie s/o
Anderson & Ailsy
age 22 S laborer
POB & POR
Spotsylvania POC
& **TERRELL**, Marcia
d/o Henry & Kezia
Terrell age 18 S
POB & POR
Spotsylvania POC;
POM Spotsylvania
28 Dec 1882 SPMR
26 Dec 1882 SPML
LEWIS, Edmond s/o
Richard & Matilda
Lewis age 25 S
laborer POB & POR
Spotsylvania POC
& **STANARD**, Dilsy
d/o Beverley &
Winney Stanard
age 22 S POB &
POR Spotsylvania
POC; POM
Fredericksburg 26
Dec 1882 FMR 25
Dec 1882 SPML
LEWIS, Frederick A.
s/o William T.&
B. Lewis age 23 S
farmer POB & POR
Spotsylvania &

DILLARD, Edith E. d/o A.W. & S. Dillard age 23 S POB & POR Spotsylvania; POM 27 Aug 1878 SPMR 26 Aug 1878 SPML

LEWIS, George s/o J. & M. Lewis age 21 S laborer POB orange POR Orange POC & **WOOLFOLK**, Milly d/o B. & E. Woolfolk S POB Spotsylvania POR Orange POC; POM Spotsylvania 6 Jan 1881 SPMR 4 Jan 1881 SPML

LEWIS, George W. s/o Stephen & Mary Lewis age 29 farmer POB & POR Spotsylvania & **LEWIS**, Mary F. d/o Robert & Jane Lewis age 29 POB & POR Spotsylvania; POM Spotsylvania 22 Jul 1873 SPMR 21 Jul 1873 SPML

LEWIS, Harvey s/o Mat & Jannie Lewis age 22 S brickmaker POB & POR Orange POC & **WOOLFOLK**, Eva d/o John & Mary Woolfolk age 20 S POB & POR Spotsylvania POC; POM Orange Grove Ch, Orange 19 Sep 1900 OMR 18 Sep 1900 SPML

LEWIS, Henry s/o John & Kitty Lewis age 25 S farmer POB & POR Spotsylvania POC & **DAY**, Sessa d/o Henry & Harriet Day age 22 S POB & POR Spotsylvania POC; POM Spotsylvania 29 Dec 1870 SPMR 23 Dec 1870 SPML

LEWIS, Henry s/o Tom Lewis & Lucy Shepherd age 66 W laborer POB Spotsylvania POR Fredericksburg POC & **TALIAFERRO**, Caroline d/o Moses & Fanny White age 56 W POB & POR Spotsylvania POC; POM Spotsylvania 25 Feb 1882 SPMR SPML

LEWIS, James s/o Edmund & Mary S. Lewis age 23 S laborer POB & POR Spotsylvania POC & **COLEMAN**, Maggie d/o Lydia Coleman age 22 S POB & POR Spotsylvania POC; POM Buleh Ch, Spotsylvania 4 Oct 1899 SPMR 2 Oct 1899 SPML

LEWIS, James s/o Edward & Amy Lewis age 45 W farmer POB & POR Spotsylvania POC & **ANDERSON**, Melvina d/o Mack & Fanny Hart age 42 W POB & POR Spotsylvania POC; POM Spotsylvania 26 Jul 1900 SPMR SPML

LEWIS, James s/o Thomas & Fanny Lewis age 25 S laborer POB & POR Spotsylvania POC & **ROBINSON**, Rosa age 33 W POB & POR Spotsylvania POC; POM

Spotsylvania 16 Jan 1889 SPMR SPML

LEWIS, James s/o Washington & Sallie Ann Lewis age 33 S laborer POB & POR Spotsylvania POC & **BROOKS**, Sara d/o Mary Jones S POB & POR Spotsylvania POC; POM Spotsylvania C.H. 17 Sep 1896 SPMR SPML

LEWIS, James s/o Madison & Margaret Lewis age 50 W laborer POB & POR Spotsylvania POC & **JOHNSON**, Linnie d/o Simon & Malvina Johnson age 30 W POB & POR Spotsylvania POC; POM Waller's Ch, Spotsylvania 11 Nov 1866 SPMR 2 Nov 1866 SPML

LEWIS, James s/o Ned (dec) & Amy Lewis (dec) age 22 farmer POC & **BANKS**, Martha J.; 4 Feb 1877 SPConsent

LEWIS, James s/o Ned & Amy Lewis age 24 S laborer POB & POR Spotsylvania POC & **BANKS**, Martha J. d/o Lewis & Eliza Banks age 22 S POB & POR Spotsylvania POC; POM Spotsylvania 6 Feb 1877 SPMR 5 Feb 1877 SPML

LEWIS, James s/o Peter & Melvina Lewis age 28 S laborer POB & POR Spotsylvania POC & **LEWIS**, Eliza d/o James & Judy Lewis age 22 S POB & POR Spotsylvania POC; POM Spotsylvania 8 Oct 1885 SPMR SPML

LEWIS, Jesse s/o M. & E. Lewis age 24 S laborer POB & POR Spotsylvania POC & **ROBINSON**, Malvina d/o H. & Amy Robinson age 20 S POB & POR Spotsylvania POC; POM Spotsylvania 21 Jun 1876 SPMR SPML

LEWIS, Jessee s/o Mat & Margaret Lewis age 50 W laborer POB & POR Spotsylvania POC & **WALKER**, Easter age 25 W POB & POR Spotsylvania POC; POM Spotsylvania 9 Nov 1875 SPMR SPML

LEWIS, John Francis s/o William F. & Mary F. Lewis age 22 S farmer POB & POR Spotsylvania & **CROSLEY**, Frances Annie d/o James & Fanny Thomas age 35 W POB & POR Spotsylvania; POM St George Ch, Fredericksburg 19 Jun 1873 FMR 18 Jun 1873 SPML

LEWIS, John H. s/o Zach & Eliza Lewis age 47 D laborer POB Orange POR

Spotsylvania POC
& **WALKER**, Delphia
d/o Dolly Walker
age 35 W laborer
POB & POR
Spotsylvania POC;
POM Spotsylvania
29 Apr 1897 SPMR
28 Apr 1897 SPML

LEWIS, John s/o
William F.&
Frances E. Lewis
age 26 S farmer
POB & POR
Spotsylvania &
JENKINS, Mary L.
d/o Albert G.&
Catharine Jenkins
age 17 S POB &
POR Spotyslvnia;
POM Spotsylvania
23 Apr 1872 SPMR
16 Apr 1872 SPML

LEWIS, John s/o John &
Kitty Lewis age
40 S laborer POB
& POR
Spotsylvania POC
& **COLEMAN**, Martha
d/o Robin & Eliza
Coleman age 25 S
POB & POR
Spotsylvania; POM
Spotsylvania 31
Aug 1877 SPMR 22
Aug 1877 SPML

LEWIS, John s/o Peter
& Hannah Lewis
age 21y 5mo S
farmer POB & POR
Spotsylvania POC
& **COLLINS**,
Adeline d/o Henry
& Lydia Slaughter
age 23 W POB &
POR Spotsylvania
POC; POM
Spotsylvania 30
Dec 1869 SPMR 25
Dece 1869 SPML

LEWIS, Joseph s/o
Henry & Melissa
Lewis age 25 S
laborer POB & POR
Spotsylvania POC
& **JOHNSON**, Carrie
d/o William &
Mary Johnson age
18 S POB & POR
Spotsylvania POC;
POM Spotsylvania
2 Aug 1899 SPMR
SPML

LEWIS, Lee s/o
Thornton & Lucy
Ann Lewis age 21
S laborer POB &
POR Spotsylvania
POC & **GARNETT**,
Mary d/o Archie &
Lettie Garnett
age 20 S POB &
POR Spotsylvania
POC; POM
Sylvannus Colored
Baptist Ch,
Spotsylvania 25
Dec 1884 SPMR 24
Dec 1884 SPML

LEWIS, Liston L. s/o
Jackson & Maria
Lewis age 30 S
laborer POB & POR
Spotsylvania POC
& **JACKSON**, Annie
M. d/o William &
Ann Jackson age
27 S POB & POR
Spotsylvania POC;
POM Spotsylvania
11 Jan 1885 SPMR
SPML

LEWIS, Marcellus s/o
B.Lewis & M.King
age 28 W laborer
POB & POR
Spotsylvania POC
& **STEWART**, Mary
d/o R.& B.Stewart
age 20 W POB &
POR Spotsylvania
POC; POM
Spotsylvania 21
Oct 1879 SPMR 20
Oct 1879 SPML

LEWIS, Mills s/o
Martha Willis age
25 S laborer POB

& POR
Spotsylvania POC
& **FRAZER**, Ella
d/o William &
Mary Frazer age
25 S POB & POR
Spotsylvania POC;
POM Spotsylvania
9 Dec 1886 SPMR 6
Dec 1886 SPML
LEWIS, Ned s/o Charles
& Melvina Lewis
age 21 S laborer
POB & POR
Spotsylvania POC
& **LEVY**, Lovely
d/o Joseph & Leah
Levy age 21 S POB
& POR
Spotsylvania POC;
POM Spotsylvania
10 Aug 1882 SPMR
7 Aug 1882 SPML
LEWIS, Ned s/o John &
Kitty Lewis age
28 W farmer POB &
POR Spotsylvania
POC & **MINER**,
Kitty d/o John &
Esther Miner age
27 S POB & POR
Spotsylvania POC;
POM Spotsylvania
3 Mar 1867 SPMR 1
Mar 1867 SPML
LEWIS, P.B. s/o P.P.&
Pamelia Lewis age
24 S carpenter
POB Orange POR
Spotsylvania &
CUNNINGHAM, Mary
E. d/o A.B.& Amy
Cunningham age 19
S POB New York
POR Spotsylvania;
POM Spotsylvania
11 May 1884 SPMR
5 May 1884 SPML
LEWIS, Philip P. &
HERNDON, Pamelia;
25 Jun 1858 OML
LEWIS, Reuben s/o
Reuben & Rose
Lewis age 42 W

laborer POB
Spotsylvania POR
Orange POC &
CARTER, Betty d/o
Abram & America
Carter age 19 S
POB & POR
Spotsylvania POC;
POM Spotsylvania
28 Dec 1898 SPMR
27 Dec 1898 SPML
LEWIS, Reuben s/o
Sandy & Melvina
Lewis age 23 S
laborer POB & POR
Spotsylvania POC
& **LEWIS**, Eliza
d/o Henry &
Melissa Lewis age
27 S POB & POR
Spotsylvania POC;
POM Spotsylvania
12 Dec 1900 SPMR
SPML
LEWIS, Reuben s/o
Reuben & Rose
Lewis age 28 S
laborer POB
Spotsylvania POR
Orange POC &
SMITH, Julia d/o
Henry & Martha
Smith age 21 S
POB & POR
Spotsylvania POC;
POM Spotsylvania
31 Dec 1885 SPMR
24 Dec 1885 SPML
LEWIS, Robert L. s/o
John & Georgia
Lewis age 24 S
laborer POB & POR
Culpeper Co POC &
JOHNSON, Barbara
E. d/o Frank &
Martha Johnson
age 19 S POB &
POR Spotsylvania
POC; POM Zion
Hill Ch,
Spotsylvania 31
Aug 1898 SPMR 24
Aug 1898 SPM

LEWIS, Robert s/o A.& M.Lewis age 21 S laborer POB & POR Spotsylvania POC & **LEWIS**, Mary d/o Margaret Lewis age 18 S POB & POR Spotsylvania POC; POM Spotsylvania 28 Dec 1876 SPMR 27 Dec 1876 SPML

LEWIS, Samuel s/o Henry & Melissa Lewis age 21 S farmer POB & POR Spotsylvania POC & **SCOTT**, Phoebe d/o Robert & Winney Scott age 18 S POB & POR Spotsylvania POC; POM Spotsylvania C.H. 27 Sep 1894 SPMR SPML

LEWIS, Samuel s/o J.& C.Lewis age 29 S laborer POB & POR Spotsylvania POC & **WHITE**, Isabella d/o S.& M.White age 30 S POB & POR Spotsylvania POC; POM their home, Spotsylvania 16 Nov 1879 SPMR 15 Nov 1879 SPML

LEWIS, Sanoy, s/o Adison & Mary Lewis age 21 S laborer POB & POR Spotsylvania POC & **MINOR**, Melvina d/o Phil & Ann Minor age 21 S POB & POR Spotsylvania POC; POM Spotsylvania 8 Mar 1876 SPMR 6 Mar 1876 SPML

LEWIS, Stephen L. s/o Stephen & Mary J.Lewis age 48 W farmer POB & POR Spotsylvania & **WHARTON**, Carrie d/o Robert & Catherine Wharton age 24 S POB & POR Spotsylvania; POM Beech Grove, Ch, Spotsylvania 3 Jan 1900 SPMR 2 Jan 1900 SPML

LEWIS, Stephen L. s/o Stephen & M.Lewis age 27 S farmer POB & POR Spotsylvania & **LEWIS**, Sarah E. d/o Robert & Jane Lewis age 33 S POB & POR Spotsylvania; POM Spotsylvania 2 May 1878 SPMR SPML

LEWIS, Thomas N. s/o Fannie Comfort age 20 S laborer POB & POR Spotsylvania POC & **MINOR**, Jane d/o Sam & Evalina Minor age 221 S POB & POR Spotsylvania POC; POM Spotsylvania 22 Dec 1885 SPMR SPML

LEWIS, Thornton s/o Thornton & Mary Lewis age 23 S laborer POB & POR Spotsylvania POC & **LEWIS**, Mary d/o William & Malvina Lewis age 17 S POB & POR Spotsylvania POC; POM Spotsylvania 21 May 1876 SPMR 20 May 1876 SPML

LEWIS, Walter s/o Mary Tyler (nee Lewis) age 24 S laborer POB & POR

Spotsylvania POC & **MONTAGUE**, Alice d/o Joshua & Fanny Montague age 17 S POB & POR Spotsylvania POC; POM Spotsylvania 23 May 1900 SPMR SPML

LEWIS, William A. s/o William F.& Mary F.Lewis age 19 S farmer POB & POR Spotsylvania & **CLARKE**, Hannah F. d/o John H.& Martha F.Clarke age 21 S POB & POR Spotsylvania; POM Spotsylvania 17 May 1876 SPMR SPML

LEWIS, William J. s/o Melvina Lewis age 21 S laborer POB & POR Spotsylvania POC & **DUVALL**, Eula Lee d/o F.W.& Sarah Duvall age 18 S POB & POR Spotsylvania POC; POM Spotsylvania C.H. 12 Apr 1884 SPMR SPML

LEWIS, William L. s/o John Wesley Lewis & Ann H.Duvall age 30 S express agent POB Prince George Co,Md POR Orange & **COLVIN**, Elizabeth F. d/o Howard Colvin & Elizabeth Henshaw age 18 S POB Culpeper Co POR Orange; POM Gordonsville,Orange 12 Apr 1866 OMR OML

LEWIS, William s/o Addison & Sarah Lewis age 25 S farmer POB & POR Spotsylvania POC & **WARE**, Rachel d/o Jacob & Clara Stanard age 20 S POB & POR Spotsylvania POC: POM New Hope CH, Spotsylvania 22 Dec 1874 SPMR 20 Dec 1874 SPML

LEWIS, William s/o G.& S.Lewis age 21 S laborer POB & POR Spotsylvania POC & **BROWN**, Emma d/o I.& M.Brown age 19 S POB & POR Spotsylvnia POC; POM Spotsylvania 15 Jan 1880 SPMR 14 Jan 1880 SPML

LIGHTFOOT, John T. s/o John & Susan Lightfoot age 22 S farmer POB Madison Co POR Madison Co & **LACY**, Lucy L. d/o Maj.J.Horace & Bettie C.Lacy age 22 S POB Stafford POR Spotsylvania; POM Ellwood, Spotsylvania 25 Oct 1882 SPMR 16 Oct 1882 SPML

LINDSAY, Henry s/o Minor Lindsay & Ann Washington age 24 S POB & POR Orange POC & **MINOR**, Sarah d/o Thornton & Louisa Poindexter age 22 W POB Spotsylvania POR Orange POC; POM Orange 28 Aug 1867 OMR 27 Aug 1867 OML

LIPSCOMB, Anderson s/o A.& E.A.Lipscomb

age 45 W laborer POB Louisa Co POR Spotsylvania POC & **ROBINSON**, Amelia d/o C.& F.Robinson age 30 S POB & POR Spotsylvania POC; POM Branch Fork Ch, Spotsylvania 23 Feb 1879 SPMR 14 Feb 1879 SPML

LIPSCOMB, Ira D. s/o Ira E.& Ann F.Lipscomb age 25 S farmer POB & POR Spotsylvania & **ANDREWS**, Sallie S. d/o John S.& Molly Andrews age 21 S POB Orange POR Spotsylvania; POM Spotsylvania 13 Dec 1866 SPMR SPML

LIPSCOMB, William J. s/o Arthur B.Lipscomb & Mary A.Strother age 29 W painter POB Campbell Co POR Orange & **FAULCONER**, Dolly M. d/o Alfred Faulconer & Madalina Bocock age 32 S POB & POR Orange; POM Orange 28 Dec 1865 OMR 27 Dec 1865 OML

LITHGOW, William & **NASH**, Mary d/o Julia T.Nash; 19 Dec 1865 SPConsent

LITHGOW, William s/o Robert & Martha Lithgow age 28 S tinner POB Philadelphia,Pa POR Spotsylvania & **NASH**, Mary F. d/o John & Julia

Nash age 21 S POB Culpeper Co POR Spotsylvania; POM Spotsylvania 28 Dec 1865 SPMR 20 Dec 1865 SPML

LIVELY, Thomas A. s/o W.T. & Mary E. Lively age 21 S farmer POB Caroline Co POR Spotsylvania & **BOERSIG**, Lizzie d/o Anthony & Kate Boersig age 16 S POB Lapeer Co, Michigan POR Spotsylvania; POM Spotsylvania 8 Jul 1890 SPMR 5 Jul 1890 SPML

LLOYD, George H. s/o James & Eliza Lloyd age 20 S farmer POB & POR Madison Co & **MARTIN**, Christianna Mary d/o Jacob Riley & Mary Hicks age 20 W POB Spotsylvania POR Orange; POM Orange 17 Oct 1867 OMR OML

LOCKETT, Robert s/o Sam & Peggy Lockett age 23 S farm laborer POB & POR Orange POC & **MURPHY**, Kittie d/o Benja Murphy age 25 S POB & POR Orange POC; POM Orange 26 Dec 1867 OMR 21 Dec 1867 OML

LOMAX, E.Ernest s/o Barnett & Sallie Lomax age 26 S tinning POB & POR Spotsylvania POC & **CARTER**, Louisa d/o Patterson &

Fanny Carter age 25 S POB & POR Spotsylvania POC; POM Sylvana Ch, Spotsylvania; 18 Oct 1892 SPMR SPML

LOMAX, Frank Jet s/o Thomas M. & Jane Lomax age 27 S farmer POB & POR Fauquier Co & STEWART, Cornelia Josephine d/o James L.& Helen E.Stewart age 20 S POB & POR Spotsylvania; POM Spotsylvania 22 May 1873 SPMR 21 May 1873 SPML

LONG, Herbert M. s/o J.& M.Long age 29 S farmer POB & POR Spotsylvania & PARKER, Julia M. d/o E.& S.Parker age 21 S POB & POR Spotsylvania; POM Spotsylvania 28 Dec 1876 SPMR 27 Dec 1876 SPML

LONG, Hubbard M. s/o Jeremiah & Mary E.Long age 49 W farmer POB & POR Spotsylvania & TALLEY, Mattie J.C. d/o Joseph & Mattie Talley age 29 S POB & POR Spotsylvania; POM Spotsylvania 19 Jan 1897 SPMR 18 Jan 1897 SPML

LONG, John H. s/o Robert & Mary Long age 19 S farmer POB & POR Spotsylvania & CURTIS, Cleopatra d/o Charles & Jane Curtis age 16 S POB & POR Spotsylvania; POM Spotsylvania 8 Dec 1868 SPMR SPML

LOVE, Thomas S. s/o William & Julia J.Love age 29 S farmer POB Matayorce Co, Texas POR Spotsylvania & BAILEY, Georgia A. d/o Charles C.& Margarett Bailey age 28 S POB & POR Spotsylvania; POM Mill Dale, Spotsylvania 28 Feb 1865 SPMR 26 Feb 1865 SPML

LOVE, William B. s/o William C.& Mary E.Love age 47 S farmer POB District of Columbia POR Culpeper Co & HIGGINS, Mary U. s/o Walter & Almeda C.Higgins age 24 S POB York Co, Maine POR Spotsylvania; POM Spotsylvania 3 Jan 1885 SPMR 31 Dec 1884 SPML

LOWERY, James T. s/o William T.& Mary Lowry age 36 S merchant POB & POR Fredericksburg & BOWMAN, Nellie G. d/o Henry & Jennette Bowman age 23 S POB & POR Spotsylvania; POM Spotsylvania 28 Jan 1891 SPMR 26 Jan 1891 SPML

LOWRY, Robert s/o Edward Lowry &

Mary Wharton age
49 S wheelwright
POB Caroline Co
POR Orange &
WRIGHT, Sarah C.
d/o Jefferson
Wright & Lucy
Wright age 24 S
POB & POR Orange;
POM Orange 27 Nov
1862 OMR OML
LOWRY, Thomas s/o Ro.
& Mildred Lowry
age 29 S POB
Stafford POR
Spotsylvania &
JONES, Harriet S.
d/o Edward & Mary
Ann Jones age 22
S POB & POR
Spotsylvania; POM
Spotsylvania 26
Jan 1856 SPMR
LOYD, E.E. s/o Robert
E.& Rhoda Loyd
age 21 S farmer
POB & POR
Spotsylvania &
BROOKS, Nelia A.
d/o Tandy W.&
Maria Brooks age
18 S POB & POR
Spotsylvania; POM
Spotsylvania
C.H.15 Sep 1892
SPMR SPML
LOYD, R.M. s/o Robert
& Rhoda Loyd age
24 S miner POB &
POR Spotsylvania
& **BROOKS**, Eliza
d/o Luther & Ella
Brooks age 16 S
POB & POR
Spotsylvania; POM
Spotsylvania 28
Dec 1897 SPMR
SPML
LOYD, Robert E. s/o
Leonard & Mary
Loyd age 37 W POB
& POR
Spotsylvania &
LANE, Rhoda F.

d/o Waller H.&
Mary I.Lane age
20 S POB & POR
Spotsylvania; POM
Spotsylvania 1869
SPMR 5 Jul 1869
SPML
LUCAS, Arthur s/o Mack
& Ann Lucas age
23 S laborer POB
& POR Caroline Co
POC & **FRY**, Martha
Ann d/o Albert
French & Sarah
A.Wise age 23 S
POB Caroline Co
POR Spotsylvania
POC; POM
Spotsylvania 12
Feb 1885 SPRM 10
Feb 1885 SPML
LUCAS, Edmund s/o Jim
Lucas & Amy Nacy
age 25 S laborer
POB & POR Orange
POC & **WEAVER**,
Jane d/o Edmund
Weaver age 28 W
POB & POR Orange
POC; POM Orange
27 May 1866 OMR
21 May 1866 OML
LUCAS, George W. s/o
William B.&
Elizabeth Lucas
age 43 W
carpenter POB &
POR Henrico Co &
CHALMERS,
Margaret A. d/o
William & Eliza
Chalmers age 41
POB Scotland POR
Spotsylvania; POM
Spotsylvania 25
Sep 1895 SPMR 24
Sep 1895 SPML
LUCAS, George W. s/o
William B. &
Elizabeth Lucas
age 45 POR
Henrico Co.,Va. &
CHALMERS,
Margaret A. s/o

William & Eliza
Chalmers age 41
POR Spotsylvania
Co.; POM
Fredericksburg 25
Sep 1895 TCF
LUCAS, Harry s/o Henry
& Keziah Lucas
age 25 W POB &
POR Spotsylvania
POC & **JACKSON**,
Maria d/o Bird &
Annie Jackson age
26 W POB Caroline
Co POR
Spotsylvania POC;
POM Bethany Ch,
Spotsylvania 1
Sep 1867 SPMR 17
Aug 1867 SPML
LUCAS, Madison s/o
Mack & Ann Lucas
age 25 S laborer
POB & POR
Caroline Co POC &
HAILSTORK, Annie
d/o John & Mary
Hailstork age 18
S POB & POR
Spotsylvania POC;
POM Long Branch
Ch 11 Jan 1894
SPMR 9 Jan 1894
SPML
LUCAS, Robert L. s/o
James & Maria
Boggs age 22 S
labore POB
Richmond, Va POR
Spotsylvania POC
& **HUNTER**, Byrdie
B. d/o Harrison &
Mine Hunter age
21 S POB Caroline
Co POR
Spotsylvania POC;
POM Spotsylvania
30 Dec 1884 SPMR
20 Dec 1884 SPML
LUCK, Ira s/o Richard
& Ellen Luck age
46 W merchant POB
& POR
Spotsylvania &

OLIVER, Sarah d/o
Charles & Mary
Oliver age 33 S
POB Spotylvania
POR Spotsylvania;
POM Spotsylvania
14 Feb 1863
(according to the
ML) 13 Feb 1863
SPML
LUCK, John A. s/o John
A.H. & Judith
C.Luck age 23 S
farmer POB & POR
Spotsylvania &
SEAY, Adra A. d/o
James W.L. & Lucy
E.Seay age 20 S
POB & POR
Spotsylvania; POM
Spotsylvania 10
Jan 1888 SPMR 3
Jan 1888 SPML
LUCK, John M. s/o
Tarlton &
Elizabeth Luck
age 44 S mechanic
POR Spotsylvania
& **LUCK**, Barbara
A. d/o Ira J.&
Catherine Luck
age 20 S POB
Louisa Co POR
Spotsylvania; POM
Spotsylvania 2
Oct 1868 SPMR
SPML
LUCK, William F. s/o
Rich & Mary Luck
age 68 W farmer
POB Louisa Co POR
Spotsylvania &
BRUMLEY, Ann E.
d/o William & Ann
Brumley age 42 S
POB & POR
Spotsylvania; POM
Spotsylvania 30
Jan 1878 SPMR
SPML
LUCK, William J. s/o
William F. &
Sarah Luck age 25
S farmer POB &

POR Spotsylvania
& **EDENTON**, Rachel
D. d/o Stephen &
Huldah Edenton
age 23 S POB &
POR Spotsylvania;
POM Spotsylvania
28 Feb 1862 SPMR
SPML
LUCUS, William E. s/o
J.Dijarnette &
L.Lucus age 35 W
laborer POB & POR
Spotsylvania POC
& **WILLIAMS**,
Bettie d/o F(?) &
B.Williams age 33
S POB & POR
Spotsylvania POC;
POM their
residence,
Spotsylvania 27
Nov 1879 SPMR 24
Nov 1879 SPML
LUMPKIN, John W. s/o
James M.& Matilda
Lumpkin age 24 S
farmer POB & POR
Spotsylvania &
CASH, Mary E. d/o
John B.&
Elizabeth Cash
age 22 S POB &
POR Spotsylvania;
POM Spotsylvania
23 Dec 1869 SPMR
20 Dec 1869 SPML
LUMSDEN, Arthur s/o
Richard & Sarah
A. Lumsden age 22
S miner POB & POR
Louisa Co &
FAULKNER, Beulah
E. d/o J.S.&
Alice Faulkner
age 18 S POB &
POR Spotsylvania;
POM Spotsylvania
17 Jul 1897 SPMR
SPML
LUMSDEN, James F. s/o
Richard M.Lumsden
& Martha Hilman
age 25 S farmer

POB Spotsylvania
POR Orange &
JACOBS, Annie E.
d/o George Jacobs
& Catharine Smith
age 24 S POB &
POR Orange; POM
Orange 20 Dec
1866 OMR 18 Dec
1866 OML
LUMSDEN, James T. s/o
T.H.& S.Lumsden
age 22 S farmer
POB & POR
Spotsylvania &
SORRELL, Virginia
C. d/o John &
S.E.Sorrell age
22 S POB & POR
Spotsylvania; POM
Spotsylvania 8
Apr 1880 SPMR 5
Apr 1880 SPML
LUMSDEN, W.A. s/o
R.M.& M.A.Lumsden
age 23 S
shoemaker POB &
POR Spotsylvania
& **LUCK**, S.E. d/o
R.A.& J.Luck age
28 S POB & POR
Spotsylvania; 26
Oct 1859 SPMR
LUMSDEN, William A.
s/o Richard M. &
Martha A. Lumsden
age 23 S
carpenter POB &
POR Spotsylvania
& **LUCK**, Lucy E.
d/o Richard A. &
Letitia Luck age
28 S POB & POR
Spotsylvania; POM
Spotsylvania 20
Oct 1859 SPMR 17
Oct 1859 SPML
LUMSDEN, William L.
s/o Thomas H.&
Sarina Lumsden
age 22 S farmer
POB & POR
Spotsylvania &
ALMOND, Malissa

E. d/o Lewis A.&
Susan F.Almond
age 20 S POB &
POR Spotsylvania;
POM Spotsylvania
21 Apr 1872 SPMR
19 Apr 1872 SPML
LYLES, John A. s/o
William H.& Ann
E.Lyles age 26 S
shoe cutter POB
Fairfax Co POR
Fredericksburg &
WHARTON, Nannie
T. d/o Robert &
Kate Wharton age
18 S POB & POR
Spotsylvania; POM
Beech Grove Ch,
Spotsylvania 14
Dec 1897 SPMR 10
Dec 1897 SPML
LYNCH, George W. s/o
Jeremiah Lynch &
Cresy Simmons age
25 S engineer on
O.& A.railroad
POB York Co, Pa
POR Alexandria,
Va & GOODWIN,
Lucy A. d/o John
Goodwin & Mary
Arnold age 23 S
POB Prince
William Co POR
Orange; POM
Gordonsville,
Orange 10 May
1866 OMR 9 May
1866 OML
MADDOX, S.G. s/o
William G.& Mary
A.Maddox age 21 S
farmer POB & POR
Hanover Co &
BEAZLEY, Mary E.
d/o Henry &
Harriet Beazley
age 20 S POB &
POR Spotsylvania;
POM Spotsylvania
22 Dec 1870 SPMR
5 Dec 1870 SPML

MADISON, James A.
physician &
HEIDEN, Lucy M.
d/o Joseph
Heiden; POM
Orange 2 Jan 1851
OMR 1 Jan 1851
OML
MADISON, James B. s/o
Dabney &
Elizabeth Madison
age 32 S school
teacher POB
Albemarle Co &
PAYNE, Annie S.
d/o Daniel &
Frances Payne age
21 S POB
Albemarle Co; POM
Orange 28 Jun
1860 OMR 23 Jun
1860 OML
MADISON, Robert L.
physician POR
Petersburg, Va &
LEE, Lititia R.;
POM Orange 3 May
1853 OMR 2 May
1853 OML
MALICHI, Augustus &
BANKHEAD,
Margaret d/o
Henry Bankhead;
11 Jun 1869
SPConsent
MALLORY, John s/o John
& Frances Mallory
age 42 W mechanic
POB Orange &
TERRILL,
Elizabeth d/o
Edmond & Susan
Terrill age 45 S
POB Orange; POM
Orange 13 Nov
1860 OMR 6 Nov
1860 OML
MALONE, George A. s/o
James Malone &
Ellen Cunningham
age 22 S
machinist POB
Saline Co, Mo POR
St.Louis, Mo &

SMITH, Frances S. d/o Ambrose A.Smith & Catharine Jacobs age 24 S POB & POR Orange; POM Orange 29 Sep 1864 OMR 27 Sep 1864 OML

MALONEY, Matthew J. s/o John & Ann Maloney age 32 S wholesale liquor dealer POB England POR Bridgeport, Connecticut & **WHITE**, Juliet d/o John & Juliet White age 21 S POB Brooklyn, Long Island POR Spotsylvania; POM Altoona near Fredericksburg 28 Oct 1891 SPMR 27 Oct 1891 SPML

MANN, John s/o John & Ann Mann age 29 S lawyer POB James City Co POR Petersburg & **BERNARD**, Catherine Frances d/o David Meade & Sally Ann Bernard age 18 S POB Petersburg POR Orange; POM Orange 8 Nov 1860 OMR 7 Nov 1860 OML

MANSFIELD, Reuben s/o John Mansfield & Lydia White age 34 W carpenter POB & POR Orange POC & **BANKS**, Lucy d/o Garrett Johnson & Nelly Berkeley age 30 W POB & POR Orange POC: POM Orange 17 Aug 1867 OMR 9 Aug 1867 OML

MARSHAL, William J. s/o Henry & N.Marshall age 29 S farmer POB & POR Spotsylvania & **THORNTON**, Indiana J. d/o Lucy J.Thornton age 20 W POB Caroline Co POR Spotsylvania; POM Spotsylvania 4 Aug 1880 SPMR 2 Aug 1880 SPML

MARSHALL, Archalus Lewis s/o James & Elizabeth Marshall age 22 S merchant POB Orange POR Barboursville & **FITZHUGH**, Estell d/o Madison & Mary F.Fitzhugh age 18 S POB Green Co POR Barboursville; POM Orange 22 May 1855 OMR

MARSHALL, Frank F. s/o A.L.& Estelle Marshall age 29 S farmer POB Culpeper Co POR Spotsylvania & **MORTON**, Bessie W. d/o Jeremiah & Charlotte W.Morton age 33 S POB Culpeper Co POR Spotsylvania; POM Spotsylvania 30 Apr 1899 SPMR 28 Apr 1899 SPML

MARSHALL, Hamilton M. s/o Joseph & Caroline Marshall age 22 S farmer POB Spotsylvania POR Stafford & **BROWN**, Susie d/o Thomas & Mary

Brown age 22 S POB Orange POR Spotsylvania; POM Spotsylvania 17 Aug 1884 SPMR 16 Aug 1884 SPML

MARSHALL, Robert W. s/o Henry & Nancy Marshall age 40 S farmer POB Caroline Co POR Spotsylvania & **HOCKADAY**, Mattie N. d/o W.W.& Catherine Hockaday age 22 S POB & POR Spotsylvania; POM Spotsylvania 12 Jun 1895 SPMR 11 Jun 1895 SPML

MARSHALL, Thomas A. s/o James & Elizabeth Marshall age 22 S POB Orange POR Barboursville & **FITZHUGH**, Louisa C. d/o James M.& Mary F.Fitzhugh age 17 S POB Green Co POR Barboursville; POM Orange 24 Dec 1857 OMR 23 Dec 1857 OML

MARTIN, A.J. s/o Alex & Sarah Martin age 49 W miller POB & POR Spotsylvania & **GARDNER**, Martha V. d/o Charles & Jane Gardiner age 40 W POB & POR Spotsylvania; POM Spotsylvania C.H. 18 Feb 1890 SPMR SPML

MARTIN, A.Payne s/o Lemuek & Eliza Martin age 34 S farmer POB & POR Culpeper Co &
SOUTHWORTH, Susan C. d/o James & Perlina Southworth age 24 S POB & POR Spotsylvania; POM Spotsylvania 24 Dec 1871 SPMR 18 Dec 1871 SPML

MARTIN, Alex J. s/o Alex & Sarah Martin age 32 S miller POB & POR Spotsylvania & **BARTLETT**, Sarah J. d/o James & Sarah A.Bartlett age 24 S POB & POR Spotsylvania; POM Poplar Spring, Spotsylvania 5 Dec 1872 SPMR 2 Dec 1872 SPML

MARTIN, James H. s/o Henry P.& Mary E.Martin age 32 S blacksmith POB Caroline Co POR Orange & **FOSTER**, Susie Z. d/o William E.& Engida Foster age 22 S POB & POR Spotsylvania; POM Unionville,Orange Co 23 Nov 1887 SPMR 21 Nov 1887 SPML

MARTIN, James s/o William & Malinda Martin age 25 S Cooper POB & POR Orange & **MARTIN**, Mary Ann d/o Thomas & Sarah Martin age 25 S POB & POR Orange; POM Orange 17 Oct 1854 OMR

MARTIN, James W. s/o Thornton & Martha A. Martin of Spotsylvania Co.

age 38 POR
Spotsylvania Co.
& **BALLARD**, Mary
Eliza d/o Thomas
& Mary Ballard of
Spotsylvania Co.
age 23 POR
Spotsylvania Co.;
POM
Fredericksburg 11
Dec 1898 TCF

MARTIN, Mallory s/o
Thomas & Sarah
Martin age 22 S
carpenter POB &
POR Orange &
BROWN, Lucy Ann
d/o John & Martha
Brown age 21 S
POB & POR Orange;
POM Orange 18 Oct
1857 OMR 17 Oct
1857 OML

MARTIN, Mallory s/o
Thomas Martin &
Sarah Collins age
31 W carpenter
POB & POR Orange
& **MARTIN** Lucilla
d/o William
Martin & Malinda
Faulconer age 21
S POB & POR
Orange; POM
Orange 28 Dec
1865 OMR 25 Dec
1865 OML

MARTIN, P.H. s/o
Patrick & Annie
Martin age 29 S
farmer POB New
York State POR
Stafford &
HASSETT, Alice J.
d/o Bartholomew &
Julia Hassett age
21 S POB Virginia
POR Spotsylvania;
POM St.Mary's Ch,
Fredericksburg 10
Nov 1886 FMR 6
Nov 1886 SPML

MARTIN, Richard H. s/o
Samuel & Eliza
Martin age 21 S
farmer POB
Fauquier Co POR
Spotsylvania &
FAULCONER, Bettie
Lewis d/o Richard
G.& Jane Swift
age 27 W POB &
POR Spotsylvania;
POM Spotsylvania
2 Dec 1869 SPMR
30 Nov 1869 SPML

MARTIN, Robert M. s/o
William & Malinda
Martin age 23 S
cooper POB & POR
Orange & **WOOD**,
Ophelia E. d/o
Thomas & Frances
Wood age 17 S POB
& POR Orange; POM
Orange 27 Oct
1859 OMR OML

MARTIN, William C. s/o
Zedekiah &
Elizabeth Martin
age 60 W farmer
POB Middlesex Co
POR Spotsylvania
& **STEPHENS**, S.S.
d/o John T.&
Susan Powell age
55 W POB & POR
Spotsylvania; POM
Spotsylvania
C.H.3 May 1894
SPMR 30 Apr 1894
SPML

MARTIN, William F. s/o
Samuel & Eliza
Martin age 34 S
farmer POB
Fauquier Co POR
Spotsylvania &
LEWIS, Ann Eliza
d/o Fleetwood &
Jane E. Lewis age
20 S POB & POR
Spotsylvania; POM
Spotsylvania 16
Jan 1873 SPMR 13
Jan 1873 SPML

MARTIN, William H. s/o
James Martin &

Sidney Willoughby age 48 W farmer POB Spotsylvania POR Orange & **POWELL**, Elizabeth H. d/o William Powell age 28 S POB Spotsylvania POR Orange; POM Orange 15 Dec 1864 OMR 5 Dec 1864 OML
MARTIN, William H. s/o Thomas & Sarah Martin age 24 S carpenter POB & POR Orange & **BROWN**, Sarah F. d/o John G.& Martha F.Brown age 17 S POB Madison POR Orange; POM Orange 23 Oct 1855 OMR
MARTIN, William J. age 22 S carpenter POR Orange & **KENNEDY**, Lucy M. d/o Hiram P.& Mary Kennedy age 27 S POB & POR Orange; POM Orange 3 Dec 1857 OMR 1 Dec 1857 OML
MASON, Charles Van s/o Charles & E.Van Mason age 28 S POB Pennsylvania POR N.Y.City ship carpenter & **BULLOCK**, L.V. d/o R.W.& M.E.Bullock age 19 S POB & POR Spotsylvania; POM Spotsylvania 6 Jan 1881 SPMR 3 Jan 1881 SPML
MASON, John E. s/o Sanders Mason & Catherine Jones age 19 S farmer POB & POR Orange & **BROWN**, Martha C. d/o John Brown & Martha F. Holbert age 22 S POB & POR Orange; POM Orange 20 Dec 1866 OMR OML
MASON, Richard R. s/o Charles & Lucy Mason age 21 S farmer POB & POR Orange & **CANADY**, Ann C. d/o James & Ann Canaday age 18 S POB & POR Orange; POM Orange 5 Apr 1855 OMR
MASON, Richard s/o Peter & Lucy Mason age 30 S mechanic POB Fauquier Co POR Orange & **MASON**, Lucy L. d/o Charles & Lucy Mason age 24 S POB & POR Orange; POM Orange 29 Dec 1858 OMR 27 Dec 1858 OML
MASON, Sanders s/o George Mason & Mildred Sanders age 62 W farmer POB & POR Orange & **BROOKING**, Susan M. d/o Benjamin Sanders & Nancy Jones age 57 W POB & POR Orange; POM Orange 5 Jun 1862 OMR 2 Jun 1862 OML
MASON, William G. & **SANDERS**, Lucy Ann; POM Orange 14 Dec 1852 OMR OML
MASSEY, C.Rosser s/o A.W.& Lucy M.Massey age 29 S physician POB & POR Spotsylvania

& **COLBERT**, Inez
E. d/o R.W.& Mary
E.Colbert age 21
S POB & POR
Spotsylvania; POM
Massaponax
Baptist Ch,
Spotsylvania 17
Feb 1897 SPMR 15
Feb 1897 SPML
MASSEY, William C. s/o
James H.&
J.Z.Massey age 24
S farmer POB &
POR Spotsylvania
& **COLEMAN**, Anna
A. d/o F.H.&
A.E.Coleman age
18 S POB & POR
Spotsylvania; POM
Spotsylvania 17
Jul 1878 SPMR 9
Jul 1878 SPML
MASTIN, Allen M. s/o
Jackson &
S.M.Mastin age 35
S farmer POB &
POR Spotsylvania
& **HALL**, Irene d/o
Horace C.& Lucy
Hall age 20 S POB
& POR
Spotsylvania; POM
Spotsylvania C.H.
8 Nov 1888 SPMR
SPML
MASTIN, Charles W. s/o
Benjamin & Betty
Mastin age 24 S
blacksmith POB &
POR Spotsylvania
& **HALL**, Ella d/o
Horace C.& Jane
E.Hall age 18 S
POB & POR
Spotsylvania; POM
Spotsylvania
C.H.2 Nov 1892
SPMR 1 Nov 1892
SPML
MASTIN, Edgar T. s/o
Thomas J.&
Elizabeth Mastin
age 25 S farmer

POB & POR
Spotsylvania &
LUMSDEN, Virginia
A. d/o Thomas H.&
Laura Lumsdon age
24 S POB & POR
Spotsylvania; POM
Spotsylvania 27
Dec 1866 SPMR 26
Dec 1866 SPML
MASTIN, Oscar J. s/o
Thomas J.&
ELizabeth Mastin
age 28 W mechanic
POB & POR
Spotsylvania &
MASSEY, Angelina
B. d/o William
B.& Maria Massey
age 23 S POB &
POR Spotsylvania;
POM Spotsylvania
13 Apr 1873 SPMR
8 Apr 1873 SPML
MATTESON, James B. s/o
Asa & Lydia
Matteson age 30 W
locomotive
engineer POB
Otsego Co, N.Y.
POR Summers
Co,W.Va & **MASTIN**,
Alice T. d/o
Benjamin &
Elizabeth
A.Mastin age 29 S
POB & POR
Spotsylvania; POM
Spotsylvania 31
Oct 1888 SPMR 29
Oct 1888 SPML
MATTHEWS, Drury C. &
ROBINSON, Martha
E.; 26 May 1856
OML
MAY, Horace G. s/o
William & Sarah
B.May age 24 S
merchant POB
Sullivan Co,
Penn. POR
Caroline Co &
RYERSON, Ada B.
d/o Peter F.&

Hetty A.Ryerson age 17 S POB New Jersey POR Caroline Co; POM Spotsylvania 2 Sep 1890 SPMR SPML

MAYNARD, James Henry s/o J.S. & Martha R.Maynard age 27 S minister POB Surry Co POR Spotsylvania & **HOLLADAY**, Mary Catherine d/o T.N.& S.B.Holladay age 21 S POB & POR Spotsylvania; POM Spotsylvania 2 May 1875 SPMR 2 Apr 1875 SPML

MAYO, William P.s/o Allen L.Mayo & **ROUTT**, Dorenda A.; 13 Oct 1851 OML

McALISTER, Richard W. s/o Henry L.& Martha J.McAlister age 21 S farmer POB Louisa Co POR Spotsylvania & **THOMAS**, Mary J. d/o John H.& Cleopatra Thomas age 20 S POB & POR Spotsylvania; POM Spotsylvani 24 Dec 1895 SPMR SPML

McALLISTER Emeul A. s/o Henry & Martha McAllister age 21 S lawyer POB Hanover Co POR Spotsylvania & **MORRIS**, Eliza Ann d/o George W.& Miley Morris age 27 S POB Caroline Co POR Spotsylvania; POM Spotsylvania 26 Mar 1890 SPMR 24 Mar 1890 SPML

McALLISTER, E. s/o H.L.& Martha McAllister age 29 W machinist POB Hanover Co POR Spotsylvania & **JETT**, Annie D. d/o Robert & Maria L.Jett age 23 S POB & POR Spotsylvania; POM Spotsylvania 13 Dec 1899 SPMR SPML

McALLISTER, Edwin C. s/o William & C.McAllister age 23 S farmer POB & POR Louisa Co & **HOCKADAY**, Sarah J. d/o R.L.& F.M. Hockaday age 21 S POB & POR Spotsylvania; POM Spotsylvania 29 Mar 1880 SPMR SPML

McCALLEY, Albert M. s/o William & Ethelinda R.McCalley age 27 S farmer POB & POR Spotsylvania & **WILKERSON**, Victoria d/o W.A.& Leah A.Wilkerson age 22 S POB & POR Spotsylvania; POM Mill Garden 22 Dec 1892 SPMR SPML

McCALLEY, James W. s/o William C.& F.M.McCalley age 29 S farmer POB & POR Spotsylvania & **DAY**, Nancie E. d/o John & Mary Day age 22 S POB Buckingham POR

Spotsylvania; POM Spotsylvania 19 Jan 1876 SPMR 18 Jan 1876 SPML

McCALLEY, Joseph M. s/o William C.& Ethalinda McCalley age 26 S carpenter POB & POR Spotsylvania & **BAKER**, Maria L. d/o B.W.& M.A.Baker age 20 S POB Louisa Co POR Spotsylvania; POM Hartwood, Spotsylvania 22 Sep 1885 SPMR 21 Sep 1885 SPML

MCCARTY, Albert J. s/o Nathaniel & Annie McCarty age 38 S farmer POB & POR Spotsylvania & **MAXWELL**, Ella d/o Charles & Ellen Maxwell age 23 S POB New Castle Co, Delaware POR Spotsylvania; POM Spotsylvania 16 Apr 1874 SPMR 14 Apr 1874 SPML

McCLARY, Charles L. s/o Tandy B.McClary & Mary F.Jacobs age 24 S blacksmith POB Orange POR Madison Co & **BLEDSOE**, Lucy d/o John Bledsoe & Peggy Perry age 22 S POB & POR Orange; POM Orange 26 Jul 1866 OMR 25 Jul 1866 OML

McCLARY, James F. s/o William & Mary McClary age 22 S boot & shoemaker POB & POR Orange & **BICKERS**, Susan A. d/o Proctor & Lucy Bickers age 24 S POB & POR Orange; POM Orange 16 Nov 1854 OMR

McCLURE, David s/o L.D.& Elizabeth E.McClure age 46 W renovating feathers(?) POB Davis Co, Kentucky POR Louisa Co & **WHEELER**, Alice A. d/o James A. & Ann Wheeler age 30 S POB & POR Spotsylvania; POM Spotsylvania C.H. 14 Apr 1890 SPMR SPML

McCOMRICK (aka McComrack), William & **NEWMAN**, Wilhelmia; POM Orange 8 Jun 1852 OMR OML

McCRACKEN, Patrick s/o Thomas & Ellen McCracken age 28 S farmer POB Ireland POR Spotsylvania & **DICKEY**, Elizabeth B. d/o James & Joanna Dickey age 41 S POB Nelson Co POR Orange; POM Orange 2 Mar 1857 OMR 28 Feb 1857 OML

McCRACKER, Michael & **ALMOND**, Martha Jane M.; 16 Dec 1856 OML

McDONALD, John s/o Thomas & Mary McDonald age 28 S conductor POB Fauquier Co POR Shenandoah Co & **CULLEN**, Mariettad/o

George & Barbara Ann Cullen age 24 S POB Shenandoah Co POR Orange; POM Orange 18 Nov 1857 OMR 17 Nov 1857 OML

McGEE, Ebenezer, D. s/o Ebenezer & Louisa McGee age 25 S farmer POB & POR Spotsylvania & **PERRY**, Berta A. d/o Edward & Sarah A.Perry age 18 S POB & POR Spotsylvania; POM Spotsylvania 29 Dec 1886 SPMR 27 Dec 1886 SPML

McGOINES, George s/o Thomas & Eliza McGoines age 35 W messenger in U.S.T. POB Ann Arundel Co,Md POR Washington D.C. POC & **COATES**, Betty L. d/o Warfield & Matilda Coates age 27 S POB & POR Spotsylvania POC; POM Spotsylvania 18 Aug 1887 SPMR SPML

McGUIRE, Richard age 29 POR Potomac, Va. & **SISSON**, Babe age 30 POR Potomac,Va.; POM Fredericksburg 28 Nov 1898 TCF

McINTOSH, Jacob s/o Albert McIntosh & Frances Ellis age 21 S laborer/farmer POB & POR Orange POC & **WASHINGTON**, Martha age 19 S POB & POR Orange POC; POM Orange 12 Aug 1866 OMR 11 Aug 1866 OML

McKENNEY, Addison L. s/o C.& F.McKenney age 51 W farmer POB & POR Spotsylvania & **THACKER**, Eliza M. d/o Charles & Malinda Beazley age 51 W POB & POR Spotsylvania; POM Caroline Co 11 Feb 1881 SPMR 7 Feb 1881 SPML

McKENNEY, John F. s/o Charles S.& Mary P.McKenney age 27 S farmer POB Shirley, Va POR Petersburg, Va & **JERRELL**, Annie V. d/o T.J.& M.S.Jerrell age 17 S POB Caroline Co POR Spotsylvania; POM Spotsylvania 20 Jul 1899 SPMR 18 Jul 1899 SPML

McMULLAN, Thomas Walker s/o James & Frances McMullen age 22 farmer POB Green Co & **BELL**, Eliza Ann d/o Francis (dec) & Mary Bell age 21 POB Orange; POM Orange 8 Feb 1854 OMR 4 Feb 1854 OML

McMULLEN, Isaac Newton s/o John & Peachy McMullen age 23 S teacher POB & POR Green Co & **BOSTON**, Annie Bettie d/o William B. & Sally Boston age 22 S POB & POR Orange; POM

Orange 29 May 1860 OMR 25 May 1860 OML

McWHIRT, Charles H. s/o George & Kate McWhirt age 25 S blacksmith POB Caroline Co POR Spotsylvania & **OLIVER**, Annie d/o Chester B.& Virginia Oliver age 22 S POB & POR Spotsylvania; POM Spotsylvania 20 Aug 1898 SPMR SPML.

McWHIRT, Joseph s/o George & Catherine McWhirt age 25 S POB & POR Caroline Co & **PAYNE**, Mary S. d/o Paircen F.& Mary S.Payne age 23 S POB & POR Spotsylvania; POM Spotsylvania 26 Dec 1889 SPMR 25 Dec 1889 SPML

McWHIRT, Walter s/o Silas & A.McWhirt age 27 S farmer POB & POR Spotsylvania & **OWENS**, Anne M. d/o Warren & S.Owens age 21 S POB & POR Spotsylvania; POM Fredericksburg 20 Feb 1878 FMR 18 Feb 1878 SPML

McWHIRT, Willard A. s/o Silas & Agnes McWhirt age 24 S farmer POB & POR Spotsylvania & **PEMBERTON**, Fanny d/o George & Ellen Butzner age 28 W POB & POR Spotsylvania; POM Salem Ch,

Spotsylvania 6 Dec 1876 SPMR 4 Dec 1876 SPML

MEADE, James N. s/o Madison Meade & Sarah E.Robinson age 30 S carpenter POB Louisa Co POR Orange **LANCASTER**, Eliza A. d/o John Lancaster & Malissa Brightwell age 25 S POB & POR Orange; POM Orange 19 Dec 1865 OMR 15 Dec 1865 OML

MEADE, Richard N. s/o Madison Meade & Sarah A, Robinson age 27 S farmer POB Louisa Co POR Orange & **LANCASTER**, Amanda C. d/o John Lancaster & Malicia Brightwell age 24 S POB & POR Orange; POM Orange 3 Oct 1867 OMR 2 Oct 1867 OML

MECHAM, Cornelius s/o Edmund & Ann Mecham age 23 S merchant & clerk POB New Orleans POR Fredericksburg & **FISHER**, Mary Ann d/o Richard & Catherine Philips age 36 W POB Orange POR Spotsylvania; POM Fredericksburg (by a Catholic priest) 11 Dec 1865 FMR 2 Dec 1865 SPML

MENDENHALL, Albert S.
s/o John Wilson &
Hannah Mendenhall
age 41 S teacher
POB Savannah,
Georgia POR near
Barboursville &
ROACH, Sarah Ann
d/o Williamson &
Sarah Ann Roach
age 22 S POB &
POR Orange; POM
Orange 23 Oct
1858 OMR OML

MERCER, Isaac s/o K.&
J.Mercer age 27 S
laborer POB & POR
Spotsylvania POC
& LEWIS, Annie
d/o Charles &
M.Lewis age 21 S
POB & POR
Spotsylvania POC;
POM Spotsylvania
10 Mar 1881 SPMR
7 Mar 1881 SPML

MERCER, John s/o
Keeling & Judy
Mercer age 25 S
laborer POB & POR
Spotsylvania POC
& CHEW, Lucy F.
d/o Tennant &
Emily Chew age 21
S POB & POR
Spotsylvania POC;
POM Spotsylvania
12 Feb 1874 SPMR
9 Feb 1874 SPML

MERCER, Nelson s/o
Keelon & Judah
Mercer age 23 S
farmer POB & POR
Spotsylvania POC
& COLEMAN, Alice
d/o Major & Eliza
Coleman age 21 S
POB & POR
Spotsylvania POC;
POM Spotsylvania
16 Feb 1882 SPMR
11 Feb 1882 SPML

MERCER, Walker s/o
Minor & Lucy

J.Mercer age 21y
6mo S farmer POB
& POR
Spotsylvania POC
& WORMLEY, Rose
d/o Tarlton &
Elzie Wormley age
19 S POB & POR
Spotsylvania POC:
POM Newland,
Spotsylvania 30
Mar 1873 SPMR 29
Mar 1873 SPML

MEREDITH, Jaquelin M.
s/o Reuben & Mary
Meredith age 22 S
farmer POB
Hanover Co POR
Stafford &
BANKHEAD, Ellen
d/o William &
Dorothea Bankhead
age 19 S POB
Caroline Co POR
Orange; POM
Orange 5 Jan 1858
OMR OML

MERSEREAU, Edgar s/o
C.B.& Deborah
Mersereau age 45
W steamboat pilot
POB Richmond
Co,New York POR
Spotsylvania &
SNELLINGS,
Columbia J. d/o
William A.& Mary
A. Snellings age
21 S POB Stafford
POR Spotsylvania;
POM Spotsylvania
12 Feb 1888 SPMR
9 Feb 1888 SPML

METZ, Philips J. s/o
John & Elizabeth
E. Metz age 24 S
machinist POB
Pennsylvania POR
Spotsylvania &
DICKINSON, Emma
L. d/o Thomas H.
& Sarah
E.Dickinson age
18 S POB & POR

Spotsylvania; POM
17 Jun 1874 SPMR
16 Jun 1874 SPML
MICHIE, James s/o
Lewis Michie &
Rachel Thomson
age 25 S
r.r.laborer POB
Louisa Co POR
Orange POC &
WALKER, Jane d/o
Joe Walker POB &
POR Orange POC;
POM Orange 23 Sep
1867 OMR OML
MICKENS, Addison s/o
James & Pattie
Mickens age 23 S
POB & POR
Spotsylvania POC
& **COLEMAN**, Lina
d/o Henry &
Louisa Coleman
age 20 S POB &
POR Spotsylvania
POC; POM
Spotsylvania 14
Dec 1882 SPMR 13
Dec 1882 SPML
MICKS, William W. s/o
Dr.William G.&
Cornelia Micks
age 35 W
bookkeeper POB
Clinton, North
Carolina POR
Spotsylvania C.H.
& **CRUTCHFIELD**,
Annie W. d/o
Corbin & Mattie
M.Crutchfield age
22 S POB & POR
Spotsylvania; POM
Spotsylvania C.H.
30 Dec 1886 SPMR
28 Dec 1886 SPML
MILLER, Andrew J. s/o
John & Anna
Miller age 28 S
POB Orange POR
Mobile, Alabama &
HANSBROUGH,
Bettie H. d/o
A.H.&

E.C.Hansbrough
age 24 S POB
Culpeper POR
Orange C.H.; POM
Orange 20 Oct
1859 OMR 19 Oct
1859 OML
MILLER, F.Theodore s/o
J.G.& W.Miller
age 26 S
photographer POB
Michigan POR
Fredericksburg &
MORRISON, Emma J.
d/o Moses & Mary
Morrison age 23 S
POB Delaware POR
Spotsylvania; POM
Presbyterian Ch,
Fredericksburg 7
Sep 1869 FMR 6
Sep 1869 SPML
MILLER, Henry s/o John
& Mary Miller age
29 S gardner POB
Germany POR
Orange & **SKINNER**,
Leanna d/o John
Skinner & ____
Webb age 30 S POB
& POR Orange; POM
Orange 5 Jun 1867
OMR 1 Jun 1867
OML
MILLER, William H. s/o
Henry & Sarah
Miller age 44 W
farmer POB
Caroline Co POR
Spotsylvania &
POUND, Lula d/o
O.W.& Mary
D.Pound age 21 S
POB Caroline Co
POR Spotsylvania;
POM Zion M.E.Ch
S., Spotsylvania
15 Dec 1891 SPMR
12 Dec 1891 SPML
MILLS, G.J. s/o T.M.&
M.S.Mills age 26
S engineer POB
Orange POR
Clifton Forge,Va

& **BULLOCK**, Minnie
R. d/o Dr.R.M.&
A.E.Bullock age
22 S POB & POR
Spotsylvania; POM
Spotsylvania 16
Dec 1886 SPMR 10
Dec 1886 SPML
MILLS, J.W. s/o W.T. &
A.Mills age 28 W
wheelwright POB
Spotsylvaia POR
Fredericksburg &
WHITE, Maggie d/o
W.A.& H.S.White
age 22 S POB &
POR Spotsylvania;
POM Spotsylvania
17 Feb 1876 SPMR
14 Feb 1876 SPML
MILLS, John B. s/o
J.W.& Eveline
Mills age 30 S
farmer POB
Hanover Co POR
Hanover Co &
McGEHEE,A.T. d/o
A.S. &
M.J.McGehee age
22 S POB Orange
POR Spotsylvania;
POM Spotsylvania
9 Feb 1882 SPMR
27 Jan 1882 SPML
MILLS, Thomas M. POB
Louisa Co &
GRAVES, Mary
S.(?); 21 Aug
1852 OML
MINER, Charles s/o
Willis & Mary
Miner age 26 S
POB Cherry Grove,
Spotsylvania POR
Spotsylvania POC
& **MINER**, Anna d/o
Joshua & Eliza
Miner age 28 S
POB & POR
Spotsylvania POC;
POM Spotsylvania
3 Jun 1886 SPMR
SPML

MINION, John M. &
SCOTT, Elizabeth
ward of George
Jacobs; 20 Dec
1852 OML
MINOR, Allen s/o Philo
& Ann Minor age
24 S farmer POB &
POR Spotsylvania
POC & **BROOKS**,
Mary Frances d/o
Allen & Sarah
Brooks age 21 S
POB & POR
Spotsylvania POC:
POM Spotsylvania
8 Mar 1873 SPMR 4
Mar 1873 SPML
MINOR, Cato s/o Joshua
& Margaret Minor
age 24 S laborer
POB & POR
Spotsylvania POC
& **BROWN**, Mollie
d/o Easter Brown
age 17 S POB &
POR Spotsylvania
POC; POM
Spotsylvania 27
Mar 1890 SPMR
SPML
MINOR, James H. s/o
James & Bella
Minor age 21 S
laborer POB & POR
Spotsylvania POC
& **BROWN**, Julia
d/o Isaac & Maria
Brown age 21 S
POB & POR
Spotsylvania POC;
POM Spotsylvania
(at their
residence) 1 Jan
1891 SPMR 31 Dec
1890 SPML
MINOR, James s/o
Jeffrey & Abbie
Minor age 32 W
laborer POB & POR
Spotsylvania POC
& **BURLEY**, Sarah
d/o Ab. & Polly
Burley age 25 S

POB & POR Spotsylvania POC; POM Spotsylvania C.H. 20 Sep 1888 SPMR SPML

MINOR, Joe s/o Ralph & Martha Minor age 22 S farmer POB & POR Spotsylvania POC & **WHITE**, Judy d/o Robert & Martha White age 21 S POB & POR Spotsylvania POC; POM Spotsylvania 27 May 1871 SPMR 26 May 1871 SPML

MINOR, John & **LEWIS**, Elibletus(?) d/o W.F. Lewis; 2_ May 1866 SPConsent

MINOR, John J. s/o James & Lucy Minor age 21 S farmer POB & POR Spotsylvania & **LEWIS**, Matilda d/o W.F. & Mary Lewis age 18 S POB & POR Spotsylvania; POM Spotsylvania 30 May 1867 SPMR 29 May 1867 SPML

MINOR, Joseph H. s/o Joseph & Julia Minor age 21 S laborer POB & POR Spotylvania POC & **STANARD**, Bertie Belle d/o Robert & Dolly Stanard age 18 S POB & POR Spotsylvania POC; POM Spotsylvania 4 Jun 1896 SPMR SPML

MINOR, Joseph s/o Ralph & Martha Minor age 48 W farmer POB & POR Spotsylvania POC & **DAVIS**, Lizzie d/o Andrew & Betsy Davis age 27 S POB & POR Spotsylvania POC; POM Spotsylvania 4 Jan 1900 SPMR 1 Jan 1900 SPML

MINOR, Micky s/o Majr(?) & E. Minor age 27 S laborer POB Louisa Co POR Spotsylvania POC & **WARE**, Rachael d/o Jacob Ware age 21 S POB & POR Spotsylvania; POM Branch Fork Ch, Spotsylvania 25 Nov 1877 SPMR 23 Nov 1877 SPML

MINOR, Philip s/o Philip & Ann Minor age 30 W POB & POR Spotsylvania POC & **DILLARD**, Annie d/o William & Margaret Lewis age 28 W POB & POR Spotsylvania POC; POM Mine Road Baptist Ch, Spotsylvania 27 Mar 1884 SPMR 26 Mar 1884 SPML

MINOR, Philip s/o Philip & Ann Minor age 23 S laborer POB & POR Spotsylvania POC & **DAVIS**, Maria d/o Alonzo & Sarah Howard age 24 S POB Louisa Co POR Spotsylvania; POM Spotsylvania 17 May 1877 SPMR 16 May 1877 SPML

MINOR, Reuben s/o William & Betsy Graves age 28 S farmer POB & POR Spotsylvania POC

& DICKINSON, Florence age 25 W POB & POR Spotsylvania POC; POM Spotsylvania 24 Nov 1866 SPMR 10 Nov 1866 SPML

MINOR, Rice s/o Scy & Millie Minor age 21 S laborer POB Caroline Co POR Spotsylvania POC & DANDRIDGE, Eliza d/o Byrd & Margaret Dandridge age 18 S POB Caroline Co POR Spotsylvania POC; POM Spotsylvania 24 Dec 1881 SPMR 21 Dec 1881 SPML

MINOR, Robert s/o Thomas & Fanny Minor age 22 S laborer POB & POR Spotsylvania POC & STEPHENS, Huldah d/o Alex Frazer & Sarah Stephens age 22 S POB & POR Spotsylvania POC; POM Spotsylvania C.H. 2 Jul 1892 SPMR SPML

MINOR, Scott s/o John & Martha Minor age 23 S laborer POB Caroline CO POR Spotsylvania POC & LEWIS, Bettie d/o Robert Lewis & Sylvia Coleman age 18 S POB & POR Spotsylvania POC POM Spotsylvania 3 Jan 1884 SPMR 1 Jan 1884 SPML

MINOR, Silas s/o Edward & Fanny Minor age 40 W laborer POB Caroline Co POR Spotsylvania POC & WIGLESWORTH, Jane d/o Walker & Judy Wiglesworth age 32 W POB & POR Spotsylvania POC; POM Spotsylvania 10 Aug 1882 SPMR 3 Aug 1882 SPML

MINOR, Thomas s/o Jack & Susan Jane Minor age 21 S laborer POB & POR Spotsylvania POC & JACKSON, Rose d/o Henry Preston & Polly Jackson age 18 S POB & POR Spotsylvania POC; POM Spotsylvania 2 Oct 1883 SPMR 1 Oct 1883 SPML

MINOR, Washington s/o Jeff. & Aby.Minor age 41 S farmer POB & POR Spotsylvania POC & JACKSON, Josephine d/o George & Rose Jackson age 18 S POB & POR Spotsylvania POC: POM Spotsylvania 19 May 1872 SPMR 14 May 1872 SPML

MITCHELL, Isaac N. s/o John Mitchell & Ella Wood age 37 W saddler POB Green Co POR Orange & JOHNS, Ann Maria d/o Mason Johns & Ann Walker age 28 S POB Albemarle Co POR Orange; POM Orange 6 Sep 1866 OMR 27 Aug 1866 OML

MITCHELL, Isaac N. s/o
John Mitchell &
Ellen Ward age 35
W saddler POB
Green Co POR
Orange &
SHOTWELL, Sarah
J. d/o Tazwell
Shotwell &
Columbia Wood age
21 S POB & POR
Orange; 20 Dec
1865 OML

MITCHELL, John C. &
LUMPKIN, Lucy W.
d/o Matilda
W.Lumpkin; 26 Aug
1862 SPConsent

MITCHELL, John C. s/o
Hickman & Judith
Mitchell age 32 W
mechanic POB &
POR Spotsylvania
& **ALSOP**, Ella d/o
Joseph M.& Susan
J.Alsop age 22 S
POB & POR
Spotsylvania; POM
Spotsylvania 21
Nov 1872 SPMR 19
Nov 1872 SPML

MITCHELL, Joseph C.
s/o John C.& Ella
S.Mitchell age 21
S farmer POB &
POR Spotsylvania
& **ARMSTRONG**, Mary
E.L. d/o Mahlon &
Romelia
W.Armstrong age
23 S POB & POR
Spotsylvania; POM
Berean L.& Advent
C.Ch,
Spotsylvania 15
Jan 1899 SPMR 13
Jan 1899 SPML

MITCHELL, Joseph s/o
Hickman & Judett
Mitchell age 22 S
farmer POB
Caroline Co POR
Spotsylvania &
BLACK, Susan C.
d/o Andrew &
Sarah E. Black
age 20 S POB &
POR Spotsylvania;
POM Spotsylvania
11 Feb 1869 SPMR
1 Feb 1869 SPML

MITCHELL, Luther R.
s/o James & Emily
Mitchell age 22 S
farmer POB & POR
Caroline Co &
MARTIN, Martha J.
d/o Alexander &
Sarah Martin age
23 S POB & POR
Spotsylvania; POM
Spotsylvania 23
Oct 1865 SPMR
SPML

MITCHELL, William D.
s/o John Mitchell
& Margaret Davis
age 27 S farmer
POB & POR Carroll
Co & **ROBINSON**,
Mary B. d/o
Richard
H.Robinson & Mary
H.Harrison age 28
S POB & POR
Orange; POM
Orange 18 Dec
1862 OMR 13 Dec
1862 OML

MITCHELL, William F.
s/o John Mitchell
& Nelly Wood age
39 S silversmith
POB Green CO POR
Orange & **DAVIS**,
M.S. d/o James
Davis & Sarah
J.Awl age 21 S
POB & POR Orange;
POM Orange 3 Oct
1867 OMR OML

MITCHELL, William F.
s/o Joseph G.&
Fanny A.Mitchell
age 24 S cashier
at Mitchell Mines
POB Philadelphia
POR Mitchell

Mines,
Spotsylvania &
HAMMOND,
Josephine C. d/o
John C.& Eliza
S.Hammond age 24
S POB Boston,
Massachusettes
POR Mitchell
Mines,
Spotsylvania; POM
Spotsylvania 5
Dec 1868 SPMR
SPML

MODENA, Benjamin J.
s/o Thomas
H.Modena & Mary
A.Hopkins age 26
S lawyer POB
Fluvanna Co POR
Orange & **GAY**,
Bettie F. d/o
William Gay &
Nancy Dorand age
22 S POB & POR
Orange; POM
Orange 29 Mar
1863 OMR 28 Mar
1863 OML

MOFFETT, George A. s/o
Samuel & Hannah
Moffett age 25 S
farmer POB & POR
Rockingham Co &
SIBERT, Mary J.
d/o R.J.&
Elizabeth Sibert
age 23 S POB
Shenandoah Co POR
Gordonsville; POM
Orange 28 Oct
1858 OMR 27 Oct
1858 OML

MONCURE, William E.
s/o John & Easter
Moncure age 28 S
farmer POB & POR
Stafford &
BANKHEAD,
Georgianna Cary
d/o William &
Dorothea
B.Bankhead age 22
S POB Caroline Co

POR Orange; POM
Orange 18 Oct
1853 OMR 17 Oct
1853 OML

MONROE, James s/o Man
Monroe age 26 S
servant POB & POR
Martin Co, N.C.
POC & **ELKINS**,
Mary Eliza d/o
Frank Elkins age
25 W POB & POR
Orange POC; POM
Orange 22 Feb
1866 OMR OML

MONT, Robert s/o John
& Matilda Mont
age 34 S farmer
POB & POR
Spotsylvania &
COLEMAN, Amy d/o
Spencer & Martha
Coleman age 21 S
POB & POR
Spotsylvania; POM
Waller's Ch,
Spotsylvania 13
Dec 1868 SPMR 12
Dec 1868 SPML

MONTACUE, Joshua s/o
G.& D.Montacue
age 22 S POB &
POR Spotsylvania
POC & **JACKSON**,
Fannie d/o Lucy
Ellis age 24 S
POB & POR
Spotsylvania POC;
POM their
residence,
Spotsylvania 2
Jun 1881 SPMR
SPML

MONTAGUE,Miles s/o
Gilbert & Dolly
Montague age 24 S
laborer POB & POR
Spotsylvania POC
& **SAMUEL**, Ella
d/o Phil & Mary
Samuel age 19 S
POB & POR
Spotsylvania POC;
POM Spotsylvania

20 Feb 1890 SPMR SPML

MONTJOY, William H. s/o James & Catherine Montjoy age 42 S farmer POB Stafford POR Prince William Co & ARNOLD, Caroline H. d/o John H. & Mary B. Arnold age 30 S POB King George Co POR Spotsylvania; POM Rocky Spring, Spotsylvania 15 Oct 1872 SPMR 14 Oct 1872 SPML

MOOBRAY, James & BROCKMAN, Mary Ann; 13 Jul 1852 OML

MOODY, Gilbert s/o Thorn & Fanny Moody age 28 S laborer POB New Kent Co POR Louisa Co POC & SHELTON, Elvira d/o Cloughf & Catherine Shelton age 23 S POB & POR Spotsylvania POC; POM Piccadilly, Spotsylvania 21 Dec 1872 SPMR 16 Dec 1872 SPML

MOORE, Charles C. s/o William C. & M.R. Moore age 30 S (F.M.G. profession ?) POB Orange & BOULWARE, Virginia A. d/o R.S. & M.C. Boulware age 21 S POB Orange; POM Orange 10 Oct 1860 OMR 9 Oct 1860 OML

MOORE, Edmund C. s/o Robert L. & Mary Moore age not certain W farmer POB & POR Orange & MOORE, Fannie B. d/o W.C. & Matilda Moore age 23 S POB & POR Orange; POM Orange 14 Aug 1855 OMR 10 Aug 1855 OML

MOORE, Harry A. s/o Allen A. & Annie M. Moore of Philadelphia, Pennsylvania age 25 POR Falmouth, Stafford Co. & ROBERSON, Katie J. d/o Charles W. & Mary F. Roberson of Falmouth age 24 POR Falmouth; POM Falmouth, Stafford Co., 3 Feb 1895 TCF

MOORE, Rolanshe s/o Thomas & Lucy Moore age 25 S physician POB & POR Memphis, Tennessee & MARTIN, Annie d/o Samuel & Eliza E. Martin age 20 S POB & POR Spotsylvania; POM Spotsylvania 30 Mar 1865 SPMR 29 Mar 1865 SPML

MOORE, William M. s/o Joseph & Mary Moore age 28 W farmer POB & POR Spotsylvania & KRONK, Etta May d/o L.M. & Lizzie Kronk age 23 S POB & POR Spotsylvania; POM Grace M.E. Ch S,

Spotsylvania 21 Jan 1900 SPMR 20 Jan 1900 SPML

MOORE, William s/o Joseph & Mary Moore age 21 farmer POB & POR Spotsylvania & **BARNES**, Annie R. d/o Eli & Mary A.Barnes age 24 S POB Beam (?) Co, Penn POR Spotsylvania; POM Maple Grove, Spotsylvania 28 Sep 1892 SPMR SPML

MORGAN, Henry s/o John & Eleanor Morgan age 70 W farmer POB Caroline Co POR Spotsylvania & **CLARKE**, Susan T. d/o William F.& Hannah Clarke age 38 S POB & POR Spotsylvania; POM Spotsylvania 28 Apr 1868 SPMR 22 Apr 1868 SPML

MORRIS, Benjamin s/o Dick & Roseanna Morris age 22 S laborer on farm POB Louisa Co POR Orange POC & **HENDERSON**, Louisa d/o Lewis Henderson age 18 S POB & POR Orange POC; 27 Oct 1867 OML

MORRIS, Frank s/o John & Lucy Morris age 21 S farmer POB & POR Louisa Co POC & **STUBBS**, Lollia d/o William & Martha Stubbs age 19 S POB & POR Spotsylvania POC; POM Branch Fork Ch, Spotsylvania 23 Jan 1898 SPMR 22 Jan 1898 SPML

MORRIS, Fred S. s/o W.F.& Ella E. Morris age 22 S farmer POB McHenry Co, Ill.POR Spotsylvania & **FARMER**, Mary E. d/o Thomas B.& Caroline B.Farmer age 17 S POB Caroline Co POR Spotsylvania; POM Spotsylvania 14 Nov 1889 SPMR 11 Nov 1889 SPML

MORRIS, George A. s/o George W.& Miley Morris age 26 S farmer POB Caroline Co POR Spotsylvania & **THACKER**, Willie S. d/o Silas J.& Mary L.Thacker age 21 S POB Hanover Co POR Spotsylvania; POM Spotsylvania C.H. 19 Dec 1883 SPMR SPML

MORRIS, James B. s/o Lewis Morris age 29 S bricklayer POB & POR Orange & **BICKERS**, Julia M. d/o Proctor & Lucy Bickers age 22 S POB & POR Orange; POM Orange 16 Nov 1854 OMR

MORRIS, James Maury s/o James M. & Ann C.Morris age 26 S farmer/planter POB Louisa Co & **PHILIPS**, Victoria E. d/o John P.& Elizabeth Philips age 21 S POB

MORRIS, John F. &
BLEDSOE, Mary
Ann; 2 Jul 1852
OML

MORRIS, John Thomas
s/o James
L.Morris &
WATSON, Frances;
12 May 1853 OML

MORRIS, Lewis C. s/o
James L.Morris &
Lavinia Battaile
age 24 S
bricklayer POB &
POR Orange &
BATTAILLE, Jane
F. d/o Mary
Battaile age 19 S
POB & POR Orange;
POM Orange 25 Dec
1860 OMR 24 Dec
1860 OML

MORRIS, Reuben J. &
BAKER, Annie M.;
POM Orange 3 Jul
1860 OMR 27 Jun
1860 OML

MORRIS, Reuben J. s/o
Benedict &
Elizabeth Morris
age 29 S
gentleman POB
Albemarle Co POR
Gordonsville,
Orange Co &
DAVIS, Sally Ann
d/o William J.&
Elizabeth W.Davis
age 19 POB Orange
POR Gordonsville;
POM Orange 13 Apr
1854 OMR 12 Apr
1854 OML

MORRIS, Richard s/o
George W.& Mollie
Morris age 26 S
farmer POB
Caroline Co POR
Spotsylvania &
SACRA, Sarah F.
d/o James C.&
Mary J.Sacra age
18 S POB & POR
Spotsylvania; POM
Spotsylvania 25
Dec 1887 SPMR 23
Dec 1887 SPML

MORRIS, William A. &
MASON, Sarah Jane
d/o Charles
Mason; POM Orange
8 Apr 1852 OMR 29
Mar 1852 OML

MORRIS, William L. s/o
G.W.& M.Morris
age 28 S farmer
POB Caroline Co
POR Spotsylvania
& **BLACK**, Sally A.
d/o Andrew &
Sarah Black age
19 S POB & POR
Spotsylvania; POM
Spotsylvania 21
Feb 1877 SPMR 19
Feb 1877 SPML

MORRISON, George H.
s/o Robert R.&
Mary A.Morrison
age 29 S
manufacturer POB
& POR
Spotsylvania &
EASTBURN, Lillian
V. d/o Oliver &
Annie Eastburn
age 21 S POB &
POR Spotsylvania;
POM Salem Ch,
Spotsylvania 16
Sep 1896 SPMR 14
Sep 1896 SPML

MORRISON, James T. s/o
James M.& Abigail
Morrison age 24 S
farmer POB New
Castle
Co,Delaware POR
Spotsylvania &
EASTBURN, Sallie
R. d/o Isaac &
Mary Eastburn age
23 S POB New
Castle
Co,Delaware POR

Spotsylvania; POM Spotsylvania 12 Dec 1867 SPMR SPML

MORRISON, Robert R. s/o M.& M.Morrison age 26 S farmer POB M.D. POR Spotsylvania & **EASTBURN**, Anna E. d/o O.& A.E.Eastburn age 24 S POB Delaware POR Spotsylvania; POM Spotsylvania 28 Feb 1878 SPMR 25 Feb 1878 SPML

MORRISON, Thomas F. s/o Moses & Mary Morrison age 25 S farmer POB Delaware POR Spotsylvania &**EASTBURN**, Maria S. d/o Oliver & A.E.Eastburn age 24 S POB Delaware POR Spotsylvania; POM Spotsylvania 3 Jun 1875 SPMR 31 May 1875 SPML

MORRISS, William L. s/o Aden C.Morriss & Milly Lee age 29 S carpenter POB & POR Orange & **GAINES**, Annie E. d/o Andrew Gaines & Frances Lee age 20 S POB & POR Orange; POM Orange 9 May 1867 OMR OML

MORSE, John s/o Ben & Charlotte Morse age 23 S laborer POB Louisa Co POR Spotsylvania POC & **CARTER**, Carrie d/o Abe & Harriet(?) Carter age 19 S POB & POR Spotsylvania

POC; POM Spotsylvania C.H. 13 Nov 1885 SPMR SPML

MOSBY, Lawrence s/o Winston & Fanny Mosby age 22 S POB & POR Orange laborer POC & **YERBER**, Rose d/o George & Penny Yerber age 18 S POB & POR Orange POC; POM Orange 18 Aug 1866 OMR OML

MOSBY, Robert s/o Winston & Fanny Mosby age 26 S laborer on farm POB & POR Orange POC & **MALLORY**, Cornelia d/o Reuben & Lucy Hackett age 28 W POB Madison Co POR Orange POC; POM Orange 21 Apr 1867 OMR 20 Apr 1867 OML

MOSS, Charles s/o Richard & Maria Moss age 20 S laborer POB & POR Spotsylvania POC & **LEWIS**, Mozelle d/o Jacob & Kiziah Lewis age 18 S POB & POR Spotsylvania POC; POM Spotsylvania 25 Jan 1891 SPMR 14 Jan 1891 SPML

MOSS, Killis s/o Dick & Mariah Moss age 21 S farmer POB & POR Spotsylvania POC & **WIGGLESWORTH**, Hardenia d/o Walker & Mary Wigglesworth age 18 S POB & POR Spotsylvania POC;

POM Waters Tavern, Spotsylvania 11 Dec 1873 SPMR (While the minister's return lists "Waters" or "Walter's" Tavern as being in Spotsylvania County, it is actually in Louisa County)20 Nov 1873 SPML

MOSS, Richard s/o Kellis & Dorcus Moss age 68 W blacksmith POB & POR Spotsylvania POC & **CLARKE**, Margaret d/o Eliza Dudley age 57 W POB & POR Spotsylvania POC; 27 Sep 1888 SPML

MOSS, Sandy s/o Richard & Maria Moss age 23 S blacksmith POB & POR Spotsylvania POC & **THORNTON**, Pamelia d/o Manuel & Dianah Thornton age 18 S POB & POR Spotsylvania POC; POM Spotsylvania 1 Feb 1872 SPMR 16 Jan 1872 SPML

MOSS, William s/o William & Maria Moss age 30 S laborer POB Culpeper Co POR Washington D.C.POC & **TAYLOR**, Anna Lee d/o Thomas & Isabella Towles age 29 D POB & POR Spotsylvania POC; POM Spotsylvania C.H.23 Nov 1894 SPMR SPML

MUDDYMAN, Edmund s/o Thomas Muddyman age 38 W mason POB England POR Orange & **MASON**, Catherine d/o Abner Clark age 35 S POB & POR Orange; POM Orange 19 Aug 1866 OMR 13 Aug 1866 OML

MUGLER, Henry J. s/o Philip & Catherine Mugler age 21 S painter POB France POR Orange & **FAUDREE**, Ellen M. d/o Joseph & Susan Faudree age 18 S POB Virginia POR Orange; POM Orange 4 Aug 1859 OMR 3 Aug 1859 OML

MUGLER, Philip s/o Philip & Catherine Mugler age 21 S painter POB Strausburg, France POR Richmond, Va & **FAUDREE**, Lucy M. d/o Joseph & Susan Faudree age 20 S POB & POR Orange; POM Orange 29 Apr 1856 OMR 24 Apr 1856 OML

MULLAN (?), John & **CROPP**, Ricey or Billy Ann ; 14 Feb 1876 SPConsent

MUNDAY, Burruss s/o Burruss & Elizabeth Munday age 31 W farmer POB Albemarle Co POR Orange & **LANCASTER**, Ann E. d/o Thomas & Mary

Lancaster age 23 S POB & POR Orange; POM Orange 21 Jan 1858 OMR 15 Jan 1858 OML

MURPHY, John G. s/o Jane Frances Murphy age 24 S laborer POB & POR Spotsylvania POC & **WHITE**, Susan d/o Moses & Eliza White age 23 S POB & POR Spotsylvania POC; POM Spotsylvania 28 Aug 1883 SPMR SPML

MURPHY, Richard s/o Thomas & Catherine Murphy age 30 S farmer POB New York City POR Spotsylvania & **RICKER**, Mary S. d/o E.& Mary S. Ricker age 26 S POB Maine POR Spotsylvania; POM Spotsylvania 30 Apr 1883 SPMR SPML

MURPHY, Thomas s/o Jane F.Murphy ("not born in wedlock") age 23 S farmer POB & POR Spotsylvania POC & **BARBOUR**, Sealey d/o George & Amie Barbour age 21 S POB & POR Spotsylvania POC; POM Spotsylvania 14 Dec 1887 SPMR 7 Dec 1887 SPML

MURPHY, William L. s/o John Murphy & Ellen Edmondson age 50 S farmer POB Fredericksburg POR Orange & **GARDNER**, Minerva d/o Ezekiah Richards & Betsy Lancaster age 41 W POB & POR Orange; POM Orange 26 Nov 1864 OMR 24 Nov 1864 OML

MURPHY, William s/o Jane F.Murphy age 22 S laborer POB & POR Spotsylvania POC & **WHITE**, Ella d/o Moses & Eliza White age 25 S POB & POR Spotsylvania POC; POM Spotsylvania 18 Jan 1887 SPMR 15 Jan 1887 SPML

MUSSELMAN, Lewis N. s/o Alexander & Lucinda Musselman age 26 S laborer POB Stafford POR Spotsylvania & **BOWLING**, Alice d/o William & Amanda Bowling age 24 S POB & POR Spotsylvania; POM Spotsylvania 13 Apr 1898 SPMR SPML

MUSSELMAN, Richard s/o Sandy & Louisa Mussleman age 24 S farmer POB Stafford POR Spotsylvania & **JETT**, Dora V. d/o James & Amanda Jett age 24 S POB & POR Spotsylvania; POM Tabernacle Ch 16 Mar 1892 SPMR 14 Mar 1892 SPML

MUSSLEMAN, William C. s/o Samuel & Bella Mussleman age 28

S farmer POB Stafford POR Spotsylvania & **JETT**, Docie J. d/o James M. & Amanda Jett age 17 S POB & POR Spotsylvania; POM Tabernacle Methodist Ch 16 Jan 1889 SPMR 14 Jan 1889 SPML

MYERS, Charlie s/o Cornelius & Patsy Myers age 27 S laborer POB & POR Fredericksburg POC & **SMITH**, Bell d/o Peter & Mary Smith age 25 S POB & POR Spotsylvania POC; POM Spotsylvania 16 Dec 1896 SPMR SPML

MYERS, Wayne s/o Charles & Sarah Myers age 26 S farmer POB Penn POR Spotsylvania & **STOVER**, Lizzie d/o Mycal & Lydia Stover age 26 S POB Penn POR Spotsylvania; POM Belvidera 28 Jan 1892 SPMR 27 Jan 1892 SPML

NELMS, Hy. P. s/o P. & C. Nelms age 38 S minister POB & POR Northumberland & **CROPP**, Sally Ann d/o S. & C. Cropp age 19 S POB Fauquier Co POR Spotsylvania; POM Spotsylvania 26 Nov 1855 SPMR

NELSON, Gabriel s/o Jeff & Winney Nelson age 24 S farmer POB Stafford POR Spotsylvania & **HART**, Susan d/o John Hart age 21 S POB & POR Spotsylvania; POM Spotsylvania 30 Nov 1868 SPMR 12 Dec 1868 SPML

NELSON, Henry s/o James & Lucinda Nelson age 28 S teamster POB & POR Spotsylvania POC & **FRAZER**, Emma d/o William & Mary Frazer age 20 S POB & POR Spotsylvania POC; POM Spotsylvania 16 Jun 1867 SPMR 11 Jun 1867 SPML

NEWMAN, George & **WILTSHIRE**, Sarah Jane; POM Orange 1 Jan 1853 OMR 27 Dec 1852 OML

NEWMAN, George s/o John Newman & Mildred Quisenberry age 40 W farmer POB & POR Orange & **JONES**, Malvina d/o James Jones & Elizabeth Overton age 36 S POB & POR Orange; POM Orange 14 Mar 1867 OMR 25 Feb 1867 OML

NEWMAN, James F. s/o George & Bettie Newman age 33y 4mo 28days S farmer POB Madison Co POR Orange & **WINSLOW**, Martha E. d/o Thompson & Eleanor Cockerille age 35y 5mo 9days W POB & POR Orange;

POM Orange 11 May 1856 OMR 10 May 1856 OML
NEWMAN, John R. s/o William S.& Lucy Newman age 35 S farmer POB & POR Orange & **RODGERS**, Margaret R. d/o Joseph & Malinda Rodgers age 24 S POB & POR Orange; POM Orange 13 Dec 1857 OMR 12 Dec 1857 OML
NEWMAN, Willie Q. s/o John R.& Margaret R.Newman age 29 S farmer POB & POR Orange & **CRAFTON**, Cora A. d/o William T.& Mary E.Crafton age 25 S POB Louisa Co POR Spotsylvania; POM Spotsylvania 20 Nov 1889 SPMR 11 Nov 1889 SPML
NEWTON, John B. s/o Willoughton Newton & Mary S.Bracker age 23 S surgeon in army POB & POR Westmoreland Co & **WILLIAMSON**, Roberta P. d/o James A.Williamson & Mary M.Page age 21 S POB Clarke Co POR Orange; POM Orange 5 Nov 1862 OMR 4 Nov 1862 OML
NICHOLAS, James s/o Ned Nicholas & Rose Wormley age 28 W farm laborer POB Culpeper Co POR Orange POC & **MYERS**, Milly d/o Jeny & Emily Myers age 22 S

POB & POR Orange POC; POM Orange 28 Dec 1866 OMR 27 Dec 1866 OML
NOLAN, Thomas & **AMES**, Alice J.; POM Orange 17 Oct 1852 OMR OML
NOLAN, W.T. s/o Z.W.& E.Nolan age 24 farmer POB Louisa Co POR Spotsylvania & **CARNER**, M.J. d/o A.& E.A.Carner age 22 POB & POR Spotsylvania; 12 Dec 1866 SPMR
NORLAN, William F. s/o Zachariah W.& Elizabeth Noeland age 24 S farmer POB Louisa Co POR Spotsylvani & **CARNER**, Mary J. d/o Allen & E.A. Carner age 23 S POB & POR Spotsylvania; POM Spotsylvania 20 Dec 1866 SPMR 12 Dec 1866 SPML
NORMAN, Joseph Thomas s/o Thomas & Frances Norman age 30 S farmer POB Culpeper & **STEWART**, Frances Cordelia d/o James & Sarah N.Stewart age 29 S POB Spotsylvania; POM Spotsylvania 1 Feb 1855 SPMR
NUSSEY, Frederick s/o F.C.& Ellen Nussey age 28 S farmer POB Blentley, England POR Spotsylvania & **WALLER**, Susan R. d/o John D.& Jane Waller age

23 S POB & POR Spotsylvania; POM Spotsylvania 5 Sep 1900 SPMR 3 Sep 1900 SPML

O'SULLIVAN, John s/o Jeremiah & Mary O'Sullivan age 24 S tinsmith POB Richmond,Va POR Orange & **ARMAND**, Josephine d/o Francis & Lucy Sarmand age 21 S POB Richmond,Va POR Orange; POM St.Thomas Ch, Orange 2 Jul 1855 OMR

OAKES, F.B. s/o M.& M.Oakes age 23 S mechanic POB Spotsylvania & **SULLIVAN**, E. d/o P.M.Sullivan age 28 S POB Spotsylvania; POM Spotsylvania 12 Nov 1855 SPMR

OAKES, Henry C. s/o John & Pricilla Oakes age 24 S farmer POB & POR Caroline Co & **LYTTLE**, Louisa J. d/o Hugh & Lucinda Satterwhite age 27 W POB & POR Spotsylvania; POM Spotsylvania 23 Nov 1871 SPMR 22 Nov 1871 SPML

OAKS, Fielding J. s/o Robert & Elizabeth Oaks age 30 S tie getter POB & POR Spotsylvania & **SULLIVAN**, Annie E. d/o Charles M.C.& Anne E.Baxter age 28 W POB & POR

Spotsylvania; POM Spotsylvania C.H. 5 Oct 1892 SPMR SPML

ODEN, S.A. s/o F.M.& A.V.Oden age 29 S musician POB Bedford Co, Va POR Louisa Co & **CANNON**, Mattie E. d/o John L.& J.Cannon age 26 S POB & POR Spotsylvania; POM Richmond 25 May 1898 SPMR SPML

OGLE, Jeremiah s/o Jerry & Harriet Ogle age 37 W porter POB Ann Arundell Co, Md POR Washington D.C.POC & **BURRUSS**. Ellen E. d/o Robert I. & Mary A.Burruss age 22 S POB & POR Spotsylvania POC; POM Spring Grove, Spotsylvania 3 Jul 1884 SPMR SPML

OGLETREE, Samuel H. s/o George T.& Nancy Ogletree age 21y 5mo S POB Spaulding Co,Ga POR Atlanta,Ga & **CASH**, Josephine d/o Robert B.& Elizabeth Cash age 19 S POB & POR Spotsylvania; POM Spotsylvania 21 Aug 1867 SPMR 17 Aug 1867 SPML

OLIVER, J.H. s/o Ellen Oliver age 25 farmer POB & POR Spotsylvania & **PILIAM**, A.E. d/o T.Piliam & B.McGee age 24

POB & POR
Spotsylvania; 7
Mar 1861 SPMR
OLIVER, Luther R. s/o
Chester & Mary
V.Oliver age 25 S
farmer POB & POR
Spotsylvania &
BRADLEY, Ida F.
d/o W.H.& Lucy
E.Bradley age 24
S POB & POR
Spotsylvania; POM
Spotsylvania 12
Nov 1896 SPMR 11
Nov 1896 SPML
OLIVER, Robert J. s/o
Charles (dec) &
M.Oliver age 24 S
mechanic POB
Spotsylvania &
WALLACE, A.E. d/o
J.& M.Wallace age
24 S POB
Spotsylvania; POM
Spotsylvania 24
Dec 1855 SPMR
OLIVER, William S. s/o
Chesterfield &
M.Virginia Oliver
age 39 S farmer
POB & POR
Spotsylvania &
PATES, Mary A.
d/o Augustus &
Clementine Pates
age 26 S POB &
POR Spotsylvania;
POM Spotsylvania
18 Aug 1897 SPMR
SPML
ORR, S.A. s/o Sample &
Eliza A.Tinder
age 31 S farmer
POB & POR
Spotsylvania &
DILLARD, Alice E.
d/o Isaiah J.&
Julia A.Dillard
age 18 S POB &
POR Spotsylvania;
POM Spotsylvania
8 Apr 1896 SPMR
SPML

ORROCK, C.A. s/o James
& Sarah A.Orrock
age 32 S farmer
POB & POR
Spotsylvania &
ROBEY, Lula B.
d/o William B.&
Mary H.Robey age
31 S POB & POR
Spotsylvania; POM
Spotsylvania 1
Jun 1898 SPMR 31
May 1898 SPML
ORROCK, J. s/o R.&
M.M. Orrock age
32 S farmer POB
Scotland POR
Spotsylvania &
WALLER, S.A. d/o
R.& E.Waller age
26 S POB & POR
Spotsylvania; 27
Jan 1859 SPML
ORROCK, James H. s/o
James & Sarah
Orrock age 25 S
farmer POB & POR
Spotsylvania &
POLLARD, Isabella
d/o Isaac & Lucy
Pollard age 23 S
POB & POR
Spotsylvania; POM
Chapel of
St.George Parish,
Spotsylvania 5
Jan 1885 SPMR 31
Dec 1884 SPML
OSBORNE, Thomas s/o
Holland Osborne &
Mary Farney(?)
age 40 S farmer
POB Orange POR
Kentucky &
FERNEYHOUGH, Mary
E. d/o John
Ferneyhough &
Jensie Darnald
age 19 S POB &
POR Orange; POM
Orange 25 Apr
1861 OMR 15 Apr
1861 OML

OSWALD, Walter C. s/o
William & Annie
Oswald age 25 S
farmer POB
Baltimore, Md POR
Spotsylvania &
WALKER, Mollie W.
d/o Robert &
E.A.Walker age 19
S POB Mecklenburg
Co POR
Spotsylvania; POM
Spotsylvania 25
Oct 1881 SPMR 24
Oct 1881 SPML
OSWALD, William W. s/o
William & Annie
A.Oswald age 33 S
farmer POB
Baltimore, Md POR
Spotsylvania &
MITCHELL, Alverta
C. d/o John C.&
Lucy W.Mitchell
age 19 S POB &
POR Spotsylvania;
POM Spotsylvania
4 Nov 1886 SPMR
SPML
OVERSTREET, James H.
s/o W.H.&
J.Overstreet age
26 S POB & POR
Bedford Co
QUISENBERRY, J.H.
age 27 S POB &
POR Spotsylvania;
POM Laurel Brook,
Spotsylvania 10
Nov 1886 SPMR 9
Nov 1886 SPML
OVERTON, Joshua s/o
William & Harriet
Overton age 22 S
laborer POB
Stafford POR
Spotsylvania POC
& **CORBIN**, Hannah
d/o Isabella
Corbin age 19 S
POB & POR
Spotsylvania POC;
POM Little Road
Baptist Ch,
Spotsylvania 7
Aug 1881 SPMR 5
Aug 1881 SPML
OVERTON, Theopilus s/o
S.& E.C.Overton
age 49 W farmer
POB & POR
SPotsylvani &
CARTER, Laetitia
d/o Lewis & Susan
C.Almond age 45 W
POB & POR
Spotsylvania; POM
Spotsylvania C.H.
9 Aug 1893 SPMR
SPML
OVERTON, William J.
s/o Joshua & Anna
Overton age 25 S
engineer POB &
POR Spotsylvania
POC & **SLAUGHTER**,
Laura B. d/o
Isabella Corbin
age 19 S POB &
POR Spotsylvania
POC; POM Parker,
Spotsylvania 28
Dec 1899 SPMR 27
Dec 1899 SPML
OWENS, Howard M. s/o
Warren & Sarah
J.Owens age 52 W
farmer POB
Stafford Co POR
Spotsylvania &
OLDS, Lucy A. d/o
Woodson Sullivan
age 30 W POB &
POR Spotsylvania;
POM Spotsylvania
C.H. 30 Jul 1888
SPMR SPML
OWENS, Howard M. s/o
Warren & Sarah
J.Owens age 33 S
farmer POB
Stafford POR
Spotsylvania &
WALLACE, Mary C.
d/o John &
Margaret Wallace
age 23 S POB &
POR Spotsylvania;

POM Spotsylvania 12 Nov 1868 SPMR 9 Nov 1868 SPML

OWENS, Lee A. d/o William Owens & Jane Chandler age 23 W farmer POB Mecklenburg Co POR Smith Co, Mississippi & **SCHUYLER**, Eliza E. d/o William Schuyker & Mary A.Sorrell age 21 S POB & POR Orange; POM Orange 9 Apr 1865 OMR 8 Apr 1865 OML

OWENS, Lewis s/o Lewis & Matilda Owens age 31 S laborer POB & POR Orange POC & **BRAXTON**, Hannah d/o Polly Gilmor age 21 S POB & POR Orange POC; POM Orange 13 Oct 1865 OMR 28 Aug 1865 OML

OWENS, O.J. s/o W.& G.J.Owens age 24 S farmer POB & POR Spotsylvania POC & **LEITCH**, Lucy A. d/o William & E.Leitch age 25 S POB & POR Spotsylvania POC; POM Spotsylvania 6 Dec 1877 SPMR 4 Dec 1877 SPML

PACE, Henry W. s/o William & Mary Pace age 28 S miner POB Albemarle Co POR Louisa Co & **BROOKS**, Minnie E. d/o Granville & Laura Brooks age 20 S POB & POR Spotsylvania; POM Spotsylvania C.H. 16 May 1900 SPMR SPML

PALMER, G.W. & **NICHOLSON**, Mary J. d/o Margaret Nicholson; 24 Dec 1873 SPConsent

PALMER, John s/o John & Joanna Palmer age 21 S POB Wayne Co, N.Y. POR Spotsylvania & **NICHOLSON**, Sarah E. d/o Charles & Margaret Nicholson age 20 S POB Montgomery Co, Pa POR Spotsylvania; POM Spotsylvania 20 Dec 1874 SPMR 18 Dec 1874 SPML

PANNILL, Baldwin s/o Jeremiah Pannill & Ann T.Payne age 23 S POB & POR Orange & **DUNN**, Mary Susan d/o Martin A.Dunn & Mary Walker age 19 S POB & POR Orange; POM Orange 20 Dec 1860 OMR 17 Dec 1860 OML

PANNILL, David & **GOODWIN**, Margaret M.; 25 Jan 1860 SPML

PANNILL, David s/o George & Susan G.Pannill age 47 W farmer POB & POR Orange & **GOODWIN**, Margaret d/o John M.& Eliza T.Goodwin age 32 S POB & POR Orange; POM Orange 26 Jan 1860 OMR 25 Jan 1860 OML

PANNILL, Philip POR Culpeper Co & **PORTER,** Martha d/o John A.Porter; 12 Jul 1851 OML

PARKER, Charles A. s/o W.A.& Olivia Parker age 21 S machinist POB & POR Spotsylvania & **MANSFIELD,** Georgie J. d/o William H.& Cordelia Mansfield age 31 S POB & POR Spotsylvania; POM Olivet M.E.Ch S, Spotsylvania 4 Feb 1894 SPMR 1 Feb 1894 SPML

PARKER, Eddie E. s/o Edgar E.& Susan Parker age 24 S farmer POB & POR Spotsylvania & **WILSON,** Ella Jane d/o Robert H.& Mary J.Wilson age 23 S POB & POR Spotsylvania; POM Zion Methodist Ch, Spotsylvania 27 Jul 1882 SPMR SPML

PARKER, F.L. s/o John F.& Annie Parker age 22 S farmer POB & POR Spotsylvania & **HIRTH,** Willey J. d/o Gottlieb & Margaret Hirth age 17 S POB & POR Spotsylvania; POM Spotsylvania C.H.2 Sep 1885 SPMR SPML

PARKER, William A. s/o Edgar & Susan M.Parker age 23 S farmer POB & POR Spotsylvania &

PAYTES, Harriet E. d/o Augusta & Clementine Paytes age 19 S POB & POR Spotsylvania; POM Spotsylvania C.H.27 Nov 1884 SPMR SPML

PARKER, William A. s/o George S.& Hardenia L.Parker age 29 S farmer POB & POR Spotsylvania & **KISHPAUGH,** Martha O. d/o John & Phoebe Kishpaugh age 18 S POB & POR Spotsylvania; POM Spotsylvania 20 Dec 1871 SPMR 18 Dec 1871 SPML

PARKER, William s/o Henry & Jane Parker age 33 S farmer POB Caroline Co POR Spotsylvania POC & **HARRORD,** Sophronia d/o Gabriel & Jane Bird age 34 W POB Essex Co POR Spotsylvania POC; POM Spotsylvania 14 Mar 1872 SPMR 9 Mar 1872 SPML

PARRAN, William S. s/o Nathaniel & Ann Parran age 25 S physician POB Hardy Co POR Barboursville & **GRAVES,** Mary Virginia d/o Charles T.& Susan Graves age 21 S POB & POR Orange; POM Orange 15 Feb 1860 OMR 10 Feb 1860 OML

PARTLOW, Benjamin H. s/o John L.Partlow &

Martha Lillard age 30 S merchant POB Rappahannock Co POR Orange & **JONES**, Edmonia H. d/o James L.Jones & Martha A.Porter age 24 S POB & POR Orange; POM Beaumont, Orange 3 Oct 1866 OMR 28 Sep 1866 OML

PARTLOW, J.L. s/o L.M.Partlow age 22 S farmer POB & POR Spotsylvania & **SCHULTZ**, Kate d/o H.& B.Schultz age 22 S POB & POR Spotsylvania; POM Spotsylvania 25 Jan 1881 SPMR 20 Jan 1881 SPML

PARTTELLO, William Z. s/o Wen P.& C.V.Partello age 21 S clerk POB Zanesville, Ohio POR Washington City & **PATTILLO**. Roza L. d/o Robert & Helen M.Pattillo age 18 S POB Mecklenburg POR Spotsylvania; POM St George Ch, Fredericksburg 9 Mar 1870 FMR 8 Mar 1870 SPML

PATES, Lewis s/o Gusty & Christine Pates age 28 S farmer POB & POR Spotsylvania & **COLLINS**, Kate d/o Dennis & Mandy Collins age 18 S POB & POR Spotsylvania; POM Spotsylvania C.H. 21 Dec 1882 SPMR 20 Dec 1882 SPML

PATTERSON, M.S. s/o A.& S.A.Patterson age 24 W farmer POB Stafford POR Spotsylvania & **SNELLINGS**, Annie J. d/o James & L.B.Snellings age 19 S POB Stafford POR Spotsylvania; POM Spotsylvania 6 Aug 1878 SPMR 3 Aug 1878 SPML

PAYNE, Albert L. s/o Albert & Margaret Payne age 23 S farmer POB & POR Spotsylvania & **MARTIN**, Julia A. d/o Linfield & Frances Martin age 17 S POB & POR Spotsylvania; POM Belair, Spotsylvania 4 Jan 1877 SPMR 1 Jan 1877 SPML

PAYNE, Allie M. s/o George & Eliza Payne age 31 S farmer POB & POR Spotsylvania & **PAYNE**, Lucie E. d/o Albert & Margaret Payne age 23 S POB & POR Spotsylvania; POM Spotsylvania 15 Aug 1888 SPMR SPML

PAYNE, Benjamin C. s/o Charles G.Payne & Mary Cooper age 22 S farmer POB & POR Orange & **COLLINS**, Elizabeth A. d/o Robert Collins & Jane Robinson age 19 S POB & POR Orange; POM Orange 21 Dec 1865 OMR 15 Dec 1865 OML

PAYNE, C.J. s/o A.J.& S.A.Payne age 34

S miller POB & POR Caroline Co & **BUTLER**, M.C. d/o J.C.& C.R.Butler age 33 S POB & POR Spotsylvania; POM County Line Ch, Caroline Co 24 May 1893 Caroline MR 22 May 1893 SPML

PAYNE, Elijah T. s/o Joseph E.& Nicy Ann Payne age 24 S farmer POB & POR Spotsylvania & **HOCKADAY**, Harriet M. d/o RiChH.& Elizabeth Hockaday age 32 S POB & POR Spotsylvania; POM Spotsylvania 4 Oct 1866 SPMR 1 Oct 1866 SPML

PAYNE, James B. s/o Jessee & C.Payne age 21 S farmer POB & POR Spotsylvania & **CLARKE**, Mattie C. d/o John H.& M.F.Clarke age 18 S POB & POR Spotsylvania; POM Spotsylvania 5 Dec 1878 SPMR SPML

PAYNE, James M. s/o Ludwell & Sally Payne age 22 S farmer POB & POR Spotsylvania & **LUCK**, Martha A.E. d/o Robert E.& Pamilia A.Payne age 20 S POB & POR Spotsylvania 18 Dec 1866 SPMR 17 Dec 1866 SPML

PAYNE, James T.& **WALLER**, Elizabeth; 31 Jan 1853 OML

PAYNE, James W. s/o Charles G.Payne & **LANCASTER**, Sarah Ann d/o James G. Lancaster; 20 Sep 1852 OML

PAYNE, John H. s/o William F.& Catherine A. Payne age 22 S farmer POB Stafford POR Spotsylvania & **HAYNES**, Roberta R. d/o Robert & Sarah Haynes age 18 S POB Spotsylvania POR Caroline Co; POM Spotsylvania C.H.8 Jan 1890 SPMR 8 Jan 1890 SPML

PAYNE, John S. s/o Richard & Mary Ann Payne age 23 S editor/publisher POB Prince William POR Orange C.H. & **THRIFT**, Virginia (aka Mary V.Thrift) d/o William & Maria Thrift age 19 POB Loudon POR Orange C.H.; POM Orange 3 Feb 1859 OMR OML

PAYNE, John T. s/o Charles Payne & Lucy Jones age 30 S lumber business POB & POR Orange & **ROACH**, Ann d/o Robert Roach & Milly Jones age 24 S POB & POR Orange; POM Orange 17 Jun 1866 OMR 15 Jun 1866 OML

PAYNE, Joseph Samuel & **DUERSON**, Lucy Ann age over 21; 8 Apr 1862 SPConsent

PAYNE, L.J. s/o Samuel H.& Elizabeth Payne age 25 S railroad employee POB Louisa Co POR Hinton Co, W.Va & **PAYNE**, Virginia D. d/o Thomas E. & Louisa Payne age 23 S POB & POR Spotsylvania; POM Spotsylvania 21 Feb 1894 SPMR 19 Feb 1894 SPML

PAYNE, Lewis s/o Thomas & Harriet Payne age 22 S farmer POB & POR Spotsylvania & **JONES**, Annie d/o Charles & Molly Jones age 22 S POB & POR Spotsylvania; POM Spotsylvania C.H.19 Dec 1893 SPMR SPML

PAYNE, Luther R. s/o Albert R.& Margaret Payne age 25 S farmer POB & POR Spotsylvania & **BURRUSS**, Emma L. d/o Leon C.& Gabriella Burruss age 18 S POB & POR Spotsylvania; POM Spotsylvania C.H.30 Dec 1884 SPMR SPML

PAYNE, Nelson W.s/o J.M.& Eliz.Payne age 36 S machinist POB & POR Spotsylvania & **CARTER**, Nora L. d/o W.N.& Lucy Carter age 22 S POB & POR Spotsylvania; POM Spotsylvania 8 Jan 1896 SPMR 6 Jan 1896 SPML

PAYNE, P.F. s/o P.W.& Susan B.Payne age 40 W farmer POB & POR Spotsylvania & **PURSLEY**, Mary T. d/o M.C.& E.Baxter age 23 W POB & POR Spotsylvania; 13 Apr 1865 SPML (ML gives the date of marriage to be 16 Apr 1865)

PAYNE, Richard J. s/o E.T.& Harriet Payne age 23 S farmer POB & POR Spotsylvania & **SATTERWHITE**, Mary A. d/o Rufus & Mary Jane Darlings age 26 W POB & POR Caroline Co; POM Spotsylvania C.H.20 Mar 1894 SPMR SPML

PAYNE, Robert P.s/o James W.& Sarah Payne age 25 S farmer POB & POR Orange & **STUBBS**, Emma J. d/o Jesse H.& Ann J.Stubbs age 19 S POB & POR Spotsylvania; POM Spotsylvania 4 Jan 1891 SPMR Jan 1891 SPML

PAYNE, Thaddeus s/o E.T.& Harriet Payne age 20 S farmer POB & POR Spotsylvania & **LONG**, Dorothea A. d/o Robert & Mary M.Long age 34 S POB & POR Spotsylvania; POM

Spotsylvania C.H. 20 Sep 1892 SPMR SPML

PAYNE, Thomas J. s/o A.R.& Margaret Payne age 33 W farmer POB & POR Spotsylvania & **GARDNER**, Josie A. d/o Nathan & Martha E.Gardner age 23 S POB & POR Spotsylvania; POM Spotsylvania C.H.23 Dec 1890 SPMR SPML

PAYNE, W.P. s/o A.R.& Margaret Payne age 23 S farmer POB & POR Spotsylvania & **PAYNE**, M.H. d/o John M.& Betsy Payne age 29 S POB & POR Spotsylvania; 27 Dec 1887 SPML

PAYNE, William J. s/o J.M.& M.A.Payne age 21 S farmer POB & POR Spotsylvania & **PAYNE**, Alice F. d/o James W.& Sara Ann Payne age 21 S POB Orange POR Spotsylvania; POM Spotsylvania 10 Jan 1889 SPMR 7 Jan 1889 SPML

PAYTES, James S. s/o Augustus & Sarah Paytes age 25 S farmer POB & POR Spotsylvania & **PERRY**, Amanda F. d/o Lewis & Frances C.Perry age 22 S POB & POR Spotsylvania; POM Spotsylvania ___,1873 SPMR 2 Jul 1873 SPML

PAYTES, Macon C. s/o Augustus & Clementine Paytes age 25 S farmer POB & POR Spotsylvania & **BUTZNER**, Julia K. d/o George & Ellen Butzner age 26 S POB & POR Spotsylvania; POM Spotsylvania 19 Jan 1887 SPMR 18 Jan 1887 SPML

PAYTES, Simeon C. s/o Jane M.Paytes age 51 W farmer POB & POR Spotsylvania & **SIMS**, Lucy B. d/o Isaac R.& M.A.Sims age 17 S POB & POR Spotsylvania; POM Spotsylvania 29 Aug 1889 SPMR SPML

PAYTON, Joseph L. s/o Robert & Sarah Payton age 40 S farmer POB Stafford POR Spotsylvania & **KELLY**, Ida B. d/o William & Sallie Kelly age 25 S POB Stafford POR Spotsylvania; POM Fredericksburg 27 Oct 1898 FMR SPML

PEACHER, A.T. s/o M.A.Peacher age 23 S farmer POB & POR Spotsylvania & **JONES**, Mary J. d/o Thomas & Mary A.Jones age 18 S POB & POR Spotsylvania; POM Spotsylvania 22 Sep 1881 SPMR 5 Sep 1881 SPML

PEACHER, George W. s/o John & Elizabeth Peacher age 17 S farmer POB & POR Spotsylvania & **SACRA**, Addie V. d/o Robert & Amanda Sacra age 18 S POB & POR Spotsylvania; POM Spotsylvania 21 Sep 1895 SPMR SPML

PEAKE, Charles R. s/o J.B.& S.J.Peake age 33 S merchant POB & POR Spotsylvania & **JERRELL**, S.B. d/o J.C.& A.M.Jerrell age 19 S POB& POR Spotsylvania; POM Spotsylvania 15 Mar 1876 SPMR 6 Mar 1876 SPML

PEARSON, Joel s/o William H.Pearson & Sarah Porter age 23 S student POB South Caroline POR Fairfield District, S.C. & **MANN**, Georgia Anna d/o William H.Mann & Arabella R.Keith age 20 S POB Albemarle Co POR Orange; POM Gordonsville, Orange 20 Aug 1866 OMR 17 Aug 1866 OML

PEATROSS, Richard D. s/o James W. & Eliza N. Peatross age 32 S carriage builder POB Caroline Co POR Spotsylvania & **GRAVES**, Mariam E. d/o Garnett & Jane F.Graves age 29 S POB & POR Spotsylvania; POM Spotsylvania 5 Nov 1874 SPMR 4 Nov 1874 SPML

PEMBERTON, Alonzo R. s/o Alonzo & Fanny PEmberton age 28 S farmer POB & POR Spotsylvania & **MORRISON**, Bessie A. d/o James T.& Sarah R.Morrison age 22 S POB & POR Spotsylvania; POM Tabernacle Ch, Spotsylvania 16 Aug 1899 SPMR 15 Aug 1899 SPML

PEMBERTON, Judson F. s/o W.R.& Melvina F.Pemberton age 43 W flagman POB Hanover Co POR Richmond, Va & **McWHIRT**, Addie B. d/o Frank & Cornelia F.McWhirt age 20 S POB & POR Spotsylvania; POM Spotsylvania 12 Aug 1896 SPMR 10 Aug 1896 SPML

PEMBERTON, Reuben A. s/o Reuben & Elizabeth Pemberton age 26 S farmer POB & POR Caroline Co & **BUTZNER**, Mary F.T. age 21 S POB Caroline Co POR Spotsylvania; POM Spotsylvania 17 Feb 1870 SPMR 16 Feb 1870 SPML

PEMBERTON, Thomas R. s/o R.B.& Kitty A.Pemberton age 25 S sawmilling POB & POR Hanover Co & **SWIFT**, Nellie d/o John H.& Mildred Swift POB & POR

Spotsylvania; POM Spotsylvania 5 Dec 1900 SPMR 4 Dec 1900 SPML

PENDLETON, G.A. s/o Robb & Martha Pendleton age 30 W farmer POB & POR Spotsylvania & **MASSEY**, Nina E. d/o A.W.& Lucy M.Massey age 20 S POB & POR Spotsylvania; POM Lebanon M.E.Ch, Spotsylvania 12 Nov 1879 SPMR 8 Nov 1879 SPML

PENDLETON, George A. s/o Robert & Martha E. Pendleton age 25 S farmer POB & POR Spotsylvania & **LANDRAM**, Annie B. d/o William & Eliza Landram age 30 S POB & POR Spotsylvania; POM Spotsylvania 18 Nov 1873 SPMR 15 Nov 1873 SPML

PENDLETON, Jackson s/o Robert & Elizabeth Pendleton age 55 W farmer POB & POR Spotsylvania & **LANDRAM**, Duley d/o William & Eliza Landram age 31 S POB & POR Spotsylvania; 27 Feb 1866 SPMR 24 Feb 1866 SPML

PENDLETON, James M. s/o Hugh C.& Melvina Pendleton age 20 S miller POB & POR Spotsylvania & **MICKLEBOROUGH**, Isabella P. d/o Taverner W.&

Sarah Holladay age 23 W POB & POR Spotsylvania; POM Spotsylvania 29 Dec 1881 SPMR SPML

PENDLETON, John H. s/o J.T.& Huldah Pendleton age 31 W farmer POB & POR Spotsylvania & **HAWKINS**, Fannie G. d/o J.H.& Fannie Hawkins age 25 S POB & POR Spotsylvania; POM Spotsylvania 10 Feb 1870 SPMR 7 Feb 1870 SPML

PENDLETON, Joseph A. s/o Hugh & Malvina Pendleton age 23 S farmer POB & POR Spotsylvania & **CARNER**, Mattie D. d/o A.& E.A.Carner age 22 S POB Green Co POR Spotsylvania; POM Spotsylvania 18 Jan 1876 SPMR 17 Jan 1876 SPML

PENDLETON, Oscar L. s/o Hugh C.& Melvina Pendleton age 24 S merchant POB & POR Spotsylvania & **HOLLADAY**, Lillie M. d/o Taverner W.& Helen Holladay age 17 S POB & POR Spotsylvania; POM Spotsylvania 26 Apr 1888 SPMR SPML

PENDLETON, Robert J. s/o Robert & M.E.Pendleton age 40 W farmer POB & POR Spotsylvania & **CARTER**, Lizzie d/o F.E.& Pamelia Carter age 19 S POB & POR Spotsylvania; POM Spotsylvania C.H. 19 Sep 1893 SPMR SPML

PENDLETON, Robert L. s/o Edmond & Lucy E.Pendleton age 46 W farmer POPB Louisa Co & **GAY**, Amy E. d/o Newton S. & Abigail H.Gay age 35 S POB Alleghany Co, Penn POR Spotsylvania; POM Mill Brook, Spotsylvania 27 Aug 1890 SPMR 26 Aug 1890 SPML

PENDLETON, Robert S. s/o Edmond & Lucy E.Pendleton age 22 S farmer POB Louisa Co POR Spotsylvania & **TINDER**, Laura E. d/o John A.& Sarah F.Tinder age 21 S POB Pike Co, Missouri POR Spotsylvania; POM Spotsylvania 31 Aug 1865 SPMR 30 Aug 1865 SPML

PENDLETON, Robert S. s/o Edmond & Lucy E.Pendleton age 38 W farmer POB Louisa Co POR Spotsylvania & **TINDER**, Samuella d/o John A.& Sarah Tinder age 30 S POB Pike Co, Missouri POR Spotsylvania; POM Spotsylvania 29 Oct 1873 SPMR 26 Oct 1873 SPML

PENDLETON, Robert s/o Robert & Martha E.Pendleton age 29 S farmer POB & POR Spotsylvania & **ROOF**, Annie d/o John & Lydia Roof age 17 S POB New York, Delaware Co POR Spotsylvania; POM Spotsylvania 15 Nov 1882 SPMR 10 Nov 1882 SPML

PENDLETON, Wilton s/o George & Harriet Pendleton age 26 S laborer POB Caroline Co POR Spotsylvania POC & **THORNTON**, Annie d/o Anthony & Mary Thornton age 20 S POB Essex Co POR Spotsylvania POC; POM New Hope Ch, Spotsylvania 28 Dec 1876 SPMR 27 Dec 1876 SPML

PERKINS, Jackson s/o Richard & Lacy Perkins age 37 W farmer POB Orange POR Spotsylvania POC & **BERKLEY**, Eliza d/o Edmond Nuckols & Jenny Fox age 25 W POB Louisa Co POR Spotsylvania POC; POM Spotsylvania 6 Sep 1868 SPMR 5 Sep 1868 SPML

PERRY, Charles A. s/o E.& S.A.Perry age 24 S farmer POB Caroline Co POR Spotsylvania & **ALSOP**, Nannie B. d/o Joseph W.& M.A.Alsop age 23 S POB & POR Spotsylvania; POM Spotsylvania 9 Jan 1879 SPMR 7 Jan 1879 SPML

PERRY, Charles R. s/o Robert B.& Lavinia Perry age 27 S POB & POR Spotsylvania & **JORDAN**, Mary A. d/o John & Virginia Jordan age 25 S POB Henrico Co, Va POR Spotsylvania; POM Spotsylvania 12 Aug 1896 SPMR 3 Aug 1896 SPML

PERRY, Charles W. s/o William S. & Mary Perry of Fredericksburg age 20 POR Fredericksburg & **SWEITZER**, Roberta M. d/o George & Eunice Sweitzer of Fredericksburg age 19 POR Fredericksburg; POM Fredericksburg 2 Jul 1895 (TCR)

PERRY, Edmund A. s/o Benjamin R.Perry & Martha White age 35 S farmer POB Perquinemons Co,N.C. POR Orange & **TERRILL**, Ellen d/o Edmund Terrill & Susan Smith age 30 S POB & POR Orange; POM Orange 23 Dec 1865 OMR 22 Dec 1865 OML

PERRY, Elijah R. s/o George Perry & Mary Brown age 23 S minister POB & POR Orange & **BOSTON**, Sophia S. d/o John Boston & Frances Waugh age 18 S POB & POR Orange; POM Orange 31 Dec 1863 OMR OML

PERRY, George W. s/o John & A.V.Perry age 30 W merchant POB & POR Spotsylvania & **BLACKLEY**, Lillian L. d/o George W.& Annie E.Blackley age 17 S POB & POR Spotsylvania; POM Zion M.E.Ch S, Spotsylvania 9 Dec 1886 SPMR 6 Dec 1886 SPML

PERRY, George W. s/o John & Martha V.Perry age 27 S merchant POB & POR Spotsylvania & **TOMPKINS**, Martha E. d/o Edmund & Bettie Tompkins age 22 S POB & POR Spotsylvania; POM Richmond, Va 1 Nov 1883 Richmond MR SPML

PERRY, James B. s/o William H.& Virginia Perry age 22 S farmer POB & POR Spotsylvania & **COLLINS**, Mary Fannie age 21 S POB & POR Spotsylvania; POM Fredericksburg 20 Dec 1888 SPMR SPML

PERRY, Lawrence s/o William Perry & Mary E.Graves age 32 S miner POB & POR Spotsylvania & **BROOKS**, Bessie d/o Mary E.Brooks age 14 S POB & POR Spotsylvania; POM Spotsylvania

C.H.9 Mar 1885 SPMR SPML

PERRY, Robert B. s/o William & Nancy Perry age 60 W laborer POB & POR Spotsylvania & **JETT**, Carrie d/o Andrew J.& Elizabeth Jett age 21 S POB & POR Spotsylvania; POM Spotsylvania 18 Nov 1896 SPMR SPML

PERRY, Silas B. s/o J.J.& Martha Perry age 26 S merchant POB & POR Spotsylvania & **EASTBURN**, Carrie Florine d/o Oliver Eastburn age 23 S POB & POR Spotsylvania; POM Tabernacle M.E.Ch S, Spotsylvania 8 Nov 1899 SPMR 7 Nov 1899 SPML

PERRY, William F. s/o William F.Perry & Augusta C.Ferris age 22 S clerk ordinance department POB New York City POR Richmond,Va & **TERRILL**, Virginia d/o Dr.Uriel Terrill & Jane Lovell age 26 S POB & POR Orange; POM Orange 2 Apr 1863 OMR OML

PERRY, William N. age 21 S farmer POB Spotsylvania & **LANCASTER**, Virginia d/o William C.& Mary F.Lancaster age 17 S POB Orange;

POM Orange 9 Aug 1860 OMR OML

PERRY, William s/o Easo.(?) & S.A.Perry age 25 S farmer POB & POR Spotsylvania & **DIGGS**, Sedonia d/o James & E.Diggs age 21 S POB & POR Spotsylvania; POM Spotsylvania 10 Jan 1878 SPMR 7 Jan 1878 SPML

PERRY, William T. s/o Robert & Lavenia Perry age 27 S farmer POB & POR Spotsylvania & **CURTIS**, Sarah E. d/o Jefferson & Sally Curtis age 20 S POB & POR Spotsylvania; POM Spotsylvania C.H. 13 Feb 1893 SPMR SPML

PETERSON, Emanuel Louis s/o Yens & Louisa F.Peterson age 31 S painter POB Copenhagen, Denmark POR Orange & **CARTER**, Hattie A. d/o F.E.& Amelia Carter age 21 S POB & POR Spotsylvania; POM Spotsylvania C.H. 15 May 1893 SPMR SPML

PETITT, Ira W. s/o Fountain P.Petitt & Martha A.Roach age 23 S bricklayer POB Albemarle Co POR Orange & **SMITH**, Serrepta A. d/o John & Lucy Smith age 22 S POB Albemarle CO POR

Orange; POM
Orange 19 Dec
1867 OMR 16 Dec
1867 OML

PETTITT, Corbin Lee
s/o Samuel
Pettitt & Louisa
Nelson age 21 S
farmer POB & POR
Fairfax Co &
LAYTON, Agnes H.
d/o Samuel Layton
& Maria Nelson
age 18 S POB &
POR Orange; POM
Orange 18 Aug
1863 OMR OML

PEYTON, James M. s/o
Minor & Ann
Peyton age 29 S
farmer POB & POR
Spotsylvania &
SACRA, Martha A.
d/o John B.&
Susan Sacra age
22 S POB & POR
Spotsylvania; POM
Spotsylvania 6
Aug 1871 SPMR 24
Jul 1871 SPML

PEYTON, John S. s/o
John Peyton &
Lydia Snyder age
44 W wheelwright
POB & POR Orange
& **NEWMAN**, Sarah
M. d/o William
Newman & Lucy
Faulconer age 45
S POB & POR
Orange; POM
Orange 13 Nov
1862 OMR 12 Nov
1862 OML

PEYTON, John W. s/o
M.& A.Peyton age
36 S farmer POB &
POR Spotsylvania
& **HUMPHRIES**,
Bettie A. d/o
Robert &
E.Humphries age
32 S POB & POR
Spotsylvania; POM
Spotsylvania 4
Dec 1879 SPMR 27
Nov 1879 SPML

PEYTON, Robert L. s/o
Minor & Ann
Peyton age 30 S
farmer POB & POR
Spotsylvania &
WILSON, Lucy H.
d/o A.H.& Sarah
Wilson age 29 S
POB & POR
Spotsylvania; POM
Spotsylvania 5
Jan 1882 SPMR 28
Dec 1881 SPML

PEYTON, Thomas J. s/o
John & Lydia
Peyton age 26 S
carpenter POB &
POR Orange &
REYNOLDS, Sarah
B. d/o William
S.& Ann Reynolds
age 23 S POB &
POR Orange; POM
Orange 27 Jul
1859 OMR 26 Jul
1859 OML
LONG, John &
HERNDON, Ann
Elizabeth; 1 Jul
1859 OML

PEYTON, William J. s/o
George H.& Ann
E.Peyton age 31 S
farmer POB & POR
Spotsylvania &
HUMPHRIES, Emma
R. d/o Eddie
Humphries age 28
S POB & POR
Spotsylvania; POM
Waller's Baptist
Ch, Spotsylvania
16 Aug 1899 SPMR
14 Aug 1899 SPML

PHILIPS, Reuben G. s/o
Zachariah
Phillips &
Susanna Coleman
age 29 S POB
Calhoun Co,
Alabama POR

Pontatock Co,
Mississippi &
HUGHES, Virginia
d/o Armistead
Hughes & Sarah
A.Sleet age 25 S
POB & POR Orange;
POM Orange 26 Nov
1863 OMR 24 Nov
1863 OML
PHILLIPS, John W. s/o
John W.& Martha
B.Phillips age 22
S farmer POB &
POR Hanover Co &
CHEWNING, Landora
H. d/o William
H.& Camillo
Chewning age 17 S
POB & POR
Spotsylvania; POM
Waller's Ch,
Spotsylvania 14
Nov 1882 SPMR 6
Nov 1882 SPML
PHILLIPS, Louis Ernest
s/o Robert A.&
Annie E.Phillips
age 23 S attorney
at law POB
Speedsville, N.Y
POR Spotylvania &
BRADLEY, Florence
Janet age 23 POB
Clinton Rock Co,
Wisconsin POR
Spotsylvania; POM
Fredericksburg 18
Aug 1885 SPMR 17
Aug 1885 SPML
PIERCE, Henry M. s/o
John Pierce &
Frances W.Tamplin
age 22 S
railroading POB
Spotsylvania POR
Orange & **ADAMS**,
Eliza Jane d/o
Robert Adams &
Mildred Mason age
22 S POB & POR
Orange; POM
Orange 23 Jan
1866 OMR 22 Jan
1866 OML
PIERCE, Oscar J. s/o
John & Frances
Pierce age 23 S
carpenter POB
Spotsylvania POR
Orange &
ANDERSON,
Charlotte N. d/o
Joseph & Mary
Anderson age 24 S
POB "Forkequire
County of Va" POR
Orange; POM
Orange 5 Apr 1855
OMR 23 Mar 1855
OML
PLACE, William Henry
s/o Henry N.&
Fanny Place age
19 S farmer POB
Connecticut POR
Spotsylvania &
ATKINS, Leonora
Lewis d/o William
L.& Sarah Atkins
age 20 S POB &
POR Spotsylvania;
POM Spotsylvania
19 Dec 1872 SPMR
16 Dec 1872 SPML
POINDEXTER, Aaron s/o
Garland & Martha
Poindexter age 37
S farmer POB &
POR Spotsylvania
POC & **RICHARDSON**,
Emily age 40 W
POB & POR
Spotsylvania POC;
POM Spotsylvania
15 Jan 1871 SPMR
13 Jan 1871 SPML
POINDEXTER, Arthur s/o
Daniel & Patsy
Poindexter age 26
S laborer POB &
POR Orange POC &
McINTOSH,
Margaret d/o
James & Matilda
McIntosh age 23 S
POB Orange POR

Spotsylvania POC;
POM Branch Fork
Ch, Spotsylvania
17 Jan 1883 SPMR
15 Jan 1883 SPML
POINDEXTER, Daniel s/o
Mary J.Allen age
21 S laborer POB
& POR
Spotsylvania POC
& **JOHNSON**,
Mildred Ann age
23 S POB & POR
Spotsylvania POC;
POM Spotsylvania
24 Aug 1886 SPMR
2 Aug 1886 SPML
POINDEXTER, Pleasant
T. s/o Garland &
Martha Poindexter
age 70 W laborer
POB & POR
Spotsylvania POC
& **HITER**, Polly
age 40 W POB &
POR Spotsylvania
POC; POM Branch
Fork Ch,
Spotsylvania 29
Aug 1890 SPMR 27
Aug 1890 SPML
POLLARD, Charles s/o
Charles Pollard
age 27 S laborer
in express office
POB Culpeper Co
POR Orange POC &
TERRILL, Helen
d/o Thornton
Terrill age 16 S
POB & POR Orange
POC; POM Orange
29 Dec 1867 OMR
28 Dec 1867 OMR
POLLARD, James s/o
Isaac & Lucy
Pollard age 31 S
farmer POB & POR
Spotsylvania &
SMITH, Ellen J.
d/o William C.&
Sarah E.Smith age
18 S POB & POR
Spotsylvania; POM
Spotsylvania 29
Feb 1888 SPMR 28
Feb 1888 SPML
POLLARD, John s/o J.&
L.Pollard age 25
S farmer POB King
George Co POR
Spotsylvania &
BUTZNER, Virginia
E. d/o George &
G.Butzner age 22
S POB & POR
Spotsylvania; POM
Spotsylvania 24
Dec 1878 SPMR 20
Dec 1878 SPML
POLLARD, Joseph s/o
Elisha & Susan
Pollard age 42 S
tobacco roller
POB Henrico Co
POR Richmond,Va
POC & **COATES**,
Martha d/o John &
Minerva Coates
age 27 S POB
Caroline Co POR
Spotsylvania POC;
POM Spotsylvania
27 Apr 1882 SPMR
SPML
POOL, Montruville s/o
A.& N.Pool age 21
S farmer POB &
POR Spotsylvania
& **EASTBURN**, Ella
d/o O.&
A.E.Eastburn age
24 S POB Delaware
POR Spotsylvania;
POM Spotsylvania
30 Dec 1880 SPMR
SPML
POOL, William s/o
Alfred & Roberta
C.Pool age 19 S
farmer POB & POR
Spotsylvania &
FLEMMING, Lucy M.
d/o B.S.&
S.A.Fleming age
18 S POB & POR
Spotsylvania; POM
Spotsylvania 13

Dec 1866 SPMR 10
Dec 1866 SPML
PORTER, Albert s/o
Moses Porter age
35 W farm laborer
POB & POR Orange
POC & **COLEMAN**,
Sylvia d/o James
Coleman age 24 S
POB & POR Orange
POC; POM Orange
29 Dec 1867 OMR
27 Dec 1867 OML
PORTER, Alexander s/o
Joshua & Hettie
Porter age 22 S
laborer POB & POR
Spotsylvania POC
& **WILLIAMS**,
Landonia d/o Jeff
& Jane Williams
age 20 S POB &
POR Spotsylvania
POC; POM
Spotsylvania 10
Sep 1890 SPMR
SPML
PORTER, John Henry s/o
Ruford Porter &
Eliza Penyman age
23 S brickmason
POB Forsythe Co,
N.C. POR Orange &
BARDEN, Alverta
Ellsworth d/o
Lewis H.Barden &
Lucy P.Faulconer
age 21 S POB &
POR Orange; POM
Orange 24 Oct
1867 OMR 21 Oct
1867 OML
PORTER, Joshua &
JOHNSON, Hetty
d/o Ann Johnson;
9 May 1868
SPConsent
PORTER, Joshua H. s/o
John & Mary
Porter age 26 W
laborer POB
Delaware POR
Spotsylvania &
HENRY, Catherine
d/o Griffin &
Mary Henry age 24
S POB & POR
Spotsylvania; POM
Courtland
Township,
Spotsylvania 26
Sep 1874
SPConsent
PORTER, Joshua s/o
John & Mary
Porter age 20
b.d.Aug 1848 S
farmer POB
Delaware state
POR Spotsylvania
POC & **JOHNSON**,
Hetty d/o John &
Ann Johnson age
20 S POB & POR
Spotsylvania POC;
POM Spotsylvania
10 May 1868 SPMR
9 May 1868 SPML
PORTER, Joshua s/o
John & Mary
Porter age 26 W
laborer POB
Newark, Delaware
POR Spotsylvania
POC & **HENRY**,
Catharine d/o
Griffin & Mary
Henry age 24 S
POB & POR
Spotsylvania POC;
POM Spotsylvania
26 Sep 1874 SPMR
SPML
PORTER, W.W. &
HIGGERSON,
Pamelia H. "of
lawful age"; 2
Feb 1867
SPConsent
POWELL, Charles T. s/o
F.& L.Powell age
27 S farmer POB &
POR Spotsylvania
& **BALLARD**, Susan
F. d/o Sanford &
Frances Ballard
age 18 S POB &
POR Spotsylvania;

POM Mt.Pleasant,
Spotsylvania 28
Dec 1877 SPMR 24
Dec 1877 SPML
POWELL, E.T. s/o John
& Mary Powell age
23 S merchant POB
King William Co
POR Ayletts, King
William Co &
CAVE, Mary A. d/o
Robert P.&
S.F.Cave age 18
POB Green Co POR
Orange; POM
Orange 15 Jan
1857 OMR OML
POWELL, Frederick D.
s/o Frank &
Louisa Powell age
23 S POB & POR
Spotsylvania &
DUNNAVANT,
Frances d/o
Archie & Mary
Dunnavant age 22
S POB & POR
Spotsylvania; POM
Spotsylvania 13
Jan 1871 SPMR 9
Jan 1871 SPML
POWELL, George H. s/o
George H.& Sarah
A.Powell age 31 S
farmer POB & POR
Spotsylvania &
HAISLIP, Mary
Willie d/o Henry
K.& Susan
A.Haislip age 21
S POB & POR
Spotsylvania; POM
Spotsylvania C.H.
1 Feb 1887 SPMR
SPML
POWELL, James C. s/o
Michael &
S.Powell age 25 S
farmer POB & POR
Spotsylvania &
JETT, Almedia d/o
John T.& Sarah
F.Jett age 19 S
POB & POR

Spotsylvania;
Spotsylvania 24
Feb 1881 SPMR 21
Feb 1881 SPML
POWELL, James L. s/o
J.L.& J.T.Powell
age 40 S farmer
POB & POR
Spotsylvania &
JONES, Carrie E.
d/o A.B.&
J.E.Jones age 21
S POB Stafford
POR Spotsylvania;
POM Massaponax
Ch, Spotsylvania
15 Jan 1879 SPMR
6 Jan 1879 SPML
POWELL, Joseph s/o
George & S.Powell
age 23(?) S
farmer POB Orange
POR Spotsylvania
& **CARTER**, Molly
d/o E.M.&
M.A.Carter age 22
S POB Caroline Co
POR Spotsylvania;
POM Spotsylvania
12 Oct 1879 SPMR
3 Oct 1879 SPML
POWELL, Josiah s/o
Thornton &
Elizabeth Powell
age 24 S farmer
POB & POR
Spotsylvania &
BYRAM, Gipsey P.
d/o Richard &
Eliza Bowling age
24 W POB & POR
Spotsylvania; POM
Spotsylvania 16
Jan 1873 SPMR
SPML
POWELL, Mason Franklin
s/o Franklin &
Louisa Powell age
26 S farmer POB &
POR Spotsylvania
& **ALLEN**, Rosa Lee
d/o Henry Thomas
& Margaret Allen
age 24 S POB

Caroline Co POR Spotsylvania; POM Cherry Grove, Spotsylvania 17 Nov 1887 SPMR SPML

POWELL, Peter B. s/o Frank & Louisa Powell age 21 S farmer POB & POR Spotsylvania & McGEE, Agnes d/o Ebenezer McGee & S.A.Stratton age 20 S POB & POR Spotsylvania; POM Spotsylvania 2 Mar 1876 SPMR 1 Mar 1876 SPML

POWELL, R.Warren s/o Dorsey & Francis Powell age 22 S laborer POB & POR Spotsylvania & POWELL, d/o Theopolus & Laura Powell age 20 S POB & POR Spotsylvania; POM Spotsylvania 26 Sep 1899 SPMR SPML

POWELL, Richard s/o Thomas & Mary Powell age 23 S POB & POR Spotsylvania & WHEELER, Lizzie d/o James W.& Mary W.Wheeler age 25 S POB & POR Spotsylvania; POM Spotsylvania 26 Dec 1900 SPMR 25 Dec 1900 SPML

POWELL, Richard s/o M.& S.Powell age 23 S farmer POB & POR Spotsylvania & TOOMBS, Mary d/o C.& T.Toombs age 23 W POB Fredericksburg POR Spotsylvania;

POM Spotsylvania 20 Dec 1877 SPMR 17 Dec 1877 SPML

POWELL, S.L. s/o Josiah & Gypsy Powell age 22 S farmer POB & POR Spotsylvania & MULLEN, Catheline d/o Daniel & Rosa Mullen age 22 S POB & POR Spotsylvania; POM Fredericksburg 14 Nov 1899 FMR 8 Nov 1899 SPML

POWELL, Thomas s/o Thomas & Mary Powell age 28 S farmer POB & POR Spotsylvania & LEECH, Lillie W. d/o William & Jennie Leech age 35 S POB & POR Spotsylvania; POM Spotsylvania 25 Aug 1897 SPMR SPML

PRATT, George G. s/o Anderson & Maria Pratt age 23 S farmer POB Caroline Co POR Spotsylvania POC & COLEMAN, Mattie d/o Minor & Louisa Coleman age 19 S POB & POR Spotsylvania POC; POM Spotsylvania 26 Dec 1895 SPMR 23 Dec 1895 SPML

PRATT, William s/o Fanny Lecoste age 24 S laborer POB & POR Spotsylvania POC & COLE, Susie d/o Alex & Sallie Cole ag 23 S POB & POR Spotsylvania POC;

POM Spotsylvania
3 Jan 1900 SPMR 1
Jan 1900 SPML
PRESTIGE, Wilson M.
s/o Campbell
Prestige & Polly
Franks age 22 S
farmer POB
Yalabasha Co,
Mississippi POR
Lafayette Co,
Mississippi &
HERNDON, Ann V.
d/o Benjamin
Herndon & Hannah
Bledsoe age 25 S
POB & POR Orange;
POM Orange 1 Sep
1863 OMR 31 Aug
1863 OML
PRESTON, Frank s/o
Enos & Mahala
Preston age 49 W
farmer POB
Chatangud Co,
N.Y. POR
Spotsylvania &
CHEWNING, Alice
Cary d/o William
H.& Camilla
Chewning age 35 S
POB & POR
Spotsylvania; POM
Waller's Ch,
Spotsylvania 22
Dec 1897 SPMR 17
Dec 1897 SPML
PRICE, Edward W. s/o
Edward & Alice
Price age 36 S
brick mason POB
England POR
Spotsylvania &
WHITAKER, Hannah
d/o George & Mary
Whitaker age 25 S
POB England POR
Spotsylvania; POM
Spotsylvania 1
Aug 1881 SPMR
SPML
PRICE, George W. &
WILHOIT, Louisa
H.; 25 Jan 1858
OML
PRICE, Robert Jr. s/o
Robert & Frances
Price age 27 S
farmer POB & POR
Spotsylvania POC
& **COATS**, Susie A.
d/o John J.&
Elzie Coats age
22 S POB & POR
Spotsylvania POC;
POM Spotsylvania
28 Dec 1893 SPMR
SPML
PRICE, Robert s/o
Thornton & Sarah
Price age 55 W
farmer POB & POR
Spotsylvania POC
& **BURRUSS**, Mary
A. d/o Annie
Williams age 45 W
POB & POR
Spotsylvania POC;
POM Caroline Co
18 Apr 1895
Caroline MR 17
Apr 1895 SPML
PRIOR, John Beverly
s/o Aaron & Alice
Prior age 62 W
farmer POB King
George Co POR
Spotsylvania POC
& **CATLETT**, Sarah
age 35 W POB &
POR Spotsylvania;
POM Spotsylvania
15 Nov 1873 SPMR
3 Nov 1873 SPML
PRIOR, William s/o
Beverly & Sally
Prior age 21 S
farmer POB & POR
Spotsylvania POC
& **AKERS**, Lucy d/o
Thorn & Ethelinda
Akers age 21 S
POB & POR
Spotsylvania POC;
POM Spotsylvania
10 Mar (no

year)SPMR 7 Mar
1870 SPML
PRITCHETT, Benjamin J.
s/o B.W.& Mildred
Pritchett age 26
S farmer POB &
POR Spotsylvania
& **PAYNE**, Roena
d/o Jesse &
Catherine Payne
age 19 S POB &
POR Spotsylvania;
12 Jun 1889 SPML
PRITCHETT, Benjamin W.
s/o William W.&
Matilda Pritchett
age 48 W farmer
POB & POR
Spotsylvania &
PERRY, Julia d/o
John & Martha
V.Perry age 34 S
POB & POR
Spotsylvania; POM
Spotsylvania 23
Apr 1885 SPMR 21
Apr 1885 SPML
PRITCHETT, Charles R.
s/o William P.&
Olivia
B.Pritchett age
25 S farmer POB &
POR Spotsylvania
& **JOHNSON**, Amanda
Q. d/o E.M.&
Sarah Johnson age
20 S POB & POR
Spotsylvania; POM
Brockenburg,
Spotsylvania 28
Feb 1900 SPMR 20
Feb 1900 SPML
PRITCHETT, Herbert M.
s/o W.W.&
M.L.Pritchett age
35 S farmer &
ALSOP, Amanda
A.F. d/o John S.&
N.Alsop age 31 S;
POM Road Side
View,
Spotsylvania 13
Apr 1876 SPMR 12
Apr 1876 SPML

PRITCHETT, John R. s/o
William W. &
Matilda Pritchett
age 28 S farmer
POB & POR
Spotsylvania &
JOHNSON, Sarah F.
d/o Eliphalet &
Sarah Johnson age
21 S POB Orange
Co POR
Spotsylvania; POM
Spotsylvania 20
Jan 1857 SPMR 5
Jan 1857 SPML
PRITCHETT, John R. s/o
H.M.& Virginia
Pritchett age 21
S farmer POB &
POR Spotsylvania
& **GLASSGOW**, Mamie
E. d/o Richard C.
Glassgow age 21 S
POB Hanover Co
POR Spotsylvania;
POM Spotsylvania
11 Jan 1900 SPMR
SPML
PRITCHETT, Joseph M.
s/o William A.&
Sarah J.Pritchett
age 25 S farmer
POB & POR
Spotsylvania &
BOWLING, Nannie
E. d/o Jeff &
Martha A.Bowling
age 18 S POB &
POR Spotsylvania;
POM Spotsylvania
C.H.27 Jul 1875
SPMR 26 Jul 1875
SPML
PRITCHETT, Joseph M.
s/o J.A.&
M.L.Pritchett age
23 S farmer POB &
POR Spotsylvania
& **WAITE**, Lucy M.
d/o William H.&
S.P.Waite age 22
S POB & POR
Spotsylvania; POM
Spotsylvania 2

Jan 1879 SPMR 31
Dec 1878 SPML

PRITCHETT, Lee D. s/o P.B.& Annie E.Pritchett age 30 S farmer POB & POR Spotsylvania & **PRICE**, Kate E. d/o Robert H.& Lucy A.Price age 23 S POB Yorkshire, England POR Spotsylvania; POM Goshen Ch, Spotsylvania 5 May 1897 SPMR 3 May 1897 SPML

PRITCHETT, Richard H. s/o Richard & M.A.Pritchett age 32 S farmer POB & POR Spotsylvania & **PEYTON**, Jane M. d/o Walter & Elizabeth Peyton age 28 S POB & POR Spotsylvania; POM Spotsylvania 8 Mar 1866 SPMR 6 Mar 1866 SPML

PRITCHETT, Thaddeus L.s/o William A.& Sarah Pritchett age 21 S farmer POB & POR Spotsylvania & **SHELTON**, Lucinda F. d/o William & Susan E.Shelton age 21 S POB & POR Spotsylvania; POM Spotsylvania 16 Nov 1881 SPMR 15 Nov 1881 SPML

PRITCHETT, Warner A. s/o Joseph A.& Nannie Pritchett age 23 S laborer POB & POR Spotsylvania & **BURRUSS**, Willie d/o W.E.L.& Martha A.Burruss age 23 S POB & POR Spotsylvania; POM Spotsylvania 28 Jun 1899 SPMR SPML

PRITCHETT, William A. s/o William W.& Martha M.Pritchett age 48 W farmer POB & POR Spotsylvania & **BOWLING**, Martha A. d/o Thomas S.& Ann A.Hicks age 33 W POB & POR Spotsylvania; POM Spotsylvania 4 Jan 1873 SPMR 3 Jan 1873 SPML

PRITCHETT, William H. s/o B.W.& M.C.Pritchett age 19 S POB & POR Spotsylvania & **LEWIS**, Adeline A. d/o Robert & Jane Lewis age 25 S POB & POR Spotsylvania; POM Spotsylvania 19 Dec 1880 SPMR 18 Dec 1880 SPML

PRITCHETT, William P. s/o Richard & Martha Pritchett age 35 S POB & POR Spotsylvania & **WAITE**, Olive B. d/o William H. & Mary Waite age 26 S POB & POR Spotsylvania; POM Spotsylvania 5 Feb 1874 SPMR 2 Feb 1874 SPML

PRITCHETT, William R. s/o P.B.& Annie E.Pritchett age 37 S farmer POB & POR Spotsylvania & **CARTER**, Irene d/o W.M.& Lucy A.Carter age 18 S POB Louisa Co POR

Spotsylvania; POM Good Hope Baptist Ch, Spotsylvania 16 Jan 1895 SPMR 7 Jan 1895 SPML

PRITCHETT, William V. s/o William P. & Martha Ann Pritchett age 22 S farmer POB & POR Spotsylvania & **PRITCHETT**, Lucy H. d/o H.M. & A.A.F. Pritchett age 21 S POB & POR Spotsylvania; POM Spotsylvania 8 Aug 1897 SPMR 7 Aug 1897 SPML

PROCTOR, George s/o Abraham Proctor & Mary A. Carter age 26 S carpenter POB & POR Orange POC & **THOMPSON**, Frances age 16 S POB & POR Orange POC; POM Orange 12 Oct 1867 OMR 11 Oct 1867 OML

PROCTOR, Olander s/o Thomas & Mary Proctor age 21 farmer POB & POR Orange & **BLEDSOE**, Mildred H. d/o John & Margaret Bledsoe age 17 POB & POR Orange; POM Orange 29 Dec 1857 OMR 26 Dec 1857 OML

PROCTOR, William s/o William & Eliza Proctor age 42 W POB & POR Caroline Co & **MILLS**, Peggie d/o James & Betsy Mills age 32 S POB & POR Spotsylvania; POM Bellvedier 3 Jul 1884 SPMR 1 Jul 1884 SPML

PROFFITT, D.J. s/o C.C. & Martha Proffitt age 21 S farmer POB Goochland Co POR Spotsylvania & **MASSEY**, Lizzie L. d/o Willliam H. & Fanny Massey age 20 S POB & POR Spotsylvania; POM Spotsylvania 6 Sep 1900 SPMR SPML

PRYOR, John s/o Beverly & Sally Pryor age 23 S farmer POB & POR Spotsylvania POC & **FRAZER**, Keziah d/o William Frazer age 20 S POB & POR Spotsylvania POC; POM Spotsylvania 22 Apr 1871 SPMR 21 Apr 1871 SPML

PRYOR, Pleasant s/o William & Mary Ann Pryor age 24 S POB & POR Orange POC & **CARTER**, Victoria d/o Alexander & Ellen Carter age 16 S POB & POR Spotsylvania POC; POM Spotsylvania 29 Dec 1874 SPMR SPML

PUGH, W.H. s/o H.W. & Elizabeth Pugh age 30 S nurseryman POB Nelson Co, Va POR Baltimore, Md & **POOL**, Nannie Irene d/o Alfred & Nannie Pool age 21 S POB & POR Spotsylvania; POM Oakland,

Spotsylvania 1 Sep 1885 SPMR 31 Aug 1885 SPML
PULLIAM, George T. s/o Thomas R.& Sarah F.Pulliam age 26 S farmer POB & POR Spotsylvania & **HAZEL**, Viola C. d/o Frank & Georgie Hazel age 18 S POB Washington D.C. POR Spotsylvania; POM Spotsylvania 4 May 1898 SPMR SPML
PULLIAM, James R. Jr. s/o James R. & Jemima Pulliam age 21 S farmer POB & POR Spotsylvania & (not listed in clerk's book and there is no original ML or MR)age 19 POB Charles Co, Md POR Spotsylvania; 17 Jan 1856 SPMR
PULLIAM, John C. s/o T.C.& Harriet Pulliam S farmer POB & POR Spotsylvania & **WIGLESWORTH**, Mattie J. d/o B.N.Wigglesworth S POB & POR Spotsylvania; POM Spotsylvania 21 Apr 1897 SPMR SPML
PULLIAM, Judson H. s/o Thomas R. & Sarah F.Pulliam age 23 S farmer POB & POR Spotsylvania & **KRONK**, Mary Hoover d/o Joseph & Barbara Kronk age 19 S POB Ohio POR Spotsylvania;

POM Spotsylvania 14 Mar 1900 SPMR SPML
PULLIAM, T.C. s/o John E.& Elizabeth Pulliam age 36 W farmer POB & POR Spotsylvania & **CHEWNING**, Jane C. d/o William V.& Pamilia Chewning age 42 S POB & POR Spotsylvania; 26 Oct 1865 SPML
PULLIAM, Thomas C. s/o Richard & R.R.Pulliam age 34 S farmer POB & POR Spotsylvania & **ROBINSON**, Harriet L. d/o Henry & Sarah Robinson age 25 S POB & POR Spotsylvania; POM Spotsylvania 18 Oct 1866 SPMR SPML
PULLIAM, Thomas R. s/o Thomas & Eliza Pulliam age 28 S farmer POB & POR Spotsylvania & **MASTIN**, Sarah d/o Elizabeth Faulconer age 27 D POB & POR Spotsylvania; POM Spotsylvania 1868 (no month or day on MR)SPMR 2 Jun 1868 SPML
PULLIAM, Willie E. s/o T.C.& Louisa Pulliam age 22 S farmer POB & POR Spotsylvania & **PARTLOW**, Ophelia E. d/o L.& Mary E.Partlow age 22 S POB & POR Spotsylvania; POM Spotsylvania 20

Dec 1871 SPMR 7
Nov 1871 SPML
QUARLES, Aaron s/o
George & Lizzie
Quarles age 24 S
laborer POB
Louisa Co POR
Spotsylvania POC
& **JOHNSTON**,
Phillis d/o
Addison & Kate
Johnston age 22 S
POB & POR
Spotsylvania POC;
POM Spotsylvania
8 May 1900 SPMR
SPML
QUARLES, Duncan M. s/o
John T. & Mary
Quarles age 22
teacher POB
Louisa Co POR
Orange &
SPOTSWOOD, Martha
P. d/o William
L.M.& Catharine
H.Spotswood age
21 POB
Spotsylvania POR
Orange; POM
Orange 21 Jul
1857 OMR 14 Jul
1857 OML
QUARLES, Frank s/o
Anderson & Rose
Quarles age 25 S
laborer POB & POR
Spotsylvania POC
& **JACKSON**, Lucy
age 22 S POB &
POR Spotsylvania
POC; POM New Hope
Ch, Spotsylvania
30 Oct 1900 SPMR
SPML
QUARLES, Thomas s/o
A.& F.Quarles age
21 S laborer POB
& POR
SPotsylvania POC
& **WILLIS**, Indy A.
d/o B.&
A.E.Willis age 16
S POB & POR

Spotsylvania POC;
POM Branch Fork,
Ch, Spotsylvania
29 Dec 1879 SPMR
27 Dec 1879 SPML
QUISENBERRY, Daniel
s/o Vivion &
Sarah Quisenberry
age 20 S farmer
POB & POR Orange
& **REYNOLDS**,
Sallie C. d/o
Joseph D.&
Elizabeth
M.Reynolds age 19
S POB & POR
Orange; POM
Orange 2 Dec 1858
OMR 29 Nov 1858
OML
QUISENBERRY, James &
SANDERS, Sarah
Frances; 19 Nov
1851 OML
QUISENBERRY, John &
ROW, Mary E. d/o
Elhanon Row; POM
Orange 23 Sep
1852 OMR 21 Sep
1852 OML
QUISENBERRY, Vivion
s/o George
Quisenberry &
Jenny Daniel age
73 W farmer POB &
POR Orange &
HERNDON,
Elizabeth d/o
Ambrose Coleman &
Frances Hilman
age 52 W POB &
POR Orange; POM
29 Nov 1866 OMR
21 Nov 1866 OML
QUISENBERRY, Vivion
s/o Vivion &
Sarah Quisenberry
age 25 POB & POR
Orange &
ROBINSON, Ann E.
d/o Thomas &
Elizabeth T.
Robinson age 19
POB & POR Orange;

POM Orange 10 Dec 1857 OMR 23 Nov 1857 OML

RABESKY, Henry s/o Philip & Anna Rabesky age 25 S blacksmith POB Germany POR Orange & **KUBE**, Mary M. d/o Henry Kube & Cathrin Ruby age 31 S POB Germany POR Orange; POM Orange 7 Sep 1865 OMR 4 Sep 1865 OML

RAFTER, James B. s/o John & Winnie Rafter age 28 S attorney POB Schenectady Co, N.Y. POR Mohawk, Herkimor Co, N.Y. & **PALMER**, Georgie B.D. d/o James E.& Susann B.Palmer age 20 S POB New York City POR Spotsylvania; POM Cool Spring, Spotsylvania 27 Nov 1871 SPMR 27 Nov 1871 SPML

RAINS, Eustace S. s/o William B. & Harriet Rains age 23 S farmer POB Stafford POR King William Co & **WILLIAMS**, Rosa B. d/o Stephen H.& Sarah C.Williams age 17 b.d.Dec 1865 S POB & POR Spotsylvania; POM Livingston Twsp, Spotsylvania 27 Dec 1882 SPMR 26 Dec 1882 SPML

RANDOLPH, John B. s/o John & Margaret Randolph age 34 W clerk, POB & POR Washington D.C. & **WHITE**, Gabreilla R. (aka Ella White) d/o A.S.& H.R.White age 25 S POB Indiana POR Spotsylvania; POM Spotsylvania 18 Mar 1878 SPMR 2 Mar 1878 SPML

RAWLINGS, Alfred B. s/o Alfred & Judith A.Rawlings age 22 S attorney POB & POR Spotsylvania & **BAILEY**, Margaret L. d/o Chancellor & Jennie E.Bailey age 22 S POB Philadelphia,Pa POR Spotsylvania; POM Spotsylvania 1 Jun 1881 SPMR 31 May 1881 SPML

RAWLINGS, Edward T. s/o Lewis & Hannah G.Rawlings age 30 general agent POB Spotsylvania POR Richmond & **PORTER**, Susan d/o John A. & Mary Porter POB & POR Orange; POM Orange 21 Feb 1856 OMR 12 Feb 1856 OML

RAWLINGS, James L. s/o Alfred & J.A.Rawlings age 25 S farmer POB & POR Spotsylvania & **BOGGS**, Clara L. d/o Lewis A.& Bettie Boggs age 24 S POB & POR Spotsylvania; POM Livingston, Spotsylvania 6 Feb 1872 SPMR 5 Feb 1872 SPML

RAWLINGS, James R. s/o J.B.& A.E.Rawlings age 25 S farmer POB & POR Spotsylvania & **CHANCELLOR**, Leona d/o M.S.& L.Chancellor age 20 POB & POR Spotsylvania; POM Spotsylvania 14 Nov 1877 SPMR 12 Nov 1877 SPML

RAWLINGS, Z.H. s/o J.B.& E.Rawlings age 25 S farmer POB Orange POR Spotsylvania & **ROWE**, B.B. d/o A.& N.Rowe age 25 S POB & POR Spotsylvania; POM Spotsylvania 1 Nov 1860 SPMR

REAMS, L.W. s/o D.& R.Reams age 34 W merchant POB & POR Powhattan Co & **JERRELL**, A.M. d/o John C.& A.M.Jerrell age 22 S POB & POR Spotsylvania; POM Spotsylvania 14 Oct 1880 SPMR 13 Oct 1880 SPML

REAMS, William B. s/o D.& R.Reams age 28 S POB Pohattan Co & **JERRELL**, Alma d/o John C.& A.M.Jerrell age 23 POB & POR Spotsylvania; POM Spotsylvania 2 Oct 1878 SPMR 3 Sep 1878 SPML

REDMAN, Gabriel s/o Harriet Redman age 24 S laborer POB & POR Spotsylvania POC & **EDLIN**, Addie d/o Thomas & Mary Edlin age 20 S POB & POR Spotsylvania POC; POM Spotsylvania 1 Mar 1894 SPMR 27 Feb 1894 SPML

REDMAN, Henry s/o Armstead Doggett & Mary Redman age 25 S farmer POB & POR Spotsylvania POC & **ARKER**, Martha d/o Hiny & Jane Parker age 16 S POB & POR Spotsylvania POC: POM Spotsylvania 18 Dec 1873 SPMR 17 Dec 1873 SPML

REED, John S. s/o Silvester & Charlotte E.Reed age 19 S farmer POB New York POR Spotsylvania & **WINTERS**, Emma A. d/o Floyd & Mary L.Robinson age 32 W POB New York POR Spotsylvania; POM Spotsylvania 13 Apr 1884 SPMR 11 Apr 1884 SPML

REED, William H. s/o Sylvester & C.E.Reed age 25 S farmer POB & POR Spotsylvania & **POWELL**, Mabel d/o Peter & Agnes E. Powell age 15 S POB & POR Spotsylvania; POM Spotsylvania C.H.25 Feb 1897 SPMR SPML

REEVES, Stafford s/o Timothy & Betsy Reeves age 26 S editor POB Hull, Yorkshire, England POR Woodville, Orange Co & **SEIDELL**.

Elizabeth A. d/o Charles Ward & Mary Seidell age 18 S POB Bucks Co, Pa POR Vancluse, Orange ; POM Orange 20 Mar 1856 OMR 19 Mar 1856 OML

REID, J.Dorsey lieutenant POR Washington city & **CHAPMAN**, Maria Louisa d/o Richard M.Chapman; POM Orange 1 Aug 1851 OMR 31 Jul 1851 OML

RENQUEST, John F. s/o A.F.& Mary E.Renquest age 29 S farmer POB Hanover Co POR Louisa Co & **MASTIN**, Lucy B. d/o James G.& Mary C.Martin age 17 S POB & POR Spotsylvania; POM Spotsylvania 30 Nov 1897 SPMR SPML

REVERE, James Holland s/o George & Marian Revere of Fredericksburg age 29 POR Fredericksburg & **BROWN**, Minnie Jane d/o Frank & Mary Brown age 24 POR Fredericksburg; POM Fredericksburg 3 Aug 1898 TCF

REYNOLDS, Benjamin F. & **WRIGHT**, Virginia T. d/o Benjamin Wright; POM Orange 4 Jul 1853 OMR 27 Jun 1853 OML

REYNOLDS, George W. s/o William & Nancy Reynolds age 30 S bricklayer POB & POR Orange & **KISHPAUGH**, Martha J. d/o John & Febia A.Kishpaugh age 20 S POB & POR Spotsylvania; POM Spotsylvania 2 Jun 1870 SPMR 28 May 1870 SPML

REYNOLDS, John W. s/o John D.Reynolds & Elizabeth Henderson age 31 S farmer POB & POR Orange & **DOWNER**, Mildred A. d/o Robert E.Downer & Frances A.Daniel age 18 S POB & POR Orange; POM Orange 31 May 1866 OMR 30 May 1866 OML

REYNOLDS, Lewis H.& **RHOADES**, Lucy; POM Orange 21 Dec 1851 OMR 19 Dec 1851 OML

REYNOLDS, Robert s/o James & Lucy Reynolds age 22 S farmer POB Caroline Co POR Spotsylvania POC & **MILLES**, Martha d/o Ralph & Harriet Milles age 21 S POB & POR Spotsylvania POC; POM Spotsylvania 26 Dec 1868 SPMR 24 Dec 1868 SPML

REYNOLDS, William G. & **ROACH**, Susan M.; POM Orange 25 Nov 1852 OMR 22 Nov 1852 OML

REYNOLDS, William H. s/o William S.Reynolds & Ann Quisenberry age 25 S farmer POB Spotsylvania POR Orange & **REYNOLDS**, Ann Wise d/o James D.Reynolds & Elizabeth Henderson age 16 S POB & POR Orange; POM Orange 14 Mar 1867 OMR 11 Mar 1867 OML

REYNOLDS, William K. s/o George Washington Reynolds & M.J.Reynolds age 23 S school teacher POB & POR Orange & **HARDING**, Irene E. d/o P.C.& C.B.Harding age 18 S POB & POR Spotsylvania; POM Spotsylvania C.H. 16 Nov 1898 SPMR 15 Nov 1898 SPML

RHOADES, John & **HATCH**, Ann Eliza d/o Henry Hatch; POM Orange 21 Dec 1851 OMR 19 Dec 1851 OML

RHOADES, Richard B. s/o Willaim Rhoades & Elizabeth Couthron age 30 S farmer POB & POR Orange & **KUBE**, Mary G. d/o John Kube age 25 S POB & POR Orange; POM Orange 29 Mar 1866 OMR 22 Mar 1866 OML

RHOADS, Clarence L. s/o Charles A.& Hannah Rhoades age 42 W farmer POB Jordan,Onondaga Co,N.Y. POR Spotsylvania & **COLE**, Lena D. d/o James & Elizabeth Cole age 29 S POB Caroline Co POR Spotsylvania; 3 Jan 1888 SPMR SPML

RHODES, John Q. s/o Richard & Martha P.Rhodes age 24 S minister POB Albemarle Co,Va POR Spotsylvania & **FLEMING**, Roberta A. d/o Alfred & Roberta C.Pool age 20 W POB & POR Spotsylvania; POM Spotsylvania 30 Nov 1871 SPMR 27 Nov 1871 SPML

RICE, Elmer E. s/o William W.& Elizabeth Rice age 25 S farmer POB Lapeer Co, Michigan POR Spotsylvania & **CLARK**, Alice B. d/o George W. & Esther V.Clark age 23 S POB & POR Spotsylvania; POM Spotsylvania 7 Dec 1898 SPMR 5 Dec 1898 SPML

RICE, Walter M. s/o William W.& Elizabeth Rice age 24 S merchant POB Lapeer Co, Michigan POR Spotsylvania & **DAVIS**, Lillie d/o Nicolas & Julia E.Davis age 16 S POB Genesee Co,

Michigan POR
Spotsylvania; POM
Spotsylvania 8
Jun 1892 SPMR 6
Jun 1892 SPML

RICHARDS, Ferdinand
s/o Richard
Richards Jr. &
QUISENBERRY,
Jannie d/o Vivion
Quisenberry; POM
Orange 9 Mar 1852
OMR 8 Mar 1852
OML

RICHARDS, George W. &
TINDER, Sarah E.;
POM Orange 30 Dec
1852 OMR 29 Dec
1852 OML

RICHARDS, John S. s/o
Fountain Richards
& Sophia Mills
age 39 S
physician POB &
POR Albemarle Co
& **WINSLOW**, Bettie
E. d/o George
Winslow & Martha
Cockrell age 26 S
POB & POR Orange;
POM Orange 22 Dec
1864 OMR 21 Dec
1864 OML

RICHARDS, John s/o
Thomas Richards &
Ann Holmes age 49
W farmer POB
Orange POR
Madison Co &
ROBINSON, Jane E.
d/o Hugh Robinson
& Susan Johnson
age 27 S POB &
POR Orange; POM
Orange 28 May
1861 OMR 25 May
1861 OML

RICHARDS, Quintus s/o
Richard & Nancy
Richards age 28 S
merchant POB
Orange POR
Crawfordville,
Georgia &
DICKINSON,
Florence M. d/o
Hugh M.&
S.C.Dickinson age
19 S POB & POR
Spotsylvania; 15
Oct 1866 SPML

RICHARDS, Richard s/o
John Richards &
Elizabeth Tinder
age 33 S
carpenter POB
Culpeper Co POR
Orange & **FAIRFAX**,
Flora d/o Robert
Dickinson & Julia
Craig age 21 W
POB Augusta Co
POR Orange; POM
Gordonsville,
Orange 13 Sep
1866 OMR OML

RICHARDS, Robinson C.
& **TINDER**,
Elizabeth L. d/o
James R.Tinder
Sr.; POM Orange
24 Dec 1851 OMR
22 Dec 1851 OML

RICHARDS, William W. &
LANCASTER, Susan;
POM Orange 2 Feb
1852 OMR 19 Jan
1852 OML

RICHARDSON, Benjamin
s/o Braddock &
Sarah Richardson
age 21 S laborer
POB & POR
Spotsylvania POC
& **HOLMES**, Celia
d/o Amanda Holmes
age 19 S POB
Clarke Co POR
Spotsylvania POC;
POM Spotsylvania
3 Jan 1884 SPMR 1
Jan 1884 SPML

RICHARDSON, George s/o
B.& S.Richardson
age 25 S laborer
POB & POR
Spotsylvaina POC
& **PENDLETON**,

Elizabeth d/o
John & D.Morton
age 26 S POB
Orange POR
Spotsylvania POC;
POM Gravel Hill,
Spotsylvania 27
Jul 1878 SPMR 26
Jul 1878 SPML
RICHARDSON, John s/o
B.& S.Richardson
age 23 S laborer
POB & POR
Spotsylvania POC
& **LEWIS**, Julia
d/o L.& M.Lewis
age 22 S POB
Louisa Co POR
Spotsylvania POC;
POM their
residence,
Spotsylvania 27
Aug 1879 SPMR 24
Aug 1879 SPML
RICHARDSON, Lee s/o
Braddock & Sarah
Richardson age 22
S laborer POB &
POR Spotsylvania
POC & **WILLIAMS**,
Fanny d/o Jackson
& Harriet
Williams age 23 S
POB Orange POR
Spotsylvania POC;
POM Fountain
Bluff,
Spotsylvania 25
Dec 1884 SPMR 24
Dec 1884 SPML
RICHARDSON, Lee s/o
William & Sarah
Richardson age 34
W laborer POB &
POR Spotsylvania
POC & **THURSTON**,
Lucy M. d/o
Samuel & Mary
Thurston age 18 S
POB Orange POR
Spotsylvania POC;
POM Spotsylvania
31 Oct 1898 SPMR
SPML

RICHARDSON, Peter s/o
George & Maria
Richardson age 51
S laborer POB
Hanover Co POR
Spotsylvania POC
& **BOXLEY**, Nancy
d/o Thornton &
Martha Boxley age
37 S POB & POR
Spotsylvania POC;
POM Spotsylvania
17 Apr 1884 SPMR
14 Apr 1884 SPML
RICHARDSON, Robert A.
& **BLEDSOE**,
Elizabeth; POM
Orange 29 Dec
1853 OMR 27 Dec
1853 OML
RICHESON, W.H. s/o
William P.& Anne
C.Richeson age 27
S farmer POB &
POR Spotsylvania
& **DURRETT**, J.T.
d/o E.V.& Mary
Durrett age 23 S
POB & POR
Spotsylvania; POM
Bethany Ch 20 Dec
1893 SPMR 19 Dec
1893 SPML
RICKER, Henry Clifford
s/o M.M.& Lucy
Ricker age 22 S
POB & POR
Spotsylvania &
THOMAS, Jennie W.
d/o William E.&
Sarah Thomas age
22 S POB & POR
Spotsylvania; POM
Tabernacle M.E.Ch
S, Spotsylvania 2
May 1899 SPMR 28
Apr 1899 SPML
RICKETTS, William H.
s/o H.Ricketts &
Elizabeth Fogg
age 25 S saddler
POB Rappahannock
Co POR Orange &
CULLEN, Emma d/o

George Cullen age 24 S POB & POR Orange; POM Orange C.H.15 Sep 1863 OMR 14 Sep 1863 OML

RIELY, Walter s/o Manoah & Cleopatra Riely age 30 S farmer POB & POR Stafford & **PATES**, Susan d/o Augustus & Clementine Pates age 22 S POB & POR Spotsylvania; POM Spotsylvania 30 Dec 1896 SPMR SPML

RIEVES, William s/o Moses Rieves & Betty Hogins age 25 W shoemaker POB Madison Co POR Orange POC & **JOHNSON**, Charlotte d/o John Johnson & Lucy Harrison age 21 S POB & POR Orange POC; POM Orange 26 Dec 1867 OMR 25 Dec 1867 OML

RINER, Jacob E. s/o Aaron Riner & Mary Plankenbaker age 31 S carpenter POB Green Co POR Louisa Co & **ROBINSON**, Martha J. d/o James Robinson & Nancy Ryan age 22 S POB Louisa Co POR Orange; POM Orange 21 Sep 1865 OMR 18 Sep 1865 OML

RINER, Jacob s/o Daniel Riner & Elizabeth Fleshman age 70 W farmer POB Madison Co POR Orange & **ESTES**, Nancy F. d/o Edward Gilbert & Susan Sandridge age 44 W POB Albemarle Co POR Orange; POM Orange 28 Apr 1867 OMR 25 Apr 1867 OML

RIXEY, James W. s/o T.C.& M.E.Rixey age 33 S farmer POB & POR Caroline Co & **SMITH**, E.L. d/o William C.& S.E.Smith age 21(?) S POB & POR Spotsylvania; POM Spotsylvania 8 Jan 1880 SPMR 5 Jan 1880 SPML

ROACH, Emanuel B. s/o Michael Roach & Angelina Ricker age 25 S farmer POB Rockingham Co POR Orange & **FAULCONER**, Mary d/o John Faulconer & Elizabeth Lee age 24 S POB & POR Orange; POM Orange 27 Jun 1867 OMR 26 Jun 1867 OML

ROACH, James s/o Robert & Mildred Roach age 26 S deputy sheriff POB & POR Orange & **ROW**, Adalade E. d/o Elahanan & Mary D.Row age 22 S POB & POR Orange; POM Orange 8 Dec 1859 OMR 28 Nov 1859 OML

ROACH, James s/o Robert Roach & Mildred Jones age 29 W sheriff of Orange Co POB & POR Orange & **HENDERSON**, Henrietta J. d/o William Henderson & Elizabeth J.Hanelson age 19 S POB Randolph Co,Mo POR Orange; POM Ellerslie, Orange 13 Aug 1863 OMR 27 Jul 1863 OML

ROACH, James s/o Robert Roach & Mildred Jones age 32 W sheriff of Orange Co POB & POR Orange & **WILLIS**, Jane G. d/o James Willis & Elizabeth Gordon age 26 S POB & POR Orange; POM Orange 19 Feb 1867 OMR 15 Feb 1867 OML

ROACH, John & **SMITH**, Lucy J.; 24 Jul 1860 OML

ROANE, John M. s/o Dr.Sam & Ann F.Roane age 25 S minister POB Middlesex Co POR Spotsylvania & **DOBYNS**, Maria L. d/o Leroy W.& Vanangus E.Dobyns age 25 S POB Essex Co POR Spotsylvania; POM Spotsylvania 18 Apr 1866 SPMR 7 Apr 1866 SPML

ROBBINS, Wilber Fiske s/o John S.Robins & Drucilla D.Conner age 32 S minister POB Accomac Co POR Culpeper & **HUME**, Bettie Thompson d/o Benjamin Hume & Mary Lower age 33 S POB & POR Orange; POM Orange 5 Mar 1867 OMR 26 Feb 2867 OML

ROBERSON, Dudley s/o Winston & Lettie Robinson age 40 W farmer POB & POR Spotsylvania POC & **CARTER**, Mattie d/o Abram & Merica age 26 S POB & POR Spotsylvania POC; POM Spotsylvania C.H.21 Oct 1886 SPMR SPML

ROBERSON, Joseph s/o Morton & Sallie Roberson age 21 S farmer POB & POR Spotsylvania POC & **ROLLS**, Martha Jane d/o Thomas & Margaret Rolls age 21 S POB Caroline Co POR Spotsylvania POC; POM Spotsylvania C.H.27 Dec 1890 SPMR SPML

ROBERTS, Andrew S. s/o J.P.Roberts & Mary l.Seal age 23 S tanner POB Madison Co POR Orange & **WATKINS**, Mollie B. d/o R.S.Watkins & Elizabeth M.Daniel age 21 S POB & POR Orange; POM Orange 1 Nov 1866 OMR OML

ROBERTS, Calvin T. s/o Henry H.& Nannie B.Roberts age 35 S lawyer POB &

POR Nelson Co, Va
& **DEJARNETTE**,
Mary A. d/o
Dr.Joseph S.&
Annie DeJarnette
age 32 S POB &
POR Spotsylvania;
POM Spotsylvania
14 Jul 1885 SPMR
11 Jul 1885 SPML
ROBERTS, Pleasant D.
s/o Mathew &
Nancy Roberts age
33 S farmer POB &
POR Nelson Co &
ATKINS, Lucy M.
d/o Joseph & Mary
Atkins age 33 S
POB & POR Orange;
POM Orange 13 Jul
1859 OMR 12 Jul
1859 OML
ROBERTS, Robert W. s/o
J.P.Roberts &
Mary L.Seal age
19 S farmer POB
Culpeper Co POR
Orange & **ESTES**,
Mildred A. d/o
James & Elizabeth
Estes age 19 S
POB & POR Orange;
POM Orange 25 Dec
1866 OMR 24 Dec
1866 OML
ROBERTS, T.W. s/o
J.W.& E.C.Roberts
age 22 S farmer
POB Goochland Co
POR Spotsylvania
& **MOORE**, S. d/o
G.& N.Moore age
21 S POB Culpeper
POR Spotsylvania;
POM Spotsylvania
29 Jan 1860 SPMR
ROBERTSON, Jame s/o
Henry Robertson &
Sarah Faulconer
age 24 S laborer
POB & POR
Spotsylvania &
WOOLFRY, Margaret
d/o Richard

Woolfry & Eveline
Sullivan age 16 S
POB Spotsylvania
POR Orange; POM
Orange 28 Dec
1860 OMR 27 Dec
1860 OML
ROBEY, Henry R. s/o
Richard & Ann
Robey age 55 W
nurseryman POB
Fredericksburg
POR Spotsylvania
& **LUCAS**, Ann E.
d/o Walker &
Sarah Lucas age
41 S POB
Fredericksburg
POR Spotsylvania;
POM
Prot.Episcopal
Ch, Spotsylvania
2 Jan 1866 SPMR
28 Dec 1865 SPML
ROBEY, William B. s/o
H.R. & Clara
Robey age 28 S
nurseryman POB &
POR Spotsylvania
& **PEAKE**, Mary H.
d/o James B.&
Louisa Peake age
29 S POB & POR
Spotsylvania; POM
Spotsylvania 6
Mar 1866 SPMR 5
Mar 1866 SPML
ROBEY, William B. s/o
H.R.& C.Robey age
41 W POB & POR
Spotsylvania &
KENDALL, Ida A.
d/o R.G.&
Virginia Kendall
age 27 S POB &
POR Spotsylvania;
POM Spotsylvania
20 Oct 1880 SPMR
19 Oct 1880 SPML
ROBEY, William B. s/o
H.R.& Clara Robey
age 28 S
nurseryman POB &
POR Spotsylvania

& **PEAKE**, Mary H. d/o James B. & Louisa Peake age 29 S POB & POR Spotsylvania; POM Spotsylvania 6 Mar 1866 SPMR 5 Mar 1866 SPML

ROBINSON, Ancyle M. s/o Larkin & Sarah A. Robinson age 26 S farmer POB Caroline Co POR Spotsylvania & **LONG**, Hardinia d/o Robert & Mary Long age 19 S POB & POR Spotsylvania; POM Spotsylvania 30 Apr 1868 SPMR 22 Apr 1868 SPML

ROBINSON, Birt s/o Dudley & Charlotte Robinson age 26 S laborer POB & POR Spotsylvania POC & **CARTER**, Matilda d/o Abram & America Carter age 22 S POB & POR Spotsylvania POC; POM Spotsylvania 27 Dec 1894 SPMR 26 Dec 1894 SPML

ROBINSON, Edward s/o Morton & Pattie Robinson ag 27 S laborer POB & POR Spotsylvania POC & **EMANUEL**, Sallie d/o Phil & Lucinda Emanuel age 21 S POB & POR Spotsylvania POC; POM Spotsylvania C.H. 17 Jun 1886 SPMR SPML

ROBINSON, Henry S. s/o F. & M. L. Robinson age 21 S farmer POB New York POR Spotsylvania & **GARDNER**, Amelia S. d/o N. & M.E. Gardner age 19 S POB & POR Spotsylvania; POM Chancellor, Spotsylvania 10 Feb 1879 SPMR 6 Feb 1879 SPML

ROBINSON, Henry s/o Henry & Sarah A. Robinson & **SPINDLE**, Virginia D. d/o Edmund J. & Mary J. Spindle age 20 S POB & POR Spotsylvania; POM Spotsylvania 18 Jan 1872 SPMR 16 Jan 1871 (possible clerk error) SPML

ROBINSON, Jacob R. s/o George & S. Robinson age 43 W farmer POB & POR Pennsylvania & **WORCESTER**, Josey d/o Thomas & C. Worcester age 24 S POB Pennsylvania POR Spotsylvania; POM Spotsylvania 6 Mar 1879 SPMR 3 Mar 1879 SPML

ROBINSON, James A. s/o William & K. Robinson age 21 S laborer POB Fredericksburg POR Spotsylvania POC & **SLAUGHTER**, Ella d/o H. & E. Slaughter age 20 S POB & POR Spotsylvania POC; POM Spotsylvania 8 Jan 1880 SPMR SPML

ROBINSON, James R. & **PAYNE**, Susan Ann

d/o Charles G.Payne; 24 Nov 1851 OML

ROBINSON, James S. s/o Thomas A.& Maria L.Robinson age 23 S merchant POB & POR Orange C.H. & **BALLARD**, Janet G. d/o Garland & Georgianna Ballard age 21 S POB & POR Orange C.H.; POM Orange 4 Aug 1858 OMR OML

ROBINSON, James s/o Waller & Sarah Robinson age 23 S laborer POB & POR Louisa Co POC & **JOHNSON**, Merian d/o Solomon & Rebecca Johnson age 17 S POB Louisa Co POR Spotsylvania POC; POM Spotsylvania 3 Jan 1877 SPMR 1 Jan 1877 SPML

ROBINSON, John J. & **PEYTON**, Georgianna; POM Orange 12 Oct 1852 OMR 11 Oct 1852 OML

ROBINSON, John s/o Henry & Sarah A.Robinson age 22 S farmer POB & POR Spotsylvania & **FULCHER**, Callie V. d/o John C.& Ann F.Fulcher age 24 S POB & POR Spotsylvania; POM Spotsylvania 23 Dec 1869 SPMR 20 Dec 1869 SPML

ROBINSON, L.B. s/o William & Eliza Robinson age 22 S farmer POB & POR King William Co &

JONES, Cappie B. d/o Eli & Mary E.Jones age 16 S POB & POR Spotsylvania; POM Spotsylvania 28 Nov 1875 SPMR

ROBINSON, Peter s/o John & G.Able age 21 S laborer POB Caroline Co POR Spotsylvania POC & **MINOR**, Bettie d/o Silas & M.Minor age 23 S POB Caroline Co POR Spotsylvania POC; POM Spotsylvania 29 Dec 1877 SPMR 28 Dec 1877 SPML

ROBINSON, S. s/o T.& Y. (or F.)Robinson age 54 W farmer POB Chesterfield Co & **SCRAIM**(?), J.T. age32 S; POM Spotsylvania 7 Mar 1858 SPMR

ROBINSON, Thomas H. s/o Joseph H.& Emily Robinson age 33 S farmer POB & POR Spotsylvania & **MASTIN**, Emma B. d/o Elijah & Eliza Mastin age 24 S POB & POR Spotsylvania; POM Spotsylvania C.H.13 Dec 1882 SPMR SPML

ROBINSON, William E. s/o James & Mary R.Robinson age 26 S farmer POB Stafford POR Fauquier Co & **ROBERSON**, Sarah E. d/o Henry & Sarah A.Roberson age 23 S POB &

POR Spotsylvania; POM Spotsylvania 25 Jan 1871 SPMR 24 Jan 1871 SPML
ROBINSON, William F. s/o Joseph B. & Mary C. Robinson age 24 S laboere POB & POR Spotsylvania & **WHITE**, Elizabeth M. d/o Alonzo & Louisa White age 17 S POB & POR Spotsylvania; POM Spotsylvania 12 May 1897 SPMR 11 May 1897 SPML
ROBINSON, Willis L. s/o Henry & S.A. Robinson age 22 S farmer POB & POR Spotsylvnania & **BURRUSS**, Olivia E. d/o James T. & Paulina P. Burruss age 23 S POB Greenfield, Illinois POR Spotsylvania; POM Spotsylvania 17 Apr 1877 SPMR 13 Apr 1877 SPML
RODGERS, Wilford M. s/o James M. & Mary M. Rodgers age 45 S shoemaker POB & POR Culpeper Co & **NASH**, Julia A. d/o Charles & Alcy Martin age 47 W POB Stafford POR Spotsylvania; POM Spotsylvania 2 Nov 1868 SPMR 31 Dec 1867 SPML
ROGERS, Charles P. POR Albemarle & **COLE**, Catharine A.; POM Orange 24 May 1853 OMR 23 May 1853 OML

ROGERS, Isaac N. & **WHITE**, Mary A.; 20 Dec 1854 OML
ROGERS, Robert H. s/o Joseph Rogers & Malinda Newman age 32 S POB & POR Orange & **TERRILL**, Emma Lovell d/o Oliver Terril & Susan Proctor age 21 S POB & POR Orange; POM Orange 21 May 1867 OMR 20 May 1867 OML
ROSE, G.W. s/o John & Mary A. Rose age 29 S farmer POB & POR King George Co & **POLLARD**, Lucy I. d/o Isaac & Lucy Pollard age 21 S POB & POR Spotsylvania; POM Spotsylvania 7 Oct 1884 SPMR 6 Oct 1884 SPML
ROSE, Marcus A. s/o Lucy Rose age 32 S farmer POB & POR Spotsylvania & **BEAZLEY**, Betty A. d/o Duerson & Clementina Beazley age 28 S POB & POR Spotsylvania; POM Spotsylvania 18 Jan 1872 SPMR 17 Jan 1872 SPML
ROSS, Henry C. s/o J. & M. Ross age 25 S laboer POB & POR Spotsylvania POC & **MORSE**, Polly d/o R. & M. Morse age 21 S POB & POR Spotsylvania POC; POM Spotsylvania 20 Dec 1877 SPMR 18 Dec 1877 SPML

ROSS, Monroe s/o George & Matilda Ross age 22 S farmer POB & POR Spotsylvania POC & **CAMPBELL**, Matilda d/o Lewis & Polly Campbell age 25 S POB & POR Spotsylvania POC; POM Spotsylvania 13 Jul 1873 SPMR 24 Dec 1872 SPML

ROSS, Robert J. s/o Robert & Matilda Ross age 50 W farmer POB Prince Edward Co, Va POR Spotsylvania POC & **COATS**, Alice d/o Fanny Coats age 37 W POB & POR Spotsylvania POC; POM St.Luke Baptist Ch, Spotsylvania 17 Nov 1897 SPMR 16 Nov 1897 SPML

ROSS, Robert James s/o Bob & Tilla Ross age 27 S farmer POB Prince Edward Co POR Spotsylvania POC & **GARNETT**, Rebecca d/o Henry & Ann Garnett age 22 S POB Essex Co POR Spotsylvania POC: POM Spotsylvania 8 Oct (no year)SPMR 8 Oct 1870 SPML

ROWE, James W. s/o Keeling Rowe & Fannie Bates age 28 S farmer POB & POR Caroline Co & **SANFORD**, Jennie B. d/o Lawrence Sanford & Lucy Walker age 21 S POB & POR Orange; POM Orange 12 Dec 1867 OMR 26 Nov 1867 OML

ROWE, John S. age about 22 deputy sheriff of Orange Co POR Orange & **WALKER**, Eliza d/o Benjamin Walker age about 22; POM Orange 20 Dec 1853 OMR 17 Dec 1853 OML

ROWLAND, William H. s/o Isaac Rowland & Winney Becksley age 26 S farmer POB Soundes Co,Ga POR Clynch(?)Co, Ga & **KNIGHT**, Ann E. d/o Lewis Knight age 25 S POB Madison Co POR Orange; POM Orange 23 Mar 1864 OMR 22 Mar 1864 OML

ROWZIE, E.G. s/o E.A.& M.Rowzie age 25 S physician POB & POR Hanover Co & **JERRELL**, J.S. d/o J.C.& M.Jerrell age 20 S POB & POR Spotsylvania; POM Spotsylvania 3 Nov 1858 SPMR

ROY, Stapleton s/o Peter & Matilda Roy age 22 S farmer POB & POR Spotsylvania POC & **WARE**, William (this is the name given on the MR & ML) d/o Cato & Sarah Ware age 21 S POB & POR Spotsylvania POC; POM Spotsylvania 9 Apr 1874 SPMR 7 Apr 1874 SPML

RUDOLPH, Frank s/o Richard & Sarah

Rudolph age 25 S minister of the gospel POB Jackson Co, N.C. POR Spotsylvania POC & **HOWARD**, Mary F. d/o Jackson & Agnes Howard age 19 S POB & POR Spotsylvania POC; POM Spotsylvania 14 Mar 1894 SPMR 12 Mar 1894 SPML

RUDOLPH, Frank s/o Wesley & Keziah Rudolph age 32 W farmer POB Cotton Valley, Jackson Co POR Spotsylvania POC & **HARVEY**, Teresa d/o Richard & Elizabeth Harvey age 18 S POB Baltimore, Md POR Spotsylvania POC; POM Spotsylvania 31 Mar 1900 SPMR SPML

RUSSELL, R.H. s/o B.& A.Russell age 232 S POB Spotsylvania & **ATKINS**, A. d/o Maria Atkins age 28 S POB King & Queen Co; POM Spotsylvania 25 Feb 1856 SPMR

SACRA, J.J. s/o Robert & Mary Sacra age 36 S miner POB & POR Spotsylvania & **BROOKS**, Lorena d/o Robert & Mary Brooks age 22 S POB & POR Spotsylvania; POM Good Hope Spotsylvania 30 Sep 1900 SPMR 29 Sep 1900 SPML

SACRA, John H. s/o James C.& Mary J.Sacra age 36 S farmer POB & POR Spotsylvania & **CLARK**, Nannie B. d/o Strother W.& Mary E.Clark age 20 S POB & POR Spotsylvania; POM Massaponax Baptist Ch, Spotsylvania 13 Dec 1899 SPMR 11 Dec 1899 SPML

SACRA, John L. s/o John B.& Mary A.Sacra age 30 S farmer POB & POR Spotsylvania & **WRENN**, Sarah C. d/o Thomas & Sarah A.F.Wrenn age 21 S POB & POR Spotsylvania; POM Spotsylvania 12 Jan 1869 SPMR 9 Jan 1869 SPML

SACRA, William s/o Charles R.& Amanda Sacra age 25 S farmer POB & POR Spotsylvania & **PEATROSS**, Clara d/o R.G.& Mary J.Peatross age 22 S POB & POR Spotsylvania; POM Spotsylvania 20 Sep 1900 SPMR SPML

SACRE, Beverley s/o Thomas J.Sacre & Lucinda Robinson age 21 S farmer POB Spotsylvania POR Orange & **CHEWNING**, Emma R. d/o C.W.Chewning & Ellen Hopkins age 21 S POB Spotsylvania POR Orange; POM Orange 20 Oct

1867 OMR 17 Oct
1867 OML
SALE, L.C. s/o William
J.& Lucy A.Sale
age 23 S merchant
POB & POR
Caroline Co &
BLACKLEY, Clara
H. d/o John W.&
S.J.Blackley age
21 S POB & POR
Spotsylvania; POM
Frederiecksburg
20 Jul 1899 SPMR
19 Jul 1899 SPML
SAMAR, John H. s/o
John Samar & Mary
L.Hill age 35 S
planter POB Bibb
Co,Ga POR
MaCon,Ga &
CARTER, Jane A.
d/o Charles
C.Taliaferro &
Louisa
G.Armistead age
25 W POB Caroline
Co POR Orange;
POM Orange 11 Jan
1864 OMR 6 Jan
1864 OML
SAMUEL, Addison L. s/o
Addison & Nancy
Samuel age 30 S
farmer POB & POR
Spotsylvania POC
& **STRAUGHAN**,
Annie (an orphan)
age 23 S POB &
POR Spotsylvania
POC; POM
Spotsylvania C.H.
18 Jan 1883 SPMR
17 Jan 1883 SPML
SAMUEL, Henry E. s/o
Addison & Nancy
Samuel age 60 W
farmer POB & POR
Spotsylvania POC
& **HAWKINS**, Junnie
d/o Rose Hawkins
age 30 S POB &
POR Spotsylvania
POC; POM
Spotsylvania 31
Aug 1898 SPMR
SPML
SAMUEL, Henry s/o
Manuel & Judy
Samuel age 47 W
farmer POB
Caroline Co POR
Spotsylvania POC
& **GOODLOE**, Sallie
d/o Billy & Abbie
Coleman age 35 W
POB & POR
Spotsylvania POC;
POM Bethany
Ch,Caroline Co 1
Dec 1867 SPMR 29
Nov 1867 SPML
SAMUEL, Henry s/o John
& Abbie Samuel
age 22 S laborer
POB & POR
Spotsylvania POC
& **WALKER**, Milly
d/o George &
Leanna Walker age
15 S POB & POR
Spotsylvania POC;
POM Spotsylvania
C.H. 19 Oct 1892
SPMR SPML
SAMUEL, John s/o H.&
C.Samuel age 30 S
farmer POB & POR
Spotsylvania POC
& **SCOTT**, Abbie
d/o L.& W.Scott
age 25 S POB &
POR Spotsylvania
POC; POM
Spotsylvania 7
Apr 1881 SPMR 4
Apr 1881 SPML
SAMUEL, John s/o Henry
& Courtney Samuel
age 40 W POB &
POR Spotsylvania
POC & **GREEN**,
Edith d/o George
& Jennie Green
age unknown S POB
& POR
Spotsylvania POC;
POM Spotsylvania

18 Apr 1900 SPMR SPML

SAMUEL, Phil s/o John & Susan Samuel age 26 W laborer POB Caroline Co POR Spotsylvania POC & **WASHINGTON**, Maria d/o Terra Washington age 26 S POB & POR Spotsylvania POC; POM Spotsylvania 8 Apr 1882 SPMR SPML

SAMUEL, Philip s/o John Pendleton & Susan Stanard age 21 S laborer POB Caroline Co POR Spotsylvania POC & **WOOMELY**, Sally d/o T.& E.Woomeley age 19 S POB Caroline Co POR Spotsylvania POC; POM Buthan Baptist Ch, Spotsylvania 8 Apr 1877 SPMR 7 Apr 1877 SPML

SAMUEL, Virgil s/o Philip & Mary Samuel age 21 S laborer POB & POR Spotsylvania POC & **JACKSON**, Elsie d/o Susan Jackson S POB & POR Spotsylvania POC; POM Spotsylvania 1 Aug 1900 SPMR SPML

SAMUEL, William Henry s/o Philip & Mary Samuel age 22 S laborer POB & POR Spotsylvania POC & **CATLETT**, Lucinda d/o Buck Lindsay & Emily Catlett age 26 S POB & POR Spotsylvania POC;

POM Spotsylvania 4 Jan 1899 SPMR SPML

SANDERS, (aka Saunders)John R. s/o Hansford & Polly Saunders age 22 S POB & POR Orange & **PAYNE**, Mary A. d/o Charles & Lucy Payne ag 24 S POB & POR Orange; POM Orange 21 Dec 1858 OMR 20 Dec 1858 OML

SANDERS, Dudley T. s/o Benjamin Sanders & Nancy Jones age 59 W miller POB & POR Orange & **BROOKING**, Mary Ann d/o Charles R.Brooking & Amanda Clark age 25 S POB & POR Orange; POM Orange 14 Feb 1865 OMR 30 Jan 1865 OML

SANDERS, James & **MASON**, Elizabeth J.; POM Orange 23 Oct 1851 OMR OML

SANDERS, John Francis s/o Dudley T.& Nann H.Sanders age 22 S POB Culpeper Co POR Orange & **MASON**, Lydia J. d/o Sanders & Catherine Mason age 19 S POB Rockingham Co POR Orange; POM Orange 22 Feb 1859 OMR 21 Feb 1859 OML

SANDERS, Thomas W. s/o Dudley T.Sanders & Mandy A.Perry age 21 S miller

POB & POR Orange
& **ADAMS**, Mildred
A. d/o Robert &
Mildred Adams age
22 S POB & POR
Orange; POM
Orange 23 Dec
1860 OMR 21 Dec
1860 OML

SANFORD, Joseph s/o
Lawrence & Apphia
Sanford age 60 W
hotel keeper &
farmer POB
Stafford POR
Spotsylvania &
LIPSCOMB, Quincey
d/o Ira E.& Ann
Lipscomb age 33 S
POB & POR
Spotsylvania; POM
Spotsylvania 18
Oct 1865 SPMR 17
Oct 1865 SPML

SANFORD, Laurence s/o
Joseph & Agnes
Sanford age 36 W
merchant POR
Fredericksburg
POR Spotsylvania
& **BAKER**,
Georgianna d/o
Bushrod Baker age
24 S POB Louisa
Co POR
Spotsylvania; POM
Spotsylvania 2
Jun 1879 SPMR 27
May 1879 SPML

SATTERWHITE, S.A. s/o
Hugh & Luncinda
Satterwhite age
23 S teacher POB
Caroline Co POR
Spotsylvania &
BEAZLEY, Ida E.
d/o Duerson &
Clem.Beazley age
18 S POB & POR
Spotsylvania; POM
Roxbury,
Spotsylvania 24
Feb 1875 SPMR
SPML

SAUNDERS, Archy G. s/o
Buckner &
P.Saunders age 26
S farmer POB
Caroline Co POR
Spotsylvania &
SURLES, Ida V.
d/o John J.&
Hester A.Surles
age 19 S POB
Caroline Co POR
Spotsylvania; POM
Fredericksburg 21
Jan 1897 FMR 20
Jan 1897 SPML

SCHOOLER, Thomas s/o
Nunly Schooler
age 41 W
blacksmith POB &
POR Spotsylvania
& **WILLOUGHBY**, E.
d/o H.L.&
E.Willoughby age
30 S POB & POR
Spotsylvania; POM
Spotsylvania 8
Jul 1877 SPMR 2
Jul 1877 SPML

SCOTT, Andrew (aka
Daniel) s/o John
Scott & Charlotte
Williams age 23 S
farm laborer POB
& POR Orange POC
& **JOHNSON**, Ellen
d/o Isaac Johnson
& Mary Smith age
21 S POB & POR
Orange POC; POM
Orange 26 Dec
1867 OMR 23 Dec
1867 OML

SCOTT, Braxton s/o
Anderson & Maria
Scott age 27 S
laborer POB Essex
Co POR
Spotsylvania POC
& **EVANS**, Patty
d/o Charles &
Betsy Evans age
20 S POB & POR
Spotsylvania POC;
22 Jan 1887 SPML

SCOTT, Frederick D.
s/o William &
Betty Dangerfield
age 28 S laborer
POB & POR
Spotsylvania POC
& **JOHNSON**, Sarah
Ann d/o Harriet
Gregory age 20 S
POB King William
Co POR
Spotsylvania POC;
POM Spotsylvania
16 Apr 1879 SPMR
SCOTT, George s/o
James Henry Scott
& Judy Scott age
21 S farmer POB &
POR Spotsylvania
POC & **WOOLFOLK**,
Sarah d/o Barnett
& Ellen Woolfolk
age 18 S POB &
POR Spotsylvania
POC; POM Branch
Fork Ch,
Spotsylvania 3
Nov 1885 SPMR
SPML
SCOTT, George s/o
Reubin & Peggy
Scott age 70 W
farmer POB & POR
Orange & **BLEDSOE**,
Rosa d/o Godfrey
& Mary Yages (?)
age 70 W POB
Madison Co POR
Orange; POM
Orange 14 Dec
1854 OMR
SCOTT, James M. s/o
James M.& Sarah
T.Scott age 33 S
physician POB &
POR Spotsylvania
& **DICKINSON**,
Sallie S.d/o
James T.Dickinson
age 27 S POB
Louisa Co POR
Spotsylvania; POM
Glenora,
Spotsylvania 24
Feb 1875 SPMR 18
Jan 1875 SPML
SCOTT, John C. s/o
William D.& Jane
Scott age 30 S
POB Spotsylvania
POR Rockbridge Co
& **HOWARD**, Maggie
M. d/o Joseph
Howard & Mary
R.Jones age 25 S
POB & POR
Spotsylvania; POM
Spotsylvania 27
Nov 1884 SPMR 25
Nov 1884 SPML
SCOTT, John Wickliffe
s/o John & Ann
Scott age 28 S
farmer POB & POR
Orange & **HACKLEY**,
Sarah F. d/o
Robert & Mary Ann
Hackley age 25 S
POB Florida POR
Orange; POM
Orange 29 Jan
1856 OMR 28 Jan
1856 OML
SCOTT, Norborne s/o
Pitt & C.Scott
age 45 S POB &
POR Spotsylvania
POC & **BOXLEY**,
Mag. d/o Monroe &
Sarah Boxley age
30 W POB Hanover
Co POR
Spotsylvania POC;
POM Spotsylvnania
7 Jun 1877 SPMR
28 May 1877 SPML
SCOTT, Shadrack R. s/o
Fannie Scott age
26 S POB & POR
Spotsylvania POC
& **BURRUSS**, Nannie
d/o Robert
J.Burruss & Mary
Ann Minor age 19
S POB & POR
Spotsylvania POC;
POM Spotsylvania

29 Dec 1881 FMR
26 Dec 1881 SPML
SCOTT, William s/o
James & Matilda
Scott age 20 S
laborer POB & POR
Spotsylvania POC
& **MONTAGUE**, Emma
d/o Gilbert &
Dolly Montague
age 19 S POB &
POR Spotsylvania
POC; POM
Spotsylvania 27
Jan 1883 SPMR
SPML
SCOVILL, George B. s/o
James C.& Marcia
S.Scovill age 28
S iron moulder
POB & POR
Watertown,
Connecticut &
HIGGINS, Harriet
W. d/o Walter &
Almeda Higgins
age 26 S POB
Fryeburg, Maine
POR Spotsylvania;
POM Spotsylvania
14 Feb 1884 SPMR
12 Feb 1884 SPML
SEALY, Fred L. s/o
William & Jane
Sealy age 23 S
farmer POB
Sinclairsville,
N.Y. POR
Spotsylvania &
SACRA, Fanny d/o
John L.& Sarah
C.Sacra age 23 S
POB & POR
Spotsylvania; POM
Spotsylvania 15
Dec 1897 SPMR 9
Dec 1897 SPML
SEATON, William s/o
Jacob & Sarah
Seaton age 40 W
mechanic POB
Frederick Co, Md
POR Spotsylvania
POC & **KNOX**, Sally
age 22 W POB
Accomac Co POR
Spotsylvania POC:
POM Spotsylvania
1 Dec 1870 SPMR
29 Nov 1870 SPML
SEAY, Charles D. s/o
Thomas W.&
Jennnie Seay age
23 S farmer POB &
POR Louisa Co &
HARRIS, Lizzie K.
d/o William H.&
Betty A.Harris
age 20 S POB &
POR Spotsylvania;
POM Spotsylvania
28 Feb 1900 SPMR
27 Feb 1900 SPML
SEAY, Charles E. s/o
James L.& Lucy
E.Seay age 21 S
farmer POB & POR
Spotsylvania &
HESTER, Mattie G.
d/o John E.&
E.H.Hester age 21
S POB & POR
Spotsylvania; POM
Spotsylvania 21
Dec 1892 SPMR 16
Dec 1892 SPML
SEAY, Henry C. s/o
Caleb & Jane Seay
age 30 S farmer
POB Hanover Co
POR Louisa Co &
TALLEY, Mary J.
d/o William A.&
Ann Robinson age
27 W POB Louisa
Co POR
Spotsylvania; POM
Spotsylvania 13
Dec 1870 SPMR
SPML
SEAY, James B. s/o
William A.& Nancy
Seay age 20 S
farmer POB & POR
Spotsylvania &
TALLEY, Sarah J.
d/o Littleton M.&
Elizabeth Talley

age 24 S POB &
POR Spotsylvania;
POM Spotsylvania
22 Dec 1870 SPMR
20 Dec 1870 SPML
SEAY, James G. s/o
James L.& Lucy
E.Seay age 22
farmer POB & POR
Spotsylvania &
HESTER, Alice d/o
James E.& Amanda
M.Hester age 18 S
POB & POR
Spotsylvania; POM
Glenora,
Spotsylvania 10
Feb 1892 SPMR 1
Feb 1892 SPML
SEAY, James L. s/o
James G.& Martha
E.Seay age 19 S
farmer POB
Hanover Co POR
Spotsylvania &
HARRIS, Lucy E.
d/o James O.&
Lucy A.Harris age
16 S POB Louisa
Co POR
Spotsylvania; POM
Louisa Co 4 Mar
1866 SPMR 2 Mar
1866 SPML
SEAY, John O. s/o
W.A.& N.A. Seay
age 23 S farmer
POB & POR
Spotsylvania &
WILLOUGHBY,
Bettie Ann d/o
J.W.&
L.Willoughby age
23 S POB & POR
Spotsylvania; POM
Spotsylvania 18
Dec 1879 SPMR 17
Dec 1879 SPML
SEAY, William J. s/o
George W.&
Elizabeth T.Seay
age 21 farmer POB
Spotsylvania POR
Hanover Co &

BUTLER, Emuella
d/o John C.&
Catherine Butler
age 21 POB & POR
Spotsylvania; POM
Spotsylvania 10
Feb 1874 SPMR 5
Feb 1874 SPML
SEAY, William W. s/o
J.L.& Lucy E.Seay
age 24 S farmer
POB & POR
Spotsylvania &
DIXON, Iola L.
d/o George Dixon
& Ida F.Wallace
age 17 S POB &
POR Spotsylvania;
POM Spotsylvania
17 Dec 1900 SPMR
SPML
SEAY, William W. s/o
William H. &
Nancy Seay age 23
S farmer POB &
POR Spotsylvania
& **WILSON**, Bettie
A. d/o Robert H.
& Mary J. Wilson
age 22 S POB &
POR Spotsylvania;
POM Spotsylvania
23 Dec 1875 SPMR
21 Dec 1875 SPML
SEAY, William W. s/o
William A.& Nancy
Seay ag 28 W
farmer POB & POR
Spotsylvania &
SIMMS, Mattie M.
d/o James S.& Ann
Eliza Simms age
22 S POB & POR
Spotsylvania; POM
Spotsylvania 2
Mar 1882 SPMR 24
Feb 1882 SPML
SEE, Edward s/o
S.R.See &
F.Rawlings age 21
S laborer POB &
POR Spotsylvania
POC & **JACKSON**,
Ann d/o M.& Ann

SEE, Jackson age 19 S POB & POR Spotsylvania POC; POM Stanfield, Spotsylvania 5 Jan 1876 SPMR 3 Jan 1876 SPML
John H. s/o Willis See & Mary Richards age 58 W farmer POB Fauquier Co POR Orange & **JONES**, Mary B. d/o A.S.Jones & Mary J.Overton age 21 S POB Petersburg,Va POR Orange; POM Orange 19 Nov 1863 OMR 18 Nov 1863 OML

SEEF (or Leef), William F. s/o Henry Leef or Seef & Julia Gambrill age 26 S engineer on O.& A.railroad POB Baltimore, Md POR Gordonsville & **GOODWIN**, Margaret C. d/o John Goodwin & Mary S. Armcol(?) age 18 S POB Prince William Co POR Gordonsville; POM Gordonsville 26 Nov 1863 OMR 24 Nov 1863 OML

SELDEN, Charles s/o M.C.& Harriet C.Selden age 37 S railway superintendent POB Powhatan Co POR Richmond, Va & **TAYLOR**, Bessie Temple d/o Dr.John R.& B.F.Taylor age 24 S POB & POR Spotsylvania; POM Trinity Ch, Fredericksburg 8 Oct 1884 FMR 7 Oct 1884 SPML

SHASPERE, Beverley s/o Sancho & Lucinda Shaspere age 26 W laborer POB & POR Spotsylvania POC & **JACKSON**, Frances d/o Charles & Nellie Jackson age 24 W POB & POR Spotsylvania POC: POM Spotsylvania 23 Sep 1875 SPMR 21 Sep 1875 SPML

SHAW, Thomas J. age 43 S engineer POB Prince William Co POR Orange & **STANARD**, Fanny P. d/o Robert Beverley Stanard & Ellen B.Stanard age 18 S POB & POR Orange; POM Orange 29 Nov 1853 OMR 28 Nov 1853 OML

SHELTON, Aleck Monroe s/o George W. & Marie A. Shelton age 24 S farmer POB Spotsylvania POR Stafford & **JETT**, Lula S. d/o John & Frances Jett age 21 S POB Stafford POR Spotsylvania; POM Fredericksburg 31 Dec 1890 FMR 29 Dec 1890 SPML

SHELTON, George C. s/o George W.& Maria Shelton age 21 S farmer POB & POR Spotsylvania & **LANDIS**, Amanda H. d/o Aaron & Mary Landis age 17 S POB Lancaster Co,

Penn POR Spotsylvania; POM Spotsylvania C.H. 24 Mar 1893 SPMR SPML

SHEPARD, Joseph s/o M.& M.Shepard age 23 S laborer POB & POR Spotsylvania POC & **JACKSON**, Priscilla d/o William & M.Jackson age 23 S POB & POR Spotsylvania POC; POM Spotsylvania 22 Jun 1878 SPMR SPML

SHEPHERD, George s/o Peter Lewis & Frances Shepherd age 22 S laborer POB & POR Spotsylvania POC & **HOPKINS**, Leanna d/o Delphia Hopkins age 18 S POB & POR Spotsylvania POC; POM Spotsylvania 7 Jan 1882 SPMR SPML

SHEPPARD, David s/o John E.& Samuela Shepperd age 27 S teamster POB Richmond,Va POR Orange & **MARTIN**, Mary d/o R.H.& Bettie L.Martin age 17 S POB & POR Spotsylvania; POM Spotsylvania 16 Dec 1894 SPMR 5 Dec 1894 SPML

SHERWOOD, James H. s/o William & Mary Sherwood age 21 S POB Alexandria POR Baltimore, Md & **BALLARD**, Ellen J. d/o Edwin & Lora Ann Frances Ballard age 21 S POB Louisa Co POR Orange; POM Orange 24 Dec 1862 OMR 17 Dec 1862 OML

SHIFLETT, Bluford P. s/o Archer & Malinda Shiflett age 24 S tailor POB Louisa Co POR Orange & **FAUDREE**, Jane C. d/o Joseph & Susan Ann Foderee age 21 S POB & POR Orange; POM Orange 4 Oct 1853 OMR OML

SHIFLETT, Waller C.(aka Sheflet) age 22 S carpenter POB Rockingham Co POR Orange & **DUVALL**, Albzerah (aka Altizerah Duvall) d/o William L.& Comfort Duvall age 15 S POB Annarundel Co,Md POR Orange; 14 Jul 1858 OML

SHIPP, John M. s/o Edward G.Shipp & Harriet Mauzey age 31 S farmer POB Green Co POR Madison Co & **MANSFIELD**, Susan M. d/o Joseph A.Mansfield & Susan M.Lindsay age 32 S POB & POR Orange; POM Orange 10 Oct 1865 OMR 3 Oct 1865 OML

SIBLEY, John L. s/o Henry & Virginia Sibley age 21 S farmer POB & POR Spotsylvania & **PAYNE**, Annie d/o

Charles R.& Mary Jones age 27 W POB & POR Spotsylvania; POM Spotsylvania 14 Dec 1898 SPMR SPML

SILCOTT, Washington s/o Abraham & Barsheba Silcott age 60 W mechanic POB Louden Co POR Hamilton,Va & **FLIPPO**, Inez B. d/o Major & A.F.Flippo age 28 S POB & POR Spotsylvania; POM Spotsylvania 1 Dec 1886 SPMR SPML

SILVER, Theodore s/o Isaac & Catherine Silver age 29 S street car driver POB Spotsylvania POR Washington D.C. & **POLLARD**, Nora d/o Isaac & Lucy Pollard age 23 S POB & POR Spotsylvania; POM Spotsylvania 1 Jan 1891 SPMR 31 Dec 1890 SPML

SILVER, Theodore s/o Isaac & Catharine Silver of Stafford Co. age 29 POR Washington D.C. & **POLLARD**, Nora d/o Isaac & Lucy Pollard of Spotsylvania Co. age 23 POR Spotsylvania Co.; POM Spotsylvania Co. 1 Jan 1891 TCF

SIMMONS, C.D. s/o Stephen W.& Laura M.Simmons age 37 S physician POB West Feliciana Parish, Louisiana POR Ascension, Penn & **PULLIAM**, L.Noel d/o J.D.& Lucy N.Pulliam age 29 S POB & POR Spotsylvania; POM Spotsylvania 24 Jan 1894 SPMR 2 Dec 1893 SPML

SIMMS, Edmund R. s/o Richard Sims & H.Q.Bullock age 27 S teacher POB Louisa Co POR Orange & **TERRILL**, Susan H. d/o John Terrill & E.E.Gibson age 20 S POB & POR Orange; POM Orange 5 Feb 1861 OMR 26 Jan 1861 OML

SIMPSON, Hugh M. s/o Hugh M.Simpson & Lucy A.Schooler age 18 S farmer POB & POR Orange & **HERNDON**, Eliza J. d/o Edward Herndon & Susan Lancaster age 25 S POB & POR Orange; POM Orange 25 Jan 1866 OMR 18 Jan 1866 OML

SIMS, Hiram A. s/o William T.Sims & Mary F.Pritchett age 24 S physician POB & POR Green Co & **YAGER**, Pamelia W. d/o Willia Yager & E.C.Whitlaw age 22 S POB & POR Orange; POM Rockingham Co 14 Feb 1867 Rockingham MR 11 Feb 1867 OML

SIMS, W.T. s/o James
R.& Julia Sims
age 34 W farmer
POB Greene Co POR
Spotsylvania &
LEWIS, Verona Z.
d/o Jack &
Harriet Lewis age
18 S POB & POR
Spotsylvania; POM
Spotsylvania
C.H.24 Dec 1885
SPMR SPML
SISSON, Elhanon B. s/o
William Sisson &
Sarah J.Row age
21 S farmer POB &
POR Culpeper Co &
ELIASON, Nannie
H. d/o William
C.Eliason & Susan
V.Pannill age 22
S POB & POR
Orange; POM
Orange 31 Jan
1867 OMR 29 Jan
1867 OML
SISSON, Landon S. s/o
David & Catherine
Sisson age 22 S
gentleman POB
Westmoreland CO
POR
Fredericksburg &
SHEARS, Matie J.
d/o John & Maria
Shears age 19 S
POB Oswego
Co,N.Y. POR
Spotsylvania 29
Sep 1870 SPMR 26
Sep 1870 SPML
SKINNER, James s/o
James A.&
S.F.Skinner age
33 S POB & POR
Caroline Co &
PERRY, Josaphine
age 25 S POB
Caroline Co POR
Spotsylvania; POM
Spotsylvania 15
Aug 1880 SPMR 14
Aug 1880 SPML

SKINNER, William H.
s/o Elijah H.&
Mary Skinner age
24 S mechanic POB
Onieda Co,N.Y.
POR Orange &
BROOKING, Jennie
E. d/o Charles &
Amanda Brooking
age 19 S POB &
POR Orange; POM
Orange 12 May
1857 OMR 8 May
1857 OML
SLACHTER, H.W. s/o
Samuel & Esther
Slachter age 38 W
undertaker POB
Prince George Co
POR Spotsylvania
& **HARFIELD**, M.K.
d/o Thaddeus &
Martha A.Harfield
age 17 S POB &
POR Spotsylvania;
POM Spotsylvania
13 Jul 1884 SPMR
12 Jul 1884 SPML
SLAUGHTER, Alexander
s/o John &
B.Slaughter age
22 S laborer POB
& POR
Spotsylvania POC
& **DOTTS**, Polly
d/o D.& E.Dotts
age 16 S POB &
POR Spotsylvania
POC; POM New Hope
Ch, Spotsylvania
27 Dec 1877 SPMR
26 Dec 1877 SPML
SLAUGHTER, Beverley
s/o Benjamin &
Charlotte
Slaughter age 39
S laborer POB &
POR Spotsylvania
POC & **WILLIAMS**,
Sallie Ann d/o
Huldah Williams
age 26 S POB &
POR Spotsylvania
POC; POM

Spotsylvania C.H.19 Oct 1886 SPMR SPML

SLAUGHTER, Charles s/o M.& S.Slaughter age 22 S laborer POB & POR Spotsylvania POC & **COLEMAN**, Coatney d/o George & H.(or K.)Coleman age 25 S POB & POR Spotsylvania POC; POM Spotsylvania 28 Dec 1879 SPMR 27 Dec 1879 SPML

SLAUGHTER, Henry s/o John & Betty Slaughter age 35 S laborer POB & POR Spotsylvania POC & **PRICE**, Caroline d/o Robert & Frankie Price age 21 S POB & POR Spotsylvania POC; POM Spotsylvania C.H.5 Aug 1886 SPMR SPML

SLEET, Philip J. s/o Philip & Ann Sleet age 32 carpenter POB near Augusta, Georgia POR Orange & **SAMUEL**, Arkansas C.V. d/o Philemon & Maria Samuel age 33 POB & POR Orange; POM Orange 24 Oct 1854 OMR 23 Oct 1854 OML

SMITH, A.T. s/o James A.& Hettie Smith age 27 S POB & POR Spotsylvania & **SMITH**, Anna L. d/o Robert K.& Eugenia L.Smith age 18 S POB Caroline Co POR Spotsylvania; POM Spotsylvania 30 Nov 1881 SPMR 28 Nov 1881 SPML

SMITH, Absalom W. s.o William & Pancy Smith age 22 S farmer POB & POR Orange & **SOUTHERLIN**, Frances d/o Alexander & Dinah Southerlin age 25 S POB & POR Orange; POM Orange 5 Dec 1858 OMR 3 Dec 1858 OML

SMITH, Anthony B. s/o Austin & Mary M.Smith age 35 S gentleman at large POB King George Co POR Spotsylvania & **HARROW**, Sarah N. d/o Charles A.& Ellen S.Harrow age 31 S POB King George Co POR Spotsylvania; POM Spotsylvania 21 Aug 1872 SPMR 20 Aug 1872 SPML

SMITH, Beverley s/o William & Betsy Smith age 24 S laborer POB & POR Spotsylvania POC & **FORCE**, Mary d/o L.& M.Force age 21 S POB & POR Spotsylvania POC; POM New Hope Ch, Spotsylvania 28 Dec 1876 SPMR 27 Dec 1876 SPML

SMITH, E.B. s/o A.& E.Smith age 38 S farmer POB West Virginia POR Spotsylvania & **HUMPHRIES**, Lavenia A. d/o

John & J.Humphries age 33 S POB & POR Spotsylvania; POM Spotsylvania 24 Feb 1878 SPMR 21 Feb 1878 SPML

SMITH, Edgar s/o Joe & A.Smith age 23 S laborer POB & POR Spotsylvania POC & **MANSFIELD**, Easter d/o Ches.& E.Mansfield age 24 S POB & POR Spotsylvania POC; POM Spotsylvania 27 Sep 1878 SPMR 26 Sep 1878 SPML

SMITH, Edward B. s/o Zed.& E.Smith age 56 W POB West Virginia POR Spotsylvania & **FAULKNER**, Alice d/o Pleasant & Frances A. Faulkner age 42 S POB & POR Spotsylvania; POM Spotsylvania 27 Sep 1894 SPMR 21 Sep 1894 SPML

SMITH, Fielding D. s/o Lewis & Louisa Smith W farmer POB & POR Spotsylvania POC & **BANKS**, Carrie d/o Frederick & Fanny Banks age 21 S POB & POR Spotsylvania POC; POM Spotsylvania 13 Nov 1895 SPMR SPML

SMITH, George W. s/o Robert K. & A.T.Smith age 39 S carpenter POB & POR Louisa Co & **KENT**, Sarah J. d/o Warner & Susan A.Kent age 24 S POB Fluvanna Co POR Spotsylvania; POM Spotsylvania 17 Dec 1872 SPMR 16 Dec 1872 SPML

SMITH, Henry s/o Joseph & Millie Smith age 40 W laborer POB & POR Spotsylvania POC & **THOMAS**, Mary Eliza d/o Eliza Thomas age 26 S POB & POR Spotsylvania POC; POM Spotsylvania C.H.24 Jan 1895 SPMR SPML

SMITH, Henry s/o Joe & Milly Smith age 21 S farmer POB & POR Spotsylvania POC & **REARELEY**, Angy d/o Jacob & Eliza Reareley age 18 S POB & POR Spotsylvania POC; POM Spotsylvania 15 Apr 1876 SPMR SPML

SMITH, Isaac s/o Joseph & Agness Smith age 22 S farmer POB & POR Spotsylvania POC & **SLAUGHTER**, Lizzie d/o Jane Slaughter age 23 S POB & POR Spotsylvania POC; POM Spotsylvania 12 Jul 1873 (possible error in day by minister) SPMR 13 Jul 1873 SPML

SMITH, J.Triplett s/o Charles H.& Evelina S.Smith age 40 S farmer POB Norfolk,Va POR Spotsylvania

& **GARNETT**, Emily
H. d/o Musco &
Mina Garnett age
35 S POB Essex
POR Spotsylvania;
POM St George Ch,
Fredericksburg 1
Oct 1867 FMR 7
Oct 1867 SPML
SMITH, J.Triplett s/o
Charles H. &
Evelina S.Smith
age 40 S farmer
POB Norfolk, Va
POR Spotsylvania
& **GARNETT**, Emily
H. d/o Musco &
Maria B.Garnett
age 35 S POB
Essex Co POR
Spotsylvania; POM
St George Ch,
Fredericksburg 10
Oct 1867 FMR 7
Oct 1867 SPML
SMITH, Jacob s/o
George & Sallie
Smith age 27 S
farmer POB
Caroline Co POR
Spotsylvania &
TAYLOR, Mary J.
d/o J.B.& Mary
Robinson age 26 W
POB & POR
Spotsylvania; POM
Spotsylvania
C.H.6 Dec 1888
SPMR SPML
SMITH, James B. s/o
William C.& &
Betty Smith age
24 S POB & POR
Spotsylvania &
YOUNG, Lucie N.
d/o William &
Jane Young age 18
S POB & POR
Spotsylvania; POM
Spotsylvania 5
Nov 1874 SPMR 3
Nov 1874 SPML
SMITH, Joe s/o
Thornton &
Lucinda Smith age
44 W farmer POB &
POR Spotsylvania
POC & **JACKSON**,
Cassandra d/o Jim
& Lucanda Jackson
age 21 S POB
Louisa Co POR
Spotsylvania POC;
POM Branch Fork
Ch, Spotsylvania
29 Dec 1874 SPMR
SPML
SMITH, John B. s/o
Braxton C.& Sarah
E.Smith age 31 S
farmer POB & POR
Spotsylvania &
SMITH, Fanny M.
d/o Joseph C.&
Martha Smith age
29 S POB & POR
Spotsylvania; POM
Spotsylvania 27
Jul 1898 SPMR
SPML
SMITH, John B. s/o J.T
& Sarah E.Smith
age 30 S farmer
POB & POR
Caroline Co &
BUTLER, Sarah A.
d/o J.C.&
Catherine Butler
age 23 S POB &
POR Spotsylvania;
POM Spotsylvania
22 Feb 1891 SPMR
17 Feb 1891 SPML
SMITH, John R. s/o
Thomas & Lucy Ann
Smith (POR
Augusta Co) age
22 S coachmaker
POR Augusta Co &
EVANS, Frances
d/o John & Nancy
Evans S POB & POR
Orange; POM
St.Thomas Ch,
Orange 3 Jul 1853
OMR 1 Jul 1853
OML

SMITH, Joseph s/o Thornton & Lucinda Ridley age 68 W laborer POB Louisa Co POR Orange POC & **LIPSCOMB**, Agness d/o Moses & Evelina Lipscomb age 18 S POB Orange POR Spotsylvania POC; POM Spotsylvania 24 Feb 1897 SPMR SPML

SMITH, Joseph s/o Thornton & Lucinda Smith age 58 W laborer POB & POR Spotsylvania POC & **GORDON**, Martha d/o Elvey Payne age 32 W POB & POR Spotsylvania POC; 31 Aug 1882 SPMR 30 Aug 1882 SPML

SMITH, Lee F. s/o Robert P.& Mary Smith age 36 S farmer POB & POR Caroline Co & **CHEWNING**, Rose E. d/o Thomas L.& Martha L.Chewning age 22 S POB & POR Spotsylvania; POM Waller's Ch, Spotsylvania 2 Nov 1898 SPMR 26 Oct 1898 SPML

SMITH, Lewis Jr. s/o Lewis & Louisa Smith age 22 S laborer POB & POR Spotsylvania POC & **BANKS**, Adeline d/o Peter & Mary Berkley age 20 S POB & POR Spotsylvania POC; POM Spotsylvania 4 May 1876 SPMR 3 May 1876 SPML

SMITH, Lewis s/o J.& R.Smith age 50 W laborer POB & POR Spotsylvania POC & **LEWIS**, Matilda d/o Sam & I.Gordon age 40 W POB & POR Spotsylvania POC; POM Spotsylvania 23 Jan 1876 SPMR 22 Jan 1876 SPML

SMITH, Lewis s/o Jesse & Rachel Smith age 72 W laborer POB & POR Spotsylvania POC & **LEWIS**, Betty Ann age 42 W POB & POR Spotsylvania; POM Spotsylvania 15 Dec 1898 SPMR 12 Dec 1898 SPML

SMITH, Lilburn M. s/o Thomas D. Smith age 55 D supt.pub.schools POB & POR Spotsylvania & **DAVIS**, Den G. d/o Dr.John W.Davis age 25 S POB & POR Spotsylvania; POM Washington D.C. 27 Feb 1900 SPMR SPML

SMITH, Lucien s/o William & Rose Smith ag 22 S laborer POB & POR Spotsylvania POC & **THOMAS**, Lannie D. d/o George D.& Leanna Walker age 21 S POB & POR Spotsylvania POC; POM Spotsylvania 5 Jan 1882 SPMR (George Dixon,minister) 4 Jan 1882 SPML

SMITH, N.F. s/o Thomas
& Nancy Smith age
26 S farmer POB &
POR Caroline Co &
ALSOP, Maggie E.
d/o Benjamin P.&
M.E.Alsop age 21
S POB & POR
Spotsylvania; POM
Spotsylvania 23
Dec 1885 SPMR 21
Dec 1885 SPML
SMITH, Richard A. s/o
William M. Smith
& Eliza Bledsoe
age 25 S farmer
POB Culpeper Co
POR Orange &
COOK, Angelina
d/o Caleb A.Smith
& Betsy Jacobs
age 29 W POB &
POR Orange; POM
Orange 16 Nov
1865 OMR OML
SMITH, Robert A. s/o
Harris & Susan
Smith age 26 S no
particular
occupation POB
Culpeper POR
Orange & **ALLISON**,
Lucy E. d/o
Robert & Mariah
Allison age 18 S
POB Culpeper POR
Orange; POM
Orange 8 Jun 1854
OMR
SMITH, Robert L. s/o
Absalom & Lucinda
Smith age 38 S
miner POB
Culpeper Co POR
Stafford & **BOASE**,
Martha J. d/o
James & Eliza
Boase age 22 S
POB Cornwall,
England POR
Spotsylvania; POM
Spotsylvania 8
Jan 1872 SPMR
SPML

SMITH, Robert L. s/o
William W.&
Frances M.Smith
age 35 S farmer
POB & POR
Spotsylvania &
HOPE, Nouraly D.
d/o Edmund & Mary
C.Hope age 18 S
POB Caroline Co
POR Spotsylvania;
POM Spotsylvania
22 Feb 1866 SPMR
20 Feb 1866 SPML
SMITH, William B. s/o
William M.Smith &
Eliza Bledsoe age
22 S farmer POB
Madison Co POR
Orange &
SUTHERLAND,
Catherine d/o
Alex Sutherland &
Dinah Howard age
24 S POB & POR
Orange; POM
Orange 24 Dec
1866 OMR 17 Dec
1866 OML
SMITH, William Brooks
s/o Benjamin H.&
Fenton B.Smith
age 45 W
newspaper
reporter POR
Norfolk,Va &
McLEOD, Mollie L.
d/o Richard A.&
Maria L.McLeod
niece of W.D.Day
age 32 S POB &
POR Spotsylvania;
POM Spotsylvania
19 Dec 1883 SPMR
13 Dec 1883 SPML
SMITH, William F. s/o
Henry Scott &
Mary Frances
Smith age 28 S
farmer POB & POR
Spotsylvania &
HARRIS, Mildred
A. d/o William
H.& Betty

SMITH, William H. s/o John W. & Ann E. Smith age 29 S merchant POB Richmond POR Fredericksburg & **JOHNSON**, Sarah Catherine d/o Richard & Pricilla Johnson age 24 S POB & POR Orange; POM Orange 7 Jul 1859 OMR 6 Jul 1859 OML

SMITH, William J. s/o Robert & Pamelia Smith age 35 S clerk in store POB Louisa Co POR Nelson Co & **PARROTT**, Lucy Jane d/o Samuel H. & Mary C. Parrott age 24 S POB Louisa Co POR Orange; POM Orange 29 Oct 1867 OMR 23 Sep 1867 OML

SMITH, William Marye s/o Yeaman & Ann C. Smith age 58 W physician POB Richmond City POR Spotsylvania & **WALKER**, Catherine d/o Alexander & Luren Walker age 41 S POB & POR Fredericksburg; POM St. George Ch, Fredericksburg 24 May 1866 FMR undated SPML

SMITH, Zedekiah s/o Zedekiah & Emily A. Harris age 19 S POB & POR Spotsylvania; POM Spotsylvania 11 Apr 1900 SPMR SPML

Smith age 21 S clerk POB Hampshire Co, Va POR Berkley Co, Va & **CHEWNING**, Vio O. d/o Oscar L. & Mary O. Chewning age 18 S POB & POR Spotsylvania; 24 Oct 1866 SPML

SNEED, William T. s/o L.W. Sneed & Elizabeth H. Woolfolk age 21 S merchant POB Louisa Co POR Orange & **GOODWIN**, Mary E. d/o Robert Goodwin & Susan H. Woolfolk age 26 S POB Louisa Co POR Orange; POM Gordonsville, Orange 6 Nov 1866 OMR 1 Nov 1866 OML

SNELLINGS, William W. s/o William A. & Mary A. Snellings age 27 W miller POB & POR Stafford & **GRIMES**, Mary M. age 18 S POB & POR Spotsylvania; POM Stafford 30 Sep 1883 STMR 29 Sep 1883 SPML

SOLAN, Emmett A. s/o John & Martha A. Solan age 26 S salesman POB & POR Fredericksburg & **BAILEY**, Florence C. d/o Chancellor & Jennie P. Bailey age 25 S POB & POR Spotsylvania; POM Mill Dale Spotsylvania 23

Apr 1890 SPMR 21
Apr 1890 SPML
SOMERVILLE, James s/o James Somerville & Helen Wallace age 43 W lawyer POB Madison Co POR Carroll Co, Mississippi & **BARBOUR**, Cornelia C. d/o Quintus Barbour & Mary E.Somerville age 29 S POB Madison Co POR Orange; POM Orange 5 Jun 1867 OMR 3 Jun 1867 OML

SORRELL, John R. s/o John & Susan Sorrell age 22 S farmer POB Louisa Co POR Spotsylvania & **MASTIN**, Amanda Jane d/o Jackson & Mildred Mastin age 22 S POB & POR Spotsylvania; POM Spotsylvania 28 Nov 1872 SPMR 26 Nov 1872 SPML

SORRELL, Joseph A. s/o Joseph A.& Ann Sorrell age 24 S farmer POB & POR Orange & **HERRING**, Sallie E. d/o Col.Frank & Lucy Saunders age 28 W POB Orange POR Spotsylvania; POM Spotsylvania C.H. 5 Nov 1884 SPMR SPML

SORRELL, Reuben s/o John Sorrell & Elizabeth Sale age 72 W farmer POB Caroline Co POR Orange & **CLARK**, Lucy C. d/o John Kimbrough & Sarah Michell age 71 W POB Hanover Co POR Orange; POM Orange 8 May 1862 OMR OML

SORRELL, William A. s/o Joseph A.& Ann Sorrell age 21 S farmer POB & POR Orange & **MASTIN**, Dora d/o James G.& Mary C.Martin age 22 S POB & POR Spotsylvania; POM Spotsylvania 16 Apr 1883 SPMR SPML

SORRILLE, Joseph C. s/o John Sorrille age 30 S carpenter POB & POR Spotsylvania & **DUNAWAY**, Ann d/o Admond Dunaway age 18 S POB & POR Orange; POM Orange 22 Nov 1857 OMR 18 Nov 1857 OML

SOUTHERLAND, James L. & **HIGGERSON**, Mary E. d/o Benjamin Higgerson; POM Orange 15 Jan 1854 OMR

SOUTHERLIN, William s/o Alexander & Diana Southerlin age 25 S laborer POB Louisa Co POR Orange & **JONES**, Sarah E. d/o Fielding & Mary Jones age 18 S POB & POR Orange; POM Orange 21 Jun 1856 OMR 20 Jun 1856 OML

SOUTHWORTH, Charles B. s/o James & Lavinia Southworth age 25 S farmer POB &

POR Spotsylvania
& **BLACKLEY**, Mary
F. d/o George D.&
Sarah Blackley
age 22 S POB &
POR Spotsylvania;
POM Spotsylvania
12 Nov 1865 SPMR
SPML
SPARKS, Michael s/o
P.& J.Sparks age
60 W laborer POB
& POR
Spotsylvania POC
& **CAMMACK**, Lucy
d/o G.& A.Cammack
age 35 S POB &
POR Spotsylvania;
pOM Spotsylvania
10 Jan 1878 SPMR
9 Jan 1878 SPML
SPENCER, George s/o
James & Louisa
Spencer age 22 S
farmer POB & POR
Spotsylvania POC
& **CRUTCHFIELD**,
Jennie d/o Robert
& Lucy
Crutchfield age
21 S POB & POR
Spotsylvania POC;
POM Branch Fork
Ch, Spotsylvania
16 Jan 1884 SPMR
7 Jan 1884 SPML
SPICER, Benjamin P.
s/o Thomas A.&
M.E.Spicer age 23
S farmer POB &
POR Hanover Co &
CARR, Minnie C.
d/o William &
Molly Carr age 21
S POB & POR
Spotsylvania; POM
Spotsylvania 25
Dec 1896 SPMR 21
Dec 1896 SPML
SPINDLE, John S. s/o
Edmond J.& Mary
J.Spindle age 27
S farmer POB &
POR Spotsylvania

& **ROBINSON**, Susie
A. d/o Henry &
S.A. Robinson age
24 S POB & POR
Spotsylvania; POM
Spotsylvania 23
Dec 1875 SPMR 21
Dec 1875 SPML
SPROULE, Charles s/o
Charles & Jane
Sproule age 53 S
farmer POB & POR
Spotsylvania POC
& **GARNETT**, Fannie
d/o Henry & Patsy
Ware age 40 W POB
& POR
Spotsylvania POC;
POM Spotsylvania
30 Jun 1897 SPMR
29 Jun 1897 SPML
STANARD, Addison s/o
James & Courtney
Stanard age 55 W
laborer POB & POR
Spotsylvania POC
& **LEWIS**, Emma d/o
Isaac & Maria
Brown age 32 W
POB & POR
Spotsylvania POC;
POM Little Road
Ch, Spotsylvania
16 Sep 1894 SPMR
15 Sep 1894 SPML
STANARD, Edward G. s/o
Addison & Jane
Stanard age 21 S
POB & POR
Spotsylvania POC
& **PENDLETON**,
Ellen d/o Frank
Pendleton age 20
S POB & POR
Spotsylvania POC;
POM Spotsylvania
15 Jan 1894 SPMR
1 Jan 1894 SPML
STANARD, Joseph s/o
Larkin & Aggy
Stanard age 21 S
farmer POB & POR
Spotsylvania POC
& **BANYAN**, Lucy

d/o William & Rachel Banyan age 19 S POB & POR Spotsylvania POC; POM Spotsylvania 15 Feb 1868 SPMR SPML

STANARD, Manuel s/o J.& B.Stanard age 21 S laborer POB Caroline Co POR Spotsylvania POC & **TURNER**, Caroline d/o M.& E.Turner age 24 S POB & POR Spotsylvnia POC; POM Spotsylvania 24 Dec 1877 SPMR SPML

STANLEY, Granville s/o Eliza Stanley age 21 S farmer POB & POR Spotsylvania & **LONG**, Lucy d/o Robert & Mary Long age 21 S POB & POR Spotsylvania; POM Spotsylvania 5 Apr 1877 SPMR 4 Apr 1877 SPML

STANLEY, RiCh C. s/o Eliza Stanley age 22 farmer POB & POR Spotsylvania & **ALSOP**, Huldah V. d/o Thomas & Elizabeth Alsop age 23 S POB & POR Spotsylvania; POM Spotsylvania 15 Nov 1865 SPMR SPML

STANLEY, William H. s/o Eliza Stanley age 19 S farmer POB & POR Spotsylvania & **LONG**, Eliza d/o Robert & Mary Long age 22 S POB & POR Spotsylvania; POM Spotsylvania 2 Jan 1868 SPMR 1 Jan 1868 SPML

STEPHENS, George H. s/o Samuel & Annie Stephens age 48 W gardner POB Dorchester Co, Md POR Spotsylvania POC & **WILLIAMS**, Josephine d/o Henry & Huldah Williams age 24 S POB & POR Spotsylvania POC; POM Spotsylvania 16 Jun 1898 SPMR SPML

STEPHENS, Harmon s/o A.& M.E.Stephens age 21 S farmer POB & POR Spotsylvania & **CURTIS**, Emma d/o James R.& E.Curtis age 21 S POB Pennsylvania POR Spotsylvania; POM Spotsylvania 17 Mar 1879 SPMR 15 Mar 1879 SPML

STEPHENS, John J. s/o William A.& Mary E.Stephens age 22 S farmer POB & POR Spotsylvania & **CHANCELLOR**, Lucie M. d/o Metzi S.& Lucie Chancellor age 18 S POB & POR Spotsylvania; POM Spotsylvania 24 Nov 1869 SPMR 23 Nov 1869 SPML

STEPHENS, Lewis E. s/o Alexander & Mary Stephens age 40 W farmer POB & POR Spotsylvania & **ALLEN**, Amanda d/o Henry T.& Margaret Allen age 17 S POB & POR Spotsylvania; POM Spotsylvania C.H. 28 Nov 1888 SPMR SPML

STEPHENS, Lewis E. s/o Alex & Mary Stephens age 21 S farmer POB & POR Spotsylvania & **WALLER**, Sallie A. d/o Benjamin P.& Betsy Waller age 22 S POB & POR Spotsylvania; POM M.E.Ch Fredericksburg 19 Jun 1866 FMR SPML

STEPHENS, Scott T. s/o J.J.& Lucy M.Stephens age 21 S merchant POB & POR Spotsylvania & **JENNINGS**, Lillie E. d/o J.C.& E.V.Jennings age 18 S POB & POR Spotsylvania; POM Spotsylvania 26 Nov 1891 SPMR 25 Nov 1891 SPML

STEPHENS, W.F. s/o Richard A.& Julia A.Stephens age 44 S farmer POB & POR Spotsylvania & **EASTBURN**, Maggie S. d/o Oliver & Anna Eastburn age 38 S POB New Castle Co, Delaware POR Spotsylvania; POM Salem Ch, Spotsylvania 3 Nov 1897 SPMR 28 Oct 1897 SPML

STEVENS, Henry W. s/o Lewis E.& Sarah A.Stephens age 21 S farmer POB & POR Spotsylvania & **STEPHENS**, Helen d/o George & Mary Stephens age 18 S POB & POR Spotsylvania; POM Fredericksburg 27 Nov 1889 FMR 20 Nov 1889 SPML

STEVENS, John F. s/o Lewis A. & Mary Stevens age 23 S farmer POB & POR Spotsylvania & **POWELL**, Sommerville d/o Michael & Susan Powell age 22 S POB & POR Spotsylvania; POM Spotsylvania 14 Jan 1868 SPMR (possible error in year by minister) 13 Jan 1869 SPML

STEVENS, Joseph L. s/o Joseph L.Stephens & Elizabeth S.Flood age 29 S planter POB Charleston, S.C. POR John's Island, S.C. & **FREEMAN**, Mary E. d/o A.R.Freeman & Mary A.Kemper age 18 S POB Culpeper Co POR Orange; POM Gordonsville 18 Oct 1864 OMR OML

STEVENS, Lewis s/o Edmond & Fanny Stevens age 30 W farmer POB & POR Spotsylvania & **ACORS**, Ema Ella d/o William & Maria Acors age 22 S POB & POR Spotsylvania; POM Spotsylvania 1 Dec 1870 SPMR 31 Nov 1870 SPML

STEVENS, Wesley s/o Indian Stevens & Virginia Bland age 35 S laborer on farm POB & POR Orange POC & **LEWIS**, Mary Ann age 31 S POB & POR Orange POC; POM Orange 25 Aug 1866 OMR OML

STEVENS, Willie E. s/o Henry & Louisa Stevens age 22 S merchant POB & POR Caroline Co & **TAYLOR**, Mary W. s/o Lewis Proctor age 24 W POB & POR Spotsylvania; POM Spotsylvania 7 Jan 1868 SPMR SPML

STEWART, Albert s/o Emanuel & Fannie Reynolds age 24 S laborer POB & POR Spotsylvania POC & **MINOR**, Laura d/o Susan Minor age 22 S POB & POR Spotsylvania POC; POM Meadowhill, Spotsylvania 2 Feb 1882 SPMR 31 Jan 1882 SPML

STEWART, Eugene E. s/o James L.& Helen E.Stewart age 26 S farmer POB & POR Spotsylvania & **LONG**, Bellzora B. d/o Jeremiah & Mary E.Long age 24 S POB & POR Spotsylvania; POM Spotsylvania 3 Aug 1882 SPMR SPML

STEWART, John P. s/o Charles & Harriet L.Stewart age 29 S farmer POB & POR Spotsylvania & **LONG**, Emma I. d/o James & A.H.Long age 30 S POB & POR Spotsylvania; POM Louisa Co 10 Mar 1870 SPMR 8 Mar 1870 SPML

STEWART, Simon s/o M.& M.Stewart age 26 S laborer POB King George Co POR Spotsylvania POC & **TAYLOR**, Milly d/o J.& C.Taylor age 18 S POB & POR Spotsylvania POC; POM Spotsylvania 8 Jan 1880 SPMR 3 Jan 1880 SPML

STEWART, William s/o R.& E.Stewart age 24 S laborer POB & POR Spotsylvania POC & **CRUTCHFIELD**, Malinda d/o S.& M.Crutchfield age 21 S POB & POR Spotsylvania POC; POM Spotsylvania 13 Feb 1879 SPMR 11 Feb 1879 SPML

STOKES, Cary B. s/o A.B. & M.J. Stokes of King George Co., Va. age 24 POR IKing George Co.,Va.& **HAYDON**, Annie C. d/o Thos.J. & Betty Haydon of Fredericksburg age 26 POR Fredericksburg; POM Fredericksburg 31 Oct 1894 TCF

STONEBRAKER, Theodore F. s/o William & Ann E. Stonebraker age

26 S farmer POB Washington Co, Md POR Spotsylvania & **CHANCELLOR**, Edmonia d/o Meltzi S.& Lucy Chancellor age 23 S POB & POR Spotsylvania; POM Spotsylvania 7 Dec 1870 SPMR 5 Dec 1870 SPML

STORY, John W. s/o William M.& Elizabeth Story age 24 S farmer POB Rappahannock Co POR Culpeper Co & **ELLEY**, Mary W. d/o John W.& Rosa L.Elley age 21 S POB & POR Spotsylvania; POM Elley's Ford Ch, Spotsylvania 22 Dec 1890 SPMR 19 Dec 1890 SPML

STOVALL, Augustus David s/o Alvin D.& Mary J.Stovall age 23 S farmer POB Georgia POR Spotsylvania & **LANE**, Nellie M. d/o J.W.& Eliza A.Lane age 20 S POB & POR Spotsylvania; POM Spotsylvania 1 Dec 1886 SPMR 26 Nov 1886 SPML

STOVIN, Charles J. s/o Charles Stovin & Mary Lewis age 54 W farmer POB Loudon Co POR Orange & **NEWMAN**, Bettie B. d/o Reuben Newman & ____ Welch age 23 S POB & POR Orange; POM Orange 5 Dec 1865 OMR 2 Dec 1865 OML

STRAHAN, Charles s/o Ebenezer Strahan & Sarah B.Holmes age 23 S merchant POB Baltimore, Md POR Fredericksburg & **MORTON**, Jennie C. d/o George W.Morton & Susan Terrell age 23 S POB & POR Orange; POM Orange 25 Jun 1863 OMR 24 Jun 1863 OML

STREET, Henry s/o James & Sarah Street (POR Chesterfield Co) age 32 W laborer POB & POR Spotsylvania POC & **WASHINGTON**, Ida d/o George & Ann Washington age 19 S POB & POR Spotsylvania POC; POM Spotsylvania 24 Sep 1891 SPMR 18 Sep 1891 SPML

STREET, Henry s/o J.& S.Street age 22 S laborer POB Chesterfield Co POR Spotsylvania POC & **COLEMAN**, Alice d/o F.& S.Coleman age 18 S POB & POR Spotsylvania POC; POM Spotsylvania 23 Apr 1876 SPMR 21 Apr 1876 SPML

STREET, Jim s/o Thornton & Fanny Street age 28 S farmer POB & POR Spotsylvania POC & **LEWIS**, Betty d/o Harry & Margaret Lewis age 18 S POB &

POR Spotsylvania
POC: POM
Spotsylvania 16
Jul 1871 SPMR 10
Jul 1971 SPML
STRINGFELLOW, Martin
S. s/o Robert R.&
Ann Stringfellow
age 24 S farmer
POB Culpeper &
WILLIS, Nellie M.
d/o Richard Henry
& Lucy Mary
Willis age 22 S
POB Orange; POM
Orange 15 Nov
1860 OMR 14 Nov
1860 OML
STRONG, Robert C. s/o
Jesse Strong &
Sarah Smith age
23 S farmer POB
Claiborne Co,
Mississippi &
HUGHES, Rebecca
A. d/o Armistead
Hughes & Sarah
A.Sleet age 22 S
POB & POR Orange;
POM Orange 29 Dec
1865 OMR 23 Dec
1865 OML
STROTHER, John s/o
Charles Strother
& Diana McDaniel
age 24 S farm
laborer POB & POR
Orange POC &
WALKER, Tamar d/o
Hoace Walker &
Cornelia Morris
age 16 S POB &
POR Orange POC;
POM Orange 27 Dec
1867 OMR 26 Dec
1867 OML
STUBBS, Andrews s/o
William & Martha
Stubbs age 21 S
laborer POB & POR
Spotsylvania POC
& **BANKS**, Irene
d/o Marshall &
Ester Banks age
19 S POB & POR
Spotsylvania POC;
POM Spotsylvania
29 Mar 1897 SPMR
SPML
STUBBS, John s/o John
& M.Stubbs ag 24
S laboere POB &
POR Spotsylvania
POC & **GORDON**,
Laura d/o Louisa
Gordon age 20 S
POB & POR
Spotsylvania POC;
POM Spotsylvania
24 Dec 1878 SPMR
23 Dec 1878 SPML
STUBBS, William Henry
s/o Jesse Stubbs
& Lucy
Crutchfield age
22 S miller POB &
POR Spotsylvania
& **CLARKE**, Martha
d/o Willis &
Margaret Clarke
age 19 S POB &
POR Spotsylvania;
POM Spotsylvnai
Dec 1867 SPMR 26
Dec 1867 SPML
STUBBS, William Henry
s/o Jesse Stubbs
& Lucy
Crutchfield age
22 S miller POB &
POR Spotsylvania
& **CLARKE**, Martha
d/o Willis &
Margaret Clarke
age 19 S POB &
POR Spotsylvania;
POM Spotsylvania
28 Dec 1867 SPMR
26 Dec 1867 SPML
SUDDUTH, George A. s/o
Thomas J.Sudduth
& Maria Spilman
age 26 S clerk
POB & POR
Culpeper Co &
NEWMAN, Mary E.
d/o Morris
D.Newman & Mary

A.Tatum age 21 S POB Madison Co POR Orange; POM Orange married by acting chaplain 13th Reg,.Va Infantry Pegrams's Brigade Early's Division A.N.Va 5 Feb 1864 OMR OML

SULLIVAN, Aurelious s/o Wiley F.& Angie Sullivan age 22 S harness maker POB & POR Spotsylvania & **COX**, Maddie L. d/o John & Sarah M.Cox age 16 S POB & POR Spotsylvania; POM Rhoadesville, Orange 11 Dec 1895 OMR 3 Dec 1895 SPML

SULLIVAN, C.N. s/o W.J.& Lucy A.Sullivan age 33 S mechanic POB Spotsylvania POR Orange & **JONES**, Mary J. d/o C.& K.Jones age 25 S POB Orange POR Spotsylvania; 6 Aug 1874 SPML

SULLIVAN, Harrison s/o Ramsay & Lucy Sullivan of Stafford Co. age 20 POR Stafford Co. & **FINES**, Ella I. d/o Virginia Fines of Stafford Co. age 27 POR Stafford Co.; POM Fredericksburg 19 Dec 1895 TCF

SULLIVAN, James R. s/o W.F.& Angelina Sullivan age 22 S farmer POB & POR Spotsylvania &

PAYTES, Dollie E. d/o S.C.& C.S.Paytes age 24 S POB & POR Spotsylvania; POM M.E.Ch S, Spotsylvania 7 Jun 1888 SPMR SPML

SULLIVAN, M.A. s/o N.(?) & S.S.Sullivan age 22 S farmer POB & POR Spotsylvania & **BAXTER**, Annie E. d/o Ann E.Baxter (father dead) ag 21 S POB & POR Spotsylvania; POM Spotsylvania 21 Apr 1883 SPMR SPML

SULLIVAN, Richard B. & **ROBINSON**. Sarah A.; 7 Apr 1857 OML

SULLIVAN, W.F. s/o Mordecai & Sarepta Sullivan age 30 S farmer POB & POR Spotsylvania & **TYLER**, Maggie L. d/o Emilly Tyler age 22 S POB & POR Spotsylvania; POM Spotsylvania C.H. 27 Jul 1893 SPMR SPML

SULLIVAN, W.F. s/o Wiley F.& Angelina Sullivan age 23 S farmer POB & POR Spotsylvania & **WOLLFREY**, Cora Lee d/o William & Ann Woolfrey age 15 S POB & POR Spotsylvania; POM Spotsylvania C.H.16 Sep 1891 SPMR SPML

SULLIVAN, W.J. s/o
Newton & Ann W.
Sullivan age 46 W
blacksmith POB &
POR Spotsylvania
& **PAYTES**, Sarah
E. d/o James &
Sarah Marton age
39 W POB
Richmond,Va POR
Spotsylvania; POM
Spotsylvania 24
Sep 1863 SPMR 23
Sep 1863 SPML
SURLES, Robert H. s/o
Robert & B.Surles
age 20 S farmer
POB & POR
Caroline Co &
GAYLE, Laura F.
d/o G.W.&
M.E.Gayle age 17
S POB Caroline Co
POR Spotsylvania;
POM Spotsylvania
28 Oct 1880 SPMR
SPML
SUTHERLIN, Thomas s/o
Robert & Jane
Sutherlin age 23
S farmer POB
Orange POR
Spotsylvania &
SULLIVAN, Ann d/o
Robert & Ann
Sullivan age 20 S
POB & POR
Spotsylvania; POM
Spotsylvania 21
Sep 1866 SPMR 18
Sep 1866 SPML
SUTTON, H.C. s/o
Robert &
Catherine Sutton
age 45 W
carpenter POB &
OPR Caroline Co &
BALL, Ann E. d/o
James C.&
Elizabeth Ball
age 30 S POB &
POR Spotsylvania;
POM Spotsylvania
3 Feb 1870 SPMR
27 Jan 1870 SPML
SUTTON, Randall B. s/o
William &
Priscilla Sutton
age 50 W farmer
POB & POR
Westmoreland Co &
HUMPHRIES, Lucie
A. d/o Joshua &
Fanny Reamy age
25 W POB Stafford
POR Spotsylvania;
POM Spotsylvania
6 May 1868 SPMR 5
May 1868 SPML
SWANN, George W. s/o
Frank Swan &
Elizabeth Duke
age 21 S farm
laborer POB
Petersburg,Va POR
Orange POC &
ROBINSON, Mary
age 26 W POB &
POR Orange POC;
POM Orange 7 Dec
1867 OMR 30 Nov
1867 OML
SWARTZ, George s/o
Frederick Swartz
& Elizabeth
Willast age 25 S
farmer POB
Germany POR
Richmond,Va &
GARNETT, Lucy M.
d/o James & Eliza
Lloyd age 25 W
POB Madison Co
POR Orange; POM
Orange 12 Jan
1864 OMR OML
SWATS, Jacob F.&
SMITH, Sarah E.;
POM Orange 24 Jul
1851 OMR 21 Jul
1851 OML
SWIFT, A.E. s/o W.T.&
O.A.Swift age 23
S saw mill
manager POB
Fredericksburg
POR Spotsylvania

& BRIGHTWELL,
L.B. d/o J.D.&
M.Brightwell age
25 S POB & POR
Spotsylvania; POM
Antioch Ch,
Spotsylvania 16
Nov 1899 SPMR 6
Nov 1899 SPML
SWIFT, Richard G. s/o
H.& E.Swift age
66 W farmer POB &
POR Spotsylvania
& , Sarah d/o
William &
N.Crawford age 63
W POB & POR
Spotsylvania; pOM
New Hope Station,
Spotsylvania 26
Sep 1878 SPMR 21
Sep 1878 SPML
SWIFT, William T. s/o
Granville & Jane
Swift age 21 S
farmer POB & POR
Spotsylvania &
MASSEY, Lucinda
d/o James O.&
Elizabeth Massey
age 27 S POB &
POR Orange; POM
Orange 25 Sep
1856 OMR 22 Sep
1856 OML
SWIFT, Willie J. s/o
William T.&
O.A.Swift age 24
S farmer POB &
POR Spotsylvania
& CHEWNING,
Lillian E. d/o
George W.& Sarah
A.Chewning age 19
S POB & POR
Spotsylvania; POM
Spotsylvania 13
Dec 1893 SPMR 4
Dec 1893 SPML
TALIAFERRO, Dabney s/o
William & Lucy
Ann Taliaferro
age 22 S laborer
POB & POR

Spotsylvania POC
& LEWIS, Susan
d/o Amelia Lewis
age 20 S POB &
POR Spotsylvania
POC; POM
Spotsylvania C.H.
18 Dec 1889 SPMR
SPML
TALIAFERRO, Ed.H. &
LUCAS, Sarah A.;
6 Feb 1855 SPMR
TALLEY, Charles A.
s/o James M.&
Lucy Talley age
33 W farmer POB &
POR Spotsylvania
& PAYNE, Annie R.
d/o F.P.& Rebecca
C.Payne age 22 S
POB & POR
Spotsylvania; POM
Goshen Ch,
Spotsylvania 14
Dec 1899 SPMR 4
Dec 1899 SPML
TALLEY, Charles A. s/o
James M.& Lucy
H.Talley age 24 S
farmer POB & POR
Spotsylvania &
GRADY, Annie B.
d/o George &
Rowena Grady age
20 S POB Stafford
POR Spotsylvania;
POM
Fredericksburg 3
Jun 1891 SPMR 1
Jun 1891 SPML
TALLEY, Charles N. s/o
Nathan & Rhoda
Talley age 25 S
farmer POB Louisa
Co POR
Spotsylvania &
PRITCHETT, Lucy
T. d/o P.B.&
Annie E.
Pritchett age 29
S POB & POR
Spotsylvania; POM
Spotsylvania 25

Nov 1884 SPMR 24
Nov 1884 SPML
TALLEY, James M. S
farmer POB & POR
Spotsylvania &
HATCH, S.C. d/o
J.A.& D.Hatch age
15 S POB Culpeper
POR Spotsylvania;
POM Spotsylvania
25 Oct 1857 SPMR
TALLEY, James M. s/o
L.M.& E.A.Talley
age 22 S farmer
POB Louisa Co POR
Spotsylvania &
HARRIS, Georgia
A. d/o Janus O. &
L.A.Harris age 20
S POB & POR
Spotsylvania; POM
Bethel Ch,
Spotsylvania 25
Dec 1879 SPMR 23
Dec 1879 SPML
TALLEY, Joe s/o
Charlotte Talley
age 19 S farmer
POB & POR
Spotsylvania POC
& **TERRELL**, Sallie
d/o John & Betsy
Terrell age 20 S
POB & POR
Spotsylvania POC;
POM Spotsylvania
17 May 1868 SPMR
SPML
TALLEY, Joseph J.J.
s/o Joseph &
Mattie E.Talley
age 21 S farmer
POB & POR
Spotsylvania &
DICKINSON, Ida V.
d/o Robert & Mary
F.Talley age 21 S
POB & POR
Spotsylvania; POM
Spotsylvania 10
May 1893 SPMR 8
May 1893 SPML
TALLEY, Martin s/o
Toby & Lucy Ann

Talley age 60 W
laborer POB
Louisa Co POR
Spotsylvania POC
& **WASHINGTON**,
Rose age 35 S POB
& POR
Spotsylvania POC;
POM Branch Fork
Ch, Spotsylvania
1 Jan 1876 SPMR
30 Dec 1875 SPML
TALLEY, Nathan B. s/o
Nathan & Rhoda
E.Talley age 31 S
farmer POB & POR
Spotsylvania &
PRITCHETT, Mollie
J. d/o P.B.&
Annie E.Pritchett
age 28 S POB &
POR Spotsylvania;
POM Spotsylvania
28 Mar 1893 SPMR
27 Mar 1893 SPML
TALLEY, Peyton G. s/o
Nathan & Prudence
W. age 23 S
farmer POB & POR
Louisa Co &
BOSTON, Fannie A.
d/o Alexander A.&
Ann Boston age 22
S POB & POR
Orange; POM
Orange 17 May
1854 OMR 1 May
1854 OML
TALLEY, Robert P. s/o
Nathan & Rhodie
E.Talley age 29 S
farmer POB & POR
Spotsylvania &
POOLE, Maggie M.
d/o W.M.& Lucy
Poole age 19 S
POB & POR
Spotsylvania; POM
Shady Grove Ch,
Spotsylvania 21
Dec 1893 SPMR 18
Dec 1893 SPML
TALLEY, W.T. s/o W.O.&
L.E.Talley age 25

S miner POB & POR
Louisa Co &
WILLOUGHBY, Lily
D. d/o W.M.&
Sarah E.
Willoughby age 23
S POB Louisa Co
POR Spotsylvania;
POM Spotsylvania
11 Mar 1898 SPMR
SPML
TALLEY, William E. s/o
Littleton M.&
Elizabeth Talley
age 22 S farmer
POB & POR
Spotsylvania &
TALLEY, Mary A.
d/o William &
Elizabeth
J.Talley age 18 S
POB & POR
Spotsylvania; POM
Spotsylvania 26
Feb 1867 SPMR 25
Feb 1867 SPML
TALLEY, William N. s/o
John C. & Mary
E.Talley age 33 S
farmer POB Louisa
Co POR
Spotsylvania &
WELCH, Virginia
E. d/o Thomas &
Annie Welch age
19 S POB & POR
Spotsylvania 24
Jan 1875 SPMR 18
Jan 1875 SPML
TALLEY, William s/o
Martin & Rose
Talley age 23 S
farmer POB & POR
Louisa Co POC &
HUNTER, Louisa
d/o Stephen &
Dren Hunter age
21 S POB & POR
Spotsylvania POC;
POM Spotsylvania
C.H. 21 Dec 1897
SPMR SPML
TATUM, Joseph H. s/o
Isham & Mary
Tatum age 25 S
teacher POB
Madison Co POR
Orange & **WOOD**,
Sarah Jane d/o
Richard & Tabitha
Wood age 25 S POB
& POR Orange; POM
Orange 23 Apr
1857 OMR 22 Apr
1857 OML
TAYLOE, George E. s/o
George P.Tayloe &
Mary Langhome age
25 S planter &
Lt.Col.C.S.A. POB
Roanoke Co POR
Marengo Co,
Alabama & **WILLIS**,
Delia S. d/o
George Willis &
Sallie J.Smith
age 20 S POB
Pensacola,
Florida POR
Orange; POM Wood
Park,Orange 9 Feb
1864 OMR OML
TAYLOR, Alexander s/o
Alexander Taylor
& Nelly Johnson
age 21 S laborer
on farm POB & POR
Orange POC &
JACKSON, Betsy
d/o Jeny &
Barbara Jackson
age 16 S POB &
POR Orange POC;
POM Orange 21 Apr
1867 OMR 20 Apr
1867 OML
TAYLOR, Benjamin W.
s/o Thomas
N.Taylor & Mary
N. Brozwell age
27 S farmer POB
Montgomery Co,
Alabama POR
Tallaporsa Co,
Alabama & **BELL**,
Minerva C. d/o
Henry C.Bell &
Elizabeth

A.Kendall age 22 S POB & POR Orange; POM Orange 21 Nov 1865 OMR 18 Nov 1865 OML

TAYLOR, Daniel s/o Ryland & Ann Taylor age 24 S laborer POB Essex Co POR Spotsylvania POC & **ROBINSON**, Emily d/o Anthony & Kitty Robinson age 24 S POB & POR Spotsylvania POC; POM Spotsylvania 20 Jan 1872 SPMR SPML

TAYLOR, Delaware s/o Silas & Mahaly Taylor age 29 W laborer POB Spotsylvania POR Partlow, Spotsylvania POC & **LEWIS**, Louisa Jane d/o Charles & Martha Lewis age 20 S POB Spotsylvania POR Partlow, Spotsylvania POC; POM Spotsylvania C.H. 29 Dec 1891 SPMR SPML

TAYLOR, George s/o William & R.Taylor age 24 S laborer POB & POR Spotsylvaia POC & **WATSON**, Mary d/o George & F.Watson age 21 S POB & POR Spotsylvania POC; POM Branch Fork Ch, Spotsylvania 27 feb 1879 SPMR 26 Feb 1879 SPML

TAYLOR, Hy s/o George & Polly Taylor age 27 S shoemaker POB Spotsylvania POR Caroline Co & **PENDLETON**, Lucy E. d/o Joel T.& Fanny Lewis age 32 W POB & POR Spotsylvania; POM Spotsylvania 11 May 1855 SPMR

TAYLOR, Isaac s/o Henry & Ann Harrison age 21 S laborer POB Louisa Co POR Spotsylvania POC & **COATES**, Susan Alice d/o Fanny Minor age 21 S POB & POR Spotsylvania POC; POM Spotsylvania 20 May 1882 SPMR SPML

TAYLOR, James s/o D.& L.Taylor age 38 S laborer POB Louisa Co POR Spotsylvania POC & **JACKSON**, Matilda d/o Sally Jackson age 25 S POB & POR Spotsylvania POC; POM Spotsylvania 6 Jul 1879 SPMR 3 Jul 1879 SPML

TAYLOR, John Edward s/o Say & Mahala Taylor age 23 (b.d.Aug 1846)S farmer POB & POR Spotsylvania POC & **ROSS**, Isabella d/o Walker & Matilda Ross age 23 S POB & POR Spotsylvania POC: POM Spotsylvania 26 Apr 1869 SPMR 10 Apr 1869 SPML

TAYLOR, John Wesley s/o John & Mary

Taylor age 26 S printer POB Pennsylvania & **HOWARD**, Ann Elizabeth d/o Thomas & Elizabeth Howard age 22 S POB Spotsylvania; POM Spotsylvania 21 Dec 1854 SPMR

TAYLOR, Lazarus s/o James & Matilda Taylor age 28 S laborer POB & POR Spotsylvania POC & **RAWLINGS**, Octabia d/o Temple & Sarah Rawlings age 22 S POB & POR Spotsylvania POC; POM Washington D.C. 2 Oct 1900 Washington MR 1 Oct 1900 SPML

TAYLOR, Lucus s/o Temple & Mary Taylor age 21 (b.d.Oct) S farmer POB Caroline Co POR Spotsylvania & **JONES**, Eliza C. d/o Burrell & Eliza Jones age 28 S POB & POR Spotsylvania; POM Spotsylvania 8 Apr 1874 SPMR 6 Apr 1874 SPML

TAYLOR, Milten C. s/o P.D.& L.K.Taylor age 23 S farmer POB & POR Spotsylvania & **PARKER**, Lelia J. d/o William & Olivia Parker age 21 S POB & POR Spotsylvania; POM Spotsylvania 7 Jul 1897 SPMR 3 Jul 1897 SPML

TAYLOR, Minor s/o Caleb & Sarah Taylor age 21 S farmer POB & POR Spotsylvania POC & **BOYD**, Maria Jane d/o Reuben & Margaret Boyd age 20 S POB Louisa Co POR Spotsylvania POC: POM Spotsylvania 29 Dec 1870 SPMR 27 Dec 1870 SPML

TAYLOR, Moses D. s/o D.& S.Taylor age 22 shoe maker POB & POR Spotsylvania POC & **TOWLES**, Anna d/o Tom Towles & Bella Lewis age 17 POB & POR Spotsylvania POC; POM Sylvana Ch, Spotsylvania 20 Feb 1881 SPMR 19 Feb 1881 SPML

TAYLOR, R.Innes s/o John R.& B.F.Taylor age 30 S farmer POB & POR Spotsylvania & **DOWNMAN**, Nannie H. d/o R.H.& M.A.Downman age 23 S POB & POR Spotsylvania; POM Idlewild, Spotsylvania 3 Oct 1876 SPMR 28 Sep 1876 SPML

TAYLOR, William J. & **LEWIS**, Frances E.; POM Spotsylvania (MR undated)SPMR 29 Jan 1859 SPML

TAYLOR, William J. s/o G.& M.Taylor age 29 S miller POB & POR Spotsylvania & **LEWIS**, Frances E. d/o J.&

B.Halley age 35 W POB & POR Spotsylvania; POM Spotsylvania 19 Jan 1859 SPML

TAYLOR, William s/o James & Jane Taylor age 23 S taylor POB & POR Stafford & **ROBINSON**, Mary J. d/o Joseph B.& Mary C.Robinson age 22 S POB & POR Spotsylvania; POM Spotsylvania 31 Dec 1884 SPMR SPML

TAYLOR, William s/o William & R.Taylor age 26 S laborer POB & POR Spotsylvania POC & **BELL**, Mary Eliza d/o T.& E.Bell age 21 S POB & POR Spotsylvania POC; POM Spotsylvania 3 Jan 1880 SPMR 30 Dec 1879 SPML

TEMPLE, James s/o Lewis & E.Temple age 48 W laborer POB & POR Caroline Co POC & **ELLIS**, Martha age 38 W POB Goochland POR Spotsylvania POC; POM Spotsylvania 14 Dec 1879 SPMR 11 Dec 1879 SPML

TEMPLER, William s/o P.& F.Templer age 23 S farmer POB Stuben Co, N.Y. POR Spotsylvania & **SULLIVAN**, R. age 23 S POB Stafford POR Spotsylvania; POM Spotsylvania 25 Feb 1867 SPMR

TERRELL, C.T. s/o Joseph C.& Ann E.Terrell age 31 S farmer POB & POR Hanover Co & **McGEE**, Fancy P. d/o Ab & M.J.McGee age 23 S POB & POR Spotsylvania; POM Spotsylvania 12 Oct 1876 SPMR 6 Oct 1876 SPML

TERRELL, Clarence L. s/o John E.& Elvira E.Terrell age 27 S farmer POB & POR Hanover Co & **MADDOX**, Lydia A. d/o L.G.& Mary E.Maddox age 27 S POB & POR Spotsylvania; POM Spotsylvania 19 Jan 1899 SPMR 11 Jan 1899 SPML

TERRELL, Joseph W. s/o David & Judy Terrell age 23 S farmer POB & POR Spotsylvania POC & **DESPOT**, Sallie d/o Murry & Louisa Despot age 19 S POB & POR Spotsylvania POC; POM Spotsylvania 5 Mar 1871 SPMR 28 Feb 1871 SPML

TERRELL, Julian s/o Sally Talley age 21 S laborer POB & POR Spotsylvania POC & **KING**, Sarah d/o Jane King age 20 S POB & POR Spotsylvania POC; POM Spotsylvania 28 Dec 1882 SPMR 27 Dec 1882 SPML

TERRELL, Lewis s/o William & Harriet

Terrell age 25 S
farmer POB Louisa
Co POR
Spotsylvania POC
& **SPENCER**, Rosa
d/o James &
Louisa Spencer
age 21 S POB &
POR Spotsylvania
POC; POM Branach
Fork Ch,
Spotsylvania 16
Jan 1884 SPMR 7
Jan 1884 SPML
TERRELL, Marion s/o
John Terrell &
Sarah Talley age
23 S laborer POB
& POR
Spotsylvania POC
& **GIBSON**, Sarah
Ella d/o Charles
& Matilda Gibson
age 18 S POB &
POR Spotsylvania
POC; POM
Spotsylvania 3
Feb 1883 SPMR 2
Feb 1883 SPML
TERRELL, William E.
s/o John G.&
E.E.Terrell age
31 S farmer POB &
POR Orange &
DICKINSON,
Florence V. d/o
James L.Dickinson
age 17 S POB
Louisa Co POR
Spotsylvania; POM
Spotsylvania 2
Mar 1876 SPMR
SPML
TERRILL, Granville s/o
Joseph & Eliza
Terrell age 58 W
farmer POB Louisa
Co & **COLEMAN**,
Laura d/o Thomas
Ellis & Joanna
Ellis (formerly
Webb) age 56 W
POB & POR
Spotsylvania POC;

POM Louisa Co 29
May 1900 Louisa
MR 4 May 1900
SPML
TERRILL, Jesse s/o
Nelson Terrill &
Patsy Payne age
22 S laborer POB
Albemarle Co POR
Orange POC &
WHITE, Lucy Ann
d/o Benjamin
White & Amy
Williams age 18 S
POB & POR Orange
POC; POM Orange
22 Oct 1867 OMR
OML
TERRILL, John s/o
Edmund & Susan
Terrill age 35 S
mechanic POB &
POR Orange &
STUBBLEFIELD,
Sarah d/o Thomas
& Mary
Stubblefield age
23 S POB & POR
Orange; POM
Orange 6 Nov 1855
OMR
THACKER, Carridon T.
s/o George W.&
Mary Thacker age
37 W railroad
official POB
Powhatan Co POB
King William Co &
BLAYDES, Emma W.
d/o J.F.&
A.V.Blaydes age
18 S POB Caroline
Co POR
Spotsylvania; POM
Spotsylvania 4
Oct 1881 SPMR 3
Oct 1881 SPML
THACKER, E.J. s/o
E.J.& Mildred
E.Thacker age 23
S farmer POB
Caroline Co POR
Spotsylvania &
COVINGTON,

Georganna d/o
Robert N.& Mary
Covington age 19
S POB Caroline Co
POR Spotsylvania;
4 Jan 1894 SPML
THACKER, Silas J.or I.
& **JONES**, Mary E.
d/o T.R.Jones S
POR Spotsylvania;
POM Spotsylvania
3 Oct 1853 SPMR
THIRSTON, Samuel s/o
Richard & Betsy
Thirston age 31 W
farmer POB Orange
POR Spotsylvania
POC & **WARD**,
Issabell d/o
Henry & Dice Ward
age 22 S POB &
POR Spotsylvania
POC; POM
Spotsylvania C.H.
12 Sep 1893 SPMR
SPML
THOMAS, Fountain s/o
Fountain & Ann
Thomas age 20 S
farmer POB & POR
Orange & **WOOD**,
Lucinda d/o James
& Rebecca Wood
age 35 S POB
Albemarle Co POR
Orange; POM
Orange 28 Apr
1856 OMR OML
THOMAS, French C. s/o
John F.& Sarah
E.Thomas age 22 S
farmer POB & POR
Spotsylvania &
TAYLOR, G.P. d/o
William L.&
T.A.Taylor age 18
S POB Caroline Co
POR Spotsylvania;
POM Roxbury,
Spotsylvania 24
Dec 1876 SPMR 21
Dec 1876 SPML
THOMAS, George W. s/o
James & Frances
E.Thomas age 24 S
farmer POB & POR
Spotsylvania &
WALLER, Mary M.
d/o William B.&
Julia B.Waller
age 21 S POB &
POR Spotsylvania;
POM Spotsylvania
19 Oct 1865 SPMR
SPML
THOMAS, Joseph A. s/o
Harrison &
Cornelia Thomas
age 30 S laborer
POB Baltimore
Co,Md POR
Spotsylvania POC
& **COLEMAN**, Hattie
d/o Minor &
Louisa Coleman
age 17 S POB &
POR Spotsylvania
POC; POM Cherry
Grove,
Spotsylvania 9
Mar 1889 SPMR 8
Mar 1889 SPML
THOMAS, Thomas E. s/o
William E. &
Amelia Thomas age
26 S farmer POB
Luzerne Co, Penn
POR Spotsylvania
& **MORRISON**, Ida
K. d/o James T.&
Sallie R.Morrison
age 21 S POB &
POR Spotsylvania;
POM Spotsylvania
30 Jul 1890 SPMR
29 Jul 1890 SPML
THOMAS, William H. s/o
Martha Ellen
Thomas age 21 S
farmer POB & POR
Spotsylvania &
HART, Virginia S.
d/o Robert J.&
M.M.Hart age 20 S
POB & POR
Spotsylvania; POM
Spotsylvania 13

THOMAS, William s/o
A.& I.Thomas age
30 W farmer POB &
POR Spotsylvania
& **STANLEY**, Eliza
d/o A.& B.Stanley
age 30 S POB &
POR Spotsylvania;
11 Apr 1861 SPMR
Sep 1876 SPMR 12
Sep 1876 SPML

THOMAS, William s/o
A.& L.Thomas age
28 S ditcher POB
& POR
Spotsylvania &
BUTLER, M.B. d/o
Thomas & E.Butler
age 30 S POB &
POR Spotsylvania;
24 Dec 1856 SPMR

THOMAS, William s/o
William & Anne
Thomas age 27 S
laborer POB
Louisa Co POR
Spotsylvania POC
& **CHILDS**, Eliza
d/o Walker &
Pricilla Childs
age 25 S POB &
POR Spotsylvania
POC; POM Waller's
Tavern
Spotsylvania
(This may be a
minister's error.
Waller's Tavern
is in Louisa Co)
23 Sep 1871 SPMR
20 Sep 1871 SPML

THOMAS, William T. s/o
Robert & Mary
M.Thomas age 30 S
farmr POB & POR
Spotsylvania &
STANLEY,
Jeannette d/o
Eliza Stanley age
30 S POB & POR
Spotsylvania; POM
Spotsylvania
C.H.13 May 1886
SPMR SPML

THOMPSON, Archibald
s/o Archibald &
Agnes Thompson
age 38 S mechanic
POB & POR
Spotsylvania POC
& **WALLACE**, Lucy
d/o Lindsey &
Ellen Wallace age
31 S POB & POR
Spotsylvania POC;
POM Glenvilla,
Spotsylvania 12
Feb 1889 SPMR 8
Feb 1889 SPML

THOMPSON, Arthur s/o
William & Mary
Thompson age 36 S
professor of
music POB England
POR Orange &
LEWIS, Kate
Lightfoot d/o
John & Mary Lewis
age 20 S POB &
POR Spotsylvania;
POM Spotsylvania
29 Apr 1896 SPMR
28 Apr 1896 SPML

THOMPSON, Charles s/o
Fife & Alice
Thompson age 23 S
laborer POB & POR
Spotsylvania POC
& **WIGLESWORTH**,
Angelina d/o
James & Matilda
Wiglesworth age
19 S POB & POR
Spotsylvania POC;
POM Spotsylvania
7 Mar 1884 SPMR 4
Mar 1884 SPML

THOMPSON, Edward M.
s/o J.R.& Mary
M.Thompson age 28
S farmer POB
Jefferson Co,N.C.
POR Spotsylvania
& **ALSOP**, Loula J.
d/o Joseph M.&
Susan J.Alsop age
28 S POB & POR
Spotsylvania; POM

Spotsylvania 5 Jun 1889 SPMR 29 May 1889 SPML

THOMPSON, Henry s/o Archie & Aggy Thompson age 23 S farmer POB & POR Spotsylvania POC & **QUARLES**, Olive d/o Olie & Juddy Quarles age 21 S POB & POR Spotsylvania; POM Spotsylvania 10 Jan 1874 SPMR 7 Jan 1874 SPML

THOMPSON, John P. s/o Philip Thompson & Sarah C.Moseley age 33 S lawyer POB & POR Owensboro, Kentucky & **CAVE**, Maria C. d/o William P.Cave & Isabella age 23 S POB New York City POR Orange; POM Montebello, Orange 19 Dec 1865 OMR OML

THOMPSON, M.A. s/o R.W.& Mary Thompson age 60 POB Louisa Co POR Spotsylvania & **BLACKLEY**, Emma d/o George D.& Sarah Blackley age originally given as 22 but changed at the direction of the bride's two brothers, G.W.& J.H Blackley, to 35 POB & POR Spotsylvania; POM Spotsylvania 4 Sep 1884 SPMR 1 Sep 1884 SPML

THOMPSON, Rawsaw M. s/o Samuel S.Thompson & Lucy A.M.Snell age 31 S carpenter POB Rutherford Co, Tennessee POR Orange & **BLEDSOE**, Roberta E. d/o S.W.Bledsoe & Jane White age 24 S POB Madison Co POR Orange; POM Orange 10 Oct 1867 OMR 7 Oct 1867 OML

THOMPSON, Reuben L. s/o Samuel Thompson & Sally Lindsay age 62 W farmer POB & POR Orange & **SORRELL**, Ann d/o Edmund Dunaway & Sally Knight age 25 W POB & POR Orange; POM Orange 30 Apr 1865 OMR 29 Apr 1865 OML

THOMPSON, Thomas G. s/o R.L.& Ann Thompson age 25 S farmer POB Orange POR Spotsylvania & **HERRING**, Susie M. d/o Robert & Sallie Herring age 18 S POB & POR Spotsylvania; POM Spotsylvania 22 Jan 1893 SPMR 19 Jan 1893 SPML

THORNTON, Jackson L. s/o Anthony Thornton & Nancy Twyman age 36 W farmer POB & POR Green Co & **MANSFIELD**, Mary L. d/o Joseph A.Mansfield & Susan A.Linsey S POB & POR Orange; POM Orange 25 Apr 1861 OMR

THORNTON, James H. s/o Anthony & Mary

Thornton age 24 S
laborer POB Essex
Co POR
Spotsylvania POC
& **MANSFIELD**,
Annis d/o Chester
& Eliza Mansfield
age 22 S POB &
POR Spotsylvania
POC ; POM
Fredericksburg 14
Dec 1882 FMR SPML
THORNTON, James H. s/o
Anthony & Mary
Thornton age 40 W
laborer POB & POR
Spotsylvania POC
& **MANUEL**, Ella
d/o Phil &
Lucinda Manuel
age 19 S POB &
POR Spotsylvania
POC; POM
Spotsylvania 2
Feb 1898 SPMR
SPML
THORNTON, John s/o
Jack & Sally
Thornton age 51 W
laborer POB & POR
Spotsylvania POC
& **LEWIS**, Mary d/o
Elizabeth Lewis
age 40 S POB
Caroline Co POR
Spotsylvania POC;
POM Spotsylvania
26 Feb 1867 SPMR
21 Feb 1867 SPML
THORNTON, Manuel s/o
M.& G.Thornton
age 72 W
blacksmith POB
Stafford POR
Spotsylvania POC
& **LEVY**, Tama age
45 W POB & POR
Spotsylvania POC;
POM Forest Hill,
Spotsylvania 26
Dec 1878 SPMR 23
Dec 1878 SPML
THORNTON, Nelson s/o
Anthony & Mary

Thornton age 23 S
farmer POB & POR
Spotsylvania POC
& **TAYLOR**, Hattie
d/o Sie & Amelia
Taylor age 21 S
POB & POR
Spotsylvania POC;
POM Spotsylvania
5 Dec 1895 SPMR
SPML
THORNTON, Peyton s/o
Anthony & Maray
Thornton age 26 S
farmer POB & POR
Spotsylvania POC
& **SCOTT**, Nannie
d/o Robert J.&
Mary A.Burruss W
POB & POR
Spotsylvania POC;
POM New Hope Ch,
Spotsylvania 18
Feb 1892 SPMR 16
Feb 1892 SPML
THURMAN, Benjamin F. &
ROUTT, Martha E.;
POM Orange 28 Sep
1852 OMR 6 Sep
1852 OML
THURMAN, John B. s/o
Edward & Agnes
R.Thurman age 31
S merchant POB
Albemarle Co POR
Albemarle Co &
SCOTT, Mildred V.
d/o James M.&
Sarah T.Scott age
26 S POB
Spotylvania POR
Spotsylvania; POM
Spotsylvania 11
Apr 1882 SPMR 10
Apr 1882 SPML
THURSTON, William s/o
Richmond & Mary
Thurston age 30 S
farmer POB Louisa
Co POR
Spotsylvania POC
& **ACORS**, Nannie
d/o Thomas &
Fanny Acors age

18 S POB & POR Spotsylvania POC; POM Hotel at Spotsylvania C.H. 27 Apr 1887 SPMR SPML

TIBBS, Gabriel s/o Gabriel & Lucy Tibbs age 21 S laborer POB Caroline Co POR Spotsylvania POC & **MINOR**, Martha d/o John & Polly Minor age 19 S POB & POR Spotsylvania POC; POM Spotsylvania 25 Jan 1877 SPMR SPML

TIBBS, William s/o G.& L.Tibbs age 30 W farmer POB Caroline Co POR Spotsylvania POC & **COLEMAN**, M. d/o S.& S.Coleman age 18 S POB & POR Spotsylvania POC; 1 Feb 1867 SPMR

TIMBERLAKE, Ellett s/o Benjamin & Melissa Timberlake age 19 S farmer POB Orange POR Culpeper Co & **GRAHAM**, Gertie L. d/o J.W.& Mary Graham age 20 S POR Spotsylvania; POM Spotsylvania 6 Oct 1896 SPMR SPML

TIMBERLAKE, James L. s/o George Timberlake & Elizabeth A.Turner age 24 S merchant POB Louisa Co POR Richmond,Va & **ESTES**, Juliett M. d/o James Estes &

Sarah Minor age 22 S POB & POR Orange; POM Orange 9 Nov 1865 OMR 31 Oct 1865 OML

TIMBERLAKE, James W. s/o Daniel Timberlake & Mary Davis age 47 W farmer POB Clarke Co POR Culpeper Co & **WALKER**, Sally Ann d/o Benjamin Walker & Betsy Henshaw age 34 S POB & POR Orange; POM Orange 11 Mar 1862 OMR 24 Feb 1862 OML

TIMBERLAKE, Richard N. s/o John M.& Joannus Timberlake age 30 S farmer POB Louisa Co POR Spotsylvania & **WATSON**, Maggie L. d/o Charles & Agnes Watson age 19 S POB & POR Spotsylvania; POM St.George Chapel, Trinity Ch, Spotsylvania 18 Jan 1888 SPMR 16 Jan 1888 SPML

TIMBY, George W. s/o E.W.& M.M.Timby age 22 S farmer POB Pennsylvania POR Spotsylvania & **BARNES**, Susan d/o E.& M.A.Barnes age 17 S POB Pennsylvania POR Spotsylvania; POM Parker's Store, Spotsylvania 25 Jan 1880 SPMR 24 Jan 1880 SPML

TINDEN, James A. s/o James & Elizabeth Tinden age 30 S farmer POB Orange & **HOPKINS**, Sarah A. d/o W.L.& M.W.Hopkins age 30 S POB Spotsylvania; POM Spotsylvania 24 Sep 1856 SPMR

TINDER, Amos E. s/o George W.Tinder & Sarah Quisenberry age 24 S farmer POB & POR Orange & **CANADAY**, Caroline F. d/o James Canaday & Ann Tinder age 22 S POB & POR Orange; POM Orange 28 Jan 1866 OMR 23 Jan 1866 OML

TINDER, Edgar A. s/o John A.Tinder & Frances Shadrack age 22 S farmer POR & POB Orange & **BROOKING**, Cassandra B. d/o Charles R.Brooking & Susan M.Sanders age 21 S POB & POR Orange; POM Orange 26 Oct 1865 OMR 23 Oct 1865 OML

TINDER, George T.& **HERNDON**, Susan d/o John Herndon Jr.; POM Orange 20 Jan 1853 OMR 18 Jan 1853 OML

TINDER, James R. & **SAUNDERS**, Emily; 12 Oct 1852 OML

TINDER, James R. s/o John & F.Tinder age 57 W gold miner POB Orange POR Spotsylvania & **ORR**, Eliza A. age 42 W POB Orange POR Spotsylvania; POM Sylvana Ch Spotsylvania 16 Jan 1881 SPMR 3 Jan 1881 SPML

TINDER, James R. s/o James R, Tinder Sr.& **TINDER**, Sarah M.; 22 Dec 1851 OMR OML

TINDER, John A. s/o David Tinder age 45 W farmer POB Louisa Co POR Spotsylvania & **TALLEY**, M.A. d/o Richard & Elizabeth Talley age 36 S POB Louisa Co POR Spotsylvania; POM Spotsylvania 10 Mar 1857 SPMR

TINDER, Thomas R. & **TINDER**, Elizabeth J. d/o Thomas Tinder; POM Orange 16 Mar 1852 OMR 13 Mar 1852 OML

TINDER, William M. (aka Waller M.) & **LANCASTER**, Sarah E. d/o Sarah Lancaster; 21 Feb 1852 OML

TISDALE, Lemuel age about 28 laborer POR Louisa Co & **ROBERSON**, Elizabeth age about 22 POR Orange; POM Orange 22 Dec 1853 OMR

TODD, Oscar B. s/o Charles & Caroline M.Todd age 25 S farmer POB & POR Spotsylvania &

STEPHENS, Sudie E. d/o William A. & Mary E.Stephens age 19 S POB & POR Spotsylvania; POM Spotsylvania 28 Jan 1869 SPMR 24 Jan 1869 SPML

TODD, Richard L. s/o Charles & Matilda Todd age 40 S farmer POB & POR Spotsylvania & **SCOTT**, Robertine T. d/o William T.& Jane Scott age 24 S POB & POR Spotsylvania; POM Spotsylvania 26 Jan 1882 SPMR 23 Jan 1882 SPML

TODD, Samuel Dick s/o Samuel & Ann Todd age 27 farmer POB Hends Co, Mississippi POR Caroline Co & **HANSBROUGH**, Sallie Milton d/o Henry M. & Mary F, Hansbrough age 20 POB Cass Co, Mo. POR Spotsylvania; POM Riverside, Spotsylvania 2 Sep 1874 SPMR 20 Aug 1874 SPML

TOMPKINS, Ed W farmer POB Caroline Co POR Spotsylvania & **BEAZLEY**, E.M. d/o C.& M.Beazley S POB & POR Spotsylvania; 18 Nov 1859 SPMR

TOMPKINS, Edward R. s/o Edward & Harriet T.Tompkins age 22 S farmer POB Goochland Co POR Spotsylvania & **BOATWRIGHT**, Mary E. d/o James A.& Mary Boatwright age 17 S POB Cumberland Co POR Spotsylvania; POM Roxbury, Spotsylvania 27 Feb 1866 SPMR 26 Feb 1866 SPML

TOMPKINS, Frank Jr. s/o Frank & Rebecca Tompkins age 27 S POB & POR Spotsylvania & **QUIMBY**, Alfa S. d/o Matthew S.& Mary J.Quimby age 20 S POB & POR Spotsylvania; POM Christ Ch, Spotsylvania 25 Aug 1885 SPMR 22 Aug 1885 SPML

TOMPKINS, George M. s/o Walker & Amy Tompkins age 27 S laboere POB & POR Caroline Co POC & **JEFFERSON**, Lucy d/o Amanda Jefferson age 19 S POB & POR Spotsylvania POC; POM Spotsylvania 23 Jan 1890 SPMR 22 Jan 1890 SPML

TOMPKINS, George s/o F.& R.M.Tompkins age 30 S farmer POB Caroline Co POR Spotsylvania & **CARNER**, Cornelia A. d/o John & M.A.Carner age 27 S POB & POR Spotsylvania; POM Zion, Spotsylvania 17 Dec 1879 SPMR 15 Dec 1879 SPML

TOMPKINS, K.K. POB & POR Fauquier Co & **WELLFORD**, E.S. POB & POR

309

Spotsylvania; 26 Jan 1864 SPMR

TOMPKINS, William F. s/o Frank & Rebecca Tompkins age 40 S farmer POB & POR Spotsylvania & **KENNEDY**, Selinda d/o William M.& Tabitha Kennedy age 27 S POB Penn POR Spotsylvania; POM Spotsylvania 10 Jun 1894 SPMR 7 Jun 1894 SPML

TOOMBS, Thomas C. s/o Thomas C.& C.C.Toombs age 21 S gentleman POB & POR Spotsylvania & **JOHNSTON**, Ruther O. d/o William E.& Sarah A.Johnston age 21 S POB & POR Spotsylvania; POM Spotsylvania 8 Feb 1867 SPMR SPML

TOOMBS, Thomas L. s/o William & Martha Toombs age 24 S farmer POB Caroline Co POR Spotsylvania & **JONES**, Virginia A. d/o Lewis & Phoebe Jones age 21 S POB Caroline Co POR Spotsylvania; POM M.E.Ch, Fredericksburg 7 Jun 1866 FMR SPML

TOWLES, Cary s/o Hannah Towles age 22 S laborer POB & POR Spotsylvania POC & **LEWIS**, Margaret d/o Julia Samuel age 23 S POB & POR Spotsylvania POC; POM Spotsylvania C.H. 21 Jun 1883 SPMR SPML

TOWLES, Frederick s/o Jack & Hannah Towles age 26 S laborer POB & POR Spotsylvania POC & **ROBINSON**, Charlotte d/o Mary Robinson age 25 S POB & POR Spotsylvania POC; POM Spotsylvania 23 Mar 1882 SPMR 22 Mar 1882 SPML

TOWLES, Nathan s/o Henry & Emily Towles age 23 W farmer POB & POR Spotsylvania POC & **FORT**, Lucy d/o Chest & Courtney Fort age 20 S POB & POR Spotsylvnai POC; POM Spotsylvania 13 Mar 1867 SPMR 4 Mar 1867 SPML

TRIBBLE, Willie N. s/o William & Ann Tribble age 32 S farmer POB & POR Spotsylvania & **DURRETT**, Fanny d/o J.J.& Margaret Durrett age 26 S POB & POR Spotsylvania; POM Spotsylvania 10 Dec 1899 SPMR 4 Dec 1899 SPML

TRICE, A.J. s/o J.L.& A.Trice age 28 S farmer POB Louisa CO & **GRAVES**, V.S. d/o C.& J.V.Graves age 28 S POB Spotsylvania; POM Spotsylvania 22 Dec 1857 SPMR

TRICE, Monroe s/o Joe
& Ann Trice age
23 S farm laborer
POB Louisa Co POR
Orange POC &
JACKSON, Ann d/o
Jacob & Cassandra
Jackson age 28 S
POB Louisa Co POR
Orange POC; POM
Orange 14 Nov
1867 OMR OML

TRIGG, J.B. s/o J.E.&
C.M.Trigg age 27
S farmer POB &
POR Spotsylvania
& **ALSOP**, Margaret
A. d/o J.M.&
S.J.Alsop age 27
S POB & POR
Spotsylvania; POM
Spotsylvania 12
May 1881 SPMR 11
May 1881 SPML

TRIGG, J.W. s/o T.& M.
Trigg age 48 W
farmer POB & POR
Spotsylvania &
HAWKINS, H.& M.
d/o T.& M.Hawkins
S POB & POR
Spotsylvania; 20
Sep 1860 SPMR

TRIGG, John W. s/o
Joseph W.& Amanda
N.Trigg age 35 S
farmer POB & POR
Spotsylvania &
HART, Alice R.
d/o Frederick &
Caroline Hart age
25 S POB Orange
POR Spotsylvania;
POM Spotsylvania
C.H.22 Sep 1885
SPMR 21 Sep 1885
SPML

TRIPLETT, Robert C.
s/o William
H.Triplett &
Ellen Hansbrough
age 33 W mechanic
POB & POR
Culpeper Co &

TOWLES, Mary C.
d/o Thomas Towles
& Catharine
Stubblefield age
40 (?) S POB
Spotsylvania POR
Orange; POM
St.Thomas Ch,
Orange C.H.28 Jul
1864 OMR OML

TRUE, Joseph A. s/o
Fielding & Nancy
True age 30 S
miller POB & POR
Spotsylvania &
LONG, Mary E. d/o
John & Manerva
Long age 18 S POB
Caroline Co POR
Spotsylvania; POM
Spotsylvania 29
Dec 1870 SPMR 28
Dec 1870 SPML

TUEL, Isaac s/o Thomas
& Mary Tuel age
24 S miller POB
Orange POR
Madison Co &
FERNEYHOUGH,
Sarah J. d/o John
& Elizabeth
Ferneyhough age
21 S POB & POR
Orange; POM
Orange 3 Mar 1857
OMR 2 Mar 1857
OML

TUEL, Socrates s/o
Thomas Tuel &
Mary A.Lee (or
See)age 28 S
carpenter POB &
POR Orange &
HUGHES, Sarah F.
age 25 S POB &
POR Orange; POM
Orange 17 May
1866 OMR OML

TULLUS, Joseph D. s/o
Rhodam &
Elizabeth Tullus
age 33 S
merchant/farmer
POB & POR

Fauquier Co &
CLARK, Mary Jane
d/o William D. &
Jane M. Clark age
25 S POB & POR
Orange; POM
Orange 3 Mar 1857
OMR 2 Mar 1857
OML

TURNER, Edmund s/o
John & Lucy
Turner age 60 W
farmer POB & POR
Spotsylvania POC
& **CHEW**, Eliza age
40 W POB & POR
Spotsylvania POC;
POM Spotsylvanias
26 May 1872 SPMR
18 May 1872 SPML

TURNER, Edward s/o
Caswell Murphy &
Fannie Turner age
21 S laborer POB
& POR
Spotsylvania POC
& **SMITH**, Mary d/o
Joe & Annie Smith
age 21 S POB &
POR Spotsylvania
POC; POM
Spotsylvania 27
Dec 1882 SPMR 26
Dec 1882 SPML

TURNER, Frank s/o
Benjamin &
America Turner
age 40 W farmer
POB Spotsylvania
POC & **DUDLEY**,
Rachel d/o Eliza
Dudley age 35 S
POB Spotsylvania
POC; POM Branch
Fork Ch,
Spotsylvania 27
Mar 1892 SPMR 23
Mar 1892 SPML

TURNER, George s/o
Nelson Turner &
Mary Green age 21
S working at saw
mill POB & POR
Orange POC &

LINDSAY, Mildred
d/o Lewis Lindsay
& Ellen Daniel
age 19 S POB &
POR Orange POC;
POM Orange 26 Dec
1867 OMR 23 Dec
1867 OML

TURNER, J.Waller &
RHOADES, Eliza;
22 Dec 1856 OML

TURNER, James s/o
William & Milly
Turner age 56 W
laborer POB
Caroline Co POR
Spotsylvania POC
& **COLEMAN**, Ann
d/o Nancy Coleman
age 51 W POB &
POR Spotsylvania
POC; POM
Spotsylvania C.H.
24 Dec 1885 SPMR
SPML

TURNER, Killis, James
& D.Turner age 25
S laborer POB
Caroline Co POR
Spotsylvania POC
& **SLAUGHTER**, Ann
d/o Bettie
Slaughter age 19
S POB & POR
Spotsylvania POC;
POM Newe Hope Ch,
Spotsylvania 27
Sep 1877 SPMR
SPML

TURNER, Nelson s/o
Nelson Turner &
Mary Green age 22
S working at
sawmill POB & POR
Orange POC &
LINDSAY,
Charlotte d/o
Lewis Lindsay &
Ellen Daniel age
18 S POB & POR
Orange POC; POM
Orange 26 Dec
1867 OMR 23 Dec
1867 OML

TURNIPSEED, H.F. s/o
William & Edith
Turnipseed age 33
S farmer POB
Montgomery
Co,Alabama POR
Bullocks Co,
Alabama &
TOMPKINS, M.A.
d/o Frank &
Rebecca
M.Tompkins age 27
S POB & POR
Spotsylvania; POM
Ormsby, Caroline
Co 6 Sep 1882
Caroline MR 4 Sep
1882 SPML

TURNLEY, Ira P. s/o
E.& M.Turnley age
29 S farmer POB &
POR Spotsylvania
& **POWELL**, C.M.
d/o J.& J.Powell
age 29 S POB &
POR Spotsylvania;
POM Spotsylvania
1 Nov 1859 SPMR

TURNLEY, James P. s/o
Ira P.&
C.M.Turnley age
28 S farmer POB &
POR Spotsylvania
& **JERRELL**, Mary
Irene age 21 S
POB & POR
Spotsylvania; POM
Hebron Baptist
Ch, Spotsylvania
17 Oct 1888 SPMR
16 Oct 1888 SPML

TWYMAN, F.C. s/o J.J.&
S.Twyman age 26 S
farmer POB & POR
Orange &
TWYMAN,M.B.
(possibly Mildred
Buford Twyman)
d/o T.(possibly
Thornhill) &
S.Twyman age 25 S
POB & POR
Spotsylvania; 21
Dec 1858 SPMR

TWYMAN, Tinsley H. s/o
Frank C.& Mildred
B.Twyman age 38 S
merchant POB
Green Co POR
Spotsylvania &
SCOTT, Fannie A.
d/o W.T.& Estelle
M.Scott age 21 S
POB & POR
Spotsylvania; POM
Spotsylvania 30
Mar 1898 SPMR 29
Mar 1898 SPML

TWYMAN, W.P. s/o A.J.
& I.J. Twyman age
29 S minister POB
Orange POR
Spotsylvania &
DUVALL, J.D.M.
d/o C.& M. Duvall
age 32 S POB &
POR Spotsylvania;
19 Jun 1860 SPMR

TYLER, Henry s/o N.&
R.Tyler age 27 S
laborer POB & POR
Spotsylvania POC
& **DUERSON**,
Harriet d/o R.&
M.Minor age 21 S
POB & POR
Spotsylvania POC;
POM Spotsylvania
13 Jan 1881 SPMR
SPML

TYLER, Jacob s/o Sarah
West age 30 S
laborer POB & POR
Spotsylvania POC
& **NELSON**,Sarah
Frances d/o
Priscilla White
age 24 S POB &
POR Spotsylvania
POC; POM
Spotsylvania 15
Oct 1887 SPMR 14
Oct 1887 SPML

TYLER, James M. s/o
James & Mary Ann
Tyler age 22 S
"pzrotechnic" POB
& POR Richmond &

313

JONES, Sallie J. d/o Samuel D.& Mary Jones age 21 S POB Hanover Co POR Spotsylvania; POM Spotsylvania 12 Dec 1865 SPMR 11 Dec 1865 SPML

TYLER, James s/o Byrd Tyler & Lucy Branden age 31 W plasterer POB HenriCo Co POR Richmond POC & **MADISON**, Mary age 21 S POB & POR Orange POC; POM Orange 17 Apr 1866 OMR 16 Apr 1866 OML

TYLER, John s/o N.& R.Tyler age 22 S laborer POB & POR Spotsylvania POC & **MINOR**, Clara d/o R.& M.Minor age 25 S POB & POR Spotsylvania POC; POM Spotsylvania 13 Jan 1881 SPMR SPML

TYLER, Peter s/o Rich & N.A.Tyler age 40 W laborer POB & POR Spotsylvania POC & **BROCK**, Frances d/o W.Brock W POB Louisa Co POR Spotsylvania POC; POM Branch Fork Ch, Spotsylvania 28 Dec 1879 SPMR 27 Dec 1879 SPML

TYLER, Samuel s/o Arch & Watsy Tyler age 24 S laborer POB & POR Spotsylvania POC & **WILLIAMS**, Mary d/o Minor & Catherine Williams age 19 S POB & POR Spotsylvania POC: POM Spotsylvania 6 Mar 1893 SPMR SPML

TYLER, Wallace s/o Mauzey Tyler & Sarah Stewart age 22 S laborer POB Fauquire Co POR Spotsylvania POC & **CARTER**, Milly d/o Eb.& Maggie Carter age 17 S POB & POR Spotsylvania POC; POM Spotsylvania 28 Dec 1882 SPMR 27 Dec 1882 SPML

UPSHER, Roots s/o Thornton & Sarah Roots Upsher age 21 S blacksmith POB & POR Spotsylvania POC & **WILLIAMS**, Susan d/o Horace & Lavinia Williams age 23 S POB Louisa Co POR Spotsylvania POC; POM Mt Zion Baptist Ch, Spotsylvania 26 Oct 1873 SPMR 25 Oct 1873 SPML

VAN HOOK, Charles Gordon s/o John & Emma Van Hook of Washington D.C. POR Washington D.C. & **GREEN**, Martha Lucas d/o James L. & Anna Green of Fredericksburg age 26 POR Fredericksburg; POM Fredericksburg 2 Apr 1891 TCF

VASS, Benjamin W. s/o Henry & Lucy J.Vass age 65 W

farmer POB & POR Spotsylvania & **QUISENBERRY**, L.E. d/o Gideon & Sallie Flippo age 66 W POB Caroline Co POR Spotsylvania; POM Rose Valley,Spotsylvania 21 Oct 1894 SPMR 2 Oct 1894 SPML

VAUGHAN, Cornelius G. s/o Paschal Vaughan & Henrietta Dowell age 25 S farmer POB Madison Co POR Orange & **YOWELL**, Cornelia Alpha d/o Abraham Yowell & Susan Utz age 20 S POB Madison Co POR Orange; POM Orange 29 Mar 1866 OMR OML

VAUGHAN, Edwin age 24 farmer POR Hanover Co & **TURNER**, Lucretia M. d/o William(dec) & Mary(dec) Turner; POM Louisa Co 7 Feb 1854 OMR

VAUGHAN, Horace L. s/o Joseph H.& Annie B.Vaughan age 26 S railraod employee POB Hanover Co POR Chester, South Car. & **TOWLES**, Nannie W. d/o Dr.T.T.& Elizabeth S.Towles age 22 S POB & POR Spotsylvania; POM Spotsylvania 10 Sep 1889 SPMR 7 Sep 1889 SPML

VAUGHAN, Joseph P. s/o Robert Vaughan & Martha Pritchett age 21 S farmer POB & POR Grayson Co & **JACOBS**, Bettie d/o Daniel Jacobs & Elmira Dempsey age 19 S POB & POR Orange; POM Orange 4 Feb 1864 OMR 1 Feb 1864 OML

VOORHEES, J.O. s/o William & Orpha M.Voorhees age 34 S farmer POB Courtland Co, New York POR Spotsylvania & **FERNEYHOUGH**, Louise M. d/o George T.& Lavinia H.Ferneyhough age 28 S POB & POR Spotsylvania; POM Summit, Spotsylvania 6 Jun 1900 SPMR 4 Jun 1900 SPML

WADDY, Henry s/o W.& J.Waddy age 24 S laborer POB & POR Spotsylvania POC & **MICHIL**, Lucy d/o A.& M.E.Michil age 22 S POB Orange POR Spotsylvania POC; POM Gravel Hill, Spotsylvania 27 Jul 1878 SPMR 26 Jul 1878 SPML

WADKINS, Wesley s/o Michael & Judy Wadkins age 24 S laborer POB & POR Spotsylvania POC & **LEWIS**, Margarett d/o Arthur & Martha Lewis age 24 S POB & POR

315

Spotsylvania POC;
POM Spotsylvania
23 Dec 1881 SPMR
21 Dec 1881 SPML
WAFFREE, Albert s/o
Anderson & Lucy
Waffree age 22 W
mechanic POB &
POR Spotsylvania
& **HAREFIELD**,
Ellen V. d/o Ann
Harefield age 22
S POB & POR
Spotsylvania; POM
Spotsylvania 1
Jul 1866 SPMR 16
Jun 1866 SPML
WAITE, Henry W. s/o
William H.&
S.P.Waite age 33
S farmer POB &
POR Spotsylvania
& **FAULCONER**,
Virginia E. d/o
P.E.&
F.A.Faulconer age
28 S POB & POR
Spotsylvania; POM
Spotsylvania 20
Feb 1879 SPMR 17
Feb 1879 SPML
WAITE, M.F. s/o
William H. &
S.Waite age 25 S
farmer POB & POR
Spotsylvania &
PULLIAM, Ophelia
d/o L.&
M.A.Partlow age
28 W POB & POR
Spotsylvania; POM
Spotsylvania 26
Oct 1879 SPMR 24
Oct 1879 SPML
WAITE, William L. s/o
William H. & Mary
Waite age 29 S
farmer POB & POR
Spotsylvania &
CHEWNING,
N.Virginia d/o
William & Manicy
Alsop age 32 W
POB Stafford POR

Spotsylvania; POM
Spotsylvania 8
Nov 1868 SPMR 7
Nov 1868 SPML
WALDEN, George A. s/o
Charles & Mary
Walden age 55 W
shoemaker POB
"State of
Pennsylvania" POR
Spotsylvania &
POWELL, Susan M.
age 36 S POB
Louisa Co POR
Spotsylvania; POM
Spotsylvania 8
Mar 1868 SPMR 7
Mar 1868 SPML
WALKER, Alexander B.
s/o Alexander S.&
Jane E.Walker age
31 S farmer POB
King George Co
POR Spotsylvania
& **WALDEN**, Susie
C. d/o George &
Susie C.Walden
age 18 S POB &
POR Spotsylvania;
POM
Fredericksburg 27
Nov 1889 FMR 25
Nov 1889 SPML
WALKER, Charles s/o
B.& Winnie Walker
age 67 W farmer
POB & POR
Spotsylvania POC
& **CARTER**, E.E.
d/o J.H.&
M.Wheeler age 38
W POB Sussex Co
POR Washington
D.C. POC; POM
Spotsylvania 15
Feb 1899 SPMR
SPML (a copy)
WALKER, Charles s/o
Barnaby & Winnie
Walker age 61 W
farmer POB & POR
Spotsylvania POC
& **CARTER**, Ella
Ellsworth d/o

J.H.& M.J.Robinson age 38 W POB Sussex Co POR Washington D.C. POC; POM Spotsylvania 24 Apr 1899 SPMR SPML

WALKER, George D. s/o George & Leanna Walker age 21 S laborer POB & POR Spotsylvania POC & **SAMUEL**, Winnie d/o John & Abbie Samuel age 19 S POB & POR Spotsylvania POC: POM Spotsylvania C.H. 31 Oct 1893 SPMR SPML

WALKER, Green s/o Zekiel & Eliza Walker age 21 S laborer at sawmill POB Brunswick Co POR Orange POC & **LINDSAY**, Mary Susan d/o Monroe Lindsay & Mary Turner age 17 S POB & POR Orange POC; POM Orange 16 Jun 1867 OMR 10 Jun 1867 OML

WALKER, James W.Jr. s/o Col.James Walker W farmer POB & POR Madison Co & **PORTER**, Mary Jane d/o Col.John & Mary Porter S POB & POR Orange; POM Orange 27 Aug 1856 OMR 26 Aug 1856 OML

WALKER, Moses s/o George Walker age 21 S farm laborer POB & POR Orange POC & **REED**, Mary Ann age 19 S POB & POR Orange POC;

POM Orange 28 Dec 1867 OMR OML

WALKER, Peter s/o Peter Walker & Fanny Crock age 51 W farmer POB & POR Orange POC & **ALEXANDER**, Hannah age 46 W POB Albemarle Co POR Orange POC; POM Orange 7 Apr 1866 OMR 29 Mar 1866 OML

WALKER, Richard s/o Charles & E.Walker age 26 S laborer POB & POR Spotsylvania POC & **WILLIS**, Jane d/o A.& S.Willis age 21 S POB & POR Spotsylvania 6 Jan 1881 SPMR 4 Jan 1881 SPML

WALKER, Samuel s/o Solomon & Frances Walker age 67 merchant/farmer POB Fauquier Co & **HAWKINS**, Elizabeth d/o Thomas & Mary Hawkins age 57 S POB Spotsylvania; POM Spotsylvania 16 Oct 1855 SPMR

WALKER, William s/o Charles & S.Walker age 22 S laborer POB & POR Spotsylvania POC & **ELLY**, Rena d/o Moris Elly & P.Washington age 21 S POB & POR Spotsylvania POC; POM Spotsylvania 25 Nov 1876 SPMR 24 Nov 1876 SPML

WALLACE, Festus D. s/o Charles & Mary Wallace age 23 S farmer POB & POR

Spotsylvania &
OWENS, Maggie J.
d/o A.M.& Mary
Owens age 21 S
POB & POR
Spotsylvania; POM
Spotsylvania C.H.
30 Dec 1891 SPMR
SPML
WALLACE, Frank s/o
Toby & Amy
Wallace age 74 W
laborer POB
Culpeper Co POR
Orange POC &
TURNER, Lavinia
d/o Johnson &
Lucy Turner age
60 W POB & POR
Orange POC; POM
Orange 16 Sep
1866 OMR 1 Sep
1866 OML
WALLACE, G.B. s/o
G.B.& Elizabeth
Wallace age 36 W
farmer POB
Fredericksburg
POR Spotsylvania
& **DIXON**, Ida F.
d/o William H.&
V.A.Perry age 32
D POB & POR
Spotsylvania; POM
Spotsylvania 7
Jul 1895 SPMR 2
Jul 1895 SPML
WALLACE, Gustavus B.
s/o G.B.&
Elizabeth Wallace
age 24 S farmer
POB
Fredericksburg
POR Spotsylvania
& **LACY**, Orilla M.
d/o J.F.& Sallie
J.Lacy age 25 S
POB Goochland Co
POR Spotsylvania;
POM Spotsylvania
21 Dec 1882 SPMR
11 Dec 1882 SPML
WALLACE, Nelson s/o
Lindsay & Millie

Wallace age 65 W
farmer POB & POR
Spotsylvania POC
& **GREEN**, Matilda
d/o Solomon Bundy
age 45 W POB
Goochland Co POR
Spotsylvania POC;
POM Spotsylvania
13 Jan 1897 SPMR
9 Jan 1897 SPML
WALLACE, Nelson s/o
Lindsey & Millie
Wallace age 57 W
laborer POB & POR
Spotsylvania POC
& **JOHNSON**,
Matilda d/o Sam &
Ellen Williams
age 40 W POB
Culpeper POR
Spotsylvania POC;
POM Spotsylvania
C.H.25 Aug 1888
SPMR SPML
WALLACE, Robert J. s/o
John & Margarett
Wallace age 44 W
farmer POB & POR
Spotsylvania &
MARTIN, Mary
Elizabeth d/o
Alexander & Sarah
Martin age 38 S
POB & POR
Spotsylvania; POM
Spotsylvania 19
Dec 1872 SPMR 18
Dec 1872 SPML
WALLER, A.B. s/o
B.P.Waller &
E.Penn age 28 S
mechanic POB &
POR Spotsylvania
& **HICKS**, M. d/o
T.S.& A.B.Hicks
age 18 S POB &
POR Spotsylvania;
POM Spotsylvania
8 May 1860 SPMR
WALLER, Edwin &
LARMAND, Lucy Ann
d/o Francis
Larmand; POM

Orange 5 Sep 1852
OMR 3 Sep 1852
OML
WALLER, George W. s/o
Dabney W. &
Caroline Waller
age 37 W farmer
POB Spotsylvania
POR Caroline Co &
DUERSON,
Elizabeth d/o
John F. & Nancy
Duerson age 40 S
POB & POR
Spotsylvania; POM
Spotsylvania 20
Feb 1872
(possible error
in year by
minister)SPMR 17
Feb 1873 SPML
WALLER, John D. s/o
Benjamin P. &
Elizabeth Waller
age 31 S POB &
POR Spotsylvania
& **WALLER**, Jane F.
d/o Richard G. &
Susan R. Buchanan
age 33 W POB &
POR Spotsylvania;
POM Spotsylvania
10 Mar 1870 SPML
9 Mar 1870 SPML
WALLER, Robert B. s/o
B. & P. Waller S
farmer POB
Spotsylvania &
TALLEY, S. d/o
R. & S. Talley age
34 S POB Louisa;
POM Spotsylvania
22 Dec 1857 SPMR
WALLER, Sidney age 40
W POB & POR
Orange POC &
ARMISTEAD,
Harriet d/o
Samuel & Hannah
Armistead age 26
W POB & POR
Orange POC; POM
St. Thomas Ch,

Orange 1 Nov 1866
OMR OML
WALLER, Thomas W. s/o
John M. & Martha
P. Waller age 22 S
farmer POB & POR
Spotsylvania &
HART, Hattie G.
d/o James C. &
Mary E. Hart age
22 S POB & POR
Spotsylvania; POM
Millbrook,
Spotsylvania 15
Nov 1870 SPMR 8
Nov 1870 SPML
WALLER, William D. s/o
John M. & Martha
P. Waller age 26 S
farmer POB & POR
Spotsylvnai &
WALLER, Olivia D.
d/o William C. &
Anne E. Waller age
26 S POB Louisa
Co POR
Spotsylvania; POM
Cedar Point,
Spotsylvania 26
Sep 1867 SPMR 20
Sep 1867 SPML
WALLINGSFORD, Asberry
M. s/o John W. &
Jane
W. Wallingsford
age 24 S farmer
POB & POR
Fredericksburg &
LANDRAM, Mollie
F. d/o John W. &
Louise Landram
age 19 S POB &
POR Spotsylvania;
POM Spotsylvania
14 Feb 1871 SPMR
13 Feb 1871 SPML
WALTERS, Geroge C. s/o
Isaac Walters &
Ann Taliaferro
age 30 S farmer
POB & POR Madison
Co & **WILHOIT**,
Pamelia Ann d/o
Curtis Wilhoit &

Louisa Harrison age 26 S POB & POR Orange; POM Orange 24 Dec 1867 OMR 19 Dec 1867 OML

WALTON, E.Payson & **SKINKER**, Jeannette C. d/o Samuel T. Skinker; POM Orange 28 Oct 1852 OMR 26 Oct 1852 OML

WARD, Henry s/o H.& P.Ward age 58 W laborer POB & POR Spotsylvania POC & **SHEPARD**, Susan d/o W.& M.Shepard age 42 S POB & POR Spotsylvania POC; POM Mt.Zion Ch, Spotsylvania 26 Oct 1879 SPMR 24 Oct 1879 SPML

WARD, Henry s/o Henry & Pamelia Ward age 48 W farmer POB & POR Spotsylvania POC & **BURWELL**, Dicey d/o Hannah Burwell age 32 W POB Lancaster Co (Va) POR Spotsylvania POC; POM Spotsylvania 5 Dec 1868 SPMR SPML

WARE, Abraham s/o Jacob & Clara Ware age 38 W laborer POB & POR Spotsylvania POC & **WILLIAMS**, Hannah d/o Buck & Lucy Williams age 27 S POB & POR Spotsylvania POC; POM New Hope Ch, Spotsylvania 26 Dec 1895 SPMR 24 Dec 1895 SPML

WARE, Abraham s/o Jacob & Clara Ware age 20 S farmer POB & POR Spotsylvania POC & **STANARD**, Rose d/o Adam & Clary Stanard age 18 S POB & POR Spotsylvania POC; POM New Hope Ch, Spotsylvania 22 Dec 1874 SPMR 21 Dec 1874 SPML

WARE, Battaile d/o Robert & Maria Ware age 22 S laborer POB & POR Spotsylvania POC & **HART**, Julia d/o Isabella Hart age 21 S POB & POR Spotsylvania POC; POM Spotsylvania 15 Mar 1883 SPMR 14 Mar 1883 SPML

WARE, Dudley s/o Robert & Maria Ware age 36 S laborer POB & POR Spotsylvania POC & **TOWLES**, Emma d/o Nat. & Lucy Towles age 29 S POB & POR Spotsylvania POC; POM Mount Zion Ch, Spotsylvania 16 Dec 1896 SPMR 15 Dec 1896 SPML

WARE, Dudley s/o Cato & Sarah Ware age 24 S laborer POB Caroline Co POR Spotsylvania POC & **MINOR**, Lucette d/o Silas & Rachel Minor age 23 S POB & POR Spotsylvania POC; POM Spotsylvania 23 Dec 1886 SPMR 21 Dec 1886 SPML

WARE, Jacob s/o J.& C.Ware age 22 S laborer POB & POR Spotsylvania POC & **WILSON**, Rose d/o John & L.Wilson age 18 S POB & POR Spotsylvania POC; POM Newe Hope, Spotsylvania 28 Dec 1880 SPMR 22 Dec 1880 SPML

WARE, James A. s/o Cato & Sarah Ware age 34 S farmer POB & POR Spotsylvania POC & **GREEN**, Gracie M. d/o W. Anderson & Maria Green age 26 S POB & POR Spotsylvania POC; POM Spotsylvania 23 Jan 1900 SPMR 20 Jan 1900 SPML

WARE, Robert C. s/o Jacob & Clara Ware age 24 S laborer POB & POR Spotsylvania POC & **FOX**, Mary L. d/o Jacob & Polly Fox age 21 S POB & POR Spotsylvania POC; POM Spotsylvania (at their residence) 20 Dec 1888 SPMR 17 Dec 1888 SPML

WARE, Robert W. s/o Robert & Maria Ware age 25 S laborer POB & POR Spotsylvania POC & **CRUMP**, Mary d/o Benjamin & Leah Crump age 21 S POB & POR Spotsylvania POC; POM Spotsylvania 4 Jan 1894 SPMR 3 Jan 1894 SPML

WARE, Thomas A. s/o N.A.& M.C.Ware age 28 S wheelwright POB & POR Louisa Co & **WILSON**, Sallie M. d/o A.H.& S.N. Wilson age 24 S POB & POR Spotsylvania; POM Road Side View, Spotsylvania 20 Dec 1877 SPMR 10 Dec 1877 SPML

WARE, Thomas s/o Dabney & Fanny Ware age 28 S laborer POB & POR Spotsylvania POC & **WILLIS**, Jennie d/o Martha Beagles age 21 S POB & POR Spotsylvania POC; POM Piney Branach Ch, Spotsylvania 6 Jul 1890 SPMR 5 Jul 1890 SPML

WARE, William Henry s/o William & Betty Ware age 22 S farmer POB & POR Spotsylvania POC & **WIGGLESWORTH**, Lovely d/o James & Matilda Wigglesworth age 21 S POB & POR Spotsylvania; POM Spotsylvania 18 Oct 1899 SPMR 16 Oct 1899 SPML

WARE, William s/o Dabney & Fannie Ware age 22 S laborer POB & POR Spotsylvania POC & **HUGHES**, Josephine d/o Susan Hughes age 19 S POB & POR

Spotsylvania POC;
POM Spotsylvania
3 Mar 1887 SPML 1
Mar 1887 SPML
WARE, William s/o J.&
Clara Ware age
22(?) S farmer
POB & POR
Spotsylvania POC
& **TURNER**, Bettie
d/o Ednd. & Ann
Turner age 16 S
POB & POR
Spotsylvania POC:
POM Spotsylvania
20 May 1875 SPMR
17 May 1875 SPML
WARREN, Edward T.H.
s/o Jehu &
Harriet Warren
age 26 S lawyer
POB Rockingham,
Va POR
Harrisonburg &
MAGRUDER,
Virginia Watson
d/o James &
Louisa Magruder
age 18 S POB
Fluvanna Co POR
Orange; POM
Orange 5 Dec 1855
OMR 3 Dec 1855
OML
WASH, A.T. s/o James &
Annie Wash age 25
S farmer POB
Hanover Co POR
Spotsylvania &
PEYTON, Ida L.
d/o James M.&
Martha A.Peyton
age 20 S POB &
POR Spotsylvania;
POM Partlow,
Spotsylvania 21
Aug 1892 SPMR 19
Aug 1892 SPML
WASHIGNTON, Willis age
27 S laborer POB
& POR
Spotsylvania POC
& **BROOKS**, Lavenia
d/o Addison &
Julia Brooks age
20 S POB Culpeper
Co POR
Spotsylvania POC;
POM Zion Hill Ch,
Spotsylvania 29
Apr 1885 SPMR 13
Apr 1885 SPML
WASHINGTON, Charles
s/o Jarrett &
Patsy Washington
age 19 S laborer
POB & POR
Spotsylvania POC
& **SAMUEL**, Lucy
Sarah d/o Phil.&
Mary Samuel age
20 S POB & POR
Spotsylvania POC;
POM Spotsylvania
27 Mar 1896 SPMR
SPML
WASHINGTON, Edmund s/o
George & Mary
Washington age 21
S farmer POB &
POR Spotsylvania
POC & **CARY**,
Margarett d/o
Wilson & Maria
Cary age 18 S POB
& POR
Spotsylvania POC;
POM Spotsylvania
17 Dec 1873 SPMR
SPML
WASHINGTON, George s/o
Dudley Washington
& Rose Bell age
33 S blacksmith
POB Albemarle Co
POC & **HESTER**,
Lucy age 28 S POB
Hanover Co POC;
POM Gordonsville,
Orange 1 Sep 1866
OMR 27 Aug 1866
OML
WASHINGTON, George T.
s/o Lewis & Lucy
A.Washington age
25 S farmer POB &
POR Spotsylvania
POC & **TAYLOR**,

Emma L. d/o Landram & Margaret Taylor age 21 S POB & POR Spotsylvania POC; POM Spotsylvania C.H. 22 Dec 1885 SPMR SPML

WASHINGTON, Jarrett s/o Jarrett & Sally Washington age 37 W farmer POB Fauquier Co POR Spotsylvania & **ELEY**, Patsy d/o Samuel & Rose Dawson age 32 W POB & POR Spotsylvania; POM Bethany Ch, Spotsylvania 2 Jun 1867 SPMR 4 Mar 1867 SPML

WASHINGTON, John Boyd s/o John & Roberta Washington age 41 S farmer POB King & Queen Co POR Caroline Co & **DEW**, Minnie M. d/o Thomas & Minnie W. Dew age 25 S POB Caroline Co POR Spotsylvania; POM Spotsylvania 19 Apr 1899 SPMR 8 Apr 1899 SPML

WASHINGTON, Moses s/o Henry George Washington & Eliza Willis age 21 S laborer on farm POB & POR Madison Co POC & **JONES**, Ann d/o Sam Jones age 21 S POB Green Co POR Orange POC; POM Orange 28 Jul 1867 OMR 26 Jul 1867 OML

WASHINGTON, Tate age 22 S farm laborer POB Louisa Co POR Orange POC & **LEWIS**, Caroline age 22 POR Orange POC; POM Orange 28 Dec 1867 OMR 27 Dec 1867 OML

WASHINGTON, W.M. s/o Benjamin & Sally Washington age 27 W laborer POB & POR Spotsylvania POC & **ANDERSON**, Deannie d/o William & Bertie Anderson age 18 S POB & POR Spotsylvania POC; POM Spotsylvania 29 Feb 1883 SPMR 28 Feb 1883 SPML

WASHINGTON, William M. s/o B. & S.Washington age 21 S laborer POB & POR Spotsylvania POC & **ADKINS**, Lucy Ann d/o Robert & M.Adkins age 20 S POB & POR Spotsylvania POC; POM Spotsylvania 20 Oct 1877 SPMR SPML

WATKINS, Lindon M. s/o R.G.(?) & E.M.Watkins age 24 S farmer POB & POR Orange & **PAYNE**, Cornelia A. d/o J.W.& S.A.Payne age 17 S POB Orange POR Spotsylvania; POM Spotsylvania 26 Feb 1878 SPMR 23 Feb 1878 SPML

WATSON, George s/o Ralph & Morillo Watson age 52 W farmer POB & POR

Spotsylvania POC & **QUARLES**, Frances d/o Harry & Katy Quarles age 35 W POB & POR Spotsylvania POC; POM Spotsylvania 1868 (no month or day on MR)SPMR 29 Dec 1868 SPML

WATSON, Thomas s/o Thomas & Isabella Watson age 36 W laborer POB & POR Spotsylvania POC & **CARTER**, Mattie d/o Warner & Eadie Carter age 25 S POB & POR Spotsylvania 22 Feb 1894 SPMR SPML

WATSON, Thomas s/o Thomas & Isabella Watson age 23 S laborer POB & POR Spotsylvania POC & **SAMUELS**, Nelly Ann d/o A.& Nancy Samuels age 20 S POB & POR Spotsylvania POC; POM Spotsylvania 11 Apr 1876 SPMR 10 Apr 1876 SPML

WATSON, Walter M. s/o Benjamin Watson & Frances Jacobs age 24 S farmer POB & POR Orange & **SANDERS**, Elizabeth R. d/o Hansford T.Sanders & Dolly Rhoades age 22 S POB & POR Orange; POM Orange 20 Dec 1860 OMR 18 Dec 1860 OML

WATTS, William M. s/o George H.& Mary A.Watts age 36 S farmer POB Richmond, Va POR Louisa Co POC & **DESPER**, Sarah d/o Robert & Lucy Crutchfield age 33 W POB & POR Spotsylvania POC; POM Spotsylvania 20 Mar 1895 SPMR 18 Mar 1895 SPML

WAUGH, Goury L. & **CLARK**, Jane D.L. d/o S.F.Clark; POM Orange 23 Dec 1852 OMR 21 Dec 1852 OML

WAUGH, Goury R. s/o Goury Waugh & Susan Wright age 39 W farmer POB & POR Orange & **COLE**, Ellen d/o John Cole & (Lucy Watkins written in at a later date) age 26 S POB & POR Orange; POM Orange 28 Feb 1867 OMR 25 Feb 1867 OML

WEATHERS, Frank s/o Henry & Martha Weathers age 27 S laborer POB & POR Spotsylvania & **WILLIAMS**, Maggie d/o Hampton & Daphna Williams age 19 S POB & POR Spotsylvania POC; POM Spotsylvania 15 Jan 1890 SPMR 11 Jan 1890 SPML

WEAVER, Reuben S. s/o John & Magdalene Weaver age 33 S cabinet maker POB Spring Creek, Rockingham Co POR Rockingham Co & **CAMMACK**, Lucy M. d/o Robert J.& Lucy J.Cammack age 32 S POB & POR Spotsylvania; POM Spotsylvania 11 Jun 1888 SPMR SPML

WEBB, Edward W. s/o James Webb age 22 S carpenter POB & POR Orange & **WEBB**, Martha J. d/o James & Rosa Webb age 17 S POB & POR Orange; POM Orange 20 Jan 1859 OMR 17 Jan 1859 OML

WEBB, Fred R. s/o John A.& Alice R.Webb age 24 S farmer POB & POR Orange & **DEMPSEY**, Callie M. d/o D.A.& Edmonia Dempsey age 20 S POB Orange POR Spotsylvania; POM Flat Run, Spotsylvania 23 Dec 1900 SPMR 17 Dec 1900 SPML

WEBB, John L. s/o William B.Webb & Martha Lancaster age 56 W farmer POB & POR Orange & **MASON**, Ann C. d/o Charles Mason & Lucy Jones age 44 S POB & POR Orange; POM Orange 27 Aug 1867 OMR 26 Aug 1867 OMR

WEBB, John M. & **JONES**, Ricey E.; 21 Dec 1857 OML

WEBB, Richard O. s/o J.W.& R.E.Webb age 24 S farmer POB Spotsylvania POR Orange & **DEMPSEY**, Minerva E. d/o P.D.& Nancy E.Dempsey age 32 S POB & POR Orange POR Spotsylvania ; POM Braeside, Spotsylvania 14 Jan 1886 SPMR 11 Jan 1886 SPML

WEBB, Spencer s/o Spencer Webb & Lila Gray age 24 S laborer on farm POB Culpeper POR Orange POC & **GRASTY**, Alverta age 18 S POB & POR Orange POC; POM Orange 25 Apr 1867 OMR OML

WEBB, William s/o Caleb & Frances Webb age 20 S carpenter POB & POR Orange & **PERRY**, Catherine W. d/o Eligey & Ann Perry S POB & POR Orange; POM Orange 22 May 1859 OMR 18 May 1859 OML

WEEDON, Charles s/o M.& R.Weedon age 38 S laborer POB Orange POR Spotsylvania POC & **JACKSON**, Elizabeth d/o S.& F.Jackson age 22 S POB & POR Spotsylvania; 29 Nov 1878 SPML

WEEDON, Thomas W. s/o Thomas W.& M.B.Weedon age 25 S merchant POB Fauquier Co POR Culpeper C.H. & **STEPHENS**, Mary F. d/o Joseph & Mary Stephens age 25 S POB & POR Orange; POM Orange 14 Jul 1858 OMR 13 Jul 1858 OML

WELCH, John s/o William & Catherine Welch age 29 S millright POB Yorkshire, England POR Baltimore, Md & **CAVELL**, Clara d/o Charles & Emma Cavill (now Emma King) age 20 S POB Fredericksburg POR Spotsylvania; POM Spotsylvania 16 May 1870 SPMR SPML

WELCH, T.N. s/o N.J.& V.Welch age 34 S lawyer POB & POR Madison Co & **DEW**, L.D. d/o P.A.(deceased)& L.A.Dew age 21 S POB Caroline Co POR Spotsylvania; POM Spotsylvania 20 May 1856 SPMR

WELLS, Davis s/o Henry & Charity Wells age 45 W minister POB Kentucky POR Alabama & **TINDER**, Lucy Ann d/o Thomas & Lucy Tinder age 35 S POB Culpeper POR Orange; POM Orange 3 Dec 1857 OMR 30 Nov 1857 OML

WEST, James Henry s/o James T.& Sarah M.West age 21 S carpenter POB & POR Spotsylvania & **DANIEL**, Susan N. d/o John L.& Ophelia Daniel age 17 S POB Orange POR Spotsylvania; POM Bethel Ch, Spotsylvania 2 Feb 1873 SPMR 1 Feb 1873 SPML

WESTER, John E. & **LLAHEWRES**(?), Eugenia; 30 Dec 1867 SPConsent

WHARTON, James L. s/o James R. & Ann E. Wharton age 23 S farmer POB & POR Spotsylvania & **STRATTON**, Josephine V. d/o J.W. Louisa Stratton age 19 S POB & POR Spotsylvania 19 Apr 1892 SPMR SPML

WHARTON, James R. s/o Robert & Nancy Wharton age 26 S farmer POB Stafford POR Spotsylvania & **JETT**, Ann E. d/o James & Kitty Jett age 25 S POB & POR Spotsylvania; POM Spotsylvania 27 Dec 1866 SPMR 26 Dec 1866 SPML

WHARTON, Milton s/o Richard & Ann L.Milton age 30 S farmer POB Stafford POR Spotsylvania & **GARNER**, Mary d/o John & Susan Powell age 30 W POB & POR Spotsylvania; POM Spotsylvania 29 Dec 1870 SPMR 24 Dec (no year given)SPML

WHARTON, Thomas H. s/o James & Ann Wharton age 20 S farmer POB & POR Spotsylvania &

STRATTON, Edna d/o John W. & Louisa Stratton age 22 S POB & POR Spotsylvania; POM Spotsylvania 3 Jul 1900 SPMR SPML

WHEELER, Caswell J. s/o Jesse & Catherine Wheeler age 48 W farmer POB & POR Spotsylvania & WHARTON, Harriet S. d/o John & Catherine Wharton age 40 W POB & POR Spotsylvania; POM Coal Hill, Spotsylvania 21 Dec 1865 SPMR 11 Dec 1865 SPML

WHEELER, Dabney C. s/o James A. & Elizabeth A. Wheeler age 25 S farmer POB & POR Spotsylvania & JONES, Mary Ellen (aka Mary Ella Jones) d/o William B. & Betsy Jones age 19 S POB & POR Spotsylvania; POM Spotsylvania 23 Dec 1873 SPMR 18 Dec 1873 SPML

WHEELER, Ed J. & TELLER, Mary J. POR Spotsylvania 22 May 1853 SPMR

WHEELER, Henry Q. s/o Sarah Wheeler age 25 S farmer POB & POR Spotsylvania & MASTIN, M.L. d/o Edgar & Virginia Mastin age 21 S POB & POR Spotsylvania; POM Spotsylvania

C.H. 7 Oct 1890 SPMR SPML

WHEELER, Ira W. s/o G.C. & A.B. Wheeler age 29 S farmer POB Louisa POR Albemarle & WALLER, D.P. d/o J.M. & D.T. Waller age 22 S POB & POR Spotsylvania; POM Spotsylvania 7 May 1857 SPMR

WHEELER, Isaiah s/o Ed. & Mary Jane Wheeler age 38 S farmer POB & POR Spotsylvania & BROOKS, Minnie Ann d/o Albert G. & Emily A. Brooks age 25 S POB & POR Spotsylvania; POM Spotsylvania 8 Nov 1899 SPMR SPML

WHEELER, J.F. s/o Sallie Wheeler age 38 S farmer POB & POR Spotsylvania & BROOKS, Catherine M. d/o Alexander & Lucy M. Brooks age 19 S POB & POR Spotsylvania; POM Spotsylvania C.H. 12 Apr 1893 SPMR SPML

WHEELER, J.R. s/o Melvina Wheeler age 42 S farmer POB & POR Spotsylvania & LLOYD, Addie age 21 S POB & POR Spotsylvania; POM Spotsylvania 17 Jun 1895 SPMR SPML

WHEELER, James W. s/o James B. & Mary Wheeler age 29 S

farmer POB & POR
Spotsylvania &
LUCK, Mary W. d/o
Richard & Lucy
Jane Luck age 25
S POB & POR
Spotsylvania; POM
Spotsylvania 21
Sep 1869 SPMR 18
Sep 1869 SPML
WHEELER, John L. s/o
James W. &
Elizabeth Ann
Wheeler age 33 S
farmer POB & POR
Spotsylvania &
WEBB, Kate Fulton
d/o James F. &
Eliza Webb age 17
S POB Richmond,Va
POR Spotsylvania;
POM Spotsylvanai
23 Jun 1875 SPMR
19 Jun 1875 SPML
WHEELER, M.Q. s/o
Edmund & Sallie
Wheeler age 26 S
farmer POB & POR
Spotsylvania &
HAILEY, Louisa F.
d/o Jesse & Sarah
Stubbs age 35 W
POB & POR
Spotsylvania; POM
Spotsylvania C.H.
24 Jul 1884 SPMR
SPML
WHEELER, Robert R. s/o
James A.&
Elizabeth Wheeler
age 26 S farmer
POB & POR
Spotsylvania &
BARRON, Maria M.
d/o Edward & Mary
Barron age 22 S
POB N.Y.POR
Spotsylvania; POM
Fredericksburg 4
Jan 1873 FMR 2
Jan 1873 SPML
WHEELER, William F.
s/o Melvina
Wheeler age 45 W

farmer POB & POR
Spotsylvania &
BROOKS, Alice M.
d/o W.D.&
B.Brooks age 35 S
POB & POR
Spotsylvania; POM
Spotsylvania 22
Jan 1891 SPMR 16
Jan 1891 SPML
WHEELER, William F.
s/o Frank England
& Malvina Wheeler
age 22 S farmer
POB & POR
Spotsylvania &
POWELL, Mary E.
d/o George &
Sarah Powell age
22 S POB & POR
Spotsylvania; POM
Spotsylvania 7
Jan 1870 SPMR 4
Jan 1870 SPML
WHITE, Benjamin s/o
Ben & Evelina
White age 25 S
farmer POB & POR
Spotsylvania POC
& **COLEMAN**, Mary
d/o Edgar & Annie
White age 24 POB
& POR
Spotsylvania POC;
POM Spotsylvania
12 Mar 1896 SPMR
SPML
WHITE, Benjamin s/o
S.& M.White age
50 W laborer POB
& POR
Spotsylvania POC
& **COLEMAN**, Annie
d/o G.Coleman age
25 S POB & POR
Spotsylvania POC;
POM Spotsylvania
16 May 1880 SPMR
15 May 1880 SPML
WHITE, H.B. s/o Elias
& Emily B.White
age 24 S clerk
POB & POR
Fluvanna Co &

WALLER, M. Jennie
d/o John M.& Ann
E. Waller age 22
S POB & POR
Spotsylvania; POM
Cedar Point,
Spotsylvania 15
Dec 1881 SPMR 5
Dec 1881 SPML

WHITE, Henry s/o Silas
& Maria White age
59 D farmer POB &
POR Spotsylvania
POC & **HART**,
Isabella d/o
Easter Hart age
45 W POB & POR
Spotsylvania POC;
POM Spotsylvania
31 Dec 1891 SPMR
30 Dec 1891 SPML

WHITE, Jacob s/o
Willis White age
23 S farm laborer
POB & POR Orange
POC & **RICHARDS**,
Emma D. d/o Dick
Richards age 22 S
POB & POR Orange
POC; POM Orange
25 Dec 1867 OMR
23 Dec 1867 OML

WHITE, Jacob s/o Jacob
& Malinda White
age 75 W laborer
POB & POR
Spotsylvania POC
& **BURWELL**,
Margaret d/o
Edmond & Lucy
Burwell age 19 S
POB & POR
Spotsylvania POC;
POM New Hope
Baptist Ch,
Spotsylvania 13
Sep 1891 SPMR 12
Sep 1891 SPML

WHITE, James s/o
Mitchell White &
Fannie Ferguson
age 20 S laborer
POB Hanover Co
POR Spotsylvania

POC & **WRIGHT**,
Mary E. d/o
William Wright &
Margaret Bozwell
age 21 S POB
Essex Co POR
Spotsylvania POC;
POM Spotsylvania
C.H. 26 Nov 1885
SPMR SPML

WHITE, Parker s/o
Richard & Betsy
White age 22 S
farmer POB & POR
Spotsylvania POC
& **WHITE**, Sarah
d/o Harry &
Matilda White age
21 W POB & POR
Spotsylvania POC;
POM Spotsylvania
29 Dec 1870 SPMR
28 Dec 1870 SPML

WHITE, Peter s/o
George & Louisa
White age 40 W
laborer POB
Louisa Co POR
Spotsylvania POC
& **TYLER**, Mary d/o
Richard & Clara
Tyler age 30 S
POB & POR
Spotsylvania POC;
POM Spotsylvania
11 Feb 1891 SPMR
10 Feb 1891 SPML

WHITE, Samuel s/o
Robin & Lucy
White age 21 S
laborer POB & POR
Spotsylvania &
GORDON, Emma d/o
Charles & Rose
Gordon age 17 S
POB & POR
Spotsylvania; POM
Spotsylvania 19
Dec 1875 SPMR 18
Dec 1875 SPML

WHITE, Thomas s/o
Robert & Rose
White age 22 S
laborer POB

Middlesex Co POR
Stafford POC &
BEVERLY, Edie d/o
Jacob Beverly &
Eliza Jackson age
22 S POB & POR
Spotsylvania POC;
POM Spotsylvania
12 Jan 1882 SPMR
SPML
WHITE, Thomas s/o Ben
& Fanny White age
38 W laborer at
steam mill POB &
POR Orange POC &
MURRAY, Phillis
age 26 W POB &
POR Orange POC;
POM Orange 9 Nov
1867 OMR 4 Nov
1867 OML
WHITE, W.F. s/o
William A.&
Harriett S.White
age 47 W farmer
POB & POR
Spotsylvania &
MITCHELL, Edna
Earl d/o Joseph
W.& Kate Mitchell
age 18 S POB &
POR Spotsylvania;
POM Salem Ch 13
Dec 1899 SPMR 12
Dec 1899 SPML
WHITE, William s/o
Alonzo & Louisa
White age 18 S
farmer POB New
Castle Co,
Delaware POR
Spotsylvania &
ROBINSON, Dora F.
d/o Joseph B.&
Mary C.Robinson
age 16 S POB
Caroline Co POR
Spotsylvania; POM
Massaponax
Baptist Ch,
Spotsylvania 16
Apr 1885 SPMR
SPML

WHITE, William s/o
Thomas & Leanna
White age 23 S
laborer POB & POR
Spotsylvania POC
& **WARE**, Rachel
d/o Jacob & Betsy
Ware age 22 W POB
& POR
Spotsylvania POC;
POM Lewis Mill,
Spotsylvania 2
Mar 1882 SPMR 28
Feb 1882 SPML
WHITFIELD, Thornton
s/o Elijah &
Susan Whitfield
age 39 W laborer
POB & POR
Fauquire Co POC &
COLEMAN, Susan M.
d/o Minor &
Louisa Coleman
age 22 S POB &
POR Spotsylvania
POC; POM
Spotsylvania 19
Jan 1888 SPMR 18
Jan 1888 SPML
WHITLOCK, Alonzo s/o
William E.&
Sallie A.Whitlock
age 23 S
blacksmith POB &
POR Spotsylvania
& **CARR**, Mamie d/o
W.S.& Marion
M.Carr POB & POR
Spotsylvania; POM
Spotsylvania
C.H.7 Dec 1898
SPMR SPML
WHITLOCK, George W.
s/o Bartholomew
H. & Mary
Whitlock age 25 S
mechanic POB
Louisa Co & **AMOS**,
Martha F. d/o
William H. &
Temperence Amos
age 28 S POB
Orange; POM
Orange 4 Nov 1860

OMR 29 Oct 1860
OML
WHITLOCK, J.D. s/o
James B.&
E.C.Whitlock age
61 W farmer POB
Louisa Co POR
Hanover Co &
HARRIS, Mollie E.
d/o R.M.C.& Mary
F.Harris age 48 S
POB & POR
Spotsylvania; POM
Shady Grove Ch,
Spotsylvania 15
Dec 1897 SPMR
SPML
WHITLOCK, James A. s/o
Thomas &
Elizabeth
Whitlock age 22 S
clerk POB Louisa
Co POR Richmond &
HAWKINS, Angelina
A. d/o Thomas R.&
Matilda Hawkins
age 24 S POB &
POR Orange; POM
Orange 14 Oct
1858 OMR 27 Sep
1858 OML
WHITLOCK, John Thomas
s/o Bartholomew
H.Whitlock & Mary
E.Hopkins age 28
S section master
on O.& A.railroad
POB Louisa Co POR
Orange & **BROWN**,
Sallie M. d/o
James O.Brown &
Sarah Cooper age
18 S POB & POR
Orange; POM
Orange 25 Jan
1866 OMR 24 Jan
1866 OML
WHITLOCK, William E.
s/o Ed.S. &
Lelietha
F.Whitlock age 25
S farmer POB
Louisa Co POR
Spotsylvania &

PENDLETON, Sallie
A. d/o Hugh &
Malvina Pendleton
age 21 S POB &
POR Spotsylvania;
POM Fair View,
Spotsylvania 29
Dec 1874 SPMR 24
Dec 1874 SPML
WHITT, Truman B. s/o
Benjamin & Rhoda
Whitt age 29 S
bridge builder
POB Montgomery Co
POR Pulaski Co &
SAMUEL, Annie B.
d/o Joseph & Ann
Samuel age 21 S
POB Essex Co POR
Spotsylvania; POM
Spotsylvania 15
Sep 1887 SPMR
SPML
WIATT, James M. s/o
Francis J.&
Elizabeth Wiatt
age 30 S farmer
POB
Fredericksburg &
RICHARDS, Marie
Ann d/o Richard
Richards Jr &
Nancy Richards
age 20 S POB
Orange; POM
Orange 23 Mar
1854 OMR
WIGGLESWORTH,
Claiborne s/o
William & Mary
Wigglesworth age
63 W farmer POB &
POR Orange &
DARNELL, Luella
d/o Benjamin &
Ann Darnell age
18 S POB & POR
Spotsylvania; POM
Spotsylvania
C.H.16 Jul 1891
SPMR SPML
WIGGLESWORTH,
Claiborne &

REYNOLDS, Eliza;
26 Sep 1853 OML
WIGGLESWORTH, H.S. s/o
Robert S.&
D.M.Wigglesworth
age 33 S farmer
POB Spotsylvania
POR Caroline Co &
BECKER, Iona d/o
Myron W.& Sallie
Becker age 19 S
POB Chatauqua
Co,N.Y. POR
Spotsylvania; POM
Spotsylvania C.H.
15 Jan 1890 SPMR
SPML
WIGLESWORTH, Alexander
s/o Henry & Mary
Wiglesworth age
21 S farmer POB &
POR Spotsylvania
POC & **COLEMAN**,
Ellen d/o Major &
Maria E. Coleman
age 19 S POB &
POR Spotsylvania
POC: POM near New
Market,
Spotsylvania
(this place is
unclear) 12 Jan
1869 SPMR 8 Jan
1869 SPML
WIGLESWORTH, Olie s/o
Alexander & Ellen
Wiglesworth age
30 S laborer POB
& POR
Spotsylvania POC
& **FOX**, Sallie d/o
Jacob & Polly Fox
age 25 S POB &
POR Spotsylvania
POC; POM
Woodstock,
Spotsylvania 16
Feb 1898 SPMR 7
Feb 1898 SPML
WIGLESWORTH,A.W. s/o
Bennett W.&
Martha Jane
Wiglesworth age
28 S farmer POB &
POR Spotsylvania
& **JERRELL**, Maggie
M. d/o Robert H.&
Nannie Jerrell
age 20 S POB &
POR Spotsylvania;
POM Spotsylvania
25 Dec 1895 SPMR
23 Dec 1895 SPML
WILKERSON, William A.
s/o Robert &
Maria Wilkerson
age 20 S farmer
POB Caroline Co
POR Spotsylvania
& **PAYNE**, Leah A.
d/o Joseph &
Maria Payne age
22 S POB & POR
Spotsylvania; POM
Spotsylvania 10
Dec 1867 SPMR 2
Dec 1867 SPML
WILKES, Robert W. s/o
Washington B.&
E.Wilkes age 30 W
minister POB
Lunenburg Co POR
DeKalb, Alabama &
CRAWFORD, S.O.
d/o J.&
L.Crawford age 22
S POB & POR
Spotsylvania; POM
Spotsylvania 29
Jan 1857 SPMR
WILLARD, H.A. s/o
H.L.& Sallie
Willard age 27 S
farmer POB & POR
Spotsylvania &
PAYNE, Lucy A.
d/o John M.Payne
age 28 S POB &
POR Spotsylvania;
POM Spotsylvania
C.H. 12 Dec 1887
SPMR SPML
WILLIAMS, Charles s/o
Troy & Martha
Williams age 23 S
laborer POB & POR
Spotsylvania POC
& **MINOR**, Grace

d/o K.& S.Minor age 18 S POB & POR Spotsylvania POC: POM Spotsylvania 3 Jan 1876 SPMR 29 Dec 1875 SPML

WILLIAMS, Charles W. s/o Lewis & Ellen Williams age 22 S farmer POB & POR Spotsylvania & **WHEELER**, Adeline d/o John & Lucy J. Wheeler age 24 S POB & POR Spotsylvania; POM Spotsylvania C.H.22 Jul 1896 SPMR SPML

WILLIAMS, Edward W. s/o Blueford & Mary Williams age 27 S farmer POB & POR Orange & **BEADLES**, Georgianna d/o James & Elizabeth Beadles age 24 S POB & POR Orange; POM Orange 13 Jul 1858 OMR 12 Jul 1858 OML

WILLIAMS, Frank s/o Daniel & Harriet Williams age 22 S hotel waiter POB Alexandria,Va POR North Point, Long Island POC & **JACKSON**, Isabella d/o Washington Jackson & Josephine Minor age 23 S POB & POR Spotsylvania POC; POM Spotsylvania 10 Aug 1898 SPMR 9 Aug 1898 SPML

WILLIAMS, J. s/o G.& M.Williams age 30 S farmer POB & POR Spotsylvania & **BURKE**, M.E. d/o F.& S.Burke age 23 S POB & POR Spotsylvania; POM Spotsylvania 2 Jan 1860 SPMR

WILLIAMS, James s/o Henry Slaughter & Bettie Williams age 22 S laborer POB & POR Spotsylvania POC & **McCALLEY**, Susan d/o Edward & Susan McCalley age 20 S POB & POR Spotsylvania POC; POM Spotsylvania 19 Dec 1894 SPMR SPML

WILLIAMS, Jefferson s/o Ben & Ailsy Williams age 63 W laborer POB & POR Spotsylvania POC & **WHITE**, Sarah d/o Harry & Matilda White POB & POR Spotsylvania POC; POM Spotsylvania 17 Oct 1888 SPMR 16 Oct 1888 SPML

WILLIAMS, John J. s/o James & Mary Williams age 21 S farmer POB & POR Spotsylvania & **HALL**, Sarah d/o Richard & Jane Hall age 34 S POB & POR Spotsylvania; POM Spotsylvania C.H. 24 May 1884 SPMR SPML

WILLIAMS, Joseph s/o W.H.& J.Williams age 24 S laborer POB & POR Spotsylvania POC & **LEVY**, Mollie d/o D.& T.Levy age 16 S POB & POR Spotsylvania POC; POM Spotsylvania 12 Jan 1876 SPMR 31 Dec 1875 SPML

WILLIAMS, Lewis B. & **BLAIR**, Charlotte J.; POM Orange 7 Dec 1852 OMR 6 Dec 1852 OML

WILLIAMS, Minor s/o Madison Carr & Millie White age 31 S railroad laborer POB Caroline Co POR Spotsylvania POC & **JACKSON**, Ann d/o Thomas & Mary Jackson age 24 S POB & POR Spotsylvania POC; POM Spotsylvania 29 Dec 1881 SPMR 28 Dec 1881 SPML

WILLIAMS, Oscar s/o Jarret & Harriet Williams age 22 S farmer POB Culpeper Co POR Spotsylvania POC & **MINOR**, Sarah Jane d/o Horace & Eliza Lomax Minor age 20 S POB & POR Spotsylvania POC; POM Spotsylvania 22 Nov 1873 SPMR 21 Nov 1873 SPML

WILLIAMS, Prince s/o Prince & Violet Williams age 49 W farmer POB & POR Spotsylvania POC & **CARTER**, Barbara d/o William & Phoebe Carter age 33 S POB & POR Spotsylvania POC; POM Spotsylvania 29 Nov 1899 SPMR SPML

WILLIAMS, Thomas s/o Hannah Bingham age 34 S laborer POB & POR Spotsylvania POC & **JOHNSON**, Sallie E. d/o William & Mary Johnson age 22 S POB & POR Spotsylvania POC; POM Spotsylvania 29 Mar 1898 SPMR SPML

WILLIAMS, Thomas s/o Jeff & Caroline Williams age 22 S laborer POB & POR Spotsylvania POC & **JONES**, Sarah d/o Fanny Jones age 18 S POB & POR Spotsylvania POC; POM Spotsylvania C.H. 8 Jan 1889 SPMR SPML

WILLIAMS, Thomas s/o Mary Williams age 24 S laborer POB & POR Spotsylvania POC & **GIBSON**, Mary L. d/o Joseph & Lavenia Gibson age 24 S POB & POR Spotsylvania POC; POM Spotsylvania 20 Mar 1900 SPMR SPML

WILLIAMS, Thomas s/o Thomas & Hannah Williams age 22 S carpenter POB & POR Fredericksburg & **JOHNSON**, Jane Frances d/o R.& P.Johnson age 20 S POB & POR Orange; POM Orange 14 Feb 1856 OMR 12 Feb 1856 OML

WILLIAMS, Thomas s/o William & S.Holladay age 26 S laborer POB & POR Spotsylvania POC & **MONTAGUE**, Julia d/o G.& D.Montague age 21 S POB & POR Spotsylvania POC; POM Spotsylvania 4 Aug 1880 SPMR SPML

WILLIAMS, Virgil s/o Minor & Kate Williams age 35 S laborer POB & POR Spotsylvania POC & **WRIGHT**, M.Ruth d/o Woodson & Louisa Wright age 19 S POB & POR Spotsylvania POC; POM "Beluh" Baptist Ch, Spotsylvania 26 Dec 1898 SPMR SPML

WILLIAMS, William G. s/o Lewis B.& Mary C.Williams age 27 S attorney POB & POR Orange & **HANSBROUGH**, Roberta B. d/o Alexander H.& Elizabeth C.Hansbrough age 19 S POB Culpeper POR Orange; POM Orange 10 Sep 1857 OMR OML

WILLIAMS, William s/o James & Frances Williams age 30 S laborer POB Stafford POR Spotsylvania & **FARMER**, Nannie d/o Robert & Nancy Farmer age 22 S POB Caroline Co POR Spotsylvania; POM Spotsylvania 16 Feb 1871 SPMR 15 Feb 1871 SPML

WILLIAMS, William T. s/o Lewis M.& L.E.Williams age 23 S farmer POB & POR Spotsylvania & **BROOKS**, Queen Victoria d/o Albert G.& Emily A.Brooks age 21 S POB & POR Spotsylvania; POM Spotsylvania C.H.24 Dec 1888 SPMR SPML

WILLIAMS, Willy s/o Caroline Williams age 25 S laborer POB & POR Spotsylvania POC & **GREEN**, Susan d/o Shelton & Mary Green age 19 S POB & POR Spotsylvania PC; POM Spotsylvania 12 Dec 1888 SPMR 11 Dec 1888 SPML

WILLIAMSON, Charles A. s/o S.D.& C.V.Williamson age 26 S farmer POB Prince Edward Co POR Spotsylvania & **PARKER**, Lucie J. d/o John F.& A.Parker age 17 S POB & POR Spotsylvania; POM Spotsylvania 25 Sep 1878 SPMr 23 Sep 1878 SPML

WILLIAMSON, D.S. s/o S.D. & C.V. Williamson age 33 W puddler in iron works POB Manchester,Va POR Campbell Co & **SMITH**, Laura d/o Mary Smith age 17

S POB Greene Co
POR Spotsylvania;
POM Spotsylvania
C.H. 1 Jul 1886
SPMR SPML
WILLIS, Addison s/o
Minor Mercer &
Hannah Willis age
24 S laborer POB
& POR
Spotsylvania POC
& **WASHINGTON**,
Alice B. d/o Ben
& Sally
Washington age 18
S POB & POR
Spotsylvania POC;
POM Spotsylvania
31 Jan 1883 SPMR
29 Jan 1883 SPML
WILLIS, Claiborne s/o
A.& S.Willis age
23 S laborer POB
& POR
Spotsylvania POC
& **FORTE**, Laura
(aka Laura Ford)
age 22 S POB &
POR Spotsylvania
POC; POM
Spotsylvania 6
Jan 1881 SPMR 4
Jan 1881 SPML
WILLIS, Isaac s/o
Larkin & Mary
Willis age 29 S
farmer POB & POR
Orange &
LIPSCOMB, Bettie
F. d/o Ira &
Nancy Lipscomb
age 27 S POB &
POR Spotsylvania;
POM Spotsylvania
1 Feb 1866 SPMR
31 Jan 1866 SPML
WILLIS, Isaac s/o S.&
M.Willis age 29 S
POB & POR Orange
& **LIPSCOMB**, B.F.
d/o J.E. &
N.Lipscomb age 27
S POB & POR
Spotsylvania; 1
Feb 1866 SPMR
WILLIS, James A. s/o
Larken & Mary
Willis age 42 W
farmer POB Orange
Co POR Culpeper
Co & **COLEMAN**,
B.H. d/o Reuben &
Mary Coleman age
31 S POB & POR
Spotsylvania; POM
Spotsylvania Jan
1868 SPMR (no day
on MR) 15 Jan
1868 SPML
WILLIS, James A. &
LEWIS, Virginia
A. aka Virginia
H.Willis; POM
Orange 12 May
1853 OMR 10 May
1853 OML
WILLIS, John Jr. s/o
John Willis &
Lucy Madison age
21 S farmer POB &
POR Orange &
ROBINSON, Lucy S.
d/o Thoams
A.Robinson &
Maria Shepherd
age 21 S POB &
POR Orange; POM
Orange 21 Jun
1866 OMR OML
WILLIS, Marion G. d/o
John C.& Mary
C.Willis age 20 S
farmer POB & POR
Orange & **GORDON**,
Lucy T. d/o
Edward H. & Fanny
Gordon age 18 S
POB Culpeper Co
POR Spotsylvania;
POM Spotsylvania
17 May 1866 SPMR
3 May 1866 SPML
WILLIS, Reuben J. s/o
Larkin Willis &
Mary Gordon age
22 S clerk POB &
POR Orange &

HOLLADAY, Rebecca A. d/o L.L.Holladay & Jane Thompson age 22 S POB Spotsylvania POR Orange; POM Orange 19 dec 1861 OMR 18 Dec 1861 OML
WILLOUGHBY, James W.M. s/o W.M.& Sarah E.Willoughby age 21 S farmer POB & POR Spotsylvania & **RONQUEST**, Mollie E. d/o A.F.& Mary E.Ronquest age 18 S POB Hanover Co POR Spotsylvania; POM Spotsylvania 19 Dec 1888 SPMR 18 Dec 1888 SPML
WILLOUGHBY, Joseph A. s/o John B.& Lucy Willoughby age 49 W POB & POR Spotsylvania & **HICKS**, Magnolia d/o H.F.& Betty Hicks age 30 S POB Madison Co POR Spotsylvania; POM Spotsylvania 17 Apr 1895 SPMR 12 Apr 1895 SPML
WILLOUGHBY, Joseph A. s/o John W.& Lucy Willoughby age 24 S farmer POB & POR Spotsylvania & **SIMMS**, Ann E. d/o Robert & Maria Hicks age 22 W POB & POR Spotsylvania; POM Spotsylvania 20 Oct 1867 SPMR 19 Oct 1867 SPML
WILLOUGHBY, R.F. s/o J.& S.Willoughby age 32 S POB & POR Spotsylvania & **JOHNSON**, E.L. d/o A.& D.Johnson age 25 S POB & POR Spotsylvania; POM Spotsylvania 5 Oct 1858 SPMR
WILLOUGHBY, Robert F. s/o Joseph & Susan Willoughby age 52 farmer POR Spotsylvania & **LEWIS**, Lucy A. d/o W.F.& Betsy Lewis age 37 POR Spotsylvania; POM Spotsylvania 1 Jan 1880 SPMR 17 Dec 1879 SPML
WILLOUGHBY, Thomas s/o John & L.Willoughby age 40 W farmer POB Spotsylvania POR Orange & **ALSOP**, R.W. d/o John S.& D.A.Alsop age 30 S POB & POR Spotsylvania; POM Spotsylvania 24 Oct 1880 SPMR 23 Oct 1880 SPML
WILLOUGHBY, Tolbert L. s/o Robert F.& Bettie Willoughby aɔe 23 S farmer POB & POR Spotsylvania & **HALL**, Ida M. d/o Thomas A.& Delia Hall age 17 S POB Brooklyn,N.Y. POR Spotsylvania; POM Spotsylvania C.H. 16 Oct 1882 SPMR SPML
WILLOUGHBY, Waller M. s/o John & Sarah Willoughby age 32 W farmer POB & POR Spotsylvania & **BIBB**, Sarah E. d/o Benjamin & Hulldah Massey age 29 W POB &

POR Spotsylvania;
POM Spotsylvania
24 Dec 1866 SPMR
17 Dec 1866 SPML
WILSHIRE, C.E. s/o
J.B.& A.Wilshire
age 20 S
plasterer POB
Orange POR
Spotsylvania &
SALE, F.A. d/o
W.& R.Sale age 18
S POB & POR
Spotsylvania; POM
Spotsylvania 25
Feb 1862 SPMR
WILSON, B.W. s/o
Robert H.& Mary
J.Wilson age 40 W
farmer POB & POR
Spotsylvania &
WRIGHT, Mattie E.
d/o James &
Lettie Wright
sister of William
Wright age 40 S
POB & POR
Spotsylvania; POM
Spotsylvania 13
Jun 1895 SPMR 4
Jun 1895 SPML
WILSON, Franklin N.
s/o Ephraim
Wilson & Anna
Smith age 21 S
farmer POB & POR
Fairfield
District, S.C. &
POINDEXTER,
Frances age 24 S
POB Louisa Co POR
Orange; POM
Orange 5 Apr 1864
OMR OML
WILSON, James s/o John
T. & Lucinda
Wilson age 25 S
farmer POB New
Orleans,
Louisiana POR
Spotsylvania &
CLARKE, Mary d/o
Washington &
Malvina Clarke

age 23 S POB &
POR Spotsylvania;
POM Spotsylvania
5 Oct 1871 SPMR 4
Oct 1871 SPML
WILSON, John s/o John
& Elizabeth
Wilson age 29 S
farmer POB
Ireland POR
Spotsylvania &
RICHARDS, Susan
E. d/o Robert &
Catherine
Richards age 22 S
POB & POR
Spotsylvania; POM
Spotsylvania 27
Nov 1866 SPMR 24
Nov 1866 SPML
WILSON, Robert D. s/o
Robert H.& Mary
Jane Wilson age
33 S farmer POB &
POR Spotsylvania
& **WILSON**, Alice
d/o A.H.& Sarah
Wilson age 29 S
POB & POR
Spotsylvania 19
Dec 1894 SPMR 14
Dec 1894 SPML
WILSON, T.G. s/o R.C.&
S.Wilson age 29 S
music teacher POB
& POR Augusta Co
& **DAVIS**, Sallie
M. d/o G.&
S.A.Davis age 28
S POB & POR
Spotsylvania; POM
Spotsylvania 19
Oct 1875 SPMR 26
Sep 1875 SPML
WILSON, Walter s/o
William & Frances
Wilson age 21 S
hotel porter POB
& POR Washington
D.C. POC &
STANARD, Cornelia
d/o Major &
Adelaide Stanard
age 21 S POB &

POR Spotsylvania
POC; POM
Spotsylvania 15
Mar 1887 SPMR
SPML
WILTSHIRE, Arthur P.
s/o John & Mary
Ann Wiltshire age
33 S farmer POB
Orange POR
Culpeper &
REYNOLDS, Lucy A.
d/o John & Susan
Reynolds age 32 S
POB & POR Orange;
POM Orange 27 Dec
1859 OMR 21 Dec
1859 OML
WILTSHIRE, Peyton s/o
William Wiltshire
& Catherine
Stratton age 44 S
wheelwright POB &
POR Orange &
CAMMACK,
Catherine A.V.
d/o William
E.Cammack &
Rebecca Mason age
26 S POB & POR
Orange; POM
Orange 7 Feb 1867
OMR 4 Feb 1867
OML
WILTSHIRE, Thomas E.
s/o Alfred &
Sallie
A.Wiltshire age
24 S farmer POB &
POR Orange &
BARNES, Dottie
d/o Eli & Mary
Ann Barnes age 20
S POB Penn POR
Spotsylvania; POM
Spotsylvania C.H.
30 Mar 1892 SPMR
SPML
WINDSOR, Thomas s/o
John & Mary
Windsor age 36 S
laborer POB King
& Queen Co POR
Spotsylvania POC

& **WILLIAMS**, Julia
d/o Gabriel &
Dollie Montague
age 25 W POB &
POR Spotsylvania
POC; POM
Spotsylvania C.H.
8 Sep 1884 SPMR
SPML
WINE, John S. s/o
Joseph &
Catherine E.Wine
age 29 S
mechanical
engineer POB
Stafford POR
Prince William Co
& **LUCK**, Jeannette
Maxie d/o John
A.H.& Catherine
Luck age 20 S POB
& POR
Spotsylvania; POM
Spotsylvania 8
Jan 1889 SPMR 4
Jan 1889 SPML
WINFIELD, John s/o
Alex.& Sally
Winfield age 40 W
laborer on farm
POB Stafford POR
Orange POC &
COFFMAN, Celia
d/o Ben & Rhoda
Coffman age 21 S
POB & POR Orange
POC; POM Orange
28 Sep 1867 OMR
23 Sep 1867 OML
WINSLOW, Thomas s/o
Moses & Lucy
Winslow age 30 S
farmer POB & POR
Orange &
WILLIAMS,
Elizabeth N. d/o
S.Bluford & Mary
Williams age 24 S
POB & POR Orange;
POM Orange 21 May
1858 OMR 18 May
1858 OML
WINSTON, Benjamin s/o
Ralph & Annie

Winston age 22 S
laborer POB
Louisa Co POR
Spotsylvania POC
& **LUCAS**,
Elizabeth d/o
Troy & Martha
Williams age 27 W
POB & POR
Spotsylvania POC;
POM Spotsylvania
C.H.4 Feb 1891
SPMR SPML
WINSTON, Bickerton,
s/o Philip &
Sarah M. Winston
age 41 W farmer
POB & POR Hanover
Co & **BANKHEAD**,
Eliza M. d/o
William &
Dorothea Bankhead
age 23 S POB
Caroline Co POR
Orange; POM
Orange 1 Jun 1858
OMR 31 May 1858
OML
WINSTON, Carter s/o
Robert & Annie
Winston age 23 S
laborer POB
Louisa Co POR
Spotsylvania POC
& **RENNOLDS**,
Catherine d/o
Frank & Martha
Reynolds age 19 S
POB & POR
Spotsylvania POC;
POM Shiloh
Baptist
Ch,Spotsylvania
28 Dec 1881 SPMR
SPML
WINSTON, Henry s/o
George & Polly
A.Winston age 30
S laborer POB &
POR Caroline Co
POC & **FRENCH**, Ida
d/o Edward & Rose
French age 23 S
POB Caroline Co

POR Spotsylvania
POC: POM Long
Branch Ch,
Caroline Co 24
Feb 1898 Caroline
MR 23 Feb 1898
SPML
WINSTON, Richard M.
s/o Philip & Jane
D.Winston age 23
S farmer POB &
POR Hanover Co &
BANKHEAD, Rosalie
S. d/o William &
Dorothea Bankhead
age 21 S POB
Caroline Co POR
Orange; POM
Orange 10 Nov
1857 OMR 9 Nov
1857 OML
WOLFREY, Thomas s/o
R.& E.Wolfrey age
22 S farmer POB &
POR Spotsylvania
& **OAKS**, Mildred
A. d/o F.B.&
E.E.Oaks age 20 S
POB & POR
Spotsylvania; POM
Spotsylvania 5
Dec 1880 SPMR 3
Dec 1880 SPML
WOLFREY, William H.
s/o Anderson &
Lucy A. Wolfrey
age 24 S farmer
POB & POR
Spotsylvania &
HASSETT, Hannah
d/o Batt & Julia
Hassett age 19 S
POB & POR
Spotsylvania; POM
Spotsylvania 30
Apr 1874 SPMR 27
Apr 1874 SPML
WOOD, Absolum s/o
Margaret Wood age
40 S miller POB
Orange & **MARTIN**,
Mary E. age 22 S
POR Orange; 26
Jan 1857 OML

WOOD, Arthur s/o James & Sarah Wood age 33 W farmer POB Louisa Co POR Spotsylvania POC & **CRUTCHFIELD**, Landonia d/o Reuben & Hettie Crutchfield age 18 S POB & POR Spotsylvania POC:POM New Hope Ch, Spotsylvania 11 Aug 1895 SPMR 8 Aug 1895 SPML

WOOD, Byron L. s/o Peter & S.J.Wood age 32 S farmer POB Tioga Co,N.Y. POR Spotsylvania & **WILLIAMS**, Amelia S. d/o William S.& Jane Williams age 32 S POB & POR Spotsylvania; POM Spotsylvania 22 Aug 1888 SPMR SPML

WOOD, Charles T. & **SMITH**, Jane E.; 27 Dec 1858 OML

WOOD, Edmund P. s/o William T.Wood & America Mitchell age 23 S saddler POB Madison Co POR Barboursville & **JOHNS**, Mildred M. d/o Mason Johns & Ann Walker age 21 S POB Albemarle Co POR Orange; POM Orange 31 Jan 1861 OMR 28 Jan 1861 OML

WOOD, Garland & **MITCHELL**, Catharine A.C. d/o Isabella M.Osbourne; 22 Dec 1852 OML

WOOD, George s/o George Wood & Ann Johnson age 22 S laborer on farm POB & POR Orange POC & **LINDSAY**, Clara d/o Abraham & Milly Lindsay age 17 S POB & POR Orange POC; POM Orange 30 Mar 1867 OMR 25 Mar 1867 OML

WOOD, John T. s/o Absalom Wood & Mary Clark age 52 S carpenter POB & POR Orange & **BERRY**, Lucy Ann age 24 S POB Culpeper CO POR Orange; POM Orange 11 Jan 1868 OMR 30 Nov 1867 OML

WOOD, Joseph T. & **WOOD**, Martha Ann; 4 Jan 1858 OML

WOOD, Laterey M. s/o John & Jane Wood age 60 W farmer POB Culpeper Co POR Fauquier Co & **BRADSHAW**, Mary A. d/o John & Susan Hatch age 45 W POB Fauquier Co POR Spotsylvania; POM Fauquier Co 26 Nov 1868 SPMR 15 Nov 1868 SPML

WOOD, Overton s/o George & Ann Wood age 32 S laborer POB & POR Spotsylvania POC & **SMITH**, Annie d/o Isaac & Sallie Smith age 28 S POB Fauquire Co POR Spotsylvania POC; POM Pilgrim Ch, Spotsylvania 23

Dec 1881 SPMR SPML

WOOD, Richard W. s/o William T.Wood & Sally Rhoades age 22 S blacksmith POB Orange POR Albemarle Co & **CLARK**, Sarah H. d/o William Clark & Frances Estes age 15 S POB & POR Orange; POM Orange 5 Mar 1867 OMR 4 Mar 1867 OML

WOOD, William B. s/o Elzy & Lucinda Wood age 21 S POB & POR Orange farmer & **THOMAS**, Frances E. d/o David Thomas & Frances Gardner age 18 S POB Albemarle Co POR Orange; POM Orange 28 Dec 1863 OMR 21 Dec 1863 OML

WOOD, Zachary s/o Zachary & Margaret Wood age 40 S miller POB & POR Orange & **HUGHES**, Nancy d/o Alexander & Elizabeth Hughes age 50 S POB & POR Orange; POM Orange 5 Oct 1854 OMR OML

WOODVILLE, Edward S. (aka Edmund S.Woodville) & **SISSON**, Miranda J.; POM Orange 15 Jul 1852 OMR 12 Jul 1852 OML

WOODWARD, Benjamin s/o Richard & martha A. Woodward age 23 S laborer POB & POR Spotsylvania POC & **LEE**, Mary d/o Julia Lee age 22 S POB & POR Spotsylvania POC; POM Spotsylvania 20 Mar 1900 SPMR 19 Mar 190 SPML

WOODWARD, Hampton s/o Richard & M.A.Woodward age 30 S farmer POB & POR Spotsylvania POC & **JACKSON**, Mary T. d/o Eliza Jackson age 24 S POB & POR Spotsylvania POC; POM Zion Hill Ch, Spotsylvania 16 Mar 1898 SPMR 15 Mar 1898 SPML

WOODWARD, Lawrence s/o Richard & Martha Woodward age 22 S farmer POB & POR Spotsylvania POC & **BROOKS**, Julia d/o Melvin & Fannie Brooks age 21 S POB & POR Spotsylvania POC; POM Zion Hill Baptist Ch, Spotsylvania 18 Dec 1900 SPMR 17 Dec 1900 SPML

WOODWARD, Othey s/o Richard & M.A. Woodward age 25 S farmer POB & POR Spotsylvania POC & **FORD**, Lizzie d/o Humphrey & Mary Young age 23 W POB & POR Spotsylvania POC; POM Spotsylvania 6 Apr 1898 SPMR SPML

WOODYARD, George M. s/o George & Mary Woodyard age 24 S street car conductor POB Fairfax Co POR Washington D.C. & **JETT**, Olive d/o John T.& Sarah F,Jett age 19 S POB & POR Spotsylvania; POM Spotsylvania 19 Aug 1891 SPMR SPML

WOOLDRIDGE, Albert B. s/o D.S.Wooldridge & M.A.Cox age 21 S student POB & POR Richmond,Va & **HANSBROUGH**, Maria S. d/o A.H. Hansbrough & E.C.Strother age 21 S POB Culpeper Co POR Orange; POM Orange C.H. 28 Oct 1863 OMR 27 Oct 1863 OML

WOOLFOLK, Clivins s/o Lavinia Woolfolk age 29 S laborer POB & POR Spotsylvania POC & **TAYLOR**, Daisy d/o Mary Taylor age 22 S POB & POR Spotsylvania POC; POM Branch Fork Ch, Spotsylvania 30 Dec 1900 SPMR 24 Dec 1900 SPML

WOOLFOLK, James T. s/o Thomas & Frances Woolfolk age 22 S farmer POB Louisa Co POR Orange & **MOORE**, Sarah M. d/o William & Mary Moore age 22 S POB & POR Orange; POM Orange 2 Sep 1857 OMR 24 Aug 1857 OML

WOOLFOLK, John s/o Aaron & Betsy Woolfolk age 21y 6mo S farmer POB & POR Orange POC & **CRUTCHFIELD**, Mary d/o Robert & Lucy Crutchfield age 21 S POB & POR Spotsylvania POC; POM Spotsylvania 28 Dec 1866 SPMR 27 Dec 1866 SPML

WOOLFOLK, Joseph s/o Barnett & Ellen Woolfolk age 23 S laborer POB & POR Spotsylvania POC & **FAULDING**, Annie age 21 S POB & POR Spotsylvania POC; POM Spotsylvania 20 Jan 1887 SPMR 15 Jan 1887 SPML

WOOLFOLK, Reuben s/o Thomas & Bettie Woolfolk age 55 W laborer POB Louisa Co POR Spotsylvania POC & **BELL**, Ellen d/o Celia Bell age 55 W POB Orange POR Spotsylvania POC; POM Spotsylvania 14 Dec 1882 SPMR 9 Dec 1882 SPML

WOOLFOLK, Robert W. ward of William E.Woolfolk & **MORTON**, Mary E. d/o George W.Morton; 16 Aug 1852 OML

WOOLFOLK, Samuel s/o Barnett & Ellen Woolfolk age 24 S laborer POB & POR Spotsylvania POC & **FAULDING**, Susan d/o Amos & Mary Faulding age 21 S

POB & POR
Spotsylvania POC;
POM Spotsylvania
22 Feb 1883 SPMR
20 Feb 1883 SPML
WOOLFOLK, Samuel s/o
Barnett & Ellen
Woolfolk age 29 W
farmer POB & POR
Spotsylvania POC
& PRICE, Jennie
d/o William &
Julia Price age
21 S POB & POR
Spotsylvania POC;
POM Spotsylvania
8 Aug 1890 SPMR 4
Aug 1890 SPML
WOOLFOLK, William T.
physician &
GOODWIN, Sally M.
d/o John
M.Goodwin; 18 Jan
1853 OML
WOOLFOLK, Willie s/o
Johnnie & Mary
Woolfolk age 22 S
farmer POB & POR
Spotsylvania POC
& WOOLFOLK,
Columbia d/o
Louvemi Woolfolk
age 21 S POB &
POR Spotsylvania
POC; POM
Spotsylvania 18
Mar 1895 SPMR
SPML
WOOLFORK, Jacob s/o
Aaron & Betsy
Woolfork age 22
(b.d.Mar 1851) S
farmer POB Orange
POR Spotsylvania
POC &
CRUTCHFIELD,
Martha d/o Robert
& Lucy
Crutchfield age
23 S POB & POR
Spotsylvania; POM
Spotsylvania 27
Dec 1872 SPMR 24
Dec 1872 SPML

WOOLFREE, John A. s/o
A.& L.Woolfree
age 25 S farmer
POB & POR
Spotsylvania &
LEITCH, Eliza A.
d/o William &
S.J.Leitch age 21
S POB & POR
Spotsylvania; POM
Spotsylvania 6
Jun 1878 SPMR 5
Jun 1878 SPML
WOOLFREY, Benjamin O.
& WOOLFREY, Mary;
26 Sep 1859 OML
WOOLFREY, Charles C.
s/o Mary
F.Woolfrey age 19
S farmer POB &
POR Spotsylvania
& CHEWNING, Laura
d/o Leanie
Chewning age 18 S
POB & POR
Spotsylvania; POM
Spotsylvania C.H.
19 Aug 1886 SPMR
SPML
WOOLFREY, Doctor
Dillworth s/o
Benjamin & Sarah
F.Woolfry age 22
S tie getter POB
Orange POR
Spotsylvania &
CHEWNING,
Wilhelmonia d/o
Philena Chewning
(mother) age 20 S
POB & POR
Spotsylvania; POM
Spotsylvania 26
Aug 1895 SPMR
SPML
WOOLFRY, Benjamin O.
s/o Henry Woolfry
& Lucy Oakes age
44 W shoemaker
POB & POR Orange
& WOOLFRY, Sarah
Frances d/o
Richard Woolfry &
Emily Sullivan

age 21 S POB &
POR Orange; POM
Orange 28 Apr
1867 OMR 27 Apr
1867 OML
WOOLFRY, James Albert
s/o Anderson &
Lucy Woolfry age
21 S cooper POB &
POR Spotsylvania
& **SCHOOLER**,
Elizabeth B. d/o
James Acores &
America C.
Schooler age 19 S
POB & POR
Spotsylvania; POM
Spotsylvania 29
Dec 1862 SPMR 28
Dec 1862 SPML
WOOLFRY, Jeremiah s/o
Richard &
Elizabeth Woolfry
age 28 S
shoemaker POB &
POR Orange &
JONES, Rebecca
d/o Elizabeth
Jones age 32 S
POB & POR Orange;
POM Orange 14 Jun
1860 OMR 4 Jun
1860 OML
WORCESTER, James T.
s/o Thomas L. &
Catherine
Worcester age 29
S farmer POB
Pittsburg, Penn
POR Spotsylvania
& **ALTENBURG**,
Julia S. d/o
David W. & Salinda
A. Altenburg age
23 S POB
Watersville,
Michigan POR
Spotsylvania; POM
Spotsylvania 29
Oct 1891 SPMR 28
Dec 1891 SPML
WORMLEY, Ellis s/o
Tarleton & Elzie
Wormley age 36 S

POB Caroline Co
POR Spotsylvania
POC & **CHILDS**,
Mary d/o Lindsay
& McKiah Childs
age 23 S POB
Caroline Co POR
Spotsylvania POC;
POM Spotsylvania
C.H. 1 Oct 1884
SPMR SPML
WORMLEY, John s/o
Hannah Wormley
age 59 W laborer
POB & POR
Spotsylvania POC
& **BANKS**, Mary
Eliza d/o Simin &
Mary Eliza Banks
age 30 S POB &
POR Spotsylvania
POC; POM
Nottingham,
Spotsylvania 26
Dec 1889 SPMR 24
Dec 1889 SPML
WORMLEY, Lewis s/o
Reuben Wormley &
Johanna Scott age
21 S laborer POB
& POR Orange POC
& **RAWLINGS**,
Louisa d/o Henry
Rawlings & Milly
Mansfield age 18
S POB & POR
Orange POC; POM
Orange 12 May
1867 OMR 11 May
1867 OML
WORMLEY, Moses s/o
Hannah Wormley
age 54 W laborer
POB & POR
Spotsylvania POC
& **BANKS**, Mary
Eliza d/o Harry
Winslow age 54 W
POB & POR
Spotsylvania POC;
POM Spotsylvania
(at their
residence) 27 Oct
1887 SPMR SPML

WORTHINGTON, Eugene s/o William & Maria Worthington age 24 S POB St.Mary's Co,Md POR Spotsylvania POC & **DAWSON**, Nannie d/o Mat & Evelina Dawson age 20 S POB & POR Spotsylvania POC; POM Spotsylvania 17 Jun 1895 SPMR SPML

WRENN, Albert s/o James Wrenn & Lucinda Mitchell age 27 S POB & POR Fairfax Co & **FOX**, Lucy d/o John Fox & A.M.Barker age 21 S POB Fairfax Co POR Orange; POM Orange 15 Feb 1866 OMR 14 Feb 1866 OML

WRENN, Edward S. s/o William & Catharine Wrenn age 52 W miner POB & POR Spotsylvania & **CHEWNING**, Ann E. d/o Garland S. & Mary A.Chewning age 30 S POB & POR Spotsylvania; POM Spotsylvania 5 Mar 1871 SPMR 3 Mar 1871 SPML

WRIGHT, Benjamin s/o Benjamin & Eliza Wright age 52 W farmer POB & POR Orange & **HAWKINS**, Cordelia L. d/o Harvey & Fannie Hawkins age 36 S POB & POR Spotsylvania; POM Wilderness, Spotsylvania 23 Oct 1888 SPMR 18 Oct 1888 SPML

WRIGHT, Curtis B. s/o Benjamin & C.A.Wright age 22 S farmer POB & POR Orange Co & **HAWKINS**, Fannie A. d/o A.B.& Lucy M.Hawkins age 21 S POB & POR Spotsylvania; POM Spotsylvania 9 Nov 1890 SPMR 7 Nov 1890 SPML

WRIGHT, Dabney s/o Dabney Wright & Sarah E.Bell age 50 W farmer POB & POR Orange & **RINER**, Sarah A.E. d/o Jacob Riner & Matilda Estes age 34 S POB & POR Orange; POM Orange 4 Apr 1865 OMR 1 Apr 1865 OML

WRIGHT, Dorsey s/o Woodson & Louisa Wright age 22 S POB & POR Spotsylvania POC & **HOLMES**, Josephine d/o Melvina Holmes age 22 S POB & POR Spotsylvania POC; POM Spotsylvania 15 Feb 1899 SPMR SPML

WRIGHT, Edwin J. s/o William H.& Susan R.Wright age 24 S mechanic POB Orange POR Spotsylvania & **BISCOE**, Mary L. d/o William E.& Catharine Biscoe age 20 S POB & POR Spotsylvania; POM Spotsylvania

23 May 1869 SPMR
30 May 1869 SPML
WRIGHT, George H. s/o
George V. & Mary
E.Wright age 24 S
railroading POB
Caroline Co POR
Richmond & **LEWIS**,
Alma A. d/o
William A. &
Hannah F.Lewis
age 19 S POB &
POR Spotsylvania;
POM Spotsylvania
16 Oct 1895 SPMR
SPML
WRIGHT, George W. &
COSBY, Martha J.;
28 Nov 1854 OML
WRIGHT, Grant s/o
Woodson & Louisa
Wright age 24 S
laborer POB & POR
Spotsylvania POC
& **SCOTT**, Lucy d/o
Robert & Winnie
Scott age 19 S
POB & POR
Spotsylvania POC;
POM Beulah
Baptist Ch,
Spotsylvania 26
Dec 1898 SPMR
SPML
WRIGHT, Jazrel &
BAYNE, Mary d/o
William Bayne S
POB & POR
Spotsylvania; POM
Spotsylvania 20
Jan 1853 SPMR
WRIGHT, John C. s/o
James C. & Jane
Wright of
Fredericksburg
age 35 POR
Fredericksburg &
SWEITZER, Maggie
d/o George &
Eunice Sweitzer
of Fredericksburg
age 17 POR
Fredericksburg;
POM

Fredericksburg 10
Feb 1891 TCF
WRIGHT, John P.R. s/o
Booker & Mary
A.Wright age 25
mechanic POB &
POR Orange &
JONES, Isabella
d/o James &
Elizabeth Jones
age 21 POB & POR
Orange; POM
Orange 9 May 1858
OMR 3 May 1858
OML
WRIGHT, John s/o James
& Sarah Wright
age 37 W farmer
POB & POR
Spotsylvania &
MASSEY, Maria L.
d/o James O.&
Elizabeth Massey
age 21 POB & POR
Orange; POM
Orange 23 Aug
1857 OMR 17 Aug
1857 OML
WRIGHT, John W. s/o
Philip & Sarah
Wright age 29 S
farmer POB & POR
Spotsylvania &
KENT, Martha C.
d/o Robert &
M.E.Hicks age 36
W POB & POR
Spotyslvaia; POM
Spotsylvania 6
Feb 1876 SPMR 2
Feb 1876 SPML
WRIGHT, Lewis s/o Wade
Wright & Rebecca
York age 27 S
gentleman at
large POB
Bridgeport,
Connecticut POR
Early Co,Ga &
WHARTON, Virginia
A. d/o Samuel
Wharton & Lucy
M.Simes age 21 S
POB & POR Orange;

347

WRIGHT, Norris s/o Woodson & Louisa Wright age 22 S laborer POB & POR Spotsylvania POC & **PRATT**, Martha d/o Anderson & Maria Pratt age 18 S POB & POR Spotsylvania POC; POM Spotsylvania 7 Feb 1896 SPMR SPML POM Orange 16 Nov 1865 OMR OML

WRIGHT, Robert J. s/o Jefferson Wright & Sarah Wright age 25 S farmer POB & POR Orange & **MASTIN**, Sarah d/o William Mastin & Kitty Wood age 21 S POB & POR Orange; POM Orange 2 Feb 1862 OMR 27 Jan 1862 OML

WRIGHT, Robert s/o James M.Wright & Martha Estes age 36 W farmer POB & POR Louisa Co & **KING**, Virginia A. d/o Absalom King & Sarah Elam age 23 S POB Louisa CO POR Orange; POM Gordonsville 25 Jan 1866 OMR 19 Jan 1866 OML

WRIGHT, Thomas J. s/o J.& L.Wright age 29 S farmer POB & POR Spotsylvania & **JERRELL**, Sunie A. d/o J.& L.Jerrell age 24 S POB & POR Spotsylvania; POM Spotsylvania 23 Dec 1879 SPMR 20 Dec 1879 SPML

WRIGHT, William E. s/o George W.& Martha J.Wright age 31 S merchant POB & POR Orange & **CHEWNING**, Mertie d/o Marcus & Sallie Chewning age 21 S POB Orange POR Spotsylvania; POM Antioch Ch, Orange Co 18 Oct 1899 OMR 16 Oct 1899 SPML

WRIGHT, William N. s/o James & Lettie Wright age 39 S farmer POB & POR Spotsylvania & **WILSON**, Rosa L. d/o B.W.Wilson age 19 S POB & POR Spotsylvania; POM Spotsylvania 4 Aug 1897 SPMR 2 Aug 1897 SPML

WYNCOOP, P.H. s/o P.& E.Wyncoop age 40 S farmer POB & POR Louden Co & **CARR**, Caroline d/o G. & M.Carr age 25 S POB & POR Spotsylvania; POM Spotsylvania 21 Nov 1865 SPMR

WYNNCOOT, Philip H. s/o Philip & Elizabeth Wynncoot age 40 S farmer POB & POR Loudon Co & **CARR**, Susan Catherine d/o George & Mary Carr age 25 S POB & POR Spotsylvania; POM Spotsylvania 21 Nov 1865 SPMR SPML

YANCEY, John W. s/o Thomas & Sarah Yancey age 51 W

farmer POB
Culpeper Co POR
Rappahannock Co &
TERRILL, Jane d/o
Urial & Jane
Terrill age 35 S
POB & POR Orange;
POM Orange 19 Oct
1854 OMR 18 Oct
1854 OML

YANCY, Anderson s/o
Wash & Zibby
Yancy age 24 S
farmer POB Louisa
Co POR
Spotsylvania POC
& **BOXLEY**, Martha
d/o Isaac & Mary
A.Boxley age 25 S
POB & POR
Spotsylvania POC;
POM Mt.Olivet Ch
1 Jan 1882 SPMR
27 Dec 1881 SPML

YATES, John B. s/o
Abner R.&
Missouri Yates
age 43 W farmer
POB & POR
Culpeper Co &
HIXSON, Martha E.
d/o J.W.& Frances
Clore age 43 W
POB Madison Co
POR Spotsylvania;
POM Spotsylvania
11 Jan 1898 SPMR
10 Jan 1898 SPML

YATES, Snowden s/o
Joseph & Sarah
Yates age about
24 S saddler POB
Fauquier Co POR
Orange & **CULLEN**,
Margaret age
about 24 S POB
Winchester, Va
POR Orange; POM
Orange 21 Nov
1854 OMR

YERBY, T.P. s/o F.&
H.Yerby age 25 S
farmer POB & POR
Spotsylvania &
DICKINSON, J.H.
d/o W.J.&
J.Dickinson age
23 S POB Caroline
Co POR
Spotsylvania; POM
Spotsylvania 19
Jul 1860 SPMR

YERBY, T.P. s/o T.&
H.Yerby age 25 S
farmer POB & POR
Spotsylvania &
DICKINSON, J.H.
d/o W.J.&
J.Dickinson age
23 S POB Caroline
Co POR
Spotsylvania; POM
Spotsylvania 19
Jul 1860 SPMR

YOUNG, Atwell s/o
Humphrey & Nancy
Young age 23 S
POB & POR
Spotsylvania &
SCHOOLER, Betty
S. d/o Martin &
Amanda Schooler
age 17 S POB &
POR Spotsylvania;
POM Spotsylvania
25 Nov 1865 SPMR
24 Nov 1865 SPML

YOUNG, Atwell s/o
Humphry & Nancy
Young age 25 W
farmer POB & POR
Spotsylvania POC
& **COOK**, Ellen d/o
William & Cath
Cook age 18 S POB
& POR
Spotsylvania POC;
POM Spotsylvania
11 Jul 1868 SPMR
SPML

YOUNG, Charles J. s/o
Charles E.& Ann
E. Young age 23 S
farmer POB & POR
Orange & **BISCOE**,
Margaret A. d/o
William E.& Susan
R. Biscoe age 18

S POB & POR
Spotsylvania; POM
Spotsylvania 21
Dec 1884 SPMR 19
Dec 1884 SPML
YOUNG, Charles O. s/o
Charles O.& Lucy
Young age 24 S
POB Spotsylvania
& **WILLIS**, Mary
Champe d/o
Richard Henry &
Lucy Mary Willis
age 20 S POB
Orange; POM
Orange 15 Nov
1860 OMR 14 Nov
1860 OML
YOUNG, Daniel &
RICHARDS, Ann;
POM Orange 2 Mar
1853 OMR 24 Jan
1853 OML
YOUNG, Edward s/o John
& Mary Young age
38 S farmer POB &
POR Orange &
WIGGLESWORTH,
Henrietta d/o
William & Mary
Wigglesworth age
30 S POB & POR
Orange; POM
Orange 29 Nov
1859 OMR 23 Nov
1859 OML
YOUNG, Jacob s/o
P.Young age 26 S
laborer POB & POR
Spotsylvania POC
& **GAINES**, Milly
d/o John & Lucy
Gaines age 24 S
POB & POR
Spotsylvania POC;
POM Spotsylvania
29 Mar 1876 SPMR
27 Mar 1876 SPML
YOUNG, Robert s/o
Robert Coleman &
Susan Young age
37 S butcher POB
Fredericksburg
POR Spotsylvania

POC & **COLBERT**,
Annie A. d/o Kate
Colbert age 24 S
POB Richmond, Va
POR Spotsylvania
POC; 6 Aug 1885
SPML
YOUNG, Tim s/o J.&
A.Young age 31 S
overseerer POR
Caroline Co &
GIBSON, Fras. d/o
J.& W.(?)Gibson
age 44 S POR
Spotsyvlania; POM
Spotsylvania 6
Aug 1857 SPMR
YOUNG, William Erasmus
s/o Humphrey &
Mary Young age 25
S laborer POB &
POR Spotsylvania
POC & **CAMMACK**,
Lizzie d/o Lucy
Cammack age 19 S
POB & POR
Spotsylvania POC;
POM Spotsylvania
17 Jan 1886 SPMR
14 Jan 1886 SPML
YOUNG, William s/o J.&
N.Young age 44 W
farmer POB
Caroline Co POR
Spotsylvania &
CHEWNING, S.E.
d/o J.&
E.Chewning age 35
S POB & POR
Spotsylvania; POM
Spotsylvania 16
Oct 1860 SPMR
YOUNG, Willie A. s/o
M.L.& Virginia
Young age 30 S
farmer POB & POR
Spotsylvania &
MILLS, Emma V.
d/o John H.&
Virginia Mills
age 23 S POB &
POR Spotsylvania;
POM Bethany
Baptist Ch 17 May

1899 SPMR 16 May
1899 SPML
YOWELL, Abraham s/o Abraham & Jane Yowell age 22 S farmer POB Green Co POR Culpeper Co & **CHILDRESS**, Sarah E. d/o G.R.(possibly Giles R.) & Sarah E.Childress age 22 S POB & POR Spotsylvania; POM Spotsylvania 19 Oct 1871 SPMR 14 Oct 1871 SPML

YOWELL, John M. s/o Abram & Martha J.Yowell age 23 S farmer POB Culpeper Co POR Madison Co & **CHILDRESS**, Alice C. d/o G.R.& Sarah E.Childress age 18 S POB & POR Spotsylvania; POM Spotsylvania 14 Nov 1871 SPMR SPML

ACORS, Addie...20
ACORS, Calahan...53
ACORS, Catherine...42
ACORS, Dorothea...177
ACORS, Ema Ella...290
ACORS, Fanny...63
ACORS, Nannie...306
ACORS, Sarah A....73
ACRES, Fannie...35
ACRES, Martha...67
ADAMS, Arianna H....82
ADAMS, Eliza Jane...246
ADAMS, Harriet...159
ADAMS, Mildred A....273
ADKINS, Dabna(?)...68
ADKINS, Lucy Ann...323
ADKINS, Nannie...68
AKERS, Lucy...251
ALEXANDER, Hannah...317
ALLEN, Amanda...289
ALLEN, Rosa Lee...249
ALLISON, Lucy E....285
ALMOND, A.N....93
ALMOND, Alverda...122
ALMOND, Jane d/o N.Sullivan...175
ALMOND, Laticia...52
ALMOND, M....62
ALMOND, Malissa E....205
ALMOND, Martha Jane M....213
ALMOND, Mary V....183
ALMOND, Susan J....192
ALRICH, Mary Ella...137
ALSOP, Amanda A.F....252
ALSOP, Ella...221
ALSOP, Emma O....46
ALSOP, Georgeanna...124
ALSOP, Huldah V....289
ALSOP, Jane F....81
ALSOP, Kitty...78
ALSOP, Loula J....304
ALSOP, Maggie E....285
ALSOP, Margaret A....311
ALSOP, Martha A. d/o Benjamin & Maria Wilson...127
ALSOP, Mary...142
ALSOP, Mary E....75
ALSOP, Mollie E....106
ALSOP, Nannie B....242
ALSOP, R.W....337
ALTENBURG, Julia S....345
AMES, Alice J....230
AMOS, Martha F....330
ANDERSON, Charlotte N....246
ANDERSON, D.J....55
ANDERSON, Deannie...323
ANDERSON, Fannie...113
ANDERSON, Melvina d/o Mack & Fanny Hart...195
ANDERSON, Sally...144
ANDREWS, E.E....171
ANDREWS, E.F....73
ANDREWS, E.S....55
ANDREWS, Elizabeth Ann...43
ANDREWS, Fanny W....86
ANDREWS, Sallie S....201
ANNS, Lizzie J....117
APPERSON, Evelina...107
APPERSON, Lucy P....144
ARMISTEAD, Hannah...190
ARMISTEAD, Harriet...319
ARMSTRONG, Mary E.L....221
ARNOLD, Caroline H....223
ARNOLD, Sallie W....47
ATKINS, A....270
ATKINS, Eliza F....3
ATKINS, Leonora Lewis...246
ATKINS, Louisa...52
ATKINS, Lucy M....265
ATKINS, Martha J....106
AUSTIN, Sallie B....154

BAILEY, Florence
    C....286
BAILEY, Georgia
    A....202
BAILEY, L.E....70
BAILEY, Margaret
    L....257
BAKER, Ann Eliza...155
BAKER, Annie M....225
BAKER, Caroline...55
BAKER, Georgianna...273
BAKER, Lillie C....51
BAKER, Maggie M....132
BAKER, Maria L....213
BAKER, Sophelia...75
BALL, Ann E....295
BALLARD, Ellen
    J....278
BALLARD, Helen
    Peyton...189
BALLARD, Janet
    G....267
BALLARD, Lucy J....124
BALLARD, Margaret...3
BALLARD, Maria...56
BALLARD, Mary E....133
BALLARD, Mary
    Eliza...209
BALLARD, Susan
    F....248
BANKHEAD, Eliza
    M....340
BANKHEAD, Ellen...216
BANKHEAD, Georgianna
    Cary...222
BANKHEAD, Margaret...206
BANKHEAD, Mary C....14
BANKHEAD, Rosalie
    S....340
BANKS, Adeline d/o
    Peter & Mary
    Berkley...284
BANKS, Carrie...282
BANKS, Ellen...189
BANKS, Ellen d/o Mary
    Galls...189
BANKS, Fanny...175
BANKS, Irene...293
BANKS, Lucy d/o
    Garrett Johnson &
    Nelly
    Berkeley...207
BANKS, Martha J....196
BANKS, Mary
    Eliza...345
BANKS, Mary Eliza d/o
    Harry
    Winslow...345
BANYAN, Lucy...288
BAPTIST, F.C....71
BAPTIST, Kate E....138
BAPTIST, Maude G....91
BARBOUR, Cornelia
    C....287
BARBOUR, Sealey...228
BARDEN, Alverta
    Ellsworth...248
BARNES, Annie R....224
BARNES, Dottie...339
BARNES, Susan...307
BARRON, Maria M....328
BARTLESON, Alithia
    C....136
BARTLETT, Sarah
    J....208
BARTLEY, Virginia
    A....183
BATTAILE, Elizabath
    B....27
BATTAILE, Martha
    Ann...157
BATTAILLE, Jane
    F....225
BAXTER, Annie E....294
BAYLOR, Rebecca...112
BAYNE, Mary...347
BEADLES, Georgianna...333
BEALE, Harriet
    H....129
BEAZLEY, Ann E....50
BEAZLEY, Betty
    A....268
BEAZLEY, E.M....309
BEAZLEY, Ida E....273
BEAZLEY, Lucy D....146
BEAZLEY, M.E....65
BEAZLEY, Mary E....206
BEAZLEY, Nannie...20
BECK, Maggie T....122
BECKER, Iona...332
BECKHAM, Lovely
    V....172
BECKHAM, Mary O....105
BECKHAM, Susan
    Ella...170

BELL, Eliza Ann...214
BELL, Elizabeth...145
BELL, Ellen...343
BELL, Jane E....131
BELL, Jane E. d/o
    Henry & Catherine
    Lumsden...132
BELL, Mary Eliza...301
BELL, Mary M....40
BELL, Mary
    Margaret...83
BELL, Minerva C....298
BERKLEY, Eliza d/o
    Edmond Nuckols &
    Jenny Fox...242
BERNARD, Catherine
    Frances...207
BERRY, Lucy Ann...341
BERRYMAN, Ella
    Lane...78
BEVERLEY, Bertie
    C....132
BEVERLEY, Bessie
    G....183
BEVERLEY, Lucy
    V....135
BEVERLEY,
    Matilda...128
BEVERLY, Edie...330
BIBB, Sarah E. d/o
    Benjamin & Hulldah
    Massey...337
BICKERS, Bettie
    A....77
BICKERS, Henrietta
    S....7
BICKERS, Julia
    M....224
BICKERS, Lucy M....31
BICKERS, Mary F....104
BICKERS, Serena...135
BICKERS, Susan
    A....213
BIRDSALL, Florence
    D....142
BISCOE, Margaret
    A....349
BISCOE, Mary L....346
BISCOE, Sallie
    Bettie...59
BLACK, Sally A....225
BLACK, Susan C....221
BLACKLEY, Clara
    H....271

BLACKLEY, Emma...305
BLACKLEY, Lillian
    L....243
BLACKLEY, Lizzie
    C....185
BLACKLEY, Mary
    F....288
BLAIR, Charlotte
    J....334
BLANKENBECKER,
    Mollie...180
BLANTON, Mary A....97
BLAYDES, Barbara
    M....50
BLAYDES, Edna...69
BLAYDES, Emma W....302
BLAYDES, Isabella
    M....125
BLAYDES, Mary E....95
BLAYDES, Mary S....166
BLAYDES, Nannie
    B....70
BLEDSOE,
    Elizabeth...262
BLEDSOE, Georgianna
    F....145
BLEDSOE, Lucy...213
BLEDSOE, Martha
    A....85
BLEDSOE, Mary
    Ann...225
BLEDSOE, Mildred
    H....254
BLEDSOE, Roberta
    E....305
BLEDSOE, Rosa d/o
    Godfrey & Mary
    Yages...274
BLEDSOE, Sarah
    Jane...163
BOASE, Martha J....285
BOATWRIGHT, Mary
    E....309
BOERSIG, Lizzie...201
BOGGS, Clara L....257
BOGGS, Eliza H....169
BOND, Lucy A....12
BOND, Lucy M....147
BOND, Martha C....147
BOON, Elizabeth...37
BOSTON, Annie
    Bettie...214
BOSTON, Clementine
    V....27

BOSTON, Fannie A....297
BOSTON, Mary E....153
BOSTON, Sophia S....243
BOSTON, Susan F....154
BOULWARE, Irene...122
BOULWARE, Virginia A....223
BOWLER, Ellen...28
BOWLER, Harriet A....93
BOWLER, Mary E....38
BOWLING, Alice...228
BOWLING, Irene C....191
BOWLING, Jane...95
BOWLING, M.E....100
BOWLING, Martha A. d/o Thomas S.& Ann A.Hicks...253
BOWLING, Nannie E....252
BOWLING, Ophelia S....129
BOWLING, S.F....166
BOWMAN, Nellie G....202
BOXLEY, Fanny...150
BOXLEY, Hardinia...8
BOXLEY, Jane...128
BOXLEY, Judith D. d/o John & Mary Lipscomb...20
BOXLEY, Mag....274
BOXLEY, Martha...349
BOXLEY, Nancy...262
BOYD, Betsy Ann...84
BOYD, Maria Jane...300
BRADLEY, Florence Janet...246
BRADLEY, Ida F....232
BRADLEY, Maria F. d/o William & Lucy Newman...188
BRADSHAW, Mary A. d/o John & Susan Hatch...341
BRAGG, Mary Y....24
BRAMHAM, Laura...3
BRAXTON, Hannah d/o Polly Gilmor...234
BRENT, Harriet M....154

BRIGHTWELL, Bettie...164
BRIGHTWELL, Bittie (aka Bettie)...164
BRIGHTWELL, L.B....296
BROADDUS, Mary R....79
BROADDUS, Mattie A....160
BROADUS, Margaret...180
BROCK, Alice...153
BROCK, Courtney...72
BROCK, Frances...314
BROCK, Nancy...88
BROCKMAN, Adaline...69
BROCKMAN, Fannie...84
BROCKMAN, Lou...126
BROCKMAN, Mary Ann...223
BROCKMAN, Sarah E....75
BROCKMAN, Virginia A....182
BROOK, Margaret E....1
BROOKE, Fanny d/o M.Hart...94
BROOKE, Margaret E....2
BROOKING, Cassandra B....308
BROOKING, Jennie E....280
BROOKING, Lucy J....2
BROOKING, Mary Ann...272
BROOKING, Mary R....81
BROOKING, Susan M. d/o Benjamin Sanders & Nancy Jones...210
BROOKS, Alice M....328
BROOKS, Allie V....35
BROOKS, Bessie...243
BROOKS, Betty A....105
BROOKS, Catherine M....327
BROOKS, Delia...34
BROOKS, Eliza...203
BROOKS, Ellen L....34
BROOKS, Esther d/o Ben & Rose Lewis...129
BROOKS, Fanny...4
BROOKS, Hattie V....11
BROOKS, Henrietta...51
BROOKS, Isadora...33

BROOKS, Isadora B....33
BROOKS, Judy...34
BROOKS, Julia...342
BROOKS, Lavenia...322
BROOKS, Lilly W....36
BROOKS, Lorena...270
BROOKS, Louisa...1
BROOKS, Lucy...105
BROOKS, Lucy A....50
BROOKS, Lucy M....32
BROOKS, Mary...178
BROOKS, Mary d/o Mary Shelton...167
BROOKS, Mary E....51
BROOKS, Mary E. d/o Sarah West...12
BROOKS, Mary Frances...218
BROOKS, Minnie Ann...327
BROOKS, Minnie E....234
BROOKS, Nannie O....35
BROOKS, Nelia A....203
BROOKS, Nettie Lee...33
BROOKS, Ollie V....35
BROOKS, Queen Victoria...335
BROOKS, Quincy I....36
BROOKS, Rosa L....115
BROOKS, Sara d/o Mary Jones...196
BROOKS, Sarah Mium...48
BROOKS, Sophia...36
BROWN, Elvira...161
BROWN, Emma...200
BROWN, Julia...172, 218
BROWN, Lilly...169
BROWN, Lucy Ann...209
BROWN, Martha C....210
BROWN, Mary D....84
BROWN, Minnie Jane d/o Frank & Mary Brown age 24 POR Fredericksburg...259
BROWN, Mollie...218
BROWN, Philippa J....103
BROWN, Sallie M....331

BROWN, Sarah F....73, 210
BROWN, Susanna...72
BROWN, Susie...207
BRUMLEY, Ann E....204
BRUMLEY, M.C....179
BRUMLEY, Mary E....158
BUCHANAN, Laura T....148
BUCHANAN, Mary A....137
BULLOCK, Alberta...22
BULLOCK, Daisy M....65
BULLOCK, Esther V....62
BULLOCK, Eva I....94
BULLOCK, Kate E....40
BULLOCK, Kate E. d/o Joseph & Catherine Kyle...40
BULLOCK, L.V....210
BULLOCK, Lily W....118
BULLOCK, Maud Gabriella...126
BULLOCK, Minnie R....218
BULLOCK, Virgie W....77
BUNDY, Either L....2
BUNLEY, Matilda...127
BUNNELL, Sallie A....177
BURKE, Lizzie T....114
BURKE, M.E....333
BURLEY, Leonora...67
BURLEY, Sarah...218
BURRUSS, Alice...31
BURRUSS, Catharine S.F....77
BURRUSS, Emma L....17, 238
BURRUSS, Mary A. d/o Annie Williams...251
BURRUSS, Nannie...274
BURRUSS, Olivia E....268
BURRUSS, Sallie E....96
BURRUSS, Willie...253
BURRUSS. Ellen E....231
BURTON, C.M....141

BURTON, Lula d/o
 Wesley & Louisa
 Stratton...96
BURTON, Mary E....174
BURWELL, Dicey...320
BURWELL,
 Margaret...329
BURWELL, Susie
 J....128
BUTLER, Annie...164
BUTLER, Emuella...276
BUTLER, M.B....304
BUTLER, M.C....237
BUTLER, Sarah A....283
BUTZNER, Julia
 K....239
BUTZNER, Mary
 F.T....240
BUTZNER, Virginia
 E....247
BYRAM, Gipsey P. d/o
 Richard & Eliza
 Bowling...249
CAFFREY, Carrie
 C....40
CAFFREY, Jenetta
 A....118
CAFFREY, Mary...96
CAMMACK, Catherine
 A.V....339
CAMMACK, Emily...102
CAMMACK, Hannah...161
CAMMACK, Julia...102
CAMMACK, Lizzie...350
CAMMACK, Lucy...192,
 288
CAMMACK, Lucy M....324
CAMMACK, Maria T....98
CAMMACK, Willie
 E....77
CAMP, Ella...102
CAMPBELL, Maggie...124
CAMPBELL,
 Matilda...269
CANADAY, Caroline
 F....308
CANADY, Ann C....210
CANNADAY, Bettie
 D....107
CANNON, E.A....106
CANNON, Mary E....62
CANNON, Mattie
 E....231

CANNON, Virginia
 A....48
CARNEAL, Martha...171
CARNEAL, Sallie
 J....133
CARNER, Cornelia
 A....309
CARNER, M.J....230
CARNER, Mary J....230
CARNER, Mattie
 D....241
CARNER, Maud L....165
CARNOHAN, Dora A....80
CARNOHAN, Fanny...50
CARNOHAN, Sallie
 I....77
CARR, Annie D....33
CARR, Betsy...83
CARR, Caroline...348
CARR, Malinda...127
CARR, Mamie...330
CARR, Minnie C....288
CARR, Sallie M....36
CARR, Susan
 Catherine...348
CARTER,...253
CARTER, Abbie...79
CARTER, Amanda...7
CARTER, Anna K....49
CARTER, Anna Lee...133
CARTER, Annie...10
CARTER, Annie E. d/o
 George W.& Mollie
 M.Beazley...18
CARTER, Barbara...334
CARTER, Betty...198
CARTER, Carrie...226
CARTER, E.E....316
CARTER, Ella Ellsworth
 d/o J.H.&
 M.J.Robinson...316
CARTER, Georgia...110
CARTER, Hattie
 A....244
CARTER, Isabelle...31
CARTER, Jane A. d/o
 Charles
 C.Taliaferro &
 Louisa
 G.Armistead...271
CARTER,
 Josephine...160
CARTER, Julia...184

CARTER, Laetitia d/o
  Lewis & Susan
  C.Almond...233
CARTER, Lizzie...241
CARTER, Lou E....27
CARTER, Louisa...201
CARTER, Luella...39
CARTER, Lydia...161
CARTER, Maria S....166
CARTER, Matilda...266
CARTER, Mattie...264,
  324
CARTER, Milly...156,
  314
CARTER, Molly...249
CARTER, Nora L....238
CARTER, Rosa...153
CARTER, Sarah N....117
CARTER, Victoria...254
CARY, Margarett...322
CARY,Evelina...86
CASH, Josephine...231
CASH, Mary E....205
CASON, Sallie M....84
CATLETT, Lucinda...272
CATLETT, Lydia...28
CATLETT, Mary...44
CATLETT, Sarah...251
CAVE, Georgianna
  V....172
CAVE, Hannah Jane...18
CAVE, Maria C....305
CAVE, Mary A....249
CAVELL, Clara...326
CAWTHORNE, M.A....56
CHALMERS, Margaret
  A....203
CHANCELLOR, Ann E....9
CHANCELLOR,
  Annastatia...184
CHANCELLOR,
  Edmonia...292
CHANCELLOR,
  Leona...258
CHANCELLOR, Lucie
  M....289
CHANCELLOR, Mary
  E....114
CHAPMAN, Emma...27
CHAPMAN, Maria
  Louisa...259
CHAPMAN, Mary...56
CHARLTON, A.E....184
CHARTTERS, F.H....5

CHARTTERS, Lucy
  P....130
CHESLEY, Frances
  E....8
CHESLEY, Mary S....87
CHEW, Eliza...312
CHEW, Elizabeth...193
CHEW, Lucy F....216
CHEW, Maria F....193
CHEW, Nannie...102
CHEW, Nicey...171
CHEWNING, Alice...52
CHEWNING, Alice
  Cary...251
CHEWNING, Amanda
  M....146
CHEWNING, Amanda
  P....157
CHEWNING, America
  E....168
CHEWNING, Ann E....346
CHEWNING, Anna
  S....170
CHEWNING, Dallie...126
CHEWNING E---nd
  J....58
CHEWNING, Ella
  V....140
CHEWNING, Emma...58
CHEWNING, Emma
  R....270
CHEWNING, Eugenia
  H....146
CHEWNING, Fannie
  L....59
CHEWNING, Fanny
  L....59
CHEWNING, Jane
  C....255
CHEWNING, Landora
  H....246
CHEWNING, Laura...344
CHEWNING, Lillian
  E....296
CHEWNING, Mary V....97
CHEWNING, Mertie...348
CHEWNING, N.Virginia
  d/o William &
  Manicy Alsop...316
CHEWNING, Nannie
  M....140
CHEWNING, Rose
  E....284
CHEWNING, S.E....350

CHEWNING, Susan F....44
CHEWNING, Vio O....286
CHEWNING, Wilhelmonia...344
CHILDRESS, Alice C....351
CHILDRESS, Sarah...88
CHILDRESS, Sarah E....351
CHILDRESS, Virginia C....2
CHILDRESS, Wilhelma C. d/o Archibald Shiflett & Barlinda Vaughn...60
CHILDS, Eliza...304
CHILDS, Mary...139, 345
CHILDS, Sallie...3
CHILDS, Susan J....108
CHILES, M.E....14
CHILTON, Almira F....88
CHILTON, Annie E....153
CHILTON, Maggie T....156
CLARK, Addie V....140
CLARK, Alice B....260
CLARK, Elizabeth...4
CLARK, Jane D.L....324
CLARK, Lucy C. d/o John Kimbrough & Sarah Michell...287
CLARK, Martha E....75
CLARK, Mary H....151
CLARK, Mary Jane...312
CLARK, Mildred...14
CLARK, Minerva A....154
CLARK, Nancy...172
CLARK, Nannie B....270
CLARK, Novella V....133
CLARK, Sarah H....342
CLARKE, Allice B....125
CLARKE, Cornelia A....179
CLARKE, Hannah F....200

CLARKE, Margaret d/o Eliza Dudley...227
CLARKE, Martha...293
CLARKE, Mary...338
CLARKE, Mattie C....237
CLARKE, Sarah J....46
CLARKE, Sue...69
CLARKE, Susan T....224
CLORE, Frances...21
COATES, Bettie M....138
COATES, Betty L....214
COATES, Martha...247
COATES, Sarah...66
COATES, Susan Alice d/o Fanny Minor...299
COATS, Alice...269
COATS, Martha V....115
COATS, Susie A....251
COBBS, Mary Ann...116
COFFMAN, Celia...339
COLBERT, Annie A....350
COLBERT, Inez E....211
COLBERT, Lillian Lyndall...45
COLDMAN, Martha...175
COLE, Ann E....143
COLE, Catharine A....268
COLE, Ellen...324
COLE, Josephine C....110
COLE, Lena D....260
COLE, Lizzie F....154
COLE, Susie...250
COLEMAN, Alice...216, 292
COLEMAN, Amy...222
COLEMAN, Ann...312
COLEMAN, Anna A....211
COLEMAN, Annie...328
COLEMAN, B.H....336
COLEMAN, Bettie S....181
COLEMAN, Coatney...281
COLEMAN, Elizabeth...145
COLEMAN, Ellen...332
COLEMAN, Emma S....122
COLEMAN, Hattie...82, 303

COLEMAN, Hettie...79
COLEMAN, Jane...15, 54
COLEMAN, Jennie d/o
  George & Martha
  Ross...127
COLEMAN, Julia A....69
COLEMAN, Julia W....90
COLEMAN, L.L....6
COLEMAN, Laura d/o
  Thomas Ellis &
  Joanna Ellis
  (formerly
  Webb)...302
COLEMAN, Lettie...6
COLEMAN, Lina...217
COLEMAN, Lizzie...109
COLEMAN, Louisa...26
COLEMAN, Lucie
  B....180
COLEMAN, Lucy
  Ann...162
COLEMAN, M....307
COLEMAN, Maggie...195
COLEMAN, Margaret...64
COLEMAN, Martha...197
COLEMAN, Martha
  A....61
COLEMAN, Martha d/o
  Wilson Green &
  Esther Chew...169
COLEMAN, Martha
  J....62
COLEMAN, Mary d/o
  Edgar & Annie
  White...328
COLEMAN, Mary
  Frances...77
COLEMAN, Mattie...250
COLEMAN, Milly...181
COLEMAN, Sally A....67
COLEMAN, Susan...38
COLEMAN, Susan
  M....330
COLEMAN, Sylvia...248
COLES, Jennie...7
COLES, Louisa...18
COLLINS, Adeline d/o
  Henry & Lydia
  Slaughter...197
COLLINS, Elizabeth
  A....236
COLLINS, Emily L....91
COLLINS, Kate...236
COLLINS, Lizzie...115
COLLINS, Mary
  Fannie...243
COLLINS, Rebecca
  E....104
COLVIN, Elizabeth
  F....200
COMFORT, Fannie...38
COMFORT, Mary d/o
  Lavenia
  Woolfolk...67
COMFORT, Nancy d/o
  Gilbert
  Baylor...112
COMFORT, Susan...54
CONLEY, Lottie
  E....183
CONNER, Martha...138
CONNER, Queen...174
CONNER, Sarah...65
COOK, Angelina d/o
  Caleb A.Smith &
  Betsy Jacobs...285
COOK, Dansy...1
COOK, Ellen...349
COOK, Julia...33
COOK, Martha...169
COOPER, Malvina
  D....29
COOPER, Mary M. d/o
  Richard & Sarah
  Brown...193
CORBIN, Hannah...233
CORNICAN, Rose...127
COSBY, Martha J....347
COVINGTON,
  Georganna...302
COWHERD, Mary
  Jane...76
COX, Isabella...158
COX, Maddie L....294
COX, S.A....124
CRAFTON, Cora A....230
CRAWFORD, Eva M.d/o
  Jerome & Maria
  Sisler...82
CRAWFORD, S.O....332
CRAWFORD, Virgie
  L....43
CROCKFORD, Rosa
  E....141
CROOKS, Elvira
  S....141
CROPP, Ricey or Billy
  Ann...227

CROPP, S.G....166
CROPP, Sally Ann...229
CROPTS, Bettie B....118
CROSLEY, Frances Annie d/o James & Fanny Thomas...196
CROUSE, Mary...12
CRUCHFIELD, Ellen...26
CRUMP, Celia...65
CRUMP, Mary...321
CRUTCHFIELD, Annie W....217
CRUTCHFIELD, Betty Ann...192
CRUTCHFIELD, Eliza...183
CRUTCHFIELD, Ellen...26
CRUTCHFIELD, Jennie...288
CRUTCHFIELD, Landonia...341
CRUTCHFIELD, Louisa...66
CRUTCHFIELD, Lula...160
CRUTCHFIELD, Malinda...291
CRUTCHFIELD, Martha...344
CRUTCHFIELD, Mary...343
CRUTCHFIELD, Mary J....90
CRUTCHFIELD, Nannie...51
CRUTCHFIELD, Sally...117
CRUTCHFIELD, Sarah...88
CULLEN, Emma...262
CULLEN, Margaret...349
CULLEN, Marietta...213
CUNNINGHAM, Fanny...93
CUNNINGHAM, Mary E....198
CURTIS, Cleopatra...202
CURTIS, Emma...289
CURTIS, Mattie L....103
CURTIS, Sarah E....244
DABNEY, Clara...10

DABNEY, M.E....8
DADE, Ann W....28
DAINGERFIELD, Matilda d/o Bob & Mariah Johnson...122
DANDRIDGE, Celia d/o Addison & Mary Lewis...153
DANDRIDGE, Eliza...220
DANDRIDGE, Louisa C....182
DANGERFIELD, Diana...123
DANIEL, Fannie S....55
DANIEL, Mary C....94
DANIEL, Susan N....326
DARNELL, Frances...7
DARNELL, Luella...331
DAUSEN, Julean...114
DAVENPORT, Della...132
DAVENPORT, Eva P....101
DAVENPORT, Jennie...104
DAVENPORT, Mary Catherine...9
DAVIS, Alice...172
DAVIS, Anna d/o Alonzo & Sarah Howard...171
DAVIS, Anner...171
DAVIS, Bettie W....122
DAVIS, Den G....284
DAVIS, Drucilla G....84
DAVIS, Ellie B....59
DAVIS, Emma...108
DAVIS, Fanny K....157
DAVIS, Harriet E....22
DAVIS, Lillie...260
DAVIS, Lizzie...219
DAVIS, Lucy M....136
DAVIS, M.S....221
DAVIS, Margaret R....30
DAVIS, Maria d/o Alonzo & Sarah Howard...219
DAVIS, Maria Jane...13
DAVIS, Mary E....131
DAVIS, Sallie M....338
DAVIS, Sally Ann...225
DAWSON, Mary Rose...37
DAWSON, Nannie...346

DAWSON, Rena d/o
   William & Susan
   Taylor...109
DAY, Fanny W. d/o John
   L.& Mary
   E.Andrews...45
DAY, Linda...57
DAY, Nancie E....212
DAY, Sessa...195
DECKER, Emma
   Iren...113
DECKER, Lucy J....44
DECKER, Mary A....29
DECKER, Prudence
   Ann...2
DeJARNETTE, Callie
   H....184
DEJARNETTE, Mary
   A....265
DEMPSEY, Callie
   M....325
DEMPSEY, Laura A....58
DEMPSEY, Lucy E....142
DEMPSEY, Minerva
   E....325
DENT, Parke P....30
DERSON,
   Georgeanna...21
DESPER, Sarah d/o
   Robert & Lucy
   Crutchfield...324
DESPOT, Sallie...301
DEW, L.D....326
DEW, Minnie M....323
DICKEN, M.A....51
DICKEN, Martha A....51
DICKERSON, Lucindy
   M....92
DICKEY, Elizabeth
   B....213
DICKINSON, Annie
   M....89
DICKINSON, Bertie
   A....135
DICKINSON, Emma
   L....216
DICKINSON, Emma
   M....126
DICKINSON, Flora
   J....105
DICKINSON,
   Florence...220
DICKINSON, Florence
   M....261
DICKINSON, Florence
   V....302
DICKINSON, Ida
   V....297
DICKINSON, J.H....349
DICKINSON,
   Lucinda...92
DICKINSON, Nelly...20
DICKINSON, Sallie
   S....274
DICKINSON, Sally
   E....10
DICKINSON, Sarah
   A....80
DIGGS, Emily...188
DIGGS, Lyla...66
DIGGS, Mary...58
DIGGS, Mildred...61
DIGGS, Sedonia...244
DILLARD, Alice
   E....232
DILLARD, Annie d/o
   William & Margaret
   Lewis...219
DILLARD, Edith
   E....195
DILLARD, Frances
   E....188
DILLARD, Hardinia A.
   d/o Lancelot &
   Nancy
   Partlow...117
DILLARD, Lottie
   R....91
DILLARD, Mary T....39
DIXON, Ida F. d/o
   William H.&
   V.A.Perry...318
DIXON, Iola L....276
DOBYNS, Maria L....264
DODD, Willie...21
DOLEN, Julia P....31
DOOLEY, Harriet A. d/o
   Robert
   Bowler...154
DORRON, Maria...21
DOTTS, Polly...280
DOUGLAS, Sarah
   A....119
DOWELL, Mary M....94
DOWNER, Lucy F....55
DOWNER, Mary B....94
DOWNER, Mildred
   A....259

DOWNEY, Mildred C. d/o
  Sanders &
  Catherine
  Mason...186
DOWNMAN, Nannie
  H....300
DOWNS, Lucie
  Elinor...179
DUDLEY, Rachel...312
DUDLEY, Rosetta...68
DUERSON, A.E....87
DUERSON, Edwina
  C....120
DUERSON,
  Elizabeth...319
DUERSON, Harriet d/o
  R.& M.Minor...313
DUERSON, Lucy
  Ann...238
DUERSON, M....40
DUERSON, Maria E....15
DUERSON, S.A....67
DUERSON, S.J....173
DUERSON, S.M....78
DUERSON, Sarah A....15
DUERSON, Virginia
  C....170
DULIN, Dicy A....59
DULIN, Martha E....95
DULIN, Mary E....96
DUNAVANT, Amelda...43
DUNAVANT, Mary L....75
DUNAWAY, Ann...287
DUNAWAY, Delpha
  O....36
DUNAWAY,
  Elizabeth...148
DUNAWAY, Emila A....32
DUNAWAY, Emily...32
DUNAWAY, Mary E....147
DUNAWAY, Sally
  J....147
DUNN, Mary Susan...234
DUNNAVANT,
  Frances...249
DUNNAVANT, Louisa...98
DURRETT, Addie...99
DURRETT, Fanny...310
DURRETT, J.T....262
DURRETT, Kate B....22
DUVALL, Albzerah...278
DUVALL, Eula Lee...200
DUVALL, J.D.M....313
DUVALL, Sarah E....121

EASTBURN, Anna
  E....226
EASTBURN, Carrie
  Florine...244
EASTBURN, Ella...247
EASTBURN, Lillian
  V....225
EASTBURN, Lizzie
  J....137
EASTBURN, Maggie
  S....290
EASTBURN, Maria
  S....226
EASTBURN, Sallie
  R....225
EDDINS, Emma J....100
EDENTON, Alice
  R....142
EDENTON, Blanche
  A....178
EDENTON, Florence
  L....90
EDENTON, M.E....111
EDENTON, Maria
  J....186
EDENTON, Mary L....130
EDENTON, Rachel
  D....205
EDENTON, Sally B....99
EDLIN, Addie...258
ELEY, Patsy...323
ELIASON, Nannie
  H....280
ELKINS, Mary
  Eliza...222
ELLEY, Ann...18
ELLEY, Mary W....292
ELLEY, Saphronia...23
ELLIS,
  Georgeanna...120
ELLIS, Laura...66
ELLIS, Maria...184
ELLIS, Martha...301
ELLIS, Mary...23
ELLIS, Maud...128
ELLIS, Sarah E....143
ELLY, Esther...178
ELLY, Rena...317
EMANUEL, Sallie...266
ENNIS, Amanda...71
ESTES, Eliza M....135
ESTES, Juliett
  M....307
ESTES, Mary E....104

ESTES, Mary T....19
ESTES, Mildred A....265
ESTES, Nancy F. d/o Edward Gilbert & Susan Sandridge...263
EUBANK, Ella W....83
EUBANK, Lucy B....40
EUBANK, Nellie G....54
EUBANK, S.H....119
EVANS, Frances...283
EVANS, Patty...273
EVANS, Sarah...143
FAIRCHILD, Laura...166
FAIRFAX, Flora d/o Robert Dickinson & Julia Craig...261
FARISH, E.J....188
FARMER, Mary E....224
FARMER, Nannie...335
FAUDREE, Ellen M....227
FAUDREE, Jane C....278
FAUDREE, Lucy M....227
FAULCONER, Annie E....23
FAULCONER, Bettie Lewis d/o Richard G. & Jane Swift...209
FAULCONER, Catherine E....187
FAULCONER, Catherine J....187
FAULCONER, Dolly M....201
FAULCONER, Emily J....144
FAULCONER, Margaret...163
FAULCONER, Margaret Elizabeth...163
FAULCONER, Mary...263
FAULCONER, Rachel V....137
FAULCONER, Susan J....163
FAULCONER, Virginia E....316
FAULDING, Annie...343
FAULDING, Susan...343
FAULKNER, Alice...282

FAULKNER, Beulah E....205
FAULKNER, J.M....4
FAULKNER, M.A....64
FAY, Dora E....81
FERNEYHOUGH, Louise M....315
FERNEYHOUGH, Mary E....232
FERNEYHOUGH, Sallie M....8
FERNEYHOUGH, Sarah J....311
FERNEYHOUGH, Susan E....83
FILE, Delia A....27
FINES, Ella I....294
FISHER, Hannah M....87
FISHER, Mary...33
FISHER, Mary Ann d/o Richard & Catherine Philips...215
FISHER, Sarah E....37
FITZHUGH, Estell...207
FITZHUGH, Louisa C....208
FITZPATRICK, Maggie...111
FLEMING, C.S.(or Q.)...60
FLEMING, E.D....182
FLEMING, Nellie E....6
FLEMING, Octavia B....43
FLEMING, Olivia J....92
FLEMING, Roberta A. d/o Alfred & Roberta C.Pool...260
FLEMMING, Lucy M....247
FLETCHER, Margaret...86, 87
FLIPPO, Frances d/o Willis & Jenny Taylor...194
FLIPPO, Inez B....279
FLIPPO, Septimia...119
FORCE, Mary...281
FORD, Caroline...169

FORD, Lizzie d/o Humphrey & Mary Young...342
FORT, Lucy...310
FORTE, Laura...336
FORTS, Fanny...68
FOSTER, Bettie J....136
FOSTER, Edmonia B....135
FOSTER, Susie Z....208
FOX, Lucy...346
FOX, Mary L....321
FOX, Sallie...332
FRAZER, E.J....12
FRAZER, Ella...198
FRAZER, Emma...229
FRAZER, Fannie C....97
FRAZER, Huldah M....68
FRAZER, Jennie C....55
FRAZER, Keziah...254
FRAZER, M.M....79
FRAZER, Martha A....162
FRAZER, Mary Ann...160
FRAZIER, Martha...151
FRAZIER, Rachel...71
FREEMAN, Mary E....290
FRENCH, Ida...340
FRY, Martha Ann d/o Albert French & Sarah A.Wise...203
FULCHER, Callie V....267
FURNEYHOUGH, Mary S....56
GABBOT, Lucinda...41
GAINES, Annie E....226
GAINES, Julia...106
GAINES, Milly...350
GALLINGER, Lucy A....142
GARDNER, Amelia S....266
GARDNER, Flossie...134
GARDNER, Josie A....239
GARDNER, Martha V....208
GARDNER, Minerva d/o Ezekiah Richards & Betsy Lancaster...228

GARNER, Mary d/o John & Susan Powell...326
GARNET, Chany...89
GARNETT, Alberta...105
GARNETT, Emily H....283
GARNETT, Fannie d/o Henry & Patsy Ware...288
GARNETT, Lelia...86
GARNETT, Louisa...149
GARNETT, Lucy E....149
GARNETT, Lucy M. d/o James & Eliza Lloyd...295
GARNETT, Mary...197
GARNETT, Mary E. d/o Larkin Willis & Mary Gordon...151
GARNETT, Rebecca...269
GAY, Amy E....242
GAY, Bettie F....222
GAYLE, B.M....29
GAYLE, Laura F....295
GAYLE, M.A....19
GAYLE, Roberta E....190
GENTRY, Susan A....181
GIBSON, Fras....350
GIBSON, Martha...162
GIBSON, Martha A.F....92
GIBSON, Mary Jane...119
GIBSON, Mary L....334
GIBSON, Sarah Ella...302
GILES, Eliza...101
GILLABERT, Mary A....151
GLASSGOW, Mamie E....252
GLENN, Susan C....98
GOODLOE, Evie...29
GOODLOE, Georgeanna d/o George & Jane Ellis...38
GOODLOE, Maudy...57
GOODLOE, Sallie...271
GOODMAN, Ethel...85
GOODWIN, Fanny D....89
GOODWIN, Lucy A....206

GOODWIN, Margaret...234
GOODWIN, Margaret C....277
GOODWIN, Margaret M....234
GOODWIN, Mary Byrd...122
GOODWIN, Mary E....286
GOODWIN, Sally M....344
GORDON, Ann...79
GORDON, B.S....20
GORDON, Blanche...73
GORDON, Emma...329
GORDON, Fanny F....123
GORDON, Laura...293
GORDON, Louisa...118
GORDON, Lucy T....336
GORDON, Martha A....114
GORDON, Martha d/o Elvey Payne...284
GORDON, Mary Alice...194
GORDON, Mary F....63
GORDON, Susan V....17
GOSS, Sarah F....149
GRADY, Annie B....296
GRADY, Lillie L....137
GRAHAM, Ellen...160
GRAHAM, Gertie L....307
GRAHAM, Josephine...61
GRASTY, Alverta...325
GRAVATT, Mary T. d/o Oliver Terrill & Susan Proctor...169
GRAVES, Ann E....31
GRAVES, Hattie F....96
GRAVES, Lucinda d/o Dick & Dinah Richards...170
GRAVES, Mariam E....240
GRAVES, Mary S....218
GRAVES, Mary Virginia...235
GRAVES, Mary Walker...76
GRAVES, Minie A....120
GRAVES, Nannie B....135

GRAVES, Rosa L....16
GRAVES, V.S....310
GRAY, Ella M....159
GRAY, Ellen...42
GREEN, Edith...271
GREEN, Gracie M....321
GREEN, Jenney...66
GREEN, Lucilla E....78
GREEN, Martha Lucas...314
GREEN, Matilda...318
GREEN, Rose Lee...103
GREEN, Susan...335
GRIMES, Mary M....286
GRIMSLEY, Mary Elizabeth...167
GROOM, Virginia Ann...23
GRUBBS, Ann E....182
GUSS, Emma...65
HACKLEY, Sarah F....274
HAILEY, Anna B....89
HAILEY, Louisa previously married...130
HAILEY, Louisa F. d/o Jesse & Sarah Stubbs...328
HAILEY, Martha A....99
HAILEY, Mary C....146
HAILEY, Sallie...91
HAILEY, Virgie Lee...181
HAILEY, Virginia T....146
HAILSTORK, Annie...204
HAISLIP, Mary Willie...249
HAISLOP, Annie O....81
HALEY, Maria P. d/o James & Mary Stephens...80
HALL, Clara I....83
HALL, Ella...211
HALL, Hattie J....185
HALL, Hattie V....52
HALL, Ida M....337
HALL, Irene...211
HALL, Lucy Mary...88
HALL, Nettie C....92
HALL, Sarah...333
HAMMOND, Josephine C....222

HANCOCK, Eliza d/o Benjamin & Sarah Johnson...112
HANEY, Angie...75
HANEY, Mary...165
HANSBROUGH, Bettie H....217
HANSBROUGH, Maria S....343
HANSBROUGH, Martha S....80
HANSBROUGH, Roberta B....335
HANSBROUGH, Sallie Milton...309
HANSFORD, Mary G....78
HANSFORD, Sallie J. d/o William Terrill & Fanny Boston...106
HARDENBERRY, Cora A....134
HARDING, Irene E....260
HAREFIELD, Clara A....32
HAREFIELD, Ellen V....316
HAREFIELD, Lucy M....51
HAREFIELD, M.S....35
HAREFIELD, Mary...33
HAREFIELD, Myrtle...32
HAREFIELD, Nellie...10
HARFIELD, Daisy V....35
HARFIELD, Eleanor...34
HARFIELD, Florence...179
HARFIELD, M.K....280
HARLOW, Lucy Mary...133
HARRIS, Bertie K....8
HARRIS, Carrie O....67
HARRIS, Elsie...64
HARRIS, Georgia A....297
HARRIS, Ida L....136
HARRIS, Lizzie K....275
HARRIS, Lucy E....276
HARRIS, Martha A....11
HARRIS, Martha Ellen...100
HARRIS, Mary C....151
HARRIS, Mildred A....285
HARRIS, Mollie E....331
HARRIS, Musette C....114
HARRIS, Patsy...173
HARRIS, Susan M....5
HARRISS, Martha C....11
HARRORD, Sophronia d/o Gabriel & Jane Bird...235
HARROW, Sarah N....281
HART, Alice R....311
HART, Bettie E....41
HART, Elizabeth...69
HART, Fannie E....32
HART, Hattie G....319
HART, Isabella...329
HART, Julia...320
HART, Leah...150
HART, Maggie M....156
HART, Martha...79
HART, Melvina...8
HART, Norma Estella...69
HART, Susan...229
HART, Virginia S....303
HARVEY, Teresa...270
HASSETT, Alice J....209
HASSETT, Hannah...340
HATCH, S.C....297
HATCH, Ann Eliza...260
HATCH, Leona S.W....145
HATCHER, Emma T....64
HAWKINS, Angelina A....331
HAWKINS, Bell...107
HAWKINS, Cordelia L....346
HAWKINS, Elizabeth...317
HAWKINS, Fannie A....346
HAWKINS, Fannie G....241
HAWKINS, H.& M....311
HAWKINS, Junnie...271

HAWKINS, Martha
 F....94
HAWKINS, Rosa L....63
HAWLEY, Lucy M....72
HAYDON, Annie C....291
HAYES, Lucy C....104
HAYNES, Alice...48
HAYNES, Amma M....48
HAYNES, Roberta
 R....237
HAYNES, Sarah N. d/o
 John & Jane
 L.Bourne...157
HAYS, Mary J....102
HAZEL, Viola C....255
HEATWELL, Bettie
 G....64
HEATWELL, Eliza...178
HEIDEN, Lucy M....206
HEISLOP, Laura...17
HENDERSON, Henrietta
 J....264
HENDERSON,
 Louisa...224
HENDERSON, Mary d/o
 S.& P.Alsop...28
HENDERSON, Mary
 J....152
HENRY, Catharine...248
HENRY, Catherine...248
HERNDON, Ann E....53
HERNDON, Ann
 Elizabeth...245
HERNDON, Ann V....251
HERNDON, Eliza
 J....279
HERNDON, Elizabeth d/o
 Ambrose Coleman &
 Frances
 Hilman...256
HERNDON, Huldah
 F....140
HERNDON, Maria
 F....141
HERNDON, Mary...187
HERNDON, Mary A....157
HERNDON, Pamelia...198
HERNDON, Susan...74,
 308
HERNDON,
 Virginia...156
HERRING, Annie
 E....116
HERRING, Apphia...145

HERRING, Fannie d/o
 Robert & Sallie
 Sorrell...32
HERRING, Fronie
 J....61
HERRING,
 Georgianna...185
HERRING, Sallie E. d/o
 Col.Frank & Lucy
 Saunders...287
HERRING, Sally
 F....107
HERRING, Susan
 F....187
HERRING, Susie
 M....305
HESTER, Alice...276
HESTER, Lucy...322
HESTER, Mattie
 G....275
HETER, Catherine...103
HICKS, Anna H....174
HICKS, Annie...13
HICKS, Ludona A....156
HICKS, M....318
HICKS, M.C....183
HICKS, Magnolia...337
HICKS, Mary F....90
HICKS, Mollie J....92
HICKS, Sally Ann...80
HICKS, Sedona Ann...95
HIGGERSON, Mary
 E....287
HIGGERSON, Pamelia
 H....248
HIGGINS, Harriet
 W....275
HIGGINS, Mary U....202
HILLMAN, Emma T....100
HILLMAN, Louisa...143
HIRTH, Willey J....235
HITER, Polly...247
HIXSON, Martha
 E....349
HOAGLAND, Susie
 H....150
HOCKADAY, Ella N....42
HOCKADAY, Harriet
 M....237
HOCKADAY, Mattie
 N....208
HOCKADAY, Sarah
 J....212
HOLLADAY, C.E....78

HOLLADAY, Emily
  Gertrude...76
HOLLADAY, Ida J....186
HOLLADAY, Ida M. d/o
  William A.& Mary
  Jennings...157
HOLLADAY, Jemima
  P....17
HOLLADAY, Julia
  R....101
HOLLADAY, Kate L....74
HOLLADAY, Lillie
  M....241
HOLLADAY, Maggie...73
HOLLADAY, Mary
  Catherine...212
HOLLADAY, Nannie
  S....110
HOLLADAY, R.R....17
HOLLADAY, Rebecca
  A....337
HOLMES, Celia...261
HOLMES, Edele...53
HOLMES,
  Josephine...346
HOLMES, Martha...66
HOLMES, Mary...114
HOLMES, Mary Ann...172
HONSER, Bettie
  T....117
HOPE, Elton
  Placett...49
HOPE, Nouraly D....285
HOPKINS, Leanna...278
HOPKINS, Sallie
  A....148
HOPKINS, Sarah
  A....308
HORD, Lucy...92
HOUSER, Lydia M....149
HOWARD, Ann
  Elizabeth...300
HOWARD, Annie L....155
HOWARD, C.L....114
HOWARD, Lucy Ann...162
HOWARD, Maggie...169
HOWARD, Maggie M. d/o
  Joseph Howard &
  Mary R.Jones...274
HOWARD, Maria d/o
  Silas Minor &
  Rachel Minor...84
HOWARD, Mary F....270
HOWARD, Mary R. d/o
  Charles & Caroline
  Todd...179
HOWARD, Mary R. d/o
  Charles & Har.
  Todd...179
HOWARD, Susan...57
HUGHES, Alice d/o
  Ellen Waugh...102
HUGHES, Jane J....153
HUGHES,
  Josephine...321
HUGHES, Nancy...342
HUGHES, Rebecca
  A....293
HUGHES, Sarah F....311
HUGHES, Virginia...246
HUME, Ann...140
HUME, Bettie
  Thompson...264
HUME, Eliza...157
HUME, Fannie P....28
HUMPHRIES, Bettie
  A....245
HUMPHRIES, Bettie
  J....47
HUMPHRIES, Emma
  R....245
HUMPHRIES, Jane...13
HUMPHRIES, Lavenia
  A....281
HUMPHRIES, Lucie A.
  d/o Joshua & Fanny
  Reamy...295
HUMPHRIES, M.T....165
HUMPHRY, Mary E. d/o
  John & Jane
  Humphries...131
HUNTER, Byrdie
  B....204
HUNTER, Louisa...298
HUTCHISON, Mattie
  E....54
IREMAN, Sallie...192
ISEMAN, Hannah...150
ISEMAN, Levinia...19
JACKSON,...277
JACKSON, Ann...191,
  276, 311, 334
JACKSON, Anna...120
JACKSON, Annie
  Bell...159
JACKSON, Annie
  M....197

JACKSON, Betsy...298
JACKSON, Caroline...128
JACKSON, Cassandra...283
JACKSON, Celia...79
JACKSON, Edna...19
JACKSON, Elizabeth...325
JACKSON, Ellen...40
JACKSON, Elsie...272
JACKSON, Emma...119
JACKSON, Fannie...1
JACKSON, Fannie d/o Lucy Ellis...222
JACKSON, Isabella...333
JACKSON, Jane...167
JACKSON, Josephine...220
JACKSON, Josephine d/o Fanny Montague...149
JACKSON, Laura D....70
JACKSON, Lucy...256
JACKSON, Margaret...2
JACKSON, Maria...204
JACKSON, Mary E....85
JACKSON, Mary T....342
JACKSON, Matilda...299
JACKSON, Priscilla...278
JACKSON, Rose...220
JACKSON, Sarah J....37
JACKSON, Tamor...155
JACKSON, Virginia...176
JACOBS, Annie E....205
JACOBS, Bettie...315
JACOBS, Elizabeth...163
JACOBS, Sarah J....187
JAMES, Bettie...164
JAMES, Ruth d/o George Sizer & Nancy Hicks...144
JEFFERSON, Lucy...309
JENINGS, Sarah H....194
JENKINS, Carrie May...176
JENKINS, Mary L....197
JENKINS, Sarah J....194
JENNINGS, Lillie E....290
JENNINGS, Susie E....155
JERDONE, Mary C....46
JERRELL, A.M....258
JERRELL, Alma...258
JERRELL, Annie V....214
JERRELL, J.S....269
JERRELL, Josie...58
JERRELL, Louisa A....108
JERRELL, Maggie M....332
JERRELL, Margaret F....173
JERRELL, Mary Irene...313
JERRELL, S.B....240
JERRELL, S.G. d/o William Cropp...98
JERRELL, Sunie A....348
JETT, Almedia...249
JETT, Ann E....326
JETT, Annie D....212
JETT, C.A....26
JETT, Carrie...244
JETT, Docie J....229
JETT, Dora V....228
JETT, Dulcie...96
JETT, Emma...13
JETT, Lula S....277
JETT, Mary L....97
JETT, Mary Lou...133
JETT, Olive...343
JETT, Rosa Catherine...177, 178
JETT, Susie D....133
JOHNS, Ann Maria...220
JOHNS, Mildred M....341
JOHNS, Sarah...108
JOHNSON, (aka Johnston) Mary...37
JOHNSON, Amanda Q....252
JOHNSON, Annie E....39
JOHNSON, Barbara E....198
JOHNSON, Betsy S....28

JOHNSON, Bettie...153
JOHNSON, Carrie...197
JOHNSON, Charlotte...263
JOHNSON, Drucilla...84
JOHNSON, E.L....337
JOHNSON, Ellen...273
JOHNSON, Emily J....176
JOHNSON, Harriet E....47
JOHNSON, Harriet E. d/o Mary Robertson...47
JOHNSON, Hetty...248
JOHNSON, Jane Frances...334
JOHNSON, Judy...189
JOHNSON, Leonora...184
JOHNSON, Linnie...196
JOHNSON, Lottie R....85
JOHNSON, Louisa...160
JOHNSON, Lucie F....59
JOHNSON, Lucy F....49
JOHNSON, Lydia...103
JOHNSON, Martha...70
JOHNSON, Mary...100, 171
JOHNSON, Mary d/o Dolly Poindexter...4
JOHNSON, Mary T....186
JOHNSON, Matilda...318
JOHNSON, Mattie...193
JOHNSON, Merian...267
JOHNSON, Mildred Ann...247
JOHNSON, Nannie...165
JOHNSON, Nicey...7
JOHNSON, Sallie E....334
JOHNSON, Sarah Ann d/o Harriet Gregory...274
JOHNSON, Sarah Catherine...286
JOHNSON, Sarah F....252
JOHNSON, Susan d/o William B.& Martha Lewis...47
JOHNSON, Virginia S....43

JOHNSON. Maria d/o Moses & Juna Coleman...149
JOHNSTON, Phillis...256
JOHNSTON, Ruther O....310
JOHNSTON, Sally...113
JONES, Amanda S....62
JONES, Angelina...62
JONES, Ann...323
JONES, Anna E....49
JONES, Annie...238
JONES, Annie J....177
JONES, Annie Laurie...25
JONES, Cappie B....267
JONES, Carrie E....249
JONES, Edmonia H....236
JONES, Eliza C....300
JONES, Frances A....38
JONES, Georgeana...53
JONES, Gillie Frances...140
JONES, Harriet S....203
JONES, Ida L....83
JONES, Isabella...347
JONES, Isadora...148
JONES, Jennie...15
JONES, Julia A....91
JONES, Leanna...40
JONES, Lelia E....5
JONES, Lizzie...116
JONES, Lucie...186
JONES, Lucy Ann...47
JONES, Magdalene L....190
JONES, Maggie A....25
JONES, Malvina...229
JONES, Martha Olivia...60
JONES, Martha T....48
JONES, Mary B....277
JONES, Mary C....35, 47
JONES, Mary C. d/o William & Ann T.Brumley...33
JONES, Mary E....303
JONES, Mary E. d/o Garland Chewning...59

JONES, Mary E.V....58
JONES, Mary
   Ellen...327
JONES, Mary J....239, 294
JONES, Mary Jane...180
JONES, Mary
   Susan...130
JONES, Mollie...116
JONES, Myrdie D....131
JONES, Pricilla
   S....180
JONES, Rebecca...345
JONES, Rebecca L....52
JONES, Ricey E....325
JONES, Sallie J....314
JONES, Sarah...48, 334
JONES, Sarah E....287
JONES, Susan H....150
JONES, Virginia
   A....20, 310
JORDAN, Mary A....243
KEETON, Mildred
   L....109
KEITH, Helen J....44
KELLY, Ida B....239
KENDALL, Ida A....265
KENDALL, Octavia
   A....85
KENDALL, Rosa V....42
KENDIG, Agness A....99
KENNEDY, Fannie...107
KENNEDY, Louisa
   W.S....157
KENNEDY, Lucy M....210
KENNEDY, Selinda...310
KENT, Martha C. d/o
   Robert &
   M.E.Hicks...347
KENT, Sarah J....282
KING, Geneva C....176
KING, Gineva
   Chase...176
KING, Ida...72
KING, Mary...106
KING, Mary P. d/o John
   & Sarah
   Haines...130
KING, Music D....182
KING, Sarah...301
KING, Virginia
   A....348
KINGER, Virginia
   W....23

KISHPAUGH, Martha
   J....259
KISHPAUGH, Martha
   O....235
KNIGHT, Ann E....269
KNIGHTEN, Barbara
   A....145
KNIGHTON, Roberta
   L....183
KNIGHTON, Virginia
   E....112
KNOX, Sally...275
KRONK, Etta May...223
KRONK, Mary
   Hoover...255
KUBE, Mary G....260
KUBE, Mary M....257
LACY, Clara E....44
LACY, E.Lee...186
LACY, Elizabeth
   Bryan...175
LACY, Lucy L....200
LACY, Orilla M....318
LANCASTER, Amanda
   C....215
LANCASTER, Ann
   E....227
LANCASTER, Eliza
   A....215
LANCASTER, Sarah
   Ann...237
LANCASTER, Sarah
   E....308
LANCASTER, Sarah Jane
   d/o James M.Jacobs
   & Lucy
   Finney...101
LANCASTER, Susan...261
LANCASTER,
   Virginia...244
LANDIS, Amanda
   H....277
LANDRAM, Annie
   B....241
LANDRAM, Bettie
   G....56
LANDRAM, Duley...241
LANDRAM, Georgeanna A.
   d/o William &
   J.A.Shepherd...70
LANDRAM, M.A....83
LANDRAM, Mary F....168
LANDRAM, Mollie
   F....319

LANDRUM, Annie F....4
LANE, Nellie M....292
LANE, Rhoda F....203
LARMAND, Lucy Ann...318
LAURENCE, Sally...139
LAUSON. Fanny d/o Charles & Rosetta Gordon...15
LAWSON, Fanny...45
LAWSON, Maggie...174
LAYTON, Agnes H....245
LEATHERS, Betsy...64
LEAVELL, Fanny G....190
LEAVELL, Ida Gayle...152
LEAVELL, Mollie A....97
LEE, Alice...163
LEE, Ann...118
LEE, Harriet E....157
LEE, Lititia R....206
LEE, Mary...342
LEE, Willieann...27
LEECH, Lillie W....250
LEITCH, Eliza A....344
LEITCH, Eliza F....130
LEITCH, Elizabeth A....142
LEITCH, Ellen E....95
LEITCH, Ida A....13
LEITCH, Lucy A....234
LEVELY, Annie M....50
LEVY, Lovely...198
LEVY, Millie A....136
LEVY, Mollie...333
LEVY, Tama...306
LEWIS, Adeline A....253
LEWIS, Aggie...155
LEWIS, Alma A....347
LEWIS, Amanda...123
LEWIS, Ann...113
LEWIS, Ann Eliza...209
LEWIS, Annie...68, 216
LEWIS, Bettie d/o Robert Lewis & Sylvia Coleman...220
LEWIS, Betty...292
LEWIS, Betty Ann...284
LEWIS, Caroline...323
LEWIS, Carrie E....58

LEWIS, Easter...14
LEWIS, Elibletus(?)...219
LEWIS, Eliza...196, 198
LEWIS, Elizabeth...9
LEWIS, Emma C....37
LEWIS, Emma d/o Isaac & Maria Brown...288
LEWIS, Ester...14
LEWIS, Fairy Belle...54
LEWIS, Fanny...72
LEWIS, Frances...159, 175
LEWIS, Frances E....300
LEWIS, Frances E. d/o J.& B.Halley...300
LEWIS, Frances s/o Willis & Jennie Taylor...15
LEWIS, Georgiana...1
LEWIS, H.E....16
LEWIS, Hettie...37
LEWIS, Julia...262
LEWIS, Kate Lightfoot...304
LEWIS, Louisa J. d/o Robert & Jane Haney...133
LEWIS, Louisa Jane...299
LEWIS, Lucy...26
LEWIS, Lucy A....337
LEWIS, Lucy A. d/o Edie Anderson...109
LEWIS, Lucy Ann...194
LEWIS, Margaret d/o Julia Samuel...310
LEWIS, Margarett...315
LEWIS, Maria...37
LEWIS, Mary...199, 306
LEWIS, Mary Ann...82, 291
LEWIS, Mary Belle...152
LEWIS, Mary E....1
LEWIS, Mary Eliza...159
LEWIS, Mary F....195
LEWIS, Matilda...219

LEWIS, Matilda d/o Sam
   & I.Gordon...284
LEWIS, Mattie...190
LEWIS, Matty...191
LEWIS, Mozelle...226
LEWIS, Nancy...102
LEWIS, Nannie...16
LEWIS, Pamilia d/o
   Herndon & Mahala
   Learndow...52
LEWIS, Ruther d/o
   Albert & Nelly
   Hambleton...70
LEWIS, Sarah d/o R.&
   A.Taylor...173
LEWIS, Sarah E....199
LEWIS, Susan...29, 95, 296
LEWIS, Verona Z....280
LEWIS, Virginia
   A....30, 336
LILLY, Eliza...168
LINDSAY, Charlotte...312
LINDSAY, Clara...341
LINDSAY, Mary Susan...317
LINDSAY, Mildred...312
LINDSAY, Susan...68
LIPSCOMB, Agness...284
LIPSCOMB, Amanda...15
LIPSCOMB, B.F....336
LIPSCOMB, Bettie F....336
LIPSCOMB, Isabella F....138
LIPSCOMB, Judy D....26
LIPSCOMB, Martha F....158
LIPSCOMB, Quincey...273
LIPSCOMB, Sallie L.
   d/o John L.& Mary
   E.Andrews...123
LIPSCOMB, Virginia C....91
LLAHEWRES(?), Eugenia...326
LLOYD, Addie...327
LOMAX, Maria...16
LOMAX, Sarah...94
LONG, Bellzora B....291

LONG, Dorothea A....238
LONG, Eliza...289
LONG, Elizabeth H. d/o
   Henry C.&
   Elizabeth
   H.Sutton...49
LONG, Emma I....291
LONG, Hardinia...266
LONG, Jane F....19
LONG, Lucy...289
LONG, Mary E....311
LONG, Ophelia E....50
LOURY, Sarah C. d/o
   Jefferson Wright &
   Sarah Wright...83
LOVING, Jane...18
LUCAS, Ann E....265
LUCAS, Elizabeth d/o
   Troy & Martha
   Williams...340
LUCAS, Sarah A....296
LUCK, Barbara A....204
LUCK, Jeannette Maxie...339
LUCK, Lucy E....205
LUCK, M.A....99
LUCK, M.F....11
LUCK, Martha A.E. d/o
   Robert E.& Pamilia
   A.Payne...237
LUCK, Mary E....11
LUCK, Mary W....328
LUCK, Mollie...186
LUCK, S.E....205
LUDLEY, Mary...174
LUMPKIN, Lucy W....221
LUMSDEN, Jane Elizabeth...18
LUMSDEN, Sarah M....76
LUMSDEN, Virginia A....211
LYTTLE, Louisa J. d/o
   Hugh & Lucinda
   Satterwhite...231
MACON, Sarah F....124
MADDOX, Lydia A....301
MADISON, Ellen...172
MADISON, Mary...314
MADISON, Nelly...183
MADISON, Sally...71
MAGRUDER, Judy...85
MAGRUDER, Virginia Watson...322

MALLORY,
    Columbia...158
MALLORY,
    Cornelia...226
MALLORY, Eveline
    T....118
MALSBERGER, Emily W.
    d/o Thomas & Mary
    Woodall...53
MANN, Georgia
    Anna...240
MANN, Lula L....98
MANN, W.M....26
MANSFIELD, Annis...306
MANSFIELD,
    Easter...282
MANSFIELD, Georgie
    J....235
MANSFIELD, Louise
    F....29
MANSFIELD, Mary
    Jane...118
MANSFIELD, Mary
    L....305
MANSFIELD, Susan
    M....278
MANUEL, Betty...67
MANUEL, Ella...306
MANUEL, Fannie...85
MARSHALL,
    Isabelle...155
MARSHALL, Lucy
    F....174
MARSHALL, Sarah
    Cordelia...169
MARTELS, Elfride
    M....74
MARTIN, Amanda...12, 13
MARTIN, Amanda
    E....109
MARTIN, Annie...223
MARTIN, Christianna
    Mary d/o Jacob
    Riley & Mary
    Hicks...201
MARTIN, Julia...173
MARTIN, Julia A....236
MARTIN, Lavinia
    E....90
MARTIN Lucilla...209
MARTIN, Lucy
    Ellen...111
MARTIN, Martha
    J....221
MARTIN, Mary...278
MARTIN, Mary Ann...208
MARTIN, Mary E....340
MARTIN, Mary
    Elizabeth...318
MARTIN, Mary J....76
MARTIN, Mary J. W...76
MARTIN, Parthenia...18
MARTIN, Sallie
    B....134
MASON, A.E....100
MASON, Aby...144
MASON, Ann C....325
MASON, Cally...168
MASON, Catherine d/o
    Abner Clark...227
MASON, Elizabeth
    J....272
MASON, Ellen A....46
MASON, Emily
    Frances...121
MASON, Lucy A....2
MASON, Lucy L....210
MASON, Lydia J....272
MASON, Sarah
    Jane...225
MASON, Sarah
    Margaret...121
MASON, Susan S....145
MASSEY, Angelina
    B....211
MASSEY, Eliza...191
MASSEY, Ella
    Maude...64
MASSEY, Lellis R. d/o
    A.B.Mastin...25
MASSEY, Lillie R. d/o
    A.B.Mastin...25
MASSEY, Lizzie
    L....254
MASSEY, Lucinda...296
MASSEY, Maria L....347
MASSEY, Nina E....241
MASSEY, S.E....20
MASTIN, Alice T....211
MASTIN, Amanda
    Jane...287
MASTIN, Bettie L....53
MASTIN, Cordelia...76
MASTIN, Dora...287

MASTIN, Eliza Ann d/o Lewis & Elizabeth Faulconer...188
MASTIN, Emma B....267
MASTIN, Lucy B....259
MASTIN, M.L....327
MASTIN, Nancy C....148
MASTIN, Sarah...348
MASTIN, Sarah d/o Elizabeth Faulconer...255
MAXWELL, Ella...213
MAZE, Ann Matilda...82
McALLISTER, Catherine...140
McCALLEY, Susan...333
McCONCHIE, Emma L....180
McGARY, Eunice L....131
McGARY, Lena E....113
McGARY, Lucy A....36
McGEE, Agnes...250
McGEE, Amanda R....166
McGEE, Anie Bell...61
McGEE, Annie Belle...62
McGEE, Fancy P....301
McGEE, Mattie L....59
McGEE, Olivia D....129
McGEHEE,A.T....218
McINTOSH, Alvia...173
McINTOSH, Margaret...246
McLEOD, Mollie L....285
McMULLEN, Ann B. d/o William B.Boston & Sarah Powell...24
McWHIRT, Addie B....240
McWHIRT, Annie...77
McWHIRT, Kate...166
MERCER, Martha...193
MEREDITH, Ursula...126
MICHIL, Lucy...315
MICKENS, Lula...69
MICKLEBOROUGH, Isabella P. d/o Taverner W.& Sarah Holladay...241
MIDDLEBROOK, Lucy C....145
MILES, Maria...168

MILES, Siller...31
MILLES, Martha...259
MILLS, Alice...162
MILLS, Ella...192
MILLS, Emma V....350
MILLS, Frances Jane...177
MILLS, Francis Jane...176
MILLS, Josephine...175
MILLS, Peggie...254
MINER, Anna...218
MINER, Kitty...198
MINNICK, Minerva Jane...170
MINOR, Addie...160
MINOR, Bettie...267
MINOR, Clara...314
MINOR, Grace...332
MINOR, Jane...199
MINOR, Julia...63
MINOR, Kitty Ann...167
MINOR, Laura...291
MINOR, Lucette...320
MINOR, Martha...307
MINOR, Melvina...199
MINOR, Sarah d/o Thornton & Louisa Poindexter...200
MINOR, Sarah Jane...334
MITCHELL, Alverta C....233
MITCHELL, Catharine A.C. d/o Isabella M.Osbourne...341
MITCHELL, Edna Earl...330
MITCHELL, Maggie B....61
MONTAGUE, Alice...200
MONTAGUE, Emma...275
MONTAGUE, Julia...335
MONTEITH, Ella...61
MOORE, Catherine...15
MOORE, E.Belle...110
MOORE, Elizabeth T....31
MOORE, Fannie B....223
MOORE, S....265
MOORE, Sarah M....343
MORGAN, Mary E....19

MORIS, Doratha Ellen
　d/o Cubid & Lucy
　Hall...33
MORRIS, Carrie...139
MORRIS, Eliza
　Ann...212
MORRIS, Margaret...16
MORRIS, Margaret
　F....87
MORRISON, Bessie
　A....240
MORRISON, Eliza
　A....131
MORRISON, Ella...56
MORRISON, Emma
　J....217
MORRISON, Ida K....303
MORSE, Elizabeth...35
MORSE, Polly...268
MORTON, Bessie
　W....207
MORTON, Fenton W....87
MORTON, Jennie
　C....292
MORTON, Mary E....343
MORTON, Sallie A....17
MORTON, Susan M....113
MOSS, Ida...73
MOSS, Lucy A....5
MOSS, Lucy Ann...5
MOSS, Mary L....30
MULLEN,
　Catheline...250
MULLEN, Maggie
　L....167
MULLEN, Mary
　Agnes...125
MURDOUGH, Lucy
　T....101
MURPHY, Joanna...135
MURPHY, Kittie...201
MURPHY, Lucinda...148
MURPHY, Maggie L....62
MURRAY, Carolina
　S....50
MURRAY, Phillis...330
MUSE, Annie E....87
MYERS, Milly...230
NALLE, Mildred
　Wallace...25
NASH, Julia A. d/o
　Charles & Alcy
　Martin...268
NASH, Mary...201

NASH, Mary F....201
NELSON, Sarah Frances
　d/o Priscilla
　White...313
NEWMAN, Jane E....16
NEWMAN, Bettie
　B....292
NEWMAN, Fanny B....15
NEWMAN, Julia...124
NEWMAN, Lucy C....190
NEWMAN, Mary E....293
NEWMAN, Sarah M....245
NEWMAN,
　Wilhelmia...213
NEWTON, Edith...12
NICHOLSON, Mary
　J....234
NICHOLSON, Sarah
　E....234
NOLAN, Mary...176
NOLAN, Mary A....176
NUSSEY, Mary J....105
OAKS, Belvedary...63
OAKS, Ella D....178
OAKS, Mildred A....340
OLDS, Lucy A....233
OLIVER, Annie...215
OLIVER, Catherine Ann
　d/o Thomas &
　M.Grinstone...152
OLIVER, Mary...55
OLIVER, Mary A....55
OLIVER, Rosa...27
OLIVER, Sarah...204
OLIVER, V.S....177
ORR, Eliza A....308
OSWALD, Annie A....6
OVERTON, Hannah...162
OWENS, Anne M....215
OWENS, Maggie J....318
OWENS, Mary J....149
PALMER, Georgie
　B.D....257
PALMORE, Sallie
　L....138
PANNILL, Louisa
　D....150
PARKER, Ann
　Maria...171
PARKER, Julia M....202
PARKER, Lelia J....300
PARKER, Lucie J....335
PARKER, Martha...258
PARKER, Mary...45

PARKER, Mollie M....147
PARROTT, Lucy Jane...286
PARROTT, Martha A....119
PARROTT, Sallie A....21
PARTLOW, Hidenia...92
PARTLOW, Matta L....60
PARTLOW, Ophelia E....255
PATES, Henrietta...115
PATES, Mary A....232
PATES, Susan...263
PATTILLO. Roza L....236
PAYNE, Alice F....239
PAYNE, Anna G....53
PAYNE, Annie d/o Charles R.& Mary Jones...278
PAYNE, Annie R....296
PAYNE, Annie S....206
PAYNE, Bettie...178
PAYNE, Betty...100
PAYNE, Cornelia A....323
PAYNE, Emma C....11
PAYNE, Estelle...185
PAYNE, Leah A....332
PAYNE, Lucie E....236
PAYNE, Lucy A....332
PAYNE, M.H....239
PAYNE, Mary A....272
PAYNE, Mary E....18
PAYNE, Mary S....215
PAYNE, Roena...252
PAYNE, Sallie N....117
PAYNE, Sarah H.B....99
PAYNE, Susan Ann...266
PAYNE, Texanar...52
PAYNE, Virginia D....238
PAYTES, Dollie E....294
PAYTES, Harriet E....235
PAYTES, M.A....179
PAYTES, Sarah E. d/o James & Sarah Marton...295
PAYTES, Sarah Frances...191

PAYTES, Virginia A....115
PEACHER, Mary F....144
PEAKE, Lucy A....91
PEAKE, Mary H....265
PEAKE, Mary H. d/o...266
PEATROSS, Clara...270
PEMBERTON, Fanny d/o George & Ellen Butzner...215
PEMBERTON, Lizzie S....81
PENDLETON, Bettie E....170
PENDLETON, Edith May...135
PENDLETON, Elizabeth d/o John & D.Morton...261
PENDLETON, Ellen...288
PENDLETON, Lily M. d/o T.W.& Helen B.Holladay...105
PENDLETON, Lucy E....152
PENDLETON, Lucy E. d/o Joel T.& Fanny Lewis...299
PENDLETON, Rosa L....4
PENDLETON, Sallie A....331
PENDLETON, Virginia...71
PERREY, Elizabeth...166
PERRY, Amanda F....239
PERRY, Berta A....214
PERRY, Catherine W....325
PERRY, Ida F....92
PERRY, Isabell...41
PERRY, Josephine...280
PERRY, Julia...252
PERRY, Mary A....80
PERRY, Mildred A....46
PETITT, Columbia F....107
PETTIS, Eliza S....31
PETTIS, Grace...162
PEYTON, Eliza P....183
PEYTON, Georgianna...267
PEYTON, Ida L....322

PEYTON, Jane M....253
PEYTON, Mattie A.E....13
PEYTON, Sallie M....50
PEYTON, T.A.R....165
PHILIPS, Victoria E....224
PIERCE, Delphia A....128
PIERCE, Eliza H....128
PIERCE, Jane...191
PIERCE, R.R....49
PILCHER, Edmonia B....177
PILIAM, A.E....231
POINDEXTER, Ann...152
POINDEXTER, Betty...162
POINDEXTER, Frances...338
POINDEXTER, Louisa...30
POINDEXTER, Maria L....125
POLLARD, Isabella...232
POLLARD, Lucy I....268
POLLARD, Nora...279
POOL, Ida A....114
POOL, Mary E....137
POOL, Nannie Irene...254
POOL, Roberta A....110
POOLE, Allie K....109
POOLE, Bertie H....83
POOLE, Maggie M....297
PORTER, Alice d/o Allen Long...159
PORTER, Fannie W....151
PORTER, Martha...235
PORTER, Mary Jane...317
PORTER, Susan...257
PORTER, Virginia O.S....143
POUND, Lula...217
POUND, M.E....111
POUND, Mattie A....120
POWELL, d/o Theopolus & Laura Powell age 20 S POB & POR Spotsylvania...250

POWELL, Alene Estelle...148
POWELL, Annie L....63
POWELL, C.M....313
POWELL, Elizabeth H....210
POWELL, Fanny...3
POWELL, Mabel...258
POWELL, Mary Ann...26
POWELL, Mary E....328
POWELL, Nancy Smith...69
POWELL, Sommerville...290
POWELL, Surella June...74
POWELL, Susan M....316
PRATT, Martha...348
PRESLEY, Emily...102
PRICE, Caroline...281
PRICE, Catherine...112
PRICE, Jennie...344
PRICE, Kate E....253
PRICE, Louisa H. d/o Curtis Wilhoit & Maria Louisa Harrison...125
PRICE, Sarah...108
PRIEST, Eliza A....103
PRITCHETT, A.B....4
PRITCHETT, Lillian May...171
PRITCHETT, Lucy H....254
PRITCHETT, Lucy T....296
PRITCHETT, Mollie J....297
PRITCHETT, Sarah C....136
PROCTOR, Bettie A....177
PROCTOR, D.E....96
PROCTOR, Ellen...72
PROCTOR, Ellen R....175
PROCTOR, M.E....19
PROCTOR, Madaline...22
PROCTOR, Mary A....96
PROCTOR, R.F....116
PRUETT, Martha E....93
PUGSLEY, Mary...161
PULLIAM, A.Myrtle...89
PULLIAM, Annie C....16

PULLIAM, Cora V....6
PULLIAM, Ivy S....82
PULLIAM, Josephine
    L....150
PULLIAM, L.Noel...279
PULLIAM, Ophelia d/o
    L.&
    M.A.Partlow...316
PURKS, Martha...12
PURSLEY, Mary T. d/o
    M.C.&
    E.Baxter...238
QUARLES, Frances...324
QUARLES, Mary...41
QUARLES, Olive...305
QUARLES, Susan...91
QUIMBY, Alfa S....309
QUIMBY, Mary J. d/o
    Charles & Harriet
    L.Stewart...178
QUISENBERRY, Ann
    F....40
QUISENBERRY,
    J.H....233
QUISENBERRY,
    Jannie...261
QUISENBERRY, L.E. d/o
    Gideon & Sallie
    Flippo...315
RAWLINGS, Clara
    L....28
RAWLINGS, Edmonia
    F....27
RAWLINGS, Fanny...46
RAWLINGS, Junie
    D....45
RAWLINGS, Kitty...127
RAWLINGS, Louisa...345
RAWLINGS, Lucy
    M....155
RAWLINGS, N.J....71
RAWLINGS,
    Octabia...300
RAWLINGS,
    Octavia...164
RAWLINGS, Sarah
    J....82
RAWLINGS,A.E....29
REARELEY, Angy...282
RECTOR, Martha...128
REDD, Ella...189
REDMAN, Mary...19
REDMOND, Jane
    Willie...104

REED, Mary Ann...317
RENNOLDS,
    Catherine...340
RENNOLDS, Rachael...76
RENOLS, Alice...44
REYNOLDS, Ann
    Wise...260
REYNOLDS, Eliza...332
REYNOLDS, Lucy
    A....339
REYNOLDS, Lucy
    Mary...95
REYNOLDS, Sallie
    C....256
REYNOLDS, Sarah
    B....245
RHOADES, Eliza...312
RHOADES, Lucy...259
RICHARDS, Ann...350
RICHARDS, Emilie
    LeG....93
RICHARDS, Emma
    D....329
RICHARDS, Marie
    Ann...331
RICHARDS, Susan
    E....338
RICHARDSON, Daisy...42
RICHARDSON,
    Emily...246
RICHARDSON, Kate
    A....158
RICHARDSON, Sarah
    F....163
RICHESON, Frances
    D....158
RICHESON, Parthania
    S....85
RICHESON, Sallie
    D....148
RICKER, Mary S....228
RILEY, Ophelia...54
RINER, Mary E....132
RINER, Sarah
    A.E....346
ROACH, Ann...237
ROACH, Sarah Ann...216
ROACH, Susan M....259
ROBERSON,
    Elizabeth...308
ROBERSON, Katie
    J....223
ROBERSON, Mandy...106

ROBERSON, Sarah
    E....267
ROBERTS, Julia...113
ROBEY, Lula B....232
ROBINSON, Amelia...201
ROBINSON, Ann...174
ROBINSON, Ann E....256
ROBINSON, Annie d/o
    Trenton Chew &
    Florence
    Minor...74
ROBINSON, Capitola B.
    d/o Eli M.& Mary
    E.Jones...110
ROBINSON,
    Caroline...56
ROBINSON,
    Charlotte...310
ROBINSON, Dora
    F....330
ROBINSON, Emily...299
ROBINSON, Harriet
    L....255
ROBINSON, Jane
    E....261
ROBINSON, Lillie
    May...90
ROBINSON, Lucy
    S....336
ROBINSON,
    Malvina...196
ROBINSON, Martha...184
ROBINSON, Martha
    E....211
ROBINSON, Martha
    J....263
ROBINSON, Mary...295
ROBINSON, Mary
    B....221
ROBINSON, Mary
    J....301
ROBINSON,
    Matilda...125
ROBINSON, Rosa...195
ROBINSON, Susie
    A....288
ROBINSON. Sarah
    A....294
RODGERS, Margaret
    R....230
ROGERS, Elizabeth
    F....106
ROLLINS,
    Catherine...94
ROLLINS, Frances d/o
    Sam & Amy
    Coleman...9
ROLLINS, Frances d/o
    Sam & Annie
    Coleman...9
ROLLS, Martha
    Jane...264
RONQUEST, Mollie
    E....337
ROOF, Annie...242
ROOSA, Annie G....80
ROSE, Olivia...76
ROSS, Hattie...9
ROSS, Isabella...299
ROSS, Virginia...70, 71
ROUTT, Dorenda
    A....212
ROUTT, Martha E....306
ROW, Adalade E....263
ROW, Mary E....256
ROWE, B.B....258
ROY, Nelly...3
RUCKER, Columbia...150
RUSSELL,
    Catherine...191
RYAN, Judith A....139
RYERSON, Ada B....211
SACRA, Addie V....240
SACRA, Alice...48
SACRA, Fanny...275
SACRA, Martha
    A....121, 245
SACRA, Mary E....98
SACRA, Mary S....100
SACRA, Mary V....111
SACRA, Nannie M....42
SACRA, Nettie B....111
SACRA, Sarah A....78
SACRA, Sarah F....225
SACROW, Mary E. d/o
    John B.& Clara
    Burruss...99
SALE, F.A....338
SAMUEL, Abbie...54
SAMUEL, Adaline
    C....31
SAMUEL, Ann d/o Katy
    Wortham...67
SAMUEL, Annie B....331
SAMUEL, Arkansas
    C.V....281
SAMUEL, Carrie V....68

SAMUEL, Ella...222
SAMUEL, L.M....13
SAMUEL, Lula B....189
SAMUEL, Winnie...317
SAMUELS, Nelly Ann...324
SANDERS, Elizabeth R....324
SANDERS, Lucy Ann...210
SANDERS, Mary C....22
SANDERS, Sarah Frances...256
SANDERS, Virginia...24
SANFORD, Agness...139
SANFORD, Jennie B....269
SANFORD, Nancy d/o Jefferson & Sarah Wright...185
SANFORD, Virginia...118
SARMAND, Josephine...231
SATTERWHITE, Mary A. d/o Rufus & Mary Jane Darlings...238
SATTERWHITE, Mary Ann...25
SAUNDERS, Emily...308
SAUNDERS, Sarah J....25
SCHOOLER, Betty S....349
SCHOOLER, Elizabeth B....345
SCHOOLER, Mattie A....129
SCHULTZ, Kate...236
SCHULZE, Anna E....93
SCHUYLER, Eliza E....234
SCHYLER, Mary E....14
SCOTT, Abbie...271
SCOTT, Ann E....116
SCOTT, Charlotte Ann Elizabeth...60
SCOTT, Elizabeth...218
SCOTT, Fannie A....313
SCOTT, Irene D....8
SCOTT, Iris...38
SCOTT, Lina A....57
SCOTT, Lucy...347

SCOTT, Lucy J. d/o Peter & Caroline Frazier...193
SCOTT, Mary H....165
SCOTT, Mary J....36
SCOTT, Mildred V....306
SCOTT, Nancy d/o Martha Johnson...51
SCOTT, Nannie d/o Robert J.& Mary A.Burruss...306
SCOTT, Phoebe...199
SCOTT, Robertine T....309
SCOTT, Sallie T.S....7
SCOTT, Susan...160
SCOTT, Willie Etta...188
SCRAIM(?), J.T....267
SEAY, Adra A....204
SEAY, Annie E....146, 147
SEAY, Emma L....92
SEAY, Mary C....120
SEE, Almyra A....42
SEE, Lucy Ellen...23
SEIDELL. Elizabeth A....258
SHACKLEFORD, Betty J....97
SHACKLEFORD, Elizabeth A....97
SHACKLEFORD, G.G....41
SHACKLEFORD, Mary Ann...158
SHACKLEFORD, Pricilla M....182
SHADLE, Edna A....131
SHEARS, Matie J....280
SHEETS, Mary Isabella Frances...182
SHELTON, Elvira...223
SHELTON, Lucinda F....253
SHELTON, Mary James...156
SHELTON, Susie J....130
SHEPARD, Susan...320
SHEPHERD, Henrietta...23

SHERMAN, Sylvia
  A....41
SHIFLETT, Sarah...112
SHIPLETT, Mildred
  Ann...156
SHOTWELL, Sarah
  J....221
SHULTZ, Lena...42
SHULZE, Mary E....190
SIBERT, Diana R....17
SIBERT, Mary J....222
SIMMS, Alverta
  V....188
SIMMS, Ann E....337
SIMMS, Betty A....137
SIMMS, Mattie M....276
SIMPSON, Elizabeth d/o
  Frances
  Shelton...192
SIMS, Lucy B....239
SISSON, Babe...214
SISSON, Miranda
  J....342
SKINKER, Jeannette
  C....320
SKINNER, Eliza
  A....120
SKINNER, Leanna...217
SLAUGHTER, Ann...312
SLAUGHTER, Courtney
  d/o George & Kitty
  Coleman...61
SLAUGHTER, Ella...266
SLAUGHTER, Laura B.
  d/o Isabella
  Corbin...233
SLAUGHTER,
  Lizzie...282
SMALLWOOD, Evelina d/o
  Thomas & Betsy
  Alsop...81
SMITH, A.O....7
SMITH, Addie E....14
SMITH, Agnes...123
SMITH, Ailsy G....34
SMITH, Angelina...75
SMITH, Ann E....39
SMITH, Anna L....281
SMITH, Anne Olivia...7
SMITH, Annie...341
SMITH, Arianna
  V....103
SMITH, Bell...229
SMITH, Bessie
  R.H....21
SMITH, Betsy d/o H.&
  M.Winsley...44
SMITH, Bettie...55
SMITH, Columbia
  C....181
SMITH, E.L....263
SMITH, Elizabeth...87
SMITH, Ellen...129
SMITH, Ellen J....247
SMITH, Elnora...193
SMITH, Fanny L....154
SMITH, Fanny M....283
SMITH, Frances
  S....207
SMITH, Ida L....39
SMITH, Inez V....192
SMITH, Jane...4
SMITH, Jane E....341
SMITH, Julia...198
SMITH, Laura...184,
  335
SMITH, Lucy J....264
SMITH, Margaret...65
SMITH, Margaret
  L....141
SMITH, Martha A....139
SMITH, Mary...73, 312
SMITH, Mary A....129
SMITH, Mary E....149
SMITH, Mary L....110
SMITH, Nancy...172
SMITH, Nannie M....90
SMITH, Polly...164
SMITH, Rowenna
  G....124
SMITH, Sallie A....127
SMITH, Sally...36
SMITH, Sarah E....295
SMITH, Sarah L....65
SMITH, Sarah M....45
SMITH, Serrepta
  A....244
SMITH, Susan J....93
SMITH, Virginia T. d/o
  John & Julia
  Curtis...132
SNEAD, Sarah A....186
SNEED, Milly...85
SNELLINGS, Annie
  J....236
SNELLINGS, Columbia
  J....216

SNOWDON, Caroline
  V....44
SOMMERVILLE, Jane
  E....22
SORRELL, Ann d/o
  Edmund Dunaway &
  Sally Knight...305
SORRELL, Edmonia
  M....80
SORRELL, Luella...81
SORRELL, Virginia
  C....205
SOUTHALL, Emma...72
SOUTHERLAND, Mary
  E....173
SOUTHERLIN,
  Elizabeth...4
SOUTHERLIN,
  Frances...281
SOUTHWORTH, Annie
  E....21
SOUTHWORTH,
  Louise...95
SOUTHWORTH, Susan
  C....208
SPENCER, Rosa...302
SPINDLE, E.A....78
SPINDLE, Virginia
  D....266
SPINDLE, Willie
  E....167
SPOTSWOOD, Martha
  P....256
STANARD, Bertie
  Belle...219
STANARD, Cora...189
STANARD,
  Cornelia...338
STANARD, Dilsy...194
STANARD, Dolly...189
STANARD,
  Elizabeth...159
STANARD, Fanny...101
STANARD, Fanny
  P....277
STANARD, Mary E....56
STANARD, Rose...320
STANARD, Winnie...116
STANLEY, Eliza...304
STANLEY,
  Jeannette...304
STANSBERRY, Julia
  Bell...109

STANSBURY, Letitia
  Y....74
STEPHENS, A....6
STEPHENS, Helen...290
STEPHENS, Huldah...220
STEPHENS, Jennie
  V....101
STEPHENS, Mary
  F....325
STEPHENS, S.S. d/o
  John T.& Susan
  Powell...209
STEPHENS, Sudie
  E....309
STEVENS, Ann M....164
STEVENS, Emma...48
STEWART, Cornelia
  Josephine...202
STEWART, Frances
  Cordelia...230
STEWART, Martha
  T....41
STEWART, Mary...197
STEWART, Mary W....194
STITZER,
  Elizabeth...45
STOVER, Lizzie...229
STRATTEN, Lula L....43
STRATTON, Edna...327
STRATTON, Josephine
  V....326
STRAUGHAN, Annie...271
STREET, Maggie...75
STUART, Malinda...2
STUBBLEFIELD,
  Sarah...302
STUBBLEFIELD,
  Susan...125
STUBBS, Emma J....238
STUBBS, Lollia...224
SULLIVAN, Ann...295
SULLIVAN, Annie E. d/o
  Charles M.C.& Anne
  E.Baxter...231
SULLIVAN, E....231
SULLIVAN, Emily
  F....16
SULLIVAN, Lenora...142
SULLIVAN, Mary...138
SULLIVAN, Mary
  F....170
SULLIVAN, R....301
SULLIVAN, Virginia
  F....176

SURLES, Ida V....273
SUTHERLAND,
    Catherine...285
SWEITZER, Maggie...347
SWEITZER, Roberta
    M....243
SWIFT, Anna C....57
SWIFT, Emma J....57
SWIFT, Irene I....136
SWIFT, M.E....3
SWIFT, Nellie...240
TALIAFERRO, Annie
    P....24
TALIAFERRO, Caroline
    d/o Moses & Fanny
    White...195
TALIAFERRO,
    Elizabeth...152
TALIAFERRO, Jane
    A....52
TALIAFERRO, Lucy
    W....27
TALIAFERRO, Mary...142
TALIAFERRO,
    Victoria...134
TALLEY, M.A....308
TALLEY, Mary A....298
TALLEY, Mary
    Alice...126
TALLEY, Mary J....176
TALLEY, Mary J. d/o
    William A.& Ann
    Robinson...275
TALLEY, Mattie
    J.C....202
TALLEY, Maud Z....124
TALLEY, Mollie E....5
TALLEY, Rosa May...132
TALLEY, S....319
TALLEY, Sarah
    E....137, 180
TALLEY, Sarah J....275
TAMPLIN, Sarah...181
TAPP, Harriet C....192
TAPP, Sarah E....23
TATE, Sarah M....77
TAYLOR, Amelia...144
TAYLOR, Ann E....115
TAYLOR, Ann M....90
TAYLOR, Anna Lee d/o
    Thomas & Isabella
    Towles...227
TAYLOR, Bessie
    Temple...277
TAYLOR, Betsy
    Hord...98
TAYLOR, Betty...179,
    180
TAYLOR, Catherine...63
TAYLOR, Daisy...343
TAYLOR, Doratha
    M....141
TAYLOR, Drusilla...158
TAYLOR, Ella...190
TAYLOR, Emma L....322
TAYLOR, G.P....303
TAYLOR, Hattie...306
TAYLOR, Isa B....39
TAYLOR, Julia...86
TAYLOR, Malvina...175
TAYLOR, Mary
    Ella...181
TAYLOR, Mary J. d/o
    J.B.& Mary
    Robinson...283
TAYLOR, Mary W. s/o
    Lewis
    Proctor...291
TAYLOR, Milly...291
TAYLOR, Polly...126
TAYLOR, Rebecca...113
TAYLOR, Rosa A....164
TAYLOR, Sallie...67
TAYLOR, Willie Ann...8
TELLER, Mary J....327
TEMPLE, Ella...5
TERRELL,
    Charlotte...53
TERRELL, Harriet A.
    d/o Armistead &
    Mary Jenkins...95
TERRELL, Marcia...194
TERRELL, Sallie...297
TERRILL, Betsy
    Veranda...121
TERRILL, Betty
    O....121
TERRILL,
    Elizabeth...206
TERRILL, Ellen...243
TERRILL, Emma
    Lovell...268
TERRILL, H.Irvin...143
TERRILL, Helen...247
TERRILL, Jane...349
TERRILL, Mary T....125
TERRILL, Sallie
    J....74

TERRILL, Susan H....279
TERRILL, Virginia...244
THACKER, Ann...49
THACKER, Eliza M. d/o Charles & Malinda Beazley...214
THACKER, Julia...45
THACKER, Martha...76
THACKER, Willie S....224
THOMAS, E.E....139
THOMAS, Ellen Douglas...175
THOMAS, Frances E....342
THOMAS, Jennie W....262
THOMAS, Lannie D....284
THOMAS, Laura...164
THOMAS, Mary Eliza...282
THOMAS, Mary J....212
THOMPKINS, Eva W....1
THOMPSON, Amanda C....22
THOMPSON, Delia...120
THOMPSON, Frances...254
THOMPSON, Maggie...30
THOMPSON, Virgie d/o Solomon & Mary Johnson...126
THORNTON, Annie...242
THORNTON, Grace...9
THORNTON, Indiana J....207
THORNTON, Malvina...155
THORNTON, Mary...161
THORNTON, Nelly...5
THORNTON, Pamelia...227
THORNTON, Rebecca...153
THRASHLY, Isabella...101
THRIFT, Virginia...237
THURSTON, Lucy M....262
TIBBS, Frances...174

TINDER, Adaline Tutt...188
TINDER, Bettie F....187
TINDER, Elizabeth J....308
TINDER, Elizabeth L....261
TINDER, Laura E....242
TINDER, Lucy Ann...326
TINDER, Lucy F....108
TINDER, Lunnuie(?) Irene...187
TINDER, Margaret...58
TINDER, Samuella...242
TINDER, Sarah E....261
TINDER, Sarah M....308
TINDER, Susan S....107
TINDER, Virginia E....60
TODD, Sallie W....94
TOMPKINS, Eva W....1
TOMPKINS, Frances B....60
TOMPKINS, M.A....313
TOMPKINS, Martha E....243
TOMPKINS, Nannie R....57
TOOMBS, Mary...250
TOWELLS, Julia Ann...24
TOWLES, Anna...300
TOWLES, Bettie C. d/o Thomas W.Gray & Sallie Lucas...119
TOWLES, Carrie C....88
TOWLES, Emma...320
TOWLES, Emma V....95
TOWLES, Lizzie W....122
TOWLES, Mary C....311
TOWLES, Nannie W....315
TRAYNHAM, Mary...156
TRAYNHAM, Menta...33
TRIBBLE, M.H....47
TRIGG, Lucy M....140
TRUEL, Margaret L....132
TURNER, Bettie...322
TURNER, Caroline...289
TURNER, Lavinia...318

TURNER, Lucretia M....315
TURNER, Mollie...136
TURNER, Rose...163
TURNLEY, Mary M....93
TURNLEY, Sarah M....25
TWYMAN, Julia D. d/o Claiborne & Mary Duvall...110
TWYMAN,M.B. (possibly Mildred Buford Twyman)...313
TYLER, Agnes A....134
TYLER, Delilah...85
TYLER, Jane...86
TYLER, Maggie L....294
TYLER, Mary...329
TYLER, Melvina...193
TYLER, Milley...79
TYLER, Rachel E....143
TYLER, Sarah d/o Abby Rodgers...10
VANNCETTER, Nancy M....58
WAITE, Lucy M....252
WAITE, Olive B....253
WALDEN, Susie C....316
WALKER, Catherine...286
WALKER, Delphia...197
WALKER, Easter...196
WALKER, Eliza...269
WALKER, Eliza J....66
WALKER, Jane...217
WALKER, Margaret...103
WALKER, Mary...161
WALKER, Milly...271
WALKER, Mollie W....233
WALKER, Rhoda...65
WALKER, Sally Ann...307
WALKER, Tamar...293
WALLACE, A.E....232
WALLACE, Lucy...304
WALLACE, Margaret S....146
WALLACE, Martha A....3
WALLACE, Mary C....233
WALLER, D.P....327
WALLER, Elizabeth...237
WALLER, Fannie Elizabeth...88

WALLER, Jane F. d/o Richard G.& Susan R.Buchanan...319
WALLER, Laura May...70
WALLER, M. Jennie...329
WALLER, Martha P....139
WALLER, Mary M....303
WALLER, Olivia D....319
WALLER, S.A....232
WALLER, Sallie A....290
WALLER, Susan R....230
WARD, Fannie...116
WARD, Issabell...303
WARE, Lucy...64
WARE, Rachael...219
WARE, Rachel...330
WARE, Rachel d/o Jacob & Clara Stanard...200
WARE, William...269
WASHINGTON, Alice B....336
WASHINGTON, Ida...292
WASHINGTON, Josephine...89
WASHINGTON, M.E....14
WASHINGTON, Maria...272
WASHINGTON, Martha...214
WASHINGTON, Mary...24
WASHINGTON, Mary Frances D....61
WASHINGTON, Nora...138
WASHINGTON, Rose...297
WASHINGTON, Rose d/o Charles & Ann Hill...109
WATKINS, Mollie B....264
WATSON, Evelina...131
WATSON, Frances...225
WATSON, Grace...159
WATSON, Ida...46
WATSON, Maggie L....307
WATSON, Mary...299
WATSON, Sarah J....107
WAYLAND, Julia A....144

WAYLAND, Kate H....87
WAYLAND, Susan C....185
WEAVER, Jane...203
WEBB, Annie E....9
WEBB, Charity...57
WEBB, Kate Fulton...328
WEBB, Maggie J....187
WEBB, Martha J....325
WEBB, Sarah A.E....144
WEEDON, M.E....1
WEEDON, Rosa...30
WELCH, Mary A....179
WELCH, Virginia E....298
WELLFORD, E.S....309
WHARTEN, Fannie P....191
WHARTON, Carrie...199
WHARTON, Harriet S....327
WHARTON, Jennie C....37
WHARTON, Mary F....25
WHARTON, Nancy d/o Thomas & Eliz. Thornton...185
WHARTON, Nannie T....206
WHARTON, Virginia A....347
WHEELER, Adeline...333
WHEELER, Alice A....213
WHEELER, Bettie J....32
WHEELER, Betty A....11
WHEELER, Eddie J....130
WHEELER, Isabel B....131
WHEELER, Laura...134
WHEELER, Lizzie...250
WHEELER, Lucy Ann...165
WHEELER, M.J....36
WHEELER, Martha Jane...49
WHITAKER, Hannah...251
WHITE, Amelia...112
WHITE, Cornelia...119
WHITE, Elizabeth M....268
WHITE, Ella...228
WHITE, Gabreilla R....257
WHITE, Georgeanna...66
WHITE, Isabella...199
WHITE, Jennie L....98
WHITE, Judy...219
WHITE, Juliet...207
WHITE, Laura...173
WHITE, Lucy Ann...302
WHITE, Maggie...218
WHITE, Maria d/o Ann Washington...41
WHITE, Mary A....268
WHITE, Mollie...43
WHITE, Molly...43
WHITE, Sarah...329, 333
WHITE, Susan...228
WHITE, Vicie...44
WHITE, Winnie B....29
WHITLOCK, Mary E....146
WHITLOCK, Mary F....10
WHITLOCK, S.L....111
WHITLOCK, Sallie B....39
WHITUS, Nannie...167
WIATT, Hannah...10
WIGGLESWORTH, Elizabeth...121
WIGGLESWORTH, Ellen...86
WIGGLESWORTH, Hardenia...226
WIGGLESWORTH, Henrietta...350
WIGGLESWORTH, Lovely...321
WIGLESWORTH, Angelina...304
WIGLESWORTH, Anna...34
WIGLESWORTH, Jane...220
WIGLESWORTH, Matilda...137
WIGLESWORTH, Mattie J....255
WIGLESWORTH, Milly...168
WILHOIT, Louisa H....251
WILHOIT, Pamelia Ann...319

WILHOIT, Sarah E....31
WILKERSON, Eliza...71
WILKERSON, Maggie...12
WILKERSON, Mary...17
WILKERSON, Victoria...212
WILKINS, Mollie...14
WILLIAMS, Amelia S....341
WILLIAMS, Ann C....72
WILLIAMS, Annie...108
WILLIAMS, Bettie...167, 168, 205
WILLIAMS, Elizabeth N....339
WILLIAMS, Fanny...262
WILLIAMS, Hannah...320
WILLIAMS, Hardenia...161
WILLIAMS, Josephine...289
WILLIAMS, Julia...35
WILLIAMS, Julia d/o Gabriel & Dollie Montague...339
WILLIAMS, Landonia...248
WILLIAMS, Lavinia...119
WILLIAMS, Lucy...38
WILLIAMS, Maggie...324
WILLIAMS, Mary...117, 314
WILLIAMS, Mary Blair...191
WILLIAMS, Mildred P....23
WILLIAMS, Nannie...20
WILLIAMS, Rosa B....257
WILLIAMS, Sallie...144
WILLIAMS, Sallie Ann...280
WILLIAMS, Sarah...171
WILLIAMS, Susan...314
WILLIAMSON, Roberta P....230
WILLIS, Delia S....298
WILLIS, Hannah E....123
WILLIS, Indy A....256
WILLIS, Isabella...141
WILLIS, Jane...317

WILLIS, Jane G....264
WILLIS, Jennie d/o Martha Beagles...321
WILLIS, Mary Champe...350
WILLIS, Mary Lewis...38
WILLIS, Nannie d/o Julia Dickerson...88
WILLIS, Nellie M....293
WILLIS, Rosa...30
WILLOUGHBY, Bettie Ann...276
WILLOUGHBY, Cornelia...129
WILLOUGHBY, E....273
WILLOUGHBY, Eddie W....147
WILLOUGHBY, Georgie...112
WILLOUGHBY, Lily D....298
WILLOUGHBY, Lucy F....147
WILLOUGHBY, Sallie E....34
WILSON, Alice...338
WILSON, Bettie A....276
WILSON, Cary Lee...22
WILSON, Ella Jane...235
WILSON, Judy d/o B.& L.William...115
WILSON, Laura J....6
WILSON, Lucy H....245
WILSON, Lucy M....186
WILSON, Mittie M....151
WILSON, Ora Washington...22
WILSON, Rosa L....348
WILSON, Rose...321
WILSON, Sallie M. d/o A.H.& S.N. Wilson age 24 S POB & POR Spotsylvania...321
WILTSHIRE, Sarah Jane...229
WINSLOW, Bettie E....261

WINSLOW, Martha E. d/o
    Thompson & Eleanor
    Cockerille...229
WINSTON, Mary...162
WINTERS, Emma A. d/o
    Floyd & Mary
    L.Robinson...258
WOLLFREY, Cora
    Lee...294
WOOD, Lizzie G....127
WOOD, Louisianna...108
WOOD, Lucinda...303
WOOD, Maria J....134
WOOD, Martha Ann...341
WOOD, Martha J....191
WOOD, Ophelia E....209
WOOD, Rebecka E....187
WOOD, Sarah Jane...298
WOODWARD, Mattie d/o
    Kate Gibson...1
WOOLFOLK, Bettie...123
WOOLFOLK,
    Columbia...344
WOOLFOLK, Eva...195
WOOLFOLK, Mary...73
WOOLFOLK, Milly...28,
    195
WOOLFOLK, Sarah...274
WOOLFREY, Mary...344
WOOLFRY,
    Margaret...265
WOOLFRY, Sarah
    Frances...344
WOOMELY, Sally...272
WORCESTER, Josey...266
WORMLEY, Hannah...19
WORMLEY, Rose...216
WORMSLEY, Elzie d/o
    Toby & Daphney
    Gibbs...86
WREN, Louisa C....182
WRENN, Mary E....99
WRENN, Sarah C....270
WRIGHT, Amanda...19
WRIGHT, Ann C....188
WRIGHT, Bettie
    E....145
WRIGHT, Emma C....89
WRIGHT, Lavinia
    A....115
WRIGHT, M.Ruth...335
WRIGHT, Mary E....329
WRIGHT, Mary V....104

WRIGHT, Mattie
    E....338
WRIGHT, Mildred
    F....104
WRIGHT, Sally Ann...18
WRIGHT, Sarah C....203
WRIGHT, Sarah d/o
    William &
    N.Crawford...296
WRIGHT, Susan R....20
WRIGHT, Virginia
    E....157
WRIGHT, Virginia
    T....259
YAGER, Pamelia
    W....279
YANCY, Elizabeth...190
YERBER, Rose...226
YERBY, Affie F....152
YERBY, Alice D....123
YOUNG, Ellen d/o
    William Cook...46
YOUNG, Emma D....97
YOUNG, Helen...151
YOUNG, Lizzie...112
YOUNG, Lucie N....283
YOUNG, Mary...161
YOUNG, Sarah E....143
YOWELL, Cornelia
    Alpha...315

____, Addison POC m POB Spotsylvania s/o Eliza owned by Darius Shackleford 23 Jul 1853 SPBR

____, Alexander POC m POB Spotsylvania s/o Fanny owned by Jas.M.Quisenberry 13 Sep 1853 SPBR

____, Alexander POC m POB Spotsylvania s/o Hannah owned by William Tompkins 10 Aug 1854 SPBR

____, Almera POC f POB Spotsylvania d/o Patty owned by John M.Waller Jan 1854 SPBR

____, Amelia POC f POB Spotsylvania d/o Phillis owned by William Holladay 3 Nov 1854 SPBR

____, Anaca POC f POB Spotsylvania d/o Louisa owned by William H.Andrews 17 Oct 1853 SPBR

____, Angelina POC f POB Spotsylvania d/o Matilda owned by John Lipscomb 8 Jan 1854 SPBR

____, Anthony POC m POB Spotsylvania s/o Caroline owned by James D.Dillard 19 Sep 1853 SPBR

____, Archie POC m POB Spotsylvania s/o Patsey owned by Spencer Coleman 2 Oct 1853 SPBR

____, Arthur POC m POB Spotsylvania s/o Betsy owned by Francis W.Coleman 27 Sep 1853 SPBR

____, Ben POC m POB Spotsylvania s/o Eda owned by Al G. Chewning 10 Jul 1854 SPBR

____, Benjamin POC m POB Meadow Hill s/o Letitia owned by John Lipscomb Mar 1856 SPBR

____, Betty POC f POB Spotsylvania d/o Matilda owned by Ann E.Duerson 7 Feb 1854 SPBR

____, Betty POC f POB Spotsylvania d/o Pheby d/o George W.Davis 8 Oct 1854 SPBR

____, Billy POC m POB Spotsylvania s/o Maria owned by William Holladay 15 Jun 1854 SPBR

____, Billy POC m POB Spotsylvania s/o Rachel owned by Patsy Quarles Apr 1854 SPBR

____, Caroline POC f POB Spotsylvania d/o Frances owned by Francis W.Conner 22 Sep 1853 SPBR

____, Caroline POC f POB Spotsylvania d/o Huldah owned by James S.Powell 1 Jul 1853 SPBR

____, Celey POC f POB Spotsylvania d/o Amelia owned by William R.Powell Oct 1853 SPBR

____, Celia d/o Captain & Amanda POC f POB Spotsylvania 8 Apr 1865 SPBR

____, Cornelius POC m POB Spotsylvania s/o Sinah owned by Bernard Phillips 15 Nov 1853 SPBR

____, Easther POC f POB Spotsylvnaia owned by William P.Bowen Dec 1853 SPBR

____, Edmund POC m POB Spotsylvania s/o Aletha owned by John F.Duerson 6 Dec 1853 SPBR

____, Edward POC m POB Spotsylvania s/o Louisa owned by Frances Johnson Oct 1853 SPBR

____, Elizabeth POC f POB Spotsylvani8a owned by Ann Proctor 6 Sep 1853 SPBR

____, Emily POC f POB Spotsylvnaia d/o Ann owned by James Pulliam 21 Dec 1853 SPBR

____, Fanny POC f POB Spotsylvania d/o Amy owned by Fanny Mason 15 Sep 1853 SPBR

____, Fleetwood POC m POB Spotsylvania s/o Ellen owned by Reuben L.Coleman 14 Aug 1853 SPBR

____, Georgeanna d/o Mary Ann s f POC POB Spotsylvania 16 May 1856 SPBR

____, Hannah s f POC POB Spotsylvania owned by John Holladay 10 Sep 1853 SPBR

____, Hardenia d/o Mary s f POC POB Spotsylvania 15 Nov 1853 SPBR

____, Hardinia s f POC POB Spotsylvania d/o Mary Ann owned by John B. Edenton 15 Nov 1853 SPBR

____, Hardinia s f POC POB Spotsylvania d/o Nancy owned by James Duerson 1 Oct 1853 SPBR

____, Harry s m POC POB Spotsylvania s/o Mary owned by Bland Gerrall 14 Oct 1853 SPBR

____, Henry s m POC POB Spotsylvania owned by Joseph M.Alsop 27 Aug 1853 SPBR

____, Hudson s m POC POB Spotsylvania s/o Betty owned byEliz.Gibson 6 Aug 1853 SPBR

____, Kate, s f POC POB Spotsylvania owned by C.A.Harrow 25 Dec 1857 SPBR

____, Katy s f POC POB Spotsylvania d/o Clara owned by John C.Pellus 26 Aug 1860 SPBR

____, Kesiah s f POC owned by John Holladay 1855 SPBR

____, Keziah s f POC POB Spotsylvania owned by Cpt.George Hambleton 29 Aug 1856 SPBR

____, Kitty POC POB Spotsylvania d/o Sidney 15 Aug 1867 SPBR

____, Kitty s f POC d/o Betsey POB Spotsylvania owned by Patsey Quarles SPBR

____, Kitty s f POC d/o Eliza Ann owned by Joseph Duerson 17 Jun 1859 SPBR

____, Kitty s f POC POB Spotsylvania d/o Eliza owned by James Duerson 1 Jul 1860 SPBR

____, Kitty s f POC POB Spotsylvania owned by Julia Taylor 15 Aug 1857 SPBR

____, Lewis POC m POB Spotsylvania s/o Celey owned by Joseph Duerson Nov 1853 SPBR

____, Lewis POC m POB Spotsylvania s/o Lucinda owned by James B.Rawlings 1 Nov 1853 SPBR

____, Lewis POC m POB Spotsylvania s/o Milly owned by Robert Hicks 15 Sep 1853 SPBR

____, Louisa POC f POB Spotsylvania d/o Charlotte owned by William E.Foster 20 Jul 1853 SPBR

____, Louisa POC f POB Spotsylvania d/o Margarett owned by Benjamin Dismukes 10 Sep 1853 SPBR

____, Margaret d/o Maria s f POC POB Spotsylvania Apr 1854 SPBR

____, Peggy POC f POB Spotsylvania POB Orange d/o Ellen owned by Robert G.Kendall 10 Oct 1853 SPBR

____, Peter POC m POB Spotsylvania d/o Charlotte s/o Eliza Goodloe Jun 1854 SPBR

____, Phoebe POC f POB Spotsylvania d/o Eliza owned by Charles G.Powell Jul 1853 SPBR

____, Rossa d/o Elzie s f owned by Ro.S.Coleman POC POB Spotsylvania Sep 1854 SPBR

____, Sarah Jane d/o Eliza s f POC POB Spotsylvania Jan 1854 SPBR

____, Theresa s f POC POB Spotsylvania d/o Matilda owned by W.S.Cropp 25 Sep 1854 SPBR

____, Thomas s m POC POB Spotsylvania owned by Cap.J.Alsop 13 Jun 1855 SPBR

____, Thomas s m POC POB Spotsylvania s/o Harriet owned by John Collins 5 Aug 1853 SPBR

____, Thomas s m POC POB Spotsylvania s/o Judy owned by George W.Davis 10 Sep 1853 SPBR

____, Thornton s m POC POB Spotsylvania owned by Julia Taylor 15 Feb 1854 SPBR

____, Thornton s m POC POB Spotsylvania s/o Amy owned by

William McKenney Apr 1855 SPBR

_____, Thornton s m POC POB Spotsylvania s/o Mary owned by John W McCalley 1 Sep 1855 SPBR

_____, Tom s m POC POB Spotsylvania s/o Ann owned by Waller Holladay Oct 1856 SPBR

ACORS, Edward Y. w m POB Spotsylvania s/o G.W.& Maria Acors 11 Apr 1856 SPBR

ACORS, Maria A. w f POB Spotsylvania d/o George W.& Maria Acors 10 Apr 1854 SPBR

ACORS, Robert H. w m POB Spotsylvania s/o John B.& Mary Acors grandson of Hez.Acors 3 Oct 1853 SPBR

ADKINS, _____ w m POB Spotsylvania s/o William L.& Mary Adkins 3 Jul 1860 SPBR

ALLEN Edward M. w m POB Spotsylvania s/o RiPOChard S.& Kate E.Allen 17 Jul 1867 SPBR

ALLEN, Jos. POC m POB Handkerchief s/o Isabell owned by M.J.Waller Mar 1856 SPBR

ALLEN, Lelia S. w f POB Spotsylvania d/o Richard S.& Kate E.Allen 17 Jul 1867 SPBR

ALMOND, Eliza L. w f POB Spotsylvania d/o James & Elizabeth Almond 23 Jan 1860 SPBR

ALMOND, Flora w f POB Spotsylvnaia d/o Barnett B.& Ann S.Almond 18 Sep 1859 SPBR

ALMOND, George G. w m POB Spotsylvania s/o Oscar F.& Sarah I.(or Q.) Almond 2 Apr 1854 SPBR

ALMOND, James w m POB Spotsylvania s/o James & Eliza Almond 12 Aug 1858 SPBR

ALMOND, Jane Mildred b.d.28 Sep 1839 d.d.15 Aug 1927 CBC

ALMOND, Laura A. w f POB Spotsylvania d/o Barnett B.& Ann S.Almond 18 Aug 1854 SPBR

ALMOND, Lewis Hy w m POB Spotsylvania s/o Lewis & Susan C.Almond 16 Aug 1858 SPBR

ALMOND, Wiatt William s/o James & Elizabeth Almond w m POB Spot 23 Nov 1859 SPBR

ALRICK, Mary E. w f POB Spotsylvania d/o John R.Alrick 25 Feb 1858 SPBR

ALSOP, A.M. b.d.16 Aug 1852 d.d.21 Jan 1934 husband to Susie M.Alsop SGMC

ALSOP, Amanda M. d/o James Alsop bond posted 7 Jan 1850 GBSP

ALSOP, Brenton B. w m POB Spotsylvania s/o Benjamin & Margaret Alsop 2 Nov 1867 SPBR

ALSOP, Clara L.
b.d.1880 d.d.1948
wife to Ollie
L.Alsop SGMC

ALSOP, Dorathea w f
d/o Jos. & Sarah
A.Alsop Sr. 11
Mar 1855 SPBR

ALSOP, Ella J. w f POB
Spotsylvania d/o
Joseph & Martha
Alsop 26 Aug 1858
SPBR

ALSOP, George G. w m
POB Spotsylvania
s/o Dr.George &
Virginia L.Alsop
12 Mar 1868 SPBR

ALSOP, James w m POB
Spotsylvania s/o
Jos.M.& Susan
J.Alsop 30 Jun
1858 SPBR

ALSOP, Lilly J.H. w f
POB Spotsylvania
d/o William &
Martha B.Alsop 3
Apr 1860 SPBR

ALSOP, Martha Bell w f
POB Spotsylvania
d/o William &
Martha B.Alsop 26
Jan 1867 SPBR

ALSOP, Nancy w f d/o
Joe W.& Martha
Alsop 18 Mar 1855
SPBR

ALSOP, Ollie L.
b.d.1877 d.d.1952
husband to Clara
L.Alsop SGMC

ALSOP, Susie M.
b.d.1858 d.d.27
Oct 1941 wife to
A.M.Alsop SGMC

ALSOP, Thomas T. w m
POB Spotsylvania
s/o Benjamin &
Margarett A.Alsop
(POR Snowden) 25
Nov 1853 SPBR

ALSOP, William L. w m
s/o William &
M.B.Alsop 18 Mar
1855 SPBR

ALSOP,_____ d/o Joseph
W.Alsop w f 1 Jul
1860 SPBR

ANDERSON, F.W. w m POB
Wallers Tavern,
Spotsylvania s/o
John &
M.P.Anderson 8
Apr 1855 SPBR

ANDERSON, Mary w f POB
Spotsylvania d/o
John & Martha
P.Anderson 25 Sep
1853 SPBR

ANDERSON, Rosa POC f
POB Spotsylvania
d/o Clifton &
Judith Anderson
20 Nov 1867 SPBR

ARNOLD,_____,s/o George
W.& S.C.Arnold w
m 14 Oct 1857
SPBR

ATWELL, Charles H. w m
POB Spotsylvania
s/o W.G.&
Margaret Atwell
15 Mar 1867 SPBR

BALDERSON, Allie w f
POB King George
Co d/o William &
Julia A.Balderson
14 Feb 1859 SPBR

BALDWIN, Mary E. w f
POB Spotsylvania
d/o Almond & Jane
Baldwin 23 Dec
1867 SPBR

BALDWIN, Sarah w f POB
Spotsylvania d/o
James & Jane
Baldwin 15 Jul
1867 SPBR

BALLARD, Charles T.
s/o Maria Ballard
bond posted 7 Feb
1842 (child is
probably under
14y) GBSP

BALLARD, James s/o
Maria Ballard
bond posted 7 Feb

1842 (child is probably under 14y) GBSP
BALLARD, Lawrence S. s/o Maria Ballard bond posted 7 Feb 1842 (child is probably under 14y) GBSP
BALLARD, Lucy L. d/o Richard W.Ballard bond posted 3 Feb 1845 GBSP
BALLARD, Margaret d/o Maria Ballard bond posted 7 Feb 1842 (child is probably under 14y) GBSP
BALLARD, Sally Ann d/o Richard W. Ballard bond posted 3 Feb 1845 GBSP
BALLARD, Sarah A. d/o Richard W.Ballard bond posted 7 Jun 1847 GBSP
BANK, William POC m POB Spotsylvania 15 Feb 1854 SPBR
BAPTIST, Kate E.D. w f d/o Ed.G. & Maria E.Baptist 9 Feb 1858 SPBR
BARITER(?), Robert w m POB Spotsylvania s/o Jacob & Ann Baxter(?) 17 Jan 1857 SPBR
BARTLESON, Anna C.Pulliam b.d.1868 d.d.1953 wife to Edwin S.Bartleson SGMC
BARTLESON, Edwin S. b.d.1865 d.d.1942 husband to Anna C.Pulliam Bartleson SGMC
BARTLESON, John W. b.d.31 Dec 1822 d.d.1 Apr 1915 husband to Susanna R.Bartleson SGMC
BARTLESON, Susanna R. b.d.11 Feb 1820 d.d.27 Apr 1918 wife to John W.Bartleson SGMC
BATTAILE, _____ w m POB Spotsylvania s/o W.C.& A.E.Battaile 15 Apr 1857 SPBR
BAXTER, Elizabeth w f POB Spotsylvania d/o Ambrose & Susan Baxter 7 Dec 1868 SPBR
BEAZLEY, Alfred P. w m POB Spotsylvania s/o Walter A.& Catherine E.Beazley 6 Sep 1853 SPBR
BEAZLEY, Ann C. w f POB Spotsylvania d/o Duerson & Clementine Beazley 11 Mar 1854 SPBR
BEAZLEY, Fanny E. w f POB Spotsylvania d/o Walter A.& Catherine Beazley 9 May 1856 SPBR
BEAZLEY, George R. w m POB Spotsylvania s/o John G.& Mary Beazley 2 Dec 1860 SPBR
BEAZLEY, John H. w m POB Spotsylvania s/o Henry & Harriet A.Beazley 16 Jul 1853 SPBR
BEAZLEY, Ovender G. w m POB Spotsylvania s/o Charles L.& Mary I.(?) Beazley 20 Jul 1854 SPBR
BEAZLEY, Thurston F. w m POB Spotsylvania s/o Walter A.&

Catherine E.Beazley 27 May 1859 SPBR
BEAZLEY, William T. w m s/o Henry & Harriet A.Beazley 2 Sep 1855 SPBR
BELL, J.Alvin b.d.28 Aug 1881 d.d.20 Sep 1963 husband to J.Cappie Bell CBC
BELL, J.Cappie b.d.14 Sep 1882 d.d.2 Dec 1954 wife to J.Alvin Bell CBC
BELL, Mary C. w f POB Spotsylvania d/o Robert & Mary Bell 5 Mar 1865 SPBR
BELL, Robert W. w m POB Spotsylvania s/o Robert H.& Mary E.Bell 12 Dec 1859 SPBR
BERTON, Benjamin W. w m POB Spotsylvania s/o Thomas Berton 5 Jan 1857 SPBR
BEVERLEY, McKen. w m POB Spotsylvania s/o James G.& A.L.Beverley 16 May 1855 SPBR
BEVERLEY, McKenzie w m POB Spotsylvania s/o James & Adranna Beverley 15 Mar 1857 SPBR
BISCOE, Lafayet w m POB Spotsylvnaia s/o W.E.& Susan R.Biscoe 28 Oct 1855 SPBR
BISCOE, Thomas Lawson s/o William E.Biscoe 6 Nov 1850 SPConsent
BISCOE, ____ s/o William E.& Susan R.Biscoe w m 16 Nov 1859 SPBR

BLACK, Hugh B. w m POB Spotsylvania s/o Andrew & Sarah E.Black 10 Mar 1854 SPBR
BLACK, Lucy B. w f POB Spotsylvnaia d/o Andrew & Sarah E.Black 28 Nov 1855 SPBR
BLAYDES, Mary S. w f d/o Jos.F.& Angelina Blaydes 2 Oct 1858 SPBR
BLEDSOE, Mary S. w f POB Spotsylvania d/o William P.& Frances A,Bledsoe 9 Oct 1856 SPBR
BOGGS, L.A. w m POB Livingston s/o L.A.& Eliza Boggs Aug 1856 SPBR
BOGGS, ____, s/o Lewis A.& Elizabeth Boggs w m 23 Dec 1857 SPBR
BOWLER, Hattie G. w f POB Spotsylvania d/o Dr.Jackson Bowler 23 Feb 1856 SPBR
BOXLEY, Hardinia w f d/o Isaac & Mary Boxley POB Locust Grove, Spotsylvania 14 Aug 1856 SPBR
BRENT, Sarah A. d.d.27 Sep 1859 age 43y SGMC
BRIGHTWELL, Fernando Cortez Todd s/o Ptolomy Brightwell (not deceased) bond posted 6 Sep 1847 (child is probably under 14y) GBSP
BRIGHTWELL, Richard S. s/o Ptolemy Brightwell (not deceased)bond

posted 4 Feb 1839
GBSP
BRIGHTWELL, Richard
Thomas s/o
Ptolomy
Brightwell (not
deceased) bond
posted 6 Sep 1847
(child is
probably under
14y) GBSP
BROADDUS, Fanny w f
POB Spotsylvania
d/o John E.&
Betty M.Broaddus
3 Dec 1860 SPBR
BROCK, Harriet A. d/o
John Brock bond 1
Oct 1849 GBSP
BROMLEY, William T.s/o
Robert & Mary
Bromley w m POB
Spot 21 Mar 1859
SPBR
BROOKE, Ella A. w f
POB Spotsylvania
d/o Francis E.7
Ella A.Brooke 3
Feb 1854 SPBR
BROOKS, _____ w f POB
Pidgeon d/o A.C.&
M.A.Brooks 14 Dec
1856 SPBR
BROOKS, _____ s/o Allen
C.& Mary A.Brooks
w m 25 Apr 1859
SPBR
BROOKS, A.M. w f POB
Spotsylvania d/o
W.D.& L.A.Brooks
22 Jan 1856 SPBR
BROOKS, Ella L. w f
POB Spotsylvania
d/o Alfred W.&
Eliza A.Brooks
Dec 1854 SPBR
BROOKS, Henrietta w f
POB Spotsylvania
d/o Allen C.&
Mary A.Brooks 14
Jan 1855 SPBR
BROOKS, Henry C. w m
s/o William D.&
Lucy A.Brooks
SPBR
BROOKS, James D. w m
POB Spotsylvania
s/o William T.&
Ann Brooks 25 Sep
1854 SPBR
BROOKS, James M. w m
POB Spotsylvania
s/o Granville &
Rebecca Brooks
Mar 1854 SPBR
BROOKS, James M. w m
s/o Granville &
Rebecca Brooks
POB Spotsylvania
Mar 1854 SPBR
BROOKS, John A. s/o
Alfred & Eliza
A.Brooks w m POB
Spotsylvania Mar
1855 SPBR
BROOKS, John A. w m
POB Spotsylvania
s/o Alfred &
Eliza A.Brooks
Mar 1855 SPBR
BROWN, Elizabeth w f
POB Spotsylvania
d/o James M.&
Mary E.Brown 8
Sep 1854 SPBR
BROWN, Isabella B. w f
POB Spotsylvania
d/o John T.&
Virginia L.Brown
8 May 1854 SPBR
BROWN, J.C. w f POB
Spotsylvania d/o
J.T.& S.V.Brown
21 Aug 1857 SPBR
BROWNE, Fran c(?) w m
POB Spotsylvania
s/o James M.&
Mary E.Browne 15
Mar 1857 SPBR
BRUMLEY, M.J. w f POB
Spotsylvania d/o
R.B.&
M.F.A.Brumley 22
Jan 1855 SPBR
BRYCE, John McDaniel w
m POB
Spotsylvania s/o

John & Mary
L.Bryce 18 May
1854 SPBR
BUCHANAN, ____ w f
POB Spotsylvania
d/o Thomas C.&
Nice A.Buchanan
Mar 1855 SPBR
BUCHANAN, Goldie P.
b.d. 23 Jan 1882
d.d.7 Nov 1973
SGMC
BUCHANAN, Henry M. w m
POB Spotsylvania
s/o Thomas C.&
Nicy A.Buchanan 7
Dec 1853 SPBR
BUCHANAN, I. w f POB
Spotsylvania d/o
T.C.&
N.A.Buchanan 27
May 1856 SPBR
BUCHANAN, J.M. w m POB
Spotsylvania s/o
William T.& Ann
Buchanan 19 Jan
1854 SPBR
BUCHANAN, James POC m
POB Spotsylvania
s/o Matilda owned
by E.T.Dillard 2
Nov 1856 SPBR
BUCHANAN, William W.
b.d.13 Mar 1868
d.d.29 Nov 1948
husband to Goldie
P.Buchanan SGMC
BUCHNER, William D. w
m POB
Spotsylvania s/o
Calhoun & Louisa
Buchner 14 Aug
1856 SPBR
BULLARD, ____ w f POB
Spotsylvania d/o
C.B.& Sarah
Bullard 13 Dec
1857 SPBR
BULLOCK, Amanda w f
POB Spotsylvania
d/o Slaughter B.&
Louisa W.Bullock
28 Dec 1854 SPBR

BULLOCK, Anna Susan w
f POB
Spotsylvania d/o
Alfred S.& Liza
Bullock 15 Oct
1859 SPBR
BULLOCK, Arthur w m
POB Spotsylvania
s/o Benjamin B.&
Mary A.Bullock 10
Nov 1868 SPBR
BULLOCK, John M. w m
POB Spotsylvania
s/o J.& A.Bullock
3 Jan 1855 SPBR
BURKE, Eliza w f POB
Spotsylvania d/o
George B.& Sarah
Burke Sep 1867
SPBR
BURRUS, Emma Lea w f
POB Spotsylvania
d/o Leon &
Grabriella Burrus
23 Mar 1867 SPBR
BURRUSS, ____ w m POB
Spotsylvania s/o
James T.&
P.Burruss (POR
Goochland Co) 20
Sep 1855 SPBR
BURRUSS, M.S. w f POB
Spotsylvania d/o
James T.& Paulina
Burruss 15 Jun
1865 SPBR
BUTLER, George T. w m
POB Spotsylvania
s/o John C.&
Catherine
R.Butler 13 May
1855 SPBR
BUTLER, Lucy Jane w f
POB Spotsylvnaia
d/o John C.&
Catherine
R.Butler 15 Dec
1867 SPBR
BUTLER, Mary Catherine
w f POB
Spotsylvania d/o
John C.&
Catherine

R.Butler 15 Jul 1859 SPBR
BUTLER, Spotsylvania w f POB Spotsylvania d/o Elijah & Susan Butler 20 Aug 1860 SPBR
BUTLER, William R. w m POB Spotsylvania s/o Calvin C.& Catherine Butler Dec 1865 SPBR
CAMMACK, Catherine Ann d/o Durrett Cammack bond posted 1 Mar 1844 GBSP
CAMMACK, Elizabeth B. d/o Durrett Cammack bond posted 1 Mar 1844 GBSP
CAMMACK, Horace A. s/o Durrett Cammack bond posted 1 Mar 1844 (child is probably under 14y) GBSP
CAMMACK, Joseph J. s/o Durrett Cammack bond posted 1 Mar 1844 (child is probably under 14y) GBSP
CAMMACK, Robert J. s/o Durrett Cammack bond posted 1 Mar 1844 (child is probably under 14y) GBSP
CAMMACK, Robert w m POB Spotsylvania s/o Robert J.& Lucy Cammack 1 Sep 1860 SPBR
CAMMACK, William R. s/o Durrett Cammack bond posted 1 Mar 1844 (child is probably under 14y) GBSP
CARNEAL, Allis d/o Atwell & Mary C.Carneal w f POB Spotsylvania 10 Apr 1868 SPBR
CARNOHAN, Leo S. w m POB Spotsylvania s/o Warren & Lucy A.Carnohan 2 Feb 1860 SPBR
CARTER, Edwin W. s/o George Carter bond posted 4 Jul 1842 GBSP
CARTER, Lucy A.C. d/o George Carter bond posted 4 Jul 1842 (child is probably under 14y) GBSP
CARTER, Robert S. s/o George Carter bond posted 4 Jul 1842 GBSP
CASH, James w m POB Spotsylvania s/o John A.& Delia M.Cash 12 Oct 1855 SPBR
CASH, Sally d/o William Cash bond posted 3 Feb 1845 GBSP
CASH, William w m POB Spotsylvania s/o James A.& Delila Cash 26 Feb 1859 SPBR
CAVELL, Frank w m POB Alexandria s/o Charles & Emma Cavell 19 Oct 1856 SPBR
CBC... Craigs Baptist Church Cemetary located in Spotsylvania County
CHANCELLOR, A.C. w m POB Spotsylvania s/o J.C.& J.Chancellor 7 Feb 1857 SPBR

CHANCELLOR, Ann d/o George Chancellor bond posted 3 Jun 1839 GBSP

CHANCELLOR, George E. s/o George Chancellor bond posted 3 Jun 1839 GBSP

CHANCELLOR, James Edgar s/o George Chancellor bond posted 3 Jun 1839 GBSP

CHANCELLOR, Melzi S. w m POB Spotsylvania s/o Melzi S.& Lucy Fox Chancellor 12 Aug 1859 SPBR

CHARTTERS, Thomas R. s/o William Chartters bond posted 2 Apr 1838 GBSP

CHEWNING, Cecil A. s/o John O.& Jarretta Chewning w m POB Spotsylvania 25 Jul 1865 SPBR

CHEWNING, Cordelia F. w f POB Spotsylvania d/o Robert O. & Mary E.Chewning 19 Dec 1853 SPBR

CHEWNING, Hiram w m POB Spotsylvania s/o William H.& Ann Chewning 4 Apr 1860 SPBR

CHEWNING, James A. w m POB Spotsylvania s/o Jos.E.& Virginia Chewning 12 Feb 1858 SPBR

CHEWNING, James C. b.d.22 Jun 1869 d.d.26 Sep 1955 husband to Maretta J.Chewning CBC

CHEWNING, John D. w m POB Spotsylvania s/o Jos.& E.S.Chewning 10 Feb 1856 SPBR

CHEWNING, M. w f POB Stafford d/o James E.& V.Chewning 24 Jun 1856 SPBR

CHEWNING, Maretta J. b.d.15 Mar 1876 d.d.15 Apr 1961 wife to James C.Chewning CBC

CHEWNING, Marght. w f POB Spotsylvania d/o James S & Emily G.Chewning 2 Sep 1860 SPBR

CHEWNING, Martha O. b.d.26 Sep 1875 d.d.18 Feb 1943 CBC

CHEWNING, Mary E. w f POB Spotsylvania d/o John S.& Margarett Chewning 20 Aug 1865 SPBR

CHEWNING, R.T. w m s/o W.R.& Clem Chewning 19 Aug 1855 SPBR

CHEWNING, William P. b.d.22 Jun 1869 d.d.3 Jan 1955 CBC

CHEWNING, William T. w m POB Spotsylvnaia s/o William H.& Ann E.Chewning 23 Aug 1855 SPBR

CHEWNING, ____, d/o John O.& Sarah I.Chewning w f 17 Jul 1857 SPBR

CLARK, Frances d/o John & Julia A.W.Clark w f POB Spotsylvania 3 Nov 1865 SPBR

CLARK, Martha w f POB Spotsylvania d/o John H.& Martha

F.Clark 1 Dec 1860 SPBR
CLARY, William s/o Henn & Sally A.Clary POC m POB Spotsylvania July 1865 SPBR
CLINE, Marie W. b.d.14 Jul 1872 d.d.15 Jul 1942 SGMC
COATS, Lucy Jane d/o John Coats bond posted 3 May 1847 GBSP
COLBERT, Mary A. w f POB Spotsylvania d/o Richard W.& Mary E.Colbert 28 Sep 1860 SPBR
COLEMAN, Early s/o J.Thomas & Early Coleman w m POB Spotsylvania 1 Jul 1865 SPBR
COLEMAN, George s/o Fontaine & Rose Coleman w m POB Spotsylvania Sep 1867 SPBR
COLEMAN, L.V. w f POB Spotsylvania d/o H.& J.T.Coleman 31 Oct 1856 SPBR
COLEMAN, Ruffin H. s/o Francis Coleman bond posted 7 Dec 1840 GBSP
COLEMAN, Ruffin s/o Francis Coleman bond posted 3 Sep 1839 GBSP
COLEMAN, Washington, William s/o Grunroy & Ellen Coleman POC m POB Spotsylvania 13 May 1865 SPBR
COLEMAN,____,d/o Ro.LaFayette & Nanniea S.Coleman w f 20 Sep 1860 SPBR
COLEMAN,____d/o Font H.& Ann E.Coleman w f 10 Dec 1859 SPBR
COLLINS, Catherine d/o D.& Amanda E. Collins w f POB Spotsylvania 7 Aug 1865 SPBR
COLLINS, John Michael s/o Dennis & Amanda E.Collins w m POB Spotsylvania 1 May 1868 SPBR
COLLIS, Mary Elizabeth d/o William Collis bond posted 6 Sep 1841 GBSP
COLVIN, Virginia w f POB Spotsylvania d/o Oliver C.Colvin 12 Oct 1855 SPBR
COOK, Matha free POC f POB Spotsylvania d/o William & Catherine Cook 15 Sep 1856 SPBR
COOK,____,d/o William & Catherine Cook free POC f 15 Aug 1859 SPBR
COSWELL, Roberta b.d.1879 d.d.1930 SGMC
COX, George T. w m POB Spotsylvania s/o John B.& Sarah M.Cox 15 Aug 1858 SPBR
CRABTREE, Joseph H. b.d.4 Feb 1865 d.d.14 Dec 1929 SGMC
CRAWFORD, Lucinda O. d/o James Crawford bond posted 4 Mar 1850 GBSP
CRAWFORD, William H. s/o James Crawford bond posted 4 Mar 1850 GBSP

CRAWFORD, Zachary L. s/o James Crawford bond posted 4 Mar 1850 GBSP

CRUMP, Barnett POC m POB Spotsylvania s/o Maria owned by Lewis A.Boggs Sep 1853 SPBR

CRUTCHFIELD, Corbin s/o Sta.Crutchfield (not deceased) bond posted 1 Jun 1846 (child is probably under 14y) GBSP

CRUTCHFIELD, Ella R. d/o Edgar M. & Lizzie M. Crutchfield w f POB Green Branch, Spotsylvania 6 May 1867 SPBR

CRUTCHFIELD, Stapleton s/o E.M. & Lizzie Crutchfield w m POB Spotsylvania 24 Aug 1868 SPBR

CURTIS, ___,d/o William H.& C. Jane Curtis w f 22 Sep 1859 SPBR

DABNEY, Mary Eliza w f POB Spotsylvania d/o Robert C.& Margaret M.Dabney 30 Jan 1860 SPBR

DABNEY, Raleigh T. w m POB Spotsylvania s/o Robert C.& Margaret M.Dabney 15 May 1854 SPBR

DAVIS, Fannie W. w f POB Spotsylvania d/o James L.& Mary F.Davis Apr 1854 SPBR

DAVIS, Frances w f POB Meadow Hill d/o James L.& Mary F.Davis 29 Apr 1856 SPBR

DAVIS, Mary C. w f POB Spotsylvania d/o John W.& Drusilla Davis 20 Nov 1867 SPBR

DAWSON, Charles M. s/o William M. & Mary Dawson 29 Jul 1852 SPConsent

DAWSON, Luther POC m POB Spotsylvnaia s/o Edward & Martha A.Dawson 27 Sep 1867 SPBR

DAWSON, Stapleton POC m POB Spotsylvania s/o Edward & Martha Dawson 15 Jun 1865 SPBR

DEMPSEY, Ann E. w f POB Spotsylvania d/o Robert & Elizabeth Dempsey 25 Dec 1853 SPBR

DICKERSON, MacHenry w m POB Spotsylvania s/o Robert H.& Mary F.Dickerson 16 or 10 Nov 1867 SPBR

DICKINSON, H.Q. w m POB Spotsylvania s/o Hugh M.& Susan C.Dickinson 29 May 1855 SPBR

DICKINSON, Katy freeborn POC POB Spotsylvania d/o William J.Dickinson 25 Jul 1859 SPBR

DICKINSON, Mary Hicks b.d.11 Dec 1836 d.d.13 Mar 1925 wife to R.H.Dickinson SGMC

DICKINSON, R.H. b.d.26 Oct 1839 d.d.11 Feb 1923 husband to Mary Hicks Dickinson SGMC

DICKINSON, Robert A.
b.d.1869 d.d.1957
SGMC
DILLARD, B. & F. w m &
f POB
Spotsylvania s/o
d/o J.R.&
M.E.Dillard 8 May
1855 SPBR
DILLARD, Buford w m
s/o George B.&
Lucy A.Dillard 2
May 1858 SPBR
DILLARD, Edith E. w f
POB Spotsylvania
d/o Alexander W.&
Emily L.Dillard 1
Jan 1855 SPBR
DILLARD, James A. w m
POB Spotsylvania
s/o Isaiah &
Julia Ann Dillard
22 Aug 1867 SPBR
DILLARD, James A. w m
POB Spotsylvania
s/o James T.&
Martha A.Dillard
2 May 1858 SPBR
DILLARD, Lewis O. w m
s/o Alex.W.&
Emily S.Dillard 2
May 1858 SPBR
DONAVANT, Lona A. w f
POB Spotsylvania
d/o Archibald &
Mary Ann Donavant
14 Feb 1854 SPBR
DOWNER, Ann d/o Larkin
Downer bond
posted 5 Apr 1847
GBSP
DOWNER, Charles M. s/o
Larkin Downer
bond posted 5 Apr
1847 GBSP
DOWNER, William C. s/o
Larkin Downer
bond posted 5 Apr
1847 GBSP
DOWNMAN, Rawley W. w
m. POB
Spotsylvania s/o
William Y.& Mary
A.Downman 10 Jul
1860 SPBR
DUERSON, ____ w m POB
Rose Hill,
Spotsylvania s/o
John J.& Jane
C.Duerson Nov
1855 SPBR
DUERSON, ____ w m POB
Spotsylvania s/o
Simon Y. & Ella
V.Duerson (POR
Woodville) 25 Mar
1855 SPBR
DUERSON, Sarah Ann d/o
Henry Duerson Jr.
bond posted 1 Mar
1841 GBSP
DUERSON, ____ d/o
Thomas L.& Mary
E.Duerson w f 28
Dec 1860 SPBR
DUNNAVANT, S.B. w f
POB Spotsylvania
d/o A.&
S.Dunnavant 16
Feb 1856 SPBR
DURRETT, ____ w f
stillborn POB
Mount Pleasant
d/o W.W.&
E.E.Durrett Nov
1856 SPBR
DURRETT, Addison W. w
m POB
Spotsylvania s/o
Frank H.&
Elizabeth Ann
Durrett 2 Apr
1858 SPBR
DURRETT, E.M. w m POB
Minorsville s/o
J.J.& S.E.Durrett
27 Nov 1856 SPBR
DURRETT, James F. w m
POB Spotsylvania
s/o F.H.&
Elizabeth
A.Durrett 5 May
1860 SPBR
DURRETT, Mary M. w f
POB Spotsylvania
d/o J.J.& Mary

E.Durrett 27 Mar 1867 SPBR
DURRETT, Virginia M. w f POB Spotsylvania d/o Jonathan J.& Susan E.Durrett Apr 1854 SPBR
DURRETT, William L. w m POB Spotsylvania s/o Franklin H.& Elizabeth A.Durrett 20 Jun 1854 SPBR
DURRETT,___ s or d/ Dr A.L.& Lou Durrett 12 Oct 1855 SPBR
DUVALL, Harriet V. d/o Frederick I.Duvall 1 Oct 1849 GBSP
DUVALL, Robert C. w m POB Spotsylvania s/o Robert A.& Maria F.Duvall 3 Jun 1855 SPBR
DUVALL, Willie Ann M. d/o Frederick I.Duvall 1 Oct 1849 GBSP
ELLIS, Lucy Ann d/o John D.Ellis bond posted 6 Mar 1837 (child was probably under 14y) GBSP
ELLIS, Lucy Ann d/o John D.Ellis bond posted 7 Oct 1844 GBSP
EMBREY,___,d/o Isaac Embrey w f 9 Feb 1859 SPBR
FARISH, John H. w m POB Spotsylvnaia s/o George R.& Sarah Farish 27 May 1859 SPBR
FARISH, William B. w m POB Spotsylvaia s/o George R.& Sarah P.Farish 13 Apr 1860 SPBR
FAULCONER, Charles M. w m POB Spotsylvania s/o John T.Emily Faulconer 29 Jul 1858 SPBR
FAULCONER, Morgan M. b.d.20 Jul 1869 d.d.30 Nov 1949 CBC
FAULCONER, Y.B. Sr. b.d.12 May 1867 d.d.3 Aug 1960 CBC
FINNEY, Allie K. b.d.1 Sep 1868 d.d.6 Dec 1952 wife to Pelham G.Finney SGMC
FINNEY, Pelham G. b.d. 11 Nov 1871 d.d.23 Jun 1954 husband to Allie K.Finney SGMC
FISHER, Brockenberry s/o Sylvanus Fisher bond posted 4 Feb 1839 GBSP
FISHER, Hiram s/o Sylvanus Fisher bond posted 4 Nov 1839 GBSP
FISHER, Jackson s/o Sylvanus Fisher bond posted 4 Feb 1839 GBSP
FISHER, Mary d/o Sylvanus Fisher bond posted 4 Nov 1839 GBSP
FISHER, Sarah A. d/o Sylvanus Fisher bond posted 4 Feb 1839 GBSP
FISHER, Sylvanus s/o Sylvanus Fisher bond posted 4 Nov 1839 GBSP
FLEMING, M.E. w f POB Spotsylvania d/o Boswell S.& Lucy

A.Fleming Aug
1855 SPBR
FLEMING, Octavis B. w
f POB
Spotsylvania d/o
Boswell S.& Lucy
A.Fleming 7 Sep
1853 SPBR
FLEMMING, Lucy M.
b.d.17 Apr 1847
d.d.16 Aug 1926
SGMC
FLIPPO, Henry L. s/o
James H.Flippo
bond posted 6 Jan
1851 GBSP
FLIPPO, James A. s/o
James H.Flippo
bond posted 6 Jan
1851 GBSP
FLIPPO, James Lewis w
m POB
Spotsylvania s/o
Joseph B.& Mary
C.Flippo 25 Jun
1854 SPBR
FLIPPO, Joseph POC m
POB Spotsylvania
s/o Rose owned by
William P.Goodwin
17 Dec 1854 SPBR
FLIPPO, Levy M. s/o
James H.Flippo
bond posted 6 Jan
1851 GBSP
FLIPPO, Major F. s/o
James H.Flippo
bond posted 6 Jan
1851 GBSP
FLIPPO, Mary E. d/o
James H.Flippo
bond posted 6 Jan
1851 GBSP
FLIPPO, Mitilda E. d/o
James H.Flippo
bond posted 6 Jan
1851 GBSP
FLIPPO, William w m
POB Spotsylvania
s/o Levi & Alice
Flippo 1 Jul 1860
SPBR
FORD, Maria POC f POB
Spotsylvania d/o
Bartlett & Jane
Ford 1867 SPBR
FOSTER, James A. s/o
William L.Foster
bond posted 1 Nov
1847 certified in
Macom Co,
Kentucky GBSP
FOSTER, Lenam b.d.1870
d.d.1966 wife to
William B.Foster
SGMC
FOSTER, Lucy Ann d/o
William L.Foster
bond posted 1 Nov
1847 certified in
Macom Co,
Kentucky GBSP
FOSTER, Rozelia T. w f
POB Spotsylvania
d/o William E.&
Engedi E.Foster
18 Jan 1854 SPBR
FOSTER, Samuel B. w m
POB Spotsylvania
s/o Fredk.C
Foster 15 Jul
1856 SPBR
FOSTER, Suda Zerrobia
w f POB
Spotsylvania d/o
William E.&
E.A.Foster Jan
1865 SPBR
FOSTER, Susanna d/o
Archibald
G.Foster bond
posted 2 May 1842
(child is
probably under
14y) GBSP
FOSTER, Thomas s/o
William L.Foster
bond posted 1 Nov
1847 certified in
Macom Co,
Kentucky GBSP
FOSTER, William B.
b.d.1862 d.d.1935
husband to Lenam
Foster SGMC
FRAZER, Ivarena S. w f
POB Spotsylvania

d/o James Frazer 25 Jul 1857 SPBR
FRAZER, John F. s/o Thomas Frazer (not deceased) bond posted 5 Feb 1838 GBSP
FRAZER, Melissa w f POB Spotsylvania d/o Frederick Frazer 1 Mar 1854 SPBR
FSC... Fletcher/Sullivan Private Cemetary located in Spotsylvania Co
FULCHER, Mary Ann d/o William H.Fulcher bond posted 1 Jun 1840 GBSP
FULCHER, Milicant M.H. child of William H.Fulcher bond posted 1 Jun 1840 GBSP
FULCHER, Nannie B. w f POB Hanover d/o John C.& Dorthula A.Fulcher 6 Oct 1853 SPBR
FULCHER, William H. w m POB Spotsylvania s/o John C.& D.A.Fulcher 6 Feb 1855 SPBR
GARDNER,___d/o Nathan & M.E.Gardner w f 1 May 1865 SPBR
GBSP.. Guardian Bonds Spotsylvania County located in clerk's office
GRADY, John W. b.d.25 Dec 1862 d.d.24 Oct 1924 husband to Sarena A.Grady CBC
GRADY, Sarena A. b.d.14 Dec 1859 d.d.15 Nov 1934 wife to John W.Grady CBC

GRAVES, Frances J. d/o Tazewell Graves bond posted 1 Sep 1845 GBSP
GREEN, Mary POC f owned by Ann Jenkins 10 Oct 1858 SPBR
HAILEY, Anne B. d/o John L.& Louisa F.Hailey w f POB Spotsylvania 17 Oct 1853 SPBR
HALL, Maury M. s/o Aaron R.& Martha Hall w m POB Spotsylvania 27 Oct 1853 SPBR
HANCOCK, Fanny J. d/o Nathl. J.& Martha Hancock w f POB Spotsylvania 19 Aug 1853 SPBR
HANCOCK,____,d/o William W.& Mary Hancock w f 29 Oct 1859 SPBR
HARRIS, Alethis C. b.d.1859 d.d.1943 wife to Lee A.Harris SGMC
HARRIS, Annie b.d.20 Sep 1838 wife to William Harris SGMC
HARRIS, Annie wife of William Harris b.d.20 Sep 1838 SGMC
HARRIS, Eugene s/o Mollie Harris Jul 1883 SPConsent
HARRIS, Lee A. b.d.1856 d.d.1946 husband to Alethia C.Harris SGMC
HARRIS, M.F. d.d.26 May 1895 age 80y wife to R.M.C.Harris SGMC
HARRIS, Magnolia V. b.d.19 Aug 1809 d.d.28 Feb 1907

wife to
R.V.Harris SGMC
HARRIS, R.M.C. d.d.26
Dec 1884 age 72y
husband to
M.F.Harris SGMC
HARRIS, Rosser V. b.d.
6 Nov 1851 d.d.22
Oct 1932 husband
to Magnolia
V.Harris SGMC
HARRIS, William b.d. 1
Feb 1836 d.d. 10
Jan 1911 husband
to Annie Harris
SGMC
HARRIS, William b.d.1
Feb 1836 d.d.10
Jan 1911 SGMC
HAZLEGROVE, Henery C.
b.d.22 Jan 1866
d.d.18 Dec 1926
husband to India
M.Hazlegrove CBC
HAZLEGROVE, India M.
b.d.13 Mar 1872
d.d.27 Oct 1947
wife to Henery
C.Hazlegrove CBC
HICKS, Mary C. d/o
Samuel Hicks (not
deceased) bond
posted 3 Nov 1845
(child is
probably under
14y) GBSP
HICKS, Sarah S. d/o
Samuel Hicks (not
deceased) bond
posted 3 Nov 1845
(child is
probably under
14y) GBSP
HICKS, Thomas Thornton
s/o Samauel Hicks
(not deceased)
bond posted 3 Nov
1845 (child is
probably under
14y) GBSP
HICKS, Wade H. s/o
Samuel Hicks (not
deceased) bond
posted 3 Nov 1845

(child is
probably under
14y) GBSP
HILMAN, Willie Alice
d/o John A.& Nana
I.Hilman w f POB
Spot 15 Apr 1859
SPBR
HOCKADAY, Mary Ann w f
POB Spotsylvnaia
d/o Richard S.&
Frances
M.Hockaday 4 Apr
1859 SPBR
HOLBERT, Nannie
Crowley b.d.19
Oct 1871 d.d.20
Sep 1961 CBC
HOLLADAY, Ellen M. d/o
James L.Holladay
bond posted 4 May
1846 GBSP
HOLLADAY, Jemima P.
d/o William
Holladay (not
deceased) bond
posted 2 Dec 1844
(child is
probably under
14y) GBSP
HOLLADAY, Nancy S. d/o
William Holladay
(not deceased)
bond posted 2 Dec
1844 (child is
probably under
14y) GBSP
HOLLADAY, Rebecca R.
d/o Willia
Holladay (not
deceased) bond
posted 2 Dec 1844
(child is
probably under
14y) GBSP
HOLLADAY, Tavenor M.
s/o William
Holladay (not
deceased) bond
posted 2 Dec 1844
(child is
probably under
14y) GBSP

HOLLADAY, William M. s/o William Holladay (not deceased) bond posted 2 Dec 1844 (child is probably under 14y) GBSP

HOLLADAY, William s/o James R.Holladay (not deceased) bond posted 2 Jun 1845 (child is probably under 14y) GBSP

HORD, Frances d/o James Hord bond posted 3 Apr 1837 GBSP

HOWELL, George N. s/o John M.Howell bond posted (child is probably under 14y) 6 Mar 1843 GBSP

HULL, Jane Minor d/o Brodie S.Hull bond posted 6 Aug 1838 GBSP

HUNTER, Stephen POC 28 Sep 1848 SPConsent

ISEMAN, Moses w m POB Spotsylvania s/o Isaac & Charlotte Iseman 30 Jun 1854 SPBR

JACKSON, Jane 27 Jan 1850 SPConsent

JERRELL, A.M. w f POB Spotsylvania d/o John C.& A.M.Jerrell 15 Sep 1858 SPBR

JERRELL, Alma d/o John C. & Ann M.Jerrell w f POB Spotsylvania 13 Jun 1854 SPBR

JOHNSON, Allen s/o Henry Johnson Mar 1850 SPConsent

JOHNSON, Mary POC f POB Spotsylvania owned by J.Long 3 Sep 1858 SPBR

JOHNSON, Mary T. d/o Thomas H.Johnson bond posted 3 May 1841 (child is probably under 14y) GBSP

JOHNSON, William T. 16 Dec 1847 SPConsent

JONES, Betty C. d/o William Jones bond posted 1 Dec 1845 GBSP

JONES, Catherine C. w f POB Spotsylvania d/o Eli M.& Mary E.Jones 27 May 1859 SPBR

JONES, Mary Ann Victoria d/o William T.Jones (not deceased) bond posted 6 Sep 1846 (child is probably under 14y) GBSP

JONES, Susan E. d/o Philip Jones bond posted 1 Oct 1838 GBSP

JONES, Virginia Alice d/o Eli M.Jones 3 Sep 1854 SPConsent

KEETON, Maggie L. w f POB Spotsylvania d/o Phillip & Louisa Keeton 19 Aug 1868 SPBR

KENDALL, Ida A. w f POB Orange d/o Robert G.& Virginia A.Kendall 8 Jul 1853 SPBR

KENDIG, _____ w m POB Spotsylvania s/o Urias P.&

409

Isabella W. Kendig 19 Dec 1855 SPBR
KENT, Ella w f POB Spotsylvania d/o John & M. Catherine Kent 21 Sep 1867 SPBR
KENT, Sarah Katherine b.d.14 May 1862 d.d.30 Mar 1912 wife to William Lee Kent SGMC
KENT, William Lee b.d.10 Aug 1862 d.d.12 Mar 1949 husband to Sarah Katherine Kent SGMC
KING, Bell w f POB Orange d/o Samuel & Ann E. King 8 Mar 1860 SPBR
KING, Franklin M. w m POB Spotsylvania s/o Samuel King 22 Oct 1856 SPBR
KINSEY, Howard G. b.d.27 Mar 1853 d.d.27 Mar 1936 married to Linda V. Kinsey SGMC
KINSEY, Linda V. b.d.20 Dec 1852 d.d.14 Aug 1941 wife to Howard G. Kinsey SGMC
KISHPAUGH, John b.d. 3 Mar 1813 d.d.4 Jul 1900 husband to Phoebe A. Kishpaugh SGMC
KISHPAUGH, Martha D. w f POB Spotsylvania d/o John & Phoeba A. Kishpaugh 25 Jul 1853 SPBR
KISHPAUGH, Phoebe A. wife of John Kishpaugh b.d.7 Oct 1819 d.d.30 Jan 1905 SGMC
LANDRAM, Joseph s/o Josiah Landram bond posted 2 Mar 1840 GBSP
LANE, Bettie E. b.d. 1851 d.d.1938 CBC
LAYTON, Horace L.E. s/o Horace Layton pond posted 6 Sep 1846 (child is probably under 14y) GBSP
LEAVELL, Arthur S.H. w m POB Spotsylvania s/o Byrd C. & Mary C. Leavell (POR Oak Grove) 30 Oct 1853 SPBR
LEWIS, Jennie Long b.d.24 Jul 1867 d.d.25 Aug 1959 SGMC
LIPSCOMB, John E. s/o Thomas H. Lipscomb (not deceased) bond posted 6 Sep 1841 GBSP
LIPSCOMB, Keren Happuch d/o Granville Lipscomb (not deceased) bond posted 3 Jan 1842 (child is probably under 14y) GBSP
LIPSCOMB, Martha E. d/o John Lipscomb bond posted 2 Apr 1838 GBSP
LIPSCOMB, Thaddeus s/o T.H. Lipscomb (not deceased) bond posted 1 Mar 1841 GBSP
LUCAS, ____ free POC s/ or d/o Eliza E. Lucas 25 Dec 1853 SPBR
LUCK, Lucy Ellen d/o Richard A. Luck bond posted 4 Feb 1850 GBSP
LUDLEY, Mary b.d. Apr 1849 SPConsent

MANSFIELD, ____ w f POB Spotsylvania d/o W.H.& C.D.Mansfield Dec 1856 SPBR
MANSFIELD, William S.P. w m POB Spotsylvania s/o William H.& Cordelia P.Mansfield 30 Jan 1854 SPBR
MARSHALL, Benjamin POC m POB Spotsylvania owned by William Chewning 10 Apr 1854 SPBR
MARTIN, Luther POC m POB Spotsylvania s/o Charlotte 10 Sep 1855 SPBR
MASSEY, Caleb Rosser w m POB Spotsylvania s/o A.W.& Lucy M.Massey 6 Jun 1867 SPBR
MASSEY, William C. w m POB Spotsylvania s/o James H.7 Jane Y.Massey 6 Aug 1853 SPBR
MASTIN, Alice w f POB Spotsylvania d/o Benjamin & Betty Mastin 21 Oct 1858 SPBR
MASTIN, Allen M. w m POB Spotsylvania s/o Jackson & Mildred Mastin 20 Aug 1853 SPBR
MASTIN, Charles M. w m POB Spotsylvania s/o Benjamin & Ann E.Mastin 27 May 1867 SPBR
MASTIN, James S. w m POB Spotsylvania s/o Benjamin & Bettie Mastin 25 Oct 1860 SPBR

McCALLEY, Allen(?) w m POB Spotsylvnaia s/o William & E.McCalley 14 Aug 1865 SPBR
McCALLEY, Robert B. w m POB Spotsylvania s/o William & E.McCally 20 Oct 1855 SPBR
McCLOUD, ____ w m POB Waller's Tavern s/o Ed. & M.L.McCloud Nov 1856 SPBR
McCLOUD, Ida L. w f POB Spotsylvania d/o Edgar & M.L.McCloud Sep 1855 SPBR
MCCRACKEN, William D.s/o Patrick & Elizabeth D.McCracken w m 28 Aug 1859 SPBR
McCUE, Virginia B. w f POB Spotsylvania d/o Charles W.& Virginia McCue 19 Aug 1860 SPBR
McGEE, Agness w f POB Spotsylvania d/o Ebeneza & Louisa McGee 25 Sep 1855 SPBR
McGEE, Agness w f POB Spotsylvania d/o Ebenezer McGee 20 May 1859 SPBR
McGEE, Henry Lee w POB Spotsylvania s/o Reubin & Mary McGee 8 Apr 1867 SPBR
McGEE, Millard w m POB Spotsylvania s/o E.& Louisa McGee 20 Sep 1854 SPBR
MCGHEE____,s/o William G.& Amanda McGhee w m 30 Oct 1859 SPBR

McKENNEY, Addison L.
s/o Champe
McKenney bond
posted 6 Sep 1841
GBSP
McKENNEY, Everett E.
s/o Champe
McKenney bond
posted 6 Sep 1841
GBSP
McKENNEY, Henry F. s/o
John McKenney
(dec) bond posted
1 Jan 1844 GBSP
McKENNEY, Jackson S.
s/o John McKenney
(dec) bond posted
1 Jan 1844 GBSP
McKENNEY, Melvin G.
s/o Champe
McKenney bond
posted 6 Sep 1841
GBSP
McKENNEY, Roberta L.
d/o Champe
McKenney bond
posted 6 Sep 1841
GBSP
McKENNEY, William W.
s/o John McKenney
(dec)bond posted
1 Jan 1844 GBSP
McWHIRT, Alfred w m
POB Spotsylvania
s/o Silas &
Agness McWhirt 15
Jun 1859 SPBR
McWHITE, Willie w m
POB Spotsylvania
s/o Jos.& Mary
G.McWhite 19 Jan
1868 SPBR
MILLS, William w m POB
Spotsylvania s/o
S.S.& Martha
E.Mills 24 Sep
1868 SPBR
MINOR, Betty w f POB
Spotsylvania d/o
James & E.Minor 7
May 1865 SPBR
MINOR, Robert D. s/o
Garret Minor bond
posted 2 Mar 1840
GBSP
MINOR, William M. s/o
Thomas W.Minor
bond posted 3 Feb
1851 GBSP
MITCHELL, Delina S.
d/o William
Mitchell bond
posted 5 Oct 1840
(child is
probably under
14y) GBSP
MITCHELL, William P.
s/o William
Mitchell bond
posted 5 Oct 1840
(child is
probably under
14y) GBSP
MORRISON, Anna M. w f
POB Baltimore d/o
Thomas & Amanda
Morrison 8 Apr
1867 SPBR
MORRISON, Ida w f POB
Spotsylvnaia d/o
James & Sallie
R.Morrison 5 Oct
1868 SPBR
MURPHEY, Martha Ann
POC f POB
Spotsylvania d/o
James H.& Julia
Ann Murphy 10 May
1867 SPBR
NOEL, Maria Hall d/o
Stapleton Noel
bond posted 7 Oct
1839 GBSP
NOEL, Mary Stapleton
d/o Stapleton
Noel bond posted
6 Jan 1840 GBSP
OLIVER, Ann A. d/o
Charles Oliver
bond posted 2 Apr
1838 GBSP
OLIVER, Caroline E.
d/o Charles
Oliver bond
posted 2 Apr 1838
GBSP

OLIVER, Jane d/o Charles Oliver bond posted 2 Apr 1838 GBSP
OLIVER, Julia P. d/o Charles Oliver bond posted 2 Apr 1838 GBSP
OLIVER, Lucy S. d/o Charles Oliver bond posted 2 Apr 1838 GBSP
OLIVER, Mary Hicks b.d.5 May 1882 d.d.21 Jan 1965 wife to William Samuel Oliver SGMC
OLIVER, Mary S. d/o Charles Oliver bond posted 2 Apr 1838 GBSP
OLIVER, Robert J. s/o Charles Oliver bond posted 2 Apr 1838 GBSP
OLIVER, William A. s/o Charles Oliver bond posted 2 Apr 1838 GBSP
OLIVER, William Samuel b.d.29 Oct 1867 d.d.28 Dec 1945 married to Mary Hicks Oliver SGMC
PARKER, Alexander s/o Winslow Parker bond posted 1 Mar 1847 GBSP
PARKER, Ann d/o Winslow Parker bond posted 1 Mar 1847 GBSP
PARKER, Elias free POC m POB Spotsylvania s/o Polly Parker 9 Apr 1854 SPBR
PARKER, Harriet P. b.d.22 Mar 1864 d.d.28 May 1939 wife to William A.Parker SGMC
PARKER, John s/o Winslow Parker bond posted 1 Mar 1847 GBSP
PARKER, Sarah d/o Winslow Parker bond posted 1 Mar 1847 GBSP
PARKER, William A. b.d.17 Mar 1860 d.d.26 Dec 1941 husband to Harriet P.Parker SGMC
PAYNE, James L. w m POB Spotsylvania s/o John M.& Elizabeth F.Payne 29 Jul 1853 SPBR
PAYTES, Florence M. b.d.4 Feb 1875 d.d.22 Dec 1955 wife to Simeon C.Paytes CBC
PAYTES, Simeon C. b.d.28 Mar 1866 d.d.9 Mar 1852 husband to Florence M.Paytes CBC
PEACHER, Mary J. b.d.1864 d.d.1935 CBC
PEAKE, Anna Maria d/o William B.Peake (not deceased) bond posted 6 Apr 1846 GBSP
PENDLETON, Calvina d/o Rice Pendleton bond posted 3 Jun 1839 GBSP
PENDLETON, Malvina R. d/o Rice Pendleton bond posted 2 Feb 1846 (child is probably under 14y) GBSP
PENDLETON, Mary d/o Rice Pendleton bond posted 3 Jun 1839 GBSP

PENDLETON, Sally A. w f POB Spotsylvania d/o Hugh C.& Malvina Pendleton 20 Sep 1853 SPBR

PEYTON, Bernard s/o John G.Peyton bond posted 2 Aug 1847 (child is probably under 14y)GBSP

PITTS, Mary E. d/o Eli Pitts bond posted 7 Mar 1842 GBSP

POOL, Adelaide d/o Alfred & Nannie Pool w f POB Spotsylvania 18 Oct 1860 SPBR

POOL, Montreville w m POB Spotsylvania s/o Alfred & Hanna Pool 13 Jun 1859 SPBR

POOL, William M. b.d.27 Mar 1848 d.d.22 Feb 1915 SGMC

POOLE, Ella E. b.d.Oct 1855 d.d.Mar 1917 wife to Monte F.Poole SGMC

POOLE, Lucy M. b.d.17 Apr 1847 d.d.16 Aug 1926 wife to William M.Poole SGMC

POOLE, Monte F. b.d.June 1860 d.d.Sep 1916 husband to Ella E.Poole SGMC

POOLE, William M. b.d.27 Mar 1848 d.d.22 Feb 1915 husband to Lucy M.Poole SGMC

POWELL, Ann E. b.d.1775 d.d.1848 wife to William Powell SGMC

POWELL, William b.d.1758 d.d.1829 husband to Ann E.Powell SGMC

PRICE, Betty Stapleton d/o Patrick H.Price (not deceased) bond posted 5 Nov 1844 (child is probably under 14y) GBSP

PRICE, Malvina d/o Patrick H.Price (not deceased) bond posted 5 Nov 1844 (child is probably under 14y) GBSP

PRITCHETT, ____ s/o P.B.& Ann E.Pritchett w m 2 Feb 1859 SPBR

PROCTOR, Rebecca F. w f POB Spotsylvania d/o Austin & Martha Ann Proctor 25 Jan 1854 SPBR

PULLIAM, ____ w f POB Spotsylvania d/o T.R.& Louisa H.Pulliam 18 Nov 1855 SPBR

PULLIAM, Fayette J. s/o David K.Pulliam (not deceased) bond posted 1 Jul 1844 (child is probably under 14y) GBSP

PULLIAM, John J. b.d.22 Jan 1844 d.d.15 Feb 1908 husband to Melissa A.Pulliam SGMC

PULLIAM, John K. w m POB Spotsylvania s/o Tobias C.R.& Louisa Pulliam 2 Feb 1854 SPBR

PULLIAM, John R. s/o John Pulliam bond posted 4 Dec 1837

(child was probably under 14y) GBSP
PULLIAM, Melissa A. b.d.11 Jan 1844 d.d.27 Feb 1907 wife to John J.Pulliam SGMC
PULLIAM, Tobias C.R. s/o John E.Pulliam bond posted 4 Nov 1839 GBSP
PULLIAM, William B. s/o David K.Pulliam (not deceased) bond posted 1 Jul 1844 (child is probably under 14y) GBSP
PULLIAM, William T. b.d.4 Feb 1872 d.d.15 May 1949 SGMC
QUISENBERRY, Mary M. w f POB Spotsylvania d/o William & Jane G.Quisenberry 15 Mar 1859 SPBR
QUISENBERRY,____d/o John & Charlotte A.Quisenberry 1867 SPBR
RAUSCH, Estella Roby b.d.27 Feb 1876 d.d.22 Sep 1962 CBC
RAWLINGS,____d/o Alfred & Judith A.Rawlings w f 10 Aug 1859 SPBR
RAWLINGS, James M. s/o James H.Rawlings bond posted 1 Oct 1849 GBSP
RAWLINGS, John Z.H.Rawlings s/o James H.Rawlings bond posted 1 Oct 1849 GBSP
RICHESON,____,s/o William P.& Ann Richeson w m 17 Aug 1859 SPBR
ROBEY, Frank O. b.d.1878 d.d.1920 CBC
ROWE,____,d/o Clack & Elizabeth Rowe w f 3 Apr 1859 SPBR
SCHULCE, William Henry s/o Henry & Elizabeth Schulce w m 5 May 1859 SPBR
SCOTT, Mary E.A. d/o Day Scott bond posted 6 Aug 1838 GBSP
SCOTT, Robert P. s/o Day Scott bond posted 6 Oct 1845 GBSP
SHELTON, Mary Ann d/o William Shelton bond posted 3 Mar 1851 GBSP
SHEPHERD, David A. s/o John M.Shepherd bond posted 5 Nov 1838 GBSP
SHEPHERD, Edward M. s/o John M.Shepherd bond posted 5 Nov 1838 GBSP
SHEPHERD, George W. s/o John M.Shepherd bond posted 5 Nov 1838 GBSP
SIMPSON, Alice M. b.d.28 May 1875 d.d.28 Feb 1957 wife to Edward F.Simpson CBC
SIMPSON, Edward F. b.d.29 Oct 1871 d.d.23 Jul 1963 husband to Alice M.Simpson CBC
SIMPSON,____s/o Joanne Simpson w m 16 Aug 1860 SPBR

SKIRVEN, Ophelia C.
  b.d.15 Mar 1873
  d.d.15 Feb 1952
  CBC
SPINDLE, Maria
  Virginia d/o
  Benjamin Spindle
  (not deceased)
  bond posted 2 Dec
  1844 (child is
  probably under
  14y) GBSP
SPINDLE, Mary
  Elizabeth d/o
  Benjamin Spindle
  (not deceased)
  bond posted 2 Dec
  1844 (child is
  probably under
  14y) GBSP
SPINDLE, Thomas
  Wiglesworth s/o
  Benjamin Spindle
  (not deceased)
  bond posted 2 Dec
  1844 (child is
  probably under
  14y) GBSP
SPINDLE, William Henry
  s/o Benjamin
  Spindle (not
  deceased) bond
  posted 2 Dec 1844
  (child is
  probably under
  14y) GBSP
STEVENSON, James W.
  s/o Richard
  S.Stevenson bond
  posted 6 Mar 1837
  GBSP
STEVENSON, William S.
  s/o Richard
  S.Stevenson bond
  posted 6 Mar 1837
  GBSP
SWIFT, Beulah K.
  b.d.10 Jun 1879
  d.d.23 Apr 1962
  CBC
TALLEY, Ida Virginia
  b.d.1870 d.d.1949
  wife to Joseph
  J.Talley SGMC

TALLEY, Joseph J.
  b.d.1872 d.d.1946
  husband to Ida
  Virginia Talley
  SGMC
TANNER, Charles D.
  b.d.1871 POB
  Oneida Co, N.Y.
  d.d.1934 PODeath
  Virginia SGMC
TAYLOR, Edmund s/o
  Henry Taylor bond
  posted 1 Nov 1847
  (child is
  probably under
  14y) GBSP
TAYLOR, Henry s/o
  Henry Taylor bond
  posted 1 Nov 1847
  (child is
  probably under
  14y) GBSP
TAYLOR, James s m POB
  Spotsylvania
  owned by William
  Hapsbrough 2 Sep
  1853 SPBR
TAYLOR, Joel H. s/o
  H.A. & S.E.Taylor
  w m POB
  Spotsylvania Jan
  1856 SPBR
TAYLOR, John s/o Henry
  Taylor bond
  posted 1 Nov 1847
  (child is
  probably under
  14y) GBSP
TAYLOR, Julia D. d/o
  Henry Taylor bond
  posted 1 Nov 1847
  (child is
  probably under
  14y) GBSP
TAYLOR, Lucy P. d/o
  Henry Taylor bond
  posted 1 Nov 1847
  (child is
  probably under
  14y) GBSP
TAYLOR, Thomas L. s/o
  Henry Taylor bond
  posted 1 Nov 1847
  (child is

probably under 14y) GBSP
TAYLOR, William P. s/o Henry Taylor bond posted 1 Nov 1847 (child is probably under 14y) GBSP
THOMAS, Caldona R. b.d.2 Dec 1878 d.d.1 Jul 1966 CBC
THOMAS, Frances Ann w f d/o Alexander & Lucy A.Thomas 31 Oct 1855 SPBR
THOMAS, ___ d/o Robert Thomas 29 Dec 1857 SPBR
THOMPSON, Nelly slave f POB Spotsylvania owned by James W.Foard(?) 1 Jun 1853 SPBR
TOMPKINS, Cornelia w f POB Spotsylvania d/o Claudius & Frances A.Tompkins 10 Jun 1859 SPBR
TOMPKINS, E.W. d/o Francis & Rebs Tompkins w f POB Prospect Hill 30 Jul 1855 SPBR
TOMPKINS, Francis T. s/o Edmund & Harriet T.Tompkins w m POB Spotsylvania 3 Aug 1853 SPBR
TOMPKINS, John M. s/o Claudius & Frances Tompkins w m POB Spotsylvania 4 Apr 1855 SPBR
TOWLER, Theret Jr. s/o Dr.Thomas T.& Elizabeth Towler w m POB Spotsylvania 6 Oct 1853 SPBR
TOWLES, Mary C. d/o Thomas Towles bond posted 7 Jan 1839 GBSP
TOWLES. Thomas R. s/o Thomas Towles bond posted 7 Jan 1839 GBSP
TRIBBLE, George W. s/o George L.& Angelina Tribble w m POB Spotsylvania 30 Aug 1855 SPBR
TRIBBLE, William A. s/o William A.& Mary A.Tribble w m POB Spotsylvania 24 Nov 1855 SPBR
TRIGG, Joseph Brock s/o Isaac W.& Catherine M.Trigg w m 29 Jan 1853 SPBR
TURNER, Austin POC m POB Spotsylvania owned by William Fife 25 Sep 1853 SPBR
TURNER, Katherine Sorrell b.d.4 Oct 1882 d.d.17 Dec 1922 FSC
TURNER, William Phillip b.d.13 Nov 1872 d.d.18 Nov 1946 FSC
TWYMAN, Mildred Buford d/o Thornhill Twyman bond posted 4 Mar 1850 GBSP
TWYMN, John James s/o Thornhill Twyman bond posted 4 Mar 1850 GBSP
TYRE, Allen H. s/o Edm.S.Spindle & Martha Tyre w f POB Spotsylvania 6 Oct 1853 SPBR

VANWORTH, Elizabeth D. d/o William H.& Elizabeth Vanworth w f 13 Dec 1859 SPBR
VASS, _____ s/o Benjamin & M.A.Vass 24 Jan 1856 SPBR
W____, Benjamin Walker s/o William A.W w m POB Spot 8 Feb 1860
W____, Ferdinand s/o William A.& Harriet S.W free POC or w m 8 Aug 1858
W____, Virginia Louisa d/o W.A.W w f 22 Mar 1855
WAKEMAN, Mabel Row b.d.30 Aug 1879 d.d.14 Apr 1974 wife to Samuel T.Wakeman SGMC
WAKEMAN, Samuel T. b.d.15 Jun 1876 d.d.3 Nov 1936 married to Mabel Row Wakeman SGMC
WALLACE, John T. s/o Charles & M.F.Wallace w m 15 Dec 1855 SPBR
WALLER, --- s/o John M.& Martha P.Waller w m 6 Jun 1855 SPBR
WALLER, Absalom C. s/o John B.Waller bond posted 6 Mar 1837 GBSP
WALLER, Absalom w m POB Spotsylvania s/o Dr. Nelson S. & M.H.Waller 16 Apr 1859 SPBR
WALLER, Benjamin L. s/o John B.Waller bond posted 6 Mar 1837 GBSP
WALLER, Dorothea T. d/o John M.Waller bond posted 6 Jan 1851 GBSP
WALLER, Douglas M. s/o Benjamin F.& Jane F. w m 8 Feb 1859 SPBR
WALLER, Lucy F. d/o John B.Waller bond posted 6 Mar 1837 GBSP
WALLER, Mildred A. d/o John M.& Elizabeth Waller w f 21 Aug 1858 SPBR
WELCH, Elizabeth d/o Thomas & Ann Welch w f 21 Apr 1854 SPBR
WELCH, _____,s/o Thomas & Ann Welch w m 1 Nov 1859 SPBR
WEST, Julia A. d/o James & Sarah M.West w f POB Spot 7 Aug 1860 SPBR
WHEELER, Cuelis s/o James A.& Elizabeath A.Wheeler w m 3 Sep 1855 SPBR
WHEELER, Sarah A.C. d/o Caswell & Huldah M.Wheeler w f 2 Sep 1855 SPBR
WHEELER, Sue J. b.d.22 Oct 1880 d.d.20 May 1960 CBC
WHEELER, Wiley F.s/o Edwin & Mary I.Wheeler 4 Feb 1854 SPBR
WHEELER, William Q.s/o Edmond & Mary J.Wheeler w m Nov 1855 SPBR
WHITIS, Laura A. d/o Michael & Betsy Ann Whitis POC f POB Spotsylvania b.d.October 1865 SPBR

WHITLOCK, Mary E.
d.d.20 Mar 1918
age 78 SGMC
WIATT, Edmonia d/o
James M & Mary
A.Wiatt w f POB
Orange 2 Jun 1855
SPBR
WIGLESWORTH, Alfred
s/o Mansfield
Wiglesworth (not
deceased) bond
posted 1 Feb 1847
GBSP
WIGLESWORTH, Almira W.
d/o Elijah
Wiglesworth bond
posted 6 Jan 1845
GBSP
WIGLESWORTH, Andrew J.
s/o Elijah
Wiglesworth bond
posted 6 Jan 1845
GBSP
WIGLESWORTH, Ann E.
d/o John
Wiglesworth bond
posted 7 Dec 1840
GBSP
WIGLESWORTH, Bennet M.
s/o Elijah
Wiglesworth bond
posted 6 Jan 1845
GBSP
WIGLESWORTH, Claiborn
s/o Claiborn
Wiglesworth bond
posted 1 Jan 1838
GBSP
WIGLESWORTH, James s/o
Claiborn
Wiglesworth bond
posted 1 Jan 1838
GBSP
WIGLESWORTH, Jane F.
d/o Elijah
Wiglesworth bond
posted 6 Jan 1845
GBSP
WIGLESWORTH, Joseph H.
s/o Mansfield
Wiglesworth (not
deceased) bond
posted 1 Feb 1847
GBSP
WIGLESWORTH, Mary d/o
Claiborn
Wiglesworth bond
posted 1 Jan 1838
GBSP
WIGLESWORTH, Mary E.
d/o Elijah
Wiglesworth bond
posted 6 Jan 1845
GBSP
WIGLESWORTH, Virginia
d/o Claiborn
Wiglesworth bond
posted 1 Jan 1838
GBSP
WIGLESWORTH, William
s/o Mansfield
Wiglesworth (not
deceased) bond
posted 1 Feb 1847
GBSP
WILLAIGHBY, Joseph s/o
Waller M.& Sarah
E.Willaighby w m
POB Spotsylvania
27 Oct 1867 SPBR
WILLAUGHBY, Percy O.
s/o James F.&
Elizabeth
Willaughby w m
POB Spot 1 Mar
1860 SPBR
WILLIAMS, A.S.d/o
W.S.& Jane
Williams w f 30
Jan 1855 SPBR
WILLIAMS, Bradberry
s/o John
P.Williams (not
deceased) bond
posted 4 Aug 1845
(child is
probably under
14y) GBSP
WILLIAMS, Clearlie S.
w f POB
Spotsylvania d/o
Stephen W.& Sarah
C.Williams 22 Oct
1859 SPBR
WILLIAMS, Mulico (?)G.
d/o William

L.Williams 19 Aug 1854 SPBR
WILLIAMS, Rosa B. d/o S.M.& Sarah C.Williams w f POB Spotsylvania Dec 1865 SPBR
WILLIAMS, Sarah Jane d/o John Williams bond posted 2 Jul 1838 GBSP
WILLIAMS, Wade Hampton s/o William S.& Jane Williams w m POB Spotsylvania 21 Aug 1867 SPBR
WILLIAMS, William M.s/o William H.& Sarah C.Williams w m 18 Oct 1854 SPBR
WILLIAMS.Charles s/o William S.& Jane Williams w m 3 Sep 1859 SPBR
WILSON, Ann Elizabeth d/o Thomas H.Wilson bond posted 6 Jul 1840 GBSP
WILSON, Lucy Mary d/o Robert H. & Jane Wilson w f POB Spotsylvania May 1867 SPBR
WILSON, Ora W. s/o W.S.& S.S. Wilson w f POB Spotsylvania 7 Apr 1858 SPBR
WILSON, Robert E.s/o Abram H.& Sarah A.Wilson w m POB Spotsylvania Sep 1867 SPBR
WILSON, Robert s/o Robert H.& Mary G.Wilson w m POB Spot 1 Aug 1860 SPBR
WILSON,____ d/o W.L.& Sally L.Wilson w f born dead 20 Oct 1855 SPBR

WILSON,____,d/o R.H.& Mary J.Wilson w f 6 May 1859 SPBR
WILTSHIRE, Fanny d/o John B.& Janae Wiltshsire w f 26 Sep 1859 SPBR
WINSLOW, Emma J.d/o Waller & Patsy Winslow POC f POB Spot 10 Aug 1865 SPBR
WOOD, Frank s/o Fleming & Lucy A.Wood w m 15 Mar 1854 SPBR
WRIGHT, Lizzie L.d/o Henry & Susan Wright w f 1855 SPBR
WRIGHT, William s/o James & Letitia Wright w m 18 Aug 1854 SPBR
WRIGHT, William s/o William Wright bond posted 5 Jul 1847 (child is probably under 14y) GBSP
WRIGHT,___, s/o John W.& Mana W.Wright w m 17 Sep 1859 SPBR
WRIGHT,Sarah A. d/o Philip & Sarah C.Wright w f 30 Sep 1854 SPBR
YERBY, Elizabeth d/o Thomas Yerby (not deceased) 4 May 1840 GBSP
YERBY, Eugena w m d.d. 15 Mar 1856 PODeath Spotsylvania age 3y POB Spotsylvania s/o John & Ella Yerby SPDeath Records
YERBY, Harriet w f d.d.1 Mar 1865 PODeath Spotsylvania age

420

1mo d/o John & E.Yerby SPDeath Records

YOUNG, ____ d/o William & Jane Young w f 25 Dec 1857 SPBR

YOUNG, Charles O. w m d.d.4 Dec 1870 PODeath Spotsylvania age 67y 10mo s/o C.& Mary Young unmarried POB Norfolk, Va SPDeath Records

YOUNG, Fanny w f d.d.26 Dec 1859 age 41 SPDeath Records

YOUNG, Lucy A. d/o William & Jane Young w f POB Spotsylvania 5 Jul 1856 SPBR

YOUNG, Mary w f PODeath C.O.Young's d.d.9 Feb 1855 age 10y POB York Co d/o Thomas & Eliz. Smith SPDeath Records

YOUNG, William S. s/o William & Jane E.Young w m POB Spotsylvania 25 Jul 1853 SPBR

YOUNG, William w m age 53 PODeath Spotsylvania (between 1853 and 1870) POB Spotsylvania s/o J.& A.Young spouse of Lucinda Young SPDeath Records

.

www.ingramcontent.com/pod-product-compliance
Lightning Source LLC
Chambersburg PA
CBHW050325230426
43663CB00010B/1744